W9-DEH-918

THE ROUGH GUIDE TO
SCOTTISH
HIGHLANDS & ISLANDS

This ninth edition updated by
**Norm Longley, Rachel Mills, Hilary Weston and
Jackie Staddon**

ROUGH
GUIDES

Contents

A NOTE TO READERS

At Rough Guides, we always strive to bring you the most up-to-date information. This book was produced during a period of continuing uncertainty caused by the Covid-19 pandemic, so please note that content is more subject to change than usual. We recommend checking the latest restrictions and official guidance.

Introduction to
Scottish Highlands & Islands

Wild and weather-beaten, the Scottish Highlands and Islands feel like another world compared to the pastoral character of much of Great Britain. With the Covid-19 pandemic shining a bigger light on domestic travel, this area is an instant winner. This is a land where the elements govern much of everyday life and the shipping forecast is more than just an aural sleeping pill. The scenery is raw and magnificent, shaped over thousands of years by geological forces, glaciers and the weather systems of the North Atlantic. Yet, experience a glorious sunset that turns the sea lochs gold or find yet another empty white-powder beach, and you'll discover the romance of the place, too. Sure, the roads can be tortuous and the weather can be grim. And let's not even start on the midges in high summer. But when the mood takes it, the Highlands and Islands have a unique glory to make the soul sing.

Although escapism accounts for much of the area's appeal, it's impossible to travel in the Highlands and Islands without being touched by the fragility of life here. The **Jacobite** defeat at Culloden in 1746 was a blow to Scottish pride generally, but it was an unmitigated disaster for the Highlands and Islands, signalling the destruction of the Highland clan system and ultimately the entire Highland way of life. The **Clearances** that followed in the nineteenth century more than halved the population, and today the Highland landscape is littered with the shells of pre-Clearance crofting communities. The **economy** struggles, too, despite government support and decades of European Union subsidies, which, following the Brexit vote, will soon be no more. And while recent census figures reveal a rise in **population**,

LOCH NEVIS, INVERIE

some of the larger islands such as Bute, Arran and Islay have suffered depopulation as the traditional Highland industries of farming, crofting and fishing no longer provide enough jobs for the younger generation. Forestry, fish-farming and the oil industry are now the bigger employers, alongside the region's other main industry – **tourism**. Since the former depends on development, and the latter on conservation, it's a fine balancing act between tapping new opportunities and maintaining traditional values: a dilemma that was voiced repeatedly in debates before the **Scottish independence referendum** in September 2014, which saw Scots vote to remain part of Great Britain.

For all that, the region is no time warp. Although tradition remains part of the weft and weave of Highlands life, you don't have to travel far to see a renewal of Highlands culture. Nowadays, shortbread and twee tearooms are out, superb super-fresh local ingredients are in, showcased at outstanding **gastropubs** and gourmet **restaurants** in some of the most remote locations. Similarly, artists have reinvigorated **traditional crafts** as more people seek a life in the slow lane and set up shop in former crofts. Even the visitor profile is changing: the tourists still come to clamber over **castles** and wrap themselves in tartan nostalgia, but just as many people now visit specifically to see whales and dolphins, to summit a Munro or wild camp their way along the West Highland Way. Nor is walking the only activity on the agenda. In recent years, the

SCOTTISH HIGHLANDS AND ISLANDS

FACT FILE

- Covering over 15,000 square miles, the Highlands and Islands house **fewer than 360,000 inhabitants** – a population density of 10 people per square mile, compared to Scotland's average of 166.
- The **shortest scheduled flight in the world** links Westray to Papa Westray in the Orkney Islands. At just one-and-a-half miles in length, the flight can take under two minutes with a tailwind.
- The **coastline** of the Highlands and Islands region is nearly 7000 miles long, and Scotland has approximately 790 **islands**, 130 of which are inhabited.
- Almost half of the 130,000 tons of **salmon** farmed in the region annually is exported, mainly to Europe.
- **George Orwell** holed up on Jura to write his dystopian futuristic novel, *1984*. He called it "an extremely ungetatable place" – perhaps why art-rock band KLF chose the island as the location to burn £1 million as an artistic statement in 1994.
- Never mind Nessie, **midges** are the real monsters of the Highlands. The tiny blood-suckers bite hardest from mid-May to August in calm cloudy conditions, and especially at dawn and dusk. There's even a Midge Forecast: ⓦmidgeforecast.co.uk.

potential of the wilderness in Britain's backyard has been realized too, as adventure-junkies explore the frontiers of Scotland's **mountains** and **coastline**; the opportunities for mountain biking, scuba diving, surfing, kitesurfing and sea-kayaking here are truly world-class, and there's also the best ice-climbing and skiing in Britain.

Of course, activities here can be a mite chillier than elsewhere, but what could be more Scottish than shrugging off a wee bit of weather?

Where to go

There's a golden rule to Highlands and Islands travel – don't try to rush. It makes no difference whether you go by public or private transport, getting around here is time-consuming: distances on land are greater than elsewhere in Britain (and there are no motorways), while visiting the islands demands coordination with ferry or plane timetables – and that's assuming the weather doesn't affect your plans. Relax the pace, however, and the journeys themselves – the spectacular train trips, the flights that scud over tiny islands, the sailings on inter-island ferries or the winding drives along scenic roads – are often as memorable as the destinations themselves. This is slow travel at its best.

The most accessible parts of the region are not far from **Glasgow** and **Edinburgh**: you can be by the banks of Loch Lomond in half an hour, or Highland Perthshire in a little over an hour. As a result, **Loch Lomond**, and the hills and wooded glens of the **Trossachs** tend to be busier than other parts of the Highlands, and while the tourist infrastructure here is hardly theme-park standard, to escape the day-trippers you need to head further north into **Perthshire** and the **Grampian hills** of Angus and Deeside where the Highland scenery is at its richest. South of Inverness the mighty **Cairngorm** massif hints at the raw wilderness Scotland still provides. To reach the lonely north and western Highlands, you'll have to cross the **Great Glen**, an ancient geological fissure that cuts across the country from **Fort William** to Inverness via **Loch Ness**, a moody stretch of water where tourists still hope to glimpse its resident monster. Yet the area with arguably the most memorable scenery of all is the jagged west coast,

A WEE DRAM

No Highland village would be complete without its **pub** (often attached to a hotel) and no pub would be complete without a line of amber **whisky** bottles glinting behind the bar. **Single malts** have grown in popularity as a new audience discovers a drink nurtured by a well-marketed mix of soft Scottish rain, Highland streams, rich peaty soil, smoke and craftsmanship.

Not only is whisky the national drink, enjoying it is often regarded as the national pastime too, lubricating any social gathering from a Highland ceilidh to a Saturday-night session. While it can be drunk neat, the truth is that a splash of water releases the whisky's flavours. It's no surprise, then, that the Scots also turn a healthy profit by bottling the country's abundant spring water and selling it around the world.

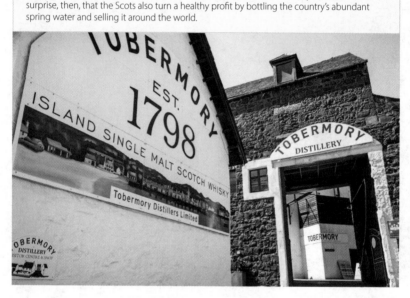

stretching from **Argyll** north to **Wester Ross** and the hills of **Assynt**. Here you'll find a beautiful coastline that feels ever wilder, ever more remote, the further north you go, not least around spectacular dome-shaped mountains such as Suilven. The north coast of Sutherland is less visited but lonelier still, with Caribbean-white beaches and an exhilarating sense of being at the edge of the world.

The Highlands are splendid, but the islands scattered off the west and north coasts are an essential part of the region's identity. As varied in size and character as accessibility, the rocky Hebrides, which necklace Scotland's Atlantic shoreline, include **Mull** and the nearby pilgrimage centre of **Iona**; **Islay** and **Jura**, famous for their wildlife and whisky; **Skye**, the most visited of the lot because of its sophisticated guesthouses and restaurants as much as the superb walking in the Cuillin mountains; and the **Western Isles**, an elongated archipelago that is still a bastion of Gaelic culture. With their rich Norse heritage, **Orkney** and **Shetland** differ not only from each other, but from the dialect and culture of mainland Scotland too. These are the most far-flung islands, buffeted by wind and sea and offering some of the country's wildest scenery, finest birdwatching and oldest archeological sites.

When to go

"There's no such thing as bad weather, only inadequate clothing", the poet laureate Ted Hughes is alleged to have said when asked why he liked holidaying on Scotland's west coast. For those who don't share Hughes' attitude, the **weather** is probably the single biggest factor to put you off visiting the Scottish Highlands and Islands. It's not that it's always bad, it's just that it is unpredictable: you could just as easily enjoy a week of fabulous sunshine in early April while the rest of the UK was sodden as suffer a week of low-lying fog and drizzle in high summer.

Almost every low-pressure system that barrels east out of the North Atlantic passes over Scotland, often forced north by the Azores' high-pressure system. The good news is that such systems tend to blow over rapidly. Out in the islands, they say you can get all four seasons in a day. And even if the weather's not necessarily good, it's generally interesting – often exhilarating or dramatic, and certainly photogenic. And when the sun finally comes out all is forgiven. A week spent in thick mist is transformed when the clouds lift to reveal a majestic mountain range or a group of islands far offshore.

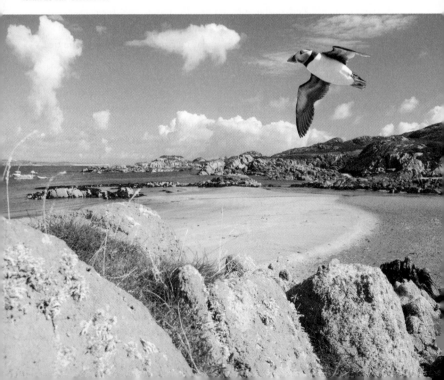

AVERAGE DAILY TEMPERATURES AND MONTHLY RAINFALL

	Jan	Feb	Mar	Apr	May	Jun	Jul	Aug	Sep	Oct	Nov	Dec
OBAN												
Max/min (°C)	7/2	8/2	9/3	12/5	15/7	17/9	18/11	18/11	16/10	13/7	10/5	8/3
Max/min (°F)	45/36	46/36	48/37	53/41	58/44	62/48	64/52	64/52	61/50	55/45	50/41	46/37
Rainfall (mm)	199	147	153	88	77	88	105	125	153	197	174	174
BRAEMAR												
Max/min (°C)	5/-2	5/-1	7/0	10/1	13/4	16/7	18/9	18/9	15/6	11/4	7/1	5/-2
Max/min (°F)	41/29	41/30	44/32	50/34	56/39	61/44	64/48	64/48	58/43	51/39	45/34	41/29
Rainfall (mm)	105	75	75	54	59	56	63	70	78	114	95	89
FORT WILLIAM												
Max/min (°C)	6/0	6/-1	7/1	10/2	14/4	16/7	17/10	17/9	15/7	11/5	8/2	6/1
Max/min (°F)	42/32	42/30	45/34	50/36	57/40	60/45	63/49	62/49	59/45	52/41	46/36	52/34
Rainfall (mm)	248	175	184	97	85	77	89	107	140	202	206	201
LERWICK												
Max/min (°C)	6/2	6/2	6/2	8/4	10/5	12/8	14/10	14/10	13/9	10/6	8/4	6/2
Max/min (°F)	43/35	43/35	43/35	46/38	51/42	54/46	58/40	58/50	55/48	51/43	46/39	43/35
Rainfall (mm)	143	121	125	71	53	58	67	84	106	142	146	143

The **summer** months of June, July and August are the high season, with local school holidays making July and early August the busiest period. Days are generally warm, but the weather is often variable. Daylight hours are long, however, and, in the far north, darkness hardly falls at all in midsummer. The warmer weather does have its drawbacks, though, in the form of clouds of **midges**, the tiny biting insects that appear around dusk, dawn and in still conditions, and can drive even the most committed adventurer mad.

Commonly, **May** and **September** provide weather as good as, if not better than, high summer. You're less likely to encounter crowds, and the mild temperatures combined with the changing **colours** of nature mean both are great for outdoor activities, particularly hiking. May is also a good month for watching nesting **seabirds**; September, however, is stalking season for deer, which can disrupt **access** to the countryside.

The months of **April** and **October** bracket the tourist season for many parts of rural Scotland. Many attractions, tourist offices and guesthouses open for business at Easter and close after the school half-term in October. If places do stay open through the winter, it's normally with reduced opening hours; the October-to-March period is also the best time to pick up **special offers** for accommodation. Note, too, that public transport will often operate on a reduced winter timetable.

Winter days, from November to March, can be crisp and bright, but are more often cold, overcast and all too short. Nevertheless, **Hogmanay** and **New Year** has traditionally been a good time to visit Scotland for partying and warm hospitality. On a clear night in winter, visitors in the far north might see displays of the **aurora borealis**, while a fall of snow in the Highlands will prompt plenty of activity in the **ski resorts**.

Author picks

The Highlands has plenty of poster places like Loch Lomond or Eilean Donan. But the most treasured memories of a country are usually more personal discoveries. Here are the favourite spots of Rough Guides' authors, who travelled to every corner of the Highlands and Islands in the cause of researching the Guide.

Seafood From the waterfront stalls in Oban (see page 67) to the gourmet restaurants on Skye (see page 278), the Highlands and Islands offer some of the finest and freshest seafood in Britain.

Island-hopping in the Small Isles If there's an easier free-wheelin' mini-adventure than a few days' bouncing between the Small Isles (see page 284), they're keeping it quiet.

Pitch perfect Only in Scotland can adventurous campers head out into Great Britain's wilds then legally pitch a tent (see page 224) in the grandest scenery.

Foula The most isolated island community in the UK, Foula (see page 389) sits 14 miles off the coast of Shetland, with thirty inhabitants, no shop, and some of the largest cliffs in the country.

WILD CAMPING NEAR ULLAPOOL
PLANE TO NORTH RONALDSAY

Flying visit The flight in an eight-seater plane to North Ronaldsay (see page 363) alone is worth it, even without a night at the ecofriendly bird observatory and the chance to visit a lighthouse or meet weavers and seaweed-eating sheep.

St Kilda The journey out by RIB is not cheap and it can be bouncy, but fifty miles off the Western Isles, St Kilda (see page 307) has the UK's biggest bird colony on its highest sea stacks.

North Coast 500 Touted as "Scotland's answer to Route 66", this truly unforgettable circular road trip (see page 216) ventures into the most remote and starkly beautiful corners of the Highlands.

Beaver Trial, Knapdale Beavers are back after 400 years' absence, and this reintroduction project at Knapdale (see page 98) offers a rare opportunity to see the creatures in the wild – if the lodges are startling, the 60ft-long dam is a feat of engineering.

> Our author recommendations don't end here. We've flagged up our favourite places – a perfectly sited hotel, an atmospheric café, a special restaurant – throughout the Guide, highlighted with the ★ symbol.

25

things not to miss

It's not possible to see everything that the Scottish Highlands and Islands have to offer in one trip – and we don't suggest you try. All entries are colour-coded and have a page reference to take you straight into the Guide, where you can find out more.

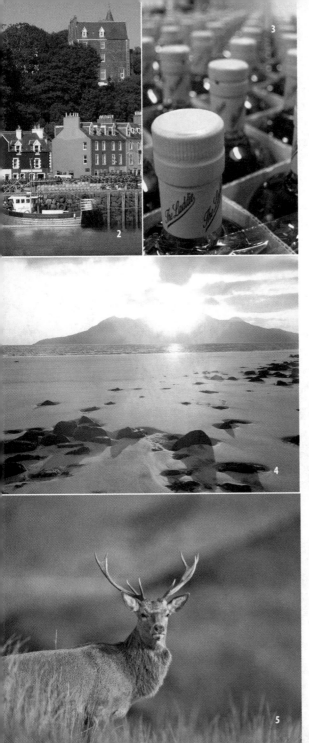

1 GLEN COE
See page 191
Scotland's most spectacular glen puts Munro summits, glacial valleys and clear waterfalls within day-trip distance of Fort William. A glorious spot for hiking, or simply absorbing the moody, poignant atmosphere.

2 TOBERMORY
See page 73
A riot of colour, Mull's chief town is the quintessential Scottish fishing port; easily the most attractive on the west coast of Scotland.

3 WHISKY ON ISLAY
See page 114
There's definitely something in the water that makes this Hebridean island home to eight distilleries. After taking a tour, you can try a wee dram (or two) for yourself.

4 EIGG
See page 287
Perfect example of a tiny Hebridean island, with a golden beach to stroll on, a hill to climb and gorgeous views across to its neighbour, Rùm.

5 ASSYNT
See page 241
Golden eagles, more deer than cows and sugarloaf mountains with poetic names like Suilven – nowhere in the Highlands is more spectacular or more exhilaratingly remote.

6 GOLF

See page 42

Anyone with half an interest in the sport shouldn't leave Scotland without taking a round, and few courses are more beautiful (or more challenging) than Machrihanish Dunes in Kintyre.

7 UP HELLY-AA

See page 374

Pack your thermals and head to Shetland in January for this spectacular Viking fire festival.

8 WEST HIGHLAND RAILWAY

See page 220

From Glasgow to Mallaig, this is one of the great railway journeys of the world – 264 miles of ever-more spectacular scenery, with steam trains in summer.

9 CALLANISH, LEWIS

See page 305

Prehistoric standing stones beside a serene loch – this Western Isles site feels steeped in ancient mystery.

10 THE CAIRNGORM MOUNTAINS

See page 164

Beguiling natural splendour, exceptional wildlife and terrific outdoor activities.

11 KNOYDART PENINSULA
See page 223
No matter whether you arrive by boat or on foot, the sense of dropping off the radar is the same in Britain's last great wilderness.

12 CALEDONIAN FOREST
See page 158
Surviving pockets of the once-great ancient Highland forest harbour magic as much as red squirrels.

13 JARLSHOF, SHETLAND
See page 383
An exceptional archeological site, taking in Iron Age, Bronze Age, Pictish, Viking and medieval remains.

14 SOUTH HARRIS BEACHES
See page 312
Take your pick of deserted golden beaches in South Harris, best of all stunning Luskentyre.

15 THE CUILLIN, SKYE
See page 274
The most spectacular mountain range on the west coast, for viewing or climbing.

13

14

15

21

22

23

21 IONA
See page 82
There's an ancient abbey and glorious beaches at the north of this beautiful island.

22 STAFFA AND THE TRESHNISH ISLES
See pages 78 and 79
The basalt columns of Staffa's Fingal's Cave and puffins on the Isle of Lunga combine to make this a superb trip.

23 ARRAN
See page 105
The most accessible of the islands, Arran offers fascinating geology, and superb walking and cycling.

24 MAESHOWE, ORKNEY
See page 334
Amazingly preserved, this five-thousand-year-old burial chamber also contains lewd Viking graffiti.

25 HIGHLAND GAMES
See page 37
Part summer sports day, part traditional gathering, these entertaining get-togethers are well worth a diversion, wherever you find one in the Highlands.

Itineraries

The following itineraries will help you to explore the drama and variety of the Highlands and Islands. Whether you're after a fortnight of island-hopping and empty beaches off the western coast, a cultural break spanning thousands of years of history, or want to discover whales and ospreys, our themed suggestions offer an insight into Scotland's stunning natural and historic wonders. These trips also give a flavour of what the region has to offer and what we can plan and book for you at www.roughguides.com/trips.

TWO WEEKS ON THE ISLANDS

While Orkney and Shetland deserve a dedicated trip, the west coast islands seem tailor-made to explore by ferry. Who needs Greece?

❶ **Mull** Embark from one of the Highlands' loveliest fishing ports, Tobermory, for one of its best wildlife adventures – whale-watching trips. See page 73

❷ **Iona** A tiny island just off Mull but almost another world, its atmosphere steeped in millennia is a pilgrimage destination. See page 82

❸ **Barra** A pipsqueak among the Western Isles whose azure seas, white beaches, mountains and sense of utter escapism deliver a concentrated dose of Hebridean magic. See page 321

❹ **The Uists** Trout-fishing doesn't get much more fun than in the half-drowned lochs of North Uist. See page 314

❺ **Lewis and Harris** The conjoined twins of the Hebrides have astonishing beaches like Luskentyre, mysterious standing stones at Callanish and a time warp back a century in the restored village of Garenin. See pages 295 and 308

❻ **Skye** Skip back to Skye to tackle the Cuillin ridge or discover Loch Coruisk by boat. Either way, your reward is fine accommodation and finer food. See page 268

❼ **Small Isles** So, what do you feel like doing today: sampling genuine island life on Eigg; discovering a barmy baronial manor on Rùm; or spotting wildlife on a stroll around tiny Muck? See page 284

WILDLIFE WONDERS

There's more here than the world's second-largest seal population and sheep galore. Here's our pick of the best Scottish animal encounters to tick off on a two-week adventure.

❶ **Beavers at Knapdale** Take the Beaver Detective Trail to see the lodges and dams of a population reintroduced in 2009. Best seasons: late spring, early summer. See page 98

Create your own itinerary with Rough Guides. Whether you're after adventure or a family-friendly holiday, we have a trip for you, with all the activities you enjoy doing and the sights you want to see. All our trips are devised by local experts who get the most out of the destination. Visit **www.roughguides.com/trips** to chat with one of our travel agents.

❷ Whales and puffins off Mull One island, two of the Highlands' finest wildlife encounters: whales on trips from Tobermory and Scotland's favourite seabird on cruises to the Treshnish Isles. Best seasons: spring, summer. See pages 74 and 79

❸ Storm petrels on Mousa, Shetland There are arctic terns, black guillemots, skuas, shags, ringed plovers and seals on Mousa. But no sight is more spectacular than 12,000 storm petrels returning at dusk to a 2000-year-old broch. Best season: summer. See page 381

❹ Dolphins in Moray Firth The world's most northerly pod of bottlenose dolphins – around two hundred strong – and groups of porpoises can be seen from a viewing point or boat on the Moray Firth. Best seasons: spring, summer. See page 206

❺ Ospreys and reindeer in the Cairngorms The must-see on any birdwatcher's checklist migrates from West Africa to breed on Loch Garten, and Britain's only herd of reindeer lives on the surrounding hills. See page 164

❻ Salmon at Pitlochry Not as spectacular as the salmon that leap up the Falls of Shin, but more fish climb the famous fish ladder at Pitlochry. Best seasons: summer, autumn. See page 143

HERITAGE IN THE HIGHLANDS

Running the gamut from remote islands to lavish estates, this route showcases the region's varied history.

❶ Mount Stuart A no-expense-spared slice of neo-Gothic baronial splendour. See page 60

❷ Iona This isolated island has been a centre of Christian culture since the sixth century. See page 82

❸ The Road to the Isles Follow in the footsteps of Bonnie Prince Charlie from Glenfinnan, or let the Jacobite steam train take the strain from Fort William to Mallaig. See page 219

❹ Kinloch Castle, Rùm A pile contemporary with Mount Stuart yet fabulously over the top, its eccentric (if slightly dilapidated) interiors capture the decadence of Edwardian shooting estates. See page 286

- ·········· TWO WEEKS ON THE ISLANDS
- ·········· WILDLIFE WONDERS
- ·········· HERITAGE IN THE HIGHLANDS

ATLANTIC

OCEAN

NORTH

SEA

NORTHERN
IRELAND

ENGLAND

NORTHERN TIP, JOHN O'GROATS

Basics

Getting there

There are numerous ways of getting to the Scottish Highlands and Islands. For most, the quickest, easiest and cheapest way is by plane. Inverness is an obvious gateway for much of the region, but you'll get a wider selection of flights to Scotland's three main international airports – Glasgow, Edinburgh and Aberdeen – each of which is only a short hop from most areas of interest.

With most airlines nowadays, how much you pay depends on how far in advance you book and how much demand there is during that period – generally speaking, the earlier you book, the cheaper the prices. That said, it's worth looking out for sales, which often start 10–12 weeks before the departure date.

If you're coming from elsewhere in Britain, from Ireland or even northwest Europe, you can reach Scotland easily enough by **train**, **bus** or **ferry** – it probably won't work out cheaper or faster than flying, but it's undoubtedly better for the environment.

From England and Wales

If you're heading out to the Highlands and Islands from **England** or **Wales**, flying is the quickest way to travel. If your ultimate destination is Argyll, Loch Lomond or the Hebrides, Glasgow is the natural gateway; for Perthshire and the Cairngorms, Edinburgh or Glasgow are good; for anywhere further north, Inverness is the best hub. **Airfares** are most competitive on popular routes such as London or Birmingham to Edinburgh and Glasgow, which can cost as little as £40 return (journey time around 1hr). Once you add on the cost of transport to the airport and flying with luggage (many budget airlines charge for all but the smallest cabin bags), the savings on the same journey overland are often minimal.

Flying with airlines such as British Airways (W brit-ishairways.com), Ryanair (W ryanair.com) and easyJet (W easyjet.com) may be quick, but coach and train fares can be pretty competitive. If you book the London–Glasgow/Edinburgh and Glasgow/Edinburgh–Inverness legs separately, return **train** fares can cost as little as £75 (journey time from 8hr), with the very cheapest tickets going on sale twelve weeks in advance. A more flexible or last-minute fare will cost two or three times that amount. Another option is the overnight **Caledonian Sleeper** (W sleeper.scot) from London Euston (daily except Sat; journey time to Inverness around 11hr); again, if you book in advance, single overnight fares cost around £50 for a reclining seat, with no saving on return fares.

The **coach** takes much longer than the train (around 11hr 30min–13hr) but costs less, with a London or Birmingham to Inverness overnight return starting for as little as £29 return.

From Ireland

Travel from Ireland is quickest by plane, with **airfares** from either Belfast or Dublin to Glasgow from as little as €45 return. Try Aer Lingus (W aerlingus.com) and Ryanair (W ryanair.com), both based in Ireland. There are good **ferry** links with Northern Ireland via Cairnryan, near Stranraer, with P&O operating up to seven sea crossings daily from Larne (2hr; single passenger without car from £27; with car from £84), and Stena Line operating up to six services daily from Belfast (2hr 15min; single passenger without car from £27; with car from £89).

From the US and Canada

If you fly nonstop to Scotland from **North America**, you'll arrive in either Glasgow or Edinburgh. The majority of cheap fares, however, route through Amsterdam, London, Manchester, Dublin or Paris. To reach any other Scottish airport, you'll definitely need to go via London, Glasgow or Edinburgh.

Figure on six to seven hours' flight time nonstop from the east coast to Glasgow, or seven hours to London plus an extra hour and a quarter from London to Glasgow or Edinburgh (not including stopover time). Add three or four hours more for travel from the west coast.

United (W united.com) flies direct from Newark Liberty International Airport in New York to Glasgow,

---

A BETTER KIND OF TRAVEL

At Rough Guides we are passionately committed to travel. We believe it helps us understand the world we live in and the people we share it with – and of course tourism is vital to many developing economies. But the scale of modern tourism has also damaged some places irreparably, and climate change is accelerated by most forms of transport, especially flying. We encourage all our authors to consider the carbon footprint of the journeys they make in the course of researching our guides.

with return fares (including taxes) from around $950. Air Canada (W aircanada.com) has direct flights to Edinburgh from Toronto. Return fares for nonstop flights (including taxes) cost around CAN$800.

From Australia and New Zealand

Flight time from **Australia** and **New Zealand** to Scotland is at least 22 hours. There's a wide variety of routes, with those touching down in Southeast Asia the quickest and cheapest on average. To reach Scotland, you usually have to change planes either in London – the most popular choice – or in another European gateway such as Paris or Amsterdam. Given the length of the journey involved, you might be better off including a night's **stopover** in your itinerary.

The cheapest scheduled flights to London are usually to be found on one of the Asian airlines, such as Malaysia Airlines (W malaysiaairlines.com) or Thai Airways (W thaiairways.com). Average **return fares** (including taxes) from eastern cities to London are Aus$1500–2000. Fares from Perth or Darwin cost around Aus$100 less. Return fares from Auckland to London range between NZ$2000 and NZ$3000 depending on the season, route and carrier.

From South Africa

There are no direct flights from **South Africa** to Scotland, so you must change planes en route. The quickest and cheapest route to take is via London, with flight time around eleven hours, usually overnight. **Return fares** from Cape Town to London are around ZAR10,000; try British Airways (W britishairways.com), South African Airways (W flysaa.com) or Virgin Atlantic (W virginatlantic.com). You'll save money if you buy the next leg of your journey to Scotland separately, through one of the budget airlines.

From mainland Europe

Ferries run by DFDS Seaways go overnight from Ijmuiden, near Amsterdam, to Newcastle (daily; 16–17hr), less than an hour's drive south of the Scottish border. High-season return fares start at around €500, for a passenger with a car and an overnight berth. The very useful Direct Ferries website (W directferries. co.uk) gives you the latest information on crossings and allows you to compare all the options. A much quicker (and usually cheaper) alternative is to fly with one of Europe's big budget carriers, such as easyJet (W easyjet.com), Ryanair (W ryanair.com) and Norwegian (W norwegian.com).

RAIL AND BUS CONTACTS

Caledonian Sleeper W sleeper.scot. Sleeper train to Glasgow, Edinburgh, Aberdeen, Inverness and Fort William.

Man in Seat 61 W seat61.com. The best train information website on the internet.

National Express T 08717 818181, W nationalexpress.com. Coaches to Scotland.

ScotRail W scotrail.co.uk. Scotland's principal domestic operator, with full route and timetable info.

Trainline W trainline.com. The best site for cheap tickets, with popular mobile app.

Traveline Scotland W travelinescotland.com. Excellent Scotland-wide journey planner, connected to the latest bus and train timetables.

Virgin W virgintrains.co.uk. Main operator from London to Scotland on both the East and West Coast routes.

FERRY COMPANIES

DFDS Seaways UK T 0871 522 9955, International T +44 330 333 0245, W dfdsseaways.co.uk.

P&O Ferries UK T 0800 130 0030, Ireland T +353 1 686 9467, W poferries.com.

Stena Line UK T 0844 770 7070, W stenaline.co.uk.

Getting around

There's no getting away from the fact that getting around the Highlands and Islands is a time-consuming business: off the main routes, public transport services are few and far between, particularly in more remote parts of Argyll, the Highland region and the Islands. With careful planning, however, practically everywhere is accessible and you'll have no trouble getting to the main tourist destinations. And in most parts of Scotland, especially if you take the scenic back roads, the low level of traffic makes driving wonderfully stress free.

By train

Scotland has a modest **rail network**, at its densest in the central belt, skeletal in the Highlands and Borders, and nonexistent in the Islands. ScotRail runs the majority of train services, reaching all the major towns, sometimes on lines rated among the great scenic routes of the world.

You can buy train **tickets** at most stations, but if the ticket office is closed, or the automatic machine isn't working, you may buy your ticket on board from the inspector using cash or a credit card. Those eligible for a national rail pass (W railcard.co.uk; £30) can

MINIBUS TOURS

Minibus tours that operate out of Edinburgh (and Glasgow) and head off into the Highlands are popular with backpackers who want a quick taste of Scotland. Aimed at the youth market, they adopt an upbeat and irreverent approach to sightseeing, as well as offering a good opportunity to get to know fellow travellers.

The current leading operator, **Haggis** (☎01315 579393, ⓦhaggisadventures.com), has bright yellow minibuses setting off daily on whistle-stop tours lasting between one and ten days, in the company of a live-wire guide. A three-day trip from Edinburgh to Skye via Loch Ness costs £135 (food and accommodation not included).

Several other companies offer similar packages, including **Macbackpackers** (☎01315 589900, ⓦmacbackpackers.com), which runs tours linking up their own hostels round the country. The popular **Rabbie's** tours (☎01312 263133, ⓦrabbies.com) don't aim squarely at the backpacker market and have a mellower outlook.

obtain discounted tickets, with up to a third off most fares. These include the **16–25 Railcard**, for full-time students and those aged between 16 and 25; the **26–30 Railcard**, the **Two Together Railcard** for two named people aged over 16 travelling together; the **Senior Railcard** for people over 60; and the **Family & Friends Railcard** which entitles up to four adults and up to four children to travel together. There's also the Club 50 (£15) scheme, offering discounted travel for those aged fifty and over.

In addition, ScotRail offers several regional passes. The most flexible is the **Spirit of Scotland Travelpass**, which gives unlimited train travel within Scotland. It's also valid on all CalMac ferries and on various buses in the remoter regions. The pass costs £149 for four days' travel in an eight-day period, or £189 for eight days' travel in a fifteen-day period. The **Highland Rover** allows unlimited train travel within the Highlands and costs £89 for four out of eight consecutive days.

On most ScotRail routes **bicycles** are carried free, but since there are only between two and six bike spaces available, it's a good idea to reserve ahead, and this is a requirement on longer journeys.

By coach and bus

The main centres of the Highlands are served by a few long-distance bus services, known across Britain as **coaches**. Scotland's national operator is **Scottish Citylink** (☎08712 663333, ⓦcitylink.co.uk). On the whole, coaches are cheaper than trains and, as a result, are very popular, so for longer journeys it's advisable to book ahead.

There are various **discounts** on offer for those with children, those under 26 or over 60, and full-time students (contact Scottish Citylink for more details), and you can also buy an **Explorer Pass**, which gives unlimited travel throughout Scotland (£45/3 days out of 5; £74/5 days out of 10; £99/8 days out of 16).

Local bus services are run by a bewildering array of companies, many of which change routes and timetables frequently. Local tourist offices can provide free timetables or you can contact **Traveline Scotland** (☎0871 200 2233, ⓦtravelinescotland.com), which provides a reliable service both online and by phone. There is also a free app available for download.

By car

In order to **drive** in Scotland you need a current full driving licence. If you're bringing your own vehicle into the country you should also carry your vehicle registration, ownership and insurance documents at all times. In Scotland, as in the rest of the UK, you **drive on the left**. Speed limits are 20–40mph in built-up areas, 70mph on motorways and dual carriageways (freeways) and 60mph on most other roads. As a rule, assume that in any area with street lighting the limit is 30mph.

In the Highlands and Islands, there are still plenty of **single-track roads** with passing places; in addition to allowing oncoming traffic to pass at these points, you should also let cars behind you overtake. These roads can be frustrating, but take care and stay alert for vehicles coming in the opposite direction, which may have been hidden by bends or dips in the road. In more remote regions, the roads are dotted with sheep, which are entirely oblivious to cars, so slow down and edge your way past; should you kill or injure one, it is your duty to inform the local farmer.

The AA (☎08008 87766, ⓦtheaa.com), RAC (☎0330 2000 999, ⓦrac.co.uk) and Green Flag (☎0800 400600, ⓦgreenflag.com) all operate 24-hour **emergency breakdown** services. You may be entitled to free assistance through a reciprocal arrangement with a motoring organization in your home country. If not, you can make use of these emergency services by joining at the roadside, but you will incur a hefty surcharge. In remote areas, you may have a long wait for assistance.

Be aware that a new drink driving limit set in 2014 (50 milligrams of alcohol per 100 millilitres of blood), bringing Scotland in line with much of Europe, means that even one pint of beer or glass of wine could leave you on the wrong side of the law.

Car rental

Car rental in Scotland is cheaper than it used to be thanks to online advance deals with comparison sites such as Ⓦ holidayautos.com. The most economical cars can be rented for as little as £25–30 a day or £110 a week, though walk-in prices will be a lot more expensive. The major chains are confined mostly to the big cities, so it may be cheaper to use small **local agencies** – we've highlighted some in the Guide. With all rentals it's worth checking the terms and conditions carefully; some rentals only allow you to drive a limited number of miles before paying extra.

Automatics are rare at the lower end of the price scale – if you want one, you should book well ahead. **Campervans** are another option, offering a wonderful sense of freedom and of course allowing you to save money on accommodation; in high season rates start at around £650 a week for a VW Campervan and £850 for a 4-berth campervan. One excellent company is Bunk Campers (Ⓦ bunkcampers.com), who have depots in Edinburgh, Coventry, the Midlands (Birmingham/Leeds) and London Heathrow). Few companies will rent to drivers with less than one year's experience and most will only rent to people over 21 or 25 and under 70 or 75 years of age.

Though **fuel** in the Highlands and Islands has always been more expensive than elsewhere in Scotland, and especially so over the last decade, the current rock-bottom oil price means much cheaper prices at the pump, for now. The recent expansion of a government subsidy scheme has also helped to bring prices more in line with the rest of the country. At the time of writing, petrol (gasoline) and diesel can be found for around £1.20 per litre, though with such a volatile market prices are likely to continue fluctuating wildly.

By ferry

Scotland has more than sixty inhabited islands, and nearly fifty of them have scheduled **ferry** links. Most ferries carry cars and vans, and, if you're driving, the vast majority can – and should – be booked in advance; there's usually a window of four to six months. There's no need to book if you're travelling on foot; simply buy your ticket at the port office or on board.

Caledonian MacBrayne aka CalMac has a virtual monopoly on services on the River Clyde and to the Hebrides, sailing to 22 islands and 4 peninsulas. They aren't quick – no catamarans or fast ferries – but with the recent introduction of the Scottish Government-sponsored RET (Road Equivalent Tariff) scheme, fares have been slashed. The ferry from Mallaig to Skye, for example, now costs £3 for foot passengers and £9.95 for cars. If you're taking more than one ferry, or aiming for a specific island grouping, you can also make significant savings with an **Island Hopscotch** ticket (there are 30 different variations to choose between). Given the notoriously fickle west coast weather, especially in winter, it's probably worth downloading the CalMac Service Status app.

Car ferries to **Orkney and Shetland** are run by NorthLink Ferries. Pentland Ferries also run a car ferry to Orkney, and John O'Groats Ferries run a summer-only passenger service to Orkney. The various Orkney islands are linked to each other by Orkney Ferries; Shetland's inter-island ferries are mostly council-run so the local tourist board (Ⓦ shetland.gov.uk/ferries) is your best bet for information. There are also numerous **small operators** round the Scottish coast that run fast RIB taxi services, day-excursion trips, and even the odd scheduled service; their contact details are given in the relevant chapters of this Guide.

FERRY COMPANIES

CalMac ☎ 08000 665000, Ⓦ calmac.co.uk
John O'Groats Ferries ☎ 01955 611353, Ⓦ jogferry.co.uk
NorthLink Ferries ☎ 08456 000449, Ⓦ northlinkferries.co.uk
Orkney Ferries ☎ 01856 872044, Ⓦ orkneyferries.co.uk
Pentland Ferries ☎ 08006 888998, Ⓦ pentlandferries.co.uk

By plane

Aside from the international airport at Inverness, there are numerous minor **airports** around the Scottish Highlands and Islands, some of which are little more than gravel airstrips. Airfares fluctuate enormously depending on demand but are generally quite expensive – if you book early enough you can fly from Glasgow to Islay for £54 one way, but leave it to the last minute and it could cost you more than twice that. Most flights within Scotland are operated by **Loganair** (Ⓦ loganair.co.uk). For inter-island flights in Shetland, you need to book direct through **Airtask** (☎ 01595 840246, Ⓦ airtask.com/shetland-islands-inter-island-service). Competition emerges from time to time, with **Eastern Airways** (Ⓦ easternairways.com) currently offering flights from Aberdeen to Stornoway and Wick.

Accommodation

In common with the rest of Britain, accommodation in the Highlands and Islands is fairly expensive. Budget travellers are well catered for, however, with numerous hostels, and those with money to spend will relish the more expensive country-house hotels. In the middle ground, however, the standard of many B&Bs, guesthouses and hotels can be disappointing. Welcoming, comfortable, well-run places do, of course, exist in all parts of the country – and you'll find the best ones listed in this Guide.

Star ratings

VisitScotland, the country's tourist board, operates a system for grading accommodation, which is updated annually. However, not every establishment participates, and you shouldn't assume that a particular B&B is no good simply because it's not on VisitScotland's lists. The tourist board uses star awards, from one to five, which are supposed to reflect the quality of welcome, service and hospitality – though it's pretty clear that places without en-suite toilets, a TV in every room, matching fabrics or packets of shortbread on the sideboard are likely to be marked down.

Booking accommodation

If you decide not to book online, most **tourist offices** will help you find accommodation and **book a room** directly, for which they normally charge a small fee. If you take advantage of this service, it's worth being clear as to what kind of place you'd prefer, as the tourist office quite often selects something quite randomly across the whole range of their membership. Bear in mind, too, that outside the main towns and cities many places are only open for the **tourist season** (Easter to Oct): you'll always find somewhere to stay outside this period, but the choice may be limited.

Hotels

Hotels come in all shapes and sizes. At the upper end of the market, they can be huge country houses and converted castles offering a very exclusive and opulent experience. Most will have a licensed bar and offer both breakfast and dinner, and often lunch as well. In the cities the increasing prevalence of modern budget hotels run by national (and international) chains may not win any prizes for aesthetics or variety, but they

ACCOMMODATION ALTERNATIVES

Useful websites that provide alternatives to standard hotel and hostel accommodation.
Airbnb Ⓦ airbnb.co.uk.
Couchsurfing Ⓦ couchsurfing.com.
onefinestay Ⓦ onefinestay.com.
Vacation Rentals by Owner Ⓦ vrbo.com.

are competitively priced and for the most part meet criteria for clean, smart, serviceable accommodation. Also making a bit of a comeback are inns (in other words, pubs), or their modern equivalent, "restaurants with rooms". These will often have only a handful of rooms, but their emphasis on creating an all-round convivial atmosphere, as well as serving top-quality food, often makes them worth seeking out.

Guesthouses and B&Bs

Guesthouses and B&Bs offer the widest and most diverse range of accommodation. VisitScotland uses the term "guesthouse" for a commercial venture that has four or more rooms, at least some of which are en suite, reserving "B&B" for a predominantly private family home that has only a few rooms to let. In reality, however, most places offer en-suite facilities, and the different names often reflect the pretensions of the owners and the cost of the rooms more than differences in service: in general, guesthouses cost more than B&Bs.

A surprising number of guesthouses and B&Bs still have decor that consists of heavy chintz and floral designs, but the location, and the chance to get an insight into the local way of life, can be some compensation. Many B&Bs, even the pricier ones, have only a few rooms, so **advance booking** is recommended, especially in the Islands.

Hostels

There's an ever-increasing number of **hostels** in the Highlands and Islands to cater for travellers – youthful or otherwise – who are unable or unwilling to pay the rates charged by hotels, guesthouses and B&Bs. Most hostels are clean and comfortable, sometimes offering doubles and even singles as well as dormitory accommodation. Others concentrate more on keeping the price as low as possible, simply providing a roof over your head and a few basic facilities. Whatever type of hostel you stay in, expect to pay £10–22 per night.

Hostelling Scotland (Ⓣ 0345 293 7373; Ⓦ hostellingscotland.org.uk) – formerly The Scottish Youth

Hostels Association – run the longest-established hostels in the Highlands and Islands. While these places sometimes occupy handsome buildings, many retain an institutionalized air. Bunk-bed accommodation in single-sex dormitories, lights out before midnight and no smoking/no alcohol policies are the norm outside the big cities. Breakfast is not normally included in the price, though most hostels have self-catering facilities.

If you're not a **member** of one of the hostelling organizations affiliated to **Hostelling International** (HI), you can pay your £15 joining fee (£6/under-25s) at most hostels. **Advance booking** is recommended, and essential at Easter, Christmas and from May to August. You can book online, in person or by phone.

The **Gatliff Hebridean Hostels Trust** or GHHT (Ⓦgatliff.org.uk) is allied to the SYHA and rents out very simple croft accommodation in the Western Isles. Accommodation is basic, and you can't book ahead, but it's unlikely you'll be turned away. Elsewhere in the Highlands and Islands, these places tend to be known as **bothies** or bunkhouses, and are usually independently run. In Shetland, **camping böds**, operated by the Shetland Amenity Trust (Ⓦcamping-bods.co.uk), offer similarly plain accommodation: you need all your usual camping equipment to stay at one (except, of course, a tent). For more details about Gatliff hostels and camping böds, see the relevant chapters in the Guide.

There are also loads of **independent hostels** across the Highlands and Islands. These are usually laidback places with no membership, fewer rules, mixed dorms and no curfew. You can find most of them in the annually updated *Independent Hostel Guide* (Ⓦindependenthostels.co.uk). Many of them are also affiliated to Scottish Independent Hostels (Ⓦhostel-scotland.co.uk), which has a programme of inspection and lists members in the *SIH Hostel Guide*, available free online.

Camping

There are hundreds of **caravan and camping parks** around the Highlands and Islands, most of which are open from April to October. The majority of sites

charge about £10–15 for two people with a car to pitch a tent, and are usually well equipped, with shops, a restaurant, a bar and, occasionally, sports facilities. Most of these, however, are aimed principally at caravans, trailers and motorhomes, and generally don't offer the tranquil atmosphere and independence that those travelling with just a tent are seeking.

That said, peaceful and **informal sites** do exist, and are described throughout this Guide, though they are few and far between. Many **hostels** allow camping, and farmers will usually let folk camp on their land for free or for a nominal sum. In this Guide, we've listed the price for a pitch (ie one tent for two people, plus a car) wherever possible; where campsites charge per person, we've listed prices in that format instead.

Scotland's relaxed land access laws allow **wild camping** in open country. The basic rule is "leave no trace", but for a guide to good practice, visit Ⓦoutdooraccess-scotland.scot.

The great majority of **caravans** are permanently moored nose to tail in the vicinity of some of Scotland's finest scenery; others are positioned singly in back gardens or amid farmland. Some can be booked for self-catering, and with prices starting at around £100 a week, this can work out as one of the cheapest options if you're travelling with kids in tow.

If you're planning to do a lot of camping at official camping and caravanning sites, it might be worthwhile joining the **Camping and Caravanning Club** (Ⓦcampingandcaravanningclub.co.uk). Membership costs £40 for the digital option and £46 for paper (with hard copies of the monthly magazine and campsite directory) if paying by direct debit entitling you to up to thirty percent discount at CCC sites. Those coming from abroad can get the same benefits by buying an international camping carnet, available from home motoring organizations or a CCC equivalent.

Self-catering

A huge proportion of visitors to the Highlands and Islands opt for **self-catering**, booking a cottage or apartment for a week and often saving themselves a considerable amount of money by doing so. In most cases, the minimum period of rental is a week, and therefore this isn't a valid option if you're aiming to tour round the country, though increasingly, with the rise of websites like Ⓦairbnb.co.uk, owners are becoming more flexible. The least you can expect to pay in the high season is around £250 per week for a place sleeping four, but something special, or somewhere in a popular tourist area, might cost £500 or more. Such is the number and variety of self-catering places on offer that we've mentioned very few in the Guide.

---

5 CAMPSITES NOT TO MISS

Blair Castle Caravan Park Blair Atholl. See page 146.

Camusdarach Campsite Camusdarach. See page 221.

Fidden Farm Campsite Fionnphort. See page 81.

Glenbrittle Campsite Glenbrittle. See page 275.

Red Squirrel Glen Coe. See page 193.

A good source of information is **VisitScotland**'s self-catering website (ⓦ visitscotland.com/accommodation/self-catering), updated frequently and listing thousands of properties. Alternatively, you could try one of the websites listed below.

SELF-CATERING AGENCIES

Cottages and Castles ☎ 01738 451610, ⓦ cottages-and-castles.co.uk. A range of self-catering properties, mostly in mainland Scotland.

Cottages ☎ 03454 268 0763, ⓦ cottages.com. Hundreds of reasonably priced properties all over Scotland.

Landmark Trust ☎ 01628 825925, ⓦ landmarktrust.org.uk. A very select number of historical properties, often in prime locations.

LHH ☎ 01381 610496, ⓦ lhhscotland.com. Attractive homes across Scotland, including mansions, castles and villas.

Mackay's Holidays ☎ 01315 501180, ⓦ mackaysholidays.com. A whole range of properties in every corner of mainland Scotland (plus Skye and Orkney), from chalets and town apartments to remote stone-built cottages.

National Trust for Scotland ☎ 01314 580200, ⓦ nts.org.uk. The NTS lets around forty of its converted historic cottages and houses, and also offers working conservation holidays.

Scottish Country Cottages ☎ 03452 680801, ⓦ scottish-country-cottages.co.uk. Superior cottages with lots of character, scattered across the Scottish mainland plus some of the Inner Hebrides.

Unique Cottages ☎ 01835 822277, ⓦ unique-cottages.co.uk. Carefully selected cottages across mainland Scotland, plus a few in the Hebrides and Orkney.

Food and drink

While Scotland isn't exactly known for its culinary heritage, the country's eating habits are changing, and from the cities to some of the furthest islands, you can often eat extremely well, with a strong emphasis on fresh, local and organic produce. The remoteness of parts of the Highlands and Islands will inevitably restrict your eating and drinking choices. It's often a good idea to plan meal locations ahead as you might find serving times restrictive or popular restaurants booked out, particularly in summer. Stocking up on picnic food from a good deli is also worthwhile.

Scottish **fish and shellfish** is the envy of Europe, with a vast array of different types of fish, prawns, lobsters, mussels, oysters, crabs and scallops found around the extensive coastline. The prevalence of fish-farming, now a significant industry in the Highlands and Islands, means that the once-treasured salmon is now widespread and relatively inexpensive. Both salmon and trout, another commonly farmed fish, are frequently served cold with bread and butter.

Scottish-reared **beef** is often delicious, especially the Aberdeen Angus breed, though Highland cattle are also rated for their depth of flavour. **Venison**, the meat of the red deer, is also popular – low in cholesterol and very tasty, it's served roasted or in casseroles, and is often cooked with juniper and red wine. Other forms of **game** include grouse, which when cooked properly is strong, dark and succulent; pheasant, a lighter meat; and the less commonly served, but still tasty, pigeon and rabbit.

In rural Scotland, attitudes towards **vegetarianism** are still some way behind the big cities. While almost all pubs and restaurants will have at least one or two vegetarian options on their menus, they're too often lazily predictable and overpriced.

Breakfast

In most hotels and B&Bs you'll be offered a **Scottish breakfast**, similar to its English counterpart of sausage, bacon and egg, but typically with the addition of black pudding (blood sausage) and potato scones. Porridge is another likely option, as is fish in the form of kippers, smoked haddock or even kedgeree. Scotland's staple drink, like England's, is **tea**, drunk strong and with milk, though **coffee** is just as readily available everywhere. However, while smart coffee shops are now a familiar feature in larger towns, execrable versions of espresso and cappuccino, as well as instant coffee, are still all too familiar.

Lunches and snacks

The most common lunchtime fare in Scotland remains the **sandwich**. A bowl or cup of hearty **soup** is a typical accompaniment, particularly in winter. A **pub lunch** is often an attractive alternative. Bar menus generally have standard, filling but unambitious options including soup, sandwiches, scampi and chips, or steak pie and chips, with vegetarians suffering from a paucity of choice. That said, some bar food is freshly prepared and filling, equalling the à la carte dishes served in the adjacent hotel restaurant. Pubs or hotel bars are among the cheapest options when it comes to eating out – in the smallest villages, these might be your only option.

Restaurants are often, though not always, open at lunchtimes, when they tend to be less busy and generally offer a shorter menu compared with their evening service: this can make for a more pleasant and less expensive experience. For morning or afternoon snacks, as well as light lunches, **tearooms**

are a common feature where you will often find decent home baking.

As for **fast food**, chip shops, or chippies, abound – the best are often found in coastal towns within sight of the fishing boats. Deep-fried battered fish is the standard choice – when served with chips it's known as a "fish supper", even if eaten at lunchtime – though everything from hamburgers to haggis suppers is normally on offer, all deep-fried, of course. Scotland is even credited with inventing the **deep-fried Mars bar**, the definitive badge of a nation with the worst heart disease statistics in Western Europe. For alternative fast food, major towns feature all the usual pizza, burger and baked potato outlets, as well as Chinese, Mexican and Indian takeaways.

Evening meals

There's no doubt that, as with the rest of the UK, eating out in the Highlands and Islands is expensive. Our restaurant listings include a mix of high-quality and budget establishments. Wine in restaurants is marked up strongly, so you'll often pay £15 for a bottle selling for £5 in the shops; house wines generally start around the £10 mark.

If you're travelling in more remote parts of the Highlands and Islands, or staying at a B&B or guest-house in the countryside, ask advice about nearby options for your **evening meal**. Many B&Bs and guesthouses will cook you dinner, but you must book ahead and indicate any dietary requirements.

As for **restaurants**, standards vary enormously, but independent restaurants using high-quality local produce are now found all over the region. Less predictable are hotel restaurants, many of which serve non-residents. Some can be very ordinary despite the descriptions on the a la carte menu. You could easily end up paying £30–40 a head for a meal with wine.

In Inverness and some of the larger towns on the mainland, you'll find a wide range of **international** cuisines including Japanese, Thai, Caribbean and Turkish, as well as the more common Indian, Chinese and Italian establishments.

Among traditional **desserts**, "clootie dumpling" is a sweet, stodgy fruit pudding bound in a cloth and cooked for hours, while Cranachan, made with toasted oatmeal steeped in whisky and folded into whipped cream flavoured with fresh raspberries, or the similar Atholl Brose, are considered more refined.

Food shopping

Most Scots get their supplies from supermarkets, but you're increasingly likely to come across good delis, farm shops and specialist **food shops**. Many stock local produce alongside imported delicacies, as well as organic fruit and veg, specialist drinks such as locally brewed beer, freshly baked bread, and sandwiches and other snacks for takeaway. Look out too for **farmers' markets** (⦿ taste-of-scotland. com/farmers-markets-in-scotland) which generally take place on Saturday and Sunday mornings; local farmers and small producers from pig farmers to cheese-makers and small smokeries set up stalls to sell their specialist lines.

Scotland is notorious for its sweet tooth, and **cakes and puddings** are taken very seriously. Bakeries with extensive displays of iced buns, cakes and cream-filled pastries are a typical feature of any Scottish high street, while home-made shortbread, scones or tablet (a hard, crystalline form of fudge) are considered great treats. In the summer, Scottish berries, in particular raspberries and strawberries, are particularly tasty.

Drinking

As in the rest of Britain, Scottish **pubs**, which originated as travellers' hostelries and coaching inns, are the main social focal points of any community. Pubs in the Highlands vary hugely, from old-fashioned inns with open fires and a convivial atmosphere to raucous theme-pubs with jukeboxes and satellite TV. Out in the islands, pubs are few and far between, with

---

CLASSIC SCOTTISH DISHES

Arbroath smokies Powerful smoked haddock.

Cullen skink Rich soup made from smoked haddock, potatoes and cream.

Haggis Flavoursome sausage meat (spiced liver, offal, oatmeal and onion) cooked inside a bag made from a sheep's stomach. Tasty and satisfying, particularly when eaten with its traditional accompaniments "bashed neeps" (mashed turnips) and "chappit tatties" (mashed potatoes).

Porridge A breakfast staple, this is properly made with oatmeal and water, and cooked with a pinch of salt. Some prefer to add milk and honey, fruit or sugar to sweeten.

Scots broth Hearty soup made with stock (usually mutton), vegetables and barley.

most drinking taking place in the local hotel bar. In some larger towns, traditional pubs are being supplemented by modern café-bars.

Scotland has very relaxed licensing laws. Pub **opening hours** are generally 11am to 11pm, but some places stay open later. Whatever time the pub closes, "last orders" will be called by the bar staff about fifteen minutes before closing time to allow "drinking-up time". In general, you have to be 16 to enter a pub unaccompanied, though some places are easy about having folk with children in, or have special family rooms and beer gardens where the kids can run free. The legal drinking age is 18.

Whisky

Whisky – *uisge beatha*, or the "water of life" in Gaelic – has been produced in Scotland, primarily in the Highlands and Islands, since the fifteenth century, but only really took off in popularity after the 1780 tax on claret made wine too expensive for most people. The taxman soon caught up with whisky, however, and drove the stills underground. Today, many distilleries operate on the site of simple cottages that once distilled the stuff illegally.

Despite the dominance of the blended whiskies such as Johnnie Walker, Bell's, Teacher's and The Famous Grouse, **single malt whisky** is infinitely superior and, as a result, a great deal more expensive. Single malts vary in character enormously depending on the amount of peat used for drying the barley, the water used for mashing and the type of oak cask used in the maturing process. Malt whisky is best drunk with a splash of water to release its distinctive flavours. The greatest concentrations of distilleries are on Speyside and Islay (whose whiskies are renowned for their smoky character), though there are distilleries popping up all over the place.

Beer

Traditional Scottish beer is a thick, dark ale known as **heavy**, served at room temperature in pints or half-pints, with a full head. Quite different in taste from English "bitter", heavy is a more robust, sweeter beer with less of an edge. All of the big-name breweries – McEwan's, Tennents, Bellhaven and Caledonian – produce a reasonable selection of heavies. However, if you really want to discover Scottish beer, look out for the products of small **local breweries**, many based in the Highlands and Islands, such as Cairngorm, the Black Isle, Arran, Fyne Ales, Isle of Skye, Orkney or Valhalla. Look out, too, for Fraoch, available mostly in bottles, a delicious, lighter-coloured ale made from heather according to an ancient recipe.

Water and soft drinks

Scotland produces a prodigious amount of **mineral water**, much of which is exported – tap water is chill, clean and perfectly palatable in most parts of the country, including the areas of the Highlands and Islands where it's tinged the colour of weak tea by peat in the ground. Locally produced **Irn-Bru**, a fizzy orange, sickly sweet concoction, has been known to outsell Coke and Pepsi in Scotland.

The media

When you're up in the Highlands and Islands, the UK's national media may seem London-based and London-biased. Most locals prefer to listen to Scottish radio programmes, read local newspapers, and – albeit to a much lesser extent – watch Scottish TV. Local papers are also avidly consumed, with the weekly papers in places like Orkney and Shetland read by virtually the entire adult population.

The press

Provincial dailies are more widely read in the Highlands and Islands than anywhere else in Britain. The biggest-selling regional title is Aberdeen's famously parochial *Press and Journal*, which has special editions for each area of the Highlands and Islands. For an insight into local life, there's the staid **weekly** *Oban Times*. More entertaining and radical is the campaigning weekly *West Highland Free Press*, printed on Skye. All carry articles in Gaelic as well as English. Further north, the lively *Shetland Times* and Orkney's sedate *Orcadian* are essential weekly reads for anyone living in or just visiting those islands.

Given the distances in the Highlands and Islands, you shouldn't always expect to find a daily newspaper arriving with your early morning cup of tea, though unless you're in a particularly remote spot or bad weather is affecting transport links, the papers are normally around by mid-morning. Most easily obtained are **Scottish newspapers**. Principal among these are the two serious dailies – *The Scotsman*, based in Edinburgh, and *The Herald*, published in Glasgow, both offering reasonable coverage of the current issues affecting Scotland, along with British and foreign news, sport, arts and lifestyle pages. They've recently been joined by *The National*, a serious, low-priced left-wing and pro-independence daily launched in 2014. A rare success in an era of dwindling circulations, the paper has filled a glaring gap in the market and provided an alternative voice for just under half of the population who voted in favour of independence in the referendum.

You should also be able to find a selection of popular tabloids, including Scotland's biggest-selling daily, the downmarket *Daily Record*, along with various national titles – from the reactionary *Sun* to the vaguely left-leaning *Daily Mirror* – which appear in specific Scottish editions.

Many **Sunday newspapers** published in London have a Scottish edition, although again Scotland has its own offerings – *Scotland on Sunday*, from the *Scotsman* stable, and the *Sunday Herald* (the only newspaper to come out in support of independence prior to the referendum), complementing its eponymous daily. Far more fun and widely read is the anachronistic *Sunday Post*, published by Dundee's D.C. Thomson publishing group. It's a wholesome paper, uniquely Scottish, and has changed little since the 1950s, since which time its two long-running cartoon strips, *Oor Wullie* and *The Broons*, have acquired cult status.

Scottish **monthlies** include the *Scottish Field*, a lowbrow version of England's *Tatler*, and the widely read *Scots Magazine*, an old-fashioned middle-of-the-road publication which promotes family values and lots of good fresh air.

TV and radio

In Scotland there are six main (sometimes called "terrestrial") **TV channels**: state-owned BBC1 and BBC2 and the Gaelic-language BBC Alba, and three commercial channels: ITV1, Channel 4 and Channel 5. **BBC Scotland** produces news programmes and a regular crop of local-interest lifestyle, current affairs, drama and comedy shows which slot into the schedules of the channels. The commercial channel ITV1 (branded in Scotland as STV) shows the same mix of talent shows, soaps and celebrity-driven programmes as the same channel south of the border, but with regional news broadcasts and some locally made shows slotted into the schedules. Channel 4 blends hard-hitting documentaries with comedy series and trashy fly-on-the-wall stuff, while downmarket Channel 5 focuses on reality shows and celebrity profiles. The vast majority of homes receive dozens of additional TV channels and radio stations through digital services like Freeview and Sky.

The **BBC radio** network broadcasts six main FM stations in Scotland, five of which are national stations originating largely from London. Only the award-winning BBC Radio Scotland offers a Scottish perspective on news, politics, arts, music, travel and sport. Gaelic-language BBC Radio nan Gàidheal, meanwhile, broadcasts news, chat, sport and music. Note that in large areas of the Highlands and Islands, some or all of these stations are impossible to receive.

A web of local **commercial radio** stations helps to fill in the gaps, mostly mixing rock and pop music with news bulletins, but a few tiny community-based stations such as Lochbroom FM in Ullapool – a place famed for its daily midge count – transmit documentaries and discussions on local issues. With a DAB **digital radio**, you can get all the main stations crackle-free along with special interest and smaller-scale stations.

SOME SCOTTISH RADIO STATIONS

BBC Radio Scotland 92–95FM, 810MW ⓦ bbc.co.uk/radioscotland. Nationwide news, sport, music, current affairs and arts.

BBC Radio nan Gàidheal 103.4FM ⓦ bbc.co.uk/scotland/alba. An opt-out from Radio Scotland, with Gaelic-language news and phone-ins, and great traditional-music shows.

Lochbroom FM 102.2 & 96.8FM ⓦ lochbroomfm.co.uk. A small local radio station broadcasting to the northwest coast from Ullapool.

Moray Firth 97.4FM, 1107MW ⓦ mfr.co.uk. Mainstream rock and pop for the Inverness area.

Nevis Radio 96.6 & 102.3FM ⓦ nevisradio.co.uk. All that's happening in Fort William and its surrounds, from the slopes of Ben Nevis.

SIBC 96.2FM ⓦ sibc.co.uk. Shetland's own independent station.

Events and spectator sports

There's a huge range of organized annual events on offer in the Highlands and Islands, reflecting both vibrant contemporary culture and well-marketed

heritage. **Many tourists will home straight in on the Highland Games and other tartan-draped theatricals, but there's more to Scotland than this: numerous regional celebrations perpetuate ancient customs. A few of the smaller, more obscure events, particularly those with a pagan bent, do not always welcome the casual visitor. The tourist board publishes a weighty list of all Scottish events on its website (Ⓦ visitscotland.com).**

Events calendar

DECEMBER–JANUARY

Dec 31 and Jan 1 Hogmanay and Ne'er Day. Traditionally more important to the Scots than Christmas, and known for the custom of "first-footing", when groups of revellers troop into neighbours' houses at midnight bearing gifts. More popular these days are huge and highly organized street parties in the larger towns.

Jan 1 Kirkwall Boys' and Men's Ba' Games, Orkney. Mass, drunken football game through the streets of the town, with the castle and the harbour the respective goals. As a grand finale the players jump into the harbour.

Last Tues in Jan Up-Helly-Aa, Lerwick, Shetland Ⓦ uphellyaa.org. Norse fire festival culminating in the burning of a specially built Viking longship. Visitors will need an invite from one of the locals, or you can buy a ticket for the Town Hall celebrations.

Jan 25 Burns Night. Scots worldwide get stuck into haggis, whisky and vowel-grinding poetry to commemorate Scotland's greatest poet, Robert Burns.

FEBRUARY

Feb Fort William Mountain Festival Ⓦ mountainfestival.co.uk. Films, lectures, guided walks and music sessions in celebration of mountain culture.

MAY

Early May Spirit of Speyside Scotch Whisky Festival Ⓦ spiritofspeyside.com. Six-day binge with pipe bands, gigs and dancing as well as distillery crawls. Shetland Folk Festival (Ⓦ shetlandfolkfestival.com). One of the liveliest and most entertaining of Scotland's round of folk festivals.

Late May Atholl Highlanders Parade at Blair Castle, Perthshire Ⓦ blair-castle.co.uk. The annual parade and inspection of Britain's last private army by their colonel-in-chief, the Duke of Atholl, on the eve of their Highland Games.

JUNE–JULY

June Beginning of the Highland Games season across the Highlands and Argyll; St Magnus Festival, Orkney Ⓦ stmagnusfestival.com. A classical and folk music, drama, dance and literature festival celebrating the islands.

July Hebridean Celtic Festival, Stornoway Ⓦ hebceltfest.com. International Celtic music festival that takes place over four days in Stornoway in the Outer Hebrides.

Tarbert Seafood Festival Ⓦ tarbertfestivals.co.uk. This weekend of gorging on seafood also sees live music and dance events around Tarbert's sheltered harbour.

Late July West Highland Yachting Week Ⓦ whyw.co.uk. A week of yacht racing and shore-based partying which moves en masse between Oban, Craobh and Tobermory.

AUGUST

Early Aug Belladrum Tartan Heart Festival, near Inverness Ⓦ tartanheartfestival.co.uk. One of Scotland's most scenic and fastest-growing music shindigs; family friendly as well.

SEPTEMBER

Early Sept Mendelssohn on Mull Ⓦ mendelssohnonmull.com. Music festival celebrating classical music. The Ben Nevis Race (for amateurs) Ⓦ bennevisrace.co.uk. Involves running to the top of Scotland's highest mountain and back again. Shinty's Camanachd Cup final Ⓦ shinty.com. The climax of the season for Scotland's own stick-and-ball game, normally held in one of the main Highland towns. Blas Ⓦ blas-festival.com. The premier Gaelic and traditional-music festival, at venues across the Highlands, though this wasn't held in 2019.

Late Sept Annual World Stone Skimming Championships, Easdale Island, near Oban Ⓦ stoneskimming.com. No previous experience is required; if you can make a stone bounce three times before sinking, you're in.

OCTOBER–NOVEMBER

Mid-Oct Tiree Wave Classic Ⓦ tireewaveclassic.co.uk. Annual event attracting windsurfers from around the world to the breezy Hebridean island. The National Mod Ⓦ ancomunn. co.uk/nationalmod. Held over nine days at a different venue each year, the Mod is a competitive festival and features all aspects of Gaelic performing arts. The Golden Spurtle World Porridge Making Championships, Carrbridge, Speyside Ⓦ goldenspurtle.com. Celebrity chefs preside over this competition, designed to find the best traditionally made porridge.

Late Oct Glenfiddich Piping and Fiddle Championships Ⓦ blairatholl.org.uk. Held at Blair Atholl for the world's top ten solo pipers.

Nov 30 St Andrew's Day. Celebrating Scotland's patron saint (Ⓦ standrewsweek.co.uk).

Highland Games

Despite their name, **Highland Games** are held all over Scotland between May and mid-September, varying in size and in the range of events they offer. The Games probably originated in the fourteenth century as a means of recruiting the best fighting men for the clan chiefs, and were popularized by **Queen Victoria** to encourage the traditional dress, music, games and dance of the Highlands; indeed, various royals still attend the Games at Braemar.

Apart from **Braemar**, the most famous games take place at **Oban** and **Cowal**, but the smaller events are often more fun – like a sort of Highland version of a school sports day. There's money to be won, too, so the Games are usually pretty competitive. The most distinctive events are known as the "heavies" – tossing the caber (pronounced "kabber"), putting the stone, and tossing the weight over the bar – all of which require prodigious strength and skill, and the wearing of a kilt. Tossing the caber is the most spectacular, when the athlete must lift an entire tree trunk up, cupping it in his hands, before running with it and attempting to heave it end over end. Just as important as the sporting events are the **piping** competitions – for individuals and bands – and **dancing** competitions, where you'll see girls as young as 3 tripping the quick, intricate steps of dances such as the Highland Fling.

Football

While **football** (soccer) is far and away Scotland's most popular spectator sport, its popularity in the Highlands and Islands is a little muted in comparison to the game's following in the Central Belt of the country. The strength of the Highland League (Ⓦ highlandfootballleague.com) was, however, recognized in the mid-1990s with the inclusion of Inverness Caledonian Thistle and Dingwall-based Ross County in the Scottish Leagues. Both teams have consistently performed way above expectations in Scotland's top division, the Scottish Premiership (Ⓦ spfl.co.uk), though Inverness are currently in the First Division. Both have also claimed their first major honours in recent years: in 2015, Inverness won the Scottish Cup – the first major trophy won by any club from the Highlands – and in 2016 Ross County won the League Cup. The **season** begins in early August and ends in mid-May, with most matches taking place on Saturday afternoons at 3pm, and also often on Sunday afternoons and Wednesday evenings. Tickets for Scottish League games cost around £25, but less for Highland League fixtures.

Shinty

Played throughout Scotland but with particular strongholds in the West Highlands and Strathspey, the game of **shinty** (the Gaelic *sinteag* means "leap")

arrived from Ireland around 1500 years ago. Until the latter part of the nineteenth century, it was played on an informal basis and teams from neighbouring villages had to come to an agreement about rules before matches could begin. However, in 1893, the **Camanachd Association** – the Gaelic word for shinty is *camanachd* – was set up to formalize the rules, and the first Camanachd Cup Final was held in Inverness in 1896. Today, shinty is still fairly close to its Gaelic roots, like the Irish game of hurling, with each team having twelve players including a goalkeeper and each goal counting for a point. The game, which bears similarities to an undisciplined version of hockey, isn't for the faint-hearted; it's played at a furious pace, with sticks – called camans or cammocks – flying alarmingly in all directions. Support is enthusiastic and vocal, and if you're in the Highlands during the season, which runs from March to October, it's well worth trying to catch a match: check with tourist offices or the local paper, or go to Ⓦ shinty.com.

Curling

The one winter sport which enjoys a strong Scottish identity is **curling** (Ⓦ scottishcurling.org), occasionally still played on a frozen outdoor rink, or "pond", though most commonly these days seen at indoor ice rinks. The game, which involves gently sliding smooth-bottomed 40lb discs of granite called "stones" across the ice towards a target circle, is said to have been invented in Scotland, although its earliest representation is in a sixteenth-century Flemish painting. Played by two teams of four, it's a highly tactical and skilful sport, enlivened by team members using brushes to sweep the ice furiously in front of a moving stone to help it travel further and straighter. If you're interested in seeing curling being played, go along to the ice rink in places such as Pitlochry or Inverness on a winter evening.

Outdoor activities

Scotland boasts a landscape that, weather conditions apart, is extremely attractive for outdoor pursuits at all levels of fitness and ambition, and legislation enacted by the Scottish Parliament has ensured a right of access to hills, mountains, lochs and rivers. Within striking distance of its cities are two national parks, remote wilderness areas and vast stretches of glens and moorland, while sea-kayakers, sailors and surfers can enjoy excellent conditions along the rugged but beautiful coastline.

MIDGES AND TICKS

Despite being only a fraction of an inch long, and enjoying a life span on the wing of just a few weeks, the **midge** (genus: *culicoides*) – a tiny biting fly prevalent in the Highlands (mainly the west coast) and Islands – is considered to be second only to the weather as the major deterrent to tourism in Scotland. There are more than thirty varieties of midge, though only half of these bite humans. Ninety percent of all midge bites are down to the female *Culicoides impunctatus* or **Highland midge** (the male does not bite), which has two sets of jaws sporting twenty teeth each; she needs a good meal of blood in order to produce eggs.

These persistent creatures can be a nuisance, but some people also have a violent allergic reaction to midge bites. The easiest way to avoid midges is to visit in the winter, since they only appear between April and October. Midges also favour still, damp, overcast or shady conditions and are at their meanest around sunrise and sunset, when clouds of them can descend on an otherwise idyllic spot. Direct sunlight, heavy rain, noise and smoke discourage them to some degree, though wind is the most effective means of dispersing them. If they appear, cover up exposed skin and get your hands on some kind of repellent. Recommendations include Autan, Eureka!, Jungle Formula (widely available from pharmacists) and the herbal remedy citronella. An alternative to repellents for protecting your face, especially if you're walking or camping, is a **midge net**, a little like a beekeeper's hat; though they appear ridiculous at first, you're unlikely to care as long as they work. The latest deployment in the battle against the midge is a gas-powered machine called a "midge magnet" which sucks up the wee beasties and is supposed to be able to clear up to an acre; the most basic unit costs between £400 and £500, but there's been a healthy take-up by pubs with beer gardens and by campsite owners.

If you're walking through long grass or bracken, there's a possibility that you may receive attention from **ticks**, tiny parasites no bigger than a pin head, which bury themselves into your skin. Removing ticks by dabbing them with alcohol, butter or oil is now discouraged; the medically favoured way of extracting them is to pull them out carefully with small tweezers. There is a very slight risk of catching some nasty diseases, such as encephalitis, from ticks. If flu-like symptoms persist after a tick bite, you should see a doctor immediately.

Walking and climbing

The Highlands and Islands offer unrivalled opportunities for **walking**, with some of the finest areas in the ownership of bodies such as the National Trust for Scotland and the John Muir Trust (Ⓦjohnmuirtrust. org); both permit year-round access. Bear in mind, though, that restrictions may be in place during lambing and deerstalking seasons. See Ⓦoutdooraccess-scotland.scot for information about **hiking safely** during the stalking season. In addition, the green signposts of the Scottish Rights of Way Society point to established paths and routes all over the country.

There are several **long-distance footpaths**, such as the well-known West Highland Way (see page 131), which take between three and seven days to walk, though you can, of course, just do a section of them. Paths are generally well signposted and well supported, with a range of services from bunkhouses to baggage-carrying services.

Numerous short walks (from accessible towns and villages) and several major walks are touched on in this Guide. However, you should only use our notes as general outlines, and always in conjunction with a good map. Where possible, we have given details of the best maps to use – in most cases one of the excellent and reliable **Ordnance Survey** (OS) series (see page 45), usually available from local tourist offices, which, along with outdoor shops, can also supply other local maps, safety advice and guidebooks/leaflets.

For relatively gentle walking in the company of knowledgeable locals, look out for guided walks offered by rangers at many National Trust for Scotland, Forestry Commission and Scottish Natural Heritage sites. These often focus on local **wildlife**, and the best can lead to some special sightings, such as a badger's sett or a golden eagle's eyrie.

WALKING INFORMATION

Ⓦ **outdooraccess-scotland.scot** All you need to know about the Scottish Outdoor Access Code, plus daily information for hillwalkers about deerstalking activities (July–Oct).

Ⓦ **walking.visitscotland.com** Official site from VisitScotland, with good lists of operators, information on long-distance footpaths, and details of deerstalking restrictions and contact phone numbers.

Ⓦ **wildlife.visitscotland.com** Highlights the fauna and flora you may spot on a walk.

WALKING CLUBS AND ASSOCIATIONS

Mountain Bothies Association Ⓦ mountainbothies.org.uk. Charity dedicated to maintaining huts and shelters in the Scottish Highlands.

Mountaineering Council of Scotland Ⓦ mountaineering.scot. The representative body for all mountain activities, with detailed information on access and conservation issues.

Ramblers Association Scotland Ⓦ ramblers.org.uk/scotland. Campaigning organization with network of local groups, and news on events and issues.

Scottish Mountaineering Club Ⓦ smc.org.uk. The largest mountaineering club in the country. A well-respected organization which publishes a popular series of mountain guidebooks.

WALKING TOUR OPERATORS

Activity Scotland Ⓣ 01887 822860, Ⓦ activityscotland.com. Highly experienced Perthshire based operator providing a wide range of adventures and activities, from horse riding and abseiling to kayaking and biking.

C-N-Do Scotland Ⓣ 01786 445703, Ⓦ cndoscotland.com. Scotland's longest-established operator, offering munro-bagging for novices and experts with qualified leaders.

G2 Outdoor Ⓣ 01540 651784, Ⓦ g2outdoor.co.uk. Personable, highly qualified adventure specialists offering gorge scrambling, hillwalking, rock climbing, canoeing and telemark skiing in the Cairngorms.

Glenmore Lodge Ⓣ 01479 861256, Ⓦ glenmorelodge.org.uk. Based within the Cairngorm National Park, and internationally recognized as a leader in outdoor skills and leadership training.

Hebridean Pursuits Ⓣ 01631 720002, Ⓦ hebrideanpursuits. org. Offers hillwalking and rock climbing in the Hebrides and West Highlands, as well as surf-kayaking and sailing trips.

Nae Limits Ⓣ 01796 482600, Ⓦ naelimits.co.uk. This excellent Perthshire-based operator offers everything from wet'n'wild rafting to bug canyoning and cliff jumping.

North-West Frontiers Ⓣ 01997 421474, Ⓦ nwfrontiers.com. Based in Ullapool, offering guided mountain trips with small groups in the northwest Highlands, Hebrides and even the Shetland Islands.

Vertical Descents Ⓣ 01397 747111, Ⓦ verticaldescents.com. Ideally located for the Glencoe and Fort William area. Activities and courses include canyoning, "funyakking" (a type of rafting) and climbing.

Walkabout Scotland Ⓣ 01312 616470, Ⓦ walkaboutscotland. com. A great way to get a taste of hiking in Scotland, from exploring Ben Lomond to the Isle of Arran. Guided day and weekend walking trips from Edinburgh with all transport included.

Wilderness Scotland Ⓣ 01479 420020, Ⓦ wildernessscotland. com. Guided, self-guided and customized adventure holidays that focus on exploring the remote and unspoiled parts of Scotland by foot, bike, sea-kayak, yacht and even on skis.

Winter sports

Skiing and **snowboarding** take place at five different locations in the Highlands – Glen Coe, the Nevis Range beside Fort William, Glen Shee, the Lecht and the Cairngorms near Aviemore. The resorts can go for months on end through the winter with insufficient snow, then see the approach roads suddenly made impassable by a glut of the stuff. When the conditions are good, Scotland's **ski resorts** have piste and off-piste areas that will challenge even the most accomplished alpine or cross-country skier.

Expect to pay up to £35 for a standard day-pass at one of the resorts, around £25 for a half-day pass (usually available from noon) or around £110 for a four-day pass; rental of skis or snowboard comes in at around £30 per day, with reductions for multi-day rentals. At weekends, in good weather with decent snow, expect the slopes to be packed with trippers from the central belt, although midweek usually sees queues dissolving. For a comprehensive rundown of all the resorts, including ticket prices and conditions, visit Ⓦ ski.visitscotland.com.

Cross-country skiing (along with the related telemark or Nordic skiing) is becoming increasingly popular in the hills around Braemar near Glenshee and the Cairngorms. The best way to get started or to find out about good routes is to contact an outdoor pursuits company that offers telemark or Nordic rental and instruction; in the Aviemore area try G2 Outdoor (see page 166). Also check out the Huntly Nordic and Outdoor Centre in Huntly, Aberdeenshire (Ⓣ 01466 794428, Ⓦ nordicski.co.uk/hnoc).

Pony trekking and horseriding

There are numerous pony trekking and riding centres across the Highlands and Islands, most approved by either the Trekking and Riding Society of Scotland (TRSS; Ⓦ ridinginscotland.com) or the British Horse Society (BHS; Ⓦ bhs.org.uk). As a rule, any centre will offer the option of **pony trekking** (leisurely ambles on sure-footed Highland ponies), **hacking** (for experienced riders who want to go for a short ride at a fast-ish pace) and **trail riding** (over longer distances, for riders who feel secure at a canter).

Cycling and mountain biking

Cycle touring is a great way to see some of the more remote parts of the Highlands and Islands. You'll find cycle shops in towns but few dedicated cycle lanes. In the countryside it can be tricky finding spare parts unless you are near one of Scotland's purpose-built mountain-bike trail centres.

Scotland is now regarded as one of the world's top destinations for **off-road mountain biking**. The Forestry Commission has established more than 1150

MUNRO-BAGGING

In recent years hillwalking in Scotland has become synonymous with "**Munro-bagging**". Munros are the hills in Scotland over 3000ft in height, defined by a list first drawn up by Sir Hugh Munro in 1891. You "bag" a Munro by walking to the top of it, and once you've bagged all 284 you can call yourself a Munroist and let your chiropodist retire in peace.

Sir Hugh's challenge is an enticing one: **3000ft** is high enough to be an impressive ascent but not so high that it's for expert mountaineers only. Nor do you need to aim to do them all – at heart, Munro-bagging is simply about appreciating the great Scottish outdoors. Munros are found across the Highlands and on two of the islands (Mull and Skye), and include many of the more famous and attractive mountains in Scotland.

However, while the Munros by definition include all the highest hills in Scotland, there isn't any quality control, and one of the loudest arguments of critics of the game (known by some as "de-baggers") is that Munro-seekers will plod up a boring pudding of a mountain because it's 3000ft high and ignore one nearby that's much more pleasing but a few feet short of the requisite mark.

Judgement is also required in a few other ways. You do have to be properly equipped, and be aware what you're tackling before you set off – the hills are hazardous in all seasons. But for many the trickiest part of Munro-bagging is getting to grips with the Gaelic pronunciation of some of the hill names. However, as it's bad form not to be able to tell the folk in the pub at the end of the day which hills you've just ticked off, beginners are encouraged to stick to peaks such as Ben Vane or Ben More, and resign themselves to the fact that Beinn Fhionnlaidh (pronounced "Byn Yoonly") and Beinn an Dothaidh (pronounced "Byn an Daw-ee") are for the really experienced.

If you want some training, you can set about the **Corbetts** (hills between 2500 and 2999ft) or even the **Donalds** (lowland hills between 2000 and 2500ft).

---

miles of excellent off-road routes. These are detailed in numerous "Cycling in the Forest" leaflets, available from Forest Enterprise offices. Alternatively, get hold of the *Scottish Mountain Biking Guide* from tourist information centres. Some of the tougher routes are best attempted on full-suspension mountain bikes, although the easier (blue/green) trails can be ridden on a standard mountain or road bike. Pocket Mountains also publish a series of compact cycling guides to the country (W pocketmountains.com).

For up-to-date information on long-distance routes, including **The Great Glen Cycle Way**, along with a list of publications detailing specific routes, contact the cyclists' campaigning group Sustrans (W sustrans. co.uk), as well as the other organizations listed here (see opposite).

Another option is to shell out on a cycling holiday package. Britain's biggest cycling organization, Cycling UK (formerly the **Cycle Touring Club**; W cyclinguk.org), provides lists of tour operators and rental outlets in Scotland, and supplies members with touring and technical advice, as well as insurance. Visit Scotland's *Cycling in Scotland* brochure is worth getting hold of, with practical advice and suggestions for itineraries around the country. The tourist board's "Cyclists Welcome" scheme gives guesthouses and B&Bs a chance to advertise that they're cyclist-friendly, and able to provide an overnight laundry service, a late meal or a packed lunch.

Travelling with bikes

Transporting your bike **by train** is a good way of getting to the interesting parts of Scotland without a lot of hard pedalling. Bikes are allowed free on ScotRail trains, but you need to book the space as far in advance as possible. Bus and coach companies, including National Express and Scottish Citylink, rarely accept cycles unless they are dismantled and boxed. Large towns and tourist centres offer **bike rental**. Expect to pay around £20 per day; more for top-notch mountain bikes. Most outlets also give good discounts for multi-day rents.

CYCLING INFORMATION

Cycle Scotland ☎ 01315 565560, W cyclescotland.co.uk. Fully organized cycle tours at all levels, with accommodation ranging from campsites to country-house hotels, and a good range of bikes available for rent, from tandems to children's bikes.

Cycling UK ☎ 01483 238301, W cyclinguk.org. Britain's largest cycling organization, and a good source of general advice; their handbook has lists of cyclist-friendly B&Bs and cafés in Scotland. Annual membership £46.50.

Forestry and Land Scotland ☎ 0300 0676000, W forestryandland.gov.scot/visit/activities/mountain-biking. The best source of information on Scotland's extensive network of forest trails – ideal for mountain biking at all levels of ability.

Full On Adventure ☎ 01479 420123, W fullonadventure.co.uk. Specialists in fully guided mountain-bike tours of the Cairngorms and Strathspey.

STAYING SAFE IN THE HILLS

Due to rapid weather changes, the **mountains** are potentially extremely **dangerous** and should be treated with respect. Every year, in every season, climbers and walkers lose their lives in the Scottish hills.

• Wear sturdy, ankle-supporting **footwear**, and wear or carry with you warm, brightly coloured and **waterproof** layered clothing, even for what appears to be an easy expedition in apparently settled weather.
• Always carry adequate **maps**, a **compass** (which you should know how to use), food, water and a whistle. If it's sunny, make sure you use **sun protection**.
• Check the **weather forecast** before you go. If the weather looks as if it's closing in, get down from the mountain fast.
• Always **leave word** with someone of your route and what time you expect to return, and remember to contact the person again to let them know that you are back.
• In an emergency, call **mountain rescue** on ☎ 999.

Highland Wildcat Trails ⓦ highlandwildcat.com. Scotland's most northerly dedicated mountain-bike centre, complete with one of the country's longest downhill tracks.

Nevis Range ⓦ ridefortwilliam.co.uk. Information on all the trails around Fort William, including the home of Scotland's World Cup downhill and cross-country tracks at Nevis Range.

Spokes ☎ 01313 132114, ⓦ spokes.org.uk. Active Edinburgh cycle campaign group with plenty of good links, and news on events and cycle-friendly developments.

WolfTrax Mountain Bike Centre ☎ 0300 0676100, ⓦ forestryandland.gov.scot/visit/laggan-wolftrax. This Central Highland bike centre near Newtonmore has almost 22 miles of routes for every standard of rider.

Golf

Golf took shape in the fifteenth century on the dunes of Scotland's east coast and today there are over four hundred golf courses, with a less elitist and more accessible approach than anywhere else in the world. It's often possible just to turn up and play, though it's sensible to phone ahead; booking is essential for the championship courses.

Public courses are owned by the local council, while **private courses** belong to a club. You can play on both – occasionally the private courses require that you are a **member** of another club, and the odd one asks for introductions from a member, but these rules are often waived for overseas visitors and all you need to do is pay a one-off fee. The cost of a round will set you back around £20 on a small nine-hole course, and more than £60 on many good-quality eighteen-hole courses. In remote areas the courses are sometimes unstaffed; just put the admission fee into the honesty box.

While many of Scotland's championship courses are in the lowlands, the Highlands' most famous links course is **Royal Dornoch** in Sutherland (ⓦ royaldor-noch.com; £100). For details on some of the others, see ⓦ visitscotlandgolf.com and ⓦ visitscotland.com/golf.

Fishing

The Highlands and Islands' serrated **coastline** – with its deep sea lochs and myriad offshore islands – ranks among the cleanest coasts in Europe. Combine this with an abundance of salmon, sea trout, brown trout and pike, acres of open space and easy access, and you have a wonderful location for game-, coarse- or sea-fishing.

No licence is needed to fish in Scotland, although nearly all land is privately owned and its fishing therefore controlled by a landlord/lady or his/her agent. Permission, however, is usually easy to obtain: permits can be bought at local tackle shops, rural post offices or through fishing clubs in the area – if in doubt, ask at the nearest tourist office. Salmon and sea trout have strict **seasons**, which usually stretch from late August to late February. Individual tourist offices will know the precise dates, or see the information and booking website ⓦ fishpal.com.

Watersports

Opportunities for **sailing** are outstanding and tainted only by the unreliability of the weather. Even in summer, the full force of the North Atlantic can be felt, and changeable conditions combined with tricky tides and rocky shores demand good sailing and navigational skills. Yacht charters are available from various ports, either bareboat or in yachts run by a skipper and crew; contact Sail Scotland (ⓦ sailscotland.co.uk) or the Association of Scottish Yacht Charterers (ⓦ asyc.co.uk).

An alternative way to enjoy the Highlands and Islands under sail is to spend a week at one of the sailing schools. Many schools, as well as small boat-rental operations dotted along the coast, rent sailing dinghies by the hour or day, as well as **windsurfing gear**, though the chilly water means you'll always need a wetsuit. The Hebridean island of Tiree is internationally renowned for its beaches and waves and has an excellent surf, windsurfing and kitesurfing school, Suds Surf (Ⓦsurfschoolscotland.co.uk).

In recent years **sea-kayaking** has witnessed an explosion in popularity, with a host of operators offering sea-kayaking lessons and expeditions across the country. Canoe Scotland (Ⓦcanoescotland.org) offers useful advice, while Glenmore Lodge (Ⓦglenmorelodge.org.uk) and Skyak Adventures (Ⓦskyakadventures.com) are highly reputable for training or tours.

Surfing

In addition to sea-kayaking, Scotland is fast gaining a reputation as a **surfing** destination. However, the northern coastline lies on the same latitude as Alaska, so the water temperature is very low: even in midsummer it rarely exceeds 15°C, and in winter can drop to as low as 7°C. The one vital accessory, therefore, is a good wetsuit (ideally a 5/3mm steamer), wetsuit boots and, outside summer, gloves and a hood, too.

Many of the best spots – such as Thurso, Tiree and the Isle of Lewis – are surrounded by stunning scenery, and you'd be unlucky to share the waves with other surfers. However, this isolation – combined with the cold water and big, powerful waves – means that many of the best locations can only be enjoyed by experienced surfers. Surf shops rent or sell equipment and provide good information about local breaks and events on the surfing scene.

Travel essentials

Costs

The Highlands and Islands are a relatively **expensive** place to visit, with travel, food and accommodation costs higher than the EU average, though this has been balanced out with a plunging pound in the wake of the Brexit vote. Given Scotland's – and the UK's – unstable political and economic climate, costs are likely to continue fluctuating for the foreseeable future. The minimum expenditure for a couple travelling on public transport, self-catering and camping, is in the region of £35 each a day, rising to around £60 per person a day if you're staying at hostels and eating the odd meal out. Staying at budget B&Bs, eating at unpretentious restaurants and visiting the odd tourist attraction means spending at least £75 each per day. If you're renting a car, staying in comfortable B&Bs or hotels and eating well, you should reckon on at least £100 a day per person.

Crime and personal safety

The **crime rate** in the Scottish Highlands and Islands is very low indeed. Even the largest urban centre, Inverness, sees very few offences committed. Out on the islands, the situation is often even more tranquil: until a fight at a wedding in 2010, the Isle of Muck (population 27) managed 50 years without a single reported crime. Should you have anything stolen or be involved in some incident that requires reporting, contact the local police station (dial ☎101 from any location); ☎999 (or ☎112) should only be used in emergencies – in other words, if someone is in immediate danger or a crime is taking place.

Discounts

Most attractions in the Highlands and Islands offer **concessions** for senior citizens, the unemployed, full-time students and children under 16, with under-5s being admitted free almost everywhere – proof of eligibility will be required in most cases. Family tickets are often available for those travelling with kids.

Once obtained, **youth/student ID cards** soon pay for themselves in savings. Full-time students are eligible for the International Student Identity Card or **ISIC** (Ⓦisic.org), which costs £12 and entitles the bearer to special air, rail and bus fares, and discounts at museums, theatres and other attractions. If you're not a student, but you're 25 or younger, you can get an International Youth Travel Card or **IYTC**, which costs the same as the ISIC and carries the same benefits.

Electricity

The current in Scotland is the **EU standard** of approximately 230v AC. All sockets are designed for British three-pin plugs, which are totally different from the rest of the EU. Adaptors are widely available at airports and electronics stores.

Emergencies

For **police**, **fire** and **ambulance** services phone ☎999.

HISTORIC ENVIRONMENT SCOTLAND AND NATIONAL TRUST FOR SCOTLAND

Many of Scotland's most treasured sights – from castles and country houses to islands, gardens and tracts of protected landscape – come under the control of the privately run **National Trust for Scotland** (ⓦ nts.org.uk) or the state-run **Historic Environment Scotland** (ⓦ historicenvironment.scot); we've quoted "**NTS**" or "**HES**" respectively for each site reviewed in this Guide. Both organizations charge an admission fee for most places, and these can be quite high, especially for the more grandiose NTS estates.

If you think you'll be visiting more than half a dozen NTS properties, or more than a dozen HES ones, it's worth taking **annual membership**, which costs around £52 (HES) or £60 (NTS), and allows free admission to their properties. In addition, HES has the **Explorer Pass**, which is valid for either 5 (£35 adult, £70 family) or 14 (£45 adult, £90 family) consecutive days.

Entry requirements

Since **Brexit** formally came to pass, there have been changes to the former free movement principles. EU, EEA and Swiss citizens are able to enter Britain with just a **passport**, without applying for a **visa**, for a stay of up to six months. Americans, Canadians, Australians, New Zealanders and citizens of many Latin American and Caribbean countries can also stay for up to six months, providing they have a return ticket and adequate funds to cover their stay. Citizens of most other countries require a visa, obtainable from the British consulate or mission office in the country of application.

Note that visa regulations are subject to frequent changes, and at the time of writing, border controls were much more stringent than usual due to the **Covid-19 pandemic**, so it's always wise to contact the nearest British embassy or high commission before you travel. If you visit ⓦ ukvisas.gov.uk, you can download the full range of **application forms** and information leaflets, and find out the contact details of your nearest embassy or consulate, as well as the rules regarding visa extensions.

In addition, an independent charity, the Immigration Advisory Service or IAS (ⓦ iasservices.org.uk), offers free and confidential advice to anyone applying for entry clearance into the UK.

Health

Pharmacists (known as chemists in Scotland) can dispense only a limited range of drugs without a doctor's prescription. Most pharmacies are open standard shop hours, though there are also late-night branches in large cities and at 24-hour supermarkets.

If your condition is serious enough, you can turn up at the Accident and Emergency (A&E) department of local **hospitals** for complaints that require immediate attention. Obviously, if it's an absolute emergency, you should ring for an ambulance (☎ 999). Air ambulances also operate in remote areas. These services are free to all

Scotland, like the rest of the UK, was hit hard by the Covid-19 pandemic, with more cases and deaths in the second wave of the virus. Check www.gov.scot for the latest updates and requirements regarding the pandemic such as mask-wearing.

Insurance

Even though EU health-care privileges apply in the UK for now (the situation could well change after the UK leaves the EU), it's a good idea to take out **travel insurance** before travelling to cover against theft, loss and illness or injury. For non-EU citizens, it's worth checking whether you are already covered before you buy a new policy. If you need to take out insurance, you might want to consider the travel insurance deal we offer.

Internet

Wi-fi is now available at most hotels, B&Bs and hostels, as well as many cafés and bars, throughout the Highlands and Islands. If you don't have your own smartphone, laptop or tablet, the tourist office should be able to help – sometimes they will have an access point – and public libraries often provide cheap or free access. Network coverage for 3G and 4G can be very patchy – and often non-existent – in the Highlands and Islands.

Laundry

Coin-operated **laundries** are still found, but are becoming less and less common. A wash followed by a spin or tumble dry costs about £3.50; a "service wash" (having your laundry done for you in a few hours) costs about £2 extra. In the more remote areas of the Highlands and Islands, you'll have to rely on hostel and campsite laundry facilities.

LGBTQ travellers

While there's no **LGBTQ scene** as such out in the Highlands and Islands, many Scots have a positive – or at least neutral – opinion of LGBTQ people, reflected in positive media coverage by the likes of the *Sunday Herald*. In more remote areas, and in particular in those areas where religious observance is high, attitudes tend to be more conservative, and gay and lesbian locals are extremely discreet about their sexuality.

Mail

A stamp for a **first-class letter** to anywhere in the British Isles currently costs 70p and should arrive the next day; second-class letters cost 61p, taking up to three days. Note that there are now size restrictions: letters over 240 x 165 x 5mm are designated as "Large letters" and are correspondingly more expensive to send. Prices to Europe and the rest of the world vary depending on the size of the item and how quickly you would like it delivered. To get an idea of how much you'll need to spend, or for general postal info, check the Royal Mail website (Ⓦ royalmail.com/ price-finder).

Note that in many parts of the Highlands and Islands there will only be one or two mail collections each day, often at lunchtime or even earlier. **Stamps** can be bought at post office counters or from newsagents, supermarkets and local shops, although they usually only sell books of four or ten stamps.

Most **post offices** are open Monday to Friday 9am–5.30pm and Saturday 9am–12.30pm. In small communities you'll find post office counters operating out of a shop, shed or even a private house, and these will often keep extremely **restricted hours**.

Maps

The most comprehensive maps of Scotland are produced by the **Ordnance Survey** or OS (Ⓦ ordnance survey.co.uk), renowned for their accuracy and clarity. If you're planning a walk of more than a couple of hours' duration, or intend to walk in the Scottish hills at all, it is strongly recommended that you carry the relevant OS map and familiarize yourself with how to navigate using it. Scotland is covered by 85 maps in the 1:50,000 (pink) **Landranger** series which show enough detail to be useful for most walkers and cyclists. There's more detail still in the full-colour 1:25,000 (orange) **Explorer** series, which covers Scotland in around 170 maps. All OS maps now also come with a smartphone download. The full Ordnance Survey range is only available at a few big-city stores or online, although in any walking district of Scotland you'll find the relevant maps in local shops or tourist offices.

Virtually every service station in Scotland stocks at least one large-format **road atlas**, covering all of Britain at around three miles to one inch, and generally including larger-scale plans of major towns. For getting between major towns and cities a sat nav or GPS-enabled smartphone is hard to beat, but you'll have less luck in rural areas, where landmarks and even entire roads can be positioned incorrectly, leading to long and sometimes expensive detours.

Money

The basic unit of **currency** in the UK is the pound sterling (£), divided into 100 pence (p). Coins come in denominations of 1p, 2p, 5p, 10p, 20p, 50p, £1 and £2. Bank of England £5, £10, £20 and £50 banknotes are legal tender in Scotland; in addition, the **Bank of Scotland** (HBOS), the **Royal Bank of Scotland** (RBS) and the **Clydesdale Bank** issue their own banknotes in all the same denominations, plus a £100 note. All Scottish notes are legal tender throughout the UK, no matter what shopkeepers south of the border might say. In general, few people use £50 or £100 notes, and shopkeepers are likely to treat them with suspicion; fear of forgeries is widespread. At the time of going to press, £1 was worth around $1.30, €1.15, Can$1.70, Aus$1.80 and NZ$1.90. For the most up-to-date exchange rates, check the useful website Ⓦ xe.com.

Credit/debit cards are by far the most convenient way to carry your money, and most hotels, shops and restaurants in Scotland accept the major brand cards. In every sizeable town in Scotland, and in some surprisingly small places too, you'll find a branch of at least one of the big Scottish high-street **banks**, usually with an **ATM** attached. However, on some islands, and in remoter parts, you may find there is only a **mobile bank** that runs to a timetable (usually available from the local post office). General **banking hours** are Monday to Friday from 9 or 9.30am to 4 or 5pm, though some branches are open until slightly later on Thursdays. Post offices charge **no commission**, have longer opening hours, and are therefore often a good place to change money and cheques. Lost or stolen credit/debit cards should be reported to the police and the following numbers: MasterCard ☎ 0800 964767; Visa ☎ 0800 891725.

Opening hours and public holidays

Traditional **shop hours** in Scotland are Monday to Saturday 9am to 5.30 or 6pm. In the bigger towns, many places now stay open on Sundays and late at night on Thursdays or Fridays. Large supermarkets typically stay open till 8pm or 10pm and a few manage 24-hour opening (excluding Sunday). However, there are also plenty of towns and villages where you'll find very little open on a Sunday, and in the Outer Hebrides in particular, the Sabbath is strictly observed. Many small towns across the Highlands and Islands also retain an "**early closing day**" – often Wednesday – when shops close at 1pm, and you'll find precious few attractions open outside the tourist season (Easter to Oct), though ruins, parks and gardens are normally accessible year-round. Note that last entrance can be an hour (or more) before the published closing time.

Phones

Public **payphones** are still occasionally found in the Highlands and Islands, though with the ubiquity of mobile phones, they're seldom used.

If you're taking your **mobile phone** with you to Scotland, check with your service provider whether your phone will work abroad and what the call charges will be. The cost of calls within the EU has decreased significantly within recent years, and roaming charges within the EU were abolished altogether on 2017. Again, though, the Brexit vote has thrown into doubt how any new law in this regard will affect the UK. Calls to destinations further afield, however, are still unregulated and can be prohibitively expensive. Unless you have a tri-band phone, it's unlikely that a mobile bought for use in the US will work outside the States and vice versa. Mobiles in Australia and New Zealand generally use the same system as the UK so should work fine. All the main UK networks cover the Highlands and Islands, though you'll still find many places in among the hills or out on the islands where there's **no signal** at all. If you're in a rural area and having trouble with reception, simply ask a local where the strongest signals are found nearby.

Beware of premium-rate numbers, which are common for pre-recorded information services – and usually have the prefix ☎ 09.

Time

Greenwich Mean Time (GMT) – equivalent to Co-ordinated Universal Time (UTC) – is used from the end of October to the end of March; for the rest of the year the country switches to **British Summer Time** (BST), one hour ahead of GMT.

Tipping

There are no fixed rules for **tipping**. If you think you've received good service, particularly in restaurants or cafés, you may want to leave a tip of ten percent of the total bill (unless service has already been included). It's not normal, however, to leave tips in pubs, although bar staff are sometimes offered drinks, which they may accept in the form of money. The only other occasions when you'll be expected to tip are in hairdressers, taxis and smart hotels, where porters, bellboys and table waiters rely on being tipped to bump up their often dismal wages.

PUBLIC HOLIDAYS

Official **bank holidays** in Scotland operate on: January 1 and 2; Good Friday; the first and last Monday in May; the last Monday in August; St Andrew's Day (Nov 30); Christmas Day (Dec 25); and Boxing Day (Dec 26). In addition, all Scottish towns have one-day holidays in spring, summer and autumn – dates vary from place to place but normally fall on a Monday. While many local shops and businesses close on these days, few tourist-related businesses observe the holidays, particularly in the summer months.

Tourist information

The official tourist board is known as **VisitScotland** (W visitscotland.com), though they have recently axed many of their tourist offices; instead there are now some 15 iCentres throughout the Highlands and Islands, effectively regional visitor centres that dispense information on the surrounding area (and invariably beyond). Opening hours are often fiendishly complex, but have been listed throughout the guide.

As well as being stacked full of souvenirs and other gifts, most TICs have a decent selection of leaflets, displays, maps and books relating to the local area. The staff are usually helpful and will do their best to help with enquiries about accommodation, local transport, attractions and restaurants, although it's worth being aware that they're sometimes reluctant to divulge information about local attractions or accommodation options that are not paid-up members of the Tourist Board, and a number of perfectly decent guesthouses and the like choose not to pay the fees.

Travellers with disabilities

Scottish attitudes towards travellers with **disabilities** still lag behind advances towards independence made in North America and Australia. Access to many public buildings has improved, with legislation ensuring that all new buildings have appropriate facilities. Some hotels and a handful of B&Bs have one or two adapted rooms, usually on the ground floor and with step-free showers, grab rails and wider doorways. It's worth keeping in mind, however, that installing ramps, lifts, wide doorways and disabled toilets is impossible in many of Scotland's older and historic buildings.

Most **trains** in Scotland have wheelchair lifts, and assistance is, in theory, available at all manned stations – see W scotrail.co.uk/plan-your-journey/ accessible-travel. Wheelchair-users (alone or with a companion) and blind or partially sighted people (with a companion only) are automatically given

> ### CALLING HOME FROM ABROAD
>
> To make an international call, dial the international access code (in Scotland it's 00), then the destination's country code, before the rest of the number. Note that the initial zero is omitted from the area code when dialling Ireland, Australia and New Zealand from abroad.
> **Australia** international access code + 61
> **Ireland** international access code + 353
> **New Zealand** international access code + 64
> **South Africa** international access code + 27
> **US and Canada** international access code + 1

thirty to fifty percent reductions on train fares (though there are usually no facilities for wheelchairs in first class), and people with other disabilities are eligible for the **Disabled Persons Railcard** (£20/ year; W disabledpersons-railcard.co.uk), which gives a third off most tickets. There are no bus discounts for disabled tourists. **Car rental** firm Avis will fit their cars (generally automatics only) with hand controls for free as long as you give them a few days' notice.

For more information and advice, contact the disability charity Capability Scotland (☎ 0131 337 9876, W capability-scotland.org.uk).

Working in Scotland

Post-Brexit, anyone intending to travel to work may require a special visa, including those from the EU, EEA or Switzerland: check if you'll need one at W gov.uk/ check-uk-visa.

Other nationals already needed a **work permit** in order to work legally in the UK, with eligibility worked out on a points-based system. There are exceptions to the above rules, and these are constantly changing, so for the latest regulations visit W gov.uk/government/ organisations/uk-visas-and-immigration.

Argyll

TOBERMORY HARBOUR, MULL

Argyll

Cut off for centuries from the rest of Scotland by the mountains and sea lochs that characterize the region, Argyll remains remote, its scatter of offshore islands forming part of the Inner Hebridean archipelago (the remaining Hebrides are dealt with in chapters 5 and 6). Geographically as well as culturally, this is a transitional area between Highland and Lowland, boasting a rich variety of scenery, from lush, subtropical gardens warmed by the Gulf Stream to flat and treeless islands on the edge of the Atlantic. And it's these islands that are the real magnet, from magnificent wildlife, endless walking possibilities and some of the world's finest whiskies. It's in the folds and twists of the countryside, the interplay of land and water and the views out to the islands that the strengths and beauties of mainland Argyll lie.

Much of mainland Argyll comprises remote peninsulas separated by a series of long sea lochs. The first peninsula you come to from Glasgow is **Cowal**, cut off from the rest of Argyll by a series of mountains including the Arrochar Alps. Nestling in one of Cowal's sea lochs is the **Isle of Bute**, whose capital, Rothesay, is probably the most appealing of the old Clyde steamer resorts. **Kintyre**, the long finger of land that stretches south towards Ireland, is possessed of some of Scotland's most alluring yet unspoilt scenery.

Arran, Scotland's most southerly big island – now strictly speaking part of North Ayrshire – is justifiably popular, with spectacular scenery ranging from the granite peaks of the north to the Lowland pasture of the south. Of the islands covered in this chapter, mountainous **Mull** is the most visited, though it's large enough to absorb the crowds, many of whom are only passing through en route to the tiny isle of **Iona**, a centre of Christian culture since the sixth century, or to **Tobermory**, the island's impossibly picturesque port (aka "Balamory"). Beautiful **Islay** draws the crowds primarily because of its fantastic whisky distilleries, while neighbouring **Jura** offers excellent walking opportunities. And, for those seeking further solitude, there's the island of **Colonsay**, with its beautiful golden sands, and the windswept islands of **Tiree** and **Coll**, which also boast great beaches and enjoy more sunny days than anywhere else in Scotland.

If you can, avoid **July** and **August**, when the crowds on Mull, Iona and Arran are at their densest – there's no guarantee the weather will be any better than during the rest of the year, and you might have more chance of avoiding the persistent **Scottish midge** (see page 39).

Brief history

The earliest man-made sites preserved in Argyll are the cluster of **Celtic** and **prehistoric remains** near Kilmartin. The region's name, however, means "Boundary of the Gaels", and refers to the Irish Celts who settled here in the fifth century AD, and whose **Kingdom of Dalriada** embraced much of what is now Argyll. Known to the Romans as *Scotti* – hence "Scotland" – it was the Irish Celts who promoted Celtic Christianity, and whose Gaelic language eventually became the national tongue. After a period of Norse invasion and settlement, the islands (and the peninsula of Kintyre) fell to the immensely powerful Somerled, who became King of the Hebrides and Lord of Argyll in the twelfth century. Somerled's successors, the MacDonalds, established Islay as their headquarters, but were in turn dislodged by Robert the Bruce. Of Bruce's allies, it was the **Campbells** who benefited most from the MacDonalds' demise and eventually, as

KILORAN BAY, COLONSAY

Highlights

❶ Mount Stuart, Bute Explore this architecturally overblown mansion set in magnificent grounds. See page 60

❷ Tobermory, Mull Archetypal fishing village, with colourful houses arranged around a sheltered harbour. See page 73

❸ Boat trip to Staffa and the Treshnish Isles Take the boat to see the "basalt cathedral" of Fingal's Cave, and then picnic amid the puffins on Lunga. See pages 78 and 79

❹ Golden beaches Kiloran Bay on Colonsay is one of the most perfect sandy beaches in Argyll, but there are plenty more on Islay, Coll and Tiree. See page 90

❺ Knapdale Explore ancient Atlantic woodland, lochs and coastline in one of Scotland's least-known but most alluring spots. See page 96

❻ Goat Fell, Arran An easy climb rewarded by spectacular views over craggy peaks to the Firth of Clyde. See page 109

❼ Whisky distilleries, Islay With eight beautifully sited distilleries to choose from, Islay is the ultimate whisky-lover's destination. See page 114

❽ Corryvreckan Whirlpool Get rocking and rolling in one of the UK's great natural phenomena. See page 120

HIGHLIGHTS ARE MARKED ON THE MAP ON PAGE 52

ARGYLL

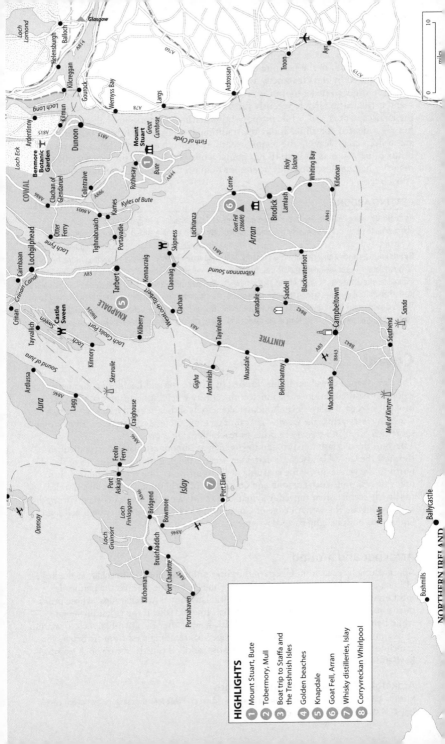

HIGHLIGHTS

1. Mount Stuart, Bute
2. Tobermory, Mull
3. Boat trip to Staffa and the Treshnish Isles
4. Golden beaches
5. Knapdale
6. Goat Fell, Arran
7. Whisky distilleries, Islay
8. Corryvreckan Whirlpool

1

the dukes of Argyll, gained control of the entire area – even today, they remain one of the largest landowners in the region.

In the aftermath of the Jacobite uprisings, Argyll, like the rest of the Highlands, was devastated by the **Clearances**, with thousands of crofters evicted from their homes in order to make room for profitable sheep farming – "the white plague" – and cattle rearing. More recently forestry plantations have dramatically altered the landscape of Argyll, while purpose-built marinas have sprouted all around the heavily indented coastline. Today the traditional industries of fishing and farming are in deep crisis, leaving the region ever more dependent on tourism and a steady influx of new settlers to keep things going, while Gaelic, once the language of the majority in Argyll, retains only a tenuous hold on the outlying islands of Islay, Coll and Tiree.

GETTING AROUND

ARGYLL

By train The one main train line in the region runs from Glasgow up to Oban, but takes in very few places covered in this chapter.

By bus Buses serve most major mainland settlements, with fairly regular services on weekdays, though usually a much-reduced service at weekends. Most of the islands have at least a handful of daily buses serving the main settlements. There's a good service from Glasgow down to Campbeltown via Arrochar, Inveraray and Tarbert. Most of the islands have at least a handful of daily buses too.

By car If you're planning to take a car across to one of the islands, it's essential that you book both your outward and return journeys as early as possible, as the ferries get booked up early, especially in summer.

By ferry CalMac (☏ 0800 066 5000, ⍵ calmac.co.uk) operate a comprehensive timetable of ferries between the islands, though this is reduced during the winter months. Individual ferry crossings are given in the relevant town accounts.

Cowal

The claw-shaped **Cowal** peninsula, formed by Loch Fyne and Loch Long, has been a popular destination since the nineteenth century when rapid steamer connections brought hordes of Glaswegian holidaymakers to its shores. It's still quickest to reach Cowal by ferry across the Clyde – by car, it's a long, though exhilarating, drive through some rich Highland scenery in order to reach the same spot.

Beyond the old-fashioned coastal towns such as **Dunoon**, the largest settlement in the area, the Cowal landscape is extremely varied, ranging from the Munros of the north to the gentle, low-lying coastline of the southwest. One way to explore it is to follow the 57-mile **Loch Lomond and Cowal Way** (⍵ lochlomondandcowalway.org), a terrifically scenic, often rugged, waymarked long-distance footpath between Portavadie and Inveruglas. The western edge of Cowal is marked by the long, narrow Loch Fyne, famous for both its kippers and oysters.

Arrochar and around

Approaching by road from Glasgow, the entry point to Cowal is **Arrochar**, at the head of Loch Long. The village itself is ordinary enough, but the area has the peninsula's most grandiose scenery, including the ambitiously named **Arrochar Alps**, whose peaks offer some of the best climbing in Argyll: Ben Ime (3318ft) is the tallest of the range, while Ben Arthur or "The Cobbler" (2891ft), named after the anvil-like rock formation at its summit, is the most distinctive (see page 55). Heading west from Arrochar, you can climb **Glen Croe**, a strategic hill pass whose saddle is called – for obvious reasons – **Rest-and-be-Thankful**.

Ardkinglas Woodland Garden and House

Just off the A83, behind the village of Cairndow · **Garden** Daily dawn–dusk · £5 · **House** April–Oct, visits by guided tour only, every Fri 2pm · £7.50 · ☏ 01499 600261, ⍵ ardkinglas.com

1

CLIMBING THE COBBLER

The jagged, triple-peaked ridge of Ben Arthur (2891ft) – better known as **The Cobbler** because of its resemblance to a cobbler bent over his work – is the most enticing of the peaks within the Argyll Forest Park. It's surprisingly accessible, with the most popular route starting from the car park at Succoth, on the road to Ardgartan. Skirting the woods, you join the Allt a' Bhalachain, which climbs steeply up to the col between the northern peak (known as The Cobbler's Wife) and The Cobbler itself. Traversing the ridge in order to ascend one or all of the three peaks is a tricky business, and the final scramble should only be attempted by experienced hikers. The total distance of the climb is only five miles, but the return trip will probably take you between five and six hours.

The wonderful **Ardkinglas Woodland Garden** contains exotic rhododendrons, azaleas, hydrangeas and a superb collection of conifers, including five so-called Champion Trees – those deemed to be the tallest or broadest examples of their kind within Britain. Indeed, the garden is home to what is still the tallest tree in the British Isles, a Grand Fir introduced by David Douglas in 1830 and now standing at a mighty 210ft. Look out, too, for the magnificent Silver Fir (159ft), typically found in Central Europe. A new addition to the gardens – and one that will appeal to kids first and foremost – is a cleverly conceived Gruffalo Trail, complete with galvanized steel characters from the much loved book.

In the southern part of the gardens stands **Ardkinglas House**, a particularly handsome Scottish Baronial mansion, built in 1907 by Robert Lorimer for the Noble family; the house was, technologically, fairly advanced for its time, and included a goods lift, central heating and the latest sanitary fittings, much of which remains unaltered to this day.

ARRIVAL AND DEPARTURE

By train Arrochar & Tarbet train station is a mile or so east of Arrochar, just off the A83 to Tarbet.
Destinations Glasgow (Mon–Sat 5–6 daily, Sun 3 daily; 1hr 20min).

ARROCHAR AND AROUND

By bus Buses stop just on the A814 near Church Rd in Arrochar.
Destinations Glasgow (6 daily; 1hr 10min); Inveraray (6 daily; 35min).

ACCOMMODATION AND EATING

Fascadail Church Rd, Arrochar ☎01301 702344, ⓦfascadail.com. A Victorian guesthouse set within its own grounds in the quieter southern part of the village, with five colourfully furnished and superbly equipped rooms. Enjoy breakfast in the dining room with glorious views across the garden. **£75**

Village Inn Shore Rd, Arrochar ☎01301 702279. If you need a bite to eat, or just fancy a pint, head for this delightful hostelry, a short walk south of the *Fascadail*. It has tables outside overlooking the loch as well as a cosy real-ale bar. Mon–Thurs & Sun 11am–11pm, Fri & Sat 11am–midnight.

Dunoon

The principal entry point into Cowal by sea is **Dunoon**. In the nineteenth century it grew from a village to a major Clyde seaside resort and favourite holiday spot for Glaswegians, but nowadays there's little to tempt you to stay, particularly with attractive countryside beckoning just beyond. That said, it is worth visiting on the last weekend in August, when the famous **Cowal Highland Gathering** (ⓦcowalgathering. com) takes place here. The largest event of its kind in the world, it culminates in the awesome spectacle of the massed pipes and drums of more than 150 bands marching through the streets.

Castle House Museum

Castle Gardens • Easter–Oct Mon–Sat 10am–4pm • £3 • ☎01369 701422, ⓦcastlehousemuseum.org.uk

The centre of town is dominated by a grassy lump of rock known as **Castle Hill**, crowned by Castle House, built in the 1820s by a wealthy Glaswegian and the subject

1

of a bitter dispute with the local populace over closure of the common land around his house. The people eventually won, and the grounds remain open to the public to this day, as does the house, which is home to the **Castle House Museum**. There's some good hands-on nature stuff for kids, and an excellent section on the Clyde steamers, as well as information about "Highland Mary", betrothed to Rabbie Burns (despite the fact that he already had a pregnant wife), who died of typhus before the pair could see through their plan to elope to the West Indies. A statue of her is in the grounds.

ARRIVAL AND INFORMATION

DUNOON

By ferry There are two ferry crossings across the Clyde from Gourock to Dunoon. The shorter, more frequent service is on Western Ferries (☎ 01369 704452, ⓦ western-ferries.co.uk) to Hunter's Quay, a mile north of the town centre. Calmac (☎ 0800 066 5000, ⓦ calmac.co.uk) operate a passenger only ferry service, which arrives at the main pier.

Destinations Gourock–Dunoon (Mon–Sat every 30min; Sun hourly; 25min); McInroy's Point–Hunter's Quay (every 20min; 20min).

By bus Buses stop on Alexandra Parade, not far from the main pier.

Destinations Colintraive (Mon–Sat 2–3 daily; 1hr); Inveraray (Mon–Sat 3 daily; 1hr 10min).

Tourist office In the absence of a tourist office, consult ⓦ visitcowal.co.uk).

ACCOMMODATION AND EATING

Abbot's Brae West Bay ☎ 01369 705021, ⓦ abbotsbrae. co.uk. Beautiful and welcoming family-run Victorian villa set in woods high above West Bay offering eight spacious rooms with wither sea or garden-facing views (one with a four-poster), though all feature evocative photographs depicting the local history. **£86**

Livingstones 58 John St ☎ 01369 703991. Despite its unappealing location next to Morrisons, this is Dunoon's one real restaurant of merit, an unpretentious bistro with nicely spaced tables and chairs offering pleasingly simple fare such as scallops with black pudding, and haggis chimichangas (£8.95); try and bag a table out in the conservatory. Tues–Sat noon–10pm.

Benmore Botanic Garden

A815, 6 miles north of Dunoon • Daily: March & Oct 10am–5pm; April–Sept 10am–6pm • £7 • ☎ 01369 706261, ⓦ rbge.org.uk • Buses #484 and #486 from Dunoon

Serenely pitched amid lush mountain scenery at the foot of Loch Eck, **Benmore Botanic Garden** is an offshoot of Edinburgh's Royal Botanic Garden. It's a beautifully laid-out garden occupying 120 acres of lush hillside, the mild, moist climate allowing a vast range of unusual plants to grow here, with different sections devoted to rainforest species native to places as exotic as China, Chile and Bhutan. The garden boasts 300 species of rhododendron and a memorably striking avenue of great redwoods, planted in 1863 and now over 150ft tall. You can also wander through a Victorian **fernery**, as impressive for its architectural features – notably a fine vaulted entrance, grotto and pool – as for the plants housed within. And look out, too, for "Puck's Hut", designed by the prolific Scottish architect Sir Robert Lorimer. Clad in various timbers and tiled with red cedar, it originally stood in Puck's Glen in the Eachaig Valley, hence the name.

Kyles of Bute

The mellower landscape of southwest Cowal, which stands in complete contrast to the bustle of Dunoon or the Highland grandeur of the Argyll Forest Park, becomes immediate as soon as you head into the area. And there are few more beautiful sights in Argyll than the **Kyles of Bute**, two slivers of water that separate Cowal from the bleak bulk of the Isle of Bute and constitute some of the best sailing territory in Scotland.

Colintraive and Tighnabruaich

Separated from the Isle of Bute by barely more than a couple of hundred yards, **Colintraive**, on the eastern Kyles, is not especially noteworthy, but you may well wind

1

WALKING UP PUCK'S GLEN

It's possible to combine a visit to Benmore Botanic Garden with one of the local **forest walks**, the most popular being a leisurely stroll up the rocky ravine of **Puck's Glen**, which begins from the car park a mile south of the gardens. Roughly two miles long, and with a total ascent of some 560ft, it's a beautiful little walk up a narrow defile enclosed by rocky walls and dense trees, and replete with rushing burns, waterfalls and footbridges.

---

up here as it's where the CalMac car ferry departs to Bute. The most popular spot from which to appreciate the Kyles, however, is along the A8003 as it rises dramatically above the sea lochs before descending to the peaceful, lochside village of **Tighnabruaich**. Peaceful that is, until the local shinty team, Kyles Athletic, takes to the field; founded in 1896, they remain one of the sport's most illustrious names despite only sporadic success in recent years, the last major victory coming in the 2012 Camanachd Cup, Scotland's most prestigious national shinty competition.

ARRIVAL AND ACTIVITIES   KYLES OF BUTE

BY FERRY

Colintraive Ferries to Bute depart from the ferry slip in the centre of the village.

Portavadie If you're driving to Kintyre, Islay or Jura, you can avoid the long haul around Loch Fyne – some seventy miles or so – by using the ferry to Tarbert from Portavadie, three miles southwest of Kames.

Destinations Portavadie–Tarbert (hourly; 25min); Colintraive–Rhubodach, Bute (every 30min; 5min).

BY BUS

Colintraive Buses drop off and pick up by the ferry slipway.
Tighnabruaich Buses stop near the post office.
Destinations Colintraive–Dunoon (Mon–Sat 2–3 daily; 1hr); Colintraive–Tighnabruaich (Mon–Sat 2 daily; 35min);

Tighnabruaich–Portavadie (Mon–Sat 3–4 daily; 25min).

ACTIVITIES

Portavadie Spa Millhouse (daily 8am–8pm; ☎01700 811075, ⓦportavadie.com; £22/day). Stunningly located on the edge of Loch Fyne, Portavadie spa comprises a beautifully designed complex of heated indoor and outdoor pools, saunas, and, best of all, an outdoor infinity pool right on the water's edge affording marvellous views out to Loch Fyne and Arran.

Sailing The Tighnabruaich Sailing School (☎01700 811717, ⓦtssargyll.co.uk) is located two miles south of the village at Carry Farm; they offer private tuition in dinghies (£69 for 3hr/£130 per day, or £49 for 3hr/£90 per day if in a group of three or more), as well as two-day sailing courses (£175).

ACCOMMODATION AND EATING

Colintraive Hotel South of the ferry slipway, Colintraive ☎01700 841207, ⓦcolintraivehotel.com. A favourite with yachties, the *Colintraive* is worth seeking out for its four crisply decorated rooms (two with views of the Kyles), as well as its delicious fresh dishes like linguini with mussels and crayfish tails in a garlic sauce. **£99**
Portavadie Spa Millhouse ☎01700 811 075, ⓦportavadie.com. There's a wide range of accommodation

here, including the *Lodge*, which offers lush, light-filled, Scandinavian-style rooms (sleeping two to four), and a mix of studio and luxury apartments (variously sleeping two to six) with open-plan living areas; for food, there's the *Marina* restaurant or, more enjoyably, the pleasingly informal *Lodge Kitchen & Bar*, offering the likes of pulled McIntyre of Bute gammon steak with fried hen's eggs, chips and mustard mayonnaise (£13). Lodge **£129**, apartments **£149–229**

Isle of Bute

The island of **Bute** is in many ways simply an extension of the Cowal peninsula, from which it is separated by the narrow Kyles of Bute. Thanks to its mild climate and its ferry link with Wemyss Bay, Bute has been a popular holiday and convalescence spot for Clydesiders for over a century. Its chief town, **Rothesay**, still rates as the most attractive seaside resort on the Clyde, although it does feel a little weary in places these days. The most compelling reason to visit Bute, however, is the chance to amble around **Mount Stuart**, one of Scotland's most singular aristocratic piles.

1

Bute's inhabitants live around the two wide bays on the island's east coast, which resembles one long seaside promenade. To escape the crowds head for the sparsely populated west coast, which, in any case, has the sandiest beaches. The best of these, six miles south of Rothesay, are **Kilchattan Bay**, which has a lovely arc of sand overlooked by a row of grand Victorian houses, and, further up the west coast, **Ettrick Bay**.

ARRIVAL AND DEPARTURE
ISLE OF BUTE

By ferry Two CalMac ferry services operate from the mainland to Bute; the main crossing is from Wemyss Bay to Rothesay, and the other is the very short crossing at the northern tip of the island, from Colintraive, in Cowal, to Rhubodach.

Destinations Colintraive–Rhubodach (every 30min; 5min); Wemyss Bay–Rothesay (every 45–60min; 35min).

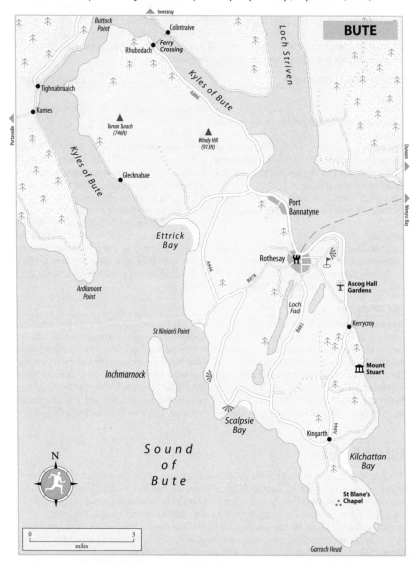

BUTE FESTIVALS

Bute stages a trio of terrific annual events; namely, the long-standing **Bute Jazz Festival** (ⓦbutejazz.com) over the May Bank Holiday, which always draws some class international artists; **Bute Fest** (ⓦbutefest.co.uk) on the last weekend of July, featuring well-established pop, rock and folk acts; and finally, its own **Highland Games** (ⓦbutehighlandgames. org) on the Saturday of the third weekend of August – this ends in a grand parade through town.

Rothesay

Bute's only town, **ROTHESAY** is a handsome Victorian resort, set in a wide sweeping bay, backed by green hills, with a classic palm-tree promenade and 1920s pagoda-style pavilion originally built to house the **Winter Gardens**; the long awaited refurbishment and reopening of this Art Deco gem in 2019 has certainly given the shorefront a new lease of life. Elsewhere, many of the buildings could use a lick of paint or two, but despite this, the town retains a certain well-worn charm.

Pavilion toilets

The Pier • Easter–Sept daily 8am–7.45pm; Oct–Easter 9am–4.45pm • 40p

Rothesay's **Victorian toilets**, built in 1899 by Twyfords, are a feast of marble, ceramics and brass so ornate that they're now one of the town's most celebrated sights. The Victorians didn't make provision for ladies' conveniences, so the women's half is a modern add-on, but if the coast is clear the attendant – attired in a neat burgundy waistcoat – will allow ladies a tour of the gents, clad in colourfully painted ceramic tiles and mosaics.

Rothesay Castle

Castle Hill St • April–Sept daily 9.30am–5.30pm; Oct–March Mon–Wed, Sat & Sun 10am–4pm • £6; HES • ☎ 01700 502691, ⓦ historicenvironment.scot

Incongruously located amid the town's backstreets stand the militarily useless, but architecturally impressive, moated ruins of **Rothesay Castle**. Built around the twelfth century, it was twice captured by the Norwegians, firstly in 1230, then in 1263; such vulnerability was the reasoning behind the unusual, almost circular, curtain wall, with its four big drum towers, only one of which remains fully intact. Look upwards inside the tower and you'll see a superbly preserved dovecot (with nesting boxes), which was a seventeenth-century addition. The wall was actually heightened in the early sixteenth century – the line is clearly identifiable in the stonework; the earlier, lower half comprises light ashlar, the upper half is darker and of rougher hew.

Bute Museum

7 Stuart St • April–Sept Mon–Sat 10.30am–3.30pm, Sun 1.30–3.30pm; Feb, March, Oct & Nov Tues–Thurs & Sat 1.30–3.30pm • £4 • ☎ 01700 505067, ⓦ butemuseum.org.uk

At first glance, **Bute Museum**, just up behind the castle, looks like your average, rather dull local-history museum, but it's well worth popping into. Inchmarnock, a tiny island to the west of Bute, provides the greatest source of treasures, not least a stunning beaded necklace made of jet, which belonged to the so-called "Queen of the Inch", whose remains were discovered in a Bronze Age cist in 1961. Look out, too, for some exquisite pieces of incised slate on which children would practise their writing or drawing, such as one depicting horses grazing; these date from around the eighth century. The museum's prize exhibit, however, is the so-called "hostage stone"; dating from the time of the Vikings, the drawing depicts a hostage-taking scene, and is believed to be the only one of its kind discovered. The local photographs make for fascinating viewing too.

1

Ascog Hall Gardens

Ascog, a mile or so east of Rothesay • Easter–Oct daily 10am–5pm • £5 • ☎ 01700 503461, ⓦ ascogfernery.com

The **Ascog Hall Gardens** is chiefly notable for its highly unusual **Victorian fernery**, a beautiful, dank place, sunk into the ground, and featuring ferns from all over the world. This one fairly recently replaced the original fernery dating from around 1870, its red, weathered sandstone walls, shade and humidity ideal conditions for cultivating these plants. The gardens themselves are a delight, featuring a truly exotic array of flowers, such as rhododendrons, wild orchids and a stunning array of blue poppies; look out, too, for the magnificent Chilean firetree. The best time to visit is spring when the aforementioned flowers are in full bloom.

ARRIVAL AND DEPARTURE ROTHESAY

By ferry The CalMac terminal is right in the middle of the Esplanade.

Destinations Wemyss Bay (every 45–60min; 35min).

By bus The main point for bus departures is Guildford Square, opposite the ferry terminal.

Destinations Kilchattan Bay (Mon–Sat hourly, 3 on Sun; 30min); Mount Stuart (Mon–Sat hourly; 15min); Rhubodach (Mon–Sat 2–3 daily; 20min).

GETTING AROUND AND INFORMATION

Tourist office Inside the Winter Gardens on Victoria St (April–May & Oct daily 10am–5pm, June & Sept daily 9.30am–5pm, July & Aug daily 9.30am–5.30pm, Nov–March Mon–Sat 10am–4pm, Sun 11am–3pm; ☎ 01700 507043, ⓦ visitbute.com). Also located here is the "Discovery Centre", which has some well-presented displays on the life and times of Bute.

ACCOMMODATION

Boat House 15 Battery Place ☎ 01700 502696, ⓦ the boathouse-bute.co.uk. Chic and utterly contemporary guesthouse with five self-contained suites furnished in cool pinks, greys and blacks and offering all the modern conveniences you could wish for. Each suite – all of which have sea views – sleeps between two and four and offers a kitchen-cum-dining room; breakfast ingredients (bread, jam, coffee, cereal) are also provided. Two-night minimum stay at weekends. £80

Bute Backpackers 36 Argyle St ☎ 01700 501876, ⓦ butebackpackers.co.uk. Conveniently located 5min walk along the seafront towards Port Bannatyne, the island's sole hostel offers reasonably furnished two- to six-bed rooms, with shared shower facilities. Breakfast is not included but there's a large kitchen for general use. Dorms £20; doubles £50

EATING AND DRINKING

Harry Haws 23–25 High St ☎ 01700 505857, ⓦ harryhawsbute.co.uk. Wholesome, warming food is the deal here, stone-baked pizzas (£9.50), steaks and slow cooked leg of lamb with buckwheat (£15.50). The interior, meanwhile, offers up some lovely, homely touches, notably framed black-and-white photos of locals and visitors to Rothesay over the years. Daily noon–9pm.

Musicker 11 High St ☎ 01700 502287, ⓦ musicker.co.uk. Funky café-cum-music retailer just across from the castle, with delicious coffee and cakes, decent veggie snacks and even better music, courtesy of the rather ace jukebox and occasional jam session. Mon–Sat 10am–5pm.

Mount Stuart

4 miles south of Rothesay • **Grounds** Daily 10am–6pm • £8.25 • **House and grounds** April–Oct daily noon–4pm • £13 • ☎ 01700 503877, ⓦ mountstuart.com

Bute's most compelling sight is **Mount Stuart**, a huge, fantasy Gothic mansion set amid acres of lush woodland gardens overlooking the Firth of Clyde, and ancestral home of the seventh marquess of Bute, also known as Johnny Bute (or, in his Formula One racing days, as Johnny Dumfries; see opposite). The building was created by the marvellously eccentric third marquess and architect Robert Rowand Anderson after a fire in 1877 destroyed the family seat. With little regard for expense, the marquess shipped in tons of Italian marble, built a railway line to transport it down the coast and employed craftsmen who had worked with William Burges on the marquess's other medieval concoction, Cardiff Castle. With 127 rooms spread out over five floors, it's on quite some scale.

JOHNNY DUMFRIES

As unlikely as it seemed, the 7th Marquess of Bute was once a hugely successful **motor racing driver**. Racing as one **Johnny Dumfries** (he was, at that time, the Earl of Dumfries), the marquess began racing in the 1980s, starting out in Formula 3 before graduating to Formula 1 in 1986, racing for the JPS Lotus team as second driver to the legendary Ayrton Senna – he raced fifteen times, compiling three points. Dumfries' greatest achievement, however, came in 1988, when he won the Le Mans 24 Hours as part of the Jaguar team. He sadly passed away in 2021. The current Marquess of Bute is John Crichton-Stuart.

The *pièce de résistance* is the columned **Marble Hall**, its vaulted ceiling and stained-glass windows decorated with the signs of the zodiac, reflecting the marquess's taste for mysticism; during World War I, the hall was used as a makeshift medical centre, some lovely photos of which you can see in the courtyard toilets. He was equally fond of animal and plant imagery; hence you'll find birds feeding on berries in the dining-room frieze, and monkeys reading (and tearing up) books and scrolls in the library. Look out also for the unusual heraldic ceiling in the drawing room, which is otherwise notable for its astonishing collection of art; casually dotted along the walls, you'll find paintings by Tintoretto, Titian and Veronese, among others. After all the heavy furnishings, there's aesthetic relief in the vast **Marble Chapel**, built entirely out of dazzling white Carrara marble, with a magnificent Cosmati floor pattern.

Upstairs, the highlight is the **Horoscope Room**, so named after the fine astrological ceiling, though do seek out the wall panels carved with occasionally amusing friezes, such as a frog playing a lute.

The grounds

There are a number of fine **walks** to be had within the vast grounds, ranging from a 45-minute stroll down through the woods to the seashore, to a more vigorous, two-hour walk taking in the **Wee Garden** and **Calvary Pond**, the latter located at the head of a small burn. Before you leave Mount Stuart, take a look at the planned village of **Kerrycroy**, just beyond the main exit. It was built by the second Marquess in the early nineteenth century, allegedly for his wife, Lady Maria North, who was missing her home town of Guildford so much that he ordered elements of it to be replicated, hence the semi-detached houses – alternately mock-Tudor and whitewashed stone – that form a crescent overlooking a pristine village green and, beyond, the sea.

ACCOMMODATION AND EATING	MOUNT STUART

Mount Stuart ☎01700 503877, ⓦmountstuart.com. Scattered around the estate are several stunning self-catering properties, each one sleeping between four and eight. Furnished to impeccably high standards, they've got more than ample space, with bright bedrooms and bathrooms, superb kitchens, and cosy open-plan living spaces complete with attractive wood burners. One week from **£350**

Bute Kitchen Main House courtyard, Mount Stuart

☎01700 505276, ⓦmountstuart.com. Mount Stuart's on-site restaurant is certainly worth making a trek to even if you're not visiting the estate. All ingredients are sourced from the island, including many from Mount Stuart's own kitchen garden, resulting in simple but scrumptious dishes like smoked salmon fishcakes with charred lemon and aioli (£6.50) and handmade haggis sausage roll with caramelised onion chutney. Daily 10am–5pm.

Kilchattan Bay and around

Six miles south of Rothesay, east-facing **Kilchattan Bay** has a lovely arc of sand overlooked by a row of grand Victorian houses. The bay is also the starting point for the wonderful **West Island Way Walk**, which runs the complete length of the island for about thirty miles, taking in coastline, farmland, moors and forests.

1

St Blane's Chapel

Just after the road turns off left to Kilchattan Bay, another road (next to the *Kingarth Hotel*) runs south to the chapel

St Blane's Chapel is a twelfth-century ruin beautifully situated in open countryside amid the foundations of an earlier Christian settlement established in the sixth century. From the car park, it's a short uphill walk through farmland; over the brow of a hill you come upon a well-built churchyard wall surrounded by mature trees. The ruined chapel sits amid a rather peculiar two-tier graveyard, the upper area reserved for the men of the parish while the women were consigned to the lower one.

Scalpsie Bay

Four miles up the coast from St Blane's is the sandy strand of **Scalpsie Bay**, which is by far the best spot on the island for **seal watching**. From the small car park on the main road, a footpath runs down to the beach, from where you walk west along the increasingly rocky shore to a couple of excellent viewing points. The many sunken timber posts dotted along the beach are the remains of World War II anti-glider defences, as the area was particularly susceptible to German invasion. Indeed, Scalpsie's military role continued right up until the end of the Cold War; the cottage near the car park was used as a listening post for enemy submarines patrolling the Firth of Clyde.

Inveraray

The traditional county town of Argyll, and a classic example of an eighteenth-century planned town, **INVERARAY** was built in the 1770s by the Duke of Argyll in order to distance his newly rebuilt castle from the hoi polloi in the town, and to establish a commercial and legal centre for the region. Inveraray has changed very little since and remains an absolute set piece of Scottish Georgian architecture, with a truly memorable setting, the brilliant white arches of Front Street reflected in the still waters of Loch Fyne.

Despite its picture-book location, there's not much more to Inveraray than its distinctive **Main Street** (perpendicular to Front Street), flanked by whitewashed terraces, which are characterized by black window casements. At the top of the street, the road divides to circumnavigate the town's Neoclassical **church**: originally the southern half served the Gaelic-speaking community, while the northern half served those who spoke English.

Inveraray Jail

Church Square • April–Oct daily 9.30am–6pm; Nov–March 10am–5pm • £12.25 • ☎ 01499 302381, ⓦ inverarayjail.co.uk

Inveraray's most enjoyable attraction is **Inveraray Jail**, comprising an attractive Georgian courthouse and two grim prison blocks. Originally built in 1820, the prison blocks ceased to function in 1889, though the courthouse continued in one form or another until 1954. The jail is now a thoroughly enjoyable museum, which graphically recounts prison conditions from medieval times to the twentieth century.

Following a trawl through some of the region's most notorious crimes, you get to listen to a **re-enactment** of a trial of the period, staged in the original semicircular courthouse of some 170 years ago. More fascinating, though, are the prisons themselves; the Old Prison housed all convicts – men, women, children, the insane – until 1849 when the New Prison was built, whose twelve cells held male prisoners only. In the courtyard stands the minute "**Airing Yards**", two caged cells where the prisoners got to exercise for an hour a day, though they were forbidden to talk to each other.

Bell Tower

The Avenue • July to mid-Sept Mon–Fri 10.30am–4.30pm • £4 • ⓦ inveraraybelltower.co.uk

The one sight that often gets overlooked in Inveraray is the **Bell Tower**, a magnificent 126ft-high, free-standing structure adjacent to All Saints Church. The tower was originally built as a war memorial, in honour of members of the Campbell clan (it was commissioned by Niall Campbell, the tenth Duke of Argyll), and not long after its completion, the bells – allegedly the second heaviest peal of ten bells in the world after those in Wells Cathedral – were cast. The bells remain the standout feature of the tower, and you can view these close up as you make your way up the dizzying spiral staircase. Having climbed the last of the 176 steps, you are rewarded with superlative views of Loch Fyne and the forested hills beyond.

Inveraray Castle

A 10min walk north of Main St • April–Oct daily 10am–5.45pm • £12.50 • ☎ 01499 302203, ⓦ inveraray-castle.com

Inveraray Castle remains the family home of the Duke of Argyll, the present (thirteenth) incumbent being Duke Torquhil Ian Campbell. Built in 1745, it was given a touch of the Loire in the nineteenth century with the addition of dormer windows and conical corner spires. In truth, the interior is fairly dull, save for a pair of Beauvais tapestries in the drawing room, and the armoury hall, whose displays of weaponry – supplied to the Campbells by the British government to put down the Jacobites – rise through several storeys. Otherwise, look out for the small exhibition on Rob Roy, complete with his belt, sporran and dirk handle.

ARRIVAL AND DEPARTURE — INVERARAY

By bus Buses stop on Front St, situated opposite the tourist office.

Destinations Campbeltown (4–5 daily; 2hr 20min); Dunoon (3 daily; 1hr 10min); Glasgow (4–6 daily; 2hr); Oban (4 daily; 1hr 5min); Tarbert (4–5 daily; 1hr 20min).

ACCOMMODATION

Inveraray Hostel Dalmally Rd ☎ 01499 302454, ⓦ inverarayhostel.co.uk. Small, low-key hostel in a low, wood-and-stone chalet-type building a short walk up the A819 to Oban (just beyond the petrol station). Single, double, twin, triple and quad rooms, all with shared shower facilities, as well as a lounge and kitchen for communal use. Breakfast £3.90. Easter to Oct. Dorms £20, doubles £46

Loch Fyne Hotel Shore Rd ☎ 01499 302980, ⓦ crerar hotels.com. Refined spa hotel out on the road to Lochgilphead offering the full complement of spa facilities (pool, hot tub, steam room and jacuzzi), in addition to a supremely comfortable range of rooms, many with a tartan theme. £125

★ **Newton Hall** Shore Rd ☎ 01499 302484, ⓦ newtonhall guesthouse.co.uk. This former church now accommodates an outstanding ensemble of six rooms, each one named after an Argyll island. Each has been conceived in a completely different style, though they're all possessed of strikingly bold colours and cool, modern furnishings; a couple of rooms have even retained the Gothic-style church windows, through which there are splendid views across the loch. £70

EATING AND DRINKING

Fyne Ales Brewery Achadunan, 1.5 miles north of Cairndow and 8.5 miles east of Inveraray ☎ 01499 600120, ⓦ fyneales.com. Friendly, family-run farm brewery superbly located in a lush valley at the head of Loch Fyne where you can sample a wide range of ales – cask, keg and bottled – in their welcoming tap room, while munching on a sausage roll; core range ales include Jarl (a former British Champion ale), Highlander and the splendidly named Hurricane Jack. Brewery tours (£7.50), including tasting, are also available. Daily 10am–6pm.

The George Hotel Main St East ☎ 01499 302111, ⓦ thegeorgehotel.co.uk. The rambling, and very convivial restaurant/bar of The George Hotel feels like a proper pub, with its flagstone flooring, log fires, and dimly lit nooks and crannies. The food is surprisingly accomplished too, such as pork belly cured in Loch Fyne whisky with pickled cabbage, though there are of course the classic pub standards. Daily 11am–11pm.

★ **Loch Fyne Oyster Bar and Shop** On the A83, 2 miles north of Cairndow and 8 miles east of Inveraray ☎ 01499 600482, ⓦ lochfyne.com. On the shores of Loch Fyne is the famous Loch Fyne Oyster Bar, which spawned the Loch Fyne chain of restaurants. The food is utterly delicious and beautifully thought out, from smoked haddock and bacon chowder to salmon fillet with smoked paprika cream and spring onions (£20). The restaurant itself oozes class, though it's anything but stuffy, but more fun is the superb marble-topped oyster bar where you can tuck into oysters (6 for £12), clams, cockles and heaps of other tasty wet stuff. The gorgeous on-site shop/deli is a great place to assemble a gourmet picnic. Reservations advised. Restaurant daily 9am–10pm; shop Mon–Sat 8.30am–6pm, Sun 9am–5pm.

Samphire 6a Arkland ☎01499 302321, ⓦsamphire seafood.com. Smart yet informal restaurant whose dazzling seafood menu features flamboyantly prepared dishes like pancetta-wrapped loin of cod with roasted pepper butter bean and chorizo ragout (£16.95), or you might just like to plump for some poached Isle of Mull scallops in a white wine and parsley sauce (£10). Closed Jan. Wed–Sun noon–2.30pm & 5–9pm.

Oban and around

The solidly Victorian resort of **OBAN** enjoys a superb setting – the island of Kerrera to the southwest providing its bay with a natural shelter – distinguished by a bizarre granite amphitheatre, dramatically lit at night, on the hilltop above the town. Despite a population of just eight thousand, it's by far the largest port in northwest Scotland, the second-largest town in Argyll, and the main departure point for ferries to the Hebrides. Although Oban is not blessed with a particularly stunning array of sights, there's more than enough to keep you entertained for a day or so, and it's one of the best places in Scotland to eat fresh seafood.

Oban lies at the centre of the coastal region known as Lorn, named after the Irish Celt Loarn, who, along with his brothers Fergus and Oengus, settled here around 500 AD. The mainland is very picturesque, although its beauty is no secret – to escape the crowds, head off and explore the nearby islands, like **Lismore** or **Kerrera**, just offshore, or to the peninsula of Appin or quiet, freshwater Loch Awe.

McCaig's Tower

Apart from the setting and views, the only truly remarkable sight in Oban is the town's landmark, **McCaig's Tower**, a stiff ten-minute climb from the quayside. Built in imitation of Rome's Colosseum, it was the brainchild of a local businessman a century ago, who had the twin aims of alleviating off-season unemployment among the local stonemasons and creating a museum, art gallery and chapel. Originally, the plan was to add a 95-foot central tower, but work never progressed further than the exterior granite walls before McCaig died. In his will, McCaig gave instructions for the lancet windows to be filled with bronze statues of the family, though no such work was ever undertaken. Instead, the folly has been turned into a sort of walled garden, providing a wonderful seaward panorama, particularly at sunset.

Oban Distillery

Stafford St • Jan–Feb & Dec daily noon–4.30pm; March–April & Oct–Nov 9.30am–5pm; May–Sept Mon–Fri 9.30am–7.30pm; last tour 1hr 15min before closing • £8 • ☎01631 572004, ⓦ discovering-distilleries.com

Oban Distillery is one of Scotland's oldest, founded in 1794 by the Stevenson brothers, and today it produces in excess of a million bottles a year of its lightly peaty malt, which is acknowledged to be a touch easier on the palate than many other whiskies produced hereabouts. The excellent 45-minute guided **tours** take in the Mash House, with four massive Scandinavian larch washbacks, and the Still House, with its beautifully proportioned copper stills – the tours end, as is the custom, with a generous dram.

Oban War and Peace Exhibition

Corran Esplanade • May–Oct Mon–Thurs 10am–6pm, Fri–Sun 10am–4pm; March, April & Nov daily 10am–4pm • Free • ☎01631 570007, ⓦ obanmuseum.org.uk

Housed in the old *Oban Times* building beside the Art Deco *Regent Hotel* on the Esplanade, the charming **War and Peace Exhibition** is stuffed full of local (and not so local) memorabilia – bizarrely, even a chunk of the Berlin Wall has ended up here. Overall, though, the emphasis is on the wartime role of the area around Oban, when it operated as a flying-boat base, mustering point for Atlantic convoys, and as a training centre for the D-Day landings. Also on display are bits of cargo (including a ladder) washed ashore from the Dutch cargo steamer, the *Breda*, which was attacked in nearby Ardmucknish Bay in 1940. It's now a popular site for wreck diving.

1

ARRIVAL AND DEPARTURE

By plane Tiny Oban Airport is six miles north of town in North Connel (☎01631 572910, ⓦobanandtheislesairports. com); the nearest train station to the airport is Connel Ferry, or take bus #405 from Oban to Barcaldine.

Destinations Coll (Wed 2 daily, Fri & Sun 1 daily; 30min); Colonsay (Thurs 2 daily); Islay (Thurs 2 daily; 40min); Tiree (Wed 2 daily; 1hr).

By train The station is on Railway Pier.

Destinations Glasgow, Queen St (4 daily; 3hr 15min).

By bus The bus station is on Station Rd, adjacent to the train station.

Destinations Appin (Mon–Sat 2–3 daily; 45min); Connel

(daily hourly; 10–15min); Cruachan (5 daily; 30min); Fort William (3 daily; 1hr 30min); Glasgow (5 daily; 3hr); Inveraray (4 daily; 1hr 10min); Kilmartin (Mon–Fri 6 daily, Sat 2 daily; 1hr 15min).

By ferry The CalMac terminal (☎01631 566688, ⓦcalmac. co.uk) is on Railway Pier, close to both the train and bus stations.

Destinations Achnacroish, Lismore (Mon–Sat 4 daily, 2 on Sun; 55min); Castlebay, Barra (daily except Wed; 4hr 45min); Coll (daily except Wed & Fri; 2hr 40min); Colonsay (daily; 2hr 15min); Craignure, Mull (9 daily; 50min); Tiree (1 daily; 3hr 40min).

INFORMATION, ACTIVITIES AND TOURS

Tourist office 3 North Pier (April, May, Sept & Oct Mon–Sat 9am–5pm, Sun 10am–5pm; June Mon–Sat 9am–6pm, Sun 10am–5pm; July & Aug Mon–Sat 9am–7pm, Sun 10am–5pm; Nov–March Mon–Sat 10am–5pm, Sun 11am–4pm; ☎01631 563122, ⓦoban.org.uk).

Bike rental Oban Cycles, 87 George St (Tues–Sat 10am–5pm; ☎01631 566033, ⓦobancyclescotland.com), rents bikes (£25/day) and also does repairs and servicing.

Diving If you fancy something a little more vigorous, head to the Puffin Dive Centre, based a mile south of Oban at Port Gallanach (☎01631 566088, ⓦpuffin.org.uk), where you can take the plunge with a fully qualified instructor (£90/2hr).

Wildlife-watching tours The best of the wildlife-watching companies hereabouts is Coastal Connection, based on Oban Pier (☎01631 565833, ⓦcoastal-connection.co.uk), who offer 2–5hr trips (£30–45) spotting bird and sea life.

ACCOMMODATION

Oban is positively heaving with **hotels** and **B&Bs**, most of them reasonably priced and many within easy walking distance of the quayside. Unlikely as it is, if you're struggling to find a place, note that there are stacks more guesthouses in Connel, five miles north.

Cologin Country Chalets 2.5 miles south of town in Lerags Glen ☎01631 564501, ⓦcologin.co.uk. Secreted away in a lush glen, this fabulous mix of one-and two-bedroom self-catering lodges and cabins provide some respite from the relative hubbub of Oban; the popular on-site Barn Bar (March–Oct) serves excellent bar meals, as well as breakfast if you can't be bothered to do your own. Per night **£150**; per week **£650**

Hawthornbank Guest House Dalriach Rd ☎01631 562041, ⓦhawthornbank.co.uk. Decent, traditional guesthouse in the lower backstreets of Oban, just across the road from the leisure centre. Its seven immaculately kept rooms, one of which has a four-poster bed, come complete with mahogany antique furnishings and a small seating area with coffee table. March–Oct. **£75**

Kilchrenan House Corran Esplanade ☎01631 562663, ⓦkilchrenanhouse.co.uk. A bright and hospitable home located near the cathedral, with sixteen rooms, variously furnished with antique furnishings, leather armchairs and tartan sofas to go alongside the tremendous sea views. March–Oct. **£75**

Oban Backpackers Breadalbane St ☎01631 562107, ⓦobanbackpackers.com. Large, friendly and colourful hostel with a range of differently sized dorms, the largest

SEE MAP PAGE 65

accommodating twelve beds. The big, open lounge-dining area has mismatched sofas, a pool table and a real fire. Breakfast £3. Dorms **£18.50**

Oban Youth Hostel Corran Esplanade ☎01631 562025, ⓦhostellingscotland.org.uk. Occupying a super seafront position in a converted Victorian house, this hostel hardly sparkles with character, but the two- to six-bed en-suite rooms are kept to a very high standard. The only downside is that it's a fair trek with a backpack from the ferry terminal. Breakfast £5.95. Doubles **£47**; dorms **£24**

★ **The Old Manse Guest House** Dalraich Rd ☎01631 564886, ⓦobanguesthouse.co.uk. There are few more welcoming places in town than this spotlessly clean Victorian villa whose five rooms (two with sea views) offer thoughtful touches all round, including CD players, complimentary sherry, and a great selection of toiletries. The breakfast is top-notch too. Mid-Feb to Oct. **£92**

CAMPSITE

Oban Caravan & Camping Park Gallanach Rd ☎01631 562425, ⓦobancaravanpark.com. Two miles southwest of Oban up a pretty glen, this is a huge, well-equipped site with lots of camping space and great views across to Kerrera, with a good chance of a breeze to blow the midges away; there are also a handful of cool pods, with a small kitchen area, that sleep two to four people. Facilities include a self-catering kitchen, TV/games lounge, BBQs and on-site shop. April to mid-Oct. Per pitch **£18**; pods from **£45**

EATING

SEE MAP PAGE 65

Oban rates as one of the finest places in Scotland to eat **fresh seafood**, with a handful of highly commendable seafood **restaurants** to choose from, not to mention several superb fish-and-chip shops. Moreover, if you're on the go, or just need a quick bite while waiting for the ferry, you'll find a cluster of excellent seafood **stalls** down by the harbour.

Coast 104 George St ☎01631 569900, ⓦcoastoban. co.uk. A slick place with a metropolitan atmosphere, serving acclaimed and original fish dishes like pan-fried fillet of hake with sea vegetables and fresh crab broth (£17.95) and Oban whisky cured hot smoked salmon. As you'd expect from one of the town's classiest outfits, the atmosphere and service are first-rate. Mon–Sat noon–2.30pm & 5.30–10pm, Sun 5.30–9.30pm.

Ee-usk North Pier ☎01631 565666, ⓦeeusk.com. Salmon mousse, sea bass with creamed leeks and savoury mash, and glistening seafood platters (£22.95 for two) are typical offerings in this bright and breezy waterfront restaurant that makes the most of the uninterrupted harbour views. Children under 12 are not allowed in the evenings. Daily noon–3pm & 5.45–10pm.

Julie's Coffee House 33 Stafford St ☎01631 565952, ⓦjuliescoffeehouse.co.uk. The pick of the many cafés hereabouts, this is a warm, friendly local with super home-baked treats – from panini to peanut butter and chocolate cheesecake – and tasty coffee. Tues–Sat 10am–5pm, also Mon in July & Aug.

★ **Oban Fish and Chips** 116 George St ☎01631 567000, ⓦobanfishandchipshop.co.uk. A cut above your average chippie, with some surprisingly sophisticated food like battered salt and pepper squid with chilli jam (£13.50) to go alongside the stock fish and chips; good ice cream too, and there's seating available. Daily 11am–11pm.

Original Green Shack Railway Pier. Long-standing and hugely popular seafood shack serving langoustine sandwiches, scallops in hot garlic butter (£9.95), mussels in white wine (£3.95), oysters, prawns, cockles and much, much more. Wooden benches available for seating. Mon–Fri & Sun 10am–6pm, Sat 10am–8pm.

Waterfront Fishouse Restaurant 1 Railway Pier ☎01631 563110, ⓦwaterfrontfishouse.co.uk. Despite the unprepossessing exterior, this is a great place rustling up impressive dishes primarily using scallops (chargrilled Isle of Mull scallops with smoked salmon and leek risotto), langoustine (crispy tails) and the best of the daily catch; alternatively, have yourself three oysters (natural, grilled or deep-fried) with a choice of dressings for £6.50. The 2-course lunch and early evening menu are a steal at £14.99. Try and bag a sea-facing table. Daily noon–2pm & 5.30–10pm.

DRINKING

SEE MAP PAGE 65

The Corryvreckan The Waterfront Centre ☎01631 568910. Although it looks and feels just like the Wetherspoons it is, this barn of a place is the town's social hub and occupies a terrific harbourfront spot; the £1.50 coffee (free refills) is just the job before a ferry crossing. Daily 7am–midnight, Fri & Sat till 1am.

Isle of Kerrera

One of the best places to escape from the crowds in Oban is the low-lying island of **Kerrera**, which shelters Oban Bay from the worst of the westerly winds. Measuring just five miles by two, the island is easily explored on foot. The island's most prominent landmark is the **Hutcheson's Monument**, best viewed, appropriately enough, from the ferries heading out of Oban, as it commemorates David Hutcheson, one of the Victorian founders of what is now Caledonian MacBrayne. The most appealing vistas, however, are from Kerrera's highest point, **Càrn Breugach** (620ft), over to Mull, the Slate Islands, Lismore, Jura and beyond.

The ferry lands roughly halfway down the east coast, at the north end of **Horseshoe Bay**, where King Alexander II died in 1249. If the weather's good and you feel like lazing by the sea, head for the island's finest sandy beach, **Slatrach Bay**, on the west coast, one mile northwest of the ferry jetty. Otherwise, there's a very rewarding trail down to the clifftop ruin of **Gylen Castle** and back to the ferry via Drove Road.

ARRIVAL AND DEPARTURE

ISLE OF KERRERA

By ferry The passenger and bicycle ferry crosses regularly (summer 8.40am & 10.30am, then every 30min until the last crossing at 5.55pm; winter every 90min; ☎01631 563665, ⓦcalmac.co.uk; £4.80 return) through the day from the mainland two miles down the Gallanach road from Oban. In summer, bus #431 from Oban train station connects with the ferry once a day.

Destinations Gallanach (every 30min; 10min).

1

ACCOMMODATION AND EATING

Kerrera Bunkhouse Lower Gylen ⊙ 01631 566367, ⓦ kerrerabunkhouse.co.uk. Located in a lovely spot a 45min walk from the ferry, this converted eighteenth-century stable building has seven beds, a bell tent with double bed and wood-burning stove, and a cowshed living space for rent by the evening. Next to the bunkhouse, the delightful tea garden – which is the island's only refreshment option – offers homemade veggie snacks, cakes and coffee. Café Easter–Sept daily 10.30am–4.30pm. Bed per person **£15**; bell tent (April–Sept) **£45**

Appin

Seventeen miles north of Oban is **Appin**, best known as the setting for Robert Louis Stevenson's *Kidnapped*, a fictionalized account of the "Appin Murder" of 1752, when Colin Campbell was shot in the back, allegedly by one of the disenfranchised Stewart clan. The name Appin derives from the Gaelic *abthaine*, meaning "lands belonging to the abbey", in this case the one on the island of Lismore, which is linked to the peninsula by passenger ferry from Port Appin.

Port Appin and Castle Stalker

Castle Stalker, A828, near Port Appin • Visits by tour only, April–Sept • £20 • ⊙ 01631 740315, ⓦ castlestalker.com

One of Argyll's most picturesque spots, **PORT APPIN** is a pretty little fishing village at the peninsula's westernmost tip, overlooking a host of tiny little islands dotted around Loch Linnhe, with Lismore and the mountains of Morvern and Mull in the background.

Framed magnificently as you wind along the single-track road to Port Appin is one of Argyll's most romantic ruined castles, the much-photographed sixteenth-century ruins of **Castle Stalker**. Privately owned, the castle can only be visited on a pre-booked tour, which departs from the boathouse and lasts for around two hours. Otherwise, there is a footpath from the *Castle Stalker View* café that winds down to a point some 200 yards from the castle, affording some cracking photo opportunities.

ARRIVAL AND DEPARTURE PORT APPIN

By ferry Ferries to Lismore depart from a small jetty at the southernmost point of the village, by the *Pierhouse Hotel*.

Destinations Lismore (hourly; 10min).

ACCOMMODATION AND EATING

Castle Stalker View Overlooking Castle Stalker ⊙ 01631 730444, ⓦ castlestalkerview.co.uk. In a tiptop position overlooking Castle Stalker, this large, light-filled café makes for a super little pit stop, serving up, among other things, fluffy jacket spuds with unusual fillings like crayfish tails or haggis and cheddar (£7.95), and a selection of baked goodies. Mid-Feb to March Wed–Sun 10am–4pm; April–Oct daily 9.30am–5pm; Nov & Dec

Thurs–Sun 10am–4pm.

Pierhouse Hotel Just a few paces from the jetty ⊙ 01631 730302, ⓦ pierhousehotel.co.uk. Perched on the waterfront, the whitewashed Pierhouse has twelve sumptuously furnished, though very pricey, rooms decorated in cool beige and mocha tones, half of which have unrivalled loch views. The hotel's sparkling seafood restaurant is highly rated in these parts too. **£150**

Isle of Lismore

Lying in the middle of Loch Linnhe, to the north of Oban, and barely rising above a hillock, the narrow island of **LISMORE** (around ten miles long and a mile wide) offers wonderful gentle walking and cycling opportunities, with unrivalled views – in fine weather – across to the mountains of Morvern, Lochaber and Mull. Legend has it that saints Columba and Moluag both fancied the skinny island as a **missionary base**, but as they raced towards it Moluag cut off his finger and threw it ashore ahead of Columba, claiming the land for himself. Of Moluag's sixth-century foundation nothing remains, but from 1236 until 1507 the island served as the seat of the **bishop of Argyll**. Lismore is one of the most fertile of the Inner Hebrides – its name derives from the Gaelic *lios* *mór*, meaning "great garden" – and before the Clearances it supported nearly 1400 inhabitants; the population today is around 150. The island's main settlement, and landing spot for the ferry, is Achnacroish.

Ionad Naomh Moluag

500yds west of Achnacroish • April–Oct daily 11am–4pm • £3.50 • ☎ 01631 760030, ⓦ lismoregaelicheritagecentre.org

To get to grips with the history of the island and its Gaelic culture, follow the signs to the Heritage Centre, **Ionad Naomh Moluag**, a turf-roofed, timber-clad building with a permanent exhibition on Lismore, a reference library, a gift shop and a café with an outdoor terrace. Your ticket also covers entry to the nearby restored nineteenth-century cottar's (landless tenant's) cottage, **Taigh Iseabal Dhaibh**, with its traditionally built stone walls, birch roof timbers and thatched roof.

Cathedral of Moluag and around

In **CLACHAN**, two and a half miles north of Achnacroish, you'll find the diminutive, whitewashed fourteenth-century **Cathedral of St Moluag**, whose choir was reduced in height and converted into the parish church in 1749; inside you can see a few of the original seats for the upper clergy, a stone basin in the south wall and several medieval doorways. Due east of the church – head north up the road and take the turning signposted on the right – the circular **Tirefour Broch**, over two thousand years old, occupies a commanding position and has walls almost 10ft thick in places.

ARRIVAL AND DEPARTURE ISLE OF LISMORE

By ferry Two ferries serve Lismore: a small CalMac car ferry from Oban to Achnacroish (Mon–Sat 4 daily, 2 on Sun; 55min), roughly halfway along the eastern coastline; and a shorter passenger- and bicycle-only crossing from Port Appin to Point, the island's north point (hourly; 10min).

GETTING AROUND AND INFORMATION

Bike rental Bike rental is available from Lismore Bikes (☎ 07376 425996; £15/day), who will deliver to the ferry upon request.

Information In the absence of a tourist office, the website ⓦ isleoflismore.com has some useful information.

ACCOMMODATION AND EATING

Bachuil ☎ 0845 4900 562, ⓦ bachuil.co.uk. Accommodation on the island is extremely limited, but this gorgeous, whitewashed country house, just north of Clachan and home of the Barons of Bachuil, has three extremely well-appointed rooms. Three-course evening meals are served for a very reasonable £20 per person. April–Sept. £120

Taynuilt

Taynuilt, eleven miles east of Oban, at the point where the River Awe flows into the sea at **Loch Etive**, is a small but sprawling village, best known for its iron-smelting works, though it's a great little spot from which to explore the loch itself.

Bonawe Iron Furnace

B845, 2 miles north of Taynuilt, just off the A85 • April–Sept daily 9.30am–5.30pm • £6; HES • ☎ 01866 822432, ⓦ historicenvironment.scot

The **Bonawe Iron Furnace** was originally founded by Cumbrian ironworkers in 1753, employing six hundred people at its height. Its decline and eventual closure, in 1876, was largely as a result of the introduction of more efficient coke-fired methods of production. During its heyday, though, the surrounding hills of birch and oak made for first-class charcoal, which was the principal fuel used to smelt iron in these early blast furnaces. The site remains hugely evocative, from the cavernous charcoal sheds with their sunken roofs, to the far smaller iron-ore sheds, one of which now has an

1

enlightening exhibition charting the development of iron making. The furnace house itself also remains largely intact, though sadly the water wheel is no more, having been sold for scrap during World War II.

Inverawe Fisheries and Smokery

A85, 1 mile east of Taynuilt • Easter–Oct & Dec daily 9am–5pm • ☎ 01866 822 808, ⓦ inverawe-fisheries.co.uk

A mile or so east up the A85 from Taynuilt, a sign invites you down a minor road to visit the tucked-away **Inverawe Fisheries and Smokery**, which has been smoking fish since 1980. Plans are afoot to allow visitors to see the smokery in action, but in the meantime there's still lots to see and do including an exhibition on traditional smoking techniques (here at Inverawe products are smoked for two days and two nights), a super little café/shop, and a couple of local trails, one of which is a very pleasant mile long riverside walk taking in a cool swing bridge; mind the cows though, they can get a little frisky.

Loch Awe

Legend has it that **Loch Awe**, twenty miles east of Oban, was created by a witch and inhabited by a monster even more gruesome than the one at Loch Ness. At more than 25 miles in length, Loch Awe is actually the longest stretch of fresh water in the country, but most travellers only encounter the loch's north end as they speed along its shores by car or train on the way to or from Oban.

Kilchurn Castle

Several tiny islands on the loch sport picturesque ruins, none more so than the fifteenth-century ruins of **Kilchurn Castle**, strategically situated on a rocky spit (once an island) at the head of the loch; although essentially just a shell, its watery setting and imposing outlines make it well worth a detour. There is no signposting, but to reach the castle there's a car park just off the A85 around two miles east of Lochawe village, from where it's a pleasant five-minute walk to the ruins.

Cruachan Power Station

A85, 19 miles east of Oban • Easter–Oct Mon–Fri 9.15am–4.45pm; Nov–March Mon–Fri 9.15am–3.45pm • Tours £7.50 • ☎ 0141 614 9105, ⓦ visitcruachan.co.uk

Constructed inside mighty Ben Cruachan (3693ft), which looms over the head of Loch Awe, **Cruachan Power Station** was built in 1965 as part of the hydroelectric network that generates around ten percent of Scotland's electricity. Thirty-minute guided tours set off every half-hour from the **visitor centre** by the loch, taking you to a viewing platform above the generating room deep inside the "hollow mountain", a 91yd-long cavern big enough to contain the Tower of London. The whole experience of visiting an industrial complex hidden within a mountain is very James Bond. Even if you don't partake in a tour, the visitor centre offers some thoroughgoing and interesting explanations of the workings of the power station and renewable energy projects, and an interactive play area for kids, while the adjoining café has marvellous loch views.

ACCOMMODATION AND EATING

Ben Cruachan Inn ☎ 01838 200880, ⓦ bencruachan inn.com. In the tiny village (hamlet really) of Loch Awe itself is this superbly renovated inn, which has a selection of colourful, tidily furnished rooms in the main building and, better still, four self-catering garden suites (sleeping up to four) in a neighbouring building. The modern bar/restaurant offers an accomplished menu. __£119__

Isle of Mull and around

The second largest of the Inner Hebrides, **MULL** is by far the most accessible: just forty minutes from Oban by ferry. As so often, first impressions largely depend on the weather – it is the wettest of the Hebrides (and that's saying something) – for without the sun the large tracts of moorland, particularly around the island's highest peak, Ben More (3169ft), can appear bleak and unwelcoming. There are, however, areas of more gentle pastoral scenery around **Dervaig** in the north and **Salen** on the east coast, and the indented west coast varies from the sandy beaches around **Calgary** to the cliffs of Loch na Keal. The most common mistake is to try and "do" the island in a day or two: flogging up the main road to the picturesque capital of **Tobermory**, then covering the fifty-odd miles between there and Fionnphort, in order to visit **Iona**. Mull is a place that will grow on you only if you have the time and patience to explore; a couple of night's here at least is recommended.

Historically, crofting, whisky distilling and fishing supported the islanders (*Muileachs*), but the population – which peaked at 10,000 – decreased dramatically in the late nineteenth century due to the Clearances and the 1846 potato famine. On Mull, it is a trend that has been reversed, mostly owing to the large influx of settlers from elsewhere in the country, which has brought the current population up to more than 2800. One of the main reasons for this resurgence is, of course, tourism – more than half a million visitors come here each year. As good a reason as any to visit Mull, and one of the main reasons why many do so, is to view the abundant **wildlife**, with the magnificent white-tailed eagles the major draw, followed by whale and dolphin watching.

ARRIVAL AND DEPARTURE

ISLE OF MULL AND AROUND

By ferry Craignure is the main ferry terminal, with a frequent daily car ferry link to Oban, though booking ahead on this route is strongly advised. A smaller and less expensive car ferry crosses daily from Lochaline on the Morvern peninsula to Fishnish, six miles northwest of Craignure. Another even smaller car ferry connects Kilchoan on the Ardnamurchan peninsula with Tobermory, the island's capital.

GETTING AROUND

By bus The two main bus routes are the #95 (#495) between Craignure and Tobermory, and the #96 (#496) between Craignure and Fionnphort, with a third route (#494) from Tobermory to Dervaig and Calgary.

By car The majority of the island's roads are single-track, with passing places, which can slow journeys down considerably; – hence patience and concentration is required when driving here.

Craignure and around

CRAIGNURE is little more than a scattering of cottages, though there is a small shop, a bar, some toilets and a CalMac ticket and **tourist office** situated opposite the pier. However, there is plenty of accommodation here, as well as a few places to eat and drink, so it is a useful place to base yourself, particularly with an early ferry to catch.

Duart Castle

A848, 3 miles south of Craignure • Daily: April 11am–4pm; May–mid-Oct 10.30am–5pm • £7.50 • ☎ 01680 812309, ⓦ duartcastle.com

---

MULL FESTIVALS

Mull stages a terrific triple-header of festivals, the first of which is the **Mendelssohn on Mull Festival** (ⓦ soundwavesscio.org.uk) at the beginning of July, a week of world-class chamber music commemorating the composer's visit here in 1829. Also in July (usually the third weekend) is the **Mull Highland Games**, and then, in October, the three-day **Mull Rally** (ⓦ mullrally.org), a major racing event around the island's fantastically winding roads.

1

Perched on a rocky promontory sticking out into the Sound of Mull, and buffeted by winds and weather, **Duart Castle** makes for a striking landmark viewed from the Oban–Craignure ferry. Duart was headquarters of the once-powerful MacLean clan from the thirteenth century, but was burnt down by the Campbells and confiscated after the 1745 rebellion. In 1911, the 26th clan chief, Fitzroy MacLean – not to be confused with the Scottish writer of the same name – managed to buy it back and restore it, and he remained here until his death, in 1936, at the ripe old age of 101 – look out for the wonderful black-and-white photos of MacLean on his 100th birthday, still looking remarkably fit even then. The banqueting room showcases some superb exhibits, particularly items belonging to Fitzroy from his time serving in the 13th Light Dragoons and 13th Hussars; keep an eye out for his dirk, passport and fob watch used during the Crimean War. Among the many gifts on display is a dazzling silver cup presented to Fitzroy from the former French president Giscard d'Estaing.

In the upstairs exhibition room you can also learn about the world scout movement; in 1959, Charles MacLean (the 27th clan chief) became Chief Scout, a role he performed with some distinction until 1971. From here, climb up to the ramparts for superlative views of the island and beyond; on a clear day, you can just make out the summit of Ben Nevis. Sir Lachlan, the current clan chief, lives in the castle annexe and you're quite likely to see him mingling among visitors. After your visit, head to the castle's pretty, barn-like tearoom, where there's an impressive array of home-made cakes on offer.

ARRIVAL AND INFORMATION   CRAIGNURE AND AROUND

By ferry The ferry terminal dominates the centre of the village, with the CalMac office located directly opposite, in the same building as the tourist office.

Destinations Oban (9 daily; 50min).
By bus Buses pick up and drop off by the main road by the ferry terminal.

Destinations Fionnphort (Mon–Sat 3–5 daily, 1 on Sun; 1hr 15min); Fishnish (4–5 daily; 15min); Salen (5–6 daily; 25min); Tobermory (5–6 daily; 50min).

Tourist office Opposite the ferry terminal in shared premises with CalMac (April–June, Sept & Oct Mon 9am–5pm, Tues–Sat 8.15am–5pm, Sun 10am–5pm; July & Aug Mon 9am–6.15pm, Tues–Sat 8.15am–6.15pm, Sun 10am–6.15pm; Nov–March Mon 9am–5pm, Tues–Sat 8.30am–5pm, Sun 10am–5pm; ☎ 01680 812377).

ACCOMMODATION AND EATING

★ **Craignure Bunkhouse** 350yds up the road towards Fionnphort ☎ 01680 812043, �🌐 craignure-bunkhouse. co.uk. Super-smart eco-designed hostel accommodating four en-suite bunk rooms, each with four or six beds (with own reading light and USB), plus a large, homely lounge with woodburner, sofas and a library of books. A self-catering kitchen, laundry and drying room complete this excellent ensemble. Bed **£24**

Craignure Inn 400yds up the road towards Fionnphort ☎ 01680 812305, �🌐 craignure-inn.co.uk. Right next to *Craignure Bunkhouse*, this eighteenth-century whitewashed inn, frequented by locals and tourists alike, is a snug little place to hole up in, be it for a pint in the bar or a meal in the adjoining restaurant; Scotch steak and ale pie (£12.95). Daily 11.30am–11pm.

Shieling Holidays Half a mile from the ferry terminal on the road to Fionnphort ☎ 01680 812496, �🌐 shieling holidays.co.uk. Set above a shingle beach, this tidy campsite also offers cool accommodation in the form of "shielings" – large, hard-top tents, some furnished and some en-suite – sleeping between two and six people; these now include shared hostel sheilings (male or female tents sleeping six), costing £20 per person. There are bikes for rent too. March–Oct. Per pitch **£18.50**; shielings from **£46**

Tobermory

Mull's chief town, **TOBERMORY**, at the northern tip of the island, is easily the most attractive fishing port on the west coast of Scotland, its clusters of brightly coloured houses and boats sheltering in a bay backed by a steep bluff. Founded in 1788 by the British Society for Encouraging Fisheries, it never really took off as a fishing port and only survived due to the steady influx of crofters evicted from other parts of the island during the Clearances. It is now the most important, and by far the most vibrant, settlement on Mull, and if you've got young kids, you'll instantly recognize it as the place where *Balamory* was filmed.

The harbour – known as **Main Street** – is one long parade of multicoloured hotels, guesthouses, restaurants and shops, and you could happily spend an hour or so meandering around. The rest of the upper town, laid out on a classic grid plan, merits a stroll too, if only for the great views over the bay.

Mull Museum

Main St • Easter–mid-Oct Mon–Sat 10am–4pm • Free • ☎ 01688 301100, �🌐 mullmuseum.org.uk

A good wet-weather retreat is the **Mull Museum**, essentially a tiny room packed with fascinating local information and artefacts. Among these is a handful of objects salvaged from the *San Juan de Sicilia*, a ship from the Spanish Armada which sank in 1588 and now lies at the bottom of Tobermory harbour; even today, it remains subject to repeated salvage attempts by locals still, somewhat optimistically, seeking gold. During World War II, Tobermory was an important naval base, in particular as a centre for the training of Escort vessels, whose job it was to protect convoy ships from being attacked by U-boats. Leading the training was one Vice Admiral Gilbert Stephenson, whose prolific and strict regime (he trained up over nine hundred ships in just four years) earned him the moniker, "The Terror of Tobermory". Such was the Admiral's notoriety that he even had a beer named after him.

Tobermory Distillery

Ledaig car park • Mon–Fri 10am–5pm, Sat & Sun 10am–4pm; tours hourly • £9.50 • ☎ 01688 302647, ⍵ tobermorydistillery.com

Founded in 1798, the minuscule **Tobermory Distillery** has had a chequered history, closing down three times since then, though today it's back in business and thriving thanks to its signature fifteen-year-old Tobermory and ten-year-old Ledaig malts.

1

WILDLIFE-WATCHING TRIPS FROM TOBERMORY

Although boat trips leave from several different places around Mull, Tobermory is as good a place as any from which to begin a **wildlife-watching tour**. Easily the best company is **Sea Life Surveys** (Easter–Oct; ☎ 01688 302916, ⓦ sealifesurveys.com), who focus on seeking out the whales (minke and even killer whales are the most common), porpoises, dolphins and basking sharks that spend time in the waters around the Hebrides; their seven-hour whale-watching trips (£90) are not recommended for under-12s, though they do offer a four-hour whale-watch trip (adult £60, child £30), while their 1.5hr Ecocruz (adult £20, child £10; family £55) is much more family oriented and includes a visit to a seal colony. For more information on the local wildlife, pop into the **Hebridean Whale and Dolphin Trust visitor centre** at 28 Main St (April–Sept daily 10.30am–4.30pm; ☎ 01688 302620, ⓦ hwdt.org), where you can also view a small exhibition. In 2019 the HWDT launched the **Hebridean Whale Trail**, a series of land-based whale watching sites along the west coast of Scotland; one of these is at Glengorm, and during the summer they run a Headland Watch excursion from here on Thursdays at 10am (£6).

Although its tour is rather drab compared to most distilleries, you do get to see the four magnificent copper stills, as well as try a dram or two at the end. As is the vogue now, they've also started producing their own gin, a rather sumptuous affair called Tobermory Hebridean Gin, concocted from local botanicals including elderflower and wild heather.

Mull Aquarium

Harbour Building, Ledaig car park • April–Oct daily 9.30am–5pm • £5.50 (day ticket) • ☎ 01688 302876, ⓦ mullaquarium.co.uk

An absolute delight, the small, community-owned **Mull Aquarium** is the first catch-and-release aquarium in Europe, meaning that all marine life – caught by local divers, fishermen and anyone else willing to head out to sea – is released back into the waters within four weeks. So, for example, you might get to see dogfish, jellyfish, sea scorpions, velvet swimming crabs or curled octopus in the half a dozen or so tanks, alongside all manner of other weird and wonderful creatures. There are touchpool stations, too, where demonstrations are given and visitors are encouraged to handle the creatures.

Glengorm Castle

5 miles northwest of Tobermory • Easter–Oct daily 10am–5pm • ☎ 01688 302932, ⓦ glengormcastle.co.uk

Dramatically overlooking the sea along a dead-end single-track road, **Glengorm Castle** is a Scots Baronial pile that's now a small luxury hotel. Although the castle is not open to the public (unless you're staying there), you can walk around their attractive walled garden or make for the longer forest, archeological and coastal trails; they also offer guided walks of varying lengths (from £20 for 2hr), though you need to book in advance. Here too is an attractively converted steading, housing a wildlife visitor centre, café and farm shop, and art gallery.

ARRIVAL AND INFORMATION   TOBERMORY

By ferry The CalMac terminal is at the far end of Main St, in the northernmost part of the bay.

Destinations Kilchoan (5–7 daily; 35min).

By bus The bus station is in the town's main Ledaig car park, by the distillery.

Destinations Calgary (Mon–Fri 4 daily, Sat 2 daily; 45min); Craignure (4–6 daily; 45min); Dervaig (Mon–Fri 4 daily, Sat 2 daily; 25min); Fishnish (2–4 daily; 40min).

Tourist information Privately run Explore Mull, located in a cabin in the Ledaig car park (April–Oct daily 9am–5pm; ☎ 01688 302875, ⓦ isle-of-mull.net), has tons of information, and also arranges accommodation and wildlife tours.

Bike Hire Cycle Mull, located at Eas Brae as you enter town (April–Oct daily 9am–5pm; ☎ 01688 302923, ⓦ cyclemull. co.uk), have both mountain bikes (£20 per day) and eBikes (£25) for hire.

1

ACCOMMODATION

Glengorm Castle 5 miles northwest of Tobermory ☎ 01688 302321, ⓦ glengormcastle.co.uk. Fairy tale, rambling Baronial mansion in a superb, secluded setting, with incredible coastal views, lovely gardens and local walks. Guests get use of the castle's wood-panelled whisky library and snooker lounge, the five large bedrooms are full of splendid features and there are self-catering cottages available too. **£140**

★ **Highland Cottage** Breadalbane St ☎ 01688 302030, ⓦ highlandcottage.co.uk. Super-luxurious B&B run by a very welcoming couple in a quiet street high above the harbour; the six modestly sized but gorgeously furnished rooms, each one named after an Argyll island, are fashioned with home comforts firmly in mind, such as shelves rammed with books. April–Oct **£170**

★ **Strongarbh House** Upper Tobermory ☎ 01688 302319, ⓦ strongarbh.com. Erstwhile bank, doctor's surgery and officer's mess, but now a fantastic and engagingly run B&B with four rooms that brilliantly combine elements of Victorian and modern; each room has an iPad for starters. There's also a library with books, newspapers and games, while complimentary tea and coffee, and cakes, are served daily between 4pm and 6pm. April–Oct. **£135**

The Tobermory Hotel 53 Main St ☎ 01688 302091, ⓦ thetobermoryhotel.com. Smallish, fairly smart hotel converted from three fishermen's cottages, hence the maze-like warren of variously configured, extremely cosy, rooms, some with coved ceilings, others with window seats, though most with a smattering of light tartan. April–Oct. **£120**

Tobermory Youth Hostel Main St ☎ 01688 302481, ⓦ hostellingscotland.org.uk. Small, friendly and superbly located on the harbourfront, with two- to- five-bed rooms, plus shared shower facilities, plus a very well-equipped kitchen, TV lounge and laundry facilities. Breakfast £4.95. Mid-March to mid-Oct. Doubles **£54**; dorms **£22**

CAMPSITE

Tobermory Camping 1.5 miles uphill from Tobermory on the B8073 to Dervaig ☎ 01688 302615, ⓦ tobermory-campsite.co.uk. Small, spruce campsite serenely situated in woodland; tents are pitched alongside the burn and there are five sweet little shepherds' huts each sleeping either two or four and with cooking facilities. Buses from Tobermory to Calgary stop here. April–Oct. Pitch **£20**; shepherds' huts **£45**

EATING

An Tobar Argyll Terrace ☎ 01688 302211, ⓦ comar. co.uk. Housed in a converted Victorian schoolhouse at the top of Back Brae, this small but attractive café doubles up as the town's principal arts centre, with a strong and imaginative programme of visual art and live music, often attracting some stellar names. The café can also be accessed via a very steep path from Main St. Tues–Sat 11am–5pm.

Café Fish The Pier ☎ 01688 301253, ⓦ thecafefish.com. Stylish harbourfront restaurant above the Calmac office sporting an all-glass frontage with superb views. Fresh from their own boat, the day's catch is prominently displayed in a large glass cabinet, which could mean anything from whole creel caught langoustines with herb garlic butter to miso and sesame glazed Mull scallops (£19.50). Mid-March to Oct daily 11am–11pm; food served noon–3pm & 5.30–10pm.

Fisherman's Pier Fish & Chip Van Fisherman's Pier ☎ 01688 301109. The friendly proprietors of this venerable takeaway van serve up all the traditional fish suppers (cod and chips £7.50), though most venture here for their scrumptious scallops and chips (£12). Mon–Sat 12.30–9pm; June–Sept also Sun.

Hebridean Lodge Baliscate ☎ 01688 301207, ⓦ hebrideanlodge.co.uk. Admittedly it doesn't look like the most enticing venue – right by the road as you enter Tobermory – and the interior, above a shop, is a little bland, but the food is beautifully cooked and tastes terrific: for example Tobermory smoked trout with beetroot jelly and fennel butter (£8.50), or spinach, goat's cheese and mushroom Wellington (£16.50). Reservations advised. Mon–Fri 6.30–10pm.

★ **Highland Cottage** Breadalbane St ☎ 01688 302030, ⓦ highlandcottage.co.uk. For a treat, look no further than this sublime guesthouse restaurant, which offers an evening four-course menu for £47.50, and which – once you've had a glass of fizz and some canapés – could feature anything from hot smoked salmon with soused cucumber to roast loin of lamb with a haggis parcel and dauphinoise potatoes, and ending with a lemon posset and home-made shortbread. Reservations only, hence there are no defined opening hours.

The Tobermory Hotel 53 Main St ☎ 01688 302091, ⓦ thetobermoryhotel.com. *The Tobermory Hotel*'s highly creditable restaurant conjures up tempting seafood dishes like Croig crab cannon balls with Thai red mayo, and pan seared seabass with grilled asparagus and lemon and chive hollandaise (£19.95). There's a pleasant, warming atmosphere about the place and the service is first-rate. Daily 6–10pm, plus Sun 1–3pm.

DRINKING

MacGochan's Ledaig car park ☎ 01688 302350, ⓦ macgochans-tobermory.co.uk. Heaving, hugely popular harbourside pub just a few paces from the distillery, with a terrific beer garden (albeit facing a car park), well-frequented restaurant-bar and occasional live music to liven things up further. Daily 11am–1am.

1

Mishnish Main St ☎01688 302500, ⓦthemishnish. co.uk. Inside the hotel of the same name, the "Mish" has been the town's most popular local watering hole for aeons, with a couple of superb snugs rammed with maritime and musical paraphernalia, and regular evenings of live music, quizzes and loads of other happenings. Daily 11am–1am.

Dervaig

The gently undulating countryside west of Tobermory, beyond the freshwater Mishnish lochs, provides some of the most beguiling scenery on the island. Added to this, the road out west, the B8073, is exceptionally dramatic. The only village of any size on this side of the island is **DERVAIG**, which nestles beside narrow Loch Chumhainn, just eight miles southwest of Tobermory, distinguished by its unusual pencil-shaped church spire and single street of dinky whitewashed cottages and old corrugated-iron shacks. Dervaig has a shop, a bookshop/café and a number of places to stay, eat and drink.

ACCOMMODATION AND EATING · DERVAIG

Am Birlinn Penmore ☎01688 400619, ⓦambirlinn. com. The cross-country road from Dervaig takes you through Penmore where you'll find this striking wood-and-glass-clad building serving up meat and seafood of the highest order: pan seared guinea fowl on puy lentils with tarragon, sherry, bacon and confit potatoes (£15.95) is one of the restaurant's typically flamboyant dishes. April–Oct Wed–Sun noon–2.30pm & 5–9pm; mid-July to Aug also Tues.

The Bellachroy Centre of village ☎01688 400314, ⓦthebellachroy.co.uk. Rugged early seventeenth-century inn with an attractive whitewashed interior, whose pull is its local real ales; the food is comforting rather than being anything particularly sophisticated; for example, shepherd's pie with parsley mash (£12.95). Daily noon–11pm; food served 12.30–2.30pm & 6–8.30pm.

Dervaig Village Hall Hostel Centre of village ☎01688 400313, ⓔdervaigbunkrooms@gmail.com. Somewhat peculiarly located inside the village hall, though certainly none the worse for it, this clean and welcoming bunkhouse offers two bunkrooms, one sleeping six, the other four, each of which has its own wet room. Bedding is provided. There's also a self-catering kitchen, sitting room and washing machine. Breakfast not included. Dorms £18

Druimnacroish Hotel 2 miles out on the Salen road ☎01688 400274, ⓦdruimnacroish.co.uk. Erstwhile farmhouse and mill, this lovely country house, pleasantly secreted away, has six amply sized and very reasonably priced rooms. Breakfast is taken in the conservatory overlooking the gardens and glen, and there's also a cosy lounge with an honesty bar. Easter–Oct. £75

Calgary

Some five miles beyond Dervaig is **CALGARY**, once a thriving crofting community, now a quiet glen which opens out onto Mull's finest sandy bay, backed by low-lying dunes and machair, with wonderful views over to Coll and Tiree. Aside from the beach, there's a super **woodland sculpture walk** entitled Calgary Art in Nature that begins at the *Calgary Farmhouse* and winds gently down through the woods to the beach. It encompasses some twenty cleverly constructed pieces of artwork hewn from various materials; bronze, copper, steel, willow and so on – a little map (£2) outlining the trail is available from the farmhouse. For the record, the city of Calgary in Canada does indeed take its name from this little village, though it was not so named by Mull emigrants, but instead by one Colonel McLeod of the North West Mounted Police, who once holidayed here. In the car park there's a super little ice cream hut (an upturned hull on stilts), which opens between April and October (noon–4/5pm).

ACCOMMODATION AND EATING · CALGARY

Calgary Back up the road from the beach ☎01688 400256, ⓦcalgary.co.uk. This delightful collection of self-catering homes includes studio lofts sleeping between two and four people, as well as other larger properties scattered around the vicinity; there's also a wooden hut with wood burning stove sleeping two. The daytime café, serving light lunches and super baked treats, is well worth venturing to, as is the adjoining art gallery. Minimum stays apply year-round. Café: April–Oct daily 10am–5pm. Kittiwake studio 2 nights £200; farmhouse per week £1300

Camping Down by the beach itself, there's a spectacular and very popular spot for camping rough; the only facilities are the basic public toilets.

1

Isle of Ulva

A chieftain to the Highlands bound/Cries "Boatman, do not tarry!/And I'll give thee a silver pound/To row us o'er the ferry!"/"Now who be ye, would cross Lochgyle/This dark and stormy water?"/"O I'm the chief of Ulva's isle,/And this, Lord Ullin's daughter."

Lord Ullin's Daughter by Thomas Campbell (1777–1844)

Around the time Poet Laureate Campbell penned this tragic poem, the population of **Ulva** (from the Norse *ulv øy*, or "wolf island") was a staggering 850, sustained by the huge quantities of kelp that were exported for glass and soap production. That was before the market for kelp collapsed and the 1846 potato famine hit, after which the remaining population was brutally evicted; numbers are currently in single figures. In 2018, Ulva was subject to a community buyout – the third Hebridean Island buyout after Eigg in 1997 and Ghiga in 2002. Purchased in somewhat controversial circumstances from the aristrocrat James Howard – whose family had owned Ulva since 1946 – the intention is, over time, to repopulate the island and regenerate the local economy by opening up new facilities. Littered with ruined crofts, it's great **walking** country, with several clearly marked paths crisscrossing the native woodland and the rocky heather moorland interior – and you're almost guaranteed to spot some of the abundant **wildlife**: at the very least deer, if not buzzards, golden eagles and even sea eagles, with seals and divers offshore.

Heritage Centre and Sheila's Cottage

You can learn more about the history of the island from the exhibition inside the **Heritage Centre** (just up from the pier on Ulva) and, nearby, the thatched smiddy housing **Sheila's Cottage**, which has been restored to the period when islander Sheila MacFadyen lived there in the first half of the last century. Originally a milkmaid, Sheila later made her living by gathering and selling winkles to locals and visitors to the island.

ARRIVAL AND INFORMATION   ISLE OF ULVA

By car To get to Ulva, which lies just a hundred yards or so off the west coast of Mull, follow the signs for "Ulva Ferry" west from Salen or south from Calgary.

By bus From April to October, the Ulva Ferry Community Bus runs a twice-daily service on Fridays, Saturdays and Sundays between Calgary and Salen, stopping at Ulva Ferry en route; this is, though, a request service, so you must phone or text by 4pm the day before (☎ 07775 531301; ⊛ ufct.co.uk).

By ferry From Ulva Ferry, a small bicycle/passenger-only ferry (£5 return; bike 50p) is available on demand (Mon–Fri 9am–5pm; June–Aug also Sun; at other times by arrangement on ☎ 01688 500226).

ACCOMMODATION AND EATING

★ **Ballygown** 3 miles from the ferry on the B8073 road towards Calgary ☎ 01688 500113, ⊛ ballygownmull. co.uk. Enchanting, family-run cottage restaurant where you feel like you're eating in their lounge – come to think of it, you pretty much are. There are typically three choices each of a starter (£5), main (£10) and dessert (£5). There might be garlic prawns, ox cheeks in red wine, or apple and plum tart, though it's the home-made haggis that most guests home in on. Unlicensed, but you're welcome to bring your own booze. April–Oct Tues–Sun 5.30–10pm; Nov–March Fri–Sun 5.30–10pm.

The Boathouse Near the ferry slip on the Ulva side ☎ 01688 500241, ⊛ theboathouseulva.co.uk. Cheery, licensed tearoom serving a selection of seafood tempters like smoked mackerel pâté (£7.50), potted crab (£9.50) and Ulva oysters, alongside home-baked cakes and coffee. Easter–Sept Mon–Fri 9am–5pm; June–Aug also Sun.

Camping There's no accommodation here, but wild camping is permitted on the island, so long as it's not within sight of any dwelling and you stay no longer than one night in the same place.

Isle of Staffa and around

Five miles southwest of Ulva, **STAFFA** is one of the most romantic and dramatic of Scotland's many uninhabited islands. On its south side, the perpendicular rock face

1

WHALES AND DOLPHINS

Watching whales, dolphins and porpoises – collectively known as cetaceans – is a growing tourist industry in Scotland. The Moray Firth (see page 206) is one of the best places in the UK to watch **bottlenose dolphins**, but the waters around the Inner Hebrides have, if anything, a wider variety of cetaceans on offer. Although there are several operators who offer whale-watching boat trips from Oban and Tobermory, it is quite possible to catch sight of marine mammals from the shore, or from a ferry. The chief problem is trying to identify what you've seen.

   The most common sightings are of **harbour porpoises**, the smallest of the marine mammals, which are about the size of an adult human and have a fairly small dorsal fin. Porpoises are easily confused with dolphins; however, if you see it leap out of the water, then you can be sure it's a dolphin, as porpoises only break the surface with their backs and fins. If you spot a whale, the likelihood is that it's a **minke whale**, which grows to about 30ft in length, making it a mere tiddler in the whale world, but a good four or five times bigger than a porpoise. Minkes are baleen whales, which is to say they have no teeth; instead, they gulp huge quantities of water and sift their food through plates of whalebone. Whales do several things dolphins and porpoises can't do, such as blowing water high into the air, and breaching, which is when they launch themselves out of the water and belly-flop down. The other whale species regularly seen in Hebridean waters is the **killer whale** or orca (there are thought to be around eight of them hereabouts), distinguished by its very tall, pointed, dorsal fin. **Basking sharks** are also fairly common in these waters. For more information, pop into the **Hebridean Whale and Dolphin Trust visitor centre** at 28 Main St in Tobermory on Mull (April–Sept daily 10.30am–4.30pm; ☎01688 302620, ⊛hwdt.org), where you can also view a small exhibition.

features an imposing series of black basalt columns, known as the Colonnade, which have been cut by the sea into cathedral-esque caverns – most notably **Fingal's Cave**. The Vikings knew about the island – the name derives from their word for "Island of Pillars" – but it wasn't until 1772 that it was "discovered" by the world. Turner painted it, Wordsworth explored it, but Mendelssohn's *Die Fingalshöhle* (the lovely "*Hebrides Overture*"), inspired by the sounds of the sea-wracked caves he heard on a visit here in 1829, did most to popularize the place – after which Queen Victoria gave her blessing, too. The polygonal basalt organ-pipes were created some sixty million years ago when a huge mass of molten basalt burst forth onto land and, as it cooled, solidified into hexagonal crystals. The same phenomenon produced the Giant's Causeway in Northern Ireland, and Celtic folk tales often link the two with rival giants Fionn mac Cumhail (Irish) and Fingal (Scottish) throwing rocks at each other across the Irish Sea.

Treshnish Isles

Northwest of Staffa lie the **Treshnish Isles**, an archipelago of uninhabited volcanic islets, none more than a mile or two across. The most distinctive is **Bac Mór**, shaped like a Puritan's hat and popularly dubbed the Dutchman's Cap. **Lunga**, the largest island, is a summer nesting place for hundreds of seabirds, in particular guillemots, razorbills and puffins; the last of these are far and away the star attraction, and, for many, the main reason for visiting. It's also a major breeding ground for seals. The two most northerly islands, **Cairn na Burgh More** and **Cairn na Burgh Beg**, have remains of ruined castles, the first of which served as a lookout post for the Lords of the Isles and was last garrisoned in the Civil War; Cairn na Burgh Beg hasn't been occupied since the 1715 Jacobite uprising.

TOURS ISLE OF STAFFA AND AROUND

Boat tours From April to October several operators offer boat trips to Staffa and the Treshnish Isles. Long-established Turus Mara, based in Penmore (☎01688 400242, ⊛turusmara. com), sets out from Ulva Ferry and charges £65 for a 6hr round trip to Staffa and the Treshnish Isles – typically including 1hr on Staffa and 2hr on Lunga; as well as a 3.5hr trip just to Staffa (£32.50). Another good outfit offering the same 6hr trip to Staffa and the Treshnish Isles is **Staffa Tours** (☎07732 912370, ⊛staffatours.com) though their boats depart from Tobermory. There's also Staffa Trips (☎01681 700755, ⊛staffatrips.co.uk), who charge £35 for passage from Iona and Fionnphort to Staffa on the MB *Iolaire*.

Ben More and around

From the southern shores of Loch na Keal, which almost splits Mull in two, rise the terraced slopes of **Ben More** (3169ft) – literally "big mountain" – a mighty extinct volcano, and the only Munro in the Hebrides outside of Skye. It's most easily climbed from Dhiseig, halfway along the loch's southern shores, though an alternative route is to climb up to the col between Beinn Fhada and A'Chioch, and approach via the mountain's eastern ridge. Further west along the shore the road carves through spectacular overhanging cliffs before heading south past the Gribun rocks, which face the tiny island of **Inch Kenneth**, where Unity Mitford lived until her death in 1948. There are great views out to Staffa and the Treshnish Isles as the road leaves the coast behind, climbing over the pass to Loch Scridain, where it eventually joins the equally dramatic Glen More road (A849) from Craignure.

If you're properly equipped for walking, you can also explore the **Ardmeanach peninsula**, to the west of the road. The area, which features a large sea cave and a fossilized tree, is NTS-owned, and there is a car park just before *Tiroran House.*

Mull Eagle Watch

April–Sept tours 11am & 2pm, booking required • £10 • ☎ 01680 812556, ⓦ mulleaglewatch.com

The largest and heaviest bird of prey, the **white-tailed eagle** (or sea eagle) became an extinct species in the British Isles in 1916, but since a successful reintroduction programme from Norway in the late 1970s, the population has thrived, and today there are currently twenty pairs of breeding eagles on Mull. In association with the RSPB, ranger-led tours currently take place at two sites: the first is the Glen Seilisdeir hide, located a short way north of Loch Scridain in the Tiroran forest, with another at West Ardhu near Dervaig – the rendezvous point is arranged at the time of booking and tours last around two hours. While a sighting is by no means guaranteed, the chances of seeing one, or more, of these magnificent birds are usually pretty good; eaglets typically hatch at the beginning of May, before fledging in August.

The Ross of Mull

Stretching for twenty miles west as far as Iona is Mull's rocky southernmost peninsula, the **Ross of Mull**, which, like much of Scotland, appears blissfully tranquil in good weather, and desolate and bleak in bad climes. Most visitors simply drive through the Ross en route to Iona, but if you have the time it's definitely worth considering exploring, or even staying in, this little-visited part of Mull.

Lochbuie

The most scenic spots on the Ross are hidden away on the south coast, starting with **LOCHBUIE**, which lies on a fertile plain beside the sea. The bay here is rugged and wide, and overlooked by the handsome peak of Ben Buie (2352ft), to the northwest. Hidden behind a patch of Scots pine are the ivy-strewn ruins of **Moy Castle**, an old MacLean stronghold; in the fields to the north is one of the few **stone circles** in the west of Scotland, dating from the second century BC, the tallest of its stones about 6ft high. A popular and fairly easy walk is the five-mile hike west from Lochbuie along the coastal path to Carsaig.

Carsaig

A rickety single-track road heads south four miles from Lochbuie to **CARSAIG**, which enjoys an idyllic setting, looking south out to Colonsay, Islay and Jura. Most folk come here either to walk east to Lochbuie, or west under the cliffs, to the **Nuns' Cave** (where nuns from Iona are alleged to have hidden during the Reformation), and then, after

1

four miles or so, at Malcolm's Point, to the spectacular **Carsaig Arches**, which were formed by eroded sea caves and are linked to basalt cliffs.

Bunessan

From Carsaig, the main road continues for another twelve miles to **BUNESSAN**, the largest village on the peninsula, roughly two-thirds of the way along the Ross. Just before the *Argyll Arms Hotel*, a road leads up to **Ardalanish Weavers** (April–Oct daily 10am–5pm, Nov–March Mon–Fri 10am–4pm, closed mid-Dec to mid-Jan; free; ☎01681 700265, ⍟ardalanish.com), where beautiful durable organic tweed is produced on Victorian looms originally from Torosay Castle. The tweed is snapped up by high-end high-street stores, and is used for the elegant couture collection displayed in the small shop; you can also buy other beautiful items here, such as scarves, rugs, wraps and blankets, though they don't come cheap. Otherwise, on weekdays, you're quite welcome to watch the girls at work in the mill. A couple of miles out of Bunessan is the wide expanse of **Ardalanish Bay**.

Fionnphort and around

The road along the Ross of Mull ends at **FIONNPHORT**, a small, not especially attractive settlement, but it does offer some handy accommodation as well as several places to eat, including the island's best restaurant; it's also where ferries ply the short route across to Iona. Around a mile and a half south of Fionnphort are the golden sands of **Fidden beach**, which looks out to the **Isle of Erraid**, where Robert Louis Stevenson is believed to have written *Kidnapped* while staying in one of the island's cottages; *Kidnapped*'s hero, David Balfour, is shipwrecked on the Torran Rocks, out to sea to the south of Erraid, beyond which lies the remarkable, stripy **Dubh Artach Lighthouse** (meaning "black stony ground" in Gaelic), built by Stevenson's father in 1867. In the book, Balfour spends a miserable time convinced that he's stranded on Erraid, which can, in fact, be reached across the sands on its eastern side at low tide.

ARRIVAL AND DEPARTURE   THE ROSS OF MULL

By bus Craignure, via Bunessan (Mon–Sat 4–5 daily, 1 on Sun; 1hr 10min).

By ferry The CalMac passenger ferry from Fionnphort to Iona is very frequent and takes just 10min (£3.50 return).

ACCOMMODATION AND EATING

UISKEN

Camping Uisken beach, two miles south of Bunessan, is a wonderful spot for wild camping, but ask permission first at *Uisken Croft* (☎01681 700307), just up the hill. Per person £2

FIONNPHORT

Fidden Farm Campsite Knockvologan Rd, Fidden ☎01681 700427. This simple, getting away from it all campsite has a wonderful location, with direct access to Fidden beach. There's a shower block, and although campfires are not allowed on site, they are allowed on the beach. May–Sept. Per person £10

★ **Ninth Wave** Bruach Mhor ☎01681 700757, ⍟ninthwaverestaurant.co.uk. For something a little special, head to this fabulous restaurant – in a renovated 200-year-old bothy – secreted away in wonderful rural isolation about a mile north of the village (it's well signposted). The owner catches and then serves up crab, lobster and other fishy treats, while the veg is supplied from their own kitchen garden, resulting in fantastic dishes like miso salt cod brandade with garden fennel slaw and fried garlic shallots. The wines (mostly organic), gins and cocktails are something special too. Three-course meal with coffee and chocolates is £48; reservations required. May–Oct Wed–Sun 7–11pm.

Seaview About 200yds up from the ferry terminal ☎01681 700235, ⍟iona-bed-breakfast-mull.com. This conscientiously run sandstone Victorian villa has five somewhat boxy, but pretty and well-equipped, rooms (with either sea or garden views) adorned with splashes of artwork. They've also got bikes for rent. Mid-March to Oct. £80

Staffa House 300yds up from the ferry terminal ☎01681 700677, ⍟staffahouse.co.uk. Handsome whitewashed building, with four light and immaculately presented rooms, and a lovely glass conservatory where breakfast is taken around a communal table looking out to the Sound of Iona. Two-night minimum stay in high season. March–Oct. £90

1 Isle of Iona

Less than a mile off the southwest tip of Mull, **IONA** – just three miles long and not much more than a mile wide – has been a place of pilgrimage for several centuries, and a place of Christian worship for more than 1400 years. For it was to this flat Hebridean island that St Columba fled from Ireland in 563 and established a monastery which was responsible for the conversion of more or less all of pagan Scotland as well as much of northern England. This history and the island's splendid isolation have lent it a peculiar religiosity; in the much-quoted words of Dr Johnson, who visited in 1773, "That man is little to be envied … whose piety would not grow warmer among the ruins of Iona."

Brief history

Whatever the truth about Columba's life, in the sixth and seventh centuries Iona enjoyed a great deal of autonomy from Rome, establishing a specifically **Celtic Christian** tradition. Missionaries were sent out to the rest of Scotland and parts of England, and Iona quickly became a respected seat of learning and artistry; the monks compiled a vast library of intricately **illuminated manuscripts** – most famously the *Book of Kells* (now on display in Trinity College, Dublin) – while the masons excelled in carving peculiarly intricate crosses. Two factors were instrumental in the demise of the Celtic tradition: a series of Viking raids, the worst of which was the massacre of 68 monks on the sands of Martyrs' Bay in 806; and relentless pressure from the established Church, beginning with the Synod of Whitby in 664, which chose Rome over the Celtic Church, and culminated in its suppression by King David I in 1144.

In 1203, Iona became part of the mainstream Church with the establishment of an **Augustinian nunnery** and a **Benedictine monastery** by Reginald, son of Somerled, Lord of the Isles. During the Reformation, the entire complex was ransacked, the contents of the library burnt and all but three of the island's 360 crosses destroyed. Although plans were drawn up at various times to turn the abbey into a Cathedral of the Isles, nothing came of them until 1899, when the (then) owner, the eighth Duke of Argyll, donated the abbey buildings to the **Church of Scotland**, who restored the abbey church for worship over the course of the next decade. Iona's modern resurgence began in 1938, when **George MacLeod**, a minister from Glasgow, established a group of ministers, students and artisans to begin rebuilding the remainder of the monastic buildings. What began as a mostly male, Gaelic-speaking, strictly Presbyterian community is today a lay, mixed and ecumenical retreat. The entire abbey complex has been successfully restored, and is now looked after by Historic Environment Scotland, while the island, apart from the church land and a few crofts, is in the care of the NTS.

Baile Mór

The passenger ferry from Fionnphort drops you off at **BAILE MÓR** (literally "Large Village"), which is in fact little more than a single terrace of cottages facing the sea. You will, though, find most things of a practical nature located here, including the island's main hotel, restaurant and shop.

Augustinian nunnery

A short walk up from the jetty lie the extensive pink-granite ruins of the fourteenth-century **Augustinian nunnery**, disused since the Reformation, though it did continue to be used as a place of burial for women. A beautifully maintained garden now occupies the cloisters, and if nothing else the complex gives you an idea of the state of the present-day abbey before it was restored.

Iona Heritage Centre

North of the Augustinian nunnery • Easter–Oct Mon–Sat 10am–5pm • £3 • ☎ 01681 700576, ⓦ ionaheritage.co.uk

In the island's former manse is the **Iona Heritage Centre**, with displays on the social history of the island over the last 200 years, including the Clearances, which nearly halved the island's population of 500 in the mid-nineteenth century. One of the more intriguing exhibits is part of the stern belonging to the *Guy Mannering*, a sailing packet on the New York to Liverpool route which sank in 1865 – indeed, it was just one of twenty or so vessels believed to have been lost in waters hereabouts around that time. At a bend in the road, just south of the manse, stands the slender, fifteenth-century **MacLean's Cross**, a fine, late medieval example of the distinctive, flowing, three-leaved foliage of the Iona school.

Iona Abbey

A 5min walk up the road from the Heritage Centre • April–Sept daily 9.30am–5.30pm; Oct–March Mon–Sat 10am–4pm; there are free daily guided tours of the abbey (the times are posted up at the ticket office) • £9; HES • ☎ 01681 700512, ⓦ historicenvironment.scot

Although no buildings remain from Columba's time, the present **Iona Abbey** dates from the arrival of the Benedictines in around 1200, though it was extensively

BAILE MÓR

■ **ACCOMMODATION**
Argyll — 2
Iona Camping — 3
Iona Hostel — 1

● **EATING**
Martyr's Bay Restaurant — 1

Dún I & the north end beaches

Shop

MacLeod Centre

Abbey Museum

The Abbey

Ticket Office

St Oran's Chapel

Reilig Odhráin

N

Bishop's House

Iona Heritage Centre

MacLean's Cross

Cottages

School

Library

Augustinian nunnery

Cottages

St Ronans Bay

Village Hall

Shops

Post Office

Finlay Ross General Store

Toilets

0 — 100
yards

Machair & Port a'Churraich

Fionnphort (Mull)

1

rebuilt in the fifteenth and sixteenth centuries, and restored virtually wholesale last century.

St Oran's Chapel

Iona's oldest building, the plain-looking eleventh-century **St Oran's Chapel**, lies south of the abbey, on the right. Legend has it that the original chapel could only be completed through human sacrifice. Oran apparently volunteered to be buried alive, and was found to have survived the ordeal when the grave was opened a few days later. Declaring that he had seen hell and it wasn't all bad, he was promptly reinterred for blasphemy.

Reilig Odhráin

Oran's Chapel stands at the centre of Iona's sacred burial ground, **Reilig Odhráin** (Oran's Cemetery), which is said to contain the graves of sixty kings of Norway, Ireland, France and Scotland, including Duncan and Macbeth. The best of the early Christian gravestones and medieval effigies that once lay in the Reilig Odhráin have been removed to the Abbey Museum and to various other locations within the complex.

Street of the Dead

Approaching the abbey from the ticket office, you cross an exposed section of the evocative medieval **Street of the Dead**, whose giant pink-granite cobbles once stretched from the abbey, past St Oran's Chapel, to the village. Beside the road stands the most impressive of Iona's Celtic high crosses, the eighth-century **St Martin's Cross**, smothered with figural scenes – the Virgin and Child at the centre, Daniel in the lions' den, Abraham sacrificing Isaac, and David with musicians in the shaft below. The reverse side features Pictish serpent-and-boss decoration. Standing directly in front of the abbey are the base of **St Matthew's Cross** (the rest of which is in the Abbey Museum) and, to the left, a concrete cast of the eighth-century **St John's Cross**, decorated with serpent-and-boss and Celtic spiral ornamental panels. Before you enter the abbey, take a look inside **St Columba's Shrine**, a small steep-roofed chamber to the left of the main entrance. Columba is believed to have been buried either here or under the rocky mound to the west of the abbey, known as Tòrr an Aba.

The Abbey

The **Abbey** itself has been simply and sensitively restored to incorporate the original elements. You can spot many of the medieval capitals in the south aisle of the choir and in the south transept, where the white marble effigies of the eighth Duke of Argyll

---

ST COLUMBA AND IONA

Legend has it that **St Columba** (Colum Cille), born in Donegal some time around 521, was a direct descendant of the semi-legendary Irish king, Niall of the Nine Hostages. A scholar and soldier priest, who founded numerous monasteries in Ireland, he is thought to have become involved in a bloody dispute with the king when he refused to hand over a copy of *St Jerome's Psalter*, copied illegally from the original owned by St Finian of Moville. This, in turn, provoked the Battle of Cúl Drebene (Cooldrumman) – also known as the **Battle of the Book** – at which Columba's forces won, though with the loss of over 3000 lives. The story goes that, repenting this bloodshed, Columba went into exile with twelve other monks, eventually settling on Iona in 563, allegedly because it was the first island he encountered from which he couldn't see his homeland. The bottom line, however, is that we know very little about Columba, though he undoubtedly became something of a cult figure after his death in 597. He was posthumously credited with miraculous feats such as defeating the Loch Ness monster – it only had to hear his voice and it recoiled in terror – and casting out snakes (and, some say, frogs) from the island. He is also famously alleged to have banned women and cows from Iona, exiling them to Eilean nam Ban (Woman's Island), just north of Fionnphort, for, as he believed, "Where there is a cow there is a woman, and where there is a woman there is mischief".

WALKING IONA

Not many day-visitors get further than the village and abbey, but it's perfectly possible to walk to the stunning sandy beaches and turquoise seas at the **north end** of the island, or up to the highest point, **Dún I**, a mere 328ft above sea level but with views on a clear day to Skye, Tiree and Jura. Alternatively, it takes about half an hour to walk over to the **machair**, or common grazing land, on the west side of Iona (also used as a rough golf course). On the edge of this is a series of pretty sandy beaches, the largest of which is the evocatively named **Camus Cúl an t-Saimh** ("Bay at the Back of the Ocean"), a crescent of pebble and shell-strewn sand with a spouting cave to the south. Those with more time (2–3hr) might hike over to the **south** of the island, where Port a'Churaich ("Bay of the Coracle", also known as St Columba's Bay), the saint's traditional landing place on Iona, is filled with smooth round rocks and multicoloured pebbles and stones. A short distance to the east is the **disused marble quarry** at Rubha na Carraig Geire on the southeasternmost point of Iona, which finally closed down in 1914.

and his wife, Ina, lie in a side chapel – an incongruous piece of Victorian pomp in an otherwise modest and tranquil place. The finest pre-Reformation effigy is that of John MacKinnon, the last abbot of Iona, who died around 1500, and now lies on the south side of the choir steps. For reasons of sanitation, the **cloisters** were placed, contrary to the norm, on the north side of the church (where running water was available); entirely reconstructed in the late 1950s, they now shelter lots of medieval grave slabs.

ARRIVAL, INFORMATION AND TOURS   ISLE OF IONA

By ferry The CalMac passenger ferry from Fionnphort is very frequent and takes just 10min (£3.50 return, bicycles free).

Information In the absence of a tourist office, ⓦ welcometoiona.com is a useful resource.

Boat tours Mark Jardine's Alternative Boat Hire is based at Lovedale Cottage, near the *Argyll Hotel* (☎01681 700537, ⓦ boattripsiona.com). The owner takes the lovely wooden gaff-rigged sailing boat *Birthe Marie* on short trips to some of the less-visited spots around the Sound of Iona and Erraid (Easter–Oct; 3hr trip £30). For details of trips across to Staffa, see page 79.

ACCOMMODATION AND EATING   SEE MAP PAGE 83

Argyll ☎01681 700334, ⓦ argyllhoteliona.co.uk. Inviting, stone-built hotel in the village's terrace of cottages overlooking the Sound of Iona, with 16 sweet, though somewhat boxy, rooms spread throughout a maze of corridors. The restaurant is first-class (for example, haunch of venison with roast Portobello mushrooms and venison and red wine ragu; £18), or you can just sup a pint out on the trim, sea-facing lawn. Feb–Oct. **£99**

Iona Camping Cnoc-Oran ☎07747 721275, ⓦ iona campsite.co.uk. Turn left at the jetty and it's a 20min walk to this super little campsite, which has a couple of showers and toilets, firepits and BBQs. You can also rent tents and sleeping bags. Per person **£6.50**

Iona Hostel Lagandorain; follow the road past the abbey for half a mile ☎01681 700781, ⓦ ionahostel.

co.uk. Terrific hostel located to the north of the island, with impeccable green credentials; five rooms sleeping two to six people, and there's a main living space filled with lovely wooden furniture and a wood-burning stove that has views out to the Treshnish Isles. They've also got a delightful shepherd's bothy tucked away on a rocky outcrop just behind the hostel. Dorms **£21**; bothy **£60**

Martyr's Bay Restaurant ☎01681 700382, ⓦ martyrs bay.co.uk. A self-service canteen by day, a fully fledged restaurant come evening; either way, the tourist hordes invariably pack this place out for steaks and seafood. Lunch meals like haddock and chips (£9.95) and baked potato with haggis are worth a punt too. Easter–Oct. Daily 10am–10pm; food served till 8pm.

Isle of Coll

Roughly thirteen miles long and three miles wide, the fish-shaped rocky island of **COLL**, with a population of around a hundred, lies less than seven miles off the coast of Mull. For the most part, this remote island is low lying, treeless and exceptionally windy, with white sandy beaches and the highest sunshine records in Scotland.

1

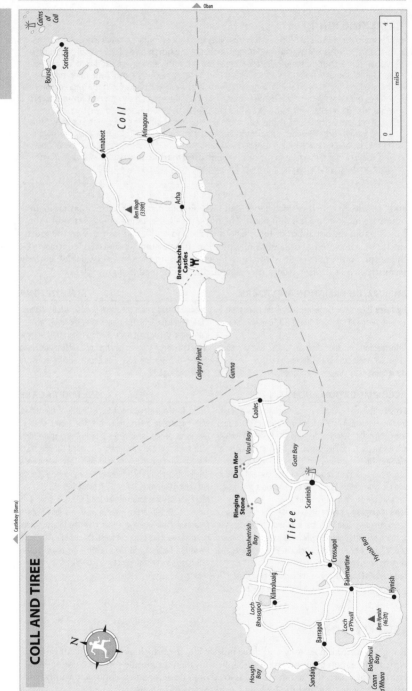

COLL AND TIREE

N

Oban

Cairns of Coll

Sorisdale
Bousd

Coll

Arinagour

Arnabost

Acha

Ben Hogh
(339ft)

Breachacha
Castles

Calgary Point

Gunna

Castlebay (Barra)

Caoles

Vaul Bay

Dun Mor

Gott Bay

Ringing
Stone

Scarinish

Tiree

Balephetrish
Bay

Hynish Bay

Kilmoluaig

Crossapol

Balemartine

Hynish

Loch
Bhasapol

Barrapol

Loch
a'Phuill

Ben Hynish
(463ft)

Hough
Bay

Sandaig

Balephuil
Bay

Ceann
a'Mhara

0   miles   4

Like most of the Hebrides, Coll was once ruled by Vikings, and didn't pass into Scottish hands until the thirteenth century. In the 1830s, the island's population peaked at 1440, but was badly affected by the Clearances, which virtually halved its population in a generation. Coll was fortunate to be in the hands of the enlightened MacLeans, but they were forced to sell in 1856 to the Stewart family, who raised the rents, forcing the island's population to move wholesale from the more fertile southeast to the northwest coast – however, overcrowding led to widespread emigration. From the northwestern tip, there's an impressive view over to the headland, the Small Isles and the Skye Cuillin beyond. The majority of visitors to Coll stay for a week in self-catering accommodation, though there are hotels and B&Bs on the islands, which should be booked in advance – as should the ferries.

Arinagour

The ferry docks at Coll's only real village, **ARINAGOUR**, whose whitewashed cottages line the western shore of Loch Eatharna, a popular safe anchorage for boats. Half the island's population lives in the village, and it's here you'll find the island's hotel and pub, post office, churches and a couple of shops. The island's petrol pump is also in Arinagour, and is run on a volunteer basis – effectively it's open when the ferry arrives.

The Breachacha castles

On the southwest coast there are two edifices, both confusingly known as **Breachacha Castle**, and both built by the MacLeans. The older, at the head of Loch Breachacha, is a fifteenth-century tower house with an additional curtain wall, now used by Project Trust overseas aid volunteers as a training centre. The less attractive "new castle", to the northwest, is made up of a central block built around 1750 and two side pavilions added a century later, now converted into holiday cottages. It was here that Dr Johnson and Boswell stayed in 1773 after a storm forced them to take refuge en route to Mull. Much of the surrounding area is now owned by the RSPB, in the hope of protecting the island's corncrakes, of which there are currently around 66 calling males; you're also likely to see white-fronted and barnacle geese, lapwings and redshanks.

ARRIVAL AND INFORMATION   ISLE OF COLL

By ferry Throughout the summer, the CalMac ferry from Oban calls daily at Coll (2hr 40min) and Tiree (3hr 40min). Destinations Barra (Wed 1 daily; 4hr); Oban (daily except Tues & Wed; 2hr 40min).

Information In the absence of a tourist office, ⓦ visitcoll. co.uk is a useful and up-to-date resource.

ACCOMMODATION AND EATING

Coll Hotel Arinagour ☎ 01879 230334, ⓦ collhotel.com. Small, family-run hotel providing refined accommodation in six rooms, four of which overlook the bay; among the many lovely touches offered is a goodie basket with biscuits, tablet and water. The hotel also offers bike rental, and can do pick-ups/drop-offs to/from the ferry. Wild camping (free) is also possible on the hill behind the hotel, but you should contact the hotel first. Creel-caught seafood forms the mainstay of a mouthwatering menu. Restaurant noon–2pm & 6–9pm. **£100**

Garden House Down a track on the left before the turn-off for the castle ☎ 01879 230374, ⓔ collcampsite@ hotmail.com. There's very basic camping at this working farm in the shelter of what was formerly a walled garden, with showers, toilets and a campers' room. April–Oct. Per pitch **£18**

Island Café Shore St ☎ 01879 230262, ⓦ theislandcafe. business.site. In the old harbour stores overlooking the bay, offering hot meals all day, though Sundays are most popular when they rustle up a superb two-course late lunch, comprising a roast and a dessert (£18), for which reservations are advised. Wed–Sat 11am–2pm & 5.30–9pm, Sun noon–6pm.

Tigh-na-Mara Arinagour Bay ☎ 01879 230354, ⓦ tighna mara.info. The "House by the Sea" is a modern guesthouse near the pier, with a selection of shared bathroom and en-suite rooms, the latter being £10 more expensive. Such is its location that there's a good chance you'll see some great wildlife while eating your breakfast. **£70**

1 Isle of Tiree

Similar in size to Coll, **TIREE**, as its Gaelic name *tir-iodh* (Land of Corn) suggests, was once known as the breadbasket of the Inner Hebrides, thanks to its acres of rich machair. Tiree's population peaked at a staggering 4450 in the 1830s, but, like Coll, it was badly affected by the Clearances, which decimated numbers. Tiree was ruthlessly cleared by its owner, the Duke of Argyll, who sent in the marines in 1885 to evict the crofters. Both islands have strong Gaelic roots, but the percentage of English-speaking newcomers is rising steadily.

Nowadays, crofting and tourism are the main sources of income for the resident population of around 750. One of the most distinctive features of Tiree is its **architecture**, in particular the large numbers of "pudding" or "spotty" houses, where only the mortar is painted white. In addition, there are numerous "white houses" (*tigh geal*) and traditional "blackhouses" (*tigh dubh*). **Wildlife**-lovers can also have a field day on Tiree, with lapwings, wheatears, redshanks, greylag geese and large, laidback brown hares in abundance. Tiree's sandy beaches attract large numbers of **windsurfers** for the Tiree Wave Classic (⊕ tireewaveclassic.co.uk) every October.

An Turas and Scarinish

An Iodhlann July & Aug Mon–Fri 11am–5pm; Sept–June Mon, Wed & Thurs 9am–1pm • £3 • ☎ 01879 220793, ⊕ aniodhlann.org.uk

The ferry calls at Gott Bay Pier, now best known for **An Turas** (The Journey), Tiree's award-winning "shelter", a structure that consists of two parallel white walls connected via a black felt section to a glass box which punctures a stone dyke and frames a sea view. Just up the road from the pier is the village of **SCARINISH**, home to a post office, a supermarket, the butcher's and the bank, with a petrol pump back at the pier. Also in Scarinish you'll find **An Iodhlann** – "haystack" in Gaelic – the island's two-roomed archive, which has an enlightening exhibition on the island's history, covering everything from the sea and settlers to saints and Vikings.

Hynish

The island's most intriguing sights lie in the bulging western half of the island, where Tiree's two landmark hills rise up. Below the higher of the two is **HYNISH** whose **harbour** was designed by Alan Stevenson – uncle of Robert Louis Stevenson – in the 1830s to transport building materials for the magnificent 157ft-tall **Skerryvore Lighthouse**, the tallest in the UK, which lies on a sea-swept reef some twelve miles southwest of Tiree. Up on the hill behind the harbour, beside the row of lighthouse keepers' houses, stands a stumpy granite signal tower, whose signals used to be the only contact the lighthouse keepers had with civilization.

Skerryvore Lighthouse Exhibition and the Treshnish Isles Exhibition

Lower Square • Daily 9am–5pm • Free, but suggested £3 donation • ☎ 01879 220045, ⊕ hebrideantrust.org

Occupying a converted smithy, the **Skerryvore Lighthouse Exhibition** recalls the Herculean effort required to erect the lighthouse, alongside many intriguing items gathered along the way. A few paces along, in some converted cowsheds, the **Treshnish Isles Exhibition** documents the wonderfully diverse array of flora and fauna to be found on the Hebridean Trust-owned islands.

Ceann a'Mhara and around

A mile or so across the golden sands of Balephuil Bay is the spectacular headland of **Ceann a'Mhara** (pronounced "kenavara"), home to thousands of seabirds, including fulmars, kittiwakes, guillemots, razorbills, shags and cormorants, with gannets and terns feeding offshore.

Taigh Iain Mhoir

Sandaig • June–Sept Mon–Fri 2–4pm • Free

In the scattered west coast settlement of **SANDAIG**, to the north of Ceann a'Mhara, three thatched white houses in a row have been turned into the **Taigh Iain Mhoir**, which gives an insight into how the majority of islanders lived in the nineteenth century, thanks to a collection of old photographs and other memorabilia.

ARRIVAL AND DEPARTURE

ISLE OF TIREE

By plane Tiree Airport (☎ 01879 220456, �🖰 hial.co.uk) is around three miles west of Scarinish. Most hosts are happy to collect you upon arrival.

Destinations Coll (Wed 1 daily; 15min); Glasgow (2 daily; 1hr); Oban (Wed 2 daily; 1hr).

By ferry Throughout the summer, the CalMac ferry from Oban calls daily at Coll (2hr 40min) and Tiree (3hr 40min). On Wednesdays (though the day may change) the ferry continues to Barra in the Western Isles, and calls in at Tiree on the way back, making a day-trip from Oban possible.

Destinations Castlebay, Barra (Wed 1 daily; 2hr 45min); Oban (1 daily; 3hr 40min).

GETTING AROUND AND INFORMATION

By minibus Tiree has a Ring'n'Ride minibus service (Mon–Sat 7am–6pm, plus Tues 7am–10pm in summer; ☎ 01879 220419) that will take you anywhere on the island, though you should book in advance; costs vary between £1.25 and £3.

Bike/car rental Based at Scarinish Pier, MacLennan Motors (☎ 01879 220555, �🖰 maclennanmotors.com) offers both car (£50/day) and bike (£10/day) rental. They can also drop cars at the airport.

Information In the absence of a tourist office, �🖰 isleof tiree.com is a useful resource.

ACCOMMODATION

Balinoe Camping Balinoe ☎ 07712 159205, �🖰 tiree campsite.co.uk. Located in the southwest of the island, six miles from Scarinish, the island's only formal campsite is well equipped with showers, toilets, a self-catering kitchen and washing/drying facilities; they've also got two, two-person pods with floor mattresses and a bothy with three single beds. April–Oct. Per pitch £24; pod £30; bothy £30

Millhouse Hostel Near Loch Bhasapol, in the northwest of the island ☎ 01879 220892, �🖰 tireemillhouse.co.uk. This superbly converted early twentieth-century barn now accommodates a colourful hostel, with two dorms each sleeping six, a couple of doubles and a triple. The excellent open-plan kitchen/lounge opens up onto a patio where you can kick back with a beer and listen to corncrakes while watching the sunset. Doubles £48; dorms £25

Scarinish Hotel Scarinish ☎ 01879 220308, �🖰 tiree scarinishhotel.com. Super location overlooking the old harbour offering eight pristine rooms (a couple with shared bathroom facilities), furnished in solid, if not spectacular, fashion. The Upper Deck lounge is a lovely spot to watch the comings and goings around the harbour. £80

Isle of Colonsay and around

Isolated between Mull and Islay, **COLONSAY** – measuring just eight miles by three – is nothing like as bleak and windswept as Coll or Tiree. Its craggy, heather-backed hills even support the occasional patch of woodland, plus a bewildering array of plant and birdlife, including wild goats and rabbits, and a very fine quasi-tropical garden. The current population of around a hundred and thirty is down from a pre-Clearance peak of nearly a thousand. With only one hotel and infrequent ferry links with the mainland, there's no fear of mass tourism taking over any time soon. That said, you can expect a discernible rise in visitor numbers during the island's three excellent festivals: the Colonsay Book Festival (�🖰 colonsaybook festival.co.uk) at the end of April; the Ceol Cholasa Folk Festival (�🖰 ceolcholasa.co.uk) in mid-September; and the two-week long Colonsay Food Festival (�🖰 colonsayfoodfest. co.uk) in October, featuring, among other things, guided walks and foraging, baking and craft workshops, and whisky tasting. The ferry terminal is at **Scalasaig**, on the east coast, where there's a post office/shop, a petrol pump, a brewery, a café and the island's hotel.

Colonsay House

Two miles north of Scalasaig • Gardens: April–Sept Wed & Fri noon–5pm, Sat 2–5pm, Oct Wed 2–4.30pm; the house itself is closed to the public • £2.50 • ☎ 01951 200316, Ⓦ colonsayholidays.co.uk

Colonsay House was built in 1722 by Malcolm MacNeil, but in 1904 the island and house were bought by Lord Strathcona, who made his fortune building the Canadian Pacific Railway (and whose descendants still own the island). He was also responsible for the house's romantically dilapidated woodland **gardens**, home to one of the most extensive rhododendron collections anywhere in Scotland. The gardens also shelter the strange eighth-century **Riasg Buidhe Cross**, which is decorated with an unusually lifelike mug shot (possibly of a monk) – ask for directions from the tearoom.

Kiloran Bay and around

To the north of Colonsay House is the island's finest sandy beach, the breathtaking **Kiloran Bay**, where spectacular breakers roll in from the Atlantic. There's another unspoilt sandy beach backed by dunes at Balnahard, two miles northeast along a rough track; en route, you might spot wild goats, choughs and even a golden eagle.

Beinn Bhreac

The island's west coast forms a sharp escarpment, quite at odds with the gentle undulating landscape that characterizes the rest of the island. Due west of Colonsay

House around **Beinn Bhreac** (456ft), the cliffs are at their most spectacular, and in their lower reaches provide a home to hundreds of seabirds, among them kittiwakes, cormorants and guillemots in spring and early summer.

Isle of Oronsay

While on Colonsay, it's worth taking a day out to visit the **Isle of Oronsay**, half a mile to the south, with its ruined Augustinian priory. The two islands are separated by "The Strand", a stretch of tidal mud flats, which act as a causeway for two hours either side of low tide (check locally for timings); you can drive over to the island at low tide, though most people park their cars and walk across. Legends (and etymology) link saints Columba and Oran with Colonsay and Oronsay, although the ruins only date back to the fourteenth century. You can, nevertheless, still make out the original church and tiny cloisters, abandoned since the Reformation and now roofless. The highlight, though, is the **Oronsay Cross**, a superb example of late medieval artistry from Iona which, along with thirty or so beautifully carved grave slabs, can be found in the restored side chapel. It takes about an hour to walk from the tip of Colonsay across The Strand to the priory (Wellington boots are a good idea).

ARRIVAL AND DEPARTURE   ISLE OF COLONSAY AND AROUND

By plane Colonsay airport is three miles west of Scalasaig (☎01951 200211, ⊚hebrideanair.co.uk).
Destinations Islay (Tues & Thurs 1 daily; 20min); Oban (Tues & Thurs 2 daily; 25min).
By ferry CalMac ferries run from Oban and once a week from Kennacraig via Islay, when a day-trip is possible, giving you around six hours on the island. Ferries also make the trip from Port Askaig on Islay.
Destinations Kennacraig (Wed 1 daily; 3hr 40min); Oban (daily except Wed & Sat; 2hr 15min); Port Askaig (Wed & Sat 1 daily; 1hr 10min).

GETTING AROUND AND INFORMATION

By minibus There's no public transport, but a minibus meets the Wednesday ferry and takes folk on a tour of the island.
Bike rental Archie McConnell (☎01951 200355) rents bikes.
Information In the absence of a tourist office, ⊚colonsay. org.uk is a useful resource.

ACCOMMODATION AND EATING

There are a couple of modern **B&Bs** to choose from, though most visitors rent **self-catering accommodation**, the majority of which is run by the estate. **Wild camping** is, of course, an option.
Backpacker's Lodge Overlooking Loch Fada about 2 miles from the ferry terminal ☎01951 200211, ⊚colonsayholidays.co.uk. The Colonsay Estate's very comfortable hostel consists of the house itself (a former gamekeeper's lodge), with lounge and real fire, and a bothy with three cabins, each sleeping two people and with a shower block outside. There's a well-equipped dining bothy too. Dorms £22; cabin £44
The Colonsay Scalasaig ☎01951 200316, ⊚colonsay holidays.co.uk. A cosy eighteenth-century inn at heart, and a short stroll from the pier, the island's only hotel, with just eight rooms, has transformed itself into a really stylish, comfortable place to stay; handily, it also has a restaurant serving decent food and a convivial bar which acts as the island's social centre. Daily noon–2.30pm & Sun 6–10pm. £105
★ **The Colonsay Pantry** Above the pier in Scalasaig ☎01951 200325, ⊚thecolonsaypantry.co.uk. Delightful seafood restaurant and bistro offering both light refreshments (tea, coffee and cake) alongside substantial and scrumptious home cooking such as smoked haddock scramble with chips (£9.95); Wednesdays and Thursdays are fish nights, and Saturday is steak night,, but in any case, you must phone ahead for any evening meals. Mon, Fri & Sat 10am–8pm, Tues 10am–3pm, Wed 10am–10pm, Thurs 10am–9pm, Sun 3–8pm.

Mid-Argyll

MID-ARGYLL loosely describes the central wedge of land south of Oban and north of Kintyre. The highlights of this gently undulating scenery lie along the sharply indented

1

and remote western coastline. Closest to Oban are the former slate mining settlements of Seil, Easdale and Luing, known collectively as the **Slate Islands**. Further south, the rich Bronze Age and Neolithic remains in the **Kilmartin Glen** comprise one of the most important prehistoric sites in Scotland. Separating Kilmartin Glen from the **Knapdale** peninsula is the **Crinan Canal**, a short cut for boats disinclined to round the Mull of Kintyre, which ends in the pint-sized, picturesque port of **Crinan**.

The Slate Islands

Eight miles south of Oban, a road heads off the A816 west to the minuscule **SLATE ISLANDS**, which at their peak in the mid-nineteenth century quarried over nine million slates annually. Today the old slate villages are sparsely populated, but their dramatic setting amid crashing waves makes for a rewarding day-trip.

Isle of Seil

The most northerly of the Slate Islands is **Seil**, a lush island separated from the mainland only by the thinnest of sea channels, which is spanned by the elegant single-arched humpback **Clachan Bridge**, built in 1793 and popularly known as the "Bridge over the Atlantic". In spring, the bridge sprouts a splendid flourish of purple fairy foxglove, which makes for a quite lovely sight. The **pub** next door to the bridge is the *Tigh na Truish* (House of the Trousers), where kilt-wearing islanders would change into trousers to conform to the post-1745 ban on Highland dress.

The main village on Seil is **Ellenabeich**, its neat white terraces of workers' cottages – featured in the film *Ring of Bright Water* – crouching below black cliffs on the westernmost tip of the island. This was once the tiny island of Eilean a'Beithich (hence "Ellenabeich"), separated from the mainland by a slim sea channel until the intensive slate quarrying succeeded in silting it up. Confusingly, the village is often referred to by the same name as the nearby island of Easdale, since they formed an interdependent community based exclusively around the slate industry.

Slate Islands Heritage Centre

Ellenabeich • April–Oct daily 10.30am–4.30pm • Free • ⓦ slateislands.org.uk

The **Slate Islands Heritage Centre**, in one of the village's little white cottages, documents the lives and times of island folk in the form of old photographs and artefacts, though mostly the emphasis is inevitably on the local quarry workings, including a model of the slate quarry as it would have been in its heyday. Moreover, and in common with many of Argyll's heritage centres, there's a dedicated genealogical department here.

Isle of Easdale

ⓦ easdale.org

Easdale remains an island, though the few hundred yards that separate it from Ellenabeich have to be dredged to keep the channel open. Up until the eve of a great storm in 1881, Easdale supported an incredible 452 inhabitants, despite being less than a mile across at any one point. That night, waves engulfed the island and flooded the quarries and the island never really recovered.

With lots of wonderfully flat stones freely available, Easdale makes the perfect venue for the annual **World Stone Skimming Championships** (ⓦ stoneskimming.com), held on the last Sunday of September. Just for the record, a legal skim qualifies as a stone that bounces twice – and if you fancy having a go, you can, as it's open to anyone.

Easdale Folk Museum

Near the main square, Easdale • April–mid-Oct 11am–4pm • £2.50 • ☎ 01852 300173, ⓦ easdalemuseum.org

Many of the village's old workers' cottages now serve as holiday homes, and one is home to the interesting **Easdale Folk Museum**, near the main square, which has

ISLANDS GALORE

Scarba is the largest of the islands around Luing, a brooding 1500-foot hulk of slate, a couple of miles wide, inhospitable and wild – most of the fifty or so inhabitants who once lived here had left by the mid-nineteenth century. The string of uninhabited islands visible west of Luing are known collectively as the **Garvellachs**, after the largest, **Garbh Eileach** (Rough Rock), which was inhabited as recently as sixty years ago. The most northerly, **Dún Chonnuill**, contains the remains of an old fort thought to have belonged to Conal of Dalriada, and **Eileach an Naoimh** (Holy Isle), the most southerly, is where the Celtic missionary Brendan the Navigator founded a community in 542, twenty years before Columba landed on Iona. Nothing survives from Brendan's day, but there are a few ninth-century remains, among them a double-beehive cell and a grave enclosure. One school of thought has it that the island is Hinba, Columba's legendary secret retreat, where he founded a monastery before settling on Iona. If you're interested in taking a boat trip to Scarba or the nearby Garvellach Islands, contact Craignish Cruises, in Ardfern (☎ 07747 023038, ⊛ craignishcruises.co.uk).

surprisingly expansive collections covering not just the local slate industry but also the island's social and military associations. It also sells a useful historical map of the island, and you can buy some interesting slate souvenirs in the shop.

Isle of Luing

⊛ isleofluing.org

South of Seil, across the narrow, treacherous Cuan Sound, lies **Luing** – pronounced "Ling" – the largest of the Slate Islands, a long, thin, fertile island which once supported more than six hundred people, but now has a third of that. During the Clearances, the population was drastically reduced to make way for cattle; Luing is still renowned for its beef and for the chocolate-brown crossbreed named after it.

Cullipool, a mile or so southwest of the ferry slipway, is the main village, its whitewashed cottages (mostly built by the slate company) dotted along the shore facing Scarba and Mull. Luing's only other village, **Toberonochy**, lies on the more sheltered east coast, three miles southeast, and boasts the same distinctive white cottages, with red-or-blue-painted door and window frames.

Atlantic Islands Centre

Cullipool • Easter–Oct Mon–Fri 10am–5pm, Sat 10am–10pm, Sun 11am–4pm; Nov–Easter daily 11am–4pm • Free • ☎ 01852 314096, ⊛ atlanticislandscentre.com

Positioned near the waterfront, the **Atlantic Islands Centre** is a superb heritage centre comprising a couple of engaging exhibitions, art space and a terrific café (see page 94). On the ground floor, a series of colourful and informative wall panels documents the forces that have shaped life on this side of the Atlantic; here too is the original lens from the Fladda Lighthouse, which was used from its inception in 1860 until 1956, when it became one of the first lighthouses in Scotland to be automated. Upstairs, the **Living History Exhibition** traces the development of the island in tandem with the local slate industry; better still are the marvellous views of Scarba, the Garvellachs and the lighthouses on Fladda and Benahua.

GETTING AROUND AND TOURS   THE SLATE ISLANDS

By ferry The Cuan Ferry runs from Seil to Luing (every 30min; 5min; £2.10 return, car £8.50 return). The passenger-only ferry from Ellenabeich to the Isle of Easdale runs more or less on demand (press the buttons in the ferry shed or phone ☎ 01852 300559).

By bike You can rent bikes from Luing Bike Hire (☎ 01852 314274; £15/day), based at Sunnybrae Caravan Park, in South Cuan on Luing.

Boat tours Three, four- and five-hour wildlife and whale-watching cruises (£52–80), as well as high-adrenaline boat trips to the Corryvreckan Whirlpool, are offered by Sealife Adventures (☎ 01852 300203 or ☎ 01631 571010, ⊛ sealife-adventures.com), whose pontoon is located just across the Clachan Bridge on Seil; depending upon the time of year, expect to see gannets, shags, kittiwakes, seals, dolphins, porpoises and sea eagles.

1

EATING AND DRINKING

Atlantic Islands Centre Café Cullipool ☎ 01852 314096, ⓦatlanticislandscentre.com. Lovely, airy café offering both great views and great food, for example hot smoked salmon panini or some home-made stilton and walnut pate with warm toast and butter (£5.95); or you could just opt for a cuppa and a chunk of home-made chocolate cake. Meals are also served on Saturday evenings, for which booking is advised. Easter–Oct Mon–Fri 10am–5pm, Sat 10am–10pm, Sun 11am–4pm; Nov–Easter daily 11am–4pm.

Oyster Bar and Restaurant Ellenabeich ☎ 01852 300121, ⓦoysterbareasdale.com. For delicious seafood – mussels in white wine (£7.95), king prawns and sweet chilli (£10.95) – or just a pint of real ale, pop inside the snug wood-panelled bar of the *Oyster* on the way to or from the ferry. April–Oct daily 11am–10pm, Nov–March same times but closed between 3–5pm.

Puffer Bar 200yds from the Folk Museum ☎ 01852 300022, ⓦpufferbarandrestaurant.co.uk. Should you wish to hang about, then you could do worse than visit the terrific *Puffer* restaurant and bar; the former serves the best of the day's fresh catch, while the latter is a convivial spot for a drink. Mon–Sat 11am–1am, Sun 12.30–11pm.

Arduaine Garden

A816, 10 miles north of Kilmartin • Daily 9.30am–dusk • £7.50; NTS • ☎ 01852 200366

A great spot at which to stop and have a picnic on the A816 from Oban to Lochgilphead is **Arduaine Garden**, overlooking Asknish Bay and the islands of Shuna, Luing, Scarba and Jura. The gardens, whose original foundations were laid in 1898, are stupendous, particularly in May and June, and have the feel of an intimate private garden, with immaculately mown lawns, lily-strewn ponds, mature woods and spectacular rhododendrons, azaleas and magnolias. In late spring, meanwhile, the wild meadow comes alive with orchids. You can follow several pathways through the gardens, one of which is the woodland walk, which leads down to the lakeshore, where there's a good chance of spotting otters, sea eagles and hen harriers.

ACCOMMODATION AND EATING

ARDUAINE GARDEN

★ **Loch Melfort Hotel** Adjacent to Arduaine Garden ☎ 01852 200233, ⓦlochmelfort.co.uk. This fine, privately run country-house hotel overlooking Asknish Bay offers a selection of beautifully appointed rooms, both in the main house and the adjoining Seaview Lodge; best of all, though, are the views, which are some of the finest in Scotland. The hotel's restaurant is outstanding (Argyll lamb with sweetbread and walnut jus; £23.50), while their sparky *Bistro* next door has cheaper alternatives, for example Loch Melfort fishcakes and home-made burgers (£11.50); you can also eat off the terrace here. Moreover, every first and third Friday evening of the month, the bistro has live music. Daily 11am–10pm. **£125**

Kilmartin Glen and around

The chief sight on the road from Oban to Lochgilphead is **KILMARTIN GLEN**, the most important prehistoric site on the Scottish mainland. The most remarkable relic is the **linear cemetery**, where several cairns are aligned for more than two miles to the south of the village of Kilmartin. These are thought to represent the successive burials of a ruling family or chieftains, but nobody can be sure. The best view of the cemetery's configuration is from the Bronze Age **Mid-Cairn**, but the Neolithic **South Cairn**, dating from around 3000 BC, is by far the oldest and the most impressive, with its large chambered tomb roofed by giant slabs.

Close to the South Cairn, the two **Temple Wood stone circles** appear to have been the architectural focus of burials in the area from Neolithic times to the Bronze Age. Visible to the south are the impressively cup-marked **Nether Largie standing stones** (no public access), the largest of which looms over 10ft high.

Cup- and ring-marked rocks are a recurrent feature of prehistoric sites in Kilmartin Glen and elsewhere in Argyll. There are many theories as to their origin: some see them as Pictish symbols, others as primitive solar calendars. The most extensive markings in the entire country are at **Achnabreck**, off the A816 towards Lochgilphead.

Kilmartin Museum

Kilmartin village • Daily: March–Oct 10am–5.30pm; Nov–Christmas 11am–4pm • £7 • ☎ 01546 510278, ⓦ kilmartin.org

Situated on high ground to the north of the Kilmartin cairns is the tiny village of **KILMARTIN**, an unremarkable place but home to the superb **Kilmartin Museum**, housed in the old manse adjacent to the village church. Not only can you learn about the various theories concerning prehistoric crannogs, henges and cairns, but you can practise polishing an axe, examine different types of wood, and listen to a variety of weird and wonderful sounds (check out the Gaelic bird imitations). Among the many remarkable exhibits is an eagle bone flute, a bronze sword from Shuna, a carved slab from the Nether Largie north cairn, and decorated querns (stones used for making flour from grain) from Barnasluagan. Note, however, that a long-awaited redevelopment of the museum finally got underway in late 2019, and is not expected to reopen until mid-2021. At 1.30pm on Wednesdays between April and October, museum staff run a superb (free) two-hour guided walk of the cairns.

Carnasserie Castle

Commanding a high ridge a mile up the road towards Oban are the ruins of **Carnasserie Castle**. Built in the 1560s by Protestant reformer John Carswell – who published the first book to be printed in Scottish Gaelic (a translation of John Knox's *Book of Common Order*) – the castle is a good example of the transition between fully fortified castles and later mansion houses, and has several original finely carved stone fireplaces and doorways, as well as numerous gun-loops and shot holes. The reward for climbing the five-storey structure is a wonderful view of Kilmartin Glen dead straight ahead.

1

Mòine Mhór and Dunadd

To the south of Kilmartin, beyond the linear cemetery, lies the raised peat bog of **Mòine Mhór** (Great Moss), now a nature reserve and home to remarkable plant, insect and birdlife. To get a close look at the sphagnum moss and wetlands, head for the Tileworks Walk, just off the A816, which includes a short boardwalk over the bog.

Mòine Mhór is best known as home to the Iron Age fort of **Dunadd**, one of Scotland's most important Celtic sites, occupying a distinctive 176ft-high rocky knoll once surrounded by the sea but currently stranded beside the winding River Add. It was here that Fergus, the first king of Dalriada – which embraced much of what is now Argyll – established his royal seat, having arrived from Ireland in around 500 AD. Its strategic position, the craggy defences and the view from the top are all impressive, but it's the **stone carvings** (albeit now fibreglass copies) between the twin summits which make Dunadd so remarkable: several lines of inscription in Ogham (an ancient alphabet of Irish origin), the faint outline of a boar, a hollowed-out footprint and a small basin. The boar and the inscriptions are probably Pictish, since the fort was clearly occupied long before Fergus got there, but the footprint and basin have been interpreted as being part of the royal coronation rituals of the kings of Dalriada. It is thought that the Stone of Destiny was used at Dunadd before being moved to Scone Palace. From the car park (well signposted from the main road), it's a fabulous little scramble to the top of the fort, whereupon you'll be rewarded with sparkling views of the Glen and Knapdale Forest.

ACCOMMODATION AND EATING
SEE MAP PAGE 95

Dunchraigaig House 1 mile south of Kilmartin ☎01546 510396, ⊛dunchraigaig.co.uk. This large detached Victorian house situated opposite the Ballymeanoch standing stones offers five spotless en-suite rooms with either woodland or Jura Island views, though its star attraction is the local pine marten, which appears at the feeding table most mornings for a bite to eat. You'll enjoy your breakfast too, while packed lunches are available upon request. March–Nov. **£90**

Kilmartin Museum Café Kilmartin Museum ☎01546 510278, ⊛kilmartin.org. Looking out across to Glebe Cairn, this is a lovely spot at which to refuel after examining the local treasures, with the likes of wild venison burger

(£8.95) and smoked salmon hoagies to feast on, as well as lots of delicious home-baked fare, not least a divine selection of cakes and buns. Daily March–Oct 10am–5.30pm; Nov to Christmas 11am–4pm.

Kings Reach B&B Dunadd View, Kilmichael Glassary ☎01546 602 306, ⊛kingsreachbedandbreakfast.co.uk. Warm and welcoming vegan guesthouse whose two large, light and impeccably kept rooms offer gorgeous views of Dunadd, as well as some fabulous sunsets; breakfast might consist of stacked pancakes, scrambled tofu on toast, or chia pudding alongside fresh fruit and yoghurts; they've also got two very well-equipped self-catering cottages (3-night minimum stay). April–Oct. **£100**

Knapdale and around

Forested **Knapdale** – from the Gaelic *cnap* (hill) and *dall* (field) – forms a buffer zone between the Kintyre peninsula and the rest of Argyll, bounded to the north by the Crinan Canal and to the south by West Loch Tarbert, and consisting of three progressively fatter fingers of land, separated by Loch Sween and Loch Caolisport. Knapdale is a little-visited area, which is surprising, as the ancient wooded landscape is among some of the most beautiful, and unique, in the country. Not only that, but there is some spectacular wildlife to observe here as well, not least thanks to the recent reintroduction of beavers to the area (see page 98).

Crinan Canal

The nine-mile-long **Crinan Canal** opened in 1801, linking Loch Fyne, at Ardrishaig south of Lochgilphead, with the Sound of Jura, thus cutting out the long and treacherous journey around the Mull of Kintyre. John Rennie's original design, although an impressive engineering feat, had numerous faults, and by 1816 Thomas

Telford was called in to take charge of the renovations. The canal runs parallel to the sea for quite some way before cutting across the bottom of Mòine Mhór and hitting a flight of locks either side of **CAIRNBAAN** (there are fifteen in total). The walk along the towpath is utterly delightful (both picturesque and not too strenuous), though you could, of course, cycle too.

The most relaxing place from which to view the canal in action is **CRINAN**, the pretty little fishing port at the canal's western end. Crinan's tiny harbour is, for the moment at least, still home to a small fishing fleet; a quick burst up through Crinan Wood to the hill above the village will give you a bird's-eye view of the sea lock and its setting.

ACCOMMODATION AND EATING   SEE MAP PAGE 95

Cairnbaan Hotel By lock no 5 on the canal, Cairnbaan ☎ 01546 603668, ⓦ cairnbaan.com. Eighteenth-century coaching inn built at the same time as the canal, which it overlooks, with twelve very accomplished and well-designed rooms. The lively restaurant-cum-bar deservedly does well from lots of passing trade from the canal, with dishes such as steamed mussels in white wine and garlic, and smoked haddock on chive mash with Kintyre cheddar (£14.50). Otherwise, just grab a pint and watch the boats pass by. Daily 11am–10pm. **£101**

Crinan Hotel ☎ 01546 830261, ⓦ crinanhotel.com. Occupying an enviable position overlooking the harbour, this mildly eccentric family-run hotel has twenty superbly conceived rooms (indeed, the hotel has its own gallery), each one named after a Scottish artist and featuring an original piece of work by that artist. All offer splendid loch views, though you're certainly paying for the privilege. **£215**

Crinan Seafood Bar Crinan Hotel ☎ 01546 830261. Reward yourself after the long canal-side walk with some steamed mussels or an Arbroath smokie (£13) washed down with a pint, at the same time as enjoying one of the most beautiful views in Scotland – especially at sunset, when the myriad islets and the distinctive Paps of Jura are reflected in the waters of the loch. Occupying the adjacent horse stables is the hotel's cheery coffee shop, serving bacon rolls, home-baked cakes, tea and coffee. Easter–Oct daily noon–12.30pm & 6–8.30pm. Café March–Oct daily 10am–5pm, Nov & Dec Sat & Sun 10am–4pm.

Knapdale Forest

South of the Crinan Canal, **Knapdale Forest** stretches virtually uninterrupted from coast to coast, across hills sprinkled with tiny lochs. There are several waymarked walks in the area to choose from: a circular, mile-long path will take you deep into the forest just past **Achnamara**, a three-mile route around **Loch Coille-Bharr**, and a two-and-a-half-mile path which runs along the canal and ascends **Dunardry** (702ft).

Tayvallich and the Taynish Nature Reserve

Continuing down the western finger of Knapdale you come to **Tayvallich**, with its attractive horseshoe bay. A short way south of Tayvallich, the road splits one-way leading to the beautiful **Taynish National Nature Reserve**, cloaked in ancient oak woodland and home to a remarkably rich variety of flora and fauna, including butterflies and dragonflies. Between May and September, an **Art Trail** is installed here, displaying the work of a dozen or so local artists, so you might see, for example, an etched glass rod suspended from a tree, or a stone seal sculpture half submerged within a pond. The trail passes through the derelict Taynish Mill and winds up near the water and the Poet's Seat, where a notebook invites visitors to jot down a poem, or a note, as they wish.

Chapel of Keills

The other road from Tayvallich leads to the medieval **Chapel of Keills**, housing a display of late medieval carved stones, and the remains of a small port where cattle used to be landed from Ireland. There's also a fine view of the **MacCormaig Islands**, the largest of which, Eilean Mór (owned by the Scottish National Party), was once a retreat of the seventh-century St Cormac.

1

> ### THE SCOTTISH BEAVER TRIAL
>
> In 2009, a colony of beavers from Norway was introduced to Knapdale Forest as part of a five-year project by the **Scottish Beaver Trial** (Ⓦ scottishbeavers.org.uk). The first beavers in the wilds of Scotland for over four hundred years, their arrival met with a rather mixed reaction, though their effect on the environment (and to a lesser degree the local economy) was closely monitored by an independent project team; following the end of the trial phase in 2016, a decision was made by the Scottish government to keep the beavers, and in the process they were granted both legal protection and native species status.
>
> From the interpretation centre at Barnluasgan (four miles west of Cairnbaan), it's a twenty-minute walk to Dubh Loch, where most of the beaver activity takes place. Here, there's a viewing platform and another rough path that cuts through to Loch Coille Bharr, the two lochs separated by a 60ft-long dam that took the beavers around four to five months to build – a quite remarkable feat of engineering. Either side of these two lochs, you'll also see their lodges, large and impressive tangles of severed branches, wood and mud.
>
> The best time to see these fascinating creatures is either at dawn or dusk, and though sightings are by no means guaranteed, there is a strong possibility that you will witness some beaver activity. Take along some binoculars, midge repellent and refreshments (you could be waiting a while), and don't bring dogs. You can follow the trail yourself or, alternatively, join one of the **free guided tours** that take place on Tuesday and Saturday evenings between June and September.

Kilberry

The bulk of Knapdale is isolated and fairly impenetrable, but it's worth persevering the fourteen miles of single-track road in order to reach **Kilberry**, where you can camp at *Port Bàn* (see below), and enjoy the fantastic sunsets and views over Jura. There's also a church worth viewing in Kilberry and a small collection of carved medieval grave-slabs.

ACCOMMODATION AND EATING ──────── TAYVALLICH AND KILBERRY

Kilberry Inn In the centre of the village ☎01880 770223, Ⓦkilberryinn.com. You'll find some of the finest food for miles around at the warm *Kilberry*, which punters flock to for its fantastically creative dishes like grilled asparagus with red wine shallots and piquillo peppers, and Gigha halibut with cauliflower, hazelnuts, capers and raisins (£22). March–Oct Tues–Sun 6–10pm, Nov & Dec Fri & Sat 6–10pm.

Port Bàn 1.5 miles north of Kilberry ☎01880 770224, Ⓦportban.com. With fantastic views and sunsets over Jura, this secluded caravan and camping site is a wonderful place to hide away for a few nights. Brilliant facilities include a shop, café, playpark and games field (with putting and crazy golf), while the nearby beach is great for mucking about on. April–Oct. Per pitch **£21**

Tayvallich Inn ☎01546 870282, Ⓦtayvallichinn.com. Beautifully sited overlooking the horseshoe-shaped Tayvallich Bay, this comely restaurant/pub has a choice seafood menu (oven baked dressed crab with apple smoked cheddar; £18), but is no less enjoyable for its ales, best supped outside on the sociable terrace. Live music first Friday of the month. Mon–Thurs & Sun 10am–11pm, Fri & Sat till 1am.

ENTERTAINMENT

Crear 1 mile north of Kilberry ☎01880 770369, Ⓦcrear. co.uk. Look out for the concerts put on at Crear, a barn that's been transformed into an artists' retreat, studio and concert hall; it attracts an impressive roster of top classical musicians.

Kintyre

But for the mile-long isthmus between West Loch Tarbert and the much smaller East Loch Tarbert, the little-visited, sparsely populated peninsula of **KINTYRE** – from the Gaelic *ceann tìre*, "land's end" – would be an island. Indeed, in the eleventh century, when the Scottish king, Malcolm Canmore, allowed Magnus Barefoot, King of Norway, to lay claim to any island he could circumnavigate by boat, Magnus dragged his boat across the Tarbert isthmus and added the peninsula to his Hebridean kingdom. During the Wars of the Covenant, the majority of the population and property was wiped out by a combination of the 1646 potato blight and the destructive attentions of the Earl of Argyll. Kintyre remained a virtual desert until the earl began his policy of transplanting Gaelic-speaking Lowlanders to the region. They probably felt quite at home here, as the southern third of the peninsula lies on the Lowland side of the Highland Boundary Fault. Despite its relative proximity to Scotland's Central Belt, Kintyre remains quiet and unfashionable; its main towns of **Tarbert** and **Campbeltown** have few obvious attractions, but that's part of their appeal.

Kintyre's bleak but often beautiful **west coast** ranks among the most exposed stretches of coastline in Argyll. Atlantic breakers pound the rocky shoreline, while the persistent westerly wind forces the trees against the hillside. However, when the weather's fine and the wind not too fierce, there are numerous deserted sandy beaches to enjoy, with great views over to Gigha, Islay, Jura and even Ireland. By way of contrast, the **east coast** of Kintyre is gentler than the west, sheltered from the Atlantic winds and in parts strikingly beautiful, with stunning views across to Arran.

ARRIVAL AND DEPARTURE · KINTYRE

By plane Campbeltown has an airport, with flights to and from Glasgow.

By bus There are regular daily buses from Glasgow to Campbeltown, via Tarbert and the west coast. Note that the bus service from Campbeltown only reaches as far as the fishing village of Carradale, some 13 miles up the coast.

By ferry Kintyre is well served with ferries: the main port is at Kennacraig, 5 miles south of Tarbert on the west coast, with ferries serving Port Askaig and Port Ellen on Islay. There are also ferries from Tarbert to Portavadie on the Cowal peninsula, from Claonaig to Lochranza on Arran, and a summer-only one from Campbeltown to Ardrossan.

Tarbert

A distinctive rocket-like church steeple heralds the fishing port of **TARBERT** (in Gaelic *An Tairbeart*, meaning "isthmus"), sheltering an attractive little bay backed by rugged hills. Tarbert's **herring industry** was mentioned in the Annals of Ulster as far back as 836 AD, though right now the local fishing industry is down to its lowest level ever. Ironically, it was local Tarbert fishermen who, in the 1830s, pioneered the method of herring fishing known as trawling, which eventually wiped out the Loch Fyne herring stocks.

Tourism is now an increasingly important source of income, and though there's little of substance to see in Tarbert itself, it's a good hub, with excellent transport links, a decent stock of accommodation, and some highly commendable seafood restaurants. Moreover, it stages two prestigious annual events: the Scottish Series yacht races in late May, and the Tarbert Seafood Festival in early July when traditional boats also hit town.

Tarbert Castle

South of town, steps lead up from Tarbert's pretty harbourfront to Robert the Bruce's fourteenth-century **castle**. The oldest part of the ivy-strewn ruins dates from around the seventh century, though the most substantial remains (albeit just two walls and with some rather ugly modern accretions) belong to the fifteenth-century Tower House, with its intact arrow slits and gun loops. The best reason to make the short

THE KINTYRE WAY

The best way to really appreciate Kintyre's remote but beguiling landscape is to tackle the **Kintyre Way**, which begins in Tarbert and zigzags its way for 100 miles down the peninsula to Southend. There are seven stages in all, mostly with moderate walking (one or two sections are more demanding), comprising hill paths, moorland, forest trails and coast. The website also has suggestions for accommodation at the end of each stage.

1

stroll up here, however, is to take in the **views**, glorious across Loch Fyne and all the way across to the Cowal peninsula.

ARRIVAL AND DEPARTURE   TARBERT

By bus Buses stop in the centre of town on Campbeltown Rd and Barmore Rd.

Destinations Campbeltown (5 daily; 1hr 15min); Claonaig (Mon–Sat 3 daily; 30min); Glasgow (5 daily; 3hr 10min); Kennacraig (5 daily; 15min); Kilberry (2 daily on schooldays;

40min); Skipness (Mon–Sat 3 daily; 35min); Tayinloan (Mon–Fri 3 daily; 30min).

By ferry The ferry terminal is on Pier Rd, a 10min walk along Harbour St.

Destinations Portavadie (hourly; 25min).

ACCOMMODATION

★ **Anchor Hotel** Harbour St ☎ 01880 820577, ⓦ lochfyne-scotland.co.uk. While this smart, harbour-facing hotel itself has thirteen perfectly accomplished rooms, it's the barge across the road that you should be heading for; brilliantly converted into four luxury cabins, you wouldn't even know you were on the water, were it not for the occasional gentle bob and swans gliding past your window at eye level. Cool, relaxing and a lot of fun. Rooms **£120**; cabins **£220**

Knap Guest House Campbeltown Rd ☎ 01880 820015, ⓦ knapguesthouse.co.uk. Handsome Victorian townhouse

with four pristine rooms leading off a beautifully appointed lounge; each room manifests a curious mixture of traditional Scottish and Asian furnishings, which somehow works very well. A little tricky to find, it's opposite the Co-op. **£90**

Struan House Harbour St ☎ 07778 742884, ⓦ struan-house-lochfyne.co.uk. Built in 1846 as a small hotel, this is now a charming six-roomed guesthouse with bespoke furnishings, grand wooden bedsteads, and some sweet little touches like bedside lamps, books and wall-mounted artwork. It's opposite the Harbour Authority building up towards the ferry terminal. **£80**

EATING AND DRINKING

Ca'Dora Harbour St ☎ 01880 820258. The pick of several cafés ranged along the seafront, which, despite looking rather dull from the outside, pulls in the punters for its comfort food such as cottage pie, and battered haddock and chips (£9), though it's renowned, above all, for its ice cream. Daily 8am–9pm.

Seabed Restaurant Harbour St ☎ 01880 820577, ⓦ lochfyne-scotland.co.uk. Complement your stay on the barge with dinner in the *Anchor Hotel*'s inviting, cheerily staffed restaurant, which offers up comforting dishes such

as Cullen skink risotto and seafood linguine (£17.95). Daily noon–9.30pm.

★ **Starfish** Castle St ☎ 01880 820733, ⓦ starfish tarbert.com. Sparkling, informally run seafood restaurant where scallops are king, literally – a plate of these will set you back £18, as will the seafood stroganoff, comprising mussels, queen scallops, salmon, and smoked and fresh haddock in a paprika sauce. Complete your meal with a classic crème caramel. March–Oct Mon–Thurs & Sun 6–10pm, Fri & Sat noon–2pm & 6–10pm.

Carradale and around

The only place of any size on the east coast is the fishing village of **Carradale**, which, according to one 1930s guide, was "popular with those who like unsophisticated resorts". The village itself is rather drab, but the tiny, very pretty harbour with its small fishing fleet, and the wide, sandy beach to the south make up for it. On the east side of the beach is **Carradale Point**, a wildlife reserve with feral goats and a good example of a vitrified fort built more than two thousand years ago on a small tidal island off the headland (best approached from the beach). There are several pleasant **walks** with good views across to Arran laid out in the woods around Carradale, for which the best starting point is the car park at Port na Storm on the road into the village. The B842 ends fourteen miles north of Carradale at **Claonaig**, little more than a slipway for the small summer car ferry to Arran.

ARRIVAL AND GETTING AROUND   CARRADALE AND AROUND

By ferry The ferry terminal is at Claonaig, fourteen miles north of Carradale.

Destinations Lochranza, Arran (8–9 daily; 30min).

Bike rental You can rent bikes, and all-terrain electric buggies, at the Network Centre, located on the road into town (£14/5hr, £20/day).

ACCOMMODATION AND EATING

Ashbank Hotel Centre of village ☏ 01583 431650, ⓦ ashbankhotel.com. A dinky little place in the heart of the village, with five boxy but comfy en-suite rooms – three with a sea view – and the Egyptian cotton bedding is something to savour. Breakfast is taken in the sweet little downstairs bar. **£75**

Carradale Bay Caravan Park Outside Carradale village ☏ 01583 431665, ⓦ carradalebay.com. The nearest campsite to town is the superbly equipped and well-sheltered *Carradale Bay Caravan Park*, right by, and with great access to, the sandy beach. Although it's predominantly a caravan site, there is a separate area to pitch tents. Easter–Oct. Per pitch **£24**

★ **Dunvalanree** Port Righ Bay ☏ 01583 431226, ⓦ dunvalanree.com. Imposing house overlooking the sheltered little bay of Port Righ, towards Carradale Point; the five rooms are of the highest order, with beautiful,

bespoke beds, though for those on a tighter budget, a couple of cheaper rooms are available (£60). The price includes a three-course dinner (excluding the two budget rooms), which is exceptional value given that you're treated to sumptuous dishes like seared scallops on pea mash with pancetta, and collops of Argyll venison with poached brambles and wild garlic pesto. The cost to non-guests is £31. Advance booking required. **£145**

Torrisdale Castle Just off the B842 a couple of miles south of Carradale ☏ 01583 431233, ⓦ torrisdalecastle. com. Within the grounds of the castle's sprawling estate are numerous self-catering properties, the most appealing of which is the Garden Cottage, cosily sleeping two and with a hot tub out back; you can sleep in the old servants' quarters of the castle itself; they've even got their own bit of beach. Per week from **£375**

Skipness

Heading north of the Claonaig ferry terminal, a dead-end road winds its way along the shore a few miles further north to the tiny village of **SKIPNESS** and the considerable ruins of the thirteenth-century **Skipness Castle** (open access; free). The castle's two surviving rooms form the base of the sixteenth-century tower; from here a slender spiral staircase leads to the roof and glorious views across the Kilbrannan Sound to Arran. To the right as you enter, the old latrine was converted into a dovecote, as evidenced by the holes in the walls on all sides.

There are also several gentle **walks** laid out in the nearby mixed woodland, up the glen, but the main reason people make the effort to visit Skipness is the wonderful *Skipness Seafood Cabin*. Here, too, is the **Skipness Smokehouse** (☏ 01880 760378; ⓦ creelers.co.uk), where you can watch all manner of foodstuffs (including salmon, kippers, duck, venison) being smoked, after which you can of course make some purchases if so desired.

ARRIVAL AND EATING   SKIPNESS

By bus Buses run between Skipness and Kennacraig via the ferry terminal at Claonaig (Mon–Sat 3 daily; 20min).

Skipness Seafood Cabin Below the castle ☏ 01880 760207, ⓦ skipnessseafoodcabin.co.uk. Little more than a hut, the Cabin has been doling out fresh local seafood for years: hot smoked salmon or crab rolls (£5), fresh oysters

(£9), grilled queen scallops (£9), langoustine, mussels and home-baked cakes are just some of the treats. There are wooden tables and bench seating from which to admire the splendid views across to Arran. End May to Sept 11am–7pm; closed Sat.

Isle of Gigha

Just six miles by one mile, **GIGHA** – pronounced "Geeya", with a hard "g" – is a low-lying, fertile island, with a population of around 150, just three miles off the west coast of Kintyre. The island's Ayrshire cattle produce over a quarter of a million gallons of milk a year to produce the island's distinctive (occasionally fruit-shaped) cheese. Like many of the smaller Hebrides, Gigha was bought and sold numerous times after its original lairds, the MacNeils, sold up, and was finally bought by the islanders themselves in 2002.

The real draw of Gigha, apart from the peace and quiet, is the white sandy beaches – including one at Ardminish, the island's only village – that dot the coastline. The ferry from Tayinloan deposits you at **ARDMINISH**, where you'll find the post office

1

and shop, and the all-denomination island church, which has some interesting stained-glass windows. Although most visitors come to Gigha for the day, it's a great place to stay.

Achamore Gardens

1.5 miles south of Ardminish • Daily dusk–dawn • £6 • ☎ 01583 505390

The main attraction on Gigha is the **Achamore Gardens**, established by the first postwar owner, Sir James Horlick of hot-drink fame. Its spectacularly colourful displays of azaleas are best seen in early summer, but elsewhere, the rhododendrons merit seeking out, as does the walled garden, with its hugely diverse collection of plants, a bamboo maze, and a superb panorama across the island's west coast and beyond to Islay and Jura. At the heart of the complex stands Achamore House itself, though this is now privately owned and off-limits to visitors.

To the southwest of the gardens, the ruins of the thirteenth-century **St Catan's Chapel** are floored with weathered medieval gravestones; the ogham stone nearby is the only one of its kind in the west of Scotland.

ARRIVAL AND INFORMATION   ISLE OF GIGHA

By ferry CalMac ferries depart more or less hourly from Tayinloan, 23 miles south of Tarbert, for the 20min crossing to Ardminish.

Gigha Activity Centre Ardminish Bay (Easter–Sept daily 10am–6pm; ☎ 07516 709249). Next to the ferry slip, this is effectively the island's information point, but is mainly concerned with renting out bikes (£10/half day, £16/day), kayaks (£10/1hr), stand-up paddle-boards (£10/1hr) and rowing boats (£20/1hr). The website, ⓦ gigha.org.uk, is also a useful resource.

ACCOMMODATION AND EATING

The Boathouse Ardminish Bay ☎ 01583 505123, ⓦ boathouseongigha.com. Inside this low dark-stone building, perched above a white sandy bay, is a gorgeous little restaurant rustling up treats like potted brown shrimp with smoked onion relish (£8) and poached Gigha halibut with chorizo and saffron potato. April–Sept daily 11.30am–9pm.

Boathouse Camping On the grass adjacent to The Boathouse ☎ 01583 505123, ⓦ boathouseongigha. com. This designated camping area, with just twenty pitches, has fantastic beach views. Facilities are limited to showers (£1) and toilets, though they sell some basic foodstuffs too. Booking ahead is essential. April–Sept. Per person £5

Gigha Hotel ☎ 01583 505254, ⓦ gighahotel.com. Just 200yds from the ferry terminal, this is the island's social hub and a very welcoming place to stay. Its twelve, largely pinewood-furnished rooms are inviting and spotlessly clean without being particularly exciting. £85

Machrihanish and around

The only major development along the entire west coast of Kintyre is **MACHRIHANISH**, at the southern end of Machrihanish Bay, the longest continuous stretch of sand in Argyll. There are two approaches to the **beach**: from Machrihanish itself, or from Westport, at the north end of the bay, where the A83 swings east towards Campbeltown; either way, the sea here is too dangerous for swimming. Machrihanish itself was once a thriving salt-producing and coal-mining centre – you can still see the miners' cottages at neighbouring Drumlemble – but now survives solely on tourism, in particular golf.

Machrihanish Golf Club and Machrihanish Dunes Golf Club

Machrihanish Golf Club Between the beach and Campbeltown Airport • Daily: April–Oct £75 per round; Oct & March £55; Nov–Feb £35 • ☎ 01586 810277, ⓦ machgolf.com **Machrihanish Dunes Golf Club** East of Campbeltown Airport • Daily: April–Oct £75 per round; Nov–March £40 • ☎ 01586 810000, ⓦ machrihanishdunes.com

Dominating the village of Machrihanish is the exposed 18-hole championship course of the **Machrihanish Golf Club**, between the beach and Campbeltown Airport on the nearby flat and fertile swathe of land known as the Laggan. One of Scotland's finest links courses (established in 1876), it plays out on a quite spectacular landscape, and is particularly notable for its first hole, which cuts across the Atlantic in dramatic fashion.

Established as recently as 2009, the sister course of Machrihanish golf course, the 18-hole **Machrihanish Dunes**, on the other side of the airport, is perhaps even more impressive. The course layout, including the tee and green positions, is dictated solely by the lie of the land.

ARRIVAL AND INFORMATION   MACHRIHANISH

By bus Buses stop in the centre of the village near the golf club.

Destinations Campbeltown (Mon–Sat 7 daily; 20min).

ACCOMMODATION AND EATING

Machrihanish Holiday Park Machrihanish Village ☎01586 810366, ⚙campkintyre.co.uk. Superbly located next to the fairways and with direct sea views, this large, fully equipped, family-run campsite has a terrific mix of caravan and tent space, as well as heated wooden wigwams (sleeping three people) and fully fitted bell tents (sleeping two adults and two children). March–Oct. Per pitch £15;

wigwams £40; bell tents (July & Aug only) £70

Old Clubhouse Pub Machrihanish Village ☎01586 810000. Overlooking the first tee, the erstwhile clubhouse is now a very agreeable village pub, frequented by golfers and locals alike, which means it's not nearly as pretentious as it might be. Good bar food and decent ales. Daily 11am–11pm.

Campbeltown

Set within a deep bay, sheltered by Davaar Island and the surrounding hills, **CAMPBELTOWN** is Kintyre's largest town with a population of around 5000. Originally known as Kinlochkilkerran (Ceann Loch Cill Chiaran), the town was renamed in the seventeenth century by the Earl of Argyll – a Campbell – when it became one of the main points for immigration from the Lowlands. As is evident from the architecture, Campbeltown's heyday was the Victorian era, when shipbuilding was going strong, coal was shipped by canal from Drumlemble, the fishing fleet was vast and Campbeltown Loch was said to be made of whisky. Nineteenth-century visitors to Campbeltown frequently found the place engulfed in a thick fog of pungent peat smoke from the town's 34 whisky distilleries. Today, only three distilleries are left to maintain this regional subgroup of single-malt whiskies.

If you're here on the third weekend of August, be prepared for the **Mull of Kintyre Music & Arts Festival** (⚙mokfest.com), which pulls in some big-name rock bands, plus some good traditional Irish and Scottish ones.

Springbank distillery

55 Longrow, but sign up at Cadenhead's whisky shop, 30–32 Union St • Mon–Sat 10am, 11.30am, 1.30pm & 3pm • £10 • ☎01586 555468, ⚙springbank.scot

Whisky-lovers shouldn't miss a visit to the **Springbank distillery**, a deeply traditional, family-owned business (founded in 1828) that produces three different single malts; indeed, it's the only distillery in Scotland to carry out the full production process on one site, from the malting to the bottling. You first get to see the malting floor (Springbank is now one of only half a dozen or so distilleries in Scotland that still does its own malting), before continuing down to the peat stacks and kiln, which again is not something you normally see on a distillery tour. Having viewed the magnificent copper stills, the tour winds up inside the capacious warehouse, which stretches for 100 yards or so. The tour ends, as is custom, with a wee tasting, but here you also get a free miniature and a glass to take away.

Burnet Building

St John St • Mon–Fri 9am–12.30pm & 1.30–4pm • Free • ☎01586 559017

Built as the town library in 1897, the **Burnett Building** is crowned by a distinctive lantern and decorated with four relief panels depicting the town's main industries

1

at the time. The building harbours a very old-fashioned one-room local **museum**, with some intriguing finds such as a gold Viking arm ring and a gorgeous jet necklace, as well as a few pieces by the acclaimed landscape painter William McTaggart. Most people, though, are drawn to the **Linda McCartney Memorial Garden**, which you should approach from Shore Street. Here, you'll find a slightly ludicrous bronze statue of Linda holding a lamb, a piece commissioned by Paul McCartney, who spent many happy times with Linda and the kids on the farm he owns near Campbeltown.

Campbeltown Heritage Centre

Big Kiln St • May–Sept Mon–Fri 11am–4pm • Donation • ☎ 01586 552775, ⊛ campbeltownheritagecentre.co.uk

The former Lorne Street Church, with its stripy bell-cote and pinnacles, has been cleverly converted into the intermittently interesting **Campbeltown Heritage Centre**. Due prominence is given to the town's once glittering industrial heritage, in particular the local fishing and whisky industries; going hand in hand with local malt production was a significant coopering industry, and at one stage there were more than sixty coopers in Campbeltown. By far the most prominent exhibit here, however, and occupying the spot where the main altar once stood, is a beautiful wooden skiff called *Yerda*, dating from 1906. Look out, too, for the model of the Victorian harbourfront with the light railway running along Hall Street.

ARRIVAL AND INFORMATION

CAMPBELTOWN

By plane Campbeltown Airport (☎ 01586 553797, ⊛ hial. co.uk) lies 3 miles west, towards Machrihanish.
Destinations Glasgow (Mon–Fri 2 daily, Sun 1; 40min).
By bus The town's main bus terminal is in front of the swimming pool on the Esplanade.
Destinations Carradale (Mon–Fri 5 daily, 4 on Sat; 45min);

Glasgow (5 daily; 4hr 15min); Machrihanish (Mon–Sat 9 daily; 20min); Southend (Mon–Sat 6 daily; 25min); Tarbert (5 daily; 1hr 10min).
By ferry The ferry terminal is on the south side of the harbour, from where it's a 5min walk into the centre.
Destinations Ardrossan (Thurs, Fri & Sun 1 daily; 2hr 40min).

ACCOMMODATION

Ardshiel Hotel Kilkerran Rd ☎ 01586 552133, ⊛ ardshiel.co.uk. A former whisky distiller's Victorian mansion situated on a lovely leafy square just a block or so back from the harbourfront. The rooms are functional more than anything else. More impressive is the hotel's glamorous, grown-up whisky bar, stocking in excess of 700 malts, well worth a visit even if you're not staying here. **£105**

Campbeltown Backpackers Big Kiln ☎ 01586 551188, ⊛ campbeltownbackpackers.co.uk. Occupying the old school house in the courtyard across from the heritage centre, this new, community-trust-run bunkhouse has sixteen firm pine beds in two dormitories, a self-catering kitchen and small lounge. There's no reception as such, so if there's no one there, pop into the heritage centre; when

that's closed just call the number on the door. Dorms **£22**

Oatfield House 3 miles down the B842 ☎ 01586 551551, ⊛ oatfield.org. A beautifully renovated whitewashed laird's house set in its own grounds on the road to Southend, retaining three rooms of some character and distinction. Guests are also free to avail themselves of the panelled dining room and parlour. **£80**

Royal Hotel Main St ☎ 0800 151 3701, ⊛ machrihanish dunes.com. Owned by the golf club, this high-end hotel sits well with the recent redevelopment of the harbourfront area, and injects a big dollop of colour into this otherwise dull street. The supremely comfortable rooms are mostly furnished in bold tartan colour schemes, with deep armchairs, big beds with thick duvets and fluffy pillows, and a host of other neat touches. **£140**

EATING AND DRINKING

Black Sheep Pub Main St ☎ 0800 151 3701. The *Royal Hotel*'s pub is by far the most enjoyable watering hole in town, with seating arranged around a shiny, semicircular bar, in addition to some outdoor tables overlooking the harbour. Some decent cask ales too. Daily 11am–1am.

Café Bluebell 6 Hall St ☎ 01586 552800. Simple-looking but warm and welcoming café opposite the tourist office offering a terrific selection of light snacks (soups, sandwiches, sausage rolls), as well as a gut-busting all-day breakfast (£7.95). Tues–Sat 9am–4.30pm, Sun 11am–4pm.

Mull of Kintyre

Most people venture south of Campbeltown to make a pilgrimage to the **Mull of Kintyre**, made famous by the mawkish number-one hit by one time local resident Paul McCartney, with the help of the Campbeltown Pipe Band. It's also infamous as the site of the RAF's worst peacetime accident when, on June 2, 1994, a Chinook helicopter on its way from Belfast to Inverness crashed, killing all 29 on board. A small memorial can be found on the hillside, not far from the **Gap** (1150ft) – after which no vehicles are allowed. The Mull is the nearest Britain gets to Ireland, just twelve miles away, and the Irish coastline appears remarkably close on fine days. There's nothing specifically to see, but the trek down to the lighthouse, itself 300ft above the ocean waves, is challengingly tortuous.

Isle of Arran

Shaped like a kidney bean and occupying centre stage in the Firth of Clyde, **Arran** is the most southerly (and therefore the most accessible) of all the Scottish islands. The Highland–Lowland dividing line passes right through its centre – hence the cliché about it being like "Scotland in miniature" – leaving the northern half sparsely populated, mountainous and bleak, while the lush southern half enjoys a much milder climate. The population of around five thousand tends to stick to the southeastern quarter of the island, leaving the west and the north relatively undisturbed.

There are two big crowd-pullers on Arran: **geology** and **golf**. The former has fascinated rock-obsessed students since Sir James Hutton came here in the late eighteenth century to confirm his theories of uniformitarianism. A hundred years later, Sir Archibald Geikie's investigations were a landmark in the study of Arran's geology, and the island remains a popular destination for university and school field trips. As for golf, Arran boasts seven courses, including three of the eighteen-hole variety at Brodick, Lamlash and Whiting Bay, and a unique twelve-hole course at Shiskine, near Blackwaterfoot.

Although **tourism** is now by far its most important industry, Arran, at twenty miles in length, is large enough to have a life of its own. While the island's post-1745 history, including the Clearances (set in motion by the local lairds, the Hamiltons), is as depressing as elsewhere in the Highlands, in recent years Arran's population has actually increased, in contrast with more remote islands.

ARRIVAL AND GETTING AROUND   **ISLE OF ARRAN**

By ferry CalMac (ⓦ calmac.co.uk) operate two year-round ferry services: one from Ardrossan in Ayrshire to Brodick (April–Oct 6–8 daily; 55min), and a smaller ferry from Claonaig on the Kintyre peninsula to Lochranza in the north (April–Oct 8–9 daily; 30min).

By bus Transport on Arran itself is pretty good: daily buses circle the island (Brodick tourist office has timetables), while the Arran Day Rider (£6.30) allows you to hop on and off as you please. Buses also link in with the two ferry services.

Brodick

The resort of **BRODICK** (from the Norse *breidr vik*, "broad bay") is a place of only moderate charm, but it does have a grand setting in a wide, sandy bay set against a backdrop of granite mountains. Its development as a tourist resort was held back for a long time by its elitist owners, the dukes of Hamilton, though nowadays, as the island's capital and main communication hub, Brodick is by far the busiest town on Arran.

The town's shops and guesthouses are spread out along the south side of the bay, along with the tourist office and the CalMac pier. Its tourist sights, meanwhile, are clustered on the west and north side of the bay, a couple of miles from the ferry terminal.

1

Arran Heritage Museum

Rosaburn • April–Oct daily 10.30am–4.30pm • £4 • ☎ 01770 302636, ⓦ arranmuseum.co.uk

Up along the road to the castle, the intermittently interesting **Arran Heritage Museum** is housed in a whitewashed eighteenth-century crofter's farm, and contains an old smiddy and a twee Victorian cottage with box-bed and range. In the old stables, the main exhibition considers the island's intriguing geological and archeological heritage – the

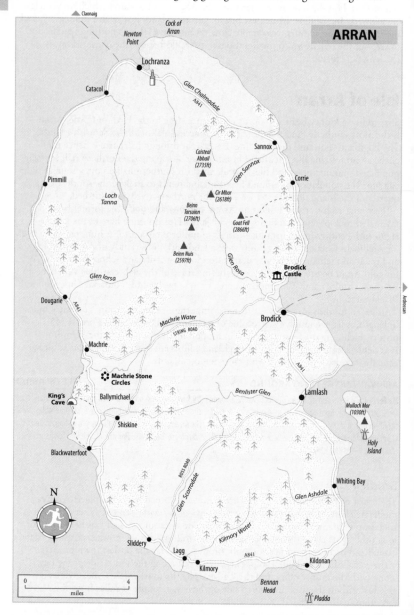

1

ARRAN ROCKS

Arran is a top destination for the country's **geology** students. First, this small island is split in two by the **Highland Boundary Fault**, and therefore contains a superb variety of rock formations, typical of both the Highlands and the Lowlands. And, second, it is the place where **Sir James Hutton** (1726–97), the "father of modern geology", came in 1787, in order to lay down research for his epic work, *A Theory of the Earth*. Even if you know very little about geology, it is possible to appreciate some of the island's more obvious features. If any of the below whets your appetite, start by getting hold of the geological booklet, *Arran and the Clyde Islands*, produced by Scottish Natural Heritage.

HUTTON'S UNCONFORMITY

The most famous location is just beyond **Newton Point**, on the north shore of Loch Ranza, where Allt Beithe stream runs into the sea. Here, two types of rocks by the shore are set virtually at right angles to one another, the older Cambrian schist dipping towards the land, while the younger Devonian sandstone slopes into the sea. This phenomenon became known as **Hutton's Unconformity**.

FOLDED ROCKS AND RAISED BEACHES

At **Imachar Point**, between Pirnmill and Dougarie, you can view in miniature the geological process known as **folding**, which affected the ancient Cambrian schist around a hundred million years ago, and, on a larger scale, resulted in the formation of mountain ranges such as those of north Arran. Another classic, more recent geological formation to be seen on Arran is **raised beaches**, formed at the end of the last Ice Age, some fifteen thousand years ago, when the sea level was much higher, and then left high and dry when the sea level dropped. The road that wraps itself around Arran runs along the flat ground that subsequently emerged from the sea. One of the best locations to observe this is at the **King's Cave**, north of Blackwaterfoot, where you can see huge sea caves stranded some distance from today's shoreline.

DOLERITE DYKES

Down on the south coast, the shoreline below **Kildonan** reveals some superb examples of **dolerite dykes**, formed when molten rock erupted through cracks in the sedimentary sandstone rocks above, around sixty million years ago. The molten rock solidified and, being harder, now stands above the surrounding sandstone, forming strange, rocky piers jutting out into the sea.

OTHER GEOLOGICAL QUIRKS

There are numerous other interesting features to look out for, such as **solidified sand dunes** and huge granite boulders, known as **erratics**, on Corrie beach in the northeast of the island, classic **glacial valleys** such as Glen Sannox, and **felsite sills** such as the one at Drumadoon, near Blackwaterfoot, in the southwest.

most notable exhibit is an incredibly well-preserved early Bronze Age cist grave, complete with intact food vessel – while another section recalls the island's prominent wartime role, as testified by the dozen or so air crashes here during the course of World War II.

Arran Visitor Centre

Home Farm • **Arran Aromatics** Daily 9.30am–6pm; factory tours June–Sept Thurs at 6pm • Free • ☎ 01770 303003, ⓦ arranaromatics. com **Island Cheese Company** Daily 9.30am–5.30pm • ☎ 01770 302788, ⓦ arranscheeseshop.co.uk

Half a mile or so up the road from the heritage museum, the **Arran Visitor Centre** incorporates a couple of superb outlets, foremost of which is **Arran Aromatics**, producers of luxury toiletries and fragrances, which you'll find in most of the more upmarket hotels and guesthouses on the island, and beyond. As well as the opportunity to participate in natural soapmaking and candlemaking, the outlet offers factory tours in the summer months. At the **Island Cheese Company**, you can see the soft, creamy Crofter's Crowdie or the piquant Arran Blue cheese being made; naturally, there's a whisky cheddar too.

1

ARRAN GOLF PASS

The **Arran Golf Pass** (⟨w⟩ golfonarran.com) currently costs £110, which is remarkable value given that it entitles you to a round on each of the island's seven courses; three 18-hole and three 9-hole courses, as well as the superb 12-hole course at Shiskine. You can buy the pass online or at any of the seven clubs and it's valid for one year meaning that you can come back and play any course that you didn't have time to on a previous visit.

Brodick Castle

2.5 miles north of town, just off the A841 · **Castle** Daily April–Oct 10am–5pm · £13.50; NTS · **Gardens** Daily 9.30am–dusk · ☎ 01770 302202

Former seat of the duke of Hamilton, **Brodick Castle** is set on a steep bank on the north side of Brodick Bay. The bulk of the castle was built in the nineteenth century, giving it a domestic rather than a military look, and the interior is decidedly dour in tone, though there are a few gems to look out for. Don't miss the portrait of the eleventh duke's faithful piper, who injured his throat on a grouse bone, was warned never to pipe again, but did so and died. There is also a handful of sketches by **Gainsborough** in the boudoir. Probably the most atmospheric room is the copper-filled Victorian kitchen, which conjures up a vision of the sweated and sweating labour required to feed the folk upstairs.

Much more attractive are the walled **gardens** and extensive grounds, a treasury of exotic plants, trees and rhododendrons, which command a superb view across the bay. There's an adventure playground for kids, but the whole area is a natural playground, with waterfalls, a giant pitcher plant that swallows thousands of midges daily, and a maze of paths. Buried in the grounds is a bizarre Bavarian-style **summerhouse** lined entirely with pine cones, one of three built by the eleventh duke to make his wife, Princess Marie of Baden, feel at home.

ARRIVAL AND INFORMATION   BRODICK

By bus The main bus station is by the ferry terminal. Destinations Blackwaterfoot (Mon–Sat 8–10 daily, 4 on Sun; 30min); Lamlash (Mon–Sat hourly, 6 on Sun; 10–15min); Lochranza (Mon–Sat 7 daily, 4 on Sun; 45min).

Tourist office By the CalMac pier (April & Oct Mon–Sat 9am–5pm; May–Sept Mon–Sat 9am–5pm, Sun 10am–5pm; Nov–March Mon–Sat 10am–4pm; ☎ 01770 303774, ⟨w⟩ visitarran.com).

ACCCOMMODATION

★ **Brodick Bunkhouse** Shore Rd ☎ 01770 302897, ⟨w⟩ brodickbunkhouse.co.uk. Sparkling bunkhouse offering brightly painted three- and six-bed dorms with spacious bunks (some are triple-height) made from wood sourced from the local sawmill; all rooms have sinks, though the wet rooms are as stylish as the dorms, and there's an honesty breakfast bar. There's no reception; you'll be emailed the code to let yourself in. **£25**

Douglas Hotel Shore Rd ☎ 01770 302968, ⟨w⟩ the douglashotel.co.uk. Virtually opposite the ferry terminal, this large and handsome sandstone building offers some of the most comfortable accommodation on the island, with a selection of bright, modern and tidily furnished rooms, in a mostly grey-checked tartan flavour, many of which have sea-facing views. **£90**

Glenartney Guest House Mayish Rd ☎ 01770 302220, ⟨w⟩ glenartney-arran.co.uk. Tucked away just uphill from the post office, this is the pick of the town's guesthouses, with a dozen immaculately presented, albeit not overly spacious, rooms. Two homely lounges and an evening bar enhance the *Glenartney's* charms, while you can expect a spectacular breakfast to see you on your way. **£86**

Glen Rosa 2 miles from town off the B880 to Blackwaterfoot ☎ 07985 566004, ⟨e⟩ glenrosacamping@ hotmail.com. Very basic, almost wild, campsite (no showers and cold water only) enjoys a wonderful setting beside a burn, with superb views across the glen. Campfires are allowed too. There's no reception; the owner will pitch up at some point and collect your money. Per person **£5**

EATING AND DRINKING

Brodick Bar and Brasserie Alma Rd ☎ 01770 302169, ⟨w⟩ brodickbar.co.uk. There's decent fare on offer at this

big, family-orientated restaurant opposite the post office. Chalked up on a huge board, the diverse menu features lots of fish and meaty treats (baked halibut with asparagus, honey-glazed belly of pork and bean casserole), while the home-made thin-crust pizzas (£10) are worth a punt. Mon–Sat noon–2.30pm & 5.30–10pm.

Crofters Shore Rd ☎ 01770 302579, ✆ croftersmusicbar. com. The fabulous music bar, with acoustic performances Mon, Wed, Fri & Sat nightly at 7.30pm (1pm on Sundays),

is actually more restaurant than drinking den, offering succulent dishes like chargrilled tuna loin with red pesto chilli, and steak burger with a blue cheese sauce (£12.50). Diners are given preference (and keep their table for the evening), but if you just fancy a pint, pop along after 9pm. Daily 9am–midnight.

Lamlash and around

With its distinctive Edwardian architecture and mild climate, **LAMLASH**, four miles south of Brodick, epitomizes the sedate charm of southeast Arran. Lamlash Bay has, in its time, sheltered King Haakon's fleet, in 1263, and, more recently, served as a naval base during both world wars.

Holy Island

The Holy Island boat runs May–Sept daily and more or less hourly, though it's subject to cancellations in windy weather • £12 return • ☎ 01770 700463, ✆ holyisland.org

The best reason for coming to Lamlash is to visit the slug-shaped hump of **Holy Island**, where a group of **Tibetan Buddhists** has established a retreat. Providing you don't dawdle, it's possible to scramble up to the top of Mullach Mór (1030ft), the island's highest point, and still catch the last boat back. En route, you might well bump into the island's most numerous residents: feral goats, Eriskay ponies, Soay sheep and rabbits.

ACCOMMODATION AND EATING   **LAMLASH AND AROUND**

Drift Inn Shore Rd ☎ 01770 600608, ✆ driftinnarran. com. Despite its undistinguished exterior, the well-regarded food at this seafront pub – homemade fishcakes or braised beef cheek in Loch Fye ale gravy (£18.95) – and its convivial beer garden, make the *Drift Inn* a fun place to hang out. Daily noon– midnight. Food noon–9pm.

Glenisle Hotel Shore Rd ☎ 01770 600559, ✆ glenisle hotel.com. High-end, if slightly overpriced, option, with

thirteen gorgeous rooms, each painted and furnished in colours that reflect those of the island itself; around half the rooms have a sea view. Terrific bistro too. **£145**

Lilybank Shore Rd ☎ 01770 600230, ✆ lilybank-arran. co.uk. This sunny roadside B&B is a typically welcoming island guesthouse, offering six floral, pastel-coloured rooms, four of which overlook the bay. **£80**

Whiting Bay

An established Clydeside resort for over a century now, **Whiting Bay**, four miles south of Lamlash, is spread out along a very pleasant bay, though it doesn't have quite the distinctive architecture of Lamlash. It is, however, a good base for walking, with the gentle hike up to the **Glenashdale Falls** probably the most popular excursion; this two-hour walk sets off from Ashdale Bridge at the southern end of the bay, for the most part passing through pretty woodland. With more time, you can branch off this path up to the **Giant's Graves**, a group of Neolithic chambered cairns. The walk is well signposted from the bridge.

GOAT FELL

Arran's most accessible peak is also the island's highest, **Goat Fell** (2866ft) – take your pick from the Gaelic, *goath*, meaning "windy", or the Norse, *geit-fjall*, "goat mountain" – which can be ascended in around four hours from Brodick or around five hours from Corrie, though it's a strenuous hike whichever way you do it; the latter route is, though, tougher.

The Coffee Pot Shore Rd ☎01770 700382. This unassuming white building on the corner of a residential street is deservedly popular for its freshly baked baguettes, quiches, and home-made cakes (many gluten-free), not to mention great coffee. Tues–Sat 10am–5pm. Closed Nov.

Kildonan

Access to the sea is tricky along the south coast, but worth the effort, as the sandy **beaches** here are among the island's finest. One place you can get down to the sea is at **Kildonan**, an attractive small village south of Lamlash, set slightly off the main road, with a good sandy beach, which you share with the local wildlife, and views out to the tiny flat island of Pladda, with its distinctive lighthouse and, in the distance, the great hump of Ailsa Craig.

Sealshore Camping ☎01770 820320, ⓦcamping arran.com. Lovely, laidback family-owned campsite also harbouring two wooden pods with an electric heater and fridge – perfect if you like it cosy. As well as its own private beach, facilities include modern shower blocks, self-catering kitchen, lounge and undercover BBQ area, plus there's an onsite shop. Buses stop at the entrance upon request. March–Oct. Two-night minimum stay for pods. Per pitch £18, pods £80

King's Cave and Machrie Moor

A couple of miles north of the village of Blackwaterfoot, a car park marks the start of a most enjoyable circular trail (2hr) to the **King's Cave**, one of several where Robert the Bruce is said to have encountered the famously patient arachnid, while hiding during his final bid to free Scotland in 1306. Inside the cave you'll find various carved symbols, typically early Christian crosses and Pictish animals. The path itself passes the site of a Bronze Age hut before descending a rocky gully to the shore, whereupon you continue along the coastline to the cave. Heading inland again, it's mostly forest en route back to the car park.

Close by, the wide expanse of **Machrie Moor** boasts a wealth of Bronze Age sites, many of which were excavated as recently as the 1980s. Entrance to the site is via the car park just off the main road; from here, it's a good thirty-minute walk (you can cycle too) across windswept, peaty moorland to a scattered group of **stone circles**, which vary from chunky boulders to slim pillars, the tallest surviving monolith being over 18ft high. The most striking configuration is at Fingal's Cauldron Seat, with two concentric circles of granite boulders; legend has it that Fingal tied his dog to one of them while cooking at his cauldron.

Machrie Tearoom Machrie Bay ☎01770 840329. After a bracing walk to the stones on Machrie Moor, make a beeline for this busy and colourful roadside tearoom that also functions as the social centre for the adjoining golf course; as well as some cracking lunch snacks (lamb and haggis burger, goat's cheese toastie), there's a scrumptious selection of home-made cakes (rhubarb and vaniila sponge, raspberry and coconut loaf) to tempt you in. Daily 9am–5pm.

Lochranza

On fair Lochranza streamed the early day/Thin wreaths of cottage smoke are upward curl'd/From the lone hamlet, which her inland bay/And circling mountains sever from the world.

The Lord of the Isles by Sir Walter Scott

The ruined castle that occupies the mud flats of the surrounding bay and the brooding north-facing slopes of the mountains that frame it make for one of the most spectacular ensembles on the island, yet **LOCHRANZA**, despite being the only place of any size in this sparsely populated area, attracts far fewer visitors than Arran's southern resorts.

WALKING IN NORTH ARRAN

Ordnance Survey Explorer map 361

The ferociously jagged and barren outline of the mountains of **north Arran** is on a par with that of the Cuillin of Skye. None of the peaks is a Munro, but they are spectacular, nevertheless, partly because they rise up so rapidly from sea level and, in fine weather, offer such wonderful views over sea and land.

One of the most popular walks is the circuit of peaks that surround Glen Rosa. The walk begins with the relatively straightforward ascent of **Goat Fell** (2866ft), which is normally approached from the grounds of Brodick Castle, to the south. From Goat Fell, you can follow a series of rocky ridges that spread out in the shape of an "H". In order to keep to the crest of the ridge, head north to the next peak of **North Goat Fell** (2657ft), and then make the sharp descent to the Saddle, a perfect spot for a rest, before making the ascent of **Cir Mhòr** (2618ft), by far the most exhilarating peak in the whole range, and the finest viewpoint of all. The next section of the walk, southwest across the knife's-edge ridge of **A'Chir**, is quite tricky due to the Bad Step, a lethal gap in the ridge, which you can avoid by dropping down slightly on the east side. Beyond A'Chir, the ascent of **Beinn Tarsuinn** (2706ft) and **Beinn Nuis** (2597ft) is relatively simple. A path leads down from the southeast face of Beinn Nuis to Glen Rosa and back to Brodick. If you don't fancy attempting A'Chir, or if the weather closes in, you can simply descend from the Saddle, or from the southwest side of Cir Mhor, to Glen Rosa.

The walk described above covers a total distance of eleven miles, with over 4600ft of climbing, and should take between eight and ten hours to complete. All walks should be approached with care, and the usual **safety precautions** should be observed (see page 42).

Arran distillery

South end of the village • Daily: March–Oct 10am–5.15pm, Nov–Feb 10am–4pm; first tour 10am (11am in winter), then hourly except 1pm • £10 • ☎ 01770 830264, ⓦ arranwhisky.com

One of the island's most popular tourist attractions these days is the **Arran distillery**, distinguished by its pagoda-style roofs at the south end of the village. Established as recently as 1995 – the first on the island since 1837 – this modern distillery produces the relatively little-known, fourteen-year-old single Arran malt. The tour itself is an entertaining and slick affair, beginning with an audiovisual presentation in a mock-up crofter's cottage, before you are led through the distillery, the highlight being the magnificent copper wash and spirit stills; two tastings are included.

ACCOMMODATION   LOCHRANZA

Lochranza Camping By the golf course ☎ 01770 830273, ⓦ arran-campsite.com. Relaxed and scenically placed campsite where red deer come to graze in the early evening. Aside from pitches, there are four pods sleeping two- to four-, each with heating and lighting, while facilities include modern shower blocks, laundry and a camper's lounge. Reception is basically the hut that doubles up as the golf clubhouse. March–Oct. Per pitch £18; pods £60

Lochranza Youth Hostel Near the castle, en route to the ferry terminal ☎ 01770 830631, ⓦ hostellingscotland. org.uk. Friendly and well-equipped SYHA hostel with three- to eight-bed dorms, plus doubles, most of which overlook the bay. Two lounges, kitchen and laundry facilities also available. Breakfast £5.95, packed lunch £6.50. March–Oct, though sometimes open at weekends in winter. Dorms £22; doubles £58

EATING AND DRINKING

Sandwich Station Opposite the CalMac slipway ☎ 07393 602806, ⓦ thesandwichstationweebly.com. If you're just passing through, or need a bite before hopping aboard the ferry, pop into this super little sandwich bar and deli, where you can get hot breakfast rolls, sandwiches (hot smoked Skipness salmon with cream cheese; £5.50), panini and home-made soups alongside a range of coffees and smoothies. March–Oct Mon–Sat 7.30am–4pm, Sun

8.45am–3.30pm.
Stags Pavilion ☎ 01770 830600, ⓦ stagspavilion. com. Warm, family-run restaurant located in an attractive pavilion at the entrance to the campsite, with sumptuous dishes like slow-roasted honey and rosemary Arran lamb (£13.95), and blackberry crème brûlée. It's not licensed but you can bring your own bottle (no corkage fee). Reservations advised. Daily except Wed 5.30–10pm.

Isle of Islay

The fertile, largely treeless island of **ISLAY** (pronounced "eye-la") is famous for one thing – single-malt **whisky**. The smoky, peaty, pungent quality of Islay whisky is unique, recognizable even to the untutored palate, and all eight of the island's distilleries will happily take visitors on a guided tour, ending with the customary tipple. Yet, despite the fame of its whiskies, Islay still remains relatively undiscovered, especially when compared with Arran, Mull or Skye, partly, perhaps, because of the two-hour ferry journey from Kennacraig on Kintyre. If you do make the effort, however, you'll be rewarded with a genuinely friendly welcome from islanders proud of their history, landscape and Gaelic culture.

In medieval times, Islay was the political centre of the Hebrides, with **Finlaggan**, near Port Askaig, the seat of the MacDonalds, Lords of the Isles. The picturesque, whitewashed villages you see on Islay today, however, date from the planned settlements founded by the Campbells in the late eighteenth and early nineteenth centuries. Apart from whisky and solitude, the other great draw is the **birdlife** –

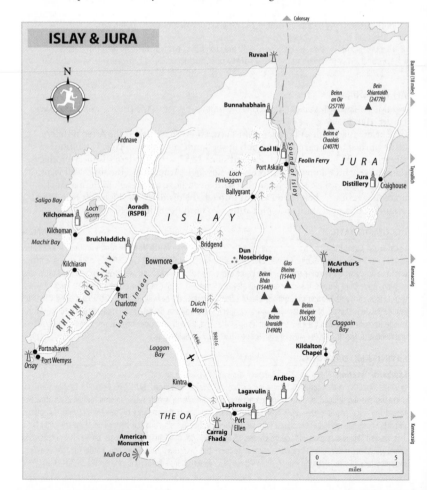

ISLAY & JURA

there's a real possibility of spotting a golden eagle, or the rare crow-like chough, and no chance of missing the white-fronted and barnacle geese that winter here in their thousands.

A great time to visit is late May for the **Feis Ile**, or Islay Festival of Malt and Music (ⓦ islayfestival.com), with whisky tasting, piping recitals, folk dancing and other events celebrating the island's Gaelic roots; you will, though, have to book accommodation months in advance.

ARRIVAL AND DEPARTURE   ISLE OF ISLAY

By plane Islay's airport (ⓣ 01496 302361, ⓦ hial.co.uk) is 5 miles north of Port Ellen on the A846.
Destinations Colonsay (Thurs 1 daily; 20min); Edinburgh (1 daily; 45min); Glasgow (Mon–Fri & Sun 2 daily, Sat 1 daily; 40min); Oban (Thurs 2 daily; 35min).

By ferry CalMac ferries from Kennacraig on Kintyre connect with both Port Ellen and Port Askaig. There's also a ferry that makes the short trip across to Jura, and, between April and September, a passenger-only ferry between Craighouse and Tayvallich on the mainland.

GETTING AROUND

By bus The island's main bus route links Port Askaig with Bridgend, from where buses continue down to Port Ellen, via Bowmore, and Portnahaven, via Port Charlotte. There is no service in Sundays.
Car rental To save on ferry fares, it's worth considering car

rental on the island itself – Islay Car Hire (ⓣ 01496 810544, ⓦ islaycarhire.com; from around £45/day) will deliver to both ferry terminals and the airport. If driving, there are filling stations at Port Askaig, Bowmore and Bridgend.

Port Ellen and around

Laid out as a planned village in 1821 by Walter Frederick Campbell, and named after his wife, **PORT ELLEN** is the chief port on Islay, with the island's largest fishing fleet and main CalMac ferry terminal. The neat, whitewashed terraces which overlook the town's bay of golden sand are pretty enough, but the strand to the north, up Charlotte Street, is dominated by the modern maltings, whose powerful odours waft across the town. Arriving at Port Ellen by boat, it's impossible to miss the unusual, square-shaped **Carraig Fhada lighthouse**, at the western entrance to the bay, erected in 1832 in memory of Walter Frederick Campbell's aforementioned wife. Just beyond the lighthouse is the prettiest bay on the island's south coast, Traigh Bhàn, or the **Singing Sands**, a perfect sandy beach peppered with jagged rocky extrusions.

The distilleries

As you head east out of Port Ellen, a dead-end road passes three **distilleries** in as many miles; however, a more relaxing – indeed, sensible – way of visiting them is to walk the new **three distilleries path**, which begins just outside Port Ellen and links all three. First up is **Laphroaig**, which, as every bottle tells you, is Gaelic for "the beautiful hollow by the bay", and, true enough, the whitewashed distillery is indeed in a gorgeous setting by the sea. Laphroaig also has the stamp of approval from Prince Charles, who famously paid a flying visit to the island in 1994, crashing an airplane of the Queen's Flight in the process.

A mile down the road lies **Lagavulin** distillery, beyond which stands **Dunyvaig Castle**, a romantic ruin on a promontory looking out to the tiny isle of Texa. Another mile further on, the traditional pagoda-style kiln roofs of **Ardbeg** distillery hove into view – in common with all Islay's distilleries, all three offer guided tours (see page 114).

Kildalton Chapel

Around four miles down the track from Ardbeg, you eventually come to the roofless ruins of the thirteenth-century **Kildalton Chapel**, which has a wonderful eighth-century Celtic ringed cross made from the local "bluestone". The quality of the scenes – some of which are more discernible than others – matches any to be found on the crosses

1

ISLAY WHISKY DISTILLERIES

It goes without saying that Islay's **whisky distilleries** are a major tourist attraction. Nowadays, every distillery offers guided tours, which usually last an hour and traditionally end with a generous dram, and occasionally a free glass. Most also offer more comprehensive tours with more tastings, and some even do warehouse tours. Phone ahead to make sure there's a tour running, as times do change frequently.

Ardbeg Port Ellen ☎ 01496 302244, ⊚ ardbeg.com. Ardbeg is traditionally considered the saltiest, peatiest malt on Islay, and that's saying something. Thoroughly overhauled and restored following its acquisition by Glenmorangie in 1997, it's a relatively small distillery by Islay's standards yet it has bags of character inside and the tour is one of the best. Moreover, its café, the *Old Kiln*, is excellent. Tours (£10) April–Oct 11am & 3pm; Feb–March & Nov to mid-Dec Mon–Fri 11am & 3pm; Old Kiln Café April–Oct daily 10am–4.30pm; Nov–March Mon–Fri 10am–4.30pm.

Bowmore School St ☎ 01496 810441, ⊚ bowmore. com. Bowmore is the most touristy of the Islay distilleries, but it is by far the most central (with unrivalled disabled access), and also one of the few still doing its own malting and kilning. Tours (£10) March–Oct Mon–Sat 10, 11, 2.30 & 3.30pm, Sun 12.30 & 2pm; Nov–Feb Mon–Sat 10.30am & 2pm.

Bruichladdich Bruichladdich ☎ 01496 850190, ⊚ bruichladdich.com. In the centre of the village of the same name, this independent distillery was rescued in 2001 by a group of whisky fanatics, but was bought out by Remy-Cointreau in 2012. Progressive and innovative, this is one distinctly cool distillery; moreover, they also produce the island's only gin, the scrumptious Botanist. Tours (£5) April–Oct Mon–Fri 10am, 1 & 4pm, Sat 10am, 1 & 3pm, Sun 11am, 1 & 2pm; Nov–March Mon–Fri 10am & 1pm, Sat 10am & 2pm.

Bunnahabhain 4 miles north of Port Askaig ☎ 01496 840557, ⊚ bunnahabhain.com. A visit to Bunnahabhain (pronounced "Bunna-have-in") is really only for whisky obsessives. The road from Port Askaig is winding, the whisky the least characteristically Islay and the distillery itself only in production for a few months each year. Tours (£7) April–Oct Mon–Sat 9.30am & 3.30pm; Nov–March Mon–Sat 10am & 2pm, Sun noon & 2pm.

carved by the monks in Iona: the Virgin and Child are on the east face, with Cain murdering Abel to the left, David fighting the lion on the top, and Abraham sacrificing Isaac on the right; on the west side amid the serpent-and-boss work are four elephant-like beasts.

ARRIVAL AND DEPARTURE

By ferry The ferry terminal is a 2min walk from the village's main through roads.
Destinations Kennacraig (3–4 daily; 2hr 20min).
By bus Buses pick up and drop off on Charlotte St in the

PORT ELLEN AND AROUND

centre of the village.
Destinations Bowmore (Mon–Sat 8 daily; 25min); Port Askaig (Mon–Sat 3 daily; 50min).

ACCOMMODATION AND EATING

Islay Hotel 18 Charlotte St ☎ 01496 300109, ⊚ theislayhotel.com. One of the finest hotels on the island, with thoroughly modern, sharp-looking rooms, and superbly equipped and very large bathrooms (two with whirlpool bathtub). The *Islay Hotel* is also Port Ellen's social hub, with a fine restaurant and a buzzy, more informal whisky bar. The former rustles up sublime dishes like pan-fried Ghigha halibut with leek risotto and brown crab fritter (£22), while at the latter you can grab a steak pie with creamy mash (£9.50) washed down with a micro-brewed beer. Restaurant: daily noon–2.30pm & 6–9pm; bar: daily 11am–11pm. **£120**

★ **Kintra Farm campsite** 3 miles northwest of Port Ellen ☎ 01496 302051, ⊚ kintrafarm-islay.co.uk. Enjoying a stunning situation at the southern tip of sandy Laggan Bay among the grassy dunes, this is not far off

wild camping at its best. Facilities are basic, but there are showers and running water as well as laundry. Once settled in, you're unlikely to bother exploring anywhere else. May–Sept. Per pitch **£16**

★ **Machrie Hotel** Port Ellen ☎ 01496 302310, ⊚ campbellgrayhotels.com. Following a long awaited refurbishment, the *Machrie* golf hotel is now once again Islay's classiest outfit; its chic, light-filled rooms and suites, boasting thick warm carpets and capacious beds with the finest linen, all have superb views, typically of the Oa Peninsula or of the course itself. The hotel's first-rate facilities also include spa, sauna and gym, and a top draw restaurant. If you have neither the time nor the energy for a full-blown round on the historic main course (£75 for 18 holes), there's the fabulous wee course. **£240**

The Oa

The most dramatic landscape on Islay is to be found in the nub of land to the southwest of Port Ellen known as **The Oa** (pronounced "O"), a windswept and inhospitable spot, much loved by illicit whisky distillers and smugglers over the centuries. Halfway along the road, a ruined church is visible to the south, testament to the area's once large population dispersed during the Clearances – several abandoned villages lie in the north of the peninsula, near **Kintra**.

American Monument

The chief target for most visitors to The Oa is the gargantuan **American Monument**, built in the shape of a lighthouse on the clifftop above the Mull of Oa. It was erected by the American National Red Cross in memory of those who died in two naval disasters that took place in 1918. The first occurred when the troop transporter SS *Tuscania*, carrying over two thousand American army personnel, was torpedoed by a German U-boat seven miles offshore in February 1918. As the lifeboats were being lowered, several ropes broke and threw the occupants into the sea, drowning 266 of those on board. The monument also commemorates those who drowned when the HMS *Otranto* was shipwrecked off Kilchoman (see page 116) in October of the same year. The memorial is inscribed with the unusual sustained metaphor: "On Fame's eternal camping ground, their silent tents are spread, while glory keeps with solemn round, the bivouac of the dead."

The RSPB-managed **Oa trail** is a lovely, and very well signposted, two-mile circular path which begins at the Upper Killeyan car park and takes in the American Monument – from where there are superb views looking east across to Kintyre and directly south to Northern Ireland, including the distinctive lump of Rathin Island – and a spectacular section of clifftop. Following the duckboards across the soggy peat, look out for choughs, golden eagles and peregrine falcons, not to mention feral goats and, down on the shore, basking seals; for a longer walk, follow the coast five miles round to or from Kintra. Alternatively, at 10am on Tuesdays between April and October, there are two-hour guided walks (£5) of the reserve starting at the car park.

Bowmore

On the other side of the monotonous peat bog of Duich Moss, on the southern shores of the tidal Loch Indaal, lies **Bowmore**, Islay's administrative capital, with a population of around eight hundred. It was founded in 1768 to replace the village of Kilarrow, which was deemed by the local laird to be too close to his own residence. It's a striking place, laid out in a grid plan rather like Inveraray, with the whitewashed terraces of Main Street climbing up the hill in a straight line from the pier on Loch Indaal.

The Round Church

High St • Daily 9am–6pm • ⓦ theroundchurch.org.uk

Built in 1767 by Daniel Campbell, then owner of the island, the town's crowning landmark is the **Round Church**, whose central tower looks uncannily like a lighthouse. Built in the round, so that the devil would have no corners in which to hide, it's well worth a look for its wood-panelled interior, lovely tiered balcony and big, central, mushroom pillar.

ARRIVAL AND INFORMATION   **BOWMORE**

By bus Buses stop on the main square, which, strangely enough, is called The Square.

Destinations Port Askaig (Mon–Sat 5–6 daily; 25min); Port Charlotte (Mon–Sat 6 daily; 25min); Port Ellen (Mon–Sat 9 daily; 25min); Portnahaven (Mon–Sat 6 daily; 50min).

Tourist office The Square, Main St (April–June & Sept–Oct Mon–Sat 10am–5pm, Sun noon–3pm; July & Aug Mon–Sat 9.30am–5.30pm, Sun 10am–4pm; Nov–March Mon–Sat 10am–3pm; ☎ 01496 305165). The staff here can help you find accommodation anywhere on the island and also on Jura.

1

ACCOMMODATION AND EATING

Bowmore House Shore St ☎01496 810324, ⓦthe bowmorehouse.co.uk. This grand-looking house, positioned on the main road entering the village, has five fabulous rooms exquisitely furnished in different styles, but all with plush carpets and plump beds, as well as sparkling bathrooms replete with luxury toiletries. There's a complimentary laundry service too. **£135**

Harbour Inn The Square ☎01496 810330, ⓦbowmore.com/harbour-inn. Smart, if unadventurously decorated, harbourside restaurant with lovely views, and serving sumptuous plates of food like black squid ink risotto with pickled crab meat (£19.90); scrummy oyster menu too (six for £12.95). Alternatively, you can warm yourself by a peat fire in the adjoining pub, where they also do lunchtime bar snacks. Daily noon–2pm & 6–10pm.

Lambeth Guesthouse Jamieson St ☎01496 810597, ⓦlambeth-guesthouse.co.uk. Just off Main St, this is a jovially run guesthouse with six modestly sized but impeccably prepared en-suite rooms. A little tricky to find: it's next to the tiny filling station, the door being around to the side. **£100**

★**Peatzeria** 22 Shore St ☎01496 810810, ⓦpeatzeria.com. The most enjoyable place to eat in Bowmore, if not the island, this cleverly titled restaurant rustles up a terrific selection of handmade stone baked pizzas (including some extravagantly priced seafood ones such as Islay Scallops: £19.95) alongside genuinely exciting Italian dishes like Fiorelli pasta stuffed with salmon and crayfish (£12.95); the space is great too, with ground floor and mezzanine seating as well as both covered and uncovered outdoor seating overlooking the water. Daily noon–10pm.

Loch Gruinart

Between October and mid-April, it's impossible to miss the island's staggeringly large wintering population of **Greenland barnacle** and **white-fronted geese**. You can see the geese just about anywhere on the island – there are an estimated 5000 white-fronted and 40,000 barnacles here (and rising) – with the largest concentrations in the fields between Bridgend and Ballygrant, and on the tidal mud flats and fields around **Loch Gruinart**. There's an RSPB-run **visitor centre** (seven miles north of Bridgend on the B8017; daily 10am–5pm; free; ☎01496 850505, ⓦrspb.org.uk/lochgruinart) at the nearby farm of Aoradh (pronounced "oorig"), with a scale model of the reserve and a sightings board, but you're better off getting yourself down to one of the two hides (both open access), just a couple of hundred yards apart from each other overlooking the salt flats and marshes at the head of the loch. The RSPB run two-hour guided walks (£5) through the reserve at 2pm on Thursdays between April and October.

The road along the western shores of Loch Gruinart to Ardnave is a good place to spot **choughs**, members of the crow family, distinguished by their curved red beaks and matching legs. Halfway along the road, there's a path off to the ruins of **Kilnave Chapel**, whose working graveyard contains a very weathered, eighth-century Celtic cross. The road ends at Ardnave Loch, beyond which lie numerous sand dunes, where seals often sun themselves, and otters sometimes fish offshore.

Machir Bay and Kilchoman

Without doubt the best **sandy beaches** on Islay are to be found on the isolated northwest coast, in particular, the lovely golden beach of **Machir Bay**, which is backed by great white-sand dunes. The sea here has dangerous undercurrents, however, and is not safe to swim in (the same goes for the much smaller **Saligo Bay**, to the north).

At the settlement of **Kilchoman**, set back from Machir Bay, beneath low rocky cliffs, where fulmars nest inland, the church is in a sorry state of disrepair. Its churchyard, however, contains a beautiful fifteenth-century cross, decorated with interlacing on one side and the Crucifixion on the other; at its base there's a wishing stone that should be turned sunwise when wishing. Across a nearby field towards the bay lies the **sailors' cemetery**, containing just 75 graves of the 400 or so who were drowned when the armed merchant cruiser HMS *Otranto* collided with another ship in its convoy in a storm in October 1918. The ship was carrying 1000 army personnel (including 665 Americans), the majority of whom made it safely to a ship that came to their aid; of the

> **ISLAY GEESE**
>
> Whisky aside, for many the other great attraction on Islay is the wonderful spectacle of thousands of **Greenland barnacle** and **white-fronted geese**. Between October and mid-April, geese dominate the landscape, feeding incessantly off the rich pasture, strolling by the shores, and flying in formation across the winter skies. In the spring, the geese hang around just long enough to snap up the first shoots of new grass, in order to give themselves enough energy to make the 2000-mile journey to Greenland, where they breed in the summer. Understandably, many local farmers are not exactly happy about the geese feeding off their land, and some receive compensation for the inconvenience.

400 who had to try and swim ashore, only 16 survived. The sailors' graves lie in three neat rows, from the cook to the captain, who has his own, much larger, gravestone.

Port Charlotte

Founded in 1828 by Walter Frederick Campbell, and named after his mother, **PORT CHARLOTTE** was originally set up to provide housing facilities for the workers of the former Lochindaal distillery, which eventually closed in 1929. It's generally agreed to be Islay's prettiest village, its immaculate whitewashed cottages clustered round a sandy cove overlooking Loch Indaal.

Museum of Islay Life

Daal Terrace • April & Oct Mon–Fri 10.30am–4.30pm; May–Sept Mon–Sat 10.30am–4.30pm, Sun 1–4.30pm • £5 • ☎ 01496 850358, ⍟ islaymuseum.org

On the northern fringe of the village, in a whitewashed former chapel, the engaging **Museum of Islay Life** is crammed to bursting with local memorabilia. As well as tantalizing snippets about eighteenth-century illegal whisky distillers, there are some terrific photos and a good library of books about the island. Best of all, though, are the displays on the SS *Tuscania* and HMS *Otranto*, both of which were sunk in the waters hereabouts during World War I. Among the exhibits from the *Tuscania* is its bell, a bunk-side cabinet, and the notebook belonging to Sergeant Malcolm McNeill, in which he records the names and conditions of those who perished, including one, he writes rather grimly, "whose body is so much decayed that it is crumbling to pieces".

Islay Natural History Trust Visitor Centre

Main St • April–Sept Mon–Fri 10am–4pm • £3.50 • ☎ 01496 850288, ⍟ islaynaturalhistory.org

The **Islay Natural History Trust Visitor Centre**, housed in the former distillery warehouse, is well worth a visit for anyone interested in the island's fauna and flora. As well as an extensive library to browse, there's lots of hands-on stuff for kids: microscopes, a touch table full of natural goodies, a sea-water aquarium, a bug world and owl pellets to examine. Tickets are valid for a week, allowing you to go back and identify things you've seen on your travels. They also organize nature rambles at 2pm each Sunday between June and September (£4), as well as wildlife adventures at 2pm on Thursdays, which could be anything from rock-pooling to beachcombing.

ARRIVAL AND DEPARTURE
PORT CHARLOTTE

By bus Buses stop just outside the *Port Charlotte Hotel*. Destinations Bowmore (Mon–Sat 6 daily; 25min); Port Wemyss (Mon–Sat 6 daily; 15min).

ACCOMMODATION AND EATING

Port Charlotte Hotel Main St ☎ 01496 850360, ⍟ port charlottehotel.co.uk. Beautifully appointed whitewashed stone hotel right in the heart of the village overlooking the beach. A handful of the ten rooms have retained their original exposed stone walls, but they're all thoughtfully designed and decorated in bold but beautiful colours. The hotel restaurant is of a similarly high order, though it's much more fun to tuck into one of their seafood lunches out on the patio, for example pan-seared Islay scallops with apple puree and black pudding crumble (£10). There's usually live music on Wednesday and Sunday evenings in the bar. Restaurant 6.30–9pm; bar noon–11pm. **£180**

Port Mòr Campsite Just outside the village out on the road to Portnahaven ☎ 01496 850441, ⓦ islandofislay. co.uk. A community-run campsite with glorious sea views and tip-top facilities: modern shower block, laundry, café and a brilliant playground for the kids. March–Nov; café 8.30am–8.30pm. Per person **£9**

Port Charlotte Youth Hostel Main St ☎ 01496 850385, ⓦ hostellingscotland.org.uk. Next door to the Natural History Trust Visitor Centre, Islay's only hostel is housed in an old bonded warehouse by the sea. It possesses a handy mix of doubles and triples all the way up to six-bed dorms, and each with shared bathroom facilities; there's also a large kitchen and common room. Breakfast £4.50. Open April–Sept. Doubles **£50**; dorms **£21.50**

Portnahaven and Port Wemyss

The main coastal road on Islay culminates seven miles south of Port Charlotte at **PORTNAHAVEN**, a fishing and crofting community since the early nineteenth century. The familiar whitewashed cottages wrap themselves prettily around the steep banks of a deep bay where seals bask on the rocks; you're guaranteed to spot some, and at pretty much any time of the year. In the distance, you can see **PORT WEMYSS**, a mile south. The communities share a little whitewashed church, located above the bay in Portnahaven, with separate doors for residents of each village.

A short way out to sea are two islands, the largest of which, Orsay, sports the **Rhinns of Islay Lighthouse**, built by Robert Louis Stevenson's father in 1825; ask around locally if you're keen to visit the island.

ARRIVAL AND DEPARTURE   PORTNAHAVEN AND PORT WEMYSS

By bus Buses make their way into the centre of both villages, dropping off first at Portnahaven.

Destinations Bowmore (Mon–Sat 6 daily; 50min); Port Charlotte (Mon–Sat 6 daily; 15min).

ACCOMMODATION AND EATING

Burnside B&B Shore St, Port Wemyss ☎ 01496 860296, ⓦ burnsidelodge.co.uk. Located just off the coastal path, this sweet little place offers two en-suite rooms of modest but tidy proportions. The friendly owner here also rustles up delectable home-baked goodies, including cupcakes and muffins, which are left in a self-service cupboard (payment via an honesty box) just outside the house, alongside hot drinks, which can be enjoyed on one of the barrel seats looking across to Rhinns Point, below which seals bask on the shore. On Wednesdays, she serves up a wonderful selection of pies. Food April–Sept daily 10am–5pm. Guesthouse March–Nov. **£98**

Loch Finlaggan

Just beyond Ballygrant, on the road to Port Askaig midway between Ballygrant and Port Askaig, a narrow road leads off north to **Loch Finlaggan**, site of a number of **prehistoric crannogs** (artificial islands) and, for four hundred years from the twelfth century, headquarters of the Lords of the Isles, semi-autonomous rulers of the Hebrides and Kintyre. The site is evocative enough, but there are, in truth, very few remains beyond the foundations. Remarkably, the palace that stood here appears to have been unfortified, a testament perhaps to the prosperity and stability of the islands in those days.

To the northeast of the loch, the **information centre** (April–Oct Mon–Sat 10.30am–4.15pm; £4; ⓦ finlaggan.org) exhibits a number of extraordinary finds uncovered on the site, notably some twelfth-century leather soles and uppers, and a thirteenth-century cast bronze figure of Christ. From the centre, a path heads down to the site itself, which is dotted with interpretive panels. Duckboards allow you to walk out across the reed beds of the loch and explore the main crannog, **Eilean Mor**, where several carved gravestones are displayed under cover in the chapel, all of which seem to support the theory that the Lords of the Isles buried their wives and children there, while having themselves interred on Iona. Further out into the loch is another smaller crannog, **Eilean na Comhairle**, originally connected to Eilean Mor by a causeway, where the Lords of the Isles are thought to have held meetings of the Council of the Isles.

Port Askaig

Islay's other ferry connection with the mainland, and its sole link with Colonsay and Jura, is from **PORT ASKAIG**, a scattering of buildings which tumbles down a little cove by the narrowest section of the Sound of Islay or Caol Ila. There's next to nothing here, save for a hotel, shop and post office.

ARRIVAL AND TOURS   PORT ASKAIG

By ferry After Port Ellen, Port Askaig is the second of the island's main ferry terminals.

Destinations Colonsay (Wed & Sat 1 daily; 1hr 10min); Feolin ferry to Jura (Mon–Sat hourly, Sun 7 daily; 5min); Kennacraig (3–4 daily; 2hr 5min).

By bus Buses depart from a spot just up from the ferry terminal.

Destinations Bowmore (Mon–Sat 5–6 daily; 25min); Port Ellen (Mon–Sat 3 daily; 50min).

Boat tours Based in Port Askaig, Islay Sea Safari (📞01496 840510, 🌐islayseasafari.co.uk) offers high-adrenaline boat trips round the distilleries in a rigid inflatable (£25/1hr, £40/2hr).

ACCOMMODATION AND EATING

★ **Ballygrant Inn** Ballygrant 📞01496 840277, 🌐ballygrant-inn.com. Incredibly hospitable, family-run affair, with seven immaculately kept rooms. Its restaurant is top-notch, serving the likes of Islay venison and red wine casserole (£13.95), though it's the brilliant bar, stocking some 400 whiskies, that's the real draw; the half a dozen tasting menus (from £22) are far superior to anything offered at the distilleries, so a visit is very much the order of the day. Look out, too, for their excellent curry night on Thursdays. Mon–Sat 11am–1am, Sun 12.30pm–midnight; food served 12.30–2.30pm & 6–9pm. £80

Kilmeny Farmhouse Ballygrant 📞01496 840668, 🌐kilmeny.co.uk. Three miles south of Port Askaig, this whitewashed farmhouse is a place that richly deserves all the superlatives it regularly receives. Antique furnishings,

locally made fabrics and slipper baths feature in some or all of the four colour-coordinated rooms. You can expect to be well pampered for the duration of your stay, and the gourmet breakfast is a real treat, comprising, among other things, poached plums, Scottish pancake stack, and smoked Argyll salmon and scrambled eggs. March–Nov. £150

Persabus Farm 1.5km inland from Port Askaig 📞01496 840243, 🌐persabus.co.uk. Out on the road to Bunnahabhain, one of the farm's outbuildings is now a delightful café-cum-pottery, where everything is handcrafted and fired on site – you can even have a go yourself, and while you're waiting for it to be set, partake in a fresh cup of coffee with a slice of scrummy home-made cake. Mon–Fri noon–4pm, Sat till 3pm.

Isle of Jura

Twenty-eight miles long and eight miles wide, the long whale-shaped island of **JURA** is one of the wildest and most mountainous of the Inner Hebrides, its entire west coast uninhabited and inaccessible except to the dedicated walker. The distinctive **Paps of Jura**, so-called because of their smooth, breast-like shape, seem to dominate every view off the west coast of Argyll, their glacial rounded tops covered in a light dusting of quartzite scree. The island's name is commonly thought to derive from the Norse *dyr-oe* (deer island) and, appropriately enough, the current deer population of 6000 outnumbers the 190 or so humans 33 to 1; other wildlife to look out for include mountain hares and eagles. With just one road, which sticks to the more sheltered eastern coast of the island, and only one hotel, a couple of B&Bs and some self-catering cottages, Jura is an ideal place to go for peace and quiet, and some great walking.

Craighouse

Anything that happens on Jura happens in the island's only real village, **CRAIGHOUSE**, eight miles up the road from Feolin Ferry. The village enjoys a sheltered setting, overlooking Knapdale on the mainland – so sheltered, in fact, that there are even a few palm trees thriving on the seafront. In terms of facilities, and things to see and do, there's a shop/post office, hotel and tearoom, plus the tiny **Isle of Jura distillery**.

Isle of Jura distillery

Opposite the Jura Hotel • Guided tours Mon–Fri 11am & 2pm, plus Sat April–Oct • £6 • ☎ 01496 820385, ⓦ jurawhisky.com

Established in 1810 by the Campbells, the **Isle of Jura distillery** has endured a somewhat chequered history. It went out of business in the early 1900s, before reopening in 1963 on the premises of the then derelict distillery. It now produces four distinctive single malts, with two notable success stories, the ten-year-old "Origin", and the sixteen-year-old "Diurachs' Own" – you'll get to sample one or both of these on one of the guided tours.

Corryvreckan Whirlpool

Between the islands of Scarba and Jura is the raging **Corryvreckan Whirlpool** (ⓦwhirlpool-scotland.co.uk), one of the world's most spectacular whirlpools – and supposedly the third largest – thought to be caused by a rocky pinnacle some 100ft below the sea. Exactly how the whirlpool appears depends on the tide and wind, but there's a potential tidal flow of over eight knots, which, when accompanied by gale-force winds, can create standing waves up to 15ft high. Inevitably there are numerous legends about the place – known as *coire bhreacain* (speckled cauldron) in Gaelic – concerning *Cailleach* (Hag), the Celtic storm goddess. From the land, the best place from which to view it is Carraig Mhor on the northern tip of Jura, though the best trips to the whirlpool – which can be quite spectacular, and hair-raising – depart from Seil (see page 93).

ARRIVAL AND DEPARTURE   ISLE OF JURA

By ferry The Feolin ferry from Port Askaig will not run if there's a strong northerly or southerly wind, so bring your toothbrush if you're coming for a day-trip. Roughly six times a day, the Jura minibus (☎01496 820314) meets

---

WALKING THE PAPS OF JURA

Ordnance Survey Explorer map 355

Perhaps the most popular of all the hillwalks on Jura is an ascent of any of the island's famous **Paps of Jura** – Beinn an Oir (2571ft), Beinn a'Chaolais (2407ft) and Beinn Shiantaidh (2477ft) – which cluster together in the south half of the island. It's possible to do a round trip from Craighouse itself, or from the Feolin ferry, but the easiest approach is from the three-arched bridge on the island's main road, three miles north of Craighouse. From the bridge, keeping to the north side of the Corran River, you eventually reach Loch an t'Siob. If you only want to climb **one Pap**, then simply climb up to the saddle between Beinn an Oir and Beinn Shiantaidh and choose which one (Beinn an Oir is probably the most interesting), returning to the bridge the same way. The trip to and from the bridge should take between five and six hours; it's hard going and care needs to be taken, as the scree is unstable.

If you want to try and bag **all three Paps**, you need to attack Beinn Shiantaidh via its southeast spur, leaving the loch at its easternmost point. This makes for a more difficult ascent, as the scree and large lumps of quartzite are tough going. Descending to the aforementioned saddle, and climbing Beinn an Oir is straightforward enough, but make sure you come off Beinn an Oir via the south spur, before climbing Beinn a'Chaolais, as the western side of Beinn an Oir is dangerously steep. Again, you can return via the loch to the three-arched bridge.

Every year, in the last bank-holiday weekend in May, hundreds of masochists take part in a **fell race** up the Paps, which the winner usually completes in three hours. Given the number of deer on Jura, it's as well to be aware of the **stalking season** (July–Feb), during which you should check with the *Jura Hotel* (see page 121) before heading out. At all times of year, you should take all the usual **safety precautions** (see page 42); beware, too, of adders, which are quite numerous on Jura.

1

GEORGE ORWELL ON JURA

In April 1946, Eric Blair (better known by his pen name of **George Orwell**), intending to give himself "six months' quiet" in which to complete his latest novel, moved to a remote farmhouse called **Barnhill**, at the northern end of Jura, which he had visited for the first time the previous year. He appears to have relished the challenge of a spartan existence here with his adopted 3-year-old son Richard, and later his sister Avril; fishing almost every night, shooting rabbits, laying lobster pots and even attempting a little farming. The book Orwell was writing, under the working title *The Last Man in Europe*, was to become *1984* (the title was arrived at by simply reversing the last two digits of the year in which it was finished – 1948). During his time on Jura, however, Orwell was suffering badly from tuberculosis, and eventually he was forced to return to London, where he died in January 1950.

Barnhill, 23 miles north of Craighouse, is as remote today as it was in Orwell's day. The road deteriorates rapidly beyond Lealt, where vehicles must be left, leaving pilgrims a four-mile walk to the house itself. Alternatively, the Richardsons of Kinauachdrachd (☎07899 912116) can organize a taxi and guided walk, and also run a bunkhouse. Orwell wrote most of the book in the bedroom (top left window as you look at the house); the place is now a self-catering cottage (☎01786 850274). If you're keen on making the journey out to Barnhill, you might as well combine it with a trip to the nearby **Corryvreckan Whirlpool**, which lies between Jura and Scarba, to the north (see page 120). Orwell nearly drowned in the whirlpool during a fishing trip in August 1947, along with his three companions (including Richard): the outboard motor was washed away, and they had to row to a nearby island and wait for several hours before being rescued by a passing fisherman.

the car ferry from Port Askaig and goes up to Inverlussa via Craighouse – phone ahead to check times.

Destinations Port Askaig (Mon–Sat every 45–60min, Sun 6 daily; 5min; £3.60 return, car £18.90 return).

By passenger ferry Between April and September, there's also a passenger ferry service (☎07768 450000, ⓦjurapassengerferry.com; £20 single) from Tayvallich, on the Argyll mainland, to Craighouse; bikes can be carried too.

Destinations Tayvallich (Mon & Wed–Sat 2 daily, Sun 1 daily; 50min).

ACCOMMODATION AND EATING

The Antlers 100yds north of the distillery ☎01496 820496. Delightful bistro restaurant that serves up burgers, sandwiches and salads for lunch, and beautifully presented Jura lamb on the one evening it's open, for which you must book. Unlicensed, but you're welcome to bring your own (corkage £3). Daily 10am–4pm, plus Fri 6.30–8.30pm.

Jura Hotel Craighouse ☎01496 820243, ⓦjurahotel. co.uk. The island's one and only hotel is not much to look at from the outside, but it's warm and friendly within and the rooms are right up to the mark. Campers are welcome to pitch tents in the field fronting the hotel, and there's a shower block (£1 per shower) and laundry facilities round the back. Unsurprisingly, it's also the centre of the island's social scene, with a restaurant, lounge-bar and pub. Bar: daily 11am–11pm. Per pitch **£5**; doubles **£110**

Caol Ila Port Askaig ☎01496 302760, ⓦmalts.com. Caol Ila (pronounced "Cull-eela"), just north of Port Askaig, is a modern distillery, the majority of whose lightly peaty malt goes into blended whiskies. Tours (£7) March–Oct Mon–Fri 9.30am & 12.30 & 3.30pm, Sat 9.30am, Sun 10.30am; Nov–Feb Tues–Sat 10.30am.

Kilchoman Rockside Farm, Bruichladdich ☎01496 850011, ⓦkilchomandistillery.com. Established in 2005 as the first new distillery on Islay for over a century, Kilchoman is a very welcoming, tiny, farm-based enterprise that grows its own barley, as well as distilling, maturing and bottling its whisky on site. Also, along with Ardbeg, this is the only distillery on the island with a café, and very lovely it is too, serving good coffee, plus home-made soup and baked goodies. Tours (£6) daily 10am 2 & 3pm. Café Mon–Sat 9.45am–5pm.

Lagavulin Port Ellen ☎01496 302749, ⓦmalts.com. Enjoying a fabulous setting in the bay of the same name, Lagavulin – which marked two hundred years of production in 2016 – is probably the classic, all-round Islay malt, with lots of smoke and peat. Tours (£8) April–Sept daily 9.30 & 11.30am & 3.30pm; March & Oct Mon–Fri 9.30am & 12.30pm, Sat & Sun 12.30pm; Nov–Feb daily 12.30pm.

Laphroaig Port Ellen ☎01496 302418, ⓦlaphroaig. com. This famous distillery, in another wonderful setting, celebrated its two-hundredth anniversary in 2015, and is another classic smoky, peaty Islay malt. The third of the island's distilleries to do its own malting, it also has a great little museum. Tours (£10) March–Oct daily 10.30 & 11.30am & 2, 2.30 & 3pm; Nov–Feb daily 11.30am & 2, & 3pm.

The Central Highlands

DRUM CASTLE IN THE SNOW

The Central Highlands

The Central Highlands lie right in the heart of Scotland, bounded by the country's two major geological fissures: the Highland Fault, which runs along a line drawn approximately from Arran to Aberdeen and marks the southern extent of Scotland's Highlands, and the Great Glen, the string of lochs that runs on a similar southwest–northeast axis between Fort William and Inverness. The appeal of the region is undoubtedly its landscape, a concentrated mix of mountain, glen, loch and moorland that responds to each season with a dramatic blend of colour and mood, combined with the outdoor activities the landscape inspires. It's also an area with a rich history, stemming in large part from the fact that along the geological divide of north and south is a significant cultural and social shift, and it is no surprise that the region is littered with castles, battlefields and monuments from the centuries of power struggle between the Highlanders and the Sassenachs, whether from lowland Scotland or south of the border.

Northwest of Glasgow, the elongated teardrop of **Loch Lomond** is the main focus of Scotland's first national park. The magnificent scenery around the loch continues east into the fabled mountains and lochs of the **Trossachs**, where hikers and mountain-bikers are drawn to explore the forested glens, and where fugitive Highlanders such as **Rob Roy** once roamed. North of the Trossachs, the massive county of **Perthshire** lies right at the heart of the Central Highlands, with **lochs Tay** and **Rannoch** stacked up across the middle of the region, each surrounded by impressive hills and progressively more remote countryside.

Further to the east are the **Grampian Mountains**. Within this range the **Angus glens**, immediately north of Perth and Dundee, are renowned for their prettiness and easy accessibility, while closer to Aberdeen the river valleys of **Deeside** and **Donside** combine the drama of peaks such as **Lochnagar** with the richly wooded glens and dramatic castles which so enchanted Queen Victoria. The northern side of the Grampians is dominated by the dramatic **Cairngorm** massif, the largest area of land over 2500ft in Britain and centre of Scotland's second national park. These hills, with their deserved reputation for superb outdoor sports in both summer and winter, are complemented by the atmospheric ancient woodlands of **Strathspey**. A little way downstream is the whisky-producing region of **Speyside**, where various trails lead you to the distilleries, home of some of the world's most famous single malts.

With no sizeable towns in the region other than useful service centres such as Callander, Pitlochry and Aviemore, **orientation** is best done by means of the traditional transport routes – many of which follow historic trading or military roads between the important population centres on the edges of the area: Glasgow, Stirling and Perth to the south, Aberdeen to the east, and Fort William and Inverness to the north. The main route on the **western** side is along the western shore of Loch Lomond, where both the A82 and the railway line wind north to Crianlarich en route to Oban and Fort William. In the **centre** of the country, the A84 cuts through the heart of the Trossachs between Stirling and Crianlarich, while the most important route to the **eastern** side is the busy A9 trunk road and the nearby railway between Perth and Inverness.

RED GROUSE IN THE CAIRNGORMS

Highlights

❶ Inchcailloch Putter out to this tranquil wooded island at the heart of Scotland's first national park. See page 130

❷ Folk music Join in a session at the bar of the Taybank in the gorgeously preserved town of Dunkeld. See page 138

❸ Scottish Crannog Centre Tour a stunning reconstructed prehistoric lake dwelling, and try your hand at Stone Age crafts. See page 141

❹ Blair Castle Observe the grand life of the Highland nobility, along with extensive parkland and the country's only private army. See page 145

❺ Schiehallion Scale Perthshire's "fairy mountain" for the views over lochs, hills, glens and moors. See page 147

❻ Rannoch Moor One of the most inaccessible places in Scotland, where hikers can discover a true sense of remote emptiness. See page 147

❼ The castles of Deeside and the Don Valley A trail of some of Scotland's finest castles, from stately piles to moody ruins. See pages 156 and 160

❽ The Cairngorms Scotland's grandest mountain massif, a place of wild animals, ancient forests, inspiring vistas – and terrific outdoor activities. See page 164

HIGHLIGHTS ARE MARKED ON THE MAP ON PAGE 126

Loch Lomond and around

The largest stretch of fresh water in Britain (23 miles long and up to five miles wide), **Loch Lomond** is the epitome of Scottish scenic splendour, thanks in large part to the ballad that fondly recalls its "bonnie, bonnie banks". The song was said to have been written by a Jacobite prisoner captured by the English, who, sure of his fate, wrote that his spirit would return to Scotland on the low road much faster than his living compatriots on the high road.

Loch Lomond is undoubtedly the centrepiece of the national park, and the most popular gateway into the park is **Balloch**, the town on the southern tip of Loch

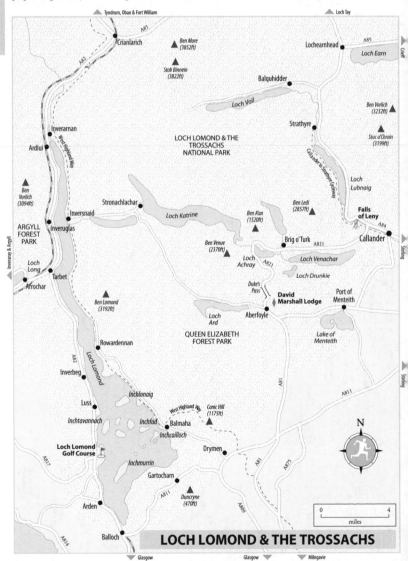

LOCH LOMOND & THE TROSSACHS

2

HIGH ROADS AND LOW ROADS AROUND LOCH LOMOND

Ordnance Survey Explorer Maps 347 & 364

The popularity of hiking and biking within **Loch Lomond and the Trossachs National Park** (ⓦlochlomond-trossachs.org) has been recognized in an initiative entitled "**4Bs**" which aims to improve the links between boats, boots (ie walking), bikes and buses around the park. Signposting and information are increasingly good, with new cycle paths and trails being set out all the time, in addition to enhanced provision for walking and nature trails. Indeed, with a seaplane and wooden mail boats operating on Loch Lomond as well as a 100-year-old steamship on Loch Katrine, getting around the park is very much part of the experience.

For those keen to take to the high road there are three obvious targets offering different levels of challenge. Most prominent, **Ben Lomond** (3192ft) is the most southerly of the "Munros" (see page 41) and one of the most popular hills in Scotland, its commanding position above Loch Lomond affording amazing views of the Highlands and Lowlands. The well-signposted route to the summit and back from Rowardennan takes five to six hours. If you're looking for an easier climb, but an equally impressive view over Loch Lomond, start at Balmaha for the ascent of **Conic Hill** (1175ft), a two- to three-hour walk through forest and hillside.

Finally, you need less than an hour to complete the ascent of **Duncryne** (470ft), a small conical hill beside Gartocharn to the east of Balloch on the south side of the loch. The route up is undemanding and the view wonderfully rewarding.

Lomond; with Glasgow city centre just nineteen miles away, both Balloch and the southwest side of the loch around **Luss** are often packed with day-trippers and tour coaches. Many of these continue up the **western side** of the loch, though the fast A82 road isn't ideal for a leisurely lochside drive.

Very different in tone, the **eastern side** of the loch, abutting the Trossachs, operates at a different pace with wooden ferryboats puttering out to a scattering of tree-covered islands off the village of **Balmaha**. Much of the eastern shore can only be reached by boat or foot, although the West Highland Way long-distance footpath (see page 131) and the distinctive peak of **Ben Lomond** ensure that even these parts are well travelled in comparison to many other areas of the Highlands.

Balloch

The main settlement by Loch Lomond is **BALLOCH** at its southwestern corner, where the water channels into the River Leven for its short journey south to the sea in the Firth of Clyde. Surrounded by housing estates and overstuffed with undistinguished guesthouses, Balloch has few redeeming features and is little more than a suburb of the factory town of Alexandria, though there are a couple of worthwhile attractions, and you can also take various loch trips from here. Across the river in the extensive mature grounds of **Balloch Castle Country Park**, there are shoreside and sylvan walks.

The Maid of the Loch

Balloch Pier • May–Sept daily 11am–4pm; Oct–April Sat & Sun 11am–4pm • Free • ⓣ01389 711865, ⓦmaidoftheloch.com

Permanently moored at Balloch pier is the 1950s **paddle steamer** *The Maid of the Loch*, for which there are plans to restore and set her afloat once again, though this is likely to take a few years yet. In the meantime you can hop aboard and find out about her glory days sailing the loch whilst enjoying a cup of tea in the onboard café.

Loch Lomond Bird of Prey Centre

Ben Lomond Way • April–Oct daily 10am–5.30pm; Nov–March Sat & Sun 10am–4pm • £8 • ⓣ01389 729239, ⓦllbopc.co.uk

By far the best reason to visit Balloch is the **Loch Lomond Bird of Prey Centre,** whose high standards of animal welfare and conservation are among the best in Scotland. There's a fantastic display of owls (Barn, Tawny, Eagle, Great Grey among them)

alongside hawks, falcons and kestrels, and a majestic Golden Eagle, many of which are tethered on the lawn, allowing visitors to get much closer to the birds than would otherwise be the case. Better still, regular flying displays are held in the adjacent field, and there's also an informative little exhibition in a small wooden cabin.

ARRIVAL AND DEPARTURE   BALLOCH

By train Balloch has a direct train connection with Glasgow Queen Street (every 30min; 50min). The station sits between the loch and the town centre.

By bus Regular buses connect Balloch with Balmaha (every 2hr; 25min) and Luss (hourly; 15min).

INFORMATION AND ACTIVITIES

Tourist office The Old Station Building opposite the modern train station contains Loch Lomond's only tourist office (daily: April–June & Sept 9.30am–5.30pm; July & Aug 9.30am–6pm; Oct–March 10am–5pm; ☎01389 753533).

Loch trips Sweeney's Cruises, in the centre of town near the bridge (☎01389 752376, ⓦsweeneyscruisesco.com), offers a choice of loch trips including a 1hr Experience Cruise of the South basin (£12), and a 2hr Island Discovery Cruise (£20).

ACCOMMODATION

Dumbain Farm Off Dumbain Crescent ☎01389 752263, ⓦdumbainfarm.co.uk. Rambling whitewashed farm with converted outbuildings, containing bright and elegant rooms with TVs and tea- and coffee-making facilities. Traditional Scottish breakfast, cooked on an Aga, with home-made jams and baking. **£70**

The eastern shore

The tranquil **eastern shore** is far better for walking and appreciating the loch's natural beauty than the overcrowded western side. It's the access point for climbing **Ben Lomond** and visiting **Inchcailloch** island, and where the minor road peters out at **Rowardennan** you can continue on foot to the village of **Inversnaid**.

Balmaha and Rowardennan

The tiny lochside settlement of **BALMAHA** lies on the Highland Boundary Fault: if you stand on the viewpoint above the pier, you can see the fault line clearly marked by the series of woody islands – many now privately owned – that form giant stepping stones across the loch. Balmaha gets very busy in summer, not least with day-trippers on the West Highland Way. Public transport ends at Balmaha, but another seven miles north through the woods brings you to the end of the road at **ROWARDENNAN**, a scattered settlement that sits below Ben Lomond.

Inchcailloch

Ferries from Balmaha (☎01360 870214, ⓦbalmahaboatyard.co.uk) operate daily 9.30am–5pm, with departures on demand; the journey takes 5min and costs £5 return

Owned by Scottish Natural Heritage, **Inchcailloch** is the closest island to Balmaha. A signposted two-mile **nature trail** loops around the island, which was extensively planted with oaks to provide bark for the local tanning industry. Along the way you'll encounter the ruins of a fourteenth-century nunnery and associated burial ground, and there's a picnic and camping site at Port Bawn on the southwestern side of the island, near a sandy beach. Until the mid-seventeenth century parishioners on the far (western) shore of Loch Lomond used to row across to Inchcailloch for Sunday services at the church linked to the nunnery. It's possible to make the short trip courtesy of the on-demand ferry service operated by MacFarlane & Son out of the Balmaha Boatyard.

Ben Lomond

Ben Lomond (3192ft) is the most southerly of the "Munros" (see page 41) and one of the most popular mountains in Scotland, its commanding position above

THE WEST HIGHLAND WAY

Ordnance Survey Explorer maps 392, 384, 377, 364, 385, 342, 347 & 348

Opened in 1980, the spectacular **West Highland Way** was Scotland's first long-distance footpath, stretching some 96 miles from Milngavie (pronounced "mill-guy"), six miles north of central Glasgow, to Fort William, where it reaches the foot of Ben Nevis, Britain's highest mountain. Today, it is by far the most popular such footpath in Scotland, and while for many the range of scenery, relative ease of walking and nearby facilities make it a classic route, others find it a little too busy in high season, particularly in comparison with the isolation of many other parts of the Highlands.

THE ROUTE

The route follows a combination of ancient **drove roads**, along which Highlanders herded their cattle and sheep to market in the Lowlands, military roads, built by troops to control the Jacobite insurgency in the eighteenth century, old coaching roads and disued railway lines. In addition to the stunning scenery, which is increasingly dramatic as the path heads north, walkers may see some of Scotland's rarer **wildlife**, including red deer, feral goats and, soaring over the highest peaks, golden eagles.

Passing through the lowlands north of Glasgow, the route runs along the eastern shores of Loch Lomond, over the Highland Boundary Fault Line, then round Crianlarich, crossing open heather moorland across the **Rannoch Moor** wilderness area. It passes close to **Glen Coe** (see page 191) before reaching **Fort William** (see page 180). Apart from a stretch between Loch Lomond and Bridge of Orchy, when the path is within earshot of the main road, this is wild, remote country: north of Rowardennan on Loch Lomond, the landscape is increasingly exposed, and you should be well prepared for changeable weather.

TACKLING THE ROUTE

Though this is emphatically not the most strenuous of Britain's long-distance walks – it passes between lofty mountain peaks, rather than over them – a moderate degree of fitness is required as there are some steep ascents. If you're looking for an added challenge, you could work a climb of Ben Lomond or Ben Nevis into your schedule. You might choose to walk individual sections of the Way (the eight-mile climb from Glen Coe up the Devil's Staircase is particularly spectacular), but to tackle the whole thing you need to set aside at least seven days; avoid a Saturday start from Milngavie and you'll be less likely to be walking with hordes of people, and there'll be less pressure on accommodation. Most walkers tackle the route from south to north, and manage between ten and fourteen miles a day, staying at hotels, B&Bs and bunkhouses en route. Camping is permitted at recognized sites.

INFORMATION

The West Highland Way Official Guide Includes a foldout map as well as descriptions of the route, with detailed cultural, historical, archeological and wildlife information. Costs £16.99.

Official website ⓦ westhighlandway.org. Gives further details about the Way, including a comprehensive accommodation list. The site also has links to tour companies and transport providers, who can take your luggage from one stopping point to the next.

Loch Lomond affording amazing views of both the Highlands and Lowlands. The well-signposted route to the summit and back from Rowardennan takes five to six hours; the alternative Ptarmigan Ridge route is only for well-equipped and fit walkers.

Inversnaid

Only walkers can continue up the lochside beyond Rowardennan, where the only settlement is seven miles north at **INVERSNAID**, made famous by a poem of the same name by Gerard Manley Hopkins about a frothing waterfall nearby ("This darksome burn, horseback brown/His rollrock highroad roaring down…").

2

By car or bus The dead-end B837 from Drymen will take you halfway up the east bank to Rowardennan, as far as you can get by car or bus (#309 from Balloch and Drymen runs to Balmaha every 2hr), while the West Highland Way sticks close to the shores for the entire length of the loch.

Ferry to Rowardennan Passenger ferries (Easter–Sept 2 daily; ☎ 01301 702356, ⓦ cruiselochlomond.co.uk) cross from Tarbert, on the west shore.

Ferry to Inversnaid It's also possible to get to or from

Inversnaid by ferry (£4 one-way/£5 return), which crosses from Inveruglas, directly opposite on the western shore. You'll have to phone the *Inversnaid Hotel* (☎ 01887 386223) to make arrangements.

National Park Centre The national park visitor centre is located beside the large car park in Balmaha (April–Sept daily 9.30am–4pm; ☎ 01389 722600, ⓦ lochlomond-trossachs.org), though it's more geared to illustrating the region's natural history than offering information.

ACCOMMODATION AND EATING

BALMAHA

Balmaha B&B and Bunkhouse Balmaha House, Main St ☎ 01360 870218, ⓦ balmaha-bunkhouse.co.uk. Welcoming West Highland Way accommodation located on the loch shore, with two B&B rooms, a well-equipped bunkhouse (£25/bed including continental breakfast) and a self-catering chalet sleeping four (£90) which overlooks the bay. **£80**

Oak Tree Inn ☎ 01360 870357, ⓦ theoaktreeinn.co.uk. Set back from the boatyard, this upscale inn offers smartly furnished doubles as well as quad rooms and a couple of two-person pods There's also a convivial pub, where food is served all day, plus the neighbouring *St Mocha* café, which, alongside superb coffee and ice cream, functions as a pop-up fish and chip shop on Friday and Saturday evenings. Café daily 9am–5pm. Doubles **£90**; pods **£120**

ROWARDENNAN

Cashel 3 miles south of Rowardennan ☎ 01360 870234, ⓦ campingintheforest.co.uk. A lovely, secluded Forestry Commission campsite on the loch shore with a decent loo block. Campers can launch craft from here onto the loch, and Ben Lomond is just four miles away. April–Oct. Per pitch **£15.50**

Clansman Bar Rowardennan Hotel, on the lake shore ☎ 01360 870273, ⓦ rowardennanhotel.co.uk. Nightlife in the area centres on this hotel's bar, which features open fires, a beer garden and weekend live music. Closed weekdays out of season. Mon–Fri 11am–9pm, Sat 11am–11pm, Sun 11am–10pm.

Rowardennan Lodge Youth Hostel A 15min walk north of the Rowardennan Hotel ☎ 01360 870259, ⓦ hostellingscotland.org.uk. A wonderfully situated SYHA hostel in a classic turreted Scots Baronial lodge with lawns running down to the shore. Four- to eight-bed dorms plus twins and a double. Dorms **£22**; doubles **£55**.

The western shore

Despite the roar of traffic hurtling along the A82, the **west bank** of Loch Lomond is an undeniably beautiful stretch of water.

Luss

LUSS is the prettiest village in the region, with its prim, identical sandstone and slate cottages garlanded in rambling roses, and its narrow sand-and-pebble strand, where there are plentiful opportunities for water-bound activities. However, its charms are no secret, and its streets and beach can become very crowded in summer. If you want to escape the hordes, pop into the parish **church**, which is a haven of peace and has a lovely ceiling made from Scots-pine rafters and some fine Victorian stained-glass windows, or make for the pier from where a number of cruises depart.

Tarbet and Inverarnan

Ten miles north of attractive Luss is the small settlement of **TARBET**, where the West Highland **train** reaches the shoreline. North of Tarbet, the A82 turns back into the narrow, winding road of old, making for slower but much more interesting driving. There's one more **train station** on Loch Lomond at Ardlui, at the mountain-framed head of the loch, but most travellers continue a couple of miles further north to **INVERARNAN**, where the *Drovers Inn* is arguably the most idiosyncratic **hotel** in Scotland.

ARRIVAL AND DEPARTURE

THE WESTERN SHORE

By bus Luss, Tarbet and Inverarnan are all stops on the Fort William–Glasgow bus route (5 daily). Journey times from Luss are 10min to Tarbet, 30min to Inverarnan, 2hr to Fort William and 1hr to Glasgow.

By ferry Between May and September, Sweeney's Cruise Co. (☎01389 752376, ⊛sweeneyscruisesco.com) operates

waterbus services between Luss and Balhama on the eastern shore (4–5 daily; 30min; £8.50 single/£12 return), and Luss and Balloch (2–3 daily; 1hr; £14 single/£20 return). From Tarbet there are ferries to Inversnaid (May–Oct 5 daily; 30min) and to the youth hostel in Rowardennan (1 daily; 45min).

ACTIVITIES AND TOURS

Bike hire and beach activities In Luss bikes can be rented (£14 for 2hr/£18 for 4hr) from Loch Lomond Leisure (☎0333 577 0715, ⊛lochlomond-scotland.com), who also have rowing and pedal boats (£25/30min), kayaks (singles and twins) and paddleboards (£20/hr) for hire.

Boat tours At Tarbet's pier over the road from the prominent *Tarbet Hotel* you can hop on an hour-long loch cruise run by Cruise Loch Lomond (☎01301 702356, ⊛cruiselochlomond.co.uk).

2

ACCOMMODATION AND EATING

LUSS

Coach House Loch Lomond Trading Company Limited ☎01436 860341. A spruce and lively tearoom serving a range of teas, cakes, ciabattas, Orkney ice cream and its own take on haggis. Daily 10am–5pm.

Loch Lomond Arms Main Road ☎01436 860420, ⊛lochlomondarmshotel.com. Graceful seventeenth-century coaching inn possessing a stock of handsome-looking rooms named after Scottish clans and furnished in muted tartan colours; some have loch views. The warming bar/restaurant is a great spot to chow down on the likes of haggis and black pudding scotch egg, and venison pie with horseradish mash (£14). **£150**

★ **Luss Seafood Bar** Pier Rd ☎01436 860341, ⊛luss-seafoodbar.com. Super-fresh seafood (langoustines,

Shetland mussels, Cumbrae oysters), plus a variety of fish products smoked in the neighbouring smokehouse, such as trout pate and salmon rillettes (£8), all served up on an outdoor terrace or in the chic modern bar. April–Oct Wed–Sun 10am–5pm.

INVERARNAN

Drover's Inn By Ardlui, North Loch Lomond ☎01301 704234, ⊛droversinn.info. The bar features a roaring fire, barmen dressed in kilts, weary hillwalkers sipping pints and bearded musicians banging out folk songs. Down the creaking corridors, past moth-eaten stuffed animals, are a number of supposedly haunted and resolutely old-fashioned rooms. Mon–Thurs & Sun 11am–11pm, Fri & Sat 11am–1am. **£94**

Crianlarich and Tyndrum

CRIANLARICH, some eight miles north of the head of Loch Lomond, is an important staging post on various transport routes, including the West Highland Railway which divides here, one branch heading due west towards Oban, the other continuing north over Rannoch Moor to Fort William. The West Highland Way long-distance footpath (see page 131) also trogs past. Otherwise, there's little reason to stop here, unless you're keen on tackling some of the steep-sided hills that rise up from the glen.

Five miles further north from here on the A82/A85, the village of **TYNDRUM** owes its existence to a minor (and very short-lived) nineteenth-century gold rush, but today supports little more than a busy service station and several characterless hotels.

ARRIVAL AND DEPARTURE

CRIANLARICH AND TYNDRUM

By train Crianlarich is well served by regular trains. Tyndrum has two train stations: the upper station serves the scenic West Highland Line, while the lower has services to and from Crianlarich and the south.

Destinations from Crianlarich Fort William (3–4 daily Mon–Sat, 1–3 on Sun; 1hr 50min); Glasgow Queen Street (6–8 daily Mon–Sat, 1–3 on Sun; 1hr 50min); Oban (3–4 daily Mon–Sat, 1–3 on Sun; 1hr 15min).

Destinations from Tyndrum Fort William (upper station 3–4 daily; 1hr 35min); Crianlarich (lower station 5 daily; 8 min); Glasgow Queen Street (lower station 5 daily Mon–Sat, 1 on Sun; 2hr 5min).

By car At Tyndrum the road divides, with the A85 heading west to Oban, and the A82 heading for Fort William via Glen Coe.

2

By The Way Hostel and Campsite Lower Station Rd, Tyndrum ☎ 01838 400333, ⊛ tyndrumbytheway.com. Right beside Tyndrum Lower railway station is a good campsite and small purpose-built bunkhouse; the cute wooden "hobbit houses" (£55) in the grounds sleep four and are self-catering. Hostel per person £20; camping per person £8

Real Food Café Main St, Tyndrum ☎ 01838 400 235, ⊛ therealfoodcafe.com. For a refreshingly different roadside dining experience, it's well worth trying the airy café on the main road serving fresh, fast food that's locally sourced and cooked to order, including fish and chips from £5.95; they've got terrific coffee and cakes too. April–Oct daily 7.30am–9pm.

The Trossachs

Often described as the Highlands in miniature, the **Trossachs** area boasts a magnificent diversity of scenery, with distinctive peaks, silvery lochs and mysterious, forest-covered slopes. It is country ripe for stirring tales of brave kilted clansmen, a role fulfilled by Rob Roy Macgregor, the seventeenth-century outlaw whose name seems to attach to every second waterfall, cave and barely discernible path. Strictly speaking, the name "Trossachs", normally translated as either "bristly country" or "crossing place", originally referred only to the wooded glen between **Loch Katrine** and Loch Achray, but today it is usually taken as being the whole area from **Callander** right up to the eastern banks of Loch Lomond, with which it has been grouped as one of Scotland's national parks.

The Trossachs' high tourist profile was largely attributable in the early days to Sir Walter Scott, whose novels *Lady of the Lake* and *Rob Roy* were set in and around the area. According to one contemporaneous account, after Scott's *Lady of the Lake* was published in 1810, the number of carriages passing Loch Katrine rose from fifty the previous year to 270. Since then, neither the popularity nor beauty of the region has waned, and in high season the place is jam-packed with coaches full of tourists as well as walkers and mountain-bikers taking advantage of the easily accessed scenery. Autumn is a better time to come, when the hills are blanketed in rich, rusty colours and the crowds are thinner. In terms of where to stay, **Aberfoyle** has a rather dowdy air while **Callander** feels somewhat overrun, and you're often better off seeking out one of the guesthouses or B&Bs tucked away in secluded corners of the region.

Aberfoyle

Each summer the sleepy little town of **ABERFOYLE**, twenty miles west of Stirling, dusts itself down for its annual influx of tourists. Though of little appeal itself, Aberfoyle's position in the heart of the Trossachs is ideal, with **Loch Ard Forest** and **Queen Elizabeth Forest Park** stretching across to Ben Lomond and Loch Lomond to the west, the long curve of Loch Katrine and Ben Venue to the northwest, and Ben Ledi to the northeast. Don't come here for lively nightlife or entertainment, but for a good, healthy blast of the outdoors.

Fairy Knowe

From Aberfoyle you might like to wander north of the village to **Doon Hill**: cross the bridge over the Forth, continue past the cemetery and then follow signs to the **Fairy Knowe** (knoll). A toadstool marker points you through oak and holly trees to the summit of the Knowe where there is a pine tree said to contain the unquiet spirit of the Reverend Robert Kirk, who studied local fairy lore and published his enquiries in *The Secret Commonwealth* (1691). Legend has it that, as punishment for disclosing supernatural secrets, he was forcibly removed to fairyland where he has languished ever since, although his mortal remains can be found in the nearby graveyard. This short walk is best at dusk, when it's at its most atmospheric.

By bus Aberfoyle is served by five buses (Mon–Sat) from/ to Stirling (45min) plus a seasonal service (late June to mid-Oct 4 daily except Wed) with Callander (25min) and Port of Menteith (10min); buses pull into the car park on Main St.

Tourist office The very helpful tourist office on Main St (April–Oct daily 10am–5pm; Nov–March daily 10am–4pm; ☎ 01877 381221) has full details of local accommodation, sights and outdoor activities.

ACCOMMODATION

Trossachs Holiday Park ☎ 01877 382614, ⊚ trossachs holidays.co.uk. This excellent family-run forty-acre park is fringed by oak and bluebell woods. Facilities include laundry, shop, games rooms and play park, and there are also bikes for rent. Per pitch **£24.50**

Lake of Menteith

About 4 miles east of Aberfoyle towards Doune

The **Lake of Menteith** is Scotland's premier fly-fishing centre, and its only lake (as opposed to loch), so named due to a historic mix-up with the word *laigh*, Scots for "low-lying ground", which applied to the whole area. Abundant with pike and brown and rainbow trout, the lake attracts anglers from all over the world, especially during the National Fly Fishing Championships each May or June. But if fishing's not your thing, there are also some secluded spots along the shore for picnics and swims. To rent fishing gear contact the Lake of Menteith Fisheries (☎ 01877 385664, ⊚ menteith-fisheries.co.uk; mid-March to Mid-Nov).

Island of Inchmahome

Lake of Menteith • Daily: April–Sept 10am–4.30pm; Oct 10am–3.30pm • £9 including ferry; HES • ⊚ historicenvironment.scot

From the northern shore of the lake, you can take a little ferry out to the **Island of Inchmahome** to explore the lovely, ruined Augustinian abbey. Founded in 1238, **Inchmahome Priory** is the most beautiful island monastery in Scotland, its remains rising tall and graceful above the trees. The masons employed to build the priory are thought to be those who built Dunblane Cathedral; certainly the western entrance there resembles that at Inchmahome. The nave of the church is roofless, but in the choir are preserved the graves of important families from the surrounding area. Most touching is a late thirteenth-century double effigy depicting Walter, the first Stewart earl of Menteith, and his countess, Mary, who, feet resting on lion-like animals, turn towards each other and embrace.

Also buried here is the adventurer and scholar Robert Bontine Cunninghame Graham, once a pal of Buffalo Bill and Joseph Conrad, and first president of the National Party of Scotland. Five-year-old Mary, Queen of Scots, was hidden at Inchmahome in 1547 before being taken to France, and there's a formal garden in the west of the island, known as Queen Mary's Bower, where legend has it she played. Traces remain of an orchard planted by the monks, but the island is thick now with oak, ash and Spanish chestnut. Visible on a nearby but inaccessible islet is the ruined castle of **Inchtalla**, the home of the earls of Menteith in the sixteenth and seventeenth centuries.

Lake of Menteith Hotel Port of Menteith ☎ 01877 385258, ⊚ lake-hotel.com. A beautiful place to stay, with an idyllic waterfront setting next to Port of Menteith's Victorian Gothic parish church. The rooms are as plush as you'd expect at this price and it also has a classy restaurant. **£150**

Queen Elizabeth Forest

The Lodge visitor centre Daily: Jan & Feb 10am–3pm; March–April & Oct–Dec 10am–4pm; May–June & Sept 10am–5pm; July & Aug 10am–6pm • Car park £3 • ☎ 01877 382258, ⊚ forestryandland.gov.scot

2

CRUISES ON LOCH KATRINE

The elegant Victorian **passenger steamer**, the SS *Sir Walter Scott* (April–Oct 4 daily; £18 return; ☎01877 376315, ⓦlochkatrine.com), has been plying the waters of Loch Katrine since 1900, chugging up to the wild country of Glengyle. It makes various **cruises** each day, one of which (the two hour sailing departing at 10.30am) makes a brief stop at Stronachlachar; the shorter hour-long cruises (£15 return) don't make any stops. The much smaller, and far less glamorous, *Lady of the Lake* cruiser makes similar trips but is cheaper (£15.50/2hr, £12.50/1hr). A popular combination is to rent a bike from the Katrinewheelz hut by the pier (£15/4hr, £20/ day; ☎01877 376366, ⓦkatrinewheelz.co.uk), take the steamer up to Stronachlachar, where the waterside *Pier Café* is an excellent place for refreshments, then **cycle** back by way of the road around the north side of the loch.

North of Aberfoyle, the A821 road to Loch Katrine winds its way into the **Queen Elizabeth Forest**, snaking up **Duke's Pass** (so-called because it once belonged to the duke of Montrose). You can walk or drive the short distance from Aberfoyle to the park's excellent **Lodge visitor centre** at David Marshall Lodge, where you can pick up maps of the walks and cycle routes in the forest, get background information on the area's flora and fauna or settle into the **café** with its splendid views out over the tree tops.

The only road in the forest open to cars is the **Achray Forest Drive**, just under two miles further on from the centre, which leads through the park and along the western shore of **Loch Drunkie** before rejoining the main road.

Adjacent to the The Lodge is the **Go Ape adventure course** (April–Oct daily 9am–5pm; Feb & March Sat & Sun 9am–5pm; £33 adults, £25 ages 10–15; ☎0845 094 9032, ⓦgoape.co.uk), which involves an extended series of 40ft-high rope bridges, Tarzan swings and high-wire slides through the forest.

Loch Katrine, Brig o'Turk and Loch Venachar

Heading down the northern side of the Duke's Pass, you come first to **Loch Achray**, tucked under Ben A'an. Look out across the loch for the small **Callander Kirk** in a lovely setting alone on a promontory. At the head of the loch a road follows the short distance through to the southern end of **Loch Katrine** at the foot of Ben Venue (2370ft). By far the best way to appreciate this atmospheric lake is to take a cruise (see box). From Loch Katrine the A821 heads due east past the tiny village of **Brig o'Turk**, before continuing along the shores of **Loch Venachar**, where *Venacher Lochside* houses an attractive café and a fishing centre offering boat rental and fly-fishing tuition.

ACCOMMODATION AND EATING — BRIG O'TURK AND LOCH KATRINE

★ **Byre Inn** Just east of Brig o'Turk ☎01877 376292, ⓦbyreinn.co.uk. A tiny country pub and classy restaurant offering mains such as fillet of cod for £10.95 and set in an old stone barn with wooden pews; it's the starting point for waymarked walks to lochs Achray, Drunkie and Venachar. There's a boules/petanque piste outside. Daily 9am–late; food served 9am–3pm & 5.30–8pm.

★ **Loch Katrine Eco Lodges** Trossachs Pier Loch Katrine ☎01877 376315, ⓦlochkatrine,com. Overlooking the water are these eight brilliantly-designed lodges, variously sleeping two- to four people, and equipped with kitchenette, toilet/shower (except for two lodges), underfloor heating and outside decking. There are also a few pitches here for tents (£14/pitch and two adults). The onsite *Steamship Café* is open for breakfast from 9am. Two-night minimum stay. Per night **£90**

Callander and around

CALLANDER, on the eastern edge of the Trossachs, sits on the banks of the River Teith at the southern end of the **Pass of Leny**, one of the key routes into the Highlands. Significantly larger than Aberfoyle, it suffers in high season for being right on the main tourist trail from Stirling through to the west Highlands. Callander first came to fame during the "Scottish Enlightenment" of the eighteenth and nineteenth centuries, with the glowing reports of the Trossachs given by Sir Walter Scott and William Wordsworth. Development was given a further boost when Queen Victoria chose to visit, and then by the arrival of the train line – long since closed – in the 1860s. Tourists have arrived in throngs ever since, as the plethora of restaurants, tearooms, gift shops and shops selling woollens and crafts testifies.

North of Callander, you can walk or ride the scenic six-mile Callander to Strathyre (Route 7) Cycleway, which forms part of the network of cycleways between the Highlands and Glasgow. The route is based on the old Caledonian train line to Oban, which closed in 1965, and runs along the western side of Loch Lubnaig.

2

ARRIVAL AND INFORMATION
CALLANDER AND AROUND

By bus Callander has bus connections with Loch Katrine (late June to mid-Oct 4 daily Thurs–Tues; 55min).

Tourist office The regional Loch Lomond and Trossachs visitor centre is at 52 Main St (☎01877 330342; daily 10am–5pm).

ACCOMMODATION

Arden House Bracklinn Rd ☎01877 330235, ⓦarden house.org.uk. A grand Victorian guesthouse in its own gardens with three period-furnished rooms and good views and woodland walks from the back door. They've even got a snooker room and putting green. There's also a self-catering studio in the grounds (from £50). April–Oct. **£100**

Callander Hostel 6 Bridgend ☎01877 331465, ⓦcallanderhostel.co.uk. Swish new hostel in a distinctive timbered building, with mountain views, a bistro and self-catering facilities, a BBQ area and bike storage. Dorms **£19**; doubles **£60**

Callander Meadows 24 Main St ☎01877 330181, ⓦcallandermeadows.co.uk. Centrally located accommodation in an attractive townhouse with three comfortable en-suite rooms and a very good restaurant. **£95**

Roman Camp Country House Hotel 182 Main St ☎01877 330003, ⓦromancamphotel.co.uk. The town's most upmarket, albeit overpriced, option is this romantic, turreted seventeenth-century hunting lodge situated in riverside gardens; you could also spend hours enjoying the rambling public areas, like the library, lounge and conservatory with a drink or two. **£160**

EATING AND DRINKING

Lade Inn Kilmahog, 1 mile west of Callander ☎01877 330152, ⓦtheladeinn.com. Pub food such as beer-battered chicken goujons (£13) can be had at this convivial inn where the owners are keen on real ales; an on-site shop sells bottled beers. Mon–Thurs noon–11pm, Fri & Sat noon–1am, Sun 12.30–10.30pm; food served noon–9pm.

★**Mhor Fish** 75–77 Main St ☎01877 330213, ⓦmhorfish.net. Sit-down or takeaway restaurant with an impressive sustainable fish policy offering delicious meals like seafood chowder (£8.50) and salt and pepper squid alongside your more traditional fish and chip suppers. Licenced too. Mid-Feb to Oct Tues–Sun noon–9pm; Nov to mid-Feb Wed–Sun same times.

Balquhidder

North of Loch Lubnaig is tiny **BALQUHIDDER**, most famous as the site of the **grave of Rob Roy** (see page 138), which is just in front of the ruined church. Framed by a low black iron fence, his grave is marked by a rough stone carved with a sword, cross and a man with a dog. Buried here too is his wife, Mary, and two sons, Coll and Robert.

ACCOMMODATION AND EATING
BALQUHIDDER

MHOR 84 Balquhidder Lochearnhead ☎01877 384646, ⓦmhor84.net. This buzzy place offers a selection of dazzling all-white rooms (including a family room with bunk) offset with subtle splashes of colour (yellow-framed mirrors, mustard-coloured throws). In addition there's a super-cool restaurant/café/bar serving scrummy breakfasts, lunches and dinners (mains £12–16). Live

folk music on Thursdays. Mon–Thurs 8am–11pm, Fri & Sat 11am–midnight, Sun 12.30pm–11pm; food served 8am–9pm. **£90**

★**Monachyle Mhor** Loch Voil, 6 miles west of Balquidder ☎01877 384622, ⓦmonachylemhor.net. This eighteenth-century farmhouse features chic rooms and a terrific restaurant with much of the food sourced

2

ROB ROY

A member of the outlawed Macgregor clan, **Rob Roy** (meaning "Red Robert" in Gaelic) was born in 1671 in Glengyle, just north of Loch Katrine, and lived for some time as a respectable cattle farmer and trader, supported by the powerful duke of Montrose. In 1712, finding himself in a tight spot when a cattle deal fell through, Rob Roy absconded with £1000, some of it belonging to the duke. He took to the hills to live as a brigand, his feud with Montrose escalating after the duke repossessed Rob Roy's land and drove his wife from their house. He was present at the Battle of Sheriffmuir during the Jacobite uprising of 1715, ostensibly supporting the Jacobites but probably as an opportunist: the chaos would have made cattle-raiding easier. Eventually captured and sentenced to transportation, Rob Roy was pardoned and returned to **Balquhidder** (see page 137), northeast of Glengyle, where he remained until his death in 1734.

Rob Roy's status as a local hero in the mould of Robin Hood should be tempered with the fact that he was without doubt a bandit and blackmailer. His life has been much romanticized, from Sir Walter Scott's 1818 novel *Rob Roy* to the 1995 film starring Liam Neeson, although the tale does serve well to dramatize the clash between the doomed clan culture of the Gaelic-speaking Highlanders and the organized feudal culture of lowland Scots, which effectively ended with the defeat of the Jacobites at Culloden in 1746. His **grave** in Balquhidder, a simple affair behind the ruined church, is mercifully free of the tartan trappings that plague parts of the Trossachs, predictably dubbed "Rob Roy Country" by the tourist board.

from the family's farm and bakery; expect sophisticated plates like Isle of Mull scallops with salsify and samphire, and Balquhidder roe deer with bramble vinaigrette (book ahead; set dinner £65). Lovely, tranquil views over Loch Voil. Daily noon–2pm & 6.45–9pm. <u>£195</u>

Perthshire

Genteel **Perthshire** is, in many ways, the epitome of well-groomed rural Scotland. First settled over eight thousand years ago, it was occupied by the Romans and then the Picts before Celtic missionaries established themselves, enjoying the amenable climate, fertile soil and ideal location for defence and trade. North and west of the county town of Perth, there are some magnificent landscapes to be discovered – snowcapped peaks falling away to forested slopes and long, deep lochs – topography that inevitably controls transport routes, influences the weather and tolerates little development. The various mountains, woods and lochs provide terrific walking and watersports, particularly through the **Strath Tay** area, dominated by Scotland's longest river, the **Tay**, which flows from **Loch Tay** past the attractive towns of **Dunkeld** and **Aberfeldy**. Further north, the countryside of **Highland Perthshire** becomes more sparsely populated and more spectacular, especially around the towns of **Pitlochry** and **Blair Atholl** and the wild expanses of **Rannoch Moor** to the west.

Dunkeld

DUNKELD, twelve miles north of Perth on the A9, was proclaimed Scotland's ecclesiastical capital by Kenneth MacAlpine in 850. Its position at the southern boundary of the Grampian Mountains made it a favoured meeting place for Highland and Lowland cultures, and the town is one of the area's most pleasant communities, with handsome whitewashed houses, appealing arts and crafts shops, and a charming cathedral.

Dunkeld cathedral

Cathedral St • Daily: April–Sept 10am–5.30pm; Oct–March 10am–4pm • Free • ☎ 01350 727249, ⦿ dunkeldcathedral.org.uk

Dunkeld's partly ruined **cathedral** is on the northern side of town, in an idyllic setting amid lawns and trees on the east bank of the Tay. As early as 570, missionaries from Iona built a wattle monastery here; construction on the current building began in the early twelfth century and continued throughout the next two hundred years, but it was more or less ruined at the time of the Reformation. The present structure consists of the fourteenth-century choir and the fifteenth-century nave; the choir, restored in 1600 (and several times since), now serves as the parish church, while the nave remains roofless apart from the clock tower. Inside, look out for the effigy of the **Wolf of Badenoch**, Robert II's son, who was born in 1343. The Wolf acquired his name and notoriety when, after being excommunicated for leaving his wife, he took his revenge by burning the towns of Forres and Elgin, and sacking the latter's cathedral.

ARRIVAL AND DEPARTURE   DUNKELD

By train The nearest train station is in nearby Birnam.
By bus Buses travelling to and from Perth (every 30min;

40min) and Inverness (5 daily; 2hr 30min) stop opposite the *Royal Dunkeld Hotel* on Atholl St, Dunkeld.

ACCOMMODATION, EATING AND DRINKING

The Bridge 10 Bridge St ☎ 01350 727068, ⓦ thebridge-bnb-dunkeld.co.uk. A soothingly decorated and extremely comfortable Georgian home located in the heart of Dunkeld with four sweet rooms. The hosts are warmly welcoming, and breakfast comes with local smoked salmon. £80

The Scottish Deli 1 Atholl St ☎ 01350 728028, ⓦ scottish-deli.com. Fill up on gourmet delights including artisan breads at this well-stocked deli, which, in the evening, morphs into a restaurant-cum-wine bar serving delicious Scottish tapas dishes such as Dunkeld smoked

salmon with oatcakes and dill mayonnaise, as well as a selection of cheese and meat boards. Daily 9.30am–6pm & 6.30–10.30pm.

★ **The Taybank** Tay Terrace ☎ 01350 727340, ⓦ the taybankdunkeld.com. A riverside beacon for music fans, who come for the regular live sessions in the convivial bar. It's also a good, simple place to eat – they serve Scottish specialities such as stovies, made from beef and potatoes, for £7.50. Mon–Thurs 11am–11pm, Fri & Sat 11am–midnight, Sun noon–11pm.

Birnam

Dunkeld is linked to its sister community, **BIRNAM**, by Thomas Telford's seven-arched bridge of 1809. This little village has a place in history thanks to Shakespeare, for it was on Dunsinane Hill, to the southeast of the village, that Macbeth declared: "I will not be afraid of death and bane/Till Birnam Forest come to Dunsinane." The **Birnam Oak**, a gnarly old character propped up by crutches which can be seen on the waymarked riverside walk, is inevitably claimed to be a survivor of the infamous mobile forest.

Birnam Arts

Station Rd • Daily 10am–4.30pm • £4 • ☎ 01350 727674, ⓦ birnamarts.com

Just like Shakespeare, children's author Beatrix Potter drew inspiration from the Birnam area, recalling her childhood holidays here when penning the Peter Rabbit stories. A Potter-themed exhibition and garden can be found in impressive **Birnam Arts**, a lively theatre, café and arts and community centre.

The Hermitage

Dunkeld and Birnam are surrounded by some lovely countryside, both along the banks of the Tay and in the deep surrounding forest. One of the most rewarding walks is the mile and a half from Birnam to **The Hermitage**, set in a grandly wooded gorge of the plunging River Braan. Here you'll find a pretty eighteenth-century folly, also known as Ossian's Hall, which was once mirrored to reflect the water – the mirrors were smashed by Victorian vandals and the folly was more tamely restored. The hall, appealing yet incongruous in its splendid setting, neatly frames a dramatic waterfall.

Loch of the Lowes

Just off the A923 • Visitor centre: March–Oct daily 10.30am–5pm; Nov–Feb Fri–Sun 10.30am–4pm • £4.50 • ☎ 01350 727337

Two miles east of Dunkeld, the **Loch of the Lowes** is a nature reserve that offers a rare chance to see breeding **ospreys**, beavers, red squirrels and a wide variety of wildfowl; the visitor centre has video-relay screens and will point you in the direction of the best vantage points.

ARRIVAL AND DEPARTURE   BIRNAM

By train The Dunkeld and Birnam train station, just south of the A9 in Birnam, is a stop on services to Inverness (8 daily; 1hr 50min) and Perth (10 daily; 20min).

By bus Direct bus services to Inverness (5 daily; 2hr 30min) and Perth (every 30min; 40min) leave from opposite the *Birnam Hotel* on Perth Rd.

ACCOMMODATION

The Merryburn Station Rd ☎ 01350 727216, ⓦ merry burn.co.uk. This old ironmonger's shop, whose many original Victorian features are still intact, has been converted into a small and inviting guesthouse, just across from Birnam Arts. Its five beautifully appointed rooms are complemented by a warming lounge bar. **£98**

Aberfeldy and around

From Dunkeld the A9 runs north alongside the Tay for eight miles to Ballinluig, a tiny village marking the turn-off along the A827 to **ABERFELDY**, a prosperous settlement of large stone houses that acts as a service centre for the wider Loch Tay area. Aberfeldy sits at the point where the Urlar Burn – lined by the silver birch trees celebrated by Robert Burns in his poem *The Birks of Aberfeldy* – flows into the River Tay.

Wade's Bridge

In Aberfeldy the Tay is spanned by the humpbacked, four-arch **Wade's Bridge**, built by General Wade in 1733 during his efforts to control the unrest in the Highlands, and one of the general's more impressive pieces of work. Overlooking the bridge from the south end is the **Black Watch Monument**, depicting a pensive, kilted soldier; it was erected in 1887 to commemorate the first muster of the Highland regiment gathered as a peacekeeping force by Wade in 1740.

Dewar's World of Whisky

Half a mile east of Aberfeldy, just off the A827 • April–Oct Mon–Sat 10am–6pm, Sun noon–4pm; Nov–March Mon–Sat 10am–4pm • Tours from £10.50 • ☎ 01887 822010, ⓦ dewars.com

The main set-piece attraction in Aberfeldy is **Dewar's World of Whisky**, at the Aberfeldy Distillery, which puts on an impressive show of describing the process of making blended whisky. If a regular tour (£10.50) doesn't satisfy, there's a **Connoisseur Tour** (£28) available for real aficionados, giving a more in-depth look around the distillery and a chance to taste (or "nose") the whisky at different stages in its life. Tour tickets also include entry to the **Heritage Museum**, which relays the history of the Dewar family and the distillery, which began production in 1898.

Castle Menzies

1 mile west of Aberfeldy, across Wade's Bridge • April–Oct Mon–Sat 10.30am–5pm, Sun 2–5pm • £7 • ☎ 01887 820982, ⓦ castlemenzies.org

West of Aberfeldy, **Castle Menzies** is an imposing, Z-shaped, sixteenth-century tower house, which until the middle of the last century was the chief seat of the Clan Menzies (pronounced "Ming-iss"). With the demise of the line, the castle was taken over by the Menzies Clan Society, which since 1971 has been involved in the lengthy process of restoring it. Much of the interior is on view, and most of it is refreshingly free of fixtures and fittings, displaying an austerity that is much more true to medieval life than many grander, furnished castles elsewhere in the country.

Highland Safaris

2 miles west of Aberfeldy, across Wade's Bridge • March–Oct daily 9am–5pm; Nov–Feb Tues–Sun 9am–5pm • Red Deer Centre £10, safaris from £45 • ☎ 01887 820071, ⓦ highlandsafaris.net

A mile or so further along the B346 from Castle Menzies, near the hamlet with the unfortunate name of Dull (twinned with Boring, Oregon, USA), is **Highland Safaris**, an excellent outfit offering a range of Land Rover trips into the heather-clad hills nearby in search of eagles, red deer and grouse. If you don't have time to partake in a safari, which range from a ninety-minute Forest Safari to a four-hour Mountain Safari Trek, you can learn more about, and feed, red deer in the paddock at the Red Deer Centre by reception. Here too you can try your hand at gold panning (£5); the fabulous on-site Safari Café serves hot lunches.

2

ARRIVAL AND DEPARTURE

ABERFELDY AND AROUND

By bus Buses stop on Chapel St in Aberfeldy, near the junction with Dunkeld St (the A827), with regular services to Perth (up to 12 daily; 1hr 25min).

ACCOMMODATION

Balnearn Guest House Crieff Rd ☎01887 820431 ⓦbalnearnhouse.co.uk. Stylish and unpretentious rooms close to the middle of town, with the added bonus of a guest lounge with log fire, drying room for your outdoor gear and homemade crepes for brekkie. **£80**

The Bunkhouse Glassie Farm, 3 miles from Aberfeldy along the winding track that starts near the footbridge ☎01887 820265, ⓦthebunkhouse.co.uk. The closest bunkhouse to Aberfeldy has small rooms that share simple showers, plus two self-catering kitchens and a communal area with magnificent views over the town. Groups only at weekends. Dorms **£19**

★ **Coshieville House** 5.5 miles west of Aberfeldy along the B846 ☎01887 830319, ⓦaberfeldybandb.com. In peaceful surroundings, this 300-year-old inn provides modern accommodation with nice touches like fresh flowers brightening up the communal areas; usefully, there's also a kitchen that guests can avail themselves of. **£84**

EATING AND DRINKING

Ailean Chraggan Across Wade's Bridge in Weem ☎01887 820346, ⓦchraggs.co.uk. This classy evening only (plus Sunday lunch) hotel restaurant offers a wonderful menu featuring the likes of venison haunch with black pudding and dark chocolate and raspberry jus (£19.50) as well as plenty of fishy mains. Mon–Sat 5–10.30pm, Sun noon–2.30pm & 5–10.30pm.

The Watermill Mill St ☎01887 822896, ⓦaberfeldy watermill.com. Aberfeldy isn't short of cafés, but the best bet for a good cup of coffee, a bowl of lunchtime soup (£5) or afternoon tea is this relaxed, superbly restored early nineteenth-century mill, with a pretty riverside garden. There's also an art gallery and inspiring bookshop. Mon–Sat 10am–5pm, Sun 11am–5pm.

Loch Tay

Aberfeldy grew up around a crossing point on the River Tay, which leaves it six miles adrift of **Loch Tay**, a fourteen-mile-long stretch of fresh water connecting the western and eastern Highlands. Rising steeply above the loch's northern edge is Ben Lawers, the tenth-highest peak in Scotland, whose mineral-rich slopes support plant life more commonly seen in the Alps or Arctic.

Kenmore

Guarding the northern end of Loch Tay is **KENMORE**, where whitewashed estate houses and well-tended gardens cluster around the gate to the extensive grounds of **Taymouth Castle**, built by the Campbells of Glenorchy in the early nineteenth century. The rocket-like eighteenth-century **church** contains an ancient "poor box" for donations and memorials to soldiers of the Black Watch Regiment.

Scottish Crannog Centre

Around half a mile from Kenmore, along the southern shore of the loch • April–Oct daily 10am–5.30pm • £10 • ☎01887 830583, ⓦcrannog.co.uk

The main attraction around Loch Tay is the **Scottish Crannog Centre**. Crannogs are Iron Age loch dwellings built on stilts over the water, with a gangway to the shore that could be lifted up to defy a hostile intruder, whether animal or human. Following

2

CLIMBING THE BEN LAWERS GROUP

Ordnance Survey Explorer map 378

Dominating the northern side of Loch Tay is moody **Ben Lawers** (3984ft), Perthshire's highest mountain; from the top there are incredible views towards both the Atlantic and the North Sea. The **ascent** – which shouldn't be tackled unless you're properly equipped for Scottish hillwalking (see page 42) – takes around three hours from the NTS car park, which you can reach by following a winding, hilly road off the A827.

The Ben Lawers range offers rich pickings for Munro-baggers, with nine hills over 3000ft in close proximity. The whole double-horseshoe-shaped ridge from Meall Greigh in the east to Meall a'Choire Leith in the northwest is too much for one day, though the eastern section from Meall Greigh (3284ft) to Beinn Ghlas (3619ft), taking in Ben Lawers, can be walked in eight to ten hours in good conditions. Standing on its own a little to the east is perhaps the prettiest of the lot, **Meall nan Tarmachan** ("The Hill of the Ptarmigan"); at 3427ft a less arduous but rewarding four-hour round-trip from the roadside, a mile or so further on from the car park.

---

underwater excavations in Loch Tay, the team here has superbly reconstructed an impressive crannog, and visitors can now walk out over the loch to the thatched wooden dwelling, complete with sheepskin rugs, wooden bowls and other evidence of how life was lived 2500 years ago. Back on dry land you can try a range of activities, from spinning yarn to making flour and starting fires.

ACCOMMODATION AND EATING   LOCH TAY

The Courtyard Just off the A827 in the centre of Kenmore ☎01887 830886, ⓦtaymouth.co.uk/restaurant. This modern brasserie beside the Kenmore golf course does a good Balti chicken (£12.95). There's also a deli/gift shop in the same complex (daily 9am–5pm). Daily 9am–late, last food orders 9pm.

Culdees Bunkhouse 4 miles along the loch's north shore in Fearnan ☎01887 830519, ⓦhostel-scotland. co.uk/hostels/culdees-bunkhouse.htm. Family-friendly bunkhouse and B&B accommodation on a spectacularly

located farm, where the emphasis is on permaculture and spiritual values. Also has a family room sleeping four (£23 per person, under-10s half price). Dorms **£18**

Kenmore Hotel On the village square ☎01887 830205, ⓦkenmorehotel.com. Reputedly Scotland's oldest inn (1752), this is by far the nicest place to stay in the area; as well as a decent stock of individually furnished rooms, there's a top draw restaurant and the Poet's Bar, which features what is believed to be a poem by Burns on the chimney breast. **£99**

Glen Lyon

North of the Ben Lawers range is **Glen Lyon** – at 34 miles long, the longest enclosed glen in Scotland – where, legend has it, the Celtic warrior Fingal built twelve castles. The narrow single-track road through the glen starts at **KELTNEYBURN**, near Kenmore, at the northern end of the loch, although a road does struggle over the hills to **Bridge of Balgie**, halfway down the glen. Either way, it's a long, winding journey.

Fortingall

A few miles from Keltneyburn, the village of **FORTINGALL** is little more than a handful of pretty thatched cottages, though locals make much of their 5000-year-old yew tree – believed (by them at least) to be the oldest living thing in Europe. The venerable tree can be found in the churchyard, with a timeline nearby listing some of the events the yew has lived through. One of these, bizarrely, is the birth of Pontius Pilate, reputedly the son of a Roman officer stationed near Fortingall.

ACCOMMODATION   GLEN LYON

Fortingall Hotel In the centre of Fortingall ☎01887 830367, ⓦfortingall.com. If you're taken by the peace and remoteness of Glen Lyon, you can stay at this attractive,

though pricey, ten-bedroom country house, which also has an excellent restaurant; it also organizes fishing and walking packages. **£190**

Killin

The mountains of **Breadalbane** (pronounced "bred-albin", from the Gaelic "braghaid Albin" meaning "high country of Scotland") loom over the southern end of Loch Tay. Glens Lochay and Dochart curve north and south respectively from the small town of **KILLIN**, right in the centre of which the River Dochart comes rushing down over the frothy **Falls of Dochart** before disgorging into Loch Tay. A short distance west of Killin the A827 meets the A85, linking the Trossachs with Crianlarich, an important waypoint on the roads to Oban, Fort William and the west coast. There's little to do in Killin itself, but it makes a convenient base for some of the area's best walks.

2

INFORMATION AND ACTIVITIES KILLIN

Tourist office On the ground floor of the old watermill by the falls (April–Oct daily 10am–4pm; ☎01567 820527, ⓦkillin.net).

Outdoor activities The helpful and enthusiastic Killin Outdoor Centre and Mountain Shop on Main St (daily 8.45am–5.45pm; ☎01567 820652, ⓦkillinoutdoor.co.uk) rents out mountain bikes (£20/4hr, £25/day), and both single and double canoes and kayaks (£20/hr).

ACCOMMODATION AND EATING

Bridge of Lochay Hotel Aberfeldy Rd ☎01567 820272, ⓦbridgeoflochayhotel.com. Traditional old whitewashed inn with twelve smart rooms (some dog-friendly) as well as a colourful restaurant serving above-average food like venison steak with wild mushrooms and redcurrant sauce (£17.95). Daily noon–9pm; food served noon–2pm & 6–8.30pm. £120

The Old Smiddy Main St ☎01567 820619, ⓦtheold smiddykillin.co.uk. Offers three neat B&B rooms near the centre of the town, two of which have views of the river and one which of which can accommodate a family of four; the room that doesn't overlook the river is cheaper (£50) The bistro-style café downstairs is a popular spot for cakes and ice creams. £60

Pitlochry

Just off the A9 and surrounded by mountains, **PITLOCHRY** is undoubtedly a useful place to find somewhere to stay or eat en route to or from the Highlands. However, there's little charm to be found on its main street, with crawling traffic and endless shops selling cut-price woollens and knobbly walking sticks to tourists, who use the town as a starting point for scenic hikes (see page 144). Far more appealing is the area south of the river, which is home to a renowned theatre and a serene botanical garden.

Explorers: the Scottish Plant Hunters Garden

Across the river from the town centre, near the theatre • April–Oct daily 10am–5pm • £4 • ☎01796 484600, ⓦwww.explorersgarden.com

If you want to escape the bustle of Pitlochry's main drag, it's worth having a wander around **Explorers: the Scottish Plant Hunters Garden**, a garden and forest area that pays tribute to Scottish botanists and collectors who roamed the world in the eighteenth and nineteenth centuries in search of new plant species. An amphitheatre in the grounds is sometimes used for outdoor performances.

Pitlochry Power Station and Dam

Armoury Road • Visitor Centre daily 9.30am–4.30pm • Free • ☎01796 484111, ⓦpitlochrydam.com

A short stroll upstream to the west of the theatre is the **Pitlochry Power Station and Dam**, a massive concrete wall that harnesses the water of artificial Loch Faskally, just north of the town, for hydroelectric power. Near the base of the dam there's a small observation cabin where you can take a peek at the underwater workings of Pitlochry's **salmon ladder**, a staircase of murky glass boxes through which you might see some nonplussed fish making their way upstream past the dam. An electronic counter shows how many of them have successfully completed the climb. You can learn more about the workings of the dam – one of nine built in the 1940 and 50s as part of the Tummel Valley Scheme – and the lifecycle of the salmon, in the excellent **visitor centre**, which also possesses a smart little café.

2

WALKS AROUND PITLOCHRY

BEN VRACKIE

Pitlochry is surrounded by good walking country. The biggest lure has to be **Ben Vrackie** (2733ft; *Ordnance Survey Explorer map 386*), which provides a stunning backdrop for the town, and deserves better than a straight up-and-down walk. However, the climb should only be attempted in settled weather conditions and if you're properly prepared (see page 42).

The direct route up the hill follows the course of the Moulin burn past the inn of the same name. Alternatively, a longer but much more rewarding circular route heads northwest out of Pitlochry, along the edge of Loch Faskally, then up the River Garry to go through the **Pass of Killiecrankie**. This is looked after by the NTS, which has a visitor centre (see page 145) providing background on the famous battle here. From the NTS centre follow the route past Old Faskally to meet the main track at Loch a'Choire. Alternatively, you can turn back here and loop around Loch Faskally instead.

BLACK SPOUT

A lovely, short hill walk from the south end of Pitlochry follows a path through oak forests along the banks of the **Black Spout** burn; when you emerge from the woods it's just a few hundred yards further uphill to the lovely Edradour Distillery (see below).

With parking available at the theatre, nearby, the dam makes a good starting point for a complete loop of the loch (around nine miles to the Pass of Killiecrankie and back).

Edradour Distillery

2.5 miles east of Pitlochry on the A924 • Mid-April–Oct Mon–Sat 10am–5pm, Nov–mid-April Mon–Fri 10am–4.30pm • £12 • ☎ 01796 472095, ⓦ edradour.com

The **Edradour Distillery** – Scotland's smallest – has an idyllic position tucked into the hills a couple of miles east of Pitlochry on the A924. Although the tour of the distillery itself isn't out of the ordinary, the lack of industrialization and the fact that the whole traditional process is done on-site give Edradour more personality than many of its rivals; indeed, if you only have time for one distillery tour in this region, make it this one.

ARRIVAL AND DEPARTURE   PITLOCHRY

By train Pitlochry is on the main train line to Inverness. The station is on Station Rd, just south of the centre. Destinations Inverness (every 1–2hr; 1hr 35min); Perth (every 1–2hr; 30min).

By bus Buses from/to Inverness (7 daily; 2hr 10min) and Perth (every 1–2hr; 40min) stop near the train station.

INFORMATION AND ACTIVITIES

Tourist office 22 Atholl Rd (April–June & Sept–Oct Mon–Sat 9.30am–5.30pm, Sun 10am–4pm; July & Aug Mon–Sat 9am–6pm, Sun 9.30am–5pm; Nov–March Mon–Sat 10am–4pm; ☎ 01796 472215). As the only office for some miles around, they have piles of information and also offer an accommodation booking service.

Bike rental For bike rental (£24/day), advice on local cycling routes, as well as general outdoor gear, try Escape Route, 3 Atholl Rd (Mon–Sat 9am–5.30pm, Sun 10am–5pm; ☎ 01796 473859, ⓦ escape-route.co.uk); they also have a repair workshop and on-site café.

ACCOMMODATION AND EATING

★ **Craigatin House and Courtyard** 165 Atholl Rd ☎ 01796 472478, ⓦ craigatinhouse.co.uk. On the northern section of the main road through town, this is an attractive, contemporary B&B with large beds, soothing decor, superb breakfasts and a pretty garden. **£110**

Fonab Castle Hotel Foss Rd, south of the river ☎ 01796 470140, ⓦ fonabcastlehotel.com. Once the headquarters of a power company, this turreted, waterside landmark has now been transformed into a luxury hotel with a spa and panoramic fine-dining restaurant. The interiors, with sparkly Swarovski wall coverings, may be a little bling for some tastes. **£195**

Moulin Hotel 11 Kirkmichael Rd, Moulin, on the outskirts of Pitlochry ☎ 01796 472196, ⓦ moulinhotel. co.uk. Pleasant old travellers' inn with fifteen rooms swathed in different coloured tartan, including some with four poster; there's also a great bar and restaurant (see below). **£105**

Moulin Inn 11 Kirkmichael Rd, Moulin, on the outskirts of Pitlochry ☎ 01796 472196, ⓦ moulinhotel.co.uk. Joined to the hotel of the same name, this restaurant serves solid Scottish dishes such as and Arbroath smokies and haggis and black pudding balls (£7.45). In a cosy, country setting at the foot of Ben Vrackie; its beers, meanwhile, are brewed just a few paces away in its own brewery. Food served daily noon–9.30pm.

Pitlochry Backpackers Hotel 134 Atholl Rd ☎ 01796 470044, ⓦ pitlochrybackpackershotel.com. Right in the centre of town, this hostel is based in a former hotel, and offers dorms, twin and double rooms (some ensuite), a communal lounge, bike storage and drying room. Breakfast £3. Dorms **£20.50**; doubles **£53.50**

ENTERTAINMENT

Pitlochry Festival Theatre Port na Craig, south side of the river ☎ 01796 484626, ⓦ pitlochryfestivaltheatre. com. On the southern edge of Pitlochry, just across the river, lies Scotland's renowned "Theatre in the Hills". A variety of productions – mostly mainstream theatre from the resident repertoire company, along with regular music events – are staged in the summer season and on ad hoc dates the rest of the year. Box office Mon–Sat 10am–8pm, Sun 10am–5pm.

Pass of Killiecrankie

NTS visitor centre: 4 miles north of Pitlochry along the A9 • Mid-April–Oct Thurs–Sun 10am–5pm • Free; parking £2 • ☎ 0844 493 2194

Four miles north of Pitlochry, the A9 cuts through the **Pass of Killiecrankie**, a breathtaking wooded gorge that falls away to the River Garry below. This dramatic setting was the site of the **Battle of Killiecrankie** in 1689, when the Jacobites crushed the forces of General Mackay. Legend has it that one soldier of the Crown, fleeing for his life, made a miraculous jump across the eighteen-foot **Soldier's Leap**, an impossibly wide chasm halfway up the gorge. Queen Victoria, visiting here 160 years later, contented herself with recording the beauty of the area in her diary.

Exhibits at the slick NTS **visitor centre**, which sits inside the boundaries of the Loch Tummel National Scenic Area, recall the battle and examine the gorge in detail. The surroundings here are thick, mature forest, full of interesting plants and creatures. If you visit during the springtime keep a lookout for the centre's webcams, which are trained on nearby nesting spots.

Blair Atholl

Three miles north of the Pass of Killiecrankie, the village of **BLAIR ATHOLL** makes for a much quieter and more idiosyncratic stop than Pitlochry. Understandably popular with day-trippers for the extravagant Blair Castle, there are also plenty of walks and bike rides to enjoy in the surrounding countryside.

Blair Castle

Just off the B8079, midway between the train station and the bridge over the River Tilt • April–Oct daily 9.30am–5.30pm (last admission 4.30pm); Nov–March occasional weekends only (see website for details) • Castle and grounds £14; grounds only £7.70 • ☎ 01796 481207, ⓦ blair-castle.co.uk

Seat of the Atholl dukedom, whitewashed, turreted **Blair Castle**, surrounded by parkland and dating from 1269, presents an impressive sight as you approach up the drive. On a self-guided tour, you get to see thirty or so rooms displaying a selection of paintings, tapestries, antique furniture and plasterwork that is sumptuous in the extreme. It begins inside the soaring **entrance hall**, with every spare inch of wood panelling covered in targes (shields), muskets and the like. There are some lesser heralded gems here too, such as an exquisite collection of items hewn from bone made by French POWs at Edinburgh Castle, and several items belonging to Queen

Victoria, among them a mourning pendant for Prince Albert and a wreath of oak leaves she wore during a three-week stay at the castle in 1844. The tour ends inside the vast **ballroom**, with its timber roof, antlers and mixture of portraits. On the hour, a piper, one of the Atholl Highlanders, plays in front of the castle; this select group was retained by the duke as his private army – a unique privilege afforded to him by Queen Victoria.

As impressive as the castle's interior are its surroundings: Highland cows graze the ancient landscaped grounds and peacocks strut in front of the castle. There is a **riding stable** from where you can take treks, and formal woodland walks take you to various parts of the castle grounds, including the walled water garden and the towering giant conifers of Diana's Grove.

Atholl Country Life Museum

A 5min walk east of the train station along the B8079 • May Sat & Sun 1–5pm; June–Oct daily 1–5pm • £4 • ☎ 01796 473035, �🌐 athollcountrylifemuseum.org.uk

The modest **Atholl Country Life Museum** offers a homespun and nostalgic look at the history of life in the local glens. In among the old photos and artefacts, the star attraction is a stuffed, full-sized Highland cow; according to the owners, it's the only one of its kind.

Blair Atholl Watermill

Ford Rd • April–Oct daily 9.30am–4pm; milling takes place Wed–Fri • Free • ☎ 01796 481321, �🌐 blairathollwatermill.com

Close to the River Tilt is Blair Atholl's **Watermill**, which dates back to 1613., and during the summertime you can wander around and witness the mill in action. Better still is a trip to the pleasant timber-beamed tearoom (see below), where you can enjoy home-baked scones and light lunches (many items are made with the mill's own flour).

INFORMATION AND ACTIVITIES   BLAIR ATHOLL

Atholl Estates Information Centre Close to the bridge over the River Tilt, a 5min walk east of the train station (April–Oct daily 9am–4.45pm; �🌐 atholl-estates.co.uk). Modern ranger station, where you can get details of the extensive network of local walks and bike rides, as well as information on surrounding flora and fauna.

Bike rental You can rent bikes (£23/day) from Blair Atholl Bike Hire (☎ 01796 481500, �🌐 blairathollbikehire.co.uk) in the reception of *Blair Castle Caravan Park* (see below).

ACCOMMODATION AND EATING

Atholl Arms Hotel On the main road, near the train station ☎ 01796 481205, ⍟ athollarms.co.uk. Grand but reasonably priced hotel with, predictably, lots of tartan amidst its thirty or so tastefully decorated rooms, some of which are pet-friendly. It's also the best place in town for a drink or a bar meal; the Atholl Highlander meat platter costs £12.95. Bar Mon–Thurs & Sun noon–10.45pm, Fri & Sat noon–11.30pm; food served daily noon–9.30pm. £105
★ **Blair Atholl Watermill** Ford Rd ☎ 01796 481321, ⍟ blairathollwatermill.com. Blair Atholl's top spot for

tea, tray bakes, toasties and bagels (snacks around £5) in a charming (and still functioning) old watermill. April–Oct daily 9.30am–4pm.

Blair Castle Caravan Park In the grounds of Blair Castle ☎ 01796 481263, ⍟ blaircastlecaravanpark. co.uk. Enormous but attractive campsite with laundry facilities, a games room and a shop selling the estate's own sausages; guests receive a discount to visit the castle. Two-night minimum stay July & Aug. Per pitch £24

Loch Tummel

West of Pitlochry, the B8019/B846 makes a memorably scenic, if tortuous, traverse of the shores of **Loch Tummel** and then Loch Rannoch. These two lochs and their adjoining rivers were much changed by the massive hydroelectric schemes built in the 1940s and 1950s, yet this is still a spectacular stretch of countryside and one that deserves leisurely exploration. **Queen's View** at the eastern end of Loch Tummel is an

RANNOCH MOOR

Rannoch Moor occupies roughly 150 square miles of uninhabited and uninhabitable peat bogs, lochs, heather hillocks, strewn lumps of granite and a few gnarled Caledonian pines, all of it over one thousand feet above sea level. Perhaps the most striking thing about the moor is its inaccessibility: one road, between Crianlarich and Glen Coe, skirts its western side, while another struggles west from Pitlochry to reach its eastern edge at Rannoch Station. The only regular form of transport is the **West Highland Railway**, which stops at **Rannoch** and, a little to the north, Corrour station, which has no road access at all. There is a simple tearoom in the station building at Rannoch, as well as a pleasant small hotel, the *Moor of Rannoch*, but even these fail to diminish the feeling of isolation. **Corrour**, meanwhile, stole an unlikely scene in the film *Trainspotting* when the four central characters headed here for a taste of the great outdoors; a wooden hostel is located a mile away on the shores of **Loch Ossian** and is only accessible on foot, making the area a great place for hikers seeking somewhere genuinely off the beaten track. From Rannoch Station it's possible to catch the train to Corrour and walk the nine miles back; it's a longer slog west to the *Kingshouse Hotel* at the eastern end of Glen Coe, the dramatic peaks of which poke up above the moor's western horizon. Determined hillwalkers will find a clutch of Munros around Corrour, including remote Ben Alder (3765ft), high above the forbidding shores of Loch Ericht.

2

obvious vantage point, looking down the loch to the misty peak of **Schiehallion**; the name comes from the Gaelic meaning "Fairy Mountain".

Schiehallion

Rising cone-like southwest of Loch Tummel to a peak of 3553ft, **Schiehallion** is a popular, fairly easy and inspiring mountain to climb (3–4hr round trip), with views on a good day to the massed ranks of Highland peaks. The path up starts at Braes of Foss, just off the B846 that links Aberfeldy with Kinloch Rannoch. You'll get a good view of the mountain from the cosy *Loch Tummel Inn* (see below).

ACCOMMODATION AND EATING   **LOCH TUMMEL**

Loch Tummel Inn About halfway along Loch Tummel, on the B8019 ☎ 01882 634272, ⊛ theinnatlochtummel. com. Beautiful stone-built inn with six gorgeous rooms which come armed with some thoughtful touches, such as shortbread and whisky upon arrival. The restaurant/bar serves real ale and rich meals like Stornoway black pudding with guinea fowl mousse, best enjoyed from the picnic benches out front which have magnificent views over the loch and Schiehallion. Food served Tues–Sat noon–2pm & 5.30–8.30pm; Sun noon–2pm. **£130**

Loch Rannoch

Beyond Loch Tummel, marking the eastern end of **Loch Rannoch**, the small community of **KINLOCH RANNOCH** doesn't see a lot of passing trade – fishermen and hillwalkers are the most common visitors. Otherwise, the only real destination here is **Rannoch railway station**, a lonely outpost on the Glasgow–Fort William West Highland train line, sixteen miles further on: the road goes no further. Here you can contemplate the bleakness of **Rannoch Moor** (see box), a wide expanse of bog, heather and wind-blown pine trees that stretches right across to the imposing entrance of Glen Coe (see page 191).

ARRIVAL AND DEPARTURE   **LOCH RANNOCH**

By train The West Highland Railway stops at Rannoch and, a little to the north, Corrour station, which has no road access at all.

Destinations (from Rannoch station) Corrour (3–4 daily; 12min); Fort William (3–4 daily; 1hr); Glasgow Queen Street (3–4 daily; 2hr 50min); London Euston (sleeper service Mon–Fri & Sun daily; 11hr–12hr 40min).

By bus A local bus service (Broons Bus #85) from Kinloch Rannoch provides connections with Rannoch railway station, sixteen miles to the west (up to 4 daily; 40min).

2

ACCOMMODATION AND EATING

LOCH RANNOCH
Macdonald Loch Rannoch Half a mile west of Kinloch Rannoch along the B846 ☎0344 879 9054, ⓦmacdonaldhotels.co.uk. This large lochside hotel offers accomplished rooms as well as a classy restaurant and two bars, including a whisky bar. Guests also have access to a leisure complex with an indoor pool and gym. **£93**

RANNOCH MOOR
★ **Corrour Station House** Corrour Station ☎01397 732236, ⓦcorrour.co.uk. Fantastically remote café, only reachable by train or on a 20-mile hike. Soups, sandwiches and fine home baking, plus venison burgers, fish and chips and the like for dinner (mains £10–15). Easter–Oct daily 8.30am–9pm.

★ **Moor of Rannoch Hotel** Rannoch Station ☎01882 633238, ⓦmoorofrannoch.co.uk. If it's isolation you want, this is the place to stay; there's no internet, radio or TV but instead open fires, board games and a big whisky selection. The five comfy en-suite rooms look out over the boggy moorland. Off-road bikes to rent (£18). **£180**

LOCH OSSIAN
Loch Ossian Youth Hostel A 1-mile walk northeast from Corrour's train station, on the shores of Loch Ossian ☎01397 732207, ⓦhostellingscotland.org.uk. Only accessible on foot, this is an excellent option for hikers seeking somewhere genuinely off the beaten track. There's a wood-lined self-catering kitchen for making basic meals, but no fridge. Dorms **£21.50**

The Angus glens

The high country in the northern part of the county of **Angus**, east of the A9 and north of the Firth of Tay, holds some of the Central Highlands' most pleasant scenery and is relatively free of tourists, most of whom tend to bypass it on their way north. Here the long fingers of the **Angus glens** – heather-covered hills tumbling down to rushing rivers – are overlooked by the southern peaks of the Grampian Mountains. Each has its own feel and devotees, **Glen Clova** being, deservedly, one of the most popular, along with **Glen Shee**, which attracts large numbers of people to its ski slopes. Handsome market towns like **Kirriemuir** and **Blairgowrie** are good bases for the area, while the tiny village of **Meigle** at the southern end of Glen Isla has Scotland's finest collection of carved Pictish stones.

Glen Shee and around

Cairnwell chairlift • Daily: April–Oct 9.30am–4.30pm; Nov–March 8.30am–5pm • £6 single, £10 return • ☎01339 741320, ⓦski-glenshee.co.uk

The upper reaches of **Glen Shee**, the most dramatic and best known of the Angus glens, are dominated by its **ski fields**, ranged over four mountains above the Cairnwell mountain pass. The resorts here may not amount to much more than gentle training slopes in comparison with those of the Alps or North America, but they all make for a fun day out for everyone from beginners to experienced skiers. During the season (Dec–March), ski lifts and tows give access to gentle beginners' slopes, while experienced skiers can try the more intimidating Tiger run. In summer the attention turns to hiking and biking with some excellent routes for both disciplines. Active types tend to overnight in Spittal of Glenshee, or twenty miles further south along the A93 in Blairgowrie, a small town at the southern end of the glen.

Spittal of Glenshee

The small settlement of **SPITTAL OF GLENSHEE** (the name derives from the same root as "hospital", indicating a refuge), though ideally situated for skiing, has little else to commend it other than the busy Gulabin Lodge Outdoor Centre. From Spittal the road climbs another five miles or so to the ski centre at the crest of the Cairnwell Pass. One of the loveliest walks (or cycle rides) hereabouts is a trek into the heart

---

SKIING IN GLEN SHEE

For information on skiing in Glen Shee, contact **Ski Glenshee** (☎ 01339 741 320, ⓦ ski-glenshee. co.uk), which also offers ski rental and lessons, as does the Gulabin Lodge Outdoor Centre, at the Spittal of Glenshee. For the latest snow and **weather conditions**, phone Ski Glenshee or check out the Ski Scotland website (ⓦ visitscotland.com/see-do/active/skiing-snowsports).

---

of Glenshee towards Glen Taitneach, which begins at the car park just beyond the humped back bridge near the outdoor centre. Although not a circular route (so you can go as far as you want), it's mostly flat, hence ideal for families, and becomes increasingly dramatic the further up the glen you go; there's a good chance of spotting Golden Eagles here too.

ACCOMMODATION AND ACTIVITIES   SPITTAL OF GLENSHEE

Dalmunzie Castle Blairgowrie ☎ 01250 885224, ⓦ dalmunzie.com. A lovely Highland retreat in a magnificent turreted mansion, which, aside from its double rooms, has four-poster bedrooms and three, rather more expensive, tower rooms, each with spectacular views; there's also first-class dining and over sixty malt whiskies to enjoy by the fireside. The entrance is just south of Gulabin Lodge Outdoor Centre, across the bridge. **£170**

Ecocamp Glenshee Blacklunans ☎ 01250 882284, ⓦ ecocampglenshee.co.uk. A fabulous, isolated retreat eight miles south of the Spittal of Glenshee offering a selection of cosy pods, shepherds huts and wagons, each sleeping between two- and four-people and with their own

fire pit. Guests are free to avail themselves of the bothy, which has all the necessary amenities for cooking, a log fire and loads of board games. **£80**

Gulabin Lodge Outdoor Centre Just off the A93 immediately north of Spittal of Glenshee ☎ 01250 885255, ⓦ gulabinoutdoors.co.uk. Snow sports are the big draw here in winter, of course, but staff can also arrange summer activities like archery, rock climbing, canoeing and canyoning. Pre-booking advised. Mountain bike hire too (£20/day). There is also clean, basic accommodation in a nineteenth-century manse, with singles, doubles and family rooms all available. **£55**

Blairgowrie

Travelling to Glen Shee from the south, you'll pass through the well-heeled little town of **BLAIRGOWRIE**, set among raspberry fields on the glen's southernmost tip and a good place to pick up information and plan your activities. Strictly two communities – Blairgowrie and **Rattray**, set on either side of the River Ericht – the town's modest claim to fame is that St Ninian once camped at Wellmeadow, a pleasant grassy triangle in the town centre.

Cateran Trail

ⓦ pkct.org/cateran-trail

The **Cateran Trail** is an ambitious, 64-mile long-distance footpath that starts in Blairgowrie then heads off on a long loop into the glens to the north following some of the drove roads used by caterans, or cattle thieves. It's a four- to five-day tramp, though of course it's possible to walk shorter sections of the way (see the website for more information).

ARRIVAL AND DEPARTURE   BLAIRGOWRIE

By bus Blairgowrie is linked by hourly bus #57 to both   Perth (50min) and Dundee (1hr).

ACCOMMODATION AND EATING

Bridge of Cally Hotel 6 miles north of town on the A93 ☎ 01250 886231, ⓦ bridgeofcallyhotel.com. Attractive medium-sized hotel right on the Cateran Trail with nicely presented rooms, some with river views, and a welcoming restaurant/bar serving intriguing dishes like peppered duck with vanilla mashed potato, and venison casserole (£20). Daily 10am–10pm; food served noon–2pm & 6–9pm. **£90**

Cargills By the river on Lower Mill St ☎ 01250 876735, ⓦ cargillsbistro.com. Popular bistro serving inexpensive daytime and evening menus, for example smoked haddock and garden pea kedgeree (£9.95); terrific breakfasts too, served until 3.30pm. Mon–Fri 8.30am–3.30pm & 5–9pm, Sat & Sun 10.30am–3.30pm & 5–9pm.

Little's 1 Riverside Rd ☎ 01250 875358, ⓦ littles

restaurant.com. Lovely little restaurant specializing in prettily presented fresh local fish, which might be, for example, marinated squid with olives or lemon sole fillet with mango chutney and straw chips (£18.95). Tues–Sat 11am–2.30pm & 5–9.30pm, Sun noon–8pm.

Meigle

Dundee Rd, Meigle • April–Sept daily 9.30am–5pm • £6; HES • ☎ 01828 640612, ⊛ historicenvironment.scot • Hourly bus #57 from Dundee to Perth passes through Meigle

Fifteen miles north of Dundee on the B954 lies the tiny settlement of **MEIGLE**, home to Scotland's most important collection of early Christian and Pictish **inscribed stones**. Housed in a modest former schoolhouse, the **Meigle Museum** displays some thirty pieces dating from the seventh to the tenth centuries, all found in and around the nearby churchyard. The majority are either gravestones that would have lain flat, or cross slabs inscribed with the sign of the cross, usually standing. Most impressive is the 7ft-tall great cross slab, said to be the gravestone of Guinevere, wife of King Arthur. The exact purpose of the stones and their enigmatic symbols is obscure, as is the reason why so many of them were found at Meigle. The most likely theory suggests that Meigle was once an important ecclesiastical centre that attracted secular burials of prominent Picts.

2

Glen Isla and around

Three and a half miles north of Meigle is **ALYTH**, near which, legend has it, Guinevere was held captive by Mordred. It's a sleepy village at the south end of **Glen Isla**, which runs parallel to Glen Shee and is linked to it by the A926. If you decide to stay in the area, the best options are in and around **Kirkton of Glenisla**, a small hamlet ten miles north of Alyth.

Reekie Linn

Close to the Bridge of Craigisla, which is a ten-minute drive north of Alyth along the B954, the River Isla narrows and then plunges some 60ft into a deep gorge to produce the classically pretty waterfall of **Reekie Linn**, or "smoking fall", so-called because of the water mist produced when the fall hits a ledge and bounces a further 20ft into a deep pool known as the Black Dub. There's a car park beside the bridge, and the waterfall is a short walk away along the river's edge.

ARRIVAL AND DEPARTURE   GLEN ISLA AND AROUND

By bus Transport connections into the glen are limited. Alyth is on the main bus routes linking Blairgowrie with Dundee.

ACCOMMODATION

Glenisla Hotel Kirkton of Glenisla ☎ 01575 582223, ⊛ glenisla-hotel.com. Cosy and refurbished, whitewashed hotel accommodating a selection of bright rooms, and which doubles as a good place for classy home-made bar food (rump steak sandwich, steak and ale pie) and convivial drinking. Food served daily noon–2.30pm & 5–8pm. **£90**

★ **West Freuchies** 1 mile east of Kirkton of Glenisla ☎ 01575 582716, ⊛ glenisla-westfreuchies.co.uk. A comfortable B&B whose first-floor rooms have views over the hills; they make their own bread for breakfast, and you might spot red squirrels in the grounds. There's also self-catering accommodation nearby in a converted mill. Approaching from Alyth, a right-hand turn leads northeast to the B&B (signposted before you reach Kirkton of Glenisla). **£76**

Kirriemuir and around

The sandstone town of **KIRRIEMUIR**, known locally as Kirrie, is set on a hill six miles northwest of Forfar on the cusp of glens Clova and Prosen. Despite the influx of hunters up for the "season", it's still a pretty special place, a haphazard confection of narrow closes, twisting wynds and steep braes. The main cluster of streets has all the appeal of an old film set, with its old-fashioned bars, tiled butcher's shop, tartan outlets and haberdasheries somehow managing to avoid being contrived and quaint.

J.M. Barrie's birthplace

9 Brechin Rd · April–mid-Oct Fri–Mon 11am–4pm · £7; NTS · ☎ 01575 572646, ⊛ nts.org.uk

Kirrie was the birthplace of **J.M. Barrie** (1860–1937). A local handloom-weaver's son, Barrie first came to notice with his series of novels about "Thrums" – a village based on his home town – and in particular *A Window in Thrums* and his third novel, *The Little Minister*. The story of **Peter Pan**, the little boy who never grew up, was penned by Barrie in 1904 – some say as a response to a strange upbringing dominated by the memory of his older brother, who died in a skating accident at the age of 13. **Barrie's birthplace**, a plain little whitewashed cottage which housed the family's ten children, has a series of small rooms decorated as they would have been during Barrie's childhood, as well as displays about his life and works.

Camera obscura

In the old cricket pavilion above town, just off West Hill Rd · April–mid-Oct Sat–Mon 11am–4pm · Donation · ☎ 01575 575885, ⊛ kirriemuircameraobscura.com

One of just three **camera obscuras** still functioning in Scotland (the others are in Edinburgh and Dumfries), this unexpected treasure is run by the local community, along with a small café. It was donated to the town, along with the cricket pavilion, in 1930 by J.M. Barrie, and offers splendid views of Strathmore and the glens: on a clear day it's possible to see as far as Ben Ledi, almost sixty miles to the west. Note that when it's raining the Camera Obscura does not operate.

Gateway to the Glens Museum

32 High St · Tues–Sat 10am–5pm · Free · ☎ 01575 526006

Standing on the main square, the handsome little Town House (the oldest building in Kirrie) has seen service as a tollbooth, court, jail, post office, police station and chemist among other things, but these days is occupied by the rewarding **Gateway to the Glens Museum**; its two floors are crammed with interactive displays and exhibits on the town and the Angus glens, including a scale model of Kirrie in 1604. There's also a cabinet full of personal effects belonging to J.M. Barrie (including the silver quill pen he used to sign the register of honorary bursaries), as well as a display celebrating the life of the town's other famous son, **Bon Scott** of the rock band AC/DC. Scott was born in Kirriemuir in 1946 before the family moved to Australia just a few years later; he then went on to become one of the most prominent rock start of his generation, first as lead singer of the Valentines, then AC/DC before his premature death in 1980. A statue of Scott on Bellies Brae, a short walk down from the museum, attracts pilgrims from far and wide.

ARRIVAL AND DEPARTURE   KIRRIEMUIR AND AROUND

By bus The hourly #20 bus runs from Kirriemuir's high   street to Forfar (15min) and Dundee (50min).

ACCOMMODATION AND EATING

Muirhouses Farm 2 miles north of town on the way to Cortachy ☎ 01575 573128, ⊛ muirhousesfarm.co.uk. Offering a proper taste of the countryside hereabouts, this is a working cattle farm with one, two-bed cottage sleeping four people; weekend stays, midweek breaks and longer stays available. **£78**

Thrums Hotel Bank St ☎ 01575 572758, ⊛ thrums hotel.co.uk. Small, family-run hotel offering nine en-suite rooms (the larger premium rooms are just £5 more) as well as unfussy lunch and evening meals; the menu includes the likes of haggis balls with mustard mayo, and steak pie with chips and veg (£9.75). Daily noon–2pm & 5–8pm. **£85**

SHOPPING

Star Rock Shop 25 The Roods ☎ 01575 218518, ⊛ starrockshop.com Pretty, old-style shop specializing in Scottish confectionery, which first opened in 1833, which make it the oldest trading sweet shop in the country. This is a nice place to try the hard, sweet and milky Scottish candy known as tablet (£2/bag). Tues–Fri 9.30am–4.30pm, Sat 10am–4.30pm.

Glen Prosen

Five miles north of Kirriemuir, the low-key hamlet of **DYKEHEAD** marks the point where **Glen Prosen** and Glen Clova divide. A mile or so up Glen Prosen, you'll find the house where Captain Scott and fellow explorer Doctor Wilson planned their ill-fated trip to Antarctica in 1910–11, with a roadside **stone cairn** commemorating the expedition. From here on, Glen Prosen remains essentially a quiet wooded backwater, with all the wild and rugged splendour of the other glens but without the crowds. To explore the area thoroughly you need to go on foot, but a good road circuit can be made by crossing the river at the tiny village of **Glenprosen** and returning to Kirriemuir along the western side of the glen via Pearsie. Alternatively, the reasonably easy four-mile **Minister's Path** links Glen Prosen with Clova. It is clearly marked and leaves from near the church in the village.

Glen Clova

With its stunning cliffs, heather slopes and valley meadows, **Glen Clova** – which in the north becomes **Glen Doll** – is one of the loveliest of the Angus glens. Although it can get unpleasantly congested in peak season, the area is still remote enough that you can leave the crowds with little effort. Wildlife is abundant, with deer on the mountains, wild hares and even grouse and the occasional buzzard. The meadow flowers on the valley floor and arctic plants on the rocks make it a botanist's paradise.

Clova

The B955 from Dykehead and Kirriemuir divides at the Gella Bridge over the swift-coursing River South Esk. Around six miles north of Gella, the two branches of the road join up once more at the hamlet of **CLOVA**, little more than the hearty *Glen Clova Hotel*. An excellent, if fairly strenuous, four-hour walk from behind the old school at the back of the hotel leads up into the mountains and around the lip of **Loch Brandy**.

WALKS FROM GLEN DOLL

Ordnance Survey Explorer maps 388 & 387

These **walks** are some of the main routes across the Grampians from the Angus glens to Deeside, many of which follow well-established old drovers' roads. All three either fringe or cross the royal estate of Balmoral, and Prince Charles's favourite mountain – **Lochnagar** – can be seen from all angles. The walks all begin from the car park at the end of the tarred road where Glen Clova meets Glen Doll; all routes should always be approached with care, and you should follow the usual safety precautions.

CAPEL MOUNTH TO BALLATER

15 miles; 7hr

Initially, the path zigzags its way up fierce slopes before levelling out to a moorland plateau, leading to the eastern end of Loch Muick. It then follows the River Muick to Ballater.

CAPEL MOUNTH ROUND TRIP

15 miles; 8hr

Follows the above route to Loch Muick, doubling back along the loch's southern shore. The dramatic Streak of Lightning path that follows Corrie Chash leads to a ruined stables below Sandy Hillock; the descent passes the waterfall by the bridge at Bachnagairn, where a gentle burn-side track leads back to Glen Doll car park.

JOCK'S ROAD TO BRAEMAR

14 miles; 7hr

A signposted path leads below Cairn Lunkhard and along a wide ridge towards the summit of Crow Craigies (3018ft). From here, the path bumps down to Loch Callater then follows the Callater Burn, eventually hitting the A93 two miles short of Braemar.

North from Clova village, the road turns into a rabbit-infested lane coursing along the riverside for four miles to the car park, a useful starting point for numerous superb **walks**. There are no other facilities beyond the village.

ACCOMMODATION AND EATING	GLEN CLOVA
Glen Clova Hotel Clova, 15 miles north of Kirriemuir along the B955 ☎ 01575 550350, ⓦ clova.com. Inviting country hotel, which also has a selection of lodges and a private fishing loch. The restaurant serves up traditional	Scottish food with a twist, such as Kentucky fried pheasant with celeriac remoulade, and venison chilli with rice (£11.95). Mon–Thurs & Sun noon–7.45pm, Fri & Sat noon–8.45pm. **£110**

Brechin

Eight miles west of Montrose, **BRECHIN** is an attractive town whose red-sandstone buildings give it a warm, welcoming feel. The chief attraction is the old **cathedral**, a building that's emboldened some (including the local football team) to proudly describe Brechin – in line with the historic definition – as a fully fledged city.

The cathedral

Bishop's Close, off the high street • Daily 9am–5pm • Free • ☎ 01356 629360, ⓦ brechincathedral.org.uk

There's been a religious building of sorts here since the arrival of evangelizing Irish missionaries in 900 AD, and the red-sandstone structure has become something of a hotchpotch of architectural styles. What you see today dates chiefly from an extensive rebuilding in 1900, with the oldest surviving part of the cathedral being the 106ft-high round tower, one of only two in Scotland. The cathedral's doorway, built 6ft above the ground for protection against Viking raids, has some notable carvings, while inside you can see various Pictish stones, illuminated by the jewel-coloured stained-glass windows.

ARRIVAL AND DEPARTURE	BRECHIN
By bus Brechin is easy to get to and from; bus #30 runs at	least once an hour to Montrose, nine miles to the east.

TOURS

Caledonian Railway tours Brechin station ☎ 01356 622992, ⓦ caledonianrailway.com. Trains operate every weekend from June to mid-September, travelling along four	miles of track from Brechin to the Bridge of Dun (£8 return). Diesel trains run on Saturdays, steam trains run on Sundays.

ACCOMMODATION

Gramarcy House 6 Airlie St ☎ 01356 622240. Bright, spacious and tastefully furnished rooms in a house set back from the main road. There's also a self-catering kitchen area	and a sunny breakfast room with bay windows. Agnes, the owner, is friendly and helpful. **£80**

Edzell and around

Travelling around Angus, you can hardly fail to notice the difference between organic settlements and planned towns that were built by landowners who forcibly rehoused local people in order to keep them under control, especially after the Jacobite uprisings. One of the better examples of the latter, **EDZELL**, five miles north of Brechin on the B966, was cleared and rebuilt with Victorian rectitude a mile to the west of its original site in the 1840s. Through the Dalhousie Arch at the entrance to the village the long, wide and ruler-straight main street is lined with prim nineteenth-century buildings, which now do a roaring trade as genteel teashops and antiques emporia.

The original village (identifiable from the cemetery and surrounding grassy mounds) lay immediately to the west of the wonderfully explorable red-sandstone ruins of Edzell Castle, itself a mile west of the planned village.

Edzell Castle

A mile west of Edzell • April–Sept daily 9.30am–5.30pm • £6; HES • ☏ 01316 688800, ⓦ historicenvironment.scot

The main part of the old castle is a good example of a comfortable tower house, where luxurious living rather than defence became a priority. However, it's the **pleasance garden** overlooked by the castle tower that makes a visit to **Edzell Castle** essential, especially in late spring and early to mid-summer. The garden was built by Sir David Lindsay in 1604, at the height of the optimistic Renaissance, and its refinement and extravagance are evident. The walls contain sculpted images of erudition: the Planetary Deities on the east side, the Liberal Arts on the south and, under floods of lobelia, the Cardinal Virtues on the west wall. In the centre of the garden, low-cut box hedges spell out the family mottoes and enclose voluminous beds of roses.

The Caterthuns

Four miles southwest of Edzell, lying either side of the lane to Bridgend, which can be reached either by carrying on along the road past the castle or by taking the narrow road at the southern end of Edzell village, are the **Caterthuns**, twin Iron Age hillforts that were probably occupied at different times. The surviving ramparts on the White Caterthun (978ft) – easily reached from the small car park below – are the most impressive, and this is thought to be the later fort, occupied by the Picts in the first few centuries AD.

ARRIVAL AND DEPARTURE
EDZELL AND AROUND

By bus Edzell is five miles north of Brechin on the B966, and linked to it by buses #21, #29 and #30.

ACCOMMODATION AND EATING

Alexandra Lodge Inveriscandye Rd ☏ 01356 648266, ⓦ alexandralodge.co.uk. Just a short walk east of the high street, this is a friendly B&B located on a quiet street in a little Edwardian lodge built in 1907; four immaculate rooms, a gut-busting breakfast and first-rate hospitality. April–Oct. **£90**

Glenesk Hotel High St ☏ 01356 647333, ⓦ glenesk hotel.com. A 38-room Victorian hotel with sweeping

gardens, a golf course and full-size snooker table, plus a pool and spa. The bar has seven hundred whiskies, at least. **£100**

Tuck Inn 44 High St ☏ 01356 648262, ⓦ tuckinnedzell. co.uk. An old-school red-painted restaurant/café, which dishes up filling fodder such as home made steak pie with veg, and haddock with chips and peas (£9.75). Eat in or take away. Mon–Fri 9am–8pm, Sat & Sun 11am-8pm.

Deeside

More commonly known as **Royal Deeside**, the land stretching west from Aberdeen along the River Dee revels in its connections with the royal family, who have regularly holidayed here, at **Balmoral**, since Queen Victoria bought the estate. Eighty thousand Scots turned out to welcome her on her first visit in 1848. Victoria adored the place and the woods were said to remind Prince Albert of Thuringia, his homeland.

Deeside is undoubtedly handsome in a fierce, craggy, Scottish way, and the royal presence has helped keep a lid on any unattractive mass development. The villages strung along the A93, the main route through the area, are well heeled and have something of an old-fashioned air. Facilities for visitors hereabouts are first class, with a number of bunkhouses and hostels, some decent hotels and plenty of castles and grounds to snoop around. It's also an excellent area for **outdoor activities**, with hiking routes into both the Grampian and Cairngorm mountains, alongside good mountain biking, horseriding and skiing.

GETTING AROUND
DEESIDE

By bus Stagecoach Bluebird buses #201, #202 and #203 from Aberdeen regularly chug along the A93, serving most of the towns on the way to Braemar. Bus #201 from Aberdeen runs to Crathes (45min), Banchory (50min), Ballater (1hr 45min), and Braemar (2hr 10min), while #202 and #203 stop at Lumphanan and Banchory respectively.

Drum Castle

Near Drumoak, 10 miles west of Aberbeen off the A93 • Jan–March & Nov–Dec Sat & Sun 10.30am–4pm; April–May & Sept–Oct Mon & Thurs–Sun 10.30am–4pm; June–Aug daily 10.30am–4pm; Garden of Historic Roses April–Oct daily 11am–5pm • £13; NTS • ☎ 01330 700334, Ⓦ nts.org.uk

Squat **Drum Castle** stands in a clearing in the ancient woods of Drum, made up of the splendid pines and oaks that covered this whole area before the shipbuilding industry precipitated mass forest clearance. The castle itself combines a 1619 Jacobean mansion with Victorian extensions and the original, huge thirteenth-century keep, which has been restored and reopened. Given by Robert the Bruce to his armour-bearer, William de Irvine, in 1323 for services rendered at Bannockburn, the castle remained in Irvine hands for 24 generations until the NTS took over in 1976.

The main part of the house is Victorian in character, with grand, antique-filled rooms and lots of family portraits. The finest room is the **library**, within the ancient tower; you'll get an even better sense of the medieval origins of the place by climbing up to the upper levels of the tower, where the battlements offer views out over the forest.

Banchory and around

BANCHORY, meaning "fair hollow", is a one-street town that essentially acts as a gateway into rural Deeside. The small local **museum** (Mon–Wed, Fri & Sat 11am–3pm; free) on Bridge Street, behind High Street, may warrant half an hour or so if you're a fan of local boy James Scott Skinner, renowned fiddler and composer of such tunes as *The Bonnie Lass o'Bon Accord*.

Crathes Castle

Crathes, 2 miles east of Banchory • Jan–March & Nov & Dec Sat & Sun 11am–4pm; April–Oct daily 10.30am–5pm; last tour 1hr before closing • £13, including access to the gardens; NTS • ☎ 01330 844525, Ⓦ nts.org.uk

Four miles west of Drum Castle and around two miles east of **Banchory** (a small town that acts as a gateway into rural Deeside), **Crathes Castle** is a splendid sixteenth-century granite tower house adorned with flourishes such as overhanging turrets, gargoyles and conical roofs. Its thick walls, narrow windows and tiny rooms loaded with heavy old furniture make Crathes rather claustrophobic, but it's enlivened by some wonderful ceilings painted with lively figures of musicians strumming their instruments; the earliest dates from 1602. The extensive grounds include a Go Ape climbing centre (see page 157).

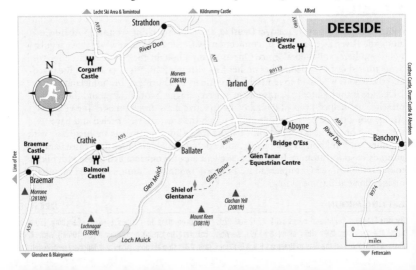

ARRIVAL AND DEPARTURE

BANCHORY AND AROUND

By bus Stagecoach Bluebird buses #201, #202 and #203 from Aberdeen bus station stop at the entrance to Crathes Estate, as well as at nearby Banchory.

INFORMATION AND ACTIVITIES

Tourist office You can pick up local tourist information from the town library on Bridge St (Mon–Wed & Fri 10am–7pm, Thurs 10am–2.30pm, Sat 10am–3pm; ☎ 01330 700441)

Go Ape Zip wires, Tarzan swings, rope ladders and skateboard zip take you through the trees in the grounds of Crathes Castle (☎ 01603 895500, ⓦ goape.co.uk).

ACCOMMODATION AND EATING

Milton Brasserie Near the entrance to Crathes Castle ☎ 01330 844566, ⓦ miltonbrasserie.com. Smart daytime brasserie in an old farm steading just across from Crathes Castle, serving moderately priced à la carte meals such as pan seared hake fillet with lemon fondant potato (£14). There's also an adjoining conservatory coffee shop serving afternoon tea. Brasserie Mon–Fri noon–3pm, Sat & Sun noon–5pm; coffee shop daily 9.30am–5pm.

Raemoir House Just over 2 miles north of Banchory ☎ 01330 824884, ⓦ raemoir.com. Glamorous country-house hotel set in spacious parkland, with decadent, individually designed rooms in either the late seventeeth-century Ha'Hoose or the main Georgian mansion, and several, grand public areas. **£195**

Tor-Na-Coille Hotel Inchmarlo Rd, Banchory ☎ 01330 822242, ⓦ tornacoille.com. Once a retreat for Charlie Chaplin and his family, *Tor-Na-Coille* has a scenic location on the town's southern edge. Some of the smart, largely tartan-decorated rooms overlook Banchory Golf Club's rolling fairways. **£115**

Ballater

Attractively hemmed in by the River Dee, the neat and ordered town of **BALLATER** was dragged from obscurity in the nineteenth century when it was discovered that waters from the local Pannanich Wells might be useful in curing scrofula. Deeside water is now back in fashion, though these days it's bottled and sold far and wide as a natural mineral water.

It was in Ballater that Queen Victoria first arrived in Deeside by train from Aberdeen back in 1848; she wouldn't allow a station to be built any closer to Balmoral, eight miles further west. Although the line has long been closed, the town's rather self-important royalism is much in evidence at the restored **train station** in the centre. The local shops that supply Balmoral with groceries and household basics also flaunt their connections, with oversized "By Appointment" crests.

If you prefer to discover the fresh air and natural beauty that Victoria came to love so much, you'll find Ballater an excellent base for local **walks and outdoor activities**. There are numerous hikes from Loch Muik (pronounced "mick"), nine miles southwest of town, including the Capel Mounth drovers' route over the mountains to Glen Doll (see page 153), and a well-worn but strenuous all-day trek up and around Lochnagar (3789ft), the mountain much painted and written about by the current Prince of Wales.

ARRIVAL AND DEPARTURE

BALLATER

By bus Buses stop at the northern end of Golf Rd, near the A93.

Destinations Aboyne (hourly; 20min); Banchory (hourly; 40min); Braemar (9 daily; 35min).

INFORMATION AND ACTIVITIES

Tourist office In the renovated former train station on Station Square (daily: July & Aug 10am–6pm; Sept–June 10am–5pm; ☎ 01339 755306, ⓦ visitballater.com).
Bike rental Good-quality bikes, including mountain bikes

and tandems, can be rented from Cycle Highlands (☎ 01339 755864, ⓦ cyclehighlands.com, daily 9am–5pm) from £35/day at The Pavilion, Victoria Rd.

ACCOMMODATION

Auld Kirk 31 Braemar Rd ☎ 01339 755762, ⓦ theauldkirk.com. As the name suggests, this pleasingly unorthodox B&B is based in a renovated church, which features an unmissable rocket-like spire. All of the seven rooms are

2

EXPLORING GLEN TANAR

Ordnance Survey Explorer map 395

Lying to the south of the Deeside town of Aboyne, the easily navigated forest tracks of **Glen Tanar** offer a taste of the changing landscape of the northeastern Highlands, passing through relatively prosperous farmland along the River Dee, through ancient woodland and then to remote grouse moors and bleak hillsides in the heart of the Grampian Mountains. Flatter than Glen Muick and without its vehicle traffic, Glen Tanar is a great place to explore on a mountain bike, although there is plenty of opportunity for walking, and there's also an **equestrian centre** in the glen, offering riding trips lasting from one hour to all day on riverside, mountain and forest horse-trails.

Leave the south Deeside road (B976) at **Bridge o'Ess**, one and a half miles southwest of Aboyne, and carry on along a tarred road on the west side of the Water of Tanar for two miles to a car park and the **Glen Tanar Visitor Centre** (daily 10am–5pm; ☎01339 886072, ⓦglentanarcharitabletrust.org). Here you can pick up details on the various routes in the glen, as well as some background on the flora and fauna of the area including efforts to protect the habitat of the rare capercaillie. If you're on **foot**, the best idea is to strike out along the clear forest tracks that follow both sides of the river, connected at various points by attractive stone bridges, allowing for easy round trips. Most of the time you are surrounded by superb old pine woodland, some of which are naturally seeded remnants of ancient Caledonian forest, with broadleafs in evidence along the river, as are wild flowers and fungi in season. The end of the glen, at **Shiel of Glentanar**, is eight miles from the car park, from where you can either retrace your path or take to the hills: **Mount Keen** (3081ft), the most easterly of Scotland's 3000ft-high mountains, looms ahead. The more ambitious can pick up the Mounth road at Shiel of Glentanar, which heads up and over Mount Keen to Invermark at the head of Glen Esk.

upstairs, leaving the ground floor free for a licensed lounge area. Attractive little coffee lounge attached too. **£125**

Ballater Caravan Park South of Anderson Rd, close to the River Dee ☎01339 755727, ⓦballatercaravanpark. com. Large campsite down by the water that mostly attracts touring caravans – tents are welcome too, though, and there are laundry and shower facilities. April–Sept. Per pitch **£14**

Ballater Hostel Bridge Square ☎01339 753752, ⓦballater-hostel.com. Excellent, friendly and well-equipped hostel tucked away off the main road. Choose between shared mixed dorms sleeping six or eight, or one of the private rooms. Excellent facilities include kitchen, communal room with wood-burning stove, bike storage and drying room. Dorms **£22**; doubles **£70**

No 45 45 Braemar Rd ☎01339 755420, ⓦno45.co.uk. Welcoming nineteenth-century house with eight good-sized doubles and twins decorated in muted tartan tones. The bar downstairs is stacked full of whisky and bottled ales, and there's also a restaurant in the large conservatory out the back. **£105**

EATING AND DRINKING

Barrel Lounge 6 Church Square ☎01339 755488. If you fancy a wee dram with the locals, pop into this pub on the main green. There's an open fire and the TV's usually on in the corner. Mon–Wed & Sun 11am–midnight, Thurs–Sat 11am–1am.

Lochnagar Indian Brasserie 2 Church Square ☎01339 755611, ⓦlochnagarindian.co.uk. A great location on the green, a warm welcome and excellent aromatic cooking, such as garlic chilli masala, and Goan lamb shank (£14.95);

book ahead. Daily noon–2pm & 5–11pm.

Riverside Cottage Café Cambus O'May, 2 miles east of Ballater ☎01339 755126, ⓦriversidecottagecafe. co.uk A cultured spot serving good coffee, snacks and light meals, as well as superb cakes (around £1.50) and bread from the award-winning Chrannach Bakery. Also offers Spanish tapas on a Friday and Saturday evening. Daily 10am–5pm, plus Fri & Sat 5.30–9pm (reduced hours in winter).

Balmoral Estate and around

8 miles west of Ballater, off the A93 • April–July daily 10am–5pm • £12; audio-tour included in admission price (additional £5 deposit required per handset); Land Rover safari £60/person for 3hr (minimum two people) • ☎01339 742534, ⓦbalmoralcastle.com

Originally a sixteenth-century tower house built for the powerful Gordon family, **Balmoral Castle** has been a royal residence since 1852, when it was converted to the Scottish Baronial mansion that stands today. The royal family traditionally spend their summer holidays here each August, but despite its fame it can be something of a disappointment even for a dedicated royalist. For the three months when the doors are nudged open, the general riffraff are permitted to view only the ballroom, an exhibition room and the grounds. With so little of the castle on view, it's worth making the most of the grounds and larger estate by following some of the country walks, heading off on a Land Rover safari (which are also available between mid-October and mid-December) or allowing the free audio-tour to guide you.

Opposite the castle's gates on the main road, the otherwise dull granite church of **Crathie**, built in 1895 with the proceeds of a bazaar held at Balmoral, is the royals' local church.

Braemar

West of Balmoral, the road rises to 1100ft above sea level in the upper part of Deeside and the village of **BRAEMAR**, situated where three passes meet and overlooked by an unremarkable **castle**. It's an invigorating, outdoor kind of place, well patronized by committed hikers, but probably best known for its Highland Games, the annual **Braemar Gathering**, on the first Saturday of September. Since Queen Victoria's day, successive generations of royals have attended and the world's most famous Highland Games have become rather an overcrowded, overblown event. You're not guaranteed to get in if you just turn up; the website (ⓦ braemargathering.org) has details of how to book tickets in advance.

Linn of Dee

A pleasant diversion from Braemar is to head six miles west to the end of the road and the **Linn of Dee**, where the river plummets savagely through a narrow rock gorge. From here there are countless walks into the surrounding countryside or up into the heart of the Cairngorms (see page 164), including the awesome Lairig Ghru pass which cuts all the way through to Strathspey.

ARRIVAL AND DEPARTURE   BRAEMAR

By bus Buses from and to Ballater (9 daily; 35min) stop on Auchendryne Square, while long-distance coaches drop package tourists in the car park opposite the *Fife Arms Hotel*.

INFORMATION AND ACTIVITIES

Tourist office In the absence of a tourist office, there's good information at ⓦ braemarscotland.co.uk.
Outdoor activities Advice on outdoor activities, as well as ski, mountain-bike and climbing equipment rental, is available from Braemar Mountain Sports (daily 9am–6pm; ☏ 01339 741242, ⓦ braemarmountainsports.com).

DEESIDE AND DONSIDE HIGHLAND GAMES

Royal Deeside is the home of the modern **Highland Games**, claiming descent from gatherings organized by eleventh-century Scottish king Malcolm Canmore to help him recruit the strongest and fittest clansmen for his army. The most famous of the local games is undoubtedly the **Braemar Gathering**, held on the first Saturday in September, which can see crowds of fifteen thousand and usually a royal or two as guest of honour. Vying for celebrity status in recent years has been the **Lonach Gathering** in nearby Strathdon on Donside, held the weekend before Braemar. For a true flavour of the spirit of Highland gatherings, however, try to get to one of the events that take place in other local towns and villages at weekends throughout July and August, where locals outnumber tourists and the competitions are guaranteed to be hard-fought and entertaining. For more information see ⓦ shga.co.uk.

2

ACCOMMODATION

Braemar Youth Hostel 21 Glenshee Rd ☎01339 741659, ⓦhostellingscotland.org.uk. SYHA hostel a short stroll from the centre in a former shooting lodge with laundry, drying room, bike storage facilities and a big communal kitchen. Feb–Oct. **£17.50**

Braemar Caravan Park Park Half a mile south of the village off Glenshee Rd ☎01339 741373, ⓦbraemar caravanpark.co.uk. Year-round caravan site which also has thirty camping pitches and half a dozen heated camping

pods sleeping four. Can get busy in the summer, so book ahead. Per pitch **£22.50**; pods **£65**

★ **Ivy Cottage Guest House** Cluniebank Rd ☎01339 741642, ⓦivycottagebraemar.co.uk. A lovely Victorian home with trim and comfortable rooms (two doubles and a twin), and a view of red squirrels and birds as you eat your breakfast. They also have two self-catering options, both with wood-burning stoves: a cottage and a bothy/studio (three nights from £200). **£80**

EATING AND DRINKING

The Gathering Place 7–9 Invercauld Rd ☎01339 741234, ⓦgatheringplacebistro.co.uk. Convivial restaurant in the heart of the village offering mouthwatering, Scottish-based cuisine, including a terrific homemade Bistro haggis puff, and a venison casserole in a red wine and port source (£18.95). Tues–Sun 5–10pm.

Taste Beside the Mar Rd roundabout ☎01339 741425, ⓦtaste-braemar.co.uk. Reliably good coffee shop and moderately priced contemporary restaurant doing home-made, gluten-free soups (served with local bread) for £3.80. Tues–Sat 10am–5pm.

The Don Valley

The quiet countryside around the **Don Valley**, once renowned for its illegal whisky distilleries and smugglers, lies at the heart of Aberdeenshire's prosperous agricultural region. From Aberdeen, the River Don winds northwest through **Inverurie**, where it takes a sharp turn west to **Alford**, then continues past ruined castles through the **Upper Don Valley** and the heather moorlands of the eastern Highlands. This remote and under-visited area is positively littered with ruined castles, Pictish sites, stones and hillforts.

Alford and around

ALFORD (pronounced "aa-ford"), 21 miles northwest of Banchory, only exists at all because it was chosen, in 1859, as the terminus for the Great North Scotland Railway. A fairly grey little town now firmly within the Aberdeen commuter belt, it's still well worth making the trip here for the Grampian Transport Museum.

Grampian Transport Museum

Main St • Daily: April–Sept 10am–5pm; Oct 10am–4pm • £10 • ☎01975 562292, ⓦgtm.org.uk

The **Grampian Transport Museum** is home to a diverse display of transport through the ages, from old tramcars and pushbikes to modern, ecofriendly cars. Notable permanent exhibits include the Craigevar Express, a strange, three-wheeled steam-driven vehicle developed by the local postman for his rounds, the last surviving Scottish-built Sentinel waggon (1913), and that famous monument to British eccentricity and ingenuity, the Sinclair C5 motorized tricycle. Many of the vehicles are taken from private collections and other museums, so they do vary from year to year.

Craigievar Castle

6 miles south of Alford on the A980 • Castle April & May Fri–Tues 10.30am–4pm; June–Sept daily 10.30am–4pm; Oct Sat & Sun 11am–3pm; grounds daily dawn–dusk • £13; NTS • ☎01339 883635, ⓦnts.org.uk

South of Alford on the A980, **Craigievar Castle** is a fantastic pink confection of turrets, gables, balustrades and cupolas bubbling over from its top three storeys. It was built in 1626 by a Baltic trader known as Willy the Merchant, who evidently allowed his whimsy to run riot. Entertainingly-led guided tours (in necessarily small groups owing to the narrow corridors and small areas) take in a number of rooms, where you can admire Jacobean woodwork and original plaster ceilings, while the grounds hold a Victorian kitchen garden and a Scottish glen garden. With a bit more time on your hands, there are a couple of lovely waymarked trails too.

ARRIVAL AND INFORMATION	ALFORD AND AROUND
By bus Stagecoach Bluebird buses #218 and #220 link Aberdeen with Alford (1hr 10min).	**Tourist information** The Grampian Transport Museum (see above) stocks loads of tourist infomation.

2

Lumsden

The A944 heads west from Alford, meeting the A97 just south of the tiny village of **LUMSDEN**, an unexpected hot spot of Scottish sculpture. A contemporary **Sculpture Walk** – heralded by a fabulous skeletal black horse at its southern end – runs parallel to the main road, coming out near the premises of the widely respected **Scottish Sculpture Workshop**, 1 Main St (Mon–Fri 9am–5pm, or by arrangement; free; ⓦssw.org.uk), very much an active workshop rather than a gallery, at the northern end of the village.

Rhynie

The village of **RHYNIE**, folded beautifully into the hills four miles north of Lumsden up the A97, is forever associated with one of the greatest Pictish memorials, the **Rhynie Man**, a remarkable 6ft-high boulder discovered in 1978, depicting a rare whole figure, clad in a tunic and holding what is thought to be a ceremonial axe. The original is in Woodhill House in Aberdeen, but there's a cast on display at the school in Rhynie, across the road from the church. A further claim to fame for the village is that the bedrock lying deep beneath it, known as **Rhynie Chert**, contains plant and insect fossils up to 400 million years old, making them some of the earth's oldest.

Tap o'Noth

A mile or so from Rhynie, along the A941 to Dufftown, a car park gives access to a path up the looming **Tap o'Noth**, Scotland's second-highest Pictish hillfort (1847ft), where substantial remnants of the wall around the lip of the summit show evidence of vitrification (fierce burning), probably to fuse the rocks together.

The Upper Don valley

Travelling west from Alford, settlements become noticeably more scattered and remote as the countryside takes on a more open, recognizably Highland appearance. The **Lecht Road**, crossing the area of bleak but wonderfully empty high country to the remote mountain village of Tomintoul (see page 177), passes the Lecht Ski Centre at 2090ft above sea level, but is frequently impassable in winter due to snow.

Kildrummy Castle

Kildrummy, 10 miles west of Alford off the A97 · **Castle** April–Sept daily 9.30am–5.30pm · £6; HES · **Gardens** April–Oct daily noon–5pm · £4.50 · ☎01975 571203, ⓦhistoricenvironment.scot

Ten miles from Alford stand the impressive ruins of the thirteenth-century **Kildrummy Castle**, where Robert the Bruce sent his wife and children during the Wars of Independence. The castle blacksmith, bribed with as much gold as he could carry, set fire to the place and it fell into English hands. Bruce's immediate family survived, but his brother was executed and the entire garrison hanged, drawn and quartered. Meanwhile, the duplicitous blacksmith was rewarded for his help by having molten gold poured down his throat. The sixth earl of Mar used the castle as the headquarters of the ill-fated Jacobite risings in 1715, but after that Kildrummy became redundant and it fell into disrepair. Beside the ruins, the separate **Kildrummy Castle Gardens** are quite a draw, boasting everything from swathes of azaleas in spring to Himalayan poppies in summer.

Lost Gallery

4 miles north of Strathdon • Wed–Mon 11am–5pm • Free • ☎ 01975 651287, ⓦ lostgallery.co.uk

Ten miles west of Kildrummy Castle, the A944 sweeps round into the parish of **Strathdon**, little more than a few buildings scattered along the roadside. Four miles north of here, up a rough track leading into Glen Nochty, lies the unexpected **Lost Gallery**, which shows work by some of Scotland's leading modern artists in a wonderfully remote and tranquil setting.

Corgarff Castle

Corgarff, 10 miles southwest of Strathdon • April–Sept daily 9.30am–5.30pm • £6; HES • ☎ 01316 688800, ⓦ historicenvironment.scot

In Corgarff, just off the A939, lies **Corgarff Castle**, an austere tower house with an unusual star-shaped curtain wall and an eventful history. Built in 1537, it was turned into a barracks in 1748, in the aftermath of Culloden, by the Hanoverian government in order to track down local Jacobite rebels; a century later, English redcoats were stationed here with the unpopular task of trying to control whisky smuggling. Today the place has been restored to resemble its days as a barracks, with stark rooms and rows of hard, uncomfortable beds – authentic touches which also extend to graffiti on the walls and peat smoke permeating the building from a fire on the upper storey.

Strathspey

Rising high in the heather-clad hills above remote Loch Laggan, forty miles due south of Inverness, the **River Spey**, Scotland's second-longest river, drains northeast towards the Moray Firth through one of the Highlands' most spellbinding valleys. Famous for its ancient forests, salmon fishing and ospreys, the area around the upper section of the river, known as **STRATHSPEY**, is dominated by the sculpted **Cairngorms**, Britain's most extensive mountain massif, unique in supporting subarctic tundra on its high plateau. Though the area has been admired and treasured for many years as one of Scotland's prime natural assets, the Cairngorms National Park was only declared in 2004. Outdoor enthusiasts flock to the area to take advantage of the superb hiking, biking, watersports and winter snows, aided by the fact that the area is easily accessible by road and rail from both the central belt and Inverness.

A string of towns and villages along the river provides useful bases for setting out into the wilder country, principal among them **Aviemore**, a rather ugly straggle of housing and hotel developments which nevertheless has a lively, youthful feel to it. It's also a good first stop for information, to sort out somewhere to stay or to find out about nearby outdoor activities, which are likely to seem very enticing after a glimpse of the stunning mountain scenery provided by the 4000ft-summit plateau of the Cairngorms. South of Aviemore, the sedate villages of **Newtonmore** and **Kingussie** are older established holiday centres, more popular with anglers and grouse hunters than canoeists and climbers.

The planned Georgian town of **Grantown-on-Spey** is an attractive alternative base for outdoor activities, with solid Victorian mansions but fewer facilities for visitors than Aviemore, while smaller settlements such as **Boat of Garten** and **Kincraig** are quieter, well-kept villages. The whole area boasts a wide choice of good-quality accommodation, particularly in the budget market, with various easy-going hostels run by and for outdoor enthusiasts.

Aviemore and around

The once-sleepy village of **AVIEMORE** was first developed as a ski and tourism resort in the mid-1960s and, over the years, fell victim to profiteering developers with scant regard for the needs of the local community. Despite recent attempts to turn things around, it remains a soulless hotchpotch of retail outlets, café-bars and characterless housing developments. That said, Aviemore is undeniably well equipped with services and facilities and is the most convenient base for the Cairngorms.

In summer, the main activities around Aviemore are walking (see page 165) and watersports, and there are great opportunities for pony trekking and fly-fishing (for the latter, the Aviemore tourist office provides a brochure outlining which permits you'll need). For both the adventurous and novice cyclist, the entire region is great for mountain biking; the Rothiemurchus Estate has several excellent (and non-technical) waymarked trails running through its extensive lands. Sailing, windsurfing and canoeing are also popular, with a specialist centre at Loch Insh providing lessons and loaning out equipment.

Wintertime sees the tourist focus switch away from the lochs and rivers and up towards the surrounding slopes, home to a well-established ski resort, a dogsled centre, and a herd of reindeer – a species reintroduced to Scotland from Scandinavia – now acting as an unlikely tourist attraction.

Strathspey Steam Railway

Aviemore Station, Dalfaber Rd · July & Aug three times daily; less regular service at other times · £15.75 return · ☏ 01479 810725,
ⓦ strathspeyrailway.co.uk

2

CAIRNGORMS NATIONAL PARK

The **Cairngorms National Park** (ⓦcairngorms.co.uk) covers almost 1750 square miles and incorporates the **Cairngorms massif**, the largest mountainscape in the UK and the only sizeable plateau in the country over 2500ft. It's the biggest national park in Britain, and while Aviemore and the surrounding area are regarded as the main point of entry, particularly for those planning outdoor activities, it's also possible to access the park from Perthshire as well as Deeside and Donside in Aberdeenshire. Crossing the range is a significant challenge: by road the only connection is the A939 Tomintoul to Cock Bridge, frequently impassable in winter due to snow. On foot the only way to avoid the high peaks is to follow the old cattle drovers' route called the **Lairig Ghru**, a very long day's walk between Inverdruie at the edge of Rothiemurchus and the Linn of Dee, near Inverey.

The name Cairngorm comes from the Gaelic *An Carm Gorm*, meaning "the blue hill" after the blueish-tinged stones found in the area, and within the park there are 52 summits over 2950ft, as well as a quarter of Scotland's native woodland and a quarter of the UK's threatened wildlife species. The conservation of the landscape's unique flora and fauna is, of course, one of the principal reasons national park status was conferred.

Vegetation in the area ranges from one of the largest tracts of ancient **Caledonian pine and birch forest** remaining in Scotland at Rothiemurchus, to subarctic tundra on the high plateau, where **alpine flora** such as starry saxifrage and the star-shaped pink flowers of moss campion peek out of the pink granite in the few months of summer that the ground is free of snow. In the pine forests of the river valleys, strikingly coloured **birds** such as crested tits, redwings and goldfinches can be observed, along with rarely seen **mammals** such as the red squirrel and pine marten. On the heather slopes above the forest, red and black grouse are often encountered, though their larger relative, the capercaillie, is a much rarer sight, having been reintroduced in 1837 after dying out in the seventeenth century. Birds of prey you're most likely to see are **osprey**, best seen at the **Abernethy Forest RSPB Reserve** (see page 168) at Loch Garten or fishing on the lochs around Aviemore, though golden eagles and peregrine falcons can occasionally be seen higher up. Venturing up to the plateau, you'll have the chance of seeing the shy **ptarmigan**, another member of the grouse family, which nests on bare rock and has white plumage during winter, or even the dotterel and snow bunting, rare visitors from the Arctic.

The main attractions of Aviemore are its outdoor pursuits, though train enthusiasts are also drawn to the restored **Strathspey Steam Railway**, which chugs the short distance between Aviemore and Broomhill, just beyond Boat of Garten village. Originally part of the Inverness & Perth Junction Railway (later the Highland Railway) which opened in 1863, the line was axed in the 1960s as a result of the infamous Beeching cuts. However, by 1978, services had been restored between Aviemore and Boat of Garten, which were then extended to Broomhill in 2002. The return journey takes an hour and a half, with glimpses of the Cairngorm Mountains visible through the trees; for the best views sit on the right-hand side leaving Aviemore.

Cairngorm Sleddog Adventure Centre

Moormore Cottage, 3 miles east of Aviemore on the Rothiemurchus Estate • Sledding Oct–April, by appointment • Museum £8; 50min sled experience £85/person; 3hr sled dog safaris £175/person; no under 12s • ☎ 07767 270526, ⓦ sled-dogs.co.uk

Between Loch Morlich and Inverdruie lies the **Cairngorm Sleddog Adventure Centre**, the UK's only sleddog centre. On a pre-booked tour of the centre's museum you can meet the centre's dogs and learn more about the history of sledding. More exhilarating are the centre's fifty-minute trips through the forest on a wheeled or ski-based sled, pulled by around ten dogs.

Cairngorm Reindeer Centre

6.5 miles southeast of Aviemore, on the road to *Glenmore Lodge* • Daily 10am–5pm • Guided excursions May–Sept 11am & 2.30pm; July & Aug also 3.30pm; rest of year 11am; closed Jan–mid-Feb • £16 • ☎ 01479 861228, ⓦ cairngormreindeer.co.uk

One of the more unusual attractions in the area, the **Cairngorm Reindeer Centre** by Loch Morlich is home to around 150 animals, some of them free-roaming. Although the reindeer here today were all born in Scotland, they are descended from a small group brought to the area from Sweden and Norway in the 1950s and 1960s. Guided hill visits entail a ninety-minute excursion up into the mountain, where you have the opportunity to stroke and hand feed the reindeer; note that the visit involves around thirty minutes of walking over fairly rough terrain – bring warm weather gear too. For those unable to partake in a hill visit, you can visit, and pet, a handful of reindeer down in the paddock by the centre (£3.50).

Cairngorm Ski Area

9 miles southeast of Aviemore • Ski season Dec–April, but varies depending on snowfall • ☎ 01479 861261, ⓦ cairngormmountain.co.uk • Buses (#31) from Aviemore wind past Inverdruie, stopping at the Coire Cas car park (April–Oct £2), near the ranger's office

By continental European and North American standards it's all on a tiny scale, but occasionally snow and sun coincide at the **Cairngorm Ski Area** high above Loch Morlich in Glenmore Forest Park to offer beginner and expert alike a great day on the pistes. The ski area is well served by public transport; from the car park at Coire Cas (2150ft), there is a **funicular railway**, and while this is the principal means of getting to the top of the ski slopes, it has been a source of controversy ever since its inception in 2001. Bitterly opposed by conservationists in the first place, it has been out of commission for some time now and there are few signs that it will reopen any time soon.

Ranger's Base

Accessed via the Coire Cas car park • Daily 9am–5pm • Free, exhibition £5

At the Cairngorm Ski Area **ranger's base**, there's a new exhibition, Cairngorm Story, which relays the history of the mountains, its climate, flora and fauna and so on. Here too you can find out about various trails, check the latest weather report and – on Thursdays between May and October – join guided walks (£10) out to the Corries. There are a couple of excellent cafés here too.

ARRIVAL AND DEPARTURE   AVIEMORE AND AROUND

By train Aviemore's train station is on Grampian Rd, just   south of the tourist office.

WALKS AROUND AVIEMORE

Ordnance Survey Explorer maps 402 & 403
Walking of all grades is a highlight of the Aviemore area, though you should heed the usual safety guidelines (see page 42). These are particularly important if you want to venture into the subarctic climatic zone of the **Cairngorms**. However, as well as the high mountain trails, there are some lovely and well-signposted low-level walks in the area.

LOCH AN EILEAN

It takes an hour or so to complete the gentle circular walk around pretty **Loch an Eilean** with its ruined castle in the Rothiemurchus Estate, beginning at the end of the back road that turns east off the B970 a mile south of Inverdruie. The helpful estate visitor centres at the lochside and by the roadside at Inverdruie provide more information on other woodland trails.

RYVOAN PASS

Another good, shortish (half-day) walk leads along a well-surfaced forestry track from Glenmore Lodge up towards the **Ryvoan Pass**, taking in An Lochan Uaine, known as the "Green Loch" and living up to its name, with amazing colours that range from turquoise to slate grey depending on the weather.

MEALL A'BHUACHALLIE

The **Glenmore Forest Park Visitor Centre** (daily 9am–5pm; ☎ 01479 861220, ⓦ forestryandland. gov.scot) by the roadside at the turn-off to *Glenmore Lodge* is the starting point for the three-hour round-trip climb of **Meall a'Bhuachaillie** (2654ft), which offers excellent views and is usually accessible year-round. The centre has information on other trails in this section of the forest.

2

Destinations Edinburgh (Mon–Sat 12 daily, 6 on Sun; 3hr); Glasgow (11 daily, 6 on Sun; 2hr 50min); Inverness (Mon–Sat 11 daily, 7 on Sun; 40min).
By bus Buses depart from outside the train station.

Destinations Cairngorm ski area (hourly; 30min); Edinburgh (6 daily; 3–4hr); Glasgow (5 daily; 2hr 40min–3hr 20min); Grantown-on-Spey (Mon–Sat every 30min–1hr, 4 on Sun; 30min); Inverness (at least 11 daily; 45min).

GETTING AROUND AND INFORMATION

By bus The most useful local bus route is the #31, which runs hourly from Aviemore to the Cairngorm Mountain Railway (see page 165) via Rothiemurchus and Loch Morlich. The #34 service is also handy, running regularly to Grantown (roughly hourly; 40min) via Boat of Garten.
Tourist office 7 The Parade, Grampian Rd (April & May Mon–Sat 9am–5pm, Sun 10am–5pm; June Mon–Sat 9am–6pm, Sun 9.30am–5pm; July & Aug Mon–Sat

9.30am–6.30pm, Sun 9.30am–6pm; Sept–March Mon, Tue & Thu–Sat 9am–5pm, Wed 10am–5pm, Sun 10am–4pm; ☎01479 810930). Offers an accommodation booking service and reams of leaflets on local attractions.
By bike Mikes Bikes, 5a Myrtlefield Shopping Centre (Mon–Sat 9.30am–5.30pm, Sun 11am–4pm; ☎01479 810478, ⓦ aviemorebikes.co.uk) has an excellent range of electric and mountain bikes for hire (£15/3hr, £20/day); they do repairs too.

ACTIVITIES

FISHING
Rothiemurchus Estate Inverdruie (☎01479 812915, ⓦ rothiemurchus.net). Has a stocked rainbow trout-fishing loch, where success is virtually guaranteed. There are various permutations for fishing here including catch and release (£27/day) and a ninety-minute lesson followed by ninety-minute's fishing costs £65.

HORSERIDING
Alvie Stables 5 miles south of Aviemore, near Kincraig (☎07831 495397, ⓦ alvie-estate.co.uk). Family-friendly riding centre set in superb countryside a short drive from Aviemore, offering 30min lessons and longer guided rides (£25/hr).

OUTDOOR TRAINING
National Outdoor Training Centre Glenmore Lodge, 8 miles east of Aviemore (☎01479 861256, ⓦ glenmore lodge.org.uk). For a crash course in surviving Scottish winters, you could do worse than try a week at the National Outdoor Training Centre, at the east end of Loch Morlich. This superbly equipped and organized centre (complete with cosy après-ski bar) offers winter and summer courses in hillwalking, mountaineering, alpine

ski-mountaineering, avalanche awareness and much more.

SKIING
G2 Outdoor Plot 10, Dalfaber Industrial Estate, Aviemore (☎01540 651784, ⓦ g2outdoor.co.uk). The experts at G2 Outdoor will provide tuition in the art of telemarking and back-country skiing (£65 for a minimum of 4 people). In summer, they also run whitewater rafting (£60) and canyoning trips, among others.
The Ski School In the Day Lodge, near the funicular railway's base station in the Cairngorm Ski Area (☎01479 811066, ⓦ theskischool.co.uk), this is your best bet for ski/board rental and lessons.

WATERSPORTS
See also G2 Outdoor in "Skiing", above.
Loch Insh Outdoor Centre 6 miles up-valley near Kincraig (☎01540 651272, ⓦ lochinsh.com). Offers a whole host of land and water-based activities, in the form of courses and trips as well as equipment hire; for example kayaks (£15/90min, £25/3hr) and mountain bikes (£35/day). To save visitors travelling back and forth from Aviemore, the centre also offers accommodation, and there's also a restaurant here.

ACCOMMODATION   SEE MAP PAGE 163

HOTELS AND B&BS
Glenmore Lodge 8 miles east of Aviemore ☎01479 861256, ⓦ glenmorelodge.org.uk. Specialist outdoor pursuits centre with excellent accommodation in en-suite twin rooms and self-catered lodges – guests can make use of the superb facilities, which include a pool, weights room, sauna and indoor climbing wall. Twins £88
Ravenscraig Guest House 141 Grampian Rd ☎01479 810278, ⓦ aviemoreonline.com. This welcoming, family-friendly B&B has a handy central location. Single, double and family rooms available, plus a wide choice of breakfast

options, including sausages bought from a local butcher. £92

HOSTELS AND BUNKHOUSES
Aviemore Bunkhouse Dalfaber Rd, next to the Old Bridge Inn ☎01479 811181, ⓦ aviemore-bunkhouse. com. A large modern place beside a cosy pub and within walking distance from the station, with six-bed dorms, plus family and private rooms; bike storage, dryer room and laundry. Dorms £23; doubles £55
Aviemore Youth Hostel 25 Grampian Rd ☎01479 810345, ⓦ hostellingscotland.org.uk. Aviemore's large

SYHA hostel, with its own bike store and drying room, has rather plain rooms but is within easy walking distance of the town centre. Dorms £17; singles £25; twins £45

Cairngorm Lodge Youth Hostel 6.5 miles east of Aviemore, by Loch Morlich ☎01479 861238, ⓦ hostellingscotland.org.uk. Located out towards the Cairngorms at Loch Morlich this old shooting lodge now accommodates a range of comfortable, if tired-looking, rooms; bike storage and drying room facilities. Closed Nov &

Dec; Jan open weekends only. Dorms £15; twins £34

CAMPING

Rothiemurchus Caravan Park 2 miles southeast of Aviemore in Coylumbridge ☎01479 812800, ⓦ rothiemurchus.net. Relaxed site for tents and caravans, nestled among tall pine trees at Coylumbridge, on the way to Loch Morlich. Per person £13

2

EATING AND DRINKING

Old Bridge Inn Dalfaber Rd, next to Aviemore Bunkhouse ☎01479 811137, ⓦ oldbridgeinn.co.uk. Fire-warmed pub that hosts regular live music sessions and serves some very creditable dishes, for example pork loin on toasted ciabatta with caramelised onions (£11). Mon–Thurs & Sun noon–midnight, Fri & Sat noon–1am; food served noon–2.30pm & 6–9pm.

The Winking Owl 123 Grampian Rd ☎01479 812368, ⓦ thewinkingowl.co. Lively brewery pub serving draught ales and beers from the nearby Cairngorm Brewery alongside classy Mediterranean/Scottish food. First-rate programme of live music too in the adjoining Bothy Bar. Mon–Thurs noon–11pm, Fri & Sat noon–1am, Sun 12.30–11pm; food served Mon–Sat noon–9.30pm, Sun 12.30–9.30pm.

Carrbridge

Worth considering as an alternative to Aviemore – particularly as a skiing base – **CARRBRIDGE** is a pleasant, quiet village about seven miles north. Look out for the spindly Bridge of Carr at the northern end of the village, built in 1717 and still making a graceful stone arch over the River Dulnain.

Landmark Forest Adventure Park

Just off the B9153 at the southern end of the village • Daily: April–mid-July & Sept & Oct 10am–5/6pm; mid-July–Aug 10am–7pm; Nov–March 10am–4pm • £21.45 (Nov–March £7.25) • ☎ 08007 313446, ⓦ landmarkpark.co.uk

The main attraction in the village is the **Landmark Forest Adventure Park**, which offers families a host of excellent outdoor and indoor activities the best of which are treetop trails, a climbing wall, and a new dinosaur kingdom complete with sound effects; elsewhere there's the Lost Labyrinth maze, Bamboozeleum (magical and illusory effects), and a couple of theme park type rides. Note that whilst the park is open year-round, some of the attractions are closed during the winter period, hence the much reduced admission fee.

ARRIVAL AND DEPARTURE   CARRBRIDGE

By train The train station is around half a mile west of the village centre, served by trains from Aviemore (5–6 daily; 10min) and Inverness (4–5 daily; 30min).

By bus Frequent buses (every 1–2hr; 15min) from/to Aviemore stop at the car park 200yds south of the river on the B9153.

ACCOMMODATION

MellonPatch Station Rd, roughly halfway between the train station and the Bridge of Carr ☎01479 841592, ⓦ mellonpatch.com. Rambling house with three, large

colour-themed rooms and friendly owners; look out, too, for woodpeckers and red squirrels in the garden. The rate includes a substantial full Scottish breakfast. £80

Boat of Garten

Seven miles northeast of Aviemore, close to the River Spey, is the attractive village of **BOAT OF GARTEN**, which has a number of good accommodation options. A short drive or pleasant walk away on the other side of the river is the northeastern shore of **Loch Garten**, famous as the nesting site of the osprey, one of Britain's rarest birds.

Abernethy Forest RSPB Reserve

2.5 miles east of Boat of Garten, on the northeastern edge of Loch Garten • Reserve open year-round; visitor centre daily: April–Aug 10am–6pm; 3hr guided walks late May–early Aug Wed 9.30am • £5; guided walks £6 • ☎ 01479 831476, ⓦ rspb.org.uk • To get here from the village, cross the Spey then take the Grantown road; the reserve is signposted to the right

A little over fifty years ago, the **osprey**, known in North America as the fish hawk, had completely disappeared from the British Isles. Then, in 1954, a single pair of these exquisite white-and-brown raptors mysteriously reappeared and built a nest in a tree half a mile or so from Loch Garten, now the location of the **Abernethy Forest RSPB Reserve**. There are now believed to be somewhere between two hundred and fifty and three hundred pairs nesting across the UK. The best time to visit is between April and August, when the ospreys return from West Africa to nest and the RSPB opens an **observation centre**, complete with powerful telescopes and CCTV monitoring of the nest. The reserve is also home to several other rare species, including the Scottish crossbill, capercaillie, whooper swan and red squirrel. Once-weekly **guided walks** leave from the observation centre, while during the spring lekking season (April to mid-May) when male capercaillie gather and joust with each other, the centre opens at 5.30am for "Caperwatch".

ARRIVAL AND DEPARTURE
BOAT OF GARTEN

By train Strathspey Steam Railway trains (July & Aug daily, less frequent at other times) stop at the attractive old station in the centre of Boat of Garten and run to Aviemore (3 daily; 15min) and Broomhill (3 daily; 25min).

By bus Buses from Aviemore run hourly to Boat of Garten (12min), stopping outside the post office on Deshar Rd.

ACCOMMODATION AND EATING

Anderson's Deshar Rd, 300yds west of the train station ☎ 01479 831466, ⓦ andersonsrestaurant.co.uk. Attractive place for lunch or dinner, serving creative dishes based on local ingredients, like pan fried salmon fillet with Mull cheddar and buttered samphire (£20). Mon & Wed–Sun noon–1.45pm & 5.30–9.30pm.

Boat Hotel Just across from the train station ☎ 01479 831258, ⓦ boathotel.co.uk. The most elegant place to stay in the village, with fresh, airy bedrooms, some of which look down the garden to the heritage railway. The hotel also has a bistro serving its own interpretations of Scottish favourites – from haggis pakora to a "Big Yin" burger. £110

★ **Fraoch Lodge** 15 Deshar Rd ☎ 01479 831331, ⓦ scotmountainholidays.com. Enthusiastically run by a couple of experienced mountaineers, this excellent hostel providing high-quality home-cooked meals (plus homemade cakes and bread) along with good facilities such as a purpose-built drying room, bike wash and bike shed. They also offer guided walking holidays. Minimum stay of two nights when booking in advance. Singles £25; twins £50

★ **Old Ferryman's House** Just east of the village, across the Spey ☎ 01479 831370. A wonderfully simple and homely B&B, with an old-school approach: a wood-burning stove, no TVs, lots of books and delicious evening meals and breakfasts. £85

Kincraig

Around **KINCRAIG**, six miles southwest of Aviemore on the B9152 towards Kingussie, there are a couple of unusual encounters with animals which offer a memorable diversion if you're not setting off on outdoor pursuits.

Highland Wildlife Park

2 miles southwest of Kincraig • Daily: July–Aug 10am–6pm; April–June, Sept & Oct 10am–5pm; Nov–March 10am–4pm; last entry 1hr before closing • £17.95 • ☎ 01540 651270, ⓦ highlandwildlifepark.org

Run by the Royal Zoological Society of Scotland, the **Highland Wildlife Park** – a combined safari park and zoo – is well worth a few hours of your time. There are some real star animals here, including four of the eight polar bears in captivity in Britain (the other four are at the Yorkshire Wildlife Park in Doncaster), snow leopards (cubs were born here in 2019), red pandas and arctic foxes – and of course, Scottish wildcats. No less enjoyable is a drive around the safari park, where you can get up close to vicuna, elk, bison and Przewalski's horses, critically endangered

CYCLISTS ON THE AVIEMORE TO BOAT OF GARTEN ROUTE

wild horses from the Mongolian steppe. There are regular talks and feeding sessions within the zoo itself, in addition to free guided tours of the park, useful if you don't have your own car.

Working Sheepdogs

Leault Farm, just off the A9 near Kincraig • June–Oct Mon–Fri & Sun 4pm • £7 • ☎ 01540 651402, ⓦ leaultworkingsheepdogs.co.uk

Nearby, the engrossing **Working Sheepdogs** demonstrations at Leault Farm afford the rare opportunity to see champion shepherd, Neil Ross, herd a flock of sheep with up to eight dogs, using a bewildering array of whistles and other commands. The fascinating 45-minute-long display also includes a chance to see traditional hand-shearing (and you can have a go yourself) and collie-pup training.

ACCOMMODATION AND EATING

KINCRAIG

Loch Insh Watersports Centre ☎ 01540 651272, ⓦ lochinsh.com. This popular activity centre has basic but practical B&B rooms, some with en-suite bathrooms, as well as an all-day restaurant serving burgers and the like for around £8. Daily 10am–8pm. **£54**

Grantown-on-Spey

Around fifteen miles northeast of Aviemore, the pretty town of **GRANTOWN-ON-SPEY** makes a good alternative base for exploring the Strathspey area. Local life is concentrated around the central square, with its attractive Georgian architecture, but there are plenty of opportunities for hiking and biking in the immediate area.

ARRIVAL AND GETTING AROUND

GRANTOWN-ON-SPEY

By bus Buses from Aviemore (roughly hourly; 35min) and Inverness (at least 2 per day Mon–Sat; 1hr 10min) stop on Grantown-on-Spey's high street.
Bike rental You'll find good bikes and decent coffee at BaseCamp Bikes (Mon 10am–5pm, Tues–Sat 9.30am–5.30pm; ☎ 01479 870050, ⓦ basecampmtb.com; £25/day), next door to the Co-op store on the town's main square; they also offer a delivery service.

ACCOMMODATION

★ **Dunallan House** Woodside Avenue ☎ 01479 872140, ⓦ dunallan.com. Large house with big double rooms – all en suite or with private facilities – and comfy, welcoming lounges to relax in. The room on the top floor, with a freestanding bathtub across the landing, is the pick of the bunch. **£100**
Garth Hotel Castle Rd, at the north end of the town square ☎ 01479 872836, ⓦ garthhotel.com. If you're after some reasonably swish accommodation, head for the large seventeenth-century *Garth Hotel*, where the restaurant serves respectable, traditional meat-based dinners. **£108**
★ **Lazy Duck Hostel** Nethy Bridge, 6 miles south of town ☎ 01479 821642, ⓦ lazyduck.co.uk. A peaceful and comfortable retreat featuring a range of quirky accommodation possibilities, for example a five-bed bunkhouse, woodman's hut and waterside lodge (both sleeping two), plus woodland camping (May–Oct). Hostel 3 days **£360**; hut and lodge 3 days **£375**; camping per pitch **£15**

EATING AND DRINKING

Craig Bar Woodside Avenue ☎ 01479 872669, ⓦ the craigbar.co.uk. Snug pub full of military aviation memorabilia, from pictures of fighter planes to dangling model aircraft. Warm yourself by the fire with a pint of real ale while you choose some food. The choice is made easy; the jovial landlord only sells pies (£8.45), made with free-range meat – and with chips of course. Mon–Fri 5pm–midnight, Sat & Sun noon–midnight.

The High Street Merchants 74 High St ☎ 01479 872246, ⓦ thehighstreetmerchants.com. An attractive wood-lined café and gallery on the high street serving organic, fairtrade and local food; lunchtime platters cost £9, while the evening menu features thin crust pizzas and burgers. Tues–Sat 10am–5pm, Sun 10am–4pm, plus Fri & Sat 5.30–10pm.

Kingussie

Twelve miles southwest of Aviemore at the head of the Strathspey Valley, **KINGUSSIE** (pronounced "king-yoos-ee") is a pleasant village best known for the free-to-access ruins of Ruthven Barracks, which stand east across the river on a hillock. The best-preserved garrison built to pacify the Highlands after the 1715 rebellion, it makes for great exploring by day and is impressively floodlit at night.

ARRIVAL AND DEPARTURE

By train Kingussie's train station is on Station Rd, just south of the A86.

Destinations Edinburgh (Mon–Sat 7 daily, 5 on Sun; 2hr 40min); Glasgow (Mon–Sat 4 daily, 2 on Sun; 2hr 30min); Inverness (Mon–Sat 12 daily, 7 on Sun; 55min); Newtonmore (Mon–Sat 5 daily, 3 on Sun; 5min).

By bus Buses arrive at and depart from near the *Duke of Gordon Hotel*, on the high street.

Destinations Edinburgh (5 daily; 3hr 30min); Inverness (Mon–Sat 8 daily, 5 on Sun; 1hr); Newtonmore (roughly hourly; 5min).

ACCOMMODATION AND EATING

★ **The Cross** North of the centre off Ardbroilach Rd ☎01540 661166, ⓦthecross.co.uk. One of the most appealing places to stay in the whole of Speyside, this relaxed but stylish restaurant with rooms is located in a converted tweed mill on the River Gynack. The restaurant is the most ambitious (and costly) in the area, where a three-course meal carefully crafted from fresh Scottish ingredients like Shetland lobster and Perthshire lamb costs £55; lunch menu £30. Daily 7–8.30pm. **£110**

The Tipsy Laird 68 High St ☎01540 661334, ⓦthetipsylaird.co.uk. No-frills pub on the high street which hosts occasional jam sessions and karaoke nights. They have a good selection of malt whiskies and offer simple bar food. Daily noon–11pm.

Newtonmore

Kingussie's closest neighbour, **NEWTONMORE**, is also its biggest rival. The two villages, separated by a couple of miles of farmland, both have long-established shinty teams that battle for dominance in the game, a fierce indigenous sport from which ice hockey and golf evolved. Newtonmore itself is notable for its top-notch folk museum, and there are plenty of rough-and-ready mountain-biking routes in the forests to the south.

Highland Folk Museum

Kingussie Rd • Daily: April–Aug 10.30am–5.30pm; Sept & Oct 11am–4.30pm • Free; donation requested • ☎01540 673551, ⓦhighlandfolk.com

Newtonmore's chief attraction is the excellent **Highland Folk Museum**, one of Scotland's most rewarding outdoor sites. Split between a 1700s Township, the Middle Village, and a working croft, you could quite easily spend half a day here wandering around the thirty odd structures, many of which have been moved from their original location. Among the highlights is the Knockbain School from Kirkhill near Inverness dating from 1925; complete with a cast-iron range and rows of ink-drenched desks, you can try your hand at writing with a fountain pen under the watchful eye of a suitably stern Victorian teacher – she'll even mark it for you. Elsewhere there's the Blackhouse from the Isle of Lewis, thickly thatched and encircled by a high stone wall so as to withstand the ferocious Atlantic weather, and Kirk's Store, where you can indulge in all your sweet-toothed fantasies.

Laggan Wolftrax

8 miles southwest of Newtonmore on the A86, just beyond the junction with the A889 from Dalwhinnie • Laggan Wolftrax Centre Easter–Oct daily 10am–5pm; Nov–Easter Sat & Sun • Free; car parking £3/day • ☎01463 791575, ⓦforestryandland.gov.scot and ⓦlagganforest.com

Laggan Wolftrax is a superb, free facility with more than twenty miles of marked mountain-biking trails to suit all abilities. The three-mile-long green route is the best place for those starting out, but expert riders might prefer the gruelling four-mile black route, which traverses a steep and rocky staircase made up of uneven slabs. The Laggan Wolftrax Centre itself has toilets, coin-operated showers and a superb café serving breakfasts and hot lunches.

ARRIVAL AND INFORMATION

NEWTONMORE

By train The train station is south of the centre on Station Rd. Destinations Edinburgh (Mon–Sat 3 daily, 2 on Sun; 2hr 30min); Glasgow (Mon–Sat 2 daily, 1 on Sun; 2hr 20min); Inverness (Mon–Sat 5 daily, 3 on Sun; 55min); Kingussie (Mon–Sat 5 daily, 3 on Sun; 5min).

By bus Buses for Edinburgh and Inverness arrive at and depart from Main St. Destinations Edinburgh (Mon–Fri 5 daily; 3hr 25min); Inverness (Mon–Sat 8 daily, 5 on Sun; 1hr 10min); Kingussie (roughly hourly; 5min).

Tourist information The volunteer-run Wildcat Centre on Main St (June–Aug Mon–Thurs 10am–4pm, Fri & Sat 10am–1pm; Sept–May Mon–Sat 10am–1pm; ☏01540 673131, ⍟wildcatcentre.org) has loads of info on the town and surrounding areas. They also run the hugely popular Wildcat Experience, which entails tracking down 132 colourfully painted model wildcats scattered around town; a wildcat trackpack, which includes brochure, map and pen, costs £10. There's also the Wildcat Trail, a 10km waymarked orbital walk around Newtonmore.

ACCOMMODATION

Coig Na Shee Laggan Rd, a 10min walk west of Main St ☏01540 670109, ⍟coignashee.co.uk. A soothingly decorated B&B in an old Edwardian hunting lodge with five bright and immaculate rooms fitted out in different colours; good value, though there is a two-night minimum stay between May and September. __£80__

★ **Where Stags Roar** Caman House, Main St ☏07876 745081, ⍟wherestagsroar.co.uk. A handful of different accommodation options, all located on, or just off, Main Street, the pick of which is The Byre; positioned just behind the Wildcat Centre, this large and cosy detached cottage features a light and spacious open-plan ground floor manifesting oak flooring and stone walls, and two en-suite bedrooms upstairs. Three nights __£379__

Speyside

Strictly speaking, the term **Speyside** refers to the entire region surrounding the River Spey, but to most people the name is synonymous with the "**whisky triangle**", stretching from just north of Craigellachie, down towards Tomintoul in the south and east to Huntly. Indeed, there are more whisky distilleries and famous brands (including Glenfiddich, Glenlivet and Macallan) concentrated in this small area than in any other part of the country. Running through the heart of the region is the River Spey, whose clean, clear, fast-running waters play a vital part in the whisky industry and are also home to thousands of salmon, making it one of Scotland's finest angling locations. Obviously fertile, the tranquil glens of the area have none of the ruggedness of other parts of the Highlands; tourism blends into a local economy kept healthy by whisky and farming, rather than dominating it.

At the centre of Speyside is the quiet market town of **Dufftown**, full of solid, stone-built workers' houses and dotted with no fewer than nine whisky distilleries. Along with the well-kept nearby villages of **Craigellachie** and **Aberlour**, it makes the best base for a tour of whisky country, whether on the official Malt Whisky Trail or more independent explorations. Fewer visitors take the chance to discover the more remote glens, such as **Glenlivet**, which push higher up towards the Cairngorm massif, nestled into which is Britain's highest village, **Tomintoul**, situated on the edge of both whisky country and a large expanse of wild uplands. The **Speyside Way**, one of Scotland's long-distance footpaths, offers the chance to enjoy the scenery of the region, as well as its whiskies, on foot.

Dufftown

The cheery community of **DUFFTOWN**, founded in 1817 by James Duff, fourth Earl of Fife, proudly proclaims itself "Malt Whisky Capital of the World" for the reason that it produces more of the stuff than any other town in Britain. A more telling statistic, perhaps, is that as a result Dufftown also reportedly raises more capital for the exchequer per head of population than anywhere else in the country. There are seven active distilleries around Dufftown, as well as a cooperage, and an extended stroll around the outskirts of the town gives a good idea of the density of whisky distilling going on, with glimpses of giant warehouses and whiffs of fermenting barley or peat smoke lingering on the breeze. On the edge of town along the A941 is the town's largest working distillery, **Glenfiddich** (see page 174).

There isn't a great deal to do in the town itself, but it's a useful starting point for orienting yourself towards the whisky trail. Dufftown's four main streets converge on its main square, scene of a lively annual party on Hogmanay when free drams are handed out to revellers. Another major event is the **Spirit of Speyside Whisky Festival** (ⓦspiritofspeyside. com), which draws whisky experts and enthusiasts to the area in early May. A separate festival, marked by special "nosing" events, takes place at the end of September.

2

SPEYSIDE

2

THE SPEYSIDE WAY

The **Speyside Way** (Ⓦ speysideway.org), with its beguiling blend of mountain, river, wildlife and whisky, is fast establishing itself as an appealing and less taxing alternative to the popular West Highland and Southern Upland long-distance footpaths. Starting at **Buckie** on the Moray Firth coast, it follows the fast-flowing River Spey from its mouth at Spey Bay south to **Aviemore** (see page 162), with branches linking it to **Dufftown**, Scotland's malt whisky capital, and **Tomintoul** on the remote edge of the Cairngorm mountains. Some 65 miles long without taking on the branch routes, the whole thing is a five- to seven-day expedition, but its proximity to main roads and small villages means that it is excellent for shorter walks or even bicycle trips, especially in the heart of **distillery** country between Craigellachie and Glenlivet; Glenfiddich, Glenlivet, Macallan and Cardhu distilleries, as well as the Speyside Cooperage, lie directly on or a short distance off the route.

Whisky Museum

24 Fife St • Mon–Fri 1–4pm • Free • ☎ 01340 821181, Ⓦ whisky.dufftown.co.uk

The tiny volunteer-run **Whisky Museum** has a slightly disorganized collection of illicit distilling equipment, most of which has been donated by local distilleries. There are also plenty of old books and photographs to help to give visitors a flavour for the industry's humble beginnings.

Keith & Dufftown Railway

Station Rd • April–Sept Sat & Sun 3 trips daily (June–Aug also on Fri) • £11 return • ☎ 01340 821181, Ⓦ keith-dufftown-railway.co.uk

Restored by enthusiasts, the old Dufftown train station is now the departure point for the **Keith & Dufftown Railway,** which uses various restored diesel locomotives to chug forty minutes through whisky country to Keith, home of the Strathisla distillery (see page 176). The Keith & Dufftown Railway originally opened in 1862 before being absorbed into the Great North of Scotland Railway in 1866; the last passenger services were withdrawn in 1968.

ARRIVAL AND INFORMATION

DUFFTOWN

By bus Buses from/to Aberlour (Mon–Sat hourly; 10–15min) and Elgin (Mon–Sat hourly; 50min) stop outside the railway station.

ACCOMMODATION

Morven On the main square ☎ 01340 820507, Ⓦ morvendufftown.co.uk. Simple B&B that's conveniently located near the Whisky Museum in the middle of town. The owners, Zoe and Lee, are first rate hosts. **£85**

Tannochbrae Guest House 22 Fife St ☎ 01340 820541, Ⓦ tannochbrae.co.uk. Pleasant and enthusiastically run former provost's house near the main square, with six comfortable en-suite rooms, a lovely restaurant, drawing room and a well-stocked whisky bar-cum-lounge. **£95**

EATING AND DRINKING

Dufftown Glassworks 16 Conval St ☎ 01340 821534, Ⓦ dufftownglassworks.com. This combined café and gallery is a smart place to sit with a coffee and a wedge of cake while you plan your trip around whisky country. The rocky road slices (£2) are scrumptious. Daily 10.30am–5pm.

Taste of Speyside 10 Balverie St, just off the main square ☎ 01340 820860, Ⓦ atasteofspeyside.com. You can sample a range of quality Scottish food at the town's most popular restaurant, where the *Table d'Hote* menu might include the likes of whisky haggis with clapshot, and herring in oatmeal; calorific brunches served between 11am and noon. Tues–Sat 11am–2pm & 6–9pm.

SHOPPING

The Whisky Shop 1 Fife St ☎ 01340 821097, Ⓦ whiskyshopdufftown.com. A mind-bogglingly well-stocked shop with over six hundred malts and umpteen beers, produced not just on Speyside but all over Scotland. Mon–Sat 10am–6pm (plus Sun March–Oct).

Craigellachie

Four miles north of Dufftown, the small settlement of **CRAIGELLACHIE** (pronounced "Craig-*ell*-ach-ee") sits above the confluence of the sparkling waters of the Fiddich and the Spey. From the village, you can look down on a beautiful iron bridge over the Spey built by Thomas Telford in 1815. The local distillery isn't open to the public (except for special events and the Spirit of Speyside Festival), though Glen Grant (see page 176) with its attractive gardens is only a few miles up the road at Rothes.

2

Speyside Cooperage

Dufftown Rd • Mon–Fri 9am–4pm (last tour 3.30pm) • £4 • ☎ 01340 871108, ⓦ speysidecooperage.co.uk

For an unusual alternative to a distillery tour, the **Speyside Cooperage** is well worth a visit. After an entertaining 4D audiovisual presentation explaining the ancient and skilled art of cooperage, you're shown onto a balcony overlooking the large workshop where you can observe the coopers crafting the oak casks for whisky.

ARRIVAL AND DEPARTURE · CRAIGELLACHIE

By bus Buses for Dufftown (hourly; 10min) arrive at and depart from Edward Avenue (the A941) in Craigellachie.

ACCOMMODATION AND EATING

Craigellachie Hotel Victoria St ☎ 01340 881204, ⓦ craigellachiehotel.co.uk. Near the River Spey, this rambling whitewashed 1893 hotel is the epitome of sumptuous Scottish hospitality, with classy cuisine, subtly modernized rooms (there's a choice between snug and comfy rooms, some of which are pet-friendly) and a bar featuring seven hundred whiskies. **£140**

Highlander Inn On Victoria St in Craigellachie ☎ 01340 881446, ⓦ whiskyinn.com. Upscale pub grub is served at basement level in this tartan-strewn pub, including locally haggis, neeps and tatties in a whisky sauce (£12.95). There are reasonable rooms on the ground floor of the inn, as well as rooms in a house opposite. Food served daily noon–2pm & 5.30–9pm. **£110**

Aberlour

Two miles southwest from Craigellachie is **ABERLOUR**, officially "Charlestown of Aberlour". Founded in 1812 by Charles Grant, its long main street, neat, flower-filled central square and well-trimmed lawns running down to the Spey have all the markings of a planned village. Though you can visit the distillery here, it's another local product – **shortbread** – that is exported in greater quantity around the world, mostly in tartan tins adorned with kilted warriors. A local baker, **Joseph Walker**, set up shop here at the turn of the twentieth century, quickly gaining a reputation for the product which seems to epitomize the Scottish sweet tooth. If you're keen, you can join the coachloads who visit the factory shop on the outskirts of the village. The town is also right on the Speyside Way (see page 174).

ARRIVAL AND ACTIVITIES · ABERLOUR

By bus Local buses from/to Craigellachie (every 30min; 5min) and Dufftown (hourly; 15min) stop on The Square, just off the high street.

Moray Monster Trails Ben Aigan car park, off the A95 near Mulben ☎ 01466 794161, ⓦ forestryandland.gov.

scot/visit/moray-monster-trails. Aberlour is just a few miles from the entrance to the extensive Moray Monster (Mountainbike) Trails at Ben Aigen, on which you can test your skills on a variety of single-track bike routes suitable for beginners through to experts.

ACCOMMODATION AND EATING

Aberlour Gardens Caravan Park ☎ 01340 871586, ⓦ aberlourgardens.co.uk. Though the campsite here is the most pleasant in the area, with its own shop specializing in local produce, it's a walk of a mile and a half from either Aberlour or Craigellachie. Closed Jan & Feb. Per pitch **£11**

Mash Tun 8 Broomfield Square ☎ 01340 881771, ⓦ mashtun-aberlour.com. The best place to eat and drink is this pleasant, traditional pub, which serves up freshly prepared bar meals (pan-fried pork £13), real ales and all the local whiskies in the heart of Aberlour near the Spey;

2

TOURING MALT WHISKY COUNTRY

Speyside is the heart of Scotland's **whisky** industry, and the presence of more than fifty **distilleries** is testimony to a unique combination of clear, clean water, a benign climate and gentle upland terrain. Yet for all the advertising-influenced visions of timeless traditions, whisky is a multimillion-pound business dominated by huge corporations, and to many working distilleries visitors are an afterthought, if not a downright nuisance. That said, plenty are located in attractive historic buildings that now go to some lengths to provide an engaging experience for visitors. Mostly this involves a tour around the essential stages in the whisky-making process, though a number of distilleries now offer pricier connoisseur tours with a tutored tasting (or **nosing**, as it's properly called) and in-depth studies of the distiller's art. Some tours have restrictions on children; typically, those under the age of eight are not allowed on tours.

There are nine distilleries on the official **Malt Whisky Trail** (⒲ maltwhiskytrail.com), a clearly signposted seventy-mile meander around the region. These are Benromach, Cardhu, Dallas Dhu Historic Distillery, Glenfiddich, Glen Grant, Glenlivet, Glen Moray, Strathisla and the Speyside Cooperage. Unless you're seriously interested in whisky, it's best to just pick out a couple that appeal. All offer a guided tour. You could cycle or walk parts of the route, using the Speyside Way. The following is a list of selected highlights from the area (not all are on the official trail).

Glendronach 8 miles northeast of Huntly ⒯ 01466 730202, ⒲ glendronachdistillery.co.uk. Off the official trail, this isolated distillery makes much of the fact that, uniquely, its stills are heated in the traditional method by coal fires. Tours £10. Daily 10am–4.30pm.

Glenfiddich On the A941 just north of Dufftown ⒯ 01340 820373, ⒲ glenfiddich.com. The biggest and slickest of all the Speyside distilleries, despite the fact that it's still owned by the same Grant family who founded it in 1887. It's a light, sweet whisky packaged in triangular bottles – unusually, the bottling is still done on the premises and is part of the £10 tours. April–Oct daily 9.30am–4pm; Nov–March daily 11am–3pm.

Glen Grant Rothes ⒯ 01340 832118, ⒲ glengrant. com. Makes a well-known, floral whisky aggressively marketed to the younger customer. The highlight here is the attractive Victorian gardens, a mix of well-tended lawns and mixed, mature trees, a tumbling waterfall and a hidden whisky safe. Tours £7.50. April–Oct Mon–Sat 9.30am–5pm, Sun 11am–5pm; Nov–March Mon–Sat 9.30am–4.30pm.

Glenlivet On the B9008 to Tomintoul ⒲ theglenlivet. com. A famous name in a lonely hillside setting. This was the first licensed distillery in the Highlands, following the 1823 act that aimed to reduce illicit distilling and smuggling. The Glenlivet 12-year-old malt is a floral, fragrant, medium-bodied whisky. Tours £12.50. Mid-March to early Nov daily 9.30am–6pm.

Macallan Near Craigellachie ⒯ 01340 318000, ⒲ themacallan.com. Small tours, and a classy whisky aged in sherry casks to give it a rich colour and flavour. Tours £15. April–Sept daily 9.30am–6pm; Oct–March Mon–Fri 9.30am–5pm.

Strathisla Keith ⒯ 01542 783044, ⒲ maltwhisky distilleries.com. A small, old-fashioned distillery claiming to be Scotland's oldest (1786); it's certainly one of the most attractive, with the River Isla rushing by. Inside there's an old-fashioned mashtun and brass-bound spirit safes. You can arrive here on one of the restored trains of the Keith & Dufftown Railway. Tours £15. Easter–Oct daily 10am–6pm; Nov–Easter daily 10am–4.30pm.

Speyside Cooperage Craigellachie ⒯ 01340 871108, ⒲ speysidecooperage.co.uk. This cooperage – which produces and repairs the casks used in whisky-making – is the only stop on the official trail that isn't a distillery, and offers fascinating glimpses of a highly skilled and vital part of the industry. Tours £4. Mon–Fri 9am–5pm.

it also has four cosy rooms and a luxury suite, all but one of which has views across the Spey. Mon–Fri noon–2pm & 6–9pm, Sat & Sun noon–9pm. **£120**

Spey Larder 96 High St ⒯ 01340 871243. There's a good range of produce on offer at this well-stocked deli, right by the village square, including olives, herbs, locally made shortbread and big bottles of ginger ale (£4.95). Mon–Sat 9am–5pm.

Glenlivet

Beyond Aberlour, the Spey and the main road both head generally southwest to Ballindalloch and, a dozen miles beyond that, Grantown-on-Spey, at the head of the Strathspey region (see page 162). South from Ballindalloch are the quieter, remote glens of the Avon (pronounced "*A'an*") and Livet rivers. Allegedly, in the days of the despised tax excisemen, the Braes of Glenlivet once held over one hundred illicit whisky stills. The (legal) distillery at **GLENLIVET** (see page 176), founded in 1824 by George Smith, is one of the most famous on Speyside, and certainly enjoys one of the more attractive settings.

ARRIVAL AND DEPARTURE   GLENLIVET

By car Public transport in this area is extremely limited, which makes having your own wheels a must. To reach the distillery from Aberlour, follow the A95 south as far as Ballindalloch (around eight miles) and then swing left onto the B9008 for the final four miles.

Tomintoul

Deep into the foothills of the Cairngorms, **TOMINTOUL** (pronounced "*tom*-in-towel") is, at 1150ft, the highest village in the Scottish Highlands, and the northern gateway to the **Lecht Ski Area** (see below). Its long, thin layout is reminiscent of a Wild West frontier town; Queen Victoria wrote that it was "the most tumble-down, poor looking place I ever saw". A spur of the Speyside Way connects Ballindalloch through Glenlivet to Tomintoul, and there are plenty of other terrific walking opportunities in the area, as well as some great routes for mountain biking.

Glenlivet Crown Estate

Visitor Centre Main St • Mon–Fri 9am–5pm • ☎ 01309 870070, ⓦ glenlivetestate.co.uk

If you've come this far it's worth exploring the **Glenlivet Crown Estate**, an extensive tract of carefully managed land abutting Tomintoul. A hugely popular recreation spot, the estate maintains a number of extensive walking and mountain bike trails and there are plenty of opportunities to spot wildlife, including reindeer; information and useful maps about its wildlife, as well as the numerous paths and trails, are available from the estate **visitor centre** at the southern end of the long main street.

ARRIVAL AND INFORMATION   TOMINTOUL

By car The only reliable way to reach Tomintoul is by car; from Grantown-on-Spey the A939 snakes east, passing Tomintoul on the way to Ballater.

ACCOMMODATION

As well as the options listed below, it's possible to **camp** beside the Glenlivet Estate ranger's office for free, though there are no facilities here whatsoever.

★ **Argyll Guest House** 7 Main St ☎ 01807 580766, ⓦ argyletomintoul.co.uk. Six spacious and comfy rooms (four of which are en-suite) and a great breakfast choice including home-made bread and porridge. The hosts give expert advice on local hiking and biking. **£64**

Smuggler's Hostel Main St ☎ 01807 580364, ⓦ the smugglershostel.co.uk. Billed as the highest hostel in the Highlands and run by the community, with six- and seven-bed dorms plus doubles and family rooms; good facilities including drying sheds, bike wash area, a well-equipped kitchen and spacious communal areas. Dorms £17; doubles **£70**

Lecht Ski Area

7 miles southeast of Tomintoul along the A939 • Open year-round • Full-day pass £28; ski rental costs £20/day from the ski school at the base station • For information on skiing and road conditions, call the base station on ☎ 01975 651440, or check ⓦ lecht.co.uk

The Lecht is the smallest and most remote of Scotland's five ski areas, but it works hard to make itself appealing with a range of winter and summer activities. While its runs include some gentle beginners' slopes, there's little really challenging for experienced skiers other than a Snowboard Fun Park, with specially built jumps and ramps. Snow-making equipment helps extend the snow season beyond January and February, while downhill bike tracks open in the summer (no bike rental on site).

The Great Glen and River Spey

BUACHAILLE ETIVE MÒR, GLEN COE

The Great Glen

The Great Glen, a major geological fault line cutting diagonally across the Highlands from Fort William to Inverness, is the defining geographic feature of the north of Scotland. A huge rift valley was formed when the northwestern and southeastern sides of the fault slid in opposite directions for more than sixty miles, while the present landscape was shaped by glaciers that only retreated around 8000 BC. The glen is impressive more for its sheer scale than its beauty, but the imposing barrier of loch and mountain means that no one can travel into the northern Highlands without passing through it. With the two major service centres of the Highlands at either end, it makes an obvious and rewarding route between the west and east coasts.

Of the **Great Glen**'s four elongated lochs, the most famous is **Loch Ness**, home to the mythical monster; lochs **Oich**, **Lochy** and **Linnhe** (the last of these a sea loch) are less renowned, though no less attractive; all four are linked by the **Caledonian Canal**. The southwestern end of the Great Glen is dominated by the town of **Fort William**, the self-proclaimed "Outdoor Capital of the UK". Situated at the heart of the Lochaber area, it is a utilitarian base, with plenty of places to stay and excellent access to a host of adventure sports. While the town itself is charmless, the surrounding countryside is a magnificent blend of rugged mountain terrain and tranquil sea loch. Dominating the scene to the south is **Ben Nevis**, Britain's highest peak, best approached from scenic Glen Nevis. The most famous and dramatic glen of all, **Glen Coe**, lies on the main A82 road half an hour's drive south of Fort William, the two separated by the coastal inlet of **Loch Leven**. Nowadays the whole area is unashamedly given over to tourism, with Fort William swamped by bus tours throughout the summer, but take a short drive from town and solitude is easy to find.

At the northeastern end of the Great Glen is the capital of the Highlands, **Inverness**, a sprawling city that hugs the northern end of the River Ness, close to the Beauly Firth; it's most often used as a springboard to more remote areas further north. Inevitably, most transport links to the northern Highlands, including Ullapool, Thurso and the Orkney and Shetland islands, pass through Inverness.

GETTING AROUND   THE GREAT GLEN

By car The main A82 road runs the length of the Great Glen, although relatively high traffic levels mean that it's not a fast or particularly easy route to drive.

By bus The Great Glen is reasonably well served by buses, with several daily services between Inverness and Fort William.

By boat The traditional and most rewarding way to travel through the Great Glen is by boat: a flotilla of kayaks,

small yachts and pleasure vessels take advantage of the Caledonian Canal and its old wooden locks during the summer.

By bike Well-marked routes make it possible to cycle all the way from Fort William to Inverness.

On foot The 79-mile Great Glen Way links Fort William with Inverness, and takes five to six days to walk in full (see page 185).

Fort William

With its stunning position on Loch Linnhe, tucked in below the snow-streaked bulk of Ben Nevis, **FORT WILLIAM** (known by the many walkers and climbers who come here as "Fort Bill") should be a gem. Sadly, the anticlimactic end point of the West Highland Way (see page 131) has had its waterfront wrecked by ribbon bungalow development

URQUHART CASTLE RUINS, LOCH NESS

Highlights

❶ Commando Memorial An exposed but dramatic place to take in sweeping views over Scotland's highest ben (Nevis) and its longest glen (the Great Glen). See page 189

❷ Glen Coe Spectacular, moody, poignant and full of history – a glorious place for hiking or simply absorbing the atmosphere. See page 191

❸ Cruise Loch Ness Chances of seeing the famous monster Nessie aren't high, but the on-board sonar images are intriguing and the scenery's fine. See page 193

❹ Glen Affric Some of Scotland's best-hidden scenery, with ancient Caledonian forests and gushing rivers. See page 198

❺ Culloden battlefield Experience the cannon-fire in a "battle immersion theatre" and tramp the heather moor where Bonnie Prince Charlie made his last stand. See page 205

❻ Dolphins of the Moray Firth Europe's most northerly school of bottle-nosed dolphin can be seen from the shore or on a boat trip. See page 206

HIGHLIGHTS ARE MARKED ON THE MAP ON PAGE 182

and an ill-advised dual carriageway. The main street and the little squares off it are more appealing, though occupied by some decidedly tacky tourist gift shops. Other than its excellent **museum**, the town is short on must-sees, but it's undeniably a convenient base for **outdoor activities** – most notably walking. Several cruises leave from the town pier every day, offering the chance to spot the marine life of Loch Linnhe, which includes seals and seabirds. Shops rent out kayaks and mountain bikes for independent exploration of the surrounding area, and local guides run mountaineering courses (in summer and

THE GREAT GLEN

HIGHLIGHTS

1. Commando Memorial
2. Glen Coe
3. Cruise Loch Ness
4. Glen Affric
5. Culloden battlefield
6. Dolphins of the Moray Firth

BLOODY TALES BEYOND THE BEAUTY

Although best known for its windswept slopes and glassy lochs, the Great Glen has a turbulent and bloody **history**. Founded in 1655 and named in honour of William III, the town of Fort William was successfully held by government troops during both of the **Jacobite risings**. The country to the southwest, meanwhile, is inextricably associated with Bonnie Prince Charlie's flight after **Culloden** (see page 205). **Glen Coe** is another historic site with a violent past, renowned as much for the infamous massacre of 1692 as for its magnificent scenery.

---

winter) on the slopes of nearby Munros. Some of the best views of these peaks can be had from **Corpach**, a small village opposite Fort William on the other side of Loch Linnhe, which also has a number of places to stay and several outdoor activities operators.

West Highland Museum

Cameron Square, just off the high street • April–Oct Mon–Sat 10am–5pm; March, Nov & Dec Mon–Sat 10am–4pm • Free • ☎ 01397 702169, ⓦ westhighlandmuseum.org.uk

Collections at the splendid and idiosyncratic **West Highland Museum** cover virtually every aspect of Highland life and the presentation is traditional, but very well done, making a refreshing change from the state-of-the-art heritage centres popping up across Scotland. You'll find treasures from the Spanish Armada, quasi-religious relics associated with Bonnie Prince Charlie and the Jacobite uprising, and the long Spanish rifle used in the Appin Murder (an event which inspired Robert Louis Stevenson's *Kidnapped*). There's even a 550kg slab of aluminium, the stuff that's processed into silver foil just five miles north of town (you'll see the huge pipes running down the mountainside), and a section on the World War II commandos, who received their famously tough training in nearby Lochaber.

The Jacobite Steam Train

At the train station on Station Square • Mid-May–Oct Mon–Fri; mid-June–mid-Sept daily; departs Fort William 10.20am, returns from Mallaig at 2.10pm; additional afternoon service (June–Aug only) departs Fort William 2.30pm, with return at 6.40pm • Return tickets £37.75 (£59.95 for first class) • ☎ 08448 504685, ⓦ westcoastrailways.co.uk

Excursions from Fort William include the 84-mile return trip to Mallaig on the **West Highland Railway Line** aboard the **Jacobite Steam Train**. Heading along the shore of Loch Eil to the west coast via historic Glenfinnan and a sinuous Victorian viaduct, the train has stunning views of the water and distant mountains, though these days it's as popular for its role in the *Harry Potter* films. The locomotives used are black and barrel-shaped machines from the 1920s and 1930s tugging younger British Rail carriages from the 1960s.

ARRIVAL AND DEPARTURE
FORT WILLIAM

By train Just across the A82 dual carriageway from the north end of the High Street you'll find Fort William's train station (one of the stops on the scenic West Highland Railway from Glasgow).

Destinations Crianlarich (Mon–Sat 4 daily, 3 on Sun; 1hr 50min); Glasgow Queen Street (Mon–Sat 3 daily, 2 on Sun; 3hr 50min); London (1 nightly; 12hr); Mallaig (Mon–Sat 4 daily, 3 on Sun; 1hr 20min).

By bus Intercity coaches from Glasgow and Inverness stop outside the train station on MacFarlane Way.

Destinations Drumnadrochit (9 daily; 1hr 25min); Edinburgh (1 daily; 4hr); Fort Augustus (9 daily; 50min); Glasgow (8 daily; 3hr); Inverness (9 Mon–Sat, 6 Sun; 2hr); Mallaig (Mon–Fri 3 daily; 1hr 20min); Oban (Mon–Sat 3 daily; 1hr 30min); Portree, Skye (4 daily; 3hr).

Tourist office 15 High St (April & May Mon–Sat 9am–5pm, Sun 10am–5pm; June Mon–Sat 9am–6pm, Sun 9.30am–5pm; July & Aug Mon–Sat 9am–6.30pm, Sun 9am–6pm; Sept & Oct Mon–Sat 9am–5pm, Sun 10am–4pm; Nov–March Mon–Sat 9am–5pm, Sun 10am–3pm; ☎ 01397 701801, ⓦ visithighlands.com). Busy and very helpful tourist office, which stocks an excellent selection of maps and guidebooks on exploring the Great Glen. Upstairs you can surf the net (£1/20min).

TOURS AND ACTIVITIES

BOAT TOURS

Crannog Cruises Town pier (☎ 01397 703786, ⓦ crannog. net/cruises). Runs 1hr 30min cruises (£17.50) from the town pier down Loch Linnhe, where you'll have the chance to spot porpoises and grey seals. Daily trips April–Sept at 10am, noon, 2pm & 4pm, plus evening cruises July & Aug Tues, Thurs & Sun 7.30pm.

MOUNTAIN BIKING

Alpine Bikes 117 High St (☎ 01397 704008, Nevis Range ☎ 01397 705825, ⓦ tiso.com/alpine). High-spec mountain

bikes are available for rent here (from £15/day). Staff know the best routes and can also issue free maps. There's a second branch at the Nevis Range gondola base station – a location that boasts forest rides and a world-championship standard downhill track.

MOUNTAINEERING

Snowgoose Mountain Centre Station Rd, Corpach (☎ 01397 772467, ⓦ highland-mountain-guides.co.uk). Set beside *Smiddy Bunkhouse* and *Blacksmith's Hostel*, this activity centre offers instruction, rental and residential

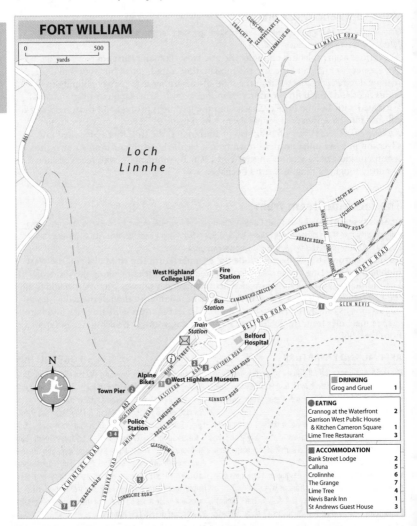

FORT WILLIAM

0 — 500
yards

Loch Linnhe

West Highland College UHI

Fire Station

Bus Station

CAMANACHD CRESCENT

Train Station

BELFORD ROAD

Belford Hospital

N

Alpine Bikes

West Highland Museum

VICTORIA ROAD

ALMA ROAD

Town Pier

KENNEDY ROAD

Police Station

CAMERON ROAD

ARGYLE ROAD

GLASDRUM RD

CONNOCHIE ROAD

GRANGE ROAD

LUNDAVRA ROAD

ACHINTORE ROAD

UNION ROAD

HIGH STREET

FASSIFERN

GLEN NEVIS

NORTH ROAD

LOCHY RD

LOCHIEL ROAD

LUNDY ROAD

WADES ROAD

ABRACH ROAD

MONTROSE RD

EARL OF INVERNESS RD

GUNS AVE

ERRACHT DR

GLENDESSARY ST

GLENMALLIE RD

KILMALLIE ROAD

A82

A861

A830

◼ **DRINKING**	
Grog and Gruel	1

⬤ **EATING**	
Crannog at the Waterfront	2
Garrison West Public House & Kitchen Cameron Square	1
Lime Tree Restaurant	3

◼ **ACCOMMODATION**	
Bank Street Lodge	2
Calluna	5
Crolinnhe	6
The Grange	7
Lime Tree	4
Nevis Bank Inn	1
St Andrews Guest House	3

THE GREAT GLEN WAY AND CYCLE PATH

Ordnance Survey Landranger maps 26, 34 and 41

The enormous cleft of the Great Glen is the most obvious – and by far the flattest – way of traversing northern Scotland from coast to coast. Stretching 79 miles, the **Great Glen Way** long-distance footpath is a relatively undemanding five-to-six-day hike that uses a combination of canal towpath and forest- and hill-tracks between Fort William and Inverness. Accommodation is readily available all the way along the route in campsites, hostels, bunkhouses and B&Bs, though in high season you should book ahead, and if you know you're going to arrive late somewhere it's worth checking that you can still get a meal either where you're staying or somewhere nearby.

There are various **guidebooks** that describe the route, including *The Great Glen Way*, published by Rucksack Readers (£11.99). For the best selection of guides, plus the relevant Ordnance Survey Landranger maps (£8.99 each) head to the tourist office in Fort William. Note, however, that forestry work can see the route diverted at short notice, so it's wise to check ⓦ highland.gov.uk/greatglenway before setting off.

Cyclists with mountain bikes or hybrids can also use the Great Glen Way, which offers a tranquil alternative to the hazardous A82 (currently the only option for those with road bikes). The route is well signposted and can be pedalled in one long day or two easier days, though of course you can tackle shorter sections. Bikes can be rented at Fort William, Banavie, Drumnadrochit and Inverness.

Whether you're cycling or walking, the suggested **direction** for following the route is from west to east, to take advantage of the prevailing southwesterly wind.

courses for activities such as mountaineering, ice-climbing and dinghy sailing. Sea-kayaking, for example, costs £60 for a full day.

West Coast Mountain Guides (ⓣ 01397 719120, ⓦ westcoast-mountainguides.co.uk). Long-established group of experienced guides who run climbing and mountaineering courses throughout the year. A five-day introduction to winter mountaineering costs £525/person.

ACCOMMODATION

The town itself isn't the most exciting place to base yourself, but Fort William's plentiful accommodation ranges from large luxury hotels to budget hostels and bunkhouses. Numerous **B&Bs** are also scattered across town, many of them in the suburb of Corpach on the other side of Loch Linnhe, three miles along the Mallaig road (served by regular buses), where you'll also find a couple of good **hostels**; try also nearby Banavie.

HOTELS AND B&BS

★ **Crolinnhe** 37 Grange Rd ⓣ 01397 703795, ⓦ crolinnhe.co.uk. Beautifully appointed guesthouse overlooking Loch Linnhe, with elegant French furniture in the rooms and attractive landscaped gardens outside. Their lakefront terrace is more Amalfi Coast than Scotland. April–Oct. __£160__

★ **The Grange** Grange Rd ⓣ 01397 705516, ⓦ grange fortwilliam.com. Top-grade accommodation in a striking old stone house, with log fires, views towards Loch Linnhe and luxurious en-suite doubles. Does vegetarian breakfasts on request. April–Oct. __£180__

Trips to Skye (and even the Swiss Alps) can also be arranged.

CANOEING AND KAYAKING

Rockhopper Unit 17, Annat Industrial Estate, Corpach (ⓣ 07739 837344, ⓦ rockhopperscotland.co.uk). Get in touch with Rockhopper for sea-kayak coaching, including half-day excursions (£50) and two-day camping trips with meals provided (£225/person).

SEE MAPS PAGE 184 AND 187

Inverlochy Castle Torlundy, 3 miles north of the town centre on the A82 ⓣ 01397 702177, ⓦ inverlochy castlehotel.co.uk. Built on the site of a thirteenth-century fortress, this is one of Scotland's grandest and most luxurious country-house hotels with fantastic (and fantastically expensive) accommodation and Michelin-star food. __£515__

★ **Lime Tree** Achintore Rd ⓣ 01397 701806, ⓦ lime treefortwilliam.co.uk. A stylish and relaxing option in an old manse, with a great modern restaurant and an excellent contemporary art gallery; they've also got the practicalities covered with a drying room, map room and bike storage. __£80__

Nevis Bank Inn Belford Rd ⓣ 01397 705721, ⓦ nevis bankinn.co.uk. The small, functional hotel rooms here are a little on the plain side but they're comfortable and quiet, and the attached restaurant is a convenient place to grab some pasta or a steak. __£140__

St Andrews Guest House Fassifern Rd ⓣ 01397 703038, ⓦ standrewsguesthouse.co.uk. Comfortable and good-value B&B in a turreted former choir school a

5min walk uphill from the high street, featuring various inscriptions and stained-glass windows. **£70**

HOSTELS AND CAMPSITES

Bank Street Lodge Bank St ☎01397 700070, ⓦbankstreetlodge.co.uk. A bright and clean if functional 43-bed hostel, handy for transport options and the town centre. Choose between dorm accommodation and a good range of en-suite rooms. Dorms **£16**, singles **£30**, doubles **£45**

Calluna Connochie Rd ☎01397 700451, ⓦfortwilliamholiday.co.uk. Well-run self-catering and hostel accommodation a 10min walk from the centre of town, configured for individual, family and group stays. Also has on-site laundry facilities and a bouldering wall. The

owners can also organize mountaineering trips. Three-night minimum stay. Dorms **£15**; doubles **£42**

★ **Great Glen Yurts** 3 miles northeast of Fort William off A82 (signposted from Torlundy) ⓦgreatglenyurts.com. Rotund and spacious, these luxury yurts occupy a magnificently peaceful setting with views of Ben Nevis. There's also a shepherd's hut and wooden cabins, and an open-sided kitchen is great for sociable evening meals. April–Oct. **£90**

Smiddy Bunkhouse and Blacksmith's Hostel Snowgoose Mountain Centre, Station Rd, Corpach ☎01397 772467, ⓦhighland-mountain-guides.co.uk. Alpine hostel and bunkhouse on the site of an old blacksmith's workshop. It's 4 miles from Ben Nevis at the southwestern end of the Caledonian Canal. Dorms **£18**

EATING AND DRINKING SEE MAP PAGE 184

Crannog at the Waterfront Town pier, just off the bypass on entering Fort William ☎01397 705589, ⓦcrannog.net. Red-roofed restaurant with lochside views and fresh seafood, including Mallaig langoustine, plus a reasonable wine list. Good lunchtime deals: the three-course lunch is £18.95. The neighbouring shack sells cullen skink for £3.50 and oysters for £2. Daily noon–2.30pm & 6–9pm.

Garrison West Public House & Kitchen Cameron Square ☎01397 701873, ⓦgarrisonwest.co.uk. Located in an old stone building in the centre of town, this is a modern but unpretentious pub serving brunch, lunch, pub dinners – they have a special "bairn's menu" for kids. There are small snacks such as stovie scones (£6) and a helping of haggis with oatcakes (£5.50) as well as meaty

burgers and veg alternatives including cauliflower and apple curry (£9.95). Cask ales and live music sessions. Daily noon–2.30pm & 5–11pm.

Lime Tree Restaurant The Old Manse, Achintore Rd ☎01397 701806, ⓦlimetreefortwilliam.co.uk/the-restaurant. Serves an excellent selection of contemporary Scottish food. Loch Etive Sea Trout costs £22.95. Daily 6–9pm.

Grog and Gruel 66 High St ☎01397 705078, ⓦgrogandgruel.co.uk. Loud and friendly, the downstairs alehouse at *Grog and Gruel* is a good bet for Scottish beer. The upstairs restaurant is more relaxed, doing mostly Mexican mains, including a spicy "hog's breath chilli" for £11.95. Mon–Wed & Sun noon–midnight, Thurs–Sat noon–1am.

Around Fort William

Any disappointment you harbour about Fort William town should be offset by the wealth of scenery and activities in its immediate vicinity. Most obvious – on a clear day, at least – is **Ben Nevis**, the most popular, though hardly the most rewarding, of Scotland's high peaks. The path up leaves from beautiful **Glen Nevis**, also a starting point for some other excellent walks of various lengths and elevations. The mountain abutting Ben Nevis is **Aonach Mhòr**, home of Scotland's most modern ski resort and an internationally renowned honeypot for downhill mountain-bike enthusiasts.

The main road travelling up the Great Glen from Fort William towards Inverness is the A82, ten miles along which is the small settlement of **Spean Bridge**, a good waypoint for getting to various remote and attractive walking areas with several backpacker hostels – in glens **Spean** and **Roy** – found along the A86 trunk road, which links the central Highlands to the A9 and the Speyside region.

Glen Nevis

A ten-minute drive south of Fort William, **GLEN NEVIS** is among the Highlands' most impressive glens: a classic U-shaped glacial valley hemmed in by steep bracken-covered slopes and swathes of blue-grey scree. With the forbidding mass of Ben Nevis rising steeply to the north, it's not surprising that the valley has served as a location in the films *Rob Roy* and *Braveheart*. Apart from its natural beauty, Glen Nevis is also the starting point for the ascent of **Ben Nevis**.

A great **low-level walk** (six miles return) runs from the end of the road at the top of Glen Nevis. The good but very rocky path leads through a dramatic gorge with impressive falls and rapids, then opens out into a secret hanging valley, carpeted with wild flowers, with a high waterfall at the far end. If you're really energetic (and properly equipped) you can walk the full twelve miles on over **Rannoch Moor** to **Corrour Station** (see page 147), where you can pick up one of four daily trains to take you back to Fort William (50min).

ARRIVAL AND INFORMATION   GLEN NEVIS

By bus Bus #42 runs from the high street in Fort William, past the Glen Nevis Visitor Centre, campsite and SYHA hostel to the Lower Falls car park (3 daily; 25min) almost five miles up the Glen Nevis road.

Glen Nevis Visitor Centre 1.5 miles southeast of Fort William along the Glen Nevis road (daily 8.30am–6pm;

☎ 01397 705922); take bus #41 (summer only) from Fort William. Staff here can give good advice on climbing the mountain. It's also worth asking for a copy of the useful leaflet *Ben Nevis: safety information for walking the mountain track*.

ACCOMMODATION AND EATING

Note that the *Achintee Farm Guest House* and *Ben Nevis Inn* are on the opposite side of the river from the main **Glen**

Nevis road from Fort William – drivers should get to these places via the Achintee road from Fort William; coming by

ACCOMMODATION	
Great Glen Yurts	1
Inverlochy Castle	3
Smiddy Bunkhouse and Blacksmith's Hostel	2

AROUND FORT WILLIAM

0   2
miles

3

ASCENT OF BEN NEVIS

Harvey's Ben Nevis Superwalker map (£13.50) is available from Fort William's tourist office and most local bookshops and outdoor stores.

Of all the walks in and around Glen Nevis, the **ascent of Ben Nevis** (4411ft), Britain's highest summit, inevitably attracts the most attention. In high summer the trail teems with hikers – around a hundred thousand trek up to the summit each year. However, this doesn't mean that the mountain should be treated casually. It can snow at the summit any day of the year and people die on the slopes, so make sure that you take the necessary precautions; in winter, of course, the mountain should be left to the experts. The most obvious **route**, a Victorian pony-path up the whaleback south side of the mountain, built to service the observatory that once stood on the top, starts from the helpful **Glen Nevis Visitor Centre**. This also sells mountain equipment and last-minute supplies, and is located a mile and a half southeast of Fort William along the Glen Nevis road. Return via the main route or, if the weather is settled and you're confident enough, make a side trip from the wide saddle into the **Allt a'Mhuilinn glen** for spectacular views of the great cliffs on Ben Nevis's north face. Allow a full day (8hr) for the climb and check the weather forecast before setting out (ⓦbennevisweather.co.uk is useful).

bus, get off at the Glen Nevis Visitor Centre and take the footbridge over the river.

Achintee Farm Guest House Achintee, across the river from the visitor centre ☎01397 702240, ⓦachintee farm.com. Friendly B&B with adjoining hostel and a rugged little stone cottage, right by the *Ben Nevis Inn* at the start of the Ben Nevis footpath. Also has drying rooms and wi-fi. Dorms **£17**; doubles **£110**

★ **Ben Nevis Inn** Achintee, across the river from the visitor centre ☎01397 701227, ⓦben-nevis-inn. co.uk. A basic and cosy bunkhouse (booking advised) in the basement of a lively 250-year-old pub at the start of the Ben Nevis footpath. The pub has a terrific atmosphere, and the menu – with ale-battered North Sea haddock for £13.50 – is especially tempting after a day on the mountain. Daily noon–11pm; food served noon–9pm. Dorms **£17**

Glen Nevis Caravan and Camping Park Half a mile past the visitor centre along the Glen Nevis road ☎01397 702191, ⓦglen-nevis.co.uk. Offers a range of lodges and rentable caravans as well as camping pitches. Gorgeous views, and facilities include hot showers, a shop and restaurant, and wheelchair-accessible bathrooms. Per pitch **£12.50**

Glen Nevis Hostel 1 mile past the visitor centre along the Glen Nevis road ☎01397 702336, ⓦhostelling scotland.org.uk/hostels/glen-nevis. This friendly hostel is an excellent base for walkers and has full catering, as well as a decent kitchen. It gets very busy in summer, so book ahead. Dorms **£15**; doubles **£27**

The Nevis Range

Situated seven miles northeast of Fort William by the A82, on the slopes of Aonach Mhòr, one of the high mountains abutting Ben Nevis, the Nevis Range is Scotland's highest ski area. The fifteen-minute gondola trip (daily: Easter–June, Sept & Oct 10am–5pm; July & Aug 9.30am–6pm; early Nov & late Dec to Easter 9am–sunset; £12.50; ⓦnevisrange.co.uk/mountain-gondola) to get here, rising 2000ft, gives an easy approach to some high-level walking as well as spectacular views from the terrace of the self-service restaurant at the top station. There's also a Discovery Centre here, providing insights into the mountain's geology and wildlife. The base station area in Torlundy, just east of Fort William, also has a café, and there's a high-wire adventure course and nature trail nearby.

ARRIVAL AND INFORMATION

THE NEVIS RANGE

By bus Bus #41 runs from Fort William's bus station four times a day (Mon–Sat; 2 on Sun).
Gondola Daily Easter–June, Sept & Oct 10am–5pm; July & Aug 9.30am–6pm; winter: 9am–sunset (closed mid-Nov to mid-Dec); £11.50 return.

Tourist information In the Mountain Discovery Centre, at the top gondola station (daily June–Aug 9.30am–6pm, Sept & Oct 10am–sunset; ☎01397 705825, ⓦnevis-range. co.uk). Has information on the history and ecology of the area.

Glen Coe and around

Glen Coe, half-an-hour's drive south of Fort William on the main A82 road to Glasgow, is one of Scotland's most inspiring places, a breathtakingly beautiful mountain valley between velvety-green conical peaks, their tops often wreathed in cloud, their flanks streaked by cascades of rock and scree. Arriving from the south across the desolate reaches of Rannoch Moor, you're likely to find the start of the glen – with **Buachaille Etive Mhòr** to the south and **Beinn a'Chrùlaiste** to the north – little short of forbidding. By the time you've reached the heart of the glen, with the three huge rock buttresses known as the **Three Sisters** on one side and the Anoach Eagach ridge on the other combining to close up the sky, you'll almost certainly want to stop. Added to the compelling emotional mix is the story of the notorious **massacre of Glen Coe** in 1692, nadir of the long-standing enmity between the clans MacDonald and Campbell (see page 192). At its western end, Glen Coe meets Loch Leven: the main road goes west and over the bridge at Ballachulish en route to Fort William

At the eastern end of Glen Coe, meanwhile, beyond the looming massif of Buachaille Etive Mhòr, the landscape opens out onto vast Rannoch Moor (see page 147). From the **Glencoe Mountain Resort** a chairlift climbs 2400ft to Meall a Bhuiridh, giving spectacular views over Rannoch Moor and to Ben Nevis. At the base station, there's a simple but pleasant café. Beyond the mountains at the eastern end of Loch Leven is the slowly reviving settlement of **Kinlochleven**, site of the world's largest indoor ice-climbing centre and a waypoint on the West Highland Way long-distance footpath (see page 131).

3

WALKS AROUND GLEN COE

Ordnance Survey Explorer map 384

Flanked by sheer-sided Munros, **Glen Coe** offers some of the Highlands' most challenging **hiking** routes, with long steep ascents over rough trails and notoriously unpredictable weather conditions that claim lives every year. The walks outlined below number among the glen's less ambitious routes, but still require a map. It's essential that you take the proper precautions, and stick to the paths, both for your own safety and the sake of the landscape, which has become badly eroded in places. For a broader selection of walks, get hold of the Ordnance Survey *Pathfinder Guide: Fort William and Glen Coe Walks* (£11.99).

DEVIL'S STAIRCASE

A good introduction to the splendours of Glen Coe is the half-day hike over the **Devil's Staircase**, which follows part of the old military road that once ran between Fort William and Stirling. The trail, part of the West Highland Way (see page 131), starts at the village of **Kinlochleven** and is marked by thistle signs, which lead uphill to the 1804ft pass and down the other side into Glen Coe.

ALLT COIRE GABHAIL

Set right in the heart of the glen, the half-day **Allt Coire Gabhail** hike starts at the car park opposite the distinctive Three Sisters massif on the main A82. This explores the so-called "Lost Valley" where the Clan MacDonald fled and hid their cattle when attacked. Once in the valley, there are superb views of the upper slopes of Bidean nan Bian, Gearr Aonach and Beinn Fhada, which improve as you continue on to its head, another twenty- to thirty-minute walk.

BUACHAILLE ETIVE BEAG

Undoubtedly one of the finest walks in the Glen Coe area that doesn't entail the ascent of a Munro is the **Buachaille Etive Beag** circuit, which follows the textbook glacial valleys of Lairig Eilde and Lairig Gartain, ascending 1968ft in only nine miles of rough trail. Park near the waterfall at **The Study** – the gorge part of the A82 through Glen Coe – and walk up the road until you see a sign pointing south to "Loch Etiveside".

VALLEY OF WEEPING

In 1692 Glen Coe (literally "valley of weeping") was the site of a notorious massacre, in which the MacDonalds were victims of an abiding government desire to suppress the clans. Fed up with what they regarded as unacceptable lawlessness, and a groundswell of Jacobitism and Catholicism, the government offered a general pardon to all those who signed an oath of allegiance to William III by January 1, 1692. When clan chief **Alastair MacDonald** missed the deadline, a plot was hatched to make an example of "that damnable sept", and **Campbell of Glenlyon** was ordered to billet his soldiers in the homes of the MacDonalds, who for ten days entertained them with traditional Highland hospitality. In the early morning of February 13, the soldiers turned on their hosts, slaying around forty and causing more than three hundred to flee in a blizzard.

Glencoe Village and around

Tucked between steep mountains, Loch Leven and the grassy banks of the River Coe, **GLENCOE VILLAGE** is an attractive place to spend a couple of days. There's a good choice of accommodation in the area, and if you fancy a break from walking, the village museum and nearby visitor centre make for pleasant distractions. Beyond the small village at the western end of the glen (a property of the NTS since the 1930s) is virtually uninhabited, and provides outstanding climbing and walking.

Glencoe Folk Museum

Main St • Easter–Aug Mon–Sat 10am–4.30pm (last admission 4pm) • £3 • ☎ 01855 811664, ⓦ glencoemuseum.com

If you have an hour to spare in Glencoe Village, it's worth paying a visit to the delightful heather-roofed **Glencoe Folk Museum**. Various games and activities for kids can be enjoyed within this cosy 1720 croft where items include a chair that reputedly once belonged to Bonnie Prince Charlie. Look out for their special storytelling events and workshops.

NTS visitor centre

1 mile east of Glencoe Village on the A82 • April–Oct 9am–4pm; Nov–Feb 10am–4pm; guided walks Easter & June–Sept (book ahead) • free, £4 for car park; guided walks £25pp; NTS • ☎ 01855 811307, ⓦ nts.org.uk/visit/places/glencoe

The attractive and ecofriendly timber **NTS visitor centre** sits in woodland a mile south of Glencoe Village. It has a good exhibition, screenings of The Glen Revealed short film, plus information about the area's natural history and conservation issues, and some entertaining material on rock- and hill-climbing through the years. There's a decent café called The Highland Coo and a gift shop, and you may be able to join a ranger-led **guided walk** of the surrounding area.

ARRIVAL AND ACTIVITIES

By bus To get to the NTS visitor centre or chairlift station from Fort William's bus station, hop on one of the Glasgow-bound Scottish Citylink coaches (up to 8 daily; 30–45min).

GLEN COE VILLAGE AND AROUND

Bus #44 from Fort William also stops at least 10 times a day (3 on Sun) at Glencoe village en route to Kinlochleven.

ACCOMMODATION AND EATING

★ **Clachaig Inn** 2.5 miles south of Glencoe Village on the minor road off the A82 ☎ 01855 811252, ⓦ clachaig.com. The liveliest, best-known hotel in the area is a great place to reward your exertions with cask-conditioned ales and heaped platefuls of food (such as Highland game pie, £13.95); they also have 23 comfy en-suite rooms. Mon–Thurs & Sun 8am–11pm, Fri 8am–midnight, Sat 8am–11.30pm. **£150**

Glencoe Hostel Adjacent to the Glencoe Independent Hostel ☎ 01855 811219, ⓦ hostellingscotland.org.uk/ hostels/glencoe. A basic but decent wood-tiled hostel with a dining area, cosy lounge and well-equipped kitchen. Dorms **£17**

Glencoe Independent Hostel North of the river ☎ 01855 811906, ⓦ glencoehostel.co.uk. Cheap and excellent independent hostel and bunkhouse in rustic whitewashed buildings, offering free wi-fi, hot showers and a laundry service. Hostel from **£14.50**, bunkhouse from **£12.50**

Red Squirrel 150m south of the turn-off to Glencoe Independent Hostel ☎01855 811256, ⓦredsquirrel campsite.co.uk. Sylvan year-round campsite, just south of the hostel on the road to *Clachaig Inn*. Campfires and pets permitted. Per pitch **£12.50**

Scorry Breac On the north side of the river ☎01855 811354, ⓦscorrybreacglencoe.com. Secluded and friendly, a short walk from the centre of Glencoe village, *Scorry Breac* has five affordable en-suite rooms, the best of which have views over the mountains. **£74**

Kinlochleven

At the easternmost end of Loch Leven, the settlement of **KINLOCHLEVEN** is, thanks to its location on the West Highland Way, steadily reviving its fortunes. For many years it was a tourism backwater best known as the site of a huge, unsightly aluminium smelter built in 1904. The tale of the area's industrial past is told in **The Aluminium Story** (same hours as tourist information centre; free), a small series of displays in the same corrugated metal building as the post office and tourist information centre. As well as being close to Glen Coe, Kinlochleven stands at the foot of the Mamore hills, popular with Munro-baggers; Fort William is a day's walk away.

The Ice Factor

Leven Rd • Mon, Wed & Fri–Sun 9am–7pm, Tues & Thurs 9am–10pm • 2.5hr ice-climbing course £48 • ☎ 01855 831100, ⓦ ice-factor.co.uk

Kinlochleven's disused aluminium smelter is now the home of an innovative indoor mountaineering centre called **The Ice Factor**. The facility includes the world's largest artificial ice-climbing wall (13.5m) as well as a range of more traditional climbing walls, plus equipment rental, a steam room and sauna. There's a bar upstairs and food is available too.

ARRIVAL AND INFORMATION

KINLOCHLEVEN

By bus The hourly #44 bus from Fort William runs to the centre of Kinlochleven (50min), passing Glencoe (35min) en route.

Tourist information In the Aluminium Story building on Linnhe Rd, in the centre of the village (Mon, Tues, Thurs & Fri 9am–12.30pm & 1.30–5.30pm, Wed & Sat

9am–1pm; ☎01855 831021). Staff at the combined post office, museum and information point can give tips on local attractions. Look out for the useful leaflet, published by Kinlochleven Community Trust, which details local walking routes.

ACCOMMODATION AND EATING

Blackwater Hostel Beside the river on Lab Rd ☎01855 831253, ⓦblackwaterhostel.co.uk. A decidedly upmarket hostel, with en-suite dorms and Hobbit-sized wooden glamping pods available for rent. You can also camp here. Dorms **£25**, glamping pod **£75**, camping per person **£20**

Edencoille Guest House Garbhein Rd ☎01855 831358, ⓦkinlochlevenbedandbreakfast.co.uk. There's fine hospitality at this Edwardian-built house where, with notice, they can organize packed lunches, evening meals and guided walking trips. **£80**

Lochleven Seafood Café 5 miles west of Kinlochleven on the B836 (north side of the loch) ☎01855 821048, ⓦlochlevenseafoodcafe.co.uk. The best place to eat near

Kinlochleven, this is a relaxed restaurant with an attractive outdoor terrace overlooking the loch. Specializes in local shellfish such as whole brown crab cooked in seawater (£12.95). Daily noon–3pm & 6–9pm.

MacDonald Hotel Fort William Rd ☎01855 831539, ⓦmacdonaldhotel.co.uk. This central hotel has ten decent en-suite bedrooms as well as cabins and a campsite, but is best visited for its Bothy Bar, where you can join fellow walkers for fish and chips (£12.50) and other pub meals. Bar Mon–Wed 12.30–11.30pm, Thurs–Sat 12.30pm–12.30am, Sun 12.30–11.15pm. Doubles **£105**; cabins for 4 **£15**; camping per person **£20**

Loch Ness and around

Twenty-three miles long, unfathomably deep, cold and often moody, **LOCH NESS** is bound by rugged heather-clad mountains rising steeply from a wooded shoreline, with attractive glens opening up on either side. Its fame, however, is based overwhelmingly on its legendary inhabitant, Nessie, the "Loch Ness monster" (see below), who encourages a steady flow of hopeful visitors to the settlements dotted along the loch, in particular **Drumnadrochit**. Nearby, the impressive ruins of **Castle Urquhart** – a favourite monster-spotting location – perch atop a rock on the lochside and attract a deluge of bus parties during the summer. Almost as busy in high season is the village of **Fort Augustus**, at the more scenic southwest tip of Loch Ness, where you can watch queues of boats tackling one of the Caledonian Canal's longest flights of locks. You'll need your own **car** to complete the whole loop around the loch, a journey that includes an impressive stretch between Fort Augustus and the high, hidden Loch Mhòr, overlooked by the imposing Monadhliath range to the south.

Away from the lochside, and seeing a fraction of Loch Ness's visitor numbers, the remote glens of **Urquhart** and **Affric** make an appealing contrast, with Affric in particular boasting narrow, winding roads, gushing streams and hillsides dotted with ancient Caledonian pine forests. The busiest of these glens to the north is the often bleak high country of Glen Moriston, a little to the southeast of Glen Affric, through which the main road between Inverness and Skye passes.

3

GETTING AROUND

LOCH NESS AND AROUND

By bus Using the A82, which runs along the western shore of Loch Ness, buses can travel the entire length of the loch, from Inverness to Fort Augustus. On the eastern side, however, regular bus services are limited to the stretch between Inverness and Foyers.

By car Although most visitors drive along the tree-lined A82 road on the western side of the loch, the sinuous, single-track B862/B852 (originally a military road built to link Fort Augustus and Fort George) that skirts the eastern shore is quieter and affords far more spectacular views.

NESSIE

The world-famous **Loch Ness monster**, affectionately known as **Nessie** (and by serious aficionados as *Nessiteras rhombopteryx*), has been a local celebrity for some time. The first mention of a mystery creature crops up in St Adamnan's seventh-century biography of **St Columba**, who allegedly calmed an aquatic animal that had attacked one of his monks. Present-day interest, however, is probably greater outside Scotland than within the country, and dates from the building of the road along the loch's western shore in the early 1930s. In 1934 the *Daily Mail* published London surgeon **R.K. Wilson**'s sensational photograph of the head and neck of the monster peering up out of the loch, and the hype has hardly diminished since. Recent encounters range from glimpses of ripples by anglers to the famous occasion in 1961 when thirty hotel guests saw a pair of humps break the water's surface and cruise for about half a mile before submerging.

Photographic evidence is showcased in two separate exhibitions located at **Drumnadrochit**, but the most impressive of these exhibits – including the renowned black-and-white movie footage of Nessie's humps moving across the water, and Wilson's original head-and-shoulders shot – have now been exposed as **fakes**. Indeed, in few other places on earth has watching a rather lifeless and often grey expanse of water seemed so compelling, or have floating logs, otters and boat wakes been photographed so often and with such excitement.

Yet while even high-tech sonar surveys carried out over the past two decades have failed to come up with conclusive evidence, it's hard to dismiss Nessie as pure myth. After all, no one yet knows where the unknown layers of silt and mud at the bottom of the loch begin and end: best estimates say the loch is over **750ft deep**, deeper than much of the North Sea, while others point to the possibilities of underwater caves and undiscovered channels connected to the sea. What scientists have found in the cold, murky depths, including pure white eels and rare arctic char, offers fertile grounds for speculation, with different theories declaring Nessie to be a remnant from the dinosaur age, a giant newt or a huge visiting Baltic sturgeon.

LOTS AND LOTS OF LOCHS AND LOCKS

Surveyed by James Watt in 1773, the **Caledonian Canal** was completed in the early 1800s by Thomas Telford to enable ships to pass between the North Sea and the Atlantic without having to navigate Scotland's treacherous northern coast. There are sixty miles between the west-coast entrance to the canal at Corpach, near Fort William, and its exit onto the Moray Firth at Inverness, although strictly speaking only 22 miles of it are bona fide canal – the other 38 exploit the Great Glen's natural string of **freshwater lochs** of Lochy, Oich and Ness.

The most famous piece of canal engineering in Scotland is the series of eight **locks** at Banavie, about a mile from the entrance at Corpach, known as Neptune's Staircase (see page 189). While the canal was originally built for freight-carrying ships and large passenger-steamers, these days it is almost exclusively used by small yachts and pleasure boats. Good spots to watch their leisurely progress are Neptune's Staircase and Fort Augustus, where four locks take traffic through the centre of the village into Loch Ness.

If you're interested in the history of the waterway, it's worth taking a look at the small **Caledonian Canal Visitor Centre**, beside the locks in Fort Augustus (see below). For more active encounters with the canal, you can set off along a section of the Great Glen Way footpath or Great Glen cycleway, both of which follow the **canal towpath** for part of their length (see page 185).

3

Fort Augustus

FORT AUGUSTUS, a tiny, busy village at the scenic southwestern tip of Loch Ness, was named after George II's son, the chubby lad who later became the "Butcher" duke of Cumberland of Culloden fame; it was built as a barracks after the 1715 Jacobite rebellion. Today, it's dominated by comings and goings along the **Caledonian Canal**, which leaves Loch Ness here, and by its large former **Benedictine abbey**, a campus of grey Victorian buildings founded on the site of the original fort in 1876. Until relatively recently this was home to a small but active community of monks, but it has now been converted into luxury flats. There are some cycling routes locally, notably along the Great Glen cycle route.

ARRIVAL AND DEPARTURE   FORT AUGUSTUS

By bus Frequent buses ply the A82, linking Fort Augustus with Drumnadrochit (35min) and Inverness (1hr) to the north, and Fort William, 30 miles south (1hr).

INFORMATION

Tourist office In the car park north of the canal (April & May Mon–Sat 9.30am–5pm, Sun 10am–4pm; June Mon–Sat 9am–5pm, Sun 10am–4pm; July & Aug Mon–Sat 9am–6pm, Sun 10am–4pm; Sept & Oct Mon–Sat 9.30am–5pm, Sun 10am–3pm; Nov–March daily 10am–3pm; ☎01320 366779). Fort Augustus's very helpful tourist office hands out useful free walking leaflets and stocks maps of the Great Glen Way (see page 185).

Caledonian Canal Visitor Centre Ardchattan House, Canalside, by the locks (daily: April–Oct 9am–5pm; Nov–March 9.30am–3.30pm; ☎01320 366493). This refurbished visitor centre is a hub in the village, with information on the locale and the canal, a shop selling local produce, a café and good accommodation.

TOURS AND ACTIVITIES

Boat tours From its berth by the Clansman Centre, near the swing bridge, Cruise Loch Ness sails five miles up Loch Ness (daily; 1hr; £15; ☎01320 366277, ⊚cruiselochness.com), using sonar technology to provide passengers with impressive live 3D imagery of the deep where underwater cave systems, salmon, cannibalistic trout (and, some would speculate, Nessie) are to be found.

Fishing The tourist office can advise you on how to obtain permits to fish the loch or nearby river.

ACCOMMODATION

Corrie Liath Market Hill, half a mile south of the centre along the A82 ☎01320 366409, ⊚corrieliath.co.uk. Small, thoughtfully managed B&B whose comfortable rooms have books and DVDs for guests to enjoy. The garden features a barbecue hut for use in the summertime. __£74__

Lovat Arms Hotel On the A82 in the centre of town ☎01456 490000, ⊚thelovat.com. Expensive hotel refurbished along ecofriendly principles and built on the site of the 1718 Kilwhimen Barracks. The brasserie serves inventive (and costly) dishes with a local focus. **£196**

★ **Lock Chambers** Ardchattan House, Canalside ⓦ scottishcanals.co.uk/destinations/fort-augustus/ airbnb-caledonian-canal-centre. The revived visitor centre now offers seven lovely en-suite rooms, bookable on Airbnb: there are doubles, a bunk room sleeping four and a family room with a double and bunks. Some rooms have canal-facing terraces, and all are tastefully and soothingly decorated. You can breakfast in the café downstairs. Doubles **£75**, bunk room **£90**, family room **£95**

Morag's Lodge Bunoich Brae, on the Loch Ness side of town ☎ 01320 366289, ⓦ moragslodge.com. The atmosphere at this pleasant and well-equipped hostel – with four- and six-bed dorms, doubles, twins and family rooms – livens up with the daily arrival of backpackers' minibus tours. They do bike hire (£20 per day including helmets and maps) and have a bothy bar for guests. Dorms **£24**, doubles **£60**

EATING AND DRINKING

Caledonian Canal Visitor Centre Café Ardchattan House, Canalside, by the locks ☎ 01320 366493). The best place for snacks – try the Loch Ness Chowder (£5) – home baking and coffee, plus local artisan ice cream. Daily: April–Oct 9am–5pm; Nov–March 9.30am–3.30pm.

The Lock Inn Canalside, opposite the Caledonian Canal Visitor Centre ☎ 01320 366302. With attractive wood-panelled interiors and a wider selection of pub meals (such as chicken curry, £11.95), *The Lock Inn* is a slightly better choice than its neighbour, *The Bothy*. Daily 11am–11pm; food served noon–3.30pm & 5.30–8.30pm.

The east side of Loch Ness

The tranquil and scenic **east side of Loch Ness** is skirted by General Wade's old military highway, now the B862/B852. From Fort Augustus, the narrow single-track road swings up, away from the lochside through the near-deserted **Stratherrick** valley, which is dotted with tiny lochans. To the east of Fort Augustus you'll pass the massive earth workings of the Glendoe Hydro Development. From here, the road drops down to rejoin the shores of Loch Ness at **FOYERS**, where there are numerous marked forest trails and an impressive waterfall.

Past **Inverfarigaig** – where a road up a beautiful, steep-sided river valley leads east over to Loch Mhor – is the sleepy village of **DORES**, nestled at the northeastern end of Loch Ness, where the whitewashed *Dores Inn* provides a pleasant pit stop.

ARRIVAL AND DEPARTURE   THE EAST SIDE OF LOCH NESS

By bus Local buses run up and down the northeast side of the loch, shuttling visitors from Inverness south to Foyers (Mon–Fri up to 5 daily; 2 on Sat; 45min).

ACCOMMODATION AND EATING

Dores Inn North of the village centre, by the loch ☎ 01463 751203, ⓦ thedoresinn.co.uk. Only 9 miles southwest of Inverness (and 11 miles north of Foyers), this old lochside pub is popular with Invernessians, who trickle out here on summer evenings for a stroll along the grey pebble beach and some monster-spotting. Seabass with king prawns costs £15.95. Mon–Thurs 10am–11pm, Fri & Sat 10am–midnight, Sun 10am–10pm.

FOYERS

Foyers House In Upper Foyers, up the track next to Waterfall Café ☎ 01456 48640, ⓦ foyershouse-lochness. com 5. Out of the way, adults-only B&B with fabulous views of the loch from its terrace. Has a self-catering kitchen and dining room. **£75**

Waterfall Café In Upper Foyers, opposite the footpath to the waterfall ☎ 01456 486233. This friendly teashop still runs a live webcam of red squirrels nesting across the road – and does delicious breakfasts, lunches and baking to boot. April–Oct Mon–Thurs 9am–5pm, Fri & Sat 9am–7pm, Sun 10am–3pm; Nov–March Mon–Thurs 9.30am–4pm, Fri & Sat 9.30am–7pm, Sun 10am–2pm.

Drumnadrochit and around

Situated above a verdant, sheltered bay of Loch Ness fifteen miles southwest of Inverness, **DRUMNADROCHIT** is the southern gateway to remote Glen Affric and the epicentre of Nessie-hype, complete with a rash of tacky souvenir shops and two rival monster exhibitions whose head-to-head scramble for punters has occasionally erupted into acrimonious exchanges, detailed with relish by the local press.

Loch Ness Centre & Exhibition

On the main A82 • Daily: Easter–June & Sept–Oct 9.30am–5pm; July & Aug 9.30am–6pm; Nov–Easter 10am–3.30pm • ☎01456 450573, ⓦ lochness.com • £8.45

Of the two major monster hubs in Drumnadrochit (the other being the Nessieland Monster Centre), the **Loch Ness Centre & Exhibition** is the better bet, offering an in-depth rundown of eyewitness accounts and information on various Nessie research projects. It does a good job, mixing "evidence" of the monster's existence with frank appraisals of pictures and sightings that turned out to be hoaxes.

Nessieland Monster Centre

Just west of the Loch Ness Centre & Exhibition on the A831 • Daily: July & Aug 9am–9pm; Sept–June 9am–5pm • £6 • ☎01456 450342, ⓦ nessieland.co.uk

Aimed mainly at families, the rather feeble **Nessieland Monster Centre** has an exhibition on monster sightings, a plastic model of Nessie for kids to clamber on, plus its own adventure playground. The wood-panelled and heavily tartanized interior of the adjacent *Loch Ness Lodge Hotel* is said to harbour a resident ghost.

Castle Urquhart

Beside Loch Ness, 2 miles southeast of Drumnadrochit and just off the A82 • Daily: April–Sept 9.30am–6pm; Oct 9.30am–5pm; Nov–March 9.30am–4.30pm • £12; HES • ☎01456 450551, ⓦ historicenvironment.scot

The thirteenth-century ruined lochside **Castle Urquhart** was built as a strategic base to guard the Great Glen. The castle was taken by Edward I of England and later held by Robert the Bruce against Edward III, only to be blown up in 1692 to prevent it from falling to the Jacobites. Today it's one of Scotland's classic picture-postcard ruins, particularly splendid at night when it's floodlit and the crowds have gone. In the small visitor centre, a short film highlights the turbulent history of the castle.

ARRIVAL AND DEPARTURE
DRUMNADROCHIT AND AROUND

By bus Drumnadrochit is served by frequent buses from Inverness (at least hourly; 30min), Fort William (up to 9 daily; 1hr 30min) and Fort Augustus (up to 10 daily; 35min). Buses stop near the post office, on the A82.

INFORMATION AND TOURS

Tourist information In the middle of the main car park in the village (April & May Mon–Sat 9.30am–5pm, Sun 10am–3pm; June Mon–Sat 9am–5pm, Sun 10am–6pm; July & Aug Mon–Sat 9am–6pm, Sun 10am–4pm; Sept & Oct Mon–Sat 9.30am–5pm, Sun 10am–3pm; Nov–March Tues–Sat 9.30am–3.30pm; ☎01456 459086).

Boat tours The sonar-equipped *Nessie Hunter* (☎01456 450395, ⓦ loch-ness-cruises.com) runs hourly trips on the loch from 9am to 6pm, from Easter to October. The hour-long cruise costs £15 and can be booked online or at the Nessieland Monster Centre.

ACCOMMODATION

Benleva Kilmore Rd, Kilmore ☎01456 450080, ⓦ benleva.co.uk. Small, basic hotel in Kilmore, a 15min walk from the monster centres of Drumnadrochit. The six en-suite rooms have tartan bedspreads and free wi-fi. **£120**

Borlum Farm A mile southeast of central Drumnadrochit, off the A82 ☎01456 450220, ⓦ borlum.com. Attractive campsite overlooking the village, with space for caravans and tents. The site is part of a popular riding school offering lessons, rides and treks (from £20/hr). they also rent out two lovely croft cottages, one with a piano. Per pitch **£10.50**, cottages weekly from **£695**

Glenkirk B&B 300m west of Nessieland Monster Centre along the A831 ☎01456 450802, ⓦ lochnessbandb. com. Bright, friendly B&B in a former church located just a few minutes' walk from the centre, with simple yet smartly decorated bedrooms. **£100**

Loch Ness Backpackers Lodge Coiltie Farmhouse, Lewiston, 1 mile south of the centre of Drumnadrochit ☎01456 450807, ⓦ lochness-backpackers.com. For a cheap bed for the night, head for this immaculate and friendly hostel, which has dorms, private rooms and good facilities including a bar and two lounges. Coming from Drumnadrochit, follow the signs to the left. Dorms **£20**; doubles **£50**

EATING AND DRINKING

Benleva Kilmore Rd, Kilmore ☎ 01456 450080. One of many hotels doing bar food, *Benleva* sets itself apart by using local beer in some of its dishes, including the steak and ale pie with chips and seasonal veg (£13.95). Mon–Thurs noon–midnight, Fri noon–1am, Sat noon–11.45pm, Sun noon–11pm.

Fiddler's Just south of the village green on the A82 ☎ 01456 450678, ⓦ fiddledrum.co.uk. Busy, friendly bar with plenty of outside seating and, it's claimed, more than five hundred single malt whiskies. The mostly meaty menu has a couple of veggie options too, including a veggie and brie burger (£13.95). Daily 12.30–2.30pm & 6–9.30pm.

Glen Affric

Due west of Drumnadrochit lies a vast area of high peaks, remote glens and few roads. The reason most folk head this way is to explore the picturesque native forests and grand mountains of **Glen Affric**, heaven for walkers, climbers and mountain bikers. Munro-baggers (see page 41) are normally much in evidence, and it's possible to tramp 25 miles all the way through Glen Affric to Shiel Bridge, on the west coast near Kyle of Lochalsh.

Cannich and Loch Affric

The main approach to Glen Affric is through the small settlement of **CANNICH**, thirteen miles west of Drumnadrochit on the A831. Cannich is a quiet and uninspiring village, but it has an excellent campsite where mountain bikes can be rented. From the car park at the head of the single-track road along the glen, ten miles southwest of Cannich, there's a selection of **walks**: the trip around **Loch Affric** will take you a good five hours but allows you to appreciate the glen and its wildlife.

ARRIVAL AND DEPARTURE — GLEN AFFRIC

By bus From July to September, Ross's Minibuses (☎ 01463 761250, ⓦ ross-minibuses.co.uk) runs scheduled services to the car park at Glen Affric from Cannich (4 on Mon, Wed & Fri; 30min); Drumnadrochit (3 on Mon, Wed & Fri; 1hr 35min) and Inverness (2 on Mon, Wed & Fri; 2hr 10min). Its vehicles will also carry bikes if given advance notice.

INFORMATION AND ACTIVITIES

Tourist information Notice boards are dotted around the glen; the Forestry Commission website (ⓦ scotland.forestry.gov.uk/visit/glen-affric) includes an interactive map showing where they're located.

Volunteering For details of volunteer work in Glen Affric helping with restoration of the woodland, get in touch with the wonderful Trees for Life charity (ⓦ treesforlife.org.uk).

ACCOMMODATION AND EATING

★ **Bog Cotton Café** At Cannich Camping & Caravan Park. The best option for food in Cannich, this welcoming chalet-like café has large windows overlooking the campsite. They serve breakfasts (including veggie) and light lunches. Planning a hike? You can buy takeaway sandwiches here for £3 too. Daily 9am–5pm.

Cannich Camping & Caravan Park In the centre of Cannich ☎ 01456 415364, ⓦ highlandcamping.co.uk. Mountain bikes can be rented (£17/day) at this pretty, shaded campsite, which has good facilities, including wi-fi

and a TV room. Per person £9, camping pod for 2 £36

Glen Affric Youth Hostel Allt Beithe, 20 miles southwest of Cannich ☎ 08452 937373, ⓦ hostellingscotland.org.uk/hostels/glen-affric. Utterly remote, this hostel near the head of Glen Affric makes a convenient if rudimentary stopover on the 25-mile hike through Glen Affric to Shiel Bridge. A wind turbine and solar panels provide the hostel with electricity, but note that you'll need to bring all your own food. Dorms £24.50; twins £29.50

Inverness

Straddling a nexus of major road and rail routes, **INVERNESS** is the busy hub of the Highlands, and an inevitable port of call if you're exploring the region by public transport. Over a hundred miles from any other major settlement yet with a population rapidly approaching 100,000, Inverness is the only city in the Highlands. Crowned by a pink crenellated **castle** and lavishly decorated with flowers, the city centre still has some hints of its medieval street layout, though unsightly concrete blocks do an efficient job of masking it. Within walking distance of the centre are peaceful spots along by the Ness, leafy parks and friendly B&Bs located in prosperous-looking stone houses.

Brief history

The sheltered harbour and proximity to the open sea made Inverness an important entrepôt and shipbuilding centre during medieval times. **David I**, who first imposed a feudal system on Scotland, erected a castle on the banks of the Ness to oversee maritime trade in the early twelfth century, promoting it to royal burgh status soon after. Bolstered by receipts from the lucrative export of leather, salmon and timber, the town grew to become the kingdom's most prosperous northern outpost, and an obvious target for the marauding Highlanders who plagued this remote border area. A second wave of growth occurred during the eighteenth century as the Highland cattle trade flourished. The arrival of the **Caledonian Canal** and **rail links** with the east and south brought further prosperity, heralding a tourist boom that reached a fashionable zenith in the Victorian era, fostered by the royal family's enthusiasm for all things Scottish.

3

Inverness Castle

Looming above the city and dominating the horizon is **Inverness Castle**, a predominantly nineteenth-century red-sandstone building perched above the river. The original castle formed the core of the ancient town, which had rapidly developed as a port trading with Europe after its conversion to Christianity by St Columba in the sixth century. Robert the Bruce wrested the castle back from the English during the Wars of Independence, destroying much of the structure in the process, and while held by the Jacobites in both the 1715 and the 1745 rebellions, it was blown up by them to prevent it falling into government hands. Today's edifice houses the **Sheriff Court** and is not open to the general public. However, there are good views down the River Ness and various plaques and statues in the grounds, including a small plinth marking the start of the 73-mile Great Glen Way.

Inverness Museum and Art Gallery

Castle Wynd • Tues–Sat 10am–5pm • Free • ☎ 01463 237114, ⓦ highlifehighland.com

Below the castle, the revamped **Inverness Museum and Art Gallery** on Castle Wynd offers an insight into the social history of the Highlands, with treasures from the times of the Picts and Vikings, taxidermy exhibits such as "Felicity" the puma, caught in Cannich in 1980, and interactive features including an introduction to the Gaelic language. It also houses the Highland Photographic archive, and has impressive temporary art exhibitions.

Old High Church

Church St, next to Leakey's bookshop • Grounds open to public; church open for Sun services 11.15am • Free • ☎ 01463 250802

The **Old High Church**, founded in 1171 and rebuilt on several occasions since, stands just back from the east bank of the river on Church Street, hemmed in by a walled graveyard. Those Jacobites who survived the massacre of Culloden were brought here and incarcerated prior to their execution in the cemetery. If you look carefully you may see the bullet holes left on gravestones by the firing squads.

Scottish Kiltmaker Visitor Centre

In the Highland House of Fraser shop at 4–9 Huntly St, on the river's west bank • Daily 9am–10pm, kilt-making demonstrations daily 9am–5pm • £2.50 • ☎ 01463 222781, ⓦ highlandhouseoffraser.com

Entered through the factory shop, the **Scottish Kiltmaker Visitor Centre** is an imaginative small attraction, complete with the outfits worn by actors for the *Braveheart* and *Rob Roy* films, which sets out everything you ever wanted to know about tartan. There's an interesting seven-minute film shown on the hour, and on weekdays you can watch various tartan products being made in the workshop. The finished products are, of course, on sale in the showroom

INVERNESS

A9 Wick, Ullapool & Edinburgh

A96 Nairn, Aberdeen & Inverness Airport

0   200
yards

LONGMAN ROAD
A82
FRIARS BRIDGE
GLEBE STREET
CHAPEL STREET
ROSE STREET
Budget
FRIARS STREET
FRIARS LANE
Library @
HUNTLY STREET
CELT STREET
KING STREET
QUEEN STREET
CHURCH STREET
SCHOOL LANE
STROTHERS LANE
Bus Station
Old High Church
POST OFFICE AVENUE
ACADEMY STREET
QUEENSGATE
Train Station
FALCON SQUARE
Eastgate Shopping Centre
MILLBURN ROAD
CROWN ROAD
CROWN AVENUE
Footbridge
Abertarff House
BANK STREET
UNION STREET
INGLIS ST
EASTGATE
CROWN CIRCUS
KENNETH STREET
GREIG STREET
DUNBAR'S STREET
KING STREET
HUNTLY STREET
BANK LANE
BARON TAYLOR'S STREET
ACADEMY STREET
HIGH ST
ARDCONNEL TERRACE
CHARLES STREET
KINGSMILLS ROAD
FAIRFIELD ROAD
Steeple
Town Hall
BRIDGE STREET
Museum & Art Gallery
Castle
CASTLE STREET
ARDCONNEL STREET
HILL STREET
REAY STREET
DENNY STREET
CROWN STREET
UNION ROAD
River Ness
PLANEFIELD ROAD
KENNETH STREET
Scottish Kiltmaker Visitor Centre (i)
YOUNG STREET NESS BRIDGE
(i)
CROWN STREET
KINGSMILLS ROAD
MONTAGUE ROW
TOMNAHURICH STREET
KENNETH STREET
ALEXANDER PLACE
NESS WALK
CASTLE ROAD
ARGYLE STREET
ARGYLE TERRACE
SOUTHSIDE PLACE
ARDROSS PLACE
ARDROSS STREET
St Andrew's Episcopal Cathedral
GORDON TERRACE
VIEW PLACE
DUFFY DRIVE
OLD EDINBURGH ROAD
COLDUTHEL ROAD
SOUTHSIDE ROAD
GLENURQUHART ROAD
MAYFIELD ROAD
NESS BANK
Eden Court Theatre
BISHOPS ROAD
HAUGH ROAD
PATON STREET
Footbridge
FRASER STREET
GORDONVILLE ROAD
COLDUTHEL ROAD
BALLIFEARY ROAD
BISHOPS PARK
NESS WALK
Ladies Walk
Godsmans Walk
BELLFIELD PARK
BALLIFEARY LANE
Ticket To Ride
Bellfield Park
ISLAND BANK ROAD
SPRINGFIELD GARDENS
N
Bught Park

7, A82 & Fort William

9 & Hospital

Bught Park
10 & Ness Islands
B862 Fort Augustus via East Loch Ness

● **EATING**	
Abstract	6
Café 1	5
Café Artysans	1
Leakey's Bookshop and Café	2
Rendezvous Café	3
Rocpool Restaurant	4

■ **ACCOMMODATION**	
Bazpackers	4
Bught Caravan and Camping Site	10
Furan Guest House	9
Glenmoriston Town House Hotel	6
Heathmount Hotel	3
Inverglen Guest House	2
Loch Ness Country House Hotel	7
Moyness House	5
Rocpool Reserve	8
SYHA Inverness	1

■ **NIGHTLIFE**	
The Ironworks	1

■ **DRINKING**	
Hootananny's	2
No 27	3

THE TRUTH ABOUT TARTAN

To much of the world, **tartan** is synonymous with Scotland. It's the natural choice of packaging for Scottish exports from shortbread and Sean Connery, and when the Scottish football team travels abroad, the high-spirited "Tartan Army" of fans is never far behind. Tartan is big business for the tourist industry, yet the truth is that romantic fiction and commercial interest have enclosed this ancient Highland art form within an almost insurmountable wall of myth.

The original form of tartan, the kind that long ago was called **Helande**, was a fine, hard and almost showerproof cloth spun in Highland villages from the wool of the native sheep, dyed with preparations of local plants. It was worn as a huge single piece of cloth, or **plaid**, which was belted around the waist and draped over the upper body, like a knee-length toga. The natural colours were clear but soft, and the broken pattern gave superb camouflage, unlike modern versions, where garish, clashing colours are often used to create impact.

TRANSFORMING TARTAN

The myth-makers were about four centuries ahead of themselves in dressing up the warriors of the film *Braveheart* in plaid: in fact tartan did not become popular in the Lowlands until the beginning of the eighteenth century, when it was adopted as the anti-Union badge of the **Jacobites**. After Culloden, a ban on the wearing of tartan in the Highlands lasted some 25 years; in that time it became a fondly held emblem for emigrant Highlanders in the colonies and was incorporated into the uniforms of the new Highland regiments in the British Army. Then **Sir Walter Scott** set to work glamorizing the clans, dressing George IV in a kilt for his visit to Edinburgh in 1822. By the time Queen Victoria set the royal seal of approval on both the Highlands and tartan with her extended annual holidays at Balmoral, the concept of tartan as formal dress rather than rough Highland wear was assured.

With the gentrification of the kilt came "rules" about the correct form of attire and the idea that every clan had its own distinguishing tartan. To have the right to wear tartan, one had to belong, albeit remotely, to a clan, and so the way was paved for the "what's-my-tartan?" lists that appear in Scottish souvenir shops. Great feats of genealogical gymnastics were performed: where lists left gaps, a marketing phenomenon of themed tartans developed, with new patterns made for different districts, companies and even football teams.

Scotsmen today will commonly wear the kilt for weddings and other formal occasions; properly made kilts, however – comprising some four yards of one hundred percent wool – are likely to set you back £300 or more, with the rest of the regalia at least doubling that figure. If the contents of your sporran don't stretch that far, most places selling kilts will rent outfits on a daily basis. The best place to find better-quality material is a recognized Highland outfitter rather than a souvenir shop: in Inverness, try the **Scottish Kiltmaker Visitor Centre** at the Highland House of Fraser shop (see page 200).

downstairs, along with all manner of Highland knitwear, woven woollies and classy Harris tweed.

Ness Islands

From **St Andrews Episcopal Cathedral**, on the west bank of the river, you can wander a mile or so upriver to the peaceful **Ness Islands**, an attractive, informal public park reached and linked by footbridges. Laid out with mature trees and shrubs, the islands are the favourite haunt of local anglers.

Caledonian Canal

Half a mile upstream from the Ness Islands park, the River Ness runs close to the **Caledonian Canal**, which was designed by Thomas Telford in the early nineteenth century as a link between the east and west coasts, joining lochs Ness, Oich, Lochy and Linnhe. Today its main use is recreational, and there are cruises through part of it to Loch Ness (see page 193), while the towpath provides relaxing walks with good views.

ARRIVAL AND DEPARTURE INVERNESS

Train station **left-luggage** lockers cost £3–5 for 24hr, depending on size (Mon–Sat 6.40am–7.50pm, Sun 10.40am–6.20pm); the left-luggage room in the bus station costs £4/item/day (Mon–Sat 8.30am–5.30pm, Sun 9am–5.30pm).

By plane Inverness airport (☏ 01667 464000) is at Dalcross, seven miles east of the city; from here, bus #11 (every 30min, 6am–11pm, 25min; £4.55; ⊛ stagecoachbus.com) goes into town, while a taxi (try Tartan Taxis on ☏ 01463 222777) costs around £15.

Destinations Belfast (6 weekly; 1hr 5min); Birmingham (Mon–Fri & Sun 1 daily; 1hr 30min); Bristol (1–2 daily; 1hr 5min); Kirkwall (Mon–Sat 1–2 daily; 45min); London Gatwick (4–5 daily; 1hr 50min); Luton (1 daily; 1hr 20min); Manchester (Mon–Fri 2 daily, Sat & Sun 1 daily; 1hr 30min); Stornoway (Mon–Fri 3–4 daily, Sat & Sun 1 daily; 40min).

By train The train station is on Station Square, just off Academy St, to the northeast of the centre.

Destinations Aberdeen (Mon–Sat 11 daily; 5 on Sun; 2hr 15min); Aviemore (Mon–Sat 11 daily, 7 on Sun; 40min); Edinburgh (Mon–Sat 8 daily, 5 on Sun; 3hr 30min); Glasgow Queen Street (3–4 daily; 3hr 20min); Kyle of Lochalsh (Mon–Sat 4 daily, 2 on Sun; 2hr 30min); London King's Cross (Mon–Fri & Sun 2 daily, 1 on Sat; 8hr–12hr 45min); Thurso (Mon–Sat 2 daily, 1 on Sun; 3hr 45min); Wick (Mon–Sat 4 daily, 1 on Sun; 4hr 20min).

By bus The main bus hub is just north of the train station, close to the public library.

Destinations Aberdeen (hourly; 3hr 50min); Aviemore (every 30min; 45min); Drumnadrochit (at least hourly; 30min); Fort Augustus (up to 9 daily; 1hr); Fort William (up to 9 daily; 2hr); Glasgow (5 daily; 3hr 25min–4hr); Kyle of Lochalsh (3 daily; 2hr); Nairn (every 20–30min; 45min); Perth (7 daily; 2hr 50min); Portree (3 daily; 3hr 15min); Thurso (Mon–Sat 5 daily, 3 on Sun; 3hr); Ullapool (2–4 daily; 1hr 25min).

GETTING AROUND

Car rental Budget, Railway Terrace, behind the train station (☏ 01463 713333).

Bike rental Ticket to Ride at The Pavilion, Bellfield Park (☏ 01463 419160, ⊛ tickettoridehighlands.co.uk), rents out decent hybrid bikes for £30/day.

INFORMATION AND ACTIVITIES

Tourist office The tourist office is in an unsightly 1960s block on Castle Wynd, a 5min walk from the train station (April & May Mon–Sat 9am–5pm, Sun 10am–5pm; June Mon–Sat 9am–6pm, Sun 9.30am–5pm; July & Aug Mon–Sat 9am–6.30pm, Sun 9.30am–6pm; Sept & Oct Mon–Sat 9am–5pm, Sun 10am–4pm; Nov–March Mon–Sat 9am–5pm, Sun 10am–3pm). It stocks a wide range of literature, including free maps of the city and its environs, and the staff can book local accommodation for a £4 fee. There's also a CalMac ferry booking office in the building (⊛ calmac.co.uk).

Outdoor equipment Tiso Outdoor Experience at 2 Henderson Rd, on the Longman Estate (Mon, Tues, Fri & Sat 9am–6pm, Wed 9.30am–6pm, Thurs 9am–7pm, Sun 10am–5pm; ☏ 01463 729171, ⊛ tiso.com), has a large range of outdoor gear to rent or buy. There's also an indoor climbing wall and a path for testing walking boots before you buy.

TOURS AND CRUISES

Inverness is the departure point for a range of day-tours and cruises to nearby attractions, including Loch Ness, Skye, Orkney and the Moray Firth, where there's a chance to spot dolphins. Inverness is also one of the few places where transport connections allow you to embark on a major grand tour of the Highlands.

LOCH NESS

Loch Ness cruises typically incorporate a visit to a monster exhibition at Drumnadrochit and Urquhart Castle. Jacobite Cruises (☏ 01463 233999, ⊛ jacobite.co.uk) runs a 3hr 30min coach trip (£30) to Loch Ness, including a 30min cruise and admission to the Loch Ness Centre & Exhibition.

THE HIGHLANDS AND SKYE

For exploring the northwest, ScotRail (☏ 0845 755 0033, ⊛ scotrail.co.uk) sells a Highland Rover pass (£81.50), offering four days of unlimited travel over eight consecutive days, with many train, ferry and coach routes included.

ORKNEY

From June to August, John O' Groats Ferries (☏ 01955 611353, ⊛ jogferry.co.uk) runs day-trips to Orkney (£68), including visits to Kirkwall, Scapa Flow and the Ring of Brodgar. Departures daily from Inverness at 7.30am.

ACCOMMODATION SEE MAP PAGE 200

HOTELS

Glenmoriston Town House Hotel 20 Ness Bank ☏ 01463 223777, ⊛ glenmoristontownhouse.com. A smart contemporary hotel by the riverside just a few minutes' walk from the town centre, with muted decor and a good dining experience on offer at *Abstract*. **£175**

Heathmount Hotel Kingsmill Rd ☎01463 235877, ☥heathmounthotel.com. Reasonably central boutique hotel with blingy but comfortable rooms, some of which have four-poster beds; all come with Sky TV and an iPod dock. **£150**

Loch Ness Country House Hotel Off the A82 Fort William Rd ☎01463 230512, ☥lochnesscountryhousehotel. co.uk. Luxurious country-house hotel, three miles southwest of central Inverness. Offers modern Scottish food, fine wines and more than two hundred malts, as well as very comfortable and spacious rooms. **£180**

Rocpool Reserve Culduthel Rd ☎01463 240089, ☥rocpool.com. Only a 10min walk south of the castle, this acclaimed hotel and restaurant has minimal but luxurious rooms (think white cotton bedsheets, subtle splashes of colour and jacuzzis in the high-end rooms), plus a swanky, French-inspired restaurant. **£355**

B&BS

Furan Guest House 100 Old Edinburgh Rd ☎01463 712094, ☥furan.co.uk. Good-value B&B a mile south of the centre, run by former hoteliers. Has a good choice of spotlessly clean rooms and a friendly resident cat. Book direct for the best rates. **£80.50**

★ **Invernglen Guest House** 7 Abertarff Rd ☎01463 716350, ☥invernglenguesthouse.co.uk. Supremely cosy and colourful rooms in a handsome villa. Smoked Scottish salmon is on the breakfast menu, and they run single-day or two-day photography workshops, with trips to nearby glens

and castles (£180/day). **£120**

★ **Moyness House** 6 Bruce Gardens ☎01463 233836, ☥moyness.co.uk. Warm, welcoming, upmarket B&B on the west side of Inverness, with original Victorian features (it was built in 1880) and a nice walled garden. **£135**

HOSTELS

Bazpackers 4 Culduthel Rd ☎01463 717663, ☥bazpackershostel.co.uk. The most cosy and relaxed of the city's hostels, with more than thirty beds, including three doubles and two twins; some dorms are mixed. Good location in an 1826 townhouse, great views and a garden, which is used for barbecues. Dorms **£26**, twins/doubles **£60**

SYHA Inverness Victoria Drive, off Millburn Rd ☎01463 231771, ☥hostellingscotland.org.uk/hostels/inverness. Big SYHA hostel with large kitchens and communal areas, plus six-bed family rooms (£155) and cheap singles (£21) in addition to the usual dorms. However, it's almost a mile from the centre, and the building is devoid of character. Dorms **£21**, twins **£47**

CAMPSITE

Bught Caravan and Camping Site Bught Park, a mile south of the centre ☎01463 236920, ☥inverness caravanpark.com. Inverness's main campsite on the west bank of the river near the sports centre. Has good facilities, but it can get very crowded at the height of the season. April–Sept. Per person **£20**

EATING

SEE MAP PAGE 200

Abstract 20 Ness Bank ☎01463 223777, ☥glen moristontownhouse.com. This award-winning French restaurant within the *Glenmoriston Town House Hotel* serves stylish French/Mediterranean/Asian fusion food; mains start at around £19. Tues–Sat 6–10pm.

Café 1 75 Castle St ☎01463 226200, ☥cafe1.net. You'll find contemporary Scottish cooking – like pan-seared venison with oven-roasted fig – in a bistro-style setting here. The restaurant's beef, lamb and pork is reared on a croft 8 miles north of Inverness. Mon–Fri noon–2.30pm & 5–9.30pm, Sat 1–3.30pm & 6–9.30pm.

Café Artysans 7 Strothers Lane ☎01463 729793, ☥cafeartysans.org.uk. An attractive social enterprise café near the bus and train stations which helps train young people in the area. It's a good bet for breakfast (granola with fruit and yogurt £2.95), or a lunchtime sandwich served on farmhouse bread (£6). Mon–Sat 8.30am–4pm.

★ **Leakey's Bookshop and Café** Church St ☎01463 239947. Prise yourself away from the old books and maps at this beautiful galleried secondhand bookshop to enjoy a cup of tea, cake or a bowl of soup (£5) at the upstairs café. Mon–Sat 10am–5.30pm.

Rendezvous Café 14a Church St ☎01463 718444, ☥rendezvous-cafe.co.uk. Good coffee and big breakfasts are served inside and out at this modern corner café, which is one of the more relaxed places for coffee and a snack in the city centre (soup £2.95). Mon–Sat 8am–4pm, Sun 9am–4pm.

Rocpool Restaurant 1 Ness Walk ☎01463 717274, ☥rocpoolrestaurant.com. Another of the city's excellent, smart-ish dining options, with a contemporary setting, attentive staff and deliciously rich food. The coriander & chilli monkfish stir fry is £25.95. Mon–Sat noon–2.30pm & 5.45–10pm.

DRINKING AND NIGHTLIFE

SEE MAP PAGE 200

Hootananny's 67 Church St ☎01463 233651, ☥hootanannyinverness.co.uk. Lively watering hole with homely food (including haggis, neeps and tatties for £10.95). Regular live music events, plus on Saturday afternoons there

are ceilidhs from 2.30–4.30pm. Mon–Thurs noon–1am, Fri & Sat noon–3am, Sun 6.30pm–midnight.

The Ironworks 122b Academy St ☎0871 789 4173, ☥ironworksvenue.com. Large live music venue with space for a thousand music fans. The place to come for touring bands, stand-up comedy and the occasional club night. See website for events and opening times.

No 27 27 Castle St ☎01463 241999, ⓦnumber27

inverness.uk. Skinny bar/restaurant with a wide range of beers (there's a new guest ale every Sunday) and burgers and pasta dishes for around £9. Mon–Thurs 11am–11pm, Fri & Sat 11am–midnight, Sun 12.30pm–11pm.

DIRECTORY

Internet Inverness Library (Mon & Tues 9am–6.30pm, Wed 10am–6.30pm, Thurs 9am–8pm, Fri 9am–6.30pm, Sat 9am–5pm), near the bus station, offers free internet access (ID required).

Medical facilities The Raigmore Hospital (☎01463 704000) is at Old Perth Rd on the southeastern outskirts of town, close to the A9.

Police 6 Burnett Rd ☎ 01463 228411.

Post office 14–16 Queensgate (Mon & Wed–Sat 9am–5.30pm, Tues 9.30am–5.30pm).

Around Inverness

A string of worthwhile sights punctuates the approach to Inverness along the main route from Aberdeen. The low-key resort of **Nairn**, with its long white-sand beaches and championship golf course, stands within striking distance of several monuments, including whimsical **Cawdor Castle**, best known for its role in Shakespeare's *Macbeth*, and **Fort George**, one of several impressive Hanoverian bastions erected in the wake of the Jacobite rebellion. The infamous battle and ensuing massacre that ended Bonnie Prince Charlie's uprising took place on the outskirts of Inverness at **Culloden**, where a visitor centre and memorial stones beside a heather-clad moor recall the gruesome events of 1746.

Northeast of Inverness is the **Moray Firth**, one of the UK's best locations for spotting dolphins (see page 206). Closer to the city, where this inlet merges with the River Ness, is the start of the Beauly Firth, a sheltered sea loch bounded by the Black Isle in the north and the wooded hills of the Aird to the south.

GETTING AROUND

AROUND INVERNESS

By bus The region's main towns are well served by public transport, but to access Cawdor Castle and Fort George outside of the peak summer season (when special tourist routes are briefly opened) you will first need to travel to Nairn and then transfer to a taxi or the local Dial-a-Bus service (☎ 01667 456066).

By car The overloaded A96 links Inverness with Nairn, 16 miles northeast, with quieter minor roads leading off it to Fort George, Cawdor Castle and Culloden. Heading northwest from Inverness, most traffic uses Kessock Bridge (the A9) to cross the Moray Firth; the A862, which skirts the shoreline and the mud flats, offers a slower, more scenic alternative.

Craig Phadrig

3 miles west of the city centre • Stagecoach bus #2 from Church St to Scorguie (Mon–Sat every 20min; 10min) then walk the final half-mile west

West of the town, on the top of **Craig Phadrig** hill, there's a vitrified **Iron Age fort**, reputed to be where the Pictish king Brude received St Columba in the sixth century. The walls of the fort were built of stone laced with timber and, when the timber was set alight, some of the stone fused to glass, becoming "vitrified". Waymarked forest trails start from the car parks at the bottom of the hill and lead up to the fort, though only the outlines of its perimeter defences are now visible, and tree planting is beginning to block some of the views.

Culloden

6 miles east of Inverness off the B9006 • Visitor centre daily: April, May, Sept & Oct 9am–5.30pm; June–Aug 9am–6pm; Nov, Dec, Feb & March 10am–4pm • £11; entrance includes an audio-guide of the site; NTS • ☎ 0844 493 2159, ⓦ nts.org.uk/culloden • Hourly Stagecoach buses run from Falcon Square near Inverness train station to the visitor centre (35min)

3

THE DOLPHINS OF THE MORAY FIRTH

The **Moray Firth**, a great wedge-shaped bay forming the eastern coastline of the Highlands, is one of only three areas of UK waters that support a resident population of **dolphins**. Around 200 of these beautiful, intelligent marine mammals live in the estuary, the most northerly breeding ground in Europe for this particular species – the bottle-nosed dolphin (*Tursiops truncatus*) – and you stand a good chance of spotting a few, either from the shore or a boat.

One of the best places in Scotland, if not in Europe, to look for them is **Chanonry Point**, on the Black Isle – a spit of sand protruding into a narrow, deep channel, where converging currents bring fish close to the surface, and thus the dolphins close to shore; a rising tide is the most likely time to see them.

Several companies run dolphin-spotting **boat trips** around the Moray Firth. However, researchers claim that the increased traffic is causing the dolphins unnecessary stress, particularly during the all-important breeding period when passing vessels are thought to force calves underwater for uncomfortably long periods. So if you decide to go on a cruise to see the dolphins, which also sometimes provides the chance of spotting minke whales, porpoises, seals and otters, make sure that the operator is a member of the Dolphin Space Programme's accreditation scheme (ⓦdolphinspace.org).

Trips with accredited operators, most of which run between April and October, are especially popular in July and August, so be sure to book them well in advance. To get from Inverness to Avoch (20min) or Cromarty (50min) with public transport, take Stagecoach bus #26 from the bus station (at least hourly) – not all services run as far as Cromarty, so check before boarding.

BOAT TOURS

Trips with these **accredited operators**, most of which operate between April and October, are especially popular in July and August, so be sure to book them well in advance. To get from Inverness to Avoch (20min) or Cromarty (50min) with public transport, take Stagecoach bus #26 from the bus station (at least hourly); note that not all services run as far as Cromarty, so check before boarding.

Dolphin Trips Avoch On the northern side of the firth in Avoch (☎01381 622383, ⓦdolphintripsavoch.co.uk).

Hourly sailings from Avoch's harbour, at the eastern end of the village, with trips lasting an hour (£20).

Ecoventures Victoria Place, Cromarty (☎01381 600323, ⓦecoventures.co.uk). Based on the Black Isle, on the northern side of the firth, Ecoventures runs 2hr wildlife cruises (£31) with the chance to spot dolphins, harbour porpoises and grey seals.

Phoenix Sea Adventures Nairn Marina (☎01667 457175, ⓦphoenix-nairn.co.uk). Runs a range of trips from Nairn Marina (from £30).

The windswept moorland of **CULLODEN** witnessed the last-ever battle on British soil when, on April 16, 1746, the Jacobite cause was finally subdued – a turning point in the history of the Scottish nation. Today, this historic site attracts more than 200,000 visitors annually. Your first stop should be the superb **visitor centre**, which hosts costumed actors and state-of-the-art audiovisual and interactive technology, all employed to tell the tragedy of Culloden through the words, songs and poetic verse of locals and soldiers who experienced it. The *pièce de résistance* is the powerful "battle immersion theatre" where visitors are surrounded by lifelike cinematography and the sounds of the raging, bloody fight.

Every April, on the Saturday closest to the date of the battle, there's a small commemorative service at Culloden. The visitor centre has a reference library and will check for you if you think you have an ancestor who died here.

Brief history

The second Jacobite rebellion began on August 19, 1745, with the raising of the Stuarts' standard at **Glenfinnan** on the west coast. Shortly after, Edinburgh fell into Jacobite hands, and Bonnie Prince Charlie began his march on London. The ruling Hanoverians had appointed the ambitious young Duke of Cumberland to command their forces, which included troops from the Lowlands and Highlands. The duke's pursuit, together with bad weather and lack of funds, eventually forced the Jacobite forces – mostly comprised of Highlanders – to retreat north. They ended up at **Culloden**, where, ill fed and exhausted after a pointless night march, they were hopelessly outnumbered by the government forces. The open, flat ground of Culloden Moor was totally unsuitable for the Highlanders' style of courageous but undisciplined fighting, which needed steep hills and lots of cover to provide the element of surprise, and they were routed.

The end of the clan system
After the battle, in which 1500 Highlanders were slaughtered (many of them as they lay wounded on the battlefield), **Bonnie Prince Charlie** fled west to the hills and islands, where fiercely loyal Highlanders sheltered and protected him. He eventually escaped to France, leaving his supporters to their fate – and, in effect, ushering in the end of the **clan system**. The clans were disarmed, the wearing of tartan and playing of bagpipes forbidden, and the chiefs became landlords greedy for higher and higher rents. The battle also unleashed an orgy of violent reprisals on Scotland, as unruly government troops raped and pillaged their way across the region; within a century, the Highland way of life had changed out of all recognition.

The battlefield
Flags mark out the positions of the two armies while simple headstones mark the **clan graves**. The **Field of the English**, for many years unmarked, is a mass grave for the fifty or so government soldiers who died (though as this government force also included Scottish infantry regiments, the term "English" is a pseudo patriotic misnomer).

Half a mile east of the battlefield, just beyond the crossroads on the main road, is the **Cumberland Stone**, thought for many years to have been the point from where the duke watched the battle. It is more likely, however, that he was much further forward and simply used the stone for shelter. Elsewhere, the restored **Leanach cottage** marks the spot where thirty injured Jacobites were burnt alive.

Cawdor Castle
14 miles northeast of Inverness off the A96 • May–Oct daily 10am–5.30pm • £12.50; £7.50 for gardens & nature trails only • ☎ 01667 404401, ⊕ cawdorcastle.com • To get here, take a train or bus from Inverness to Nairn (several per hour; 20–45min), then pick up a taxi for the final 6 miles (around £15) – book ahead with Taxi 24/7 Nairn (☎ 01667 459595) and a driver will meet you at the bus station; a cheaper but less reliable option is Nairn's Dial-a-Bus service (☎ 01667 456066), which must be booked by 6pm the day before you wish to travel

The pretty village of **CAWDOR**, eight miles east of Culloden, is the site of **Cawdor Castle**, a setting intimately linked to Shakespeare's *Macbeth*: the fulfilment of the witches' prediction that Macbeth was to become thane of Cawdor sets off his tragic desire to be king. Though visitors arrive here in their droves each summer because of the site's dramatic associations, the castle, which dates from the early fourteenth century, could not possibly have witnessed the grisly eleventh-century events on which the Bard's drama was based. However, the immaculately restored monument – a fairy-tale affair of towers, turrets, hidden passageways, dungeons, gargoyles and crenellations whimsically shooting off from the original keep – is still well worth a visit. Outside is a 1620 walled kitchen garden, a formal flower garden and a rambling 1960s wild garden.

Fort George
13 miles northeast of Inverness, near Ardersier • Daily: April–Sept 9.30am–5.30pm; Oct–March 10am–4.30pm • £9; HES • ☎ 01667 460232, ⊕ historicenvironment.scot • There are no scheduled bus services to Fort George – as with Cawdor Castle (see above), the best bet is to take a bus or train from Inverness to Nairn, where you can pick up a taxi or local Dial-a-Bus service for the final stretch

Eight miles of undulating coastal farmland separate Cawdor Castle from **Fort George**, an old Hanoverian bastion with walls a mile long, considered by military architectural historians to be one of the finest fortifications in Europe. Crowning a sandy spit that juts into the middle of the Moray Firth, it was built between 1747 and 1769 as a base for George II's army, in case the Highlanders should attempt to rekindle the Jacobite flame. By the time of its completion, however, the uprising had been firmly quashed and the fort has been used ever since as barracks; note the armed sentries at the main entrance and the periodic crack of live gunfire from the nearby firing ranges. The dog cemetery commemorates regimental hounds, and there's a small café.

Walking on the northern, grass-covered casemates, which look out into the estuary, you may be lucky enough to see a school of bottlenose **dolphins** (see page 206) swimming in with the tide. This is also a good spot for birdwatching: a colony of kittiwakes occupies the fort's slate rooftops.

3

Nairn

One of the driest and sunniest places in the whole of Scotland, **NAIRN**, sixteen miles east of Inverness, began its days as a peaceful community of fishermen and farmers. The former spoke Gaelic, the latter English, allowing James VI to boast that a town in his kingdom was so large that people at one end of the main street could not understand those at the other end. Nairn became popular in Victorian times, when the train line offered a convenient link to its revitalizing sea air and mild climate, and today the 11,000-strong population still relies on tourism, with all the ingredients for a traditional seaside holiday – sandy beach, ice-cream shops and fish-and-chip stalls. The town has two championship golf courses, and Thomas Telford's **harbour** is filled with leisure craft rather than fishing boats.

Nairn Museum

Viewfield House, King St • May–Oct Mon–Fri 10am–4.30pm, Sat 10am–1pm (last admission 30min before closing) • £4 • ☎ 01667 456791, ⓦ nairnmuseum.co.uk

The **Nairn Museum** provides a general insight into the history and prehistory of the area: the **Fishertown Room** illustrates the parsimonious and puritanical life of the fishing families, while the weapon-filled **Military Room** includes information on the battles of Culloden and Auldearn.

ARRIVAL AND DEPARTURE   NAIRN

By train Nairn's railway station is just south of the centre, where Chattan Drive meets Cawdor St. Services run every 1–2hr from/to Aberdeen (2hr), Elgin (25min), Forres (10min) and Inverness (20min).

By bus Buses arrive at and depart from a car park on King St, just south of the police station.

Destinations Aberdeen (hourly; 3hr 15min); Elgin (every 30min; 45min); Forres (every 30min; 25min); Inverness (every 20min; 45min).

GETTING AROUND AND INFORMATION

Tourist information There's a tourist information point within the Nairn Community & Arts Centre on King St (Mon–Thurs 8.30am–10pm, Fri 8.30am–late, Sat 8.30am–5pm, Sun 9am–1pm & 5–9pm; ☎ 01667 453476, ⓦ nairncc. co.uk). Their handy "Welcome to Nairn" map is worth picking up.

ACCOMMODATION AND EATING

Boath House Auldearn, 2 miles east of Nairn ☎ 01667 454896, ⓦ boath-house.com. The most luxurious place to stay in the area, this is a fine Georgian country house set in magnificent gardens, with its own Michelin-starred restaurant that draws upon organic produce and regional dairy, fish and meat suppliers. For an affordable taste of such luxury, book a lunchtime table (three courses for £30). Note that there is only one sitting for dinner. Daily 12.30–1.15pm & 7.30pm. **£295**

★ **Cawdor House** 7 Cawdor St ☎ 01667 455855,

ⓦcawdorhousenairn.co.uk. A bright and attractive B&B set in a fine 1850s villa, conveniently located between the train station and the main shopping street. Good choice of breakfasts, with vegetarians well catered for. **£105**

The Classroom 1 Cawdor St ⓣ01667 455999, ⓦthe classroombistro.com. Nairn's most popular bar/restaurant, serving tasty light bites, lunches and dinners. Try the house salad with sun-blushed tomatoes and chargrilled chicken (£6.50); mains start at £16.50. Mon–Sat 10am–late, Sun 11am–late.

The north and northwest Highlands

EILEAN DONAN CASTLE

The north and northwest Highlands

As you drive along a single-track road, with bagpipes blaring on Gaelic radio and only sheep and stags for company, the bleak yet beautiful north and northwest Highlands feels like nowhere else in Britain. Here the weather is as changing as the scenery: a combination of bare mountains, remote glens, dark lochs and tumbling rivers surrounded on three sides by a magnificent coastline. Although the landscape, along with its tranquillity and space, is the main attraction, so too is the enduring sense of remoteness; the vast peat bogs in the north are among the most extensive and unspoilt wilderness areas in Europe, and some of the west-coast crofting villages can still only be reached by boat.

Different weather conditions and cultural histories give each of the three coastlines a distinct character. For many visitors, the Highlands' **west coast** is the reason to visit Scotland. The Vikings, who ruled the region in the ninth century, called it the "South Land", from which the modern district of Sutherland takes its name. After Culloden, the Clearances emptied most of the inland glens of the far north, and left the population clinging to the coastline, which is the main reason to come. Cut by fjord-like **sea lochs**, it is scalloped by white-sand **beaches** or **waterfalls** in high, shattered cliffs, with **mountains** sweeping up from the shoreline. Weather fronts roll over rapidly, but when the sun shines, the sparkle of the sea, the rich colours in the clear light and the clarity of the views to the Hebrides are pure magic. With exhilarating scenery everywhere you look, this isolated region has historically seen far fewer visitors than the rest of Scotland, but the wiggling single-track roads are slowly getting busier as touring visitors from around the world flock to complete the new **North Coast 500** road trip. The north and northwest Highlands also provide some of the best **cycling**, **walking** and **sea-kayaking** in Britain, superlative trout and salmon **fishing**, and wildlife by the ton. In fact the only issues are the west coast's predictably unpredictable **weather**, and **midges** that drive even the locals to distraction from June to August.

The most visited part of the west coast is the stretch between Kyle of Lochalsh and Ullapool. This is **Wester Ross**, with quintessentially west-coast scenes of beautiful coast set against some of Scotland's most impressive mountains and Skye and the Western Isles on the horizon. The obvious highlights are the mountainscape of **Torridon**, **Gairloch**'s sandy beaches, the botanic gardens at **Inverewe**, and **Ullapool** itself, a bustling fishing town and launchpad for the Outer Hebrides. However, press on north or south and you get a truer sense of the isolation that makes this coast so special. Traversed by few roads, the remote northwest is wild and bleak. Villages in the southwest tend to be more sheltered, but they are separated by some of the most extensive wilderness areas in Britain – lonely peninsulas like **Ardnamurchan**, **Glenelg** or **Knoydart**, a magnificently untamed expanse with no road access and the remotest pub in mainland Britain.

The other coasts receive fewer visitors, and of the two the **north coast** is more popular. Stretching from **Cape Wrath** at the very northwest tip of the mainland to **John O'Groats**, it is even more rugged than the west, its sheer cliffs and white-sand bays bearing the brunt of frequently fierce Atlantic storms. The only town here is the surfing hub **Thurso**, jumping-off point for the main ferry service to Orkney.

All of this makes the fertile **east coast** of the Highlands such a surprise. Stretching north from Inverness to the old herring port of **Wick**, it is a place of rolling moors, green fields and woodlands which run down to the sandy beaches of the **Black Isle** and **Cromarty** and **Dornoch firths**. If the west coast is about raw nature, the east is one of

DUNNET HEAD LIGHTHOUSE

Highlights

❶ **North Coast 500** This circular route loops around the entire north and northwest Highlands; an unforgettable ride. See page 216

❷ **West Highland Railway** Ride the rails of Britain's most scenic train journey from Glasgow to Mallaig via Fort William for scenery that's more spectacular by the mile. See page 220

❸ **Knoydart** Thrilling remoteness is not the only reason to visit Britain's last wilderness – there's also its most isolated pub. See page 223

❹ **Ceilidhs** An impromptu night of music and song in the pub best expresses the vitality of modern Highland culture – try *Ceilidh Place* in Ullapool or Knoydart's *Old Forge*. See page 240

❺ **Suilven** A glimpse of the fantastical sugarloaf outline of this iconic mountain is reason enough to travel to Assynt. See page 242

❻ **Foodie Lochinver** The Highlands' foodie capital offers everything from slap-up pies to Scottish tapas. See page 242

❼ **Dunnet Head** Come to the true tip of mainland Britain, all remote red cliffs and empty seascapes to Orkney. See page 253

❽ **Cromarty** A mix-and-match of handsome Georgian townhouses and cute cottages all packaged up in a friendly coastal town. See page 256

HIGHLIGHTS ARE MARKED ON THE MAP ON PAGE 214

THE NORTH & NORTHWEST HIGHLANDS

HIGHLIGHTS

1. North Coast 500
2. West Highland Railway
3. Knoydart
4. Ceilidhs
5. Suilven
6. Foodie Lochinver
7. Dunnet Head
8. Cromarty

"SCOTLAND'S ANSWER TO ROUTE 66": THE NORTH COAST 500

Unveiled in 2014 as "Scotland's answer to Route 66", the **North Coast 500** touring route was created to tempt visitors up to this most remote corner of mainland Scotland, and it seems to be working. While driving or cycling in the north Highlands, you'll be asked "are you doing the North Coast 500?" on a daily basis, and you probably are doing at least a stretch of it, even if you didn't know it. There are few alternative ways of getting around this part of Scotland, and certainly none more impressive than this mainly single-track route hugging the coastal edges of the north Highlands.

With Inverness, Applecross, Durness and John O'Groats forming the four cardinal points of the route, pretty much everything in this chapter is covered by the North Coast 500. If you are on a mission to tour the full five hundred miles, try to incorporate **Plockton**, **Achiltibuie** and **Cromarty** – and if time permits, **Skye** – into your itinerary; all short detours from the designated route but highlights of the region. See ⓦnorthcoast500.com for more information on the official route.

---

human history: **Golspie**'s Sutherland Monument and castle, **Dornoch**'s fourteenth-century sandstone cathedral, relics of the **Picts** and several sites linked to the **Clearances**.

GETTING AROUND
THE HIGHLANDS

Getting around the **Highlands**, particularly the remoter parts, can be tricky without your own transport. **Bus services** are sporadic and often cease entirely on Sunday. Most sizeable villages have a petrol station or 24-hour fuel supply (typically card payment only), although these are few and far between in the west and north, so fill up early and be prepared for higher prices. Bear in mind, too, that the Highlands' single-track roads are far from fast; remember to pull in to let faster drivers behind overtake.

Morvern to Knoydart: the "Rough Bounds"

Its Gaelic name *Garbh-chiochan* translates as the "**Rough Bounds**", implying a region geographically and spiritually apart, and the southwest corner of the Highlands is indeed remote and sparsely populated. From the empty district of **Morvern** to the isolated **Knoydart** peninsula are lonely mountains and moors, a rocky, indented coast studded with white beaches, and wonderful views to Mull, Skye and other islands. It's scenery that begs you to spend time exploring on foot.

Morvern

Bounded on three sides by sea lochs and in the north by desolate Glen Tarbet, the mountainous **Morvern peninsula** lies at the southwest corner of the Rough Bounds. Many inhabitants of St Kilda were settled here when the island was abandoned, and the landscape can seem bleak until the coast reveals views to Mull.

Lochaline

Most visitors only travel through the Morvern peninsula to get to **LOCHALINE** (pronounced "loch-*aa*lin") on the **Sound of Mull**, little more than a scattering of houses around a small pier built as a work-for-food scheme during famine in 1846. From here, a small ferry chugs to **Fishnish** – the shortest crossing to Mull from the mainland and cheaper than the Oban–Craignure crossing with a car. The town is also the departure point for excellent wreck-diving and snorkelling excursions in the Sound of Mull.

ARRIVAL AND DEPARTURE
MORVERN

By bus Shiel Buses (☎01967 431272, ⓦshielbuses.co.uk) runs a service (#506) between Kilchoan and Fort William Mon–Sat (2hr 30min), plus another service (#507) Fort William and Drimnin via Lochaline (Mon–Fri school term time, Tue & Thurs school holidays).

By ferry To save the long journey around Loch Eil into the peninsula, a ferry nips across to Ardgour from Corran Ferry, 9 miles south of Fort William, every 20–30min (Mon–Sat 6.30am–9.30pm, Sun 8.45am–9.30pm; 10min; £8.50 car,

bikes and passengers free; ☎ 01855 841243, ⓦ highland. gov.uk/homepage/62/corran_ferry). In addition, Calmac operate a car ferry between Lochaline and Fishnish on Mull (☎ 01854 612358, ⓦ calmac.co.uk; Mon–Sat 7am–6.35pm, Sun 8.45am–5.45pm; 15min).

ACTIVITIES

Lochaline Dive Centre Lochaline ☎ 01967 421627, ⓦ lochalinedivecentre.co.uk. Based in the village centre, this outfit specializes in underwater archeology on local wrecks, and provides drift, shallow, scenic and shore dives, and snorkelling excursions. Also offers air filling and cylinder rental, plus a four-star lodge and the *O2 Café*.

EATING

★ **Whitehouse Restaurant** Lochaline ☎ 01967 421777, ⓦ thewhitehouserestaurant.co.uk. Morvern's (and one of the Highlands') finest restaurants, the simple style here belies outstanding modern European cooking that showcases local meat and seafood like smoked mussels and hand-dived scallops. A range of two-to- six course taster menus, starting at a two-course lunch menu for £32, with dinner menus starting from £56 for four courses. Booking essential. Easter–Oct Tues–Sat noon–2pm & 6–9pm.

The Ardnamurchan peninsula

The **Ardnamurchan peninsula** is the most westerly point on the British mainland. Once ruled by Norse invaders, the peninsula lost most inhabitants during the Clearances and only a handful of crofting settlements cling to the coastline. Yet with its empty beaches and sea vistas, Ardnamurchan is an inspiring place. A single-track road threads down its length, a superb route with a real sense of transition from ancient mossy oak forest to salt-sprayed moorland as you approach the sea. It's not fast, but this is slow travel at its best, with a huge variety of wildlife and scenery to make **walking** a pleasure.

4

Strontian and Salen

Actually part of the near-roadless regions of **Sunart** and **Ardgour**, **STRONTIAN** serves as a gateway base for the peninsula. The village's moment of fame came in 1722, when local lead mines yielded the first-ever traces of **strontium**, which was named after the village; indeed it's claimed that this is the only village named after an element in the periodic table.

The hamlet of **SALEN**, spread around another sheltered notch on the loch's shore, marks the turn-off for Ardnamurchan Point: from here it's 25 miles of scenic driving beside Loch Sunart. The turf-roofed **Garbh Eilean Wildlife Hide** (free access) five miles west of Strontian is an opportunity to peer for seals, seabirds and the occasional eagle; on Mondays between Easter and October you'll find a knowledgeable ranger on-hand to help spot wildlife.

Ardnamurchan Natural History Visitor Centre

2 miles west of Glenborrodale • Easter–Oct Mon–Sat 8.30am–5pm, Sun 9am–5pm • £2 • ☎ 01972 500209, ⓦ ardnamurchannaturalhistorycentre.com

The **Ardnamurchan Natural History Visitor Centre**, a small, child-friendly natural history centre, introduces the flora, fauna and geology of Ardnamurchan. The centre is in a timber "Living Building" designed to allow in wildlife – pine martens nest within the walls, long-eared bats occasionally hang from the rafters and a glass wall descends into a wildlife pond. Otherwise there are the usual wildlife displays, a beautifully shot film, plus cameras trained on whatever's most interesting – the pine martens, perhaps, or a heronry opposite.

Kilchoan and Ardnamurchan Lighthouse

Lighthouse exhibition April–Oct daily 10am–5pm • £5 • **Lighthouse tour** April–Oct daily 11am–4pm • £6 • ☎ 01972 510210, ⓦ ardnamurchanlighthouse.com

KILCHOAN is Ardnamurchan's main village – a modest crofting settlement which straggles along the Sound of Mull. From here, the road continues to **Ardnamurchan Point**, the most westerly point in mainland Britain, marked by a 118ft-high **lighthouse**. The lighthouse buildings house a small café and an **exhibition** on local history, while tours – which are very worthwhile though do book ahead – go up the tower to see the lighting mechanism.

Sanna Bay

Explore the area around Kilchoan to find myriad coves, beaches and headlands. The finest beach is **Sanna Bay**, about three miles northeast of the lighthouse, a white strand with unforgettable views of the Small Isles. Incidentally, the road there crosses the crater of what was the largest volcano in prehistoric Britain, still visible on a map in the northwest peninsula.

ARRIVAL AND DEPARTURE THE ARDNAMURCHAN PENINSULA

By bus A single service (Mon–Sat; ☎01967 431272) that begins at Fort William (currently 1.50pm) and goes via Corran Ferry to reach Strontian (50min), before continuing to Kilchoan (2hr 40min); the bus from Kilchoan to Fort William currently departs at 7.50am.

By ferry A CalMac (⊚calmac.co.uk) car ferry operates between Tobermory (Mull) and Kilchoan (Mon–Sat 7 daily, plus Sun May–Aug 5 daily; 35min).

By car The single-track road from Salen to Ardnamurchan Point is 25 miles long; allow just over an hour in each direction.

INFORMATION AND ACTIVITIES

Strontian tourist office The Oakwood Tourism and Crafts Centre on the village green (Easter–Oct Mon–Fri 10am–4pm, Sat 10am–1pm; ☎01967 402443, , ⊚moidart.com) has some good local information.

Kilchoan tourist office In the community centre on Pier Road down towards the ferry slip (Easter–Oct Mon–Fri 9am–5pm, Sat 9.30am–5pm; Nov–March 10am–4pm; ☎01972 510711, ⊚ardnamurchan.com); there's a tea

room here too, and it also hosts a crafts and produce market a couple of times a month between April and October.

Ardnamurchan Charters ☎01972 500208, ⊚www. west-scotland-marine.com. Operates wildlife-watching trips from Laga Bay, near Acharacle, to observe dolphins, seals, basking sharks, whales and possibly sea eagles. Also runs trips around the Isle of Carna (⊚isleofcarna.co.uk) and has self drive motor boats for hire.

ACCOMMODATION AND EATING

Accommodation isn't plentiful and in summer you're advised to **book** through local tourist offices for **B&Bs** (see above). **Food** options are also limited; Strontian has a couple of modest cafés. The useful *Ferry Stores* in Kilchoan (Mon–Sat 9am–1pm & 2–5.30pm) carries fresh local produce when available – ideal for the most westerly picnic tables on mainland Britain at Ardnamurchan Point. Note that fuel is available from pumps opposite the *Ferry Stores*.

STRONTIAN

Ariundle Centre 1 mile north of Strontian ☎01967 402279, ⊚ariundlecentre.co.uk. This tearoom and bunkhouse is a godsend for walkers and cyclists. Expect inexpensive fresh lunches and dinner such as beef casserole in Glenfinnan ale, and local ales and spirits in the convivial bar. Modern bunkhouse has dorms, family rooms and twins, all en suite; it's set among woods a mile from the centre – turn right across Strontian bridge. Extra £7 for breakfast at bunkhouse. Food served 8am–10pm. Dorms £20

SALEN

Resipole Farm 2.5 miles east of Salen ☎01967 431235, ⊚resipole.co.uk. This is a well-maintained spot, with a

camping and caravan park plus two, three-person wooden pods with heating and electricity (two night min stay), and year-round self-catering accommodation in lodges (one week min). Facilities include a laundry and a basic store. April–Oct. Per pitch £20, pods £55

Salen Hotel Salen ☎01967 431661, ⊚salenhotel. co.uk. Less a small hotel than a restaurant with three smart rooms above – tastefully furnished where modern flair meets antiques – and simpler comfy rooms in the cheaper chalet. The restaurant offers a Scottish gastropub menu, for example haggis and whisky cream pot with salad and oatcakes, and a Scottish fish platter with hot and cold salmon and herring (mains £11–14). Breakfast by prior arrangement. Easter–Oct daily 8–9am, 12.30–2.30pm & 5.30–11pm; Nov–Easter Thurs–Sun 8–9am, 12.30–2.30pm & 5.30–8pm. £100

KILCHOAN

★ **Ardnamurchan Campsite** Ormsaigbeg ☎01972 510766, ⊚ardnamurchancampsite.com. Cracking views, plus campfires on the beach of a laudably back-to-basics, kid-friendly campsite behind the loch – pure magic at sunset and usually spared summer midges by a breeze;

freshly baked goodies delivered each morning too. Find it past the *Ferry Stores*. Easter–Sept. Per person **£10** **Puffin Café** 500m from the Ferry Stores ☏ 07379 352067, ⓦ puffincoffee.co.uk. Colourful, artfully-decorated café (the owner is a sliversmith) just off the main road which takes its coffee pretty seriously and so should you – it's delicious, as are the homebaked cakes and scones; toasties and pizza too. Mon–Fri 10am–4pm, Sat & Sun 10am–5pm.

Acharacle and Glenuig

At the eastern end of Ardnamurchan, just northwest of Salen where the A861 heads north towards the district of Moidart, the main settlement is **ACHARACLE**, a nondescript crofting village set back from **Loch Shiel**. The reason to swing through is **Castle Tioram** (pronounced "cheerum"), one of Scotland's most atmospheric monuments. Perched on a promontory above **Loch Moidart** and accessed via a sandy causeway (its Gaelic name means "dry land"), the thirteenth-century fortress was the seat of the MacDonalds of Clanranald until it was destroyed by their chief in 1715 to prevent it falling into Hanoverian hands. There's no entry into the castle (three miles north of Acharacle), but for a slice of picture-postcard romantic Scotland, it's hard to beat.

Keep going north on the A861 and you'll roll through woods to arrive at **GLENUIG**, gathered on a picturesque inlet on the Sound of Arisaig. Barely a hamlet, it makes a fine base for walking, sea-kayaking (see below) – or partying, when the community centre hosts gigs every other Saturday (listings on ⓦ glenuig.org.uk).

ARRIVAL AND DEPARTURE   ACHARACLE AND GLENUIG

By bus Buses go from Fort William (Mon–Sat 1 daily) to Acharacle (1hr 30min) and Glenuig (1hr 10min).
By boat Loch Shiel Cruises runs trips to Acharacle from Glenfinnan at the head of Loch Shiel (April–Oct Wed & Sat; £23 single; ☏ 07946 842732, ⓦ highlandcruises.co.uk).
Sea-kayaking The owner of the *Glenuig Inn* (see below) runs full-day trips in the Sound of Arisaig costing £95.

ACCOMMODATION AND EATING

Glenuig Inn Glenuig ☏ 01687 470219, ⓦ glenuig.com. A refurbished inn that ticks all boxes: an excellent hostel with single beds, not bunks; smarter ensuite rooms in an annexe; and local beers plus well-priced bar food – lamb kofta kebabs, root vegetable curries and home-made burgers, all around £12. Daily noon–9pm; food served 6–8.30pm. Dorms **£45**, doubles **£125**

The Road to the Isles

The "**Road to the Isles**" from Fort William to Mallaig, followed by the West Highland Railway and the winding A830, traverses the mountains and glens of the Rough Bounds before breaking out near **Arisaig** onto a coast of sheltered inlets, white-sand beaches and wonderful views to the islands of Rùm, Eigg, Muck and Skye. This is a country commonly associated with **Bonnie Prince Charlie**, whose adventures of 1745–46 began on this stretch of coast with his gathering of the clans at **Glenfinnan** and ended here too, when he embarked near Arisdale and fled into French exile.

Glenfinnan

This sleepy village may be spectacularly sited at the head of Loch Shiel, but it's the local history that draws most visitors to **GLENFINNAN**, since it was here that Bonnie Prince Charlie raised his standard and rallied forces before the ill-fated march on London. That said, nowadays just as many visitors come to see the imposing arched viaduct, as crossed by the *Hogwarts Express* in the *Harry Potter* films.

Glenfinnan Monument and Visitor Centre

Centre of the village • Daily: March & Oct 9.30am–5pm; April–Sept 9am–7pm; Nov–Feb 10am–4pm • £4; NTS • ☏ 01397 722250 • ⓦ nts.org.uk

THE WEST HIGHLAND RAILWAY

A fixture in lists of the world's most scenic train journeys, the brilliantly engineered **West Highland Railway** runs from Glasgow to Mallaig via Fort William. The line is in two sections: the southern part travels from **Glasgow** Queen Street station, up the banks of Loch Lomond to **Crianlarich**, then around Beinn Odhar on a horseshoe of viaducts to cross **Rannoch Moor**, where the track had to be laid on a mattress of tree roots, brushwood and thousands of tons of earth and ashes. You're out in the wilds here, the line long having diverged from the road. The route then swings into Glen Roy, passing through the **Monessie Gorge** to enter **Fort William**.

Leg two, from Fort William to Mallaig, is even more spectacular. Shortly after leaving Fort William the railway crosses the Caledonian Canal beside Neptune's Staircase at **Benavie**, before travelling along Locheil and crossing the 21-arch viaduct at **Glenfinnan**, where passengers get to live out *Harry Potter* fantasies. Then it's on to the coast, with views of the Small Isles and Skye before journeys end at **Mallaig**. You can book tickets through Ⓦ scotrail. co.uk. Between May and October, this leg of the route is also served by the **Jacobite Steam Train** (Ⓦ westcoastrailways.co.uk).

The spot where the Young Pretender raised his battle standard on August 19, 1745, is marked by one of Scotland's most iconic structures, **Glenfinnan Monument**, a 60ft column crowned with a Highland clansman in full battle dress, erected as a tribute by Alexander Macdonald of Glenaladale in 1815. It's a beautiful, brooding spot at the head of the loch that's best appreciated from a viewpoint behind the **Visitor Centre**. After admiring the view, pop inside for an account of the '45 uprising through to the rout at Culloden.

Glenfinnan Station Museum

Centre of the village • Daily April–mid-Oct 9am–5pm & by appointment • £1 • ☎ 01397 722295, Ⓦ glenfinnanstationmuseum.co.uk

Glenfinnan proudly hosts one of the most spectacular parts of the **West Highland Railway** line (see above), which chuffs over the 21-arched Loch nan Uamh **viaduct** built in 1901. You might recognize it from *Harry Potter* films, in which it is crossed by the *Hogwarts Express* – Loch Shiel itself serves as the "Dark Lake" seen from the ramparts of Hogwarts.

Head to the **Glenfinnan Station Museum** to learn more about the history of this section of the railway – no surprise that the gift shop is stuffed with *Harry Potter* merchandise. Enthusiastic rail buffs can also stay the night or dine here (see page 221).

The museum also marks the start of a pleasant 30-minute circular walk, which leads right up to the viaduct before curling back into the village centre. Time your ramble well and it might coincide with the Jacobite Steam Train chugging by (around 10.45am and 3pm during the summer months).

ARRIVAL AND DEPARTURE
GLENFINNAN

By train A direct service links Fort William to Glenfinnan (Mon–Sat 4 daily, Sun 3 daily; 35min).

INFORMATION AND TOURS

Tourist information The Visitor Centre (see above) is a good source of local information, as is the website Ⓦ road-to-the-isles.org.uk.

Loch Shiel Cruises ☎ 07946 842732, Ⓦ highlandcruises. co.uk. Runs boat trips to view the superb scenery between April and October. Cruises embark from a jetty near *Glenfinnan House Hotel*, signposted off the main road half a mile west of the monument.

ACCOMMODATION AND EATING

Glenfinnan House Hotel Centre of the village, signposted off A830 ☎ 01397 722235, Ⓦ glenfinnanhouse.com. Traditional furnishings, smoky open fires and stunning views – including the Glenfinnan Monument and, on a clear day, Ben Nevis – at this upscale lochside hotel. The menu includes pan-fried fillet of trout and a "hot pot" of haggis (mains £13–18), while the lively bar is the best option for a drink in the village, serving real ales from Glenfinnan Brewery. **£155**

Prince's House Centre of the village, on the A830 ☎ 01397 722246, ⓦ glenfinnan.co.uk. This seventeenth-century former coaching inn offers homely rooms – the best at the front nod to Highlands tradition – and a warm welcome to match. The fine restaurant offers a seasonal, fresh menu, or there's gastropub grub in the Stage House bar; expect West Coast hot smoked salmon, lamb and venison (mains £12–16). March–Dec; food served Easter–Sept daily 11am–3pm & 7–10pm. **£145**

Sleeping Car Glenfinnan station ☎ 01397 722295, ⓦ glenfinnanstationmuseum.co.uk. A 1958 camping coach is now a (very) mini-bunkhouse with two twin compartments (bunk beds), a family compartment for four, plus a kitchen, lounge and bathroom – a memorable if rather cosy place to stay. Linen costs extra. The adjacent *Dining Car* is open for light lunches from April to Sept (Mon–Sat 9am–5pm, Sun from 10am; phone ahead for evening meals). Compartment **£35**, single **£20**

Arisaig

The little coastal village of **ARISAIG** (meaning "the Safe Place" in Gaelic) is an appealingly drowsy place scattered around a sandy bay. The only specific attraction in the village is the sweet little **Land, Sea and Islands Visitor Centre**, which doubles up as the village's tourist information centre.

Stretching for eight miles or so north of Arisaig along the road signposted "Alternative Coastal Route" is a string of stunning white-sand, azure-water **beaches**: summer holiday favourites backed by flowery machair and with views out to Eigg and Rùm. Pretty **Traigh** beach is your spot to collect cowrie shells, but larger and more celebrated is **Camusdarach Beach** a mile or so north, where the beach scenes of the films *Local Hero* and *Highlander* were shot. If it's busy, head for two intimate beaches that lie over the headlands on either side.

4

Land, Sea and Islands Visitor Centre

April–Oct Mon–Sat 10am–6pm, Sun 11–5pm; Nov–March Sat 10am–4pm, Sun 11am–4pm, Mon 10am–1pm • Free • ☎ 01687 450771, ⓦ arisaiginfo.org.uk

This small, volunteer-run community project, occupying the site of the old village smiddy, has some wonderful displays pertaining to crofting life, local characters and the area's role as a base for Special Operations during World War II; some 3000 agents were secretly trained here during World War II. Among the more curious items is part of a sperm whale's vertebrae washed ashore in 2013, and a coconut also discovered on the shoreline two years later. There's also a small research library of wildlife and walks – swot up before walking to a seal colony at nearby **Rhumach**, reached via a single-track lane heading west out of Arisaig.

ARRIVAL AND DEPARTURE
ARISAIG

By train Direct services run from Fort William to Arisaig (Mon–Sat 4 daily, Sun 3 daily; 1hr 5min).
By boat Arisaig Marine (☎ 01687 450224, ⓦ arisaig.co.uk)

sails from Arisaig marina to Eigg (£18), Rùm (£20) and Muck (£25) at 11am daily, from late April to late Sept.

ACTIVITIES

Arisaig Sea Kayak Centre ☎ 07858 214985, ⓦ arisaig seakayakcentre.co.uk. Based at the *Arisaig Hotel*, this operator offers trips every day in season for all levels starting at £50 for a 3-hour guided trip.

ACCOMMODATION AND EATING

Arisaig Hotel Arisaig ☎ 01687 450210, ⓦ arisaighotel. co.uk. Comfortable enough old coaching inn on the waterfront harbouring reasonably modern rooms, most with sea views. The jolly Crofter's Bar repares a solid pub menu at good prices plus Highland real ales on draught, and there are live music sessions on Friday nights and Sunday afternoons. Daily 12.30–2.30pm & 6–9pm. **£110**

★ **Camusdarach Campsite** Camusdarach ☎ 01687 450221, ⓦ camusdarach.co.uk. By far the loveliest

campsite in the area, its neat fields a pleasing balance of eco-emptiness and modern facilities, all spread behind sands so white they've featured in films. Glamping pods (sleeping up to five) available for those who would rather not brave the elements. Decent takeaway pizzas and proper coffees available. April–Sept. Per person **£15**, per pod **£50**

Old Library Lodge and Restaurant Arisaig ☎ 01687 450651, ⓦ oldlibrary.co.uk. This old stone building,

4

IN THE FOOTSTEPS OF BONNIE PRINCE CHARLIE

The Road to the Isles is steeped in the tragic tale of **Bonnie Prince Charlie**'s failed rebellion. Having landed on the Western Isles, he set foot on the Scottish mainland on the sands of **Borrodale** at Loch nan Uamh (Loch of Caves) near Arisaig on July 25, 1745. He had been promised ten thousand French troops to back a claim to the British throne on behalf of his father, the Old Pretender. Instead he arrived with only seven companions – the "Seven Men of Moidart", commemorated at Kinlochmoidart by a line of beech trees (now reduced in number). For a week he gauged support, then took an old hill route to **Dalilea**, on the north shore of Loch Shiel, and on August 19 rowed to the head of the loch at **Glenfinnan**. At a position marked by the Glenfinnan monument, the young rebel prince, surrounded by two hundred loyal clansmen, waited to see if Cameron of Loch Shiel would arrive. Without the support of this powerful chief, the Stuarts' claim to the throne would have been folly. Late in the day, Cameron backed the uprising with eight hundred men. The prince raised his red-and-white silk colours, proclaimed his father as King James III of England and marched on London. Only a handful of the soldiers would return.

If Charles's original visit to Arisaig and Moidart was full of optimism, his return was desperate. By summer 1746 he was on the run, his armies routed at Culloden and a £30,000 bounty on his head. Yet none of the Highlanders the prince called on for food, favours or hiding turned him in, and his fortitude and bravery in those months earned much respect. Fleeing from Culloden down the Great Glen, he passed through Arisaig en route to the Western Isles, desperately hoping for a French ship to rescue him. On South Uist, **Flora MacDonald** extracted him from a tight squeeze, but still on the run he landed back on the mainland again at **Mallaigvaig**, near Mallaig.

It was swarming with soldiers, so he returned to **Borrodale**, this time hiding in a large cave, then fled to Lochaber, dodging patrols and hiding in caves near **Loch Arkaig** and on the slopes of Ben Alder, by **Loch Ericht**. Finally, some hope: a French frigate, *L'Heureux*, was off the west coast. Charles dashed back to Arisaig and from a promontory in **Loch nan Uamh** on September 19, 1746, half a mile east of where he'd landed fourteen months before, he clambered into the French shoreboat. It was his last footfall in Scotland and he died, an embittered alcoholic, in Rome. A cairn on the shore between Lochailort and Arisaig village (on A380) marks the spot. The best place to learn more of the prince's doomed campaign is on the site of his final defeat, **Culloden**.

formerly the stables for the Arisaig estate's horses, is not much to look at from the outside but its six rooms here are perfectly agreeable; the best ones overlook the bay. The popular dining room, meanwhile, offers upscale Scottish dishes: cullen skink or delicious crab sandwiches for lunch (around £8), and Atlantic halibut steak with white wine and crab for supper (£15.95). Mid-Feb to Oct noon–2.30pm & 6–9pm. £120

The Tea Room Arisaig marina ☎ 01687 450224. Although more of a gift shop/chandlery than a café, this is a splendid spot – with floor-to-ceiling windows offering views down the loch – for coffees, simple toasties and baked potatoes priced around a fiver. May–Sept Mon–Sat 9am–4pm, July & Aug till 5pm.

Mallaig

The fate of **MALLAIG**, 47 miles west of Fort William, is to be seen as somewhere to go through, not to. Before the railway arrived in 1901 it consisted of a few cottages. Now in season it's full of visitors as the main embarkation point for ferries to Skye, the Small Isles and Knoydart. Even if not especially pretty, it is a solid town given a workaday honesty by its local **fishing** industry – it once had one of Europe's busiest herring ports and the harbour remains the source of the village's wealth.

Mallaig Heritage Centre

Beside the train station • April, May, June & Oct Mon–Sat 11am–4pm; July & Aug daily 11am–6pm, Sept Mon–Fri 10am–4pm, Sat & Sun noon–4pm, Nov–March Mon–Thurs noon–4pm • £2.50 • ☎ 01687 462085, ⊕ mallaigheritage.org.uk

Apart from the hubbub of the harbour, the town's only sight is **Mallaig Heritage Centre** – nothing to quicken the pulse but worth a browse for displays on the area's past and information about lifeboats, fishing and the highland galleys that once plied the waters of the Inner Hebrides and descend directly from Viking longships.

ARRIVAL AND DEPARTURE | MALLAIG

BY TRAIN
A direct service arrives from Fort William (4 daily; 1hr 25min) and Glasgow (Mon–Sat 3 daily; 5hr 30min), via Glenfinnan and Arisaig.

BY BUS
There are regular buses from Fort William to Mallaig via Glenfinnan and Arisaig (Mon–Fri 4 daily, Sat & Sun 1 daily; 1hr 10min).

BY FERRY
The CalMac ticket office (☎01687 462403, ⓦcalmac.co.uk) is at the main ferry terminal.

To/from Skye Regular services shuttle between Mallaig and Armadale (Mon–Sat 9 daily, Sun 6 daily; 30min). Car reservations are essential in peak season.

To/from the Small Isles There are services between Mallaig and Eigg (1 daily except Wed; 1hr 15min); Rùm (Mon, Wed, Fri, Sat & Sun 1 daily; 1hr 20min); Muck (Tues, Thurs, Fri, Sat & Sun 1 daily; 1hr 40min–2hr); and Canna (Mon, Wed, Fri, Sat & Sun; 1 daily; 2hr 30min).

To/from Knoydart Western Isles Cruises (☎01687 462233, ⓦwesternislescruises.co.uk) sails from Mallaig to Inverie (April–Oct Mon–Sat 4 daily, Sun 3 daily; Nov–March Mon–Fri 4 daily, Sat & Sun 2 daily; 25min; £20 return).

ACCOMMODATION

Mallaig Backpackers Main St ☎01687 462764, ⓦmallaigbackpackers.co.uk. 100m south of the train station, this relaxed, independent modern hostel has two mixed dorms, a small kitchen and a lounge. Reception is in the *Tea Garden* restaurant (see below). Dorms £22

Seaview Main St ☎01687 462059, ⓦseaviewguest housemallaig.com. Snug dimensions and surprisingly smart decor – tasteful shades of taupe and grey with a leaning towards modest boutique – set the tone in this central B&B with harbour views from five of the six rooms. March–Oct. £80

West Highland Hotel ☎01687 462210, ⓦwest highlandhotel.co.uk. Uphill from the harbour, this traditional pile has been thoughtfully refurbished over recent years, with spacious rooms, some with bespoke furnishings and king-size beds. The Superior rooms provide sea or harbour views. March to mid-Oct. £90

EATING AND DRINKING

★**The Old Quay Bakehouse** Old Quay ☎01687 462808. For a coffee and croissant hit before boarding the ferry, look no further than this fantastic bakery, which also doles out a variety of breads (including sourdough and foccacia) and truly scrumptious handmade pizza. Marvellous. Tues–Fri 9am–3pm, Sat 9am–4pm.

Cornerstone Main St ☎01687 462306, ⓦseafood restaurantmallaig.com. A simple first-floor restaurant that's the locals' choice for classic seafood – expect a daily soup and a menu of fresh fish (haddock and chips, Arisaig mussels), excellently prepared and fairly priced at around £10–15. March to mid-Oct Mon–Sat noon–2.30pm & 5.30–9.30pm.

Tea Garden Main St ☎01687 462764, ⓦmallaig

backpackers.co.uk. Park yourself out on the flower-filled terrace of this popular hostel and tuck into a surprisingly decent bistro menu featuring the likes of Mallaig kippers, salt and pepper squid, and pints of prawns (£12.50). Mid-March to mid-Nov daily 9am–6pm.

Terrace Restaurant ☎01687 462210, ⓦwesthighland hotel.co.uk. In the *West Highland Hotel*, this is Mallaig's fine-dining address with stunning sea views and super, modern Scottish cooking: Wester Ross smoked salmon roulade, and pave of Mallaig cod with roasted red pepper dressing feature plus locally landed fish and chips. Start (or end) with one of over a hundred whiskies in the bar. Easter–late Oct. Noon–2.30pm & 6–10pm.

The Knoydart peninsula

Touted as "Britain's last great wilderness", the very thought of the **Knoydart peninsula** stirs the imagination. The fact that it is inaccessible by car is part of the allure – to reach the heart of the peninsula, you either catch a **boat** from Mallaig or **hike** across rugged moorland, sleeping in stone bothies (marked on OS maps). The scenery is superb, flanked by **Loch Nevis** ("Loch of Heaven") and the fjord-like **Loch Hourn** ("Loch of Hell") and three Munros sweeping straight up from the sea. Unsurprisingly, the peninsula has long attracted walkers. But with increasingly comfortable

WALKING INTO KNOYDART

Ordnance Survey Explorer maps 413 and 398

There are two main **hiking routes** into Knoydart. The trailhead for the first is **Kinloch Hourn** at the far east end of Loch Hourn (turn south off the A87 six miles west of Invergarry). From Kinloch Hourn, a well-marked path winds around the coast on the south side of Loch Hourn to Barisdale, where there's a year-round bothy and wild camp (bothy (max two nights) £4 (honesty box), campsite £1), before continuing ten miles to Inverie; expect 18–20 hours' walk in total. The second path into Knoydart starts from the west end of **Loch Arkaig**, approaching the peninsula via Glen Dessary. Hardened walkers reckon on knocking off the eighteen-mile journey in one long summer's day. The rest of us should set aside two. Either way, take wet-weather gear, a good map, plenty of food, warm clothes and a good sleeping bag, and leave your name and expected time of arrival with someone when you set off.

accommodation, it is also gaining a cachet among holiday-makers in search of escapism: a place to slow down for a few days' self-imposed exile from modernity.

Brief history

At the end of the eighteenth century, around a thousand people eked out a living from this inhospitable terrain through crofting and fishing. **Evictions** in 1853 began a dramatic decrease in the population, which continued to dwindle through the twentieth century as a succession of landowners ran the estate as a hunting and shooting playground, prompting a famous land raid in 1948 by a group of crofters known as the "**Seven Men of Knoydart**", who claimed ownership of portions of the estate. Although their bid failed, their cause was invoked when the crofters of Knoydart finally achieved a **community buyout** in 1999. An offer to provide the money from theatre impresario Cameron Mackintosh was rejected because locals were wary of giving up control.

Inverie

Most of the peninsula's hundred or so occupants live in the sleepy hamlet of **INVERIE**. Spread along Loch Nevis, it has a pint-sized post office and shop (with wi-fi), a ranger post with tips on local walks and wildlife, a pleasant tearoom and mainland Britain's most remote pub, *The Old Forge*. You're here for the Tolkienesque scenery, for walks and for the thrill of dropping off the radar.

ARRIVAL AND DEPARTURE
THE KNOYDART PENINSULA

By boat Western Isles Cruises (☎ 01687 462233, ⓦ western islescruises.co.uk) sails from Mallaig to Inverie (April–Oct Mon–Sat 4 daily, Sun 3 daily; Nov–March Mon–Fri 4 daily, Sat & Sun 2 daily; 25min; £20 return).

On foot It's a two-day hike into Knoydart; our box (see above) gives details.

INFORMATION AND ACTIVITIES

Tourist information A ranger post (☎ 01687 462242) beside *The Old Forge* has information on the Knoydart Foundation, and on local and wildlife. The adjoining shop sells walking leaflets plus local goods, from wild venison to woolly blankets.

Mountain biking Two mountain-bike trails – a 1.5-mile red-grade route and a 500yd blue-grade route – loop around Inverie. Knoydart Carbon Cycle rents bikes from the village centre (☎ 01687 462242; £12).

ACCOMMODATION

Most beds are in Inverie, with a growing number of self-catering options (see ⓦ knoydart-foundation.com). You can **camp** on Long Beach, east of Inverie centre, for a £5 donation to the Knoydart Foundation – pay the ranger or leave it in an honesty box at the campsite. The turf-roofed compost toilet, mountain water supply and cabin shelter make for a comfortable enough stay. Firewood (£4.50) for use in the fire-pits is available at the campsite, and visitors may be able to use the showers in the *Knoydart Bunkhouse* for a small charge.

★ **Doune Knoydart** 6 miles northwest of Inverie (owners collect guests by boat from Mallaig) ☎01687 462667, ⚇doune-knoydart.co.uk. This may be the ultimate Highland getaway, with en-suite doubles in restored pine-clad crofts behind a bay. As well as isolation and views, its lovely owners provide superb cooking (also available for non-guests; call ahead). Minimum three nights. Full board. Easter–Sept. **£200**

The Gathering Inverie ☎01687 460051, ⚇thegathering knoydart.co.uk. Relaxed sophistication in a modern, ecofriendly B&B just west of the wharf that feels like self-contained accommodation (the owner lives opposite; each room sleeps up to four. Superb views and sensational breakfasts. Bring swimming gear to enjoy the hot tub with a view. **£110**

Knoydart Foundation Bunkhouse Half a mile east of the pier, Inverie ☎01687 462163, ⚇knoydart-foundation.com. The well-run community hostel is on an old farm near Long Beach. Dorms are large, facilities include a kitchen and laundry, and there's internet access in a comfy lounge with a woodburner. Dorms **£20**

EATING AND DRINKING

Knoydart Pottery & Tearoom Inverie ☎01687 460191. A lovely spot to lose a few hours (or a long wet day): choose from sofas, a long communal table or the outdoor decking with the best loch view in Knoydart. Isla and Rhona serve up breakfast rolls, home-made soups and gluten-free home baking for around £5–8. Easter–Oct Mon–Fri 9am–5pm, Sat 11am–3pm; Nov–Easter Mon–Fri 10am–4pm.

★ **The Old Forge** Inverie ☎01687 462267, ⚇theold forge.co.uk. Britain's most isolated pub remains one of Scotland's finer boozers, fuelled by a convivial atmosphere and wonderful sense of remoteness. Impressive bar meals feature local seafood – Loch Nevis scallops on a leek fondue (£18.95), fish and chips £11.95 – and terrific loch views. Regular live music sessions add to the conviviality here. March–Oct daily except Wed 11.30am–midnight, Nov–Feb daily; food served noon–2.30pm & 6–9pm.

Kyle of Lochalsh and around

Prior to the construction of the Skye Bridge in 1995, the **Kyle of Lochalsh** was Skye's main ferry port, but these days it's mainly used as a terminus for the train route from Inverness. Nearby, the photogenic **Eilean Donan Castle** sits on the glassy shores of **Loch Duich**. Both are fixtures on the tourist trail, which makes the remote **Glenelg** peninsula to the south side of Loch Duich all the more inspiring. A few miles north of Kyle of Lochalsh, the village of **Plockton** is a lovely spot, with a superb setting on **Loch Carron**, a long inlet which acts as a dividing line between Kyle of Lochalsh and the splendours of Wester Ross to the north.

Kyle of Lochalsh

Truth be told, traffic has little reason to stop in **KYLE OF LOCHALSH**, especially since Skye or Plockton nearby offer more appealing accommodation. One good reason to pause here is the *Seaprobe Atlantis*, the UK's only semi-submersible **glass-bottom boat** (see below).

ARRIVAL AND ACTIVITIES   KYLE OF LOCHALSH

By train It's a glorious journey from Inverness to Kyle of Lochalsh (Mon–Sat 4 daily, Sun 1 daily; 2hr 35min); trains stop at Plockton (15min from Kyle) en route.

By bus Reservations are recommended for all services (☎0870 550 5050, ⚇citylink.co.uk). Buses stop on the waterfront at the old slipway.
Destinations Fort William (7 daily; 1hr 55min); Glasgow (5 daily; 5hr 15min); Inverness (8 daily; 2hr); Kyleakin, Skye (6 daily; 5min).

Boat tours The glass-bottom *Seaprobe Atlantis* (☎01471 822716 or ☎0800 980 4846, ⚇seaprobeatlantis.com) leads summer trips to protected seal and bird colonies on Seal Island (1hr; £15) or over the World War II wreck of HMS *Port Napier* (1hr 15min; £18).

EATING

Buth Bheag By the old ferry wharf ☎01599 534002. A charming takeaway shack where fish and seafood from the owner's boat goes into big sandwiches and salad boxes – a bargain at £3–6. Also prepares cullen skink, and home baking. Easter to Christmas Tues–Fri 10am–5pm, Sat noon–4pm.

Loch Duich

Skirted on its northern shore by the A87, **Loch Duich** features prominently on the tourist trail: coach tours from all over the world thunder down from **SHIEL BRIDGE** en route to Skye and one of Scotland's most iconic castles, Eilean Donan. Not that it's just the happy hordes who visit: at the end of the loch is Glen Shiel, flanked by the **Five Sisters of Kintail** – a classic tough trek that ticks off three Munros (see page 41).

Eilean Donan Castle

Beside A87 near the village of Dornie • Daily: April–Oct 10am–6pm, Nov–March 10am–4pm • £10 • ☎ 01599 555202, ⓦ eileandonancastle.com

After Edinburgh's fortress, **Eilean Donan Castle** has to be the most photographed monument in Scotland. Located on the A87 guarding the confluence of lochs Alsh, Long and Duich, its tower rises on an islet, joined to the shore by a stone bridge and set against a backdrop of mountains. Small wonder it has featured in *Highlander* and the James Bond adventure *The World is Not Enough*. The castle was established in 1230 by Alexander II to protect the area from the Vikings but was destroyed during the Jacobite uprising of 1719. It was rebuilt between 1912 and 1932 by a British army officer, John Macrae-Gilstrap, because of the Macrae clan's ancestral links to the area. Hence its three floors, including the banqueting hall, the bedrooms and the troops' quarters, are re-creations rather than originals, though the Jacobite and clan relics on display are all original; this includes a toddy ladle belonging to Bonnie Prince Charlie, as well as a lock of his hair, displayed in cabinets in the impressive-looking Billeting Room, which manifests a superb barrel-vaulted ceiling. Hand held audio guides (included in the entrance fee) do an excellent job of making sense of it all.

ARRIVAL AND DEPARTURE

By bus Citylink bus #917 (3 daily) stops at Eilean Donan Castle, about halfway between Inverness (1hr 50min) and Portree (1hr 20min).

ACCOMMODATION AND EATING   **LOCH DUICH**

All the Goodness Half a mile north of Eilean Donan ☎ 01599 555221, ⓦ allthegoodness.co.uk. Delightful artisan food store and coffeeshop, selling home-baked cakes and biscuits. Teas, coffees and hot choccy to take away, or sit on the decking outside to enjoy views across to Eilean Donan. May–Sept Wed–Sun 9am–3.30pm.

Kintail Lodge Hotel Shiel Bridge ☎ 01599 511275, ⓦ kintaillodgehotel.co.uk. A Victorian pile on the loch's east shore with nine comfortable, if slightly dated, hotel rooms plus simple twins and singles in the *Trekkers' Lodge*. Its *Kintail Bar* serves good pub grub such as steak-and-ale pie or beer battered haddock and chips (£12.95). Food served noon–2.30pm & 6–9.30pm. Dorms £17, hotel doubles £140, lodge twins £34

Shielbridge Caravan Park & Campsite Off the A87, just south of Shiel Bridge ☎ 01599 511221, ⓦ shielbridgecaravanpark.co.uk. It's pretty basic, but its superb location at the west end of Glen Shiel beneath the Five Sisters makes this a great spot to bed down for the night; reception is in the (handy) little shop just before the site proper. Late March to Oct. Per person £7.50

SYHA Ratagan Youth Hostel Ratagan, 2 miles south of Shiel Bridge ☎ 01599 511243, ⓦ hostellingscotland. org.uk. Superbly sited on the loch, with views across to the Five Sisters. Traditional in public areas, but dorms, sleeping three-to ten people, are more IKEA-esque. Kitchen/diner, lounge, laundry and bike storage facilities. March–Oct. Dorms £19.50, doubles £54

The Glenelg peninsula

Even though summer traffic trickles through for the Kylerhea ferry to Skye, sleepy **Glenelg peninsula** remains a quiet backwater jutting into the Sound of Sleat – one benefit of being on a road to nowhere. Indeed, the peninsula has probably changed little since Gavin Maxwell wrote about it in his otter novel *Ring of Bright Water* and he disguised its pristine coast by calling it "Camusfearnà". The landward approach is equally impressive on a road that switchbacks over the Mam Ratagan Pass (1115ft), rewarding drivers with spectacular views over the **Five Sisters** massif. The main village,

---

HIKING IN GLEN SHIEL

Ordnance Survey Explorer map 414

The mountains of **Glen Shiel**, rising dramatically from sea level to over 3000ft in less than a couple of miles, offer some of the best hiking routes in Scotland. Taking in a bumper crop of Munros, the classic **Five Sisters traverse** is claimed by some walkers to be the best day-walk in Scotland. Allow ten hours to complete the whole 12-mile route, which starts at a lay-by off the A87 in Glen Shiel. The distinctive chain of mountains across the glen from the Five Sisters is the **Kintail Ridge**, with breathtaking views south across Knoydart and the islands of the west. It's another full-day trek, beginning from the *Cluanie Inn* on the A87.

Don't underestimate either of these two routes: walkers come unstuck here every year, so only attempt them if you're confident in your walking experience, and have a map and a compass.

GLENELG, is an appealingly soporific spot – a row of whitewashed houses, surrounded by trees, that shows little indication of its time as a strategic centre in the 1700s, when a large barracks kept clans in check. The ruins of Bernera Barracks are on the left as you approach the ferry.

Glenelg Brochs

Nearly two miles south of Glenelg, a left turn up Glen Beag leads to the **Glenelg Brochs**, one of the best-preserved Iron Age monuments in Scotland. Its spectacular circular towers – Dun Telve and Dun Troddan – in a sheltered valley are thought to have been erected around two thousand years ago to protect surrounding settlements from raiders.

Arnisdale

A lonely backroad beyond Glenelg village snakes southeast through a scattering of old crofting hamlets, timber forests and views of Skye and Eigg that grow more spectacular at each bend. Eventually you drop down to the shore of Loch Hourn at **ARNISDALE**, actually two hamlets in the bosom of the mountains: **Camusbane**, a traditional crofting settlement ranged behind a pebble beach; and **Corran** a mile further, a minuscule, whitewashed fishing hamlet huddled around a river mouth. Display boards in the latter's **Ceilidh House and Heritage Centre** (always open; free) relate local history, including that of Mansion House between the hamlets, built by Valentine Fleming, father of James Bond author Ian.

ARRIVAL AND DEPARTURE
          THE GLENELG PENINSULA

By bus MacRae Kintail bus service (Mon, Tues & Fri 1 daily; ☏ 01599 511384) operates from Kyle of Lochalsh to Glenelg (50min; request on boarding) and Arnisdale (1hr 40min; booking essential) via Shiel Bridge.

By ferry The six-car Glenelg–Kylerhea turntable ferry (daily: Easter–Oct 10am–6pm; June–Aug till 7pm; ☏ 01599 522313, ⓦ skyeferry.co.uk) shuttles to and from Skye every 20min, taking 5min.

ACCOMMODATION AND EATING

The Glenelg Inn Glenelg ☏ 01599 522273, ⓦ glenelg-inn.com. Snug, eclectic, with a fire in the grate and a spectacular lochside setting to boot. Comfortable rooms and a decent gastropub menu that showcases local seafood – smoked mackerel pate with toast, langoustines in paprika and garlic butter (£18.95) – confirm this is a class act. Live music every Wednesday. Daily Easter–Oct, bar only Nov–Easter;

Thurs–Sun; food served 12.30–2.30pm & 6–9.30pm. £120

Sheena's Tea Hut End of the road, Corran ☏ 01599 522336. Probably Britain's most remote cuppa, and well worth the journey. This charmingly ramshackle corrugated hut, now run by local legend Sheena's daughter, Lorraine, serves up cockle-warming soups, toasties and cakes, plus fish and chips (£6.50). A true one-off. Mon–Fri & Sun 10am–5pm.

Plockton

With its picture-postcard cottages curved behind a tiny harbour and views across Loch Carron to mountains, **PLOCKTON** is one of the most picturesque settlements on the

4

west coast. Until the end of the eighteenth century, Am Ploc, as the settlement was then known, was just another crofting hamlet. Then a local laird transformed it with a prosperous fishery, funding a planned village that was renamed "Plocktown". It's packed in high season with yachties – a popular regatta fills the bay over a fortnight from late July – artsy second-home owners with easels in tow, and visiting families squelching over the seabed at low tide to take a turn around the small island. It may look familiar to first-time visitors – its flower- and palm-filled seafront featured in cult horror film *The Wicker Man*.

ARRIVAL AND DEPARTURE
PLOCKTON

By train Trains from Inverness stop in Plockton (2hr 20min; Mon–Sat 4 daily, Sun 1 daily) before continuing on to Kyle of Lochalsh (15min).

INFORMATION AND ACTIVITIES

Tourist information In the absence of a tourist office, try ⓦ visitplockton.com.

Calum's Seal Trips Between Easter and October, this long-running outfit runs seal-watching trips – expect "better views than the QE2" aboard this pretty, traditional cruiser. Perhaps true if you like seals (1hr; £12 or free if no seals; ☎ 01599 544306 or 07761 263828, ⓦ calums-sealtrips. com).

ACCOMMODATION

An Caladh 25 Harbour St ☎ 01599 544356. Anna and Bob's whitewashed fisherman's cottage is one of the best of Plockton's many B&Bs, with sea views from front rooms – though not en suites in all. __£65__

Duncraig Castle Turn-off midway between Duirnish and Plockton ☎ 01599 544295, ⓦ duncraigcastle.com. On the opposite side of the bay from Plockton village in a truly stunning setting, this grand Baronial pile has just completed a top-to-bottom renovation. The impressive suite of individually designed rooms come with sumptuous beds and Egyptian cotton, and free standing baths and underfloor heating in the bathrooms. You'll not want for anything. __£260__

Plockton Hotel 41 Harbour St ☎ 01599 544274, ⓦ plocktonhotel.co.uk. This friendly, small hotel provides cosy, contemporary-cottage decor in rooms, of which the best come with a view at the front. A four-room annexe on the harbour appeals for its shared kitchen as much as its cheaper rates that still include breakfast. Well-stocked pub downstairs, with a wee grassy beer garden overlooking the bay. Annexe __£90__, doubles __£140__

Station Bunkhouse Opposite train station ☎ 01599 544235, ✉ mickcoe@btinternet.com. A pleasant wee bunkhouse bang opposite the railway station, with rather cramped six-bed dorms and better four-bed dorms popular with families, all below a pleasant open-plan kitchen and living area. Check-in is at the same owner's *Nessun Dorma* B&B next door. Dorms __£18__

EATING AND DRINKING

Plockton Inn Innes St ☎ 01599 544222, ⓦ plocktoninn. co.uk. The locals' choice offers excellent lunches like watercress and sweet-potato soup or smoked trout pâté, then a fine evening menu including haggis and clapshot (£11.95) and their famous Plockton prawns (£18.50). Good vegetarian options and music on Tues and Thurs evenings. Daily 11am–11.30pm; food served noon–2.30pm & 6–9pm.

Plockton Shores 30 Harbour St ☎ 01599 544263. Metropolitan-styled café-restaurant that starts the day as a relaxed coffee and lunch stop, then shifts up a gear for Modern Scottish dishes like scallops in a lime, ginger and honey glaze (£15.95). Rotating exhibition of local artwork adorns the walls. Mid-March to Oct Tues–Sat 9.30am–9pm & Sun noon–9pm, Nov–March Wed–Sat 10am–8.15pm, Sun noon–2.15pm.

Loch Carron

North of Plockton are the twin sea lochs of **Loch Kishorn**, so deep it was once used as an oil-rig construction site, and **Loch Carron**, which cuts far inland to **STRATHCARRON**, a useful rail link between Kyle of Lochalsh and Torridon, but little else.

Attadale Gardens

2.5 miles south of Strathcarron • April–Oct Mon–Sat 10am–5pm • £8 • ☎ 01520 722603, ⓦ attadalegardens.com

Made up of twenty artistically landscaped acres, **Attadale Gardens** are ranked among Scotland's finest by horticultural aficionados, yet they remain little visited compared to the country's larger National Trust properties. They are, though, utterly charming, the highlights being a stunning fernery – complete with Victorian drain – the nearby Rhododendron Dell, with trees perched precariously on rock ledges, a cleverly conceived sunken garden and an abundant kitchen garden. For kids (well, adults too), there's a delightful sculpture trail (mostly bronze animals), while, for a pause in proceedings, pop your head into the honesty café where you can grab a hot drink and a cake or an ice cream.

Lochcarron

With supermarkets, cafés, a bank and fuel set along a long whitewashed seafront, **LOCHCARRON** represents a considerable hub hereabouts. While it's of more use than interest, two crafty sights warrant a pause. A mile north of town on the main road, the **Smithy Community Hub** (see below), a nineteenth-century smithy and forge, is open erratically in season but has become a focus for local **crafts collectives** selling their wares. More celebrated are the tartans of **Lochcarron Weavers** (Easter–Oct Mon–Sat 9am–5pm; Nov–Easter Mon–Fri 10am–4pm; ☎01520 722212, ⓦlochcarron.co.uk), five miles south of the Community Hub towards Strome Castle, where you can see weaving demonstrations, and buy fabrics and clothing.

ARRIVAL AND INFORMATION   **LOCHCARRON**

By rail Strathcarron is on the splendid Kyle of Lochalsh–Inverness line (Mon–Sat 4 daily, Sun 1 daily): trains run from/to Inverness (1hr 50min) and Kyle (40min).
By bus Timetables are coordinated so that buses meet train arrivals at Strathcarron. Services run to Lochcarron from

Shieldaig (Mon–Sat 1 daily; 35min) and Torridon (Mon–Sat 1 daily; 1hr; call ☎01520 722682 to request).
Tourist information Tourist information desk in the Smithy Community Hub (March–Sept Mon–Sat 11am–4pm, ☎01520 722952).

ACCOMMODATION AND EATING

★**Kishorn Seafood Bar** Kishorn, 6 miles northwest of Lochcarron ☎01520 733240, ⓦkishornseafoodbar. co.uk. A baby-blue, lodge-like café often named in the top-ten British seafood restaurants for local and fresh seafood and it's not difficult to see why with dishes like peppered mackerel fillet, smoke roasted salmon with dill sauce, and scallops with garlic and wakame seaweed (£13.50) on the menu. Outdoor seating available. March to mid-July & mid-Sept to Oct Sat–Thurs 10am–5pm,

Fri 10am–9pm; mid-July to mid-Sept Mon–Sat 10am–9pm, Sun 10am–5pm.
Old Manse Church St, Lochcarron ☎01520 722208, ⓦtheoldmanselochcarron.com. Floral fabrics, pine furniture and wrought-iron beds – country style rules in the five spacious en-suite rooms of the *Old Manse*, on the road to Strome Castle. Perhaps its real appeal is the location before the loch – £10 extra buys you a room with a view. **£70**

Wester Ross

The western seaboard of the old county of Ross-shire, **Wester Ross** is where the west coast ups the ante. Here, all the classic elements of Scotland's **coastal scenery** – craggy mountains, sandy beaches, whitewashed crofting cottages and shimmering island views – come together. Settlements such as **Applecross** and the peninsulas north and south of **Gairloch** maintain a simplicity and sense of isolation outside of peak season. There is some tough but wonderful **hiking** in the mountains around **Torridon** and **Coigach**, while **boat trips** and the prolific marine life and birdlife draw nature-lovers. The hub of activity is **Ullapool**, a proper fishing town and ferry port whose modest size ranks as a metropolis in these parts.

The Applecross peninsula

The **Applecross peninsula** sounds bucolic; the English-sounding name is a corruption of the Gaelic *Apor Crosan*, meaning "estuary". Yet the approach from the south – up a glacial U-shaped valley and over the **Bealach na Bà** ("Pass of the Cattle") at 2054ft – is one of the classic drives and cycle pistes of the Highlands. With a sticker-strewn sign at the base warning off large vehicles and learner drivers (heed the advice!), this former drovers' road provides the greatest road ascent in the UK, with a 1:5 gradient and switchbacks worthy of the Alps. Views across the Minch to Raasay and Skye more than compensate – assuming the weather plays ball. The other way in, from the north, is a beautiful coast road that meanders from Shieldaig on Loch Torridon, past scattered crofting villages and with gorgeous seascapes.

Applecross

The sheltered, fertile coast around **APPLECROSS** village, where an Irish missionary Maelrhuba founded a monastery in 673 AD, is a surprise after experiencing the wilds that surround it. Though popular in peak season, it feels exhilaratingly remote, with little to do but visit the excellent pub, potter along lanes, paddle a kayak or build sandcastles on the beach. A small **Heritage Centre** (April–Oct Mon–Sat noon–4pm; ⊚applecrossheritage.org.uk) near the site of St Maelrhuba's monastery, and beside Clachan church, showcases local history, and several **waymarked trails** along the shore are great for walking off lunch. Come towards the end of July for the barnstormin' annual Applecross Highland Games.

ARRIVAL AND DEPARTURE   APPLECROSS

By bus The Dial-A-Bus (☎01520 722205) takes passengers from Applecross to Inverness, with stop-offs in Lochcarron, Shieldaig and Kishorn.

INFORMATION AND ACTIVITIES

Tourist information In the absence of a tourist office consult ⊚applecross.uk.com or ⊚visitapplecross.com. Otherwise, the *Applecross Campsite* (see below) is the best place to pick up brochures.
Mountain & Sea Guides ☎01520 722734, ⊚apple

cross.uk.com/msg. Located by the fuel pumps, this company organizes mountain walking and climbing adventures, plus sea-kayaking, from half-day tasters to overnight wild-camping trips.

ACCOMMODATION AND EATING

Applecross Campsite East of the centre ☎01520 744268, ⊚visitapplecross.com. A popular, well-run two-field site above the village – the furthest field is the quietest – that also provides basic cabins sleeping four, with electricity and heating. The Flower Tunnel common area is a splendid spot to while away an afternoon. No fires allowed. March–Oct. Camping per person **£11**, cabins **£45**

★ **Applecross Inn** On the waterfront ☎01520 744262, ⊚applecrossinn.co.uk. The heart of the community provides seven pretty, cottagey en-suites in the eaves, all with sea views. In the lively bar downstairs are Highland ales and freshly prepared classic pasta dishes plus divine seafood like Applecross Bay prawns with lemon and garlic butter, and king scallops with crispy bacon (£22). Outside, the *Applecross Inn-Side Out* food truck serves up quality fish and chips (£9), coffee, cakes and ice cream during

the summer. Reservations recommended in season. Daily noon–11pm; food served noon–9pm. **£150**
Hartfield House Hostel Down a long track, 1 mile north of the village ☎01520 744333, ⊚hartfieldhouse. org.uk. New hostel set in an old hunting lodge with a good mix of singles, doubles/twins and triple rooms, plus a bunkhouse. Kitchen/diner and communal lounge plus bike storage area. Closed Jan & Feb. Dorms **£25**, doubles **£70**
The Walled Garden Signposted northeast of the bay ☎01520 744440, ⊚applecrossgarden.co.uk. Head here to enjoy delicious food in the laidback atmosphere of a walled Victorian garden. Gutbusting Scottish breakfasts (£10), generous slices of divine home-made cake, with mouthwatering dishes like seafood linguine with Applecross smoked salmon and shellfish (£15) available in the afternoon/evening. March–Oct daily 8.30am–8.30pm.

Loch Torridon

Loch Torridon marks the northern boundary of the Applecross peninsula and a transition into some awe-inspiring scenery. From the water rise the mountains of **Liathach** (3643ft) and **Beinn Eighe** (3314ft), shapely hulks of reddish, 750-million-

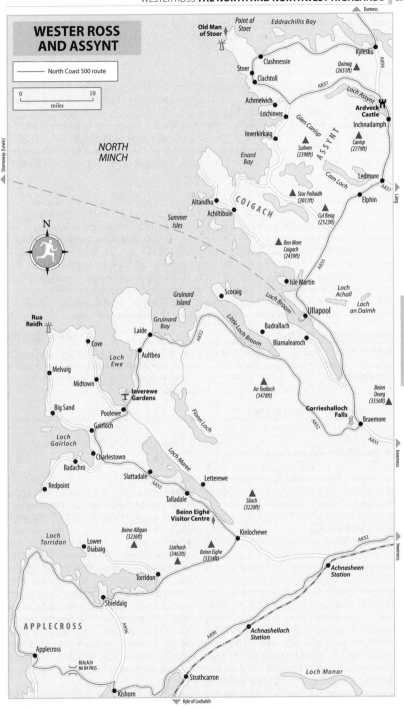

WESTER ROSS AND ASSYNT

North Coast 500 route

0   10
miles

Durness

Point of Stoer
Eddrachillis Bay
Old Man of Stoer
Kylesku
A894
Clashnessie
Stoer
Quinag (2651ft)
Clachtoll
A837
Loch Assynt
Achmelvich
Ardveck Castle
Lochinver
Inchnadamph
Inverkirkaig
Glen Canisp
Canisp (2779ft)
ASSYNT
NORTH MINCH
Enard Bay
Suilven (2398ft)
Ledmore
Cam Loch
Stac Pollaidh (2011ft)
Elphin
Altandhu
COIGACH
Cul Beag (2523ft)
Achiltibuie
A835
Summer Isles
Ben More Coigach (2439ft)
N
Isle Martin
Loch Achall
Scoraig
Loch Broom
Loch an Daimh
4
Gruinard Island
Little Loch Broom
Ullapool
Rua Reidh
Laide
Gruinard Bay
Badrallach
Cove
A832
Blarnalearoch
Loch Ewe
Aultbea
An Teallach (3478ft)
Beinn Dearg (3556ft)
Melvaig
Inverewe Gardens
Midtown
Corrieshalloch Falls
Braemore
Big Sand
Poolewe
Fionn Loch
A832
Gairloch
A835
Loch Gairloch
Charlestown
Loch Maree
Badachro
Slattadale
Letterewe
Redpoint
A832
Slioch (3220ft)
Talladale
Beinn Eighe Visitor Centre
Beinn Alligan (3236ft)
Kinlochewe
A832
Lower Diabaig
Liathach (3463ft)
Beinn Eighe (3314ft)
Loch Torridon
Torridon
Achnasheen Station
Shieldaig
APPLECROSS
A896
Achnashellach Station
Applecross
A890
BEALACH NA BA PASS
Strathcarron
Loch Monar
Kishorn
Kyle of Lochalsh

Stornoway (Lewis)
Lairg
Inverness

year-old white quartzite. Around fifteen thousand acres of the massif are under the protection of the National Trust for Scotland, which makes this superb walking country, with a trio of Munros to bag.

Shieldaig

Smuggled off the main road on the shore of Loch Torridon, pretty **SHIELDAIG** ("herring bay") is a gentle, and little visited, spot – until the Shieldaig Fete and Rowing Regatta livens things up with some wacky boat races over the first weekend in August. A track winding north up the peninsula from the village makes for an enjoyable stroll. Otherwise, simply enjoy the view to **Shieldaig Island**, managed by the National Trust for Scotland; in 2009 a pair of sea eagles pitched up on the island and have remained here ever since – stay patient and you may catch a glimpse of these magnificent birds.

Torridon

TORRIDON village, at the east end of the loch, marks where the road heads inland through spectacular Glen Torridon to Kinlochewe (see page 233). The village itself – thirty or so houses and a shop – straggles along the loch beneath the mountains, making it a fine launchpad for hikes (see page 233). A **Countryside Centre** (April–Sept Sun–Fri 10am–5pm; donation requested; NTS; ☎01445 791221, ☒nts.org.uk/visit/ places/torridon) at the turning into the village provides advice on mountain walks plus information on geology, flora and fauna. In a large paddock a short walk from the centre are thirty or so red deer, which you can feed (food is available from the centre), and there's also a small museum (same hours) nearby which has information on the history and management of the animal, which are abundant in the region.

4

ARRIVAL AND ACTIVITIES

LOCH TORRIDON

By bus The Dial-A-Bus (☎01520 722205) from Strathcarron calls at Shieldaig and Torridon (Mon–Sat 1 daily).
Torridon Activities 1 mile south of turn-off into village ☎01445 791242, ☒thetorridon.com/adventure. An operator based at the *Torridon Hotel* (see below) provides the full range of local fun: guided walks, gorge scrambling, coasteering and climbing, plus kayaking and even clay pigeon shooting.

ACCOMMODATION AND EATING

SHIELDAIG

★ **Shieldaig Camping and Cabins** Temperance Brae ☎01520 755224, ☒shieldaigcampingandcabins.co.uk. In a wonderful, elevated position near the primary school at the village's north end, this pristine new campsite has nicely spaced pitches, in addition to a couple of cabins, plus a modern shower/toilet block; the views (from most pitches at least) are fabulous. **£21**
★ **Tigh-an-Eilean** On the waterfront ☎01520 755251, ☒tighaneilean.co.uk. Faultless service and utter relaxation in a lovely small hotel on the waterfront with classy country accommodation plus a sensational restaurant, although this is for residents only; expect the likes of west coast sea bream with a Provençal tomato confit on innovative daily menus. Non-residents, though, can eat in the attached *Shieldaig Bar and Coastal Kitchen*, which rustles up top-notch bistro dishes like the famous seafood stew (£21), hot smoked salmon from the nearby smokehouse, and wood-fired pizzas (£8–12); alternatively, just grab a beer, park yourself on the lawn opposite and savour the views across to Shieldaig Island Bar Feb–New

Year daily 11am–11pm; food served March–Oct daily 6–9pm. **£145**

TORRIDON

Camping area A wild camp is located beside the turning into the village next to the SYHA hostel. Dishwashing and a shower are in an adjacent public toilet. Beware the midges in summer, though.
★ **Torridon Hotel** 1.5 miles southwest of turn-off into village ☎01445 791242, ☒thetorridon.com. This Victorian hunting lodge is one of the west coast's grandest stays. Sympathetically styled where boutique meets baronial in public areas and Master rooms; Classics are more up to date, while the 1887 Suite is pure indulgence. The elegant *1867* restaurant offers a six-course tasting menu (£80) and a three-curse *table d'hote* menu (£62.50), within which you can expect gems such as Loch Torridon oyster veloute or Scrabster landed monkfish cheek with samphire. The whisky bar, meanwhile, has 350-plus malts (tasting session £30). **£245**
Torridon Inn Next to the Torridon Hotel ☎01445

WALKS AROUND TORRIDON

Ordnance Survey Explorer map 433

The Torridon area offers a wealth of fantastic **walks**. If you're relatively inexperienced but want to do the magnificent ridge walk along the **Liathach** (pronounced "lee-ach") massif, or the strenuous traverse of **Beinn Eighe** (pronounced "ben ay"), you can join a National Trust Ranger Service guided hike (July & Aug weekdays via Torridon Countryside Centre; £25; ☎01445 791221).

For those confident to go it alone, one of many possible routes takes you behind Liathach and down the pass, **Coire Dubh**, to the main road in Glen Torridon. This covers thirteen miles and takes in superb landscapes: weather permitting, you can make the rewarding diversion up to the **Coire Mhic Fhearchair**, widely regarded as the most spectacular corrie in Scotland. Allow the whole day.

Even in rough weather, the seven-mile hike up the coast from **Lower Diabaig**, ten miles northwest of Torridon village, to **Redpoint** is a rewarding one, and on a clear day the views across to Raasay and Applecross are wonderful. For any of these walks, ensure you are properly equipped with waterproofs, warm clothing, provisions and a map.

791242, ⊛thetorridon.com/inn. More cyclist- and walker-friendly than the neighbouring *Torridon Hotel* (same owners), with neat, modern en-suites. Bar-bistro serves regional ales and good gastropub cooking – mixed bean and garden vegetable cassoulet, haddock and chips with mushy peas (£13). Feb–Easter Mon–Sat 8am–9pm, Sun till 5pm; Easter–Dec daily 8am–9pm; food served noon–2pm & 6–8pm. **£120**

Torridon Youth Hostel Start of village, 100yds from turn-off ☎01445 791284, ⊛hostellingscotland.org. uk. Though the Seventies-vintage municipal building is no looker, this hostel is spacious and a popular choice with hikers and bikers thanks to a location beneath the peaks. Four-to eight bed dorms plus twins as well as the usual kitchen, laundry and drying room facilities. March–Oct & Thurs–Sun Nov & Feb. Dorms **£22**, doubles **£60**

Loch Maree

About eight miles north of Loch Torridon, **Loch Maree**, dotted with Caledonian-pine-covered islands, is one of the area's scenic highlights, best viewed from the A832 road that drops down to its southeastern tip through Glen Docherty; try to time your journey here with early dawn or dusk, when red deer take over the land. At the southeastern end of the loch, the A896 from Torridon meets the A832 from Achnasheen at small **KINLOCHEWE**, a good base if you're heading into the hills.

Beinn Eighe Nature Reserve

The A832 skirts the southern shore of Loch Maree, passing the **Beinn Eighe Nature Reserve**, Britain's oldest national nature reserve, set up in 1951. Parts of the reserve are forested with Caledonian pine, which once covered the whole country, and it is home to pine martens, wildcats, buzzards and golden eagles. A mile north of Kinlochewe, the **Beinn Eighe Visitor Centre** (March–Oct daily 10am–5pm; ☎01445 760254, ⊛nnr. scot) on the A832, has an excellent exhibition on the reserve courtesy of wall-bound panoramic displays, as well as free leaflets covering local **walks**. Two walks start from the Coille na Glas-Leitir Trails car park just over a mile north of the visitor centre: a mile-long trail into ancient pine woodland and a 3.5-mile track into the mountains.

ACCOMMODATION AND EATING   LOCH MAREE

Kinlochewe Hotel On A832, centre of village ☎01445 760253, ⊛kinlochewehotel.co.uk. A traditional hotel dating back to 1850 with a warm welcome and a fantastic line in regional ales and pub classics (garlic mushrooms, steak and onion burger). Rooms , which include a couple of economy rooms with shared bathrooms (£90), are comfy

enough. An annexe holds a very basic twelve-bed self-catering bunkhouse, with triple-deck bunks in one room (bedding not included). Dorm **£20**, doubles **£110**

The Gorse Bush Torrisdale Rd ☎01445 760423, ⊛thegorsebush.com. This brightly decorated, refurbed old village hall is always a good stop before or after the hills, serving filled rolls for lunch (grilled scallops, slow roasted pork) for between £7–11, and superb dinners, perhaps sweet onion tart with wild mushrooms or steamed sea trout with crab bisque (mains £15–20)..A well-placed log-burner guarantees to warm the cockles. Feb–Nov Thurs–Sun noon–8pm.

Gairloch and around

Cheerful and unpretentious, **GAIRLOCH** thrives as a low-key holiday resort, with several sandy beaches for the bucket-and-spade brigade, some good coastal walks within easy reach and an abundance of wildlife cruise operators that pray for passing minke whales. The township is divided into distinct areas spread along Loch Gairloch: to the south, in **Flowerdale Bay**, is Charlestown with the harbour; west, at the turn-off to Melvaig, **Achtercairn** is the centre of Gairloch; and along the north side of the bay is the crofting area of **Strath**. Near the *Old Inn* in Charlestown, the **Sòlas Gallery** (May–Oct Tues–Fri 1–5pm; ☎01445 712626, ⊛solasgallery.co.uk) is worth a stop for its ceramics and watercolours inspired by the Highlands landscapes. A 1.5-mile walk (round trip) tracks the Flowerdale River through a woodland glen to a waterfall.

Gairloch Museum

On the A382 just before the turn-off into Achtercairn • April–Oct Mon–Sat 10am–6pm, Thurs til 8pm • £5 • ☎01445 712287, ⊛gairlochmuseum.org

Occupying a former nuclear bunker – hence the chilly grey concrete walls – the superb **Gairloch Museum** houses eclectic displays of traditional Highland life, from a mock-up crofthouse to one of the largest Fresnel lenses ever constructed from the nearby Rua Reidh Lighthouse. Perhaps the museum's most prestigious display, however, is the so-called Poolewe Hoard, discovered by crofter Hector Maciver in 1877 and comprising a rich collection of Bronze Age items (axeheads, rings and ornamental objects) thought to date from around 570 BC.

Big Sand and Melvaig

The area's real attraction is its **coastline**. There's a **beach** just north of the harbour in Charlestown, a crescent of pure sand, or a more impressive stretch a few miles around the north side of the bay at **Big Sand** – it's cleaner, quieter and a mite more pebbly. The B8021 terminates at the crofting hamlet of **Melvaig**, where a community-funded replacement for the legendary but now-closed *Melvaig Inn* is currently in the pipeline.

Rua Reidh and around

From Melvaig, a private track heads three miles to **Rua Reidh** (pronounced "roo-a-ray"), where a fully operational lighthouse houses a hostel in its keepers' quarters. Around the headland lies beautiful **Camas Mòr** beach, from where a marked footpath tracks inland (southeast) beneath a sheer scarp slope, past a string of lochans and ruined crofts to **MIDTOWN** on the east side of the peninsula, four miles north of Poolewe on the B8057. Allow half a day, though be aware that few buses travel back from Poolewe (check times on ☎01445 712255).

Badachro

On the south side of Loch Gairloch, a single-track lane (built with the Destitution Funds raised during the nineteenth-century potato famine) winds past wooded coves and inlets along the loch to **BADACHRO**, a secluded, former fishing village with a wonderful pub (see page 236).

Redpoint

Beyond Badachro, the road winds five miles further to **REDPOINT**, with beautiful beaches of peach-coloured sand on either side of the headland and great views to Raasay, Skye and the Western Isles. It also marks the trailhead for the wonderful coast walk to Lower Diabaig. Even if you don't fancy a full-blown hike, follow the path a mile or so to find an exquisite **beach** on the south side of the headland.

ARRIVAL AND INFORMATION

By bus Public transport is minimal and requires careful planning. Bus stops for all services are at the *Old Inn*, Charlestown, as well as Achtercairn and Strath.
Destinations Inverness (Mon–Sat 1 daily; also ScotBus June–Sept Mon–Sat 1 daily; 2hr 45min); Poolewe (Mon, Wed & Sat 1 daily; 15min); Ullapool (Mon, Wed, Thurs & Sat

GAIRLOCH AND AROUND

1 daily; 1hr 10min).
Tourist information The superb, community-run Gale Centre in Achtercairn (Mon–Fri 9.30am–5pm, Sat 10am–4pm, Sun 11am–3pm; ☎ 01445 712071, ⓦ galeaction forum.co.uk) has stacks of information as well as a gallery and splendid little café.

ACTIVITIES

BOAT TRIPS

Gairloch prides itself on wildlife cruises from its harbour. Orcas and minke whales migrate past from late spring to late summer; porpoise and dolphins are common year-round, and seal-spottings near enough guaranteed. All operators are located on the harbour at Charlestown.
Gairloch Marine Life Centre & Cruises Charlestown ☎ 01445 712636, ⓦ porpoise-gairloch.co.uk. The bay's largest operator runs three different trips a day (1hr/£15, 2hr/£30 and 4hr/£60), aboard two vessels which deploy a mini-sub for underwater pictures and a hydrophone to pick up audio. Its visitor centre (Easter–Oct daily 10am–4pm) has displays of local sea life.

Hebridean Whale Cruises Charlestown ☎ 01445 712458, ⓦ hebridean-whale-cruises.co.uk. As well as in-shore cruises, the longest-established operator runs trips (Easter–Oct; call for winter cruises; from £49.50) in a high-speed RIB that allows it to reach further offshore into the North Minch out to the Shiant Isles off Lewis.

PONY TREKKING

Gairloch Trekking Centre Croft 3, Red Point ☎ 01445 741743, ⓦ gairlochtrekkingcentre.co.uk. Lead-rein rides for young or inexperienced riders (£14/30mins, £25/1hr), plus longer hacks (1hr £25; 2hr £50) along the beach or through pretty Highland scenery, between Easter and Oct (closed Thurs).

ACCOMMODATION

GAIRLOCH

Old Inn Signposted off A832, Charlestown ☎ 01445 712006, ⓦ theoldinn.net. Country character abounds in the rooms of this former coaching inn set off the main road beside the Flowerdale River. Expect pretty patchwork-style quilts or tartan headboards in cosy en-suite rooms. **£120**

BIG SAND

Gairloch Sands Youth Hostel On B8021, 2.5 miles west of Gairloch ☎ 01445 712219, ⓦ hostellingscotland.org. uk. This former hunting lodge is spectacularly sited above the foreshore, with vast views to Skye from its lounge. It dates back to 1880 and rather shows its age. April–Sept. Dorms **£20**, doubles **£48**
Sands Caravan and Camping On B8021, 3.5 miles west of Gairloch ☎ 01445 712152, ⓦ sandscaravanand camping.co.uk. The best – and by far the largest – of the

area's campsites, with pitches behind the dunes for sea views. Also rents "wigwams" – actually Scandi-style cabins for up to five with electricity, heating and a fire-pit. Laundry facilities, plus kayak (£25/day) and bike rental (£18/day). There's a well-stocked shop, while the cosy on-site *Barn Café* serves evening meals (reserve ahead) and there's a terrific pizza truck for takeaways. March–Nov. Per pitch **£22**, wigwams for two **£50**

RUA REIDH

Rua Reidh Lighthouse Rua Reidh ☎ 01445 771263, ⓦ stayatalighthouse.co.uk. Epic seascapes to the Hebrides in the only lighthouse hostel on Britain's west coast (see page 234), with four rooms (one room sleeps four) manifesting homely decorative touches and private bathrooms. Breakfasts, packed lunches and a buffet supper (£10) available. Easter–Oct. **£110**

EATING AND DRINKING

GAIRLOCH

Mountain Coffee Company Achtercairn ☎ 01445 712316. Here's an unusual find for a small Highlands town – a relaxed café with a global backpacker vibe. Coffees, mammoth-sized scones and toasted bagels with fresh

fillings, plus a good bookshop on-site and rooms upstairs. Easter–Nov daily 9am–6pm; Dec–Easter Mon–Sat 10am–4pm.
Old Inn Signposted off A832, Charlestown ☎ 01445 712006, ⓦ theoldinn.net. Flagstone floors and stone

4

walls provide character in a sympathetically modernized coaching inn. Posh-pub specials such as shellfish bisque and chicken liver parfait (mains £12–14), plus beers of the on-site microbrewery, provide the sustenance. Easter–Nov daily 11am–11pm; food served noon–2.30pm & 5–8.30pm.

BADACHRO

★ **Badachro Inn** ☎ 01445 741225, ⊛ badachroinn.

com. Settle onto the terrace with a plate of creel-caught langoustine (£16.95) or a bowl of smoked haddock and garden pea risotto (£13) and this pub by the old harbour is as fine a place as you'll find for a sunny afternoon. Inside are real ales, excellent malts and a fire for chill evenings. Look out for otters at dawn and dusk. April–Oct daily noon–midnight, Sun noon–11pm; Nov–March Wed–Sun same hours; food served weekdays noon–3pm & 6–9pm, Sat & Sun noon–3pm.

Poolewe

It's a short hop over the headland from Gairloch to the sleepy village of **POOLEWE** at the sheltered southern end of Loch Ewe. During World War II, the Arctic convoy embarked from here and the deep-water loch remains one of only three berths for nuclear submarines. One of the area's best **walks** begins nearby, signposted from the lay-by viewpoint on the A832, a mile south. It takes a couple of hours to follow the easy trail across open moorland to the shores of **Loch Maree** (see page 233), then the car park at Slattadale, seven miles southeast of Gairloch. Double-check timetables (☎ 01445 712255), but you should be able to continue along the loch shore to catch the Wester bus from Inverness back to Poolewe from the *Loch Maree Hotel* just after 7pm (Tues, Thurs & Fri only).

Inverewe Gardens

Half a mile north of Poolewe on A832 · **Gardens** Daily: Jan–May & Sept 9.30am–5pm; June–Aug 9.30am–6pm; Oct 9.30am–4pm; Nov–mid-Dec 10am–4pm · **Restaurant** April–Oct daily 10.30am–5pm · £12.50; NTS · ☎ 01445 781229, ⊛ nts.org.uk

Most visitors arrive in Poolewe for **Inverewe Gardens**, a subtropical-style oasis of foliage and riotously colourful compared to the wild coast. The gardens were the brainchild of **Osgood MacKenzie** who collected plants from all over the world for his spectacular, curved walled garden, which still forms the nucleus of the complex. Protected from Loch Ewe's salt breezes by Scots pine, rowan, oak, beech and birch trees, the fragile plants flourished on rich soil brought as ballast on Irish ships, and by the time MacKenzie died in 1922, his garden sprawled over the peninsula, surrounded by a hundred acres of woodland. Today a network of paths and walkways wanders through more than a dozen gardens featuring exotic plant collections from as far afield as Chile, China, Tasmania and the Himalayas. Mid-May to mid-June is the best time to see the rhododendrons and azaleas, while the herbaceous garden reaches its peak in July and August, as does the wonderful Victorian vegetable and flower garden beside the sea. You'll quite likely see plenty of wildlife too, including otters and seals, and herons nesting in the trees down by Camas Bay. Between April and September there are free **guided walks** at 1.30pm each day (except Sun), and the self-service restaurant offers up sandwiches and soups, with hot grub during the height of summer. Visitors can also explore the opulent Inverewe House, which, with its original furnishings, feel happily lived in.

ARRIVAL AND DEPARTURE

POOLEWE

By bus There's a bus to Poolewe from Gairloch (15min; Mon, Wed & Sat 7.45am; Tues, Thurs, Fri & Sat 7.45pm).

ACCOMMODATION AND EATING

Inverewe Gardens Camping & Caravanning Centre of Poolewe on A832 ☎ 01445 781249, ⊛ camping andcaravanningclub.co.uk. As trim a site as usual from a member of the Camping & Caravanning Club and largely

occupied by motorhomes. Facilities are well maintained and a few pitches in a shady corner allow campers to wake up to loch views. Easter–Oct. Per pitch **£30.65**

★ **Pool House Hotel** Centre of Poolewe on A832

☎ 01445 781272, **ⓦ** pool-house.co.uk. Once the residence of Inverewe Gardens' Osgood MacKenzie, the Harrison family home remains one of the Highlands' most elegantly opulent small hotels – think rich fabrics, family antiques and art, loch views and a serene sense of calm. Don't be surprised if you struggle to leave the lounge. Dinner for residents is served on Wed, Fri & Sat. Easter– Oct. **£275**

Poolewe to Ullapool

At **LAIDE**, nine miles north of Poolewe, the road skirts the shores of **Gruinard Bay**. It's a great drive, offering fabulous views and, at the inner end of the bay, some excellent sandy beaches before you swing east, tracking high above Little Loch Broom, with gorgeous views to mountains opposite – **Badrallach**, seven miles from a left-turn at the head of the loch, is a magical spot to drop off the radar.

Inland, the route joins the A835 at **Braemore Junction**, above the head of Loch Broom. Easily accessible from a lay-by on the A835, the spectacular 160ft **Falls of Measach** plunge through the mile-long **Corrieshalloch Gorge**, formed by glacial meltwaters. After walking for five minutes you'll reach a Victorian suspension bridge that spans the chasm, offering a vertiginous view of the falls and gorge, whose 197ft vertical sides are draped in wych elm, goat willow and bird cherry.

ACCOMMODATION   **POOLEWE TO ULLAPOOL**

★ **Badrallach** Croft 9, Badrallach **☎** 01854 633281, **ⓦ** badrallach.com. Views, space and pure escapism literally at the end of the road. Alongside the campsite are beds in a snug bothy and B&B in a sweet two-bedroom cottage (3 night minimum stay). Excellent ecofriendly facilities. With fishing rod and kayak rental, too, this deserves a few days. Per pitch **£15**, bothy **£8**, cottage per night **£50**

Ullapool

ULLAPOOL, the northwest's principal town, is an appealing place spread across a sheltered arm of land in Loch Broom – a perfect base for exploring the northwest Highlands. Here you'll find all the cultural life of the only town worth the title in the region, with a penchant for barnstorming live music nights and a few excellent restaurants. Founded by the British Fisheries Society at the height of the herring boom in 1788, the grid-plan town remains an important fishing centre, which gives it a salty authenticity despite the hundreds of visitors who pass through in high season, bound north or to catch the **ferry** to Stornoway on Lewis.

Ullapool Museum

7–8 West Argyle St • Easter–Oct Mon–Sat 10am–5pm • £4 • **☎** 01854 612987, **ⓦ** ullapoolmuseum.co.uk

The only conventional attraction in town is the small but engaging **Ullapool Museum**, which occupies the old, Thomas Telford commissioned parish church, as evidenced by the pulpit, pews and gallery all still *in situ*. By way of artefacts, photographs and audiovisual displays it offers a marvellous insight into crofting, fishing and the sea, local weather and emigration. During the Clearances, Ullapool was one of the ports through which evicted crofters left to start new lives abroad – it also has some genealogy resources. The museum also offers local history walks (£4) at 11am on Thursdays between mid-July and mid-September.

Isle Martin

ⓦ islemartin.org

Three miles northwest of Ullapool in Loch Broom, **Isle Martin** was inhabited on and off for a few thousand years – they say it was named after a follower of St Columba, who may be under a fifth-century gravestone in the old graveyard – until the last crofting families called it a day in 1949. Gifted to the RSPB in 1999, the four-hundred-acre island is a romantic spot to be a temporary castaway, with beaches, walks and views to the cliffs of Beinn Mhor Coigach and the Summer Isles. Bothy-style accommodation is available in the *Croft House* (£60 for the night) or bunk rooms in the *Mill House* (£20 per person). It's now possible to visit the island courtesy of a community-run passenger boat, which currently operates on Fridays, Saturdays and Sundays in July and August (£10). Otherwise, you can visit with your own boat (a donation is required) or via a RIB trip with Seascape Expeditions (see below).

Summer Isles

During summer, the *M.V. Shearwater* steamer (May to early Sept Mon–Sat Mon–Sat 1am & 1.30pm; £35; ☎01854 612472, ⓦsummerqueen.co.uk) and the RIB-safari operator Seascape Expeditions (Easter–Sept, depending on weather; £30; ☎01854 633708, ⓦsea-scape.co.uk), run wildlife cruises and trips to the **Summer Isles**, twelve miles west of Ullapool, to view seabird colonies, grey seals, dolphins, porpoises and the occasional whale. Whether slow and stately or fast and full-on in caves, it's a trip worth taking (weather permitting).

ARRIVAL AND INFORMATION   **ULLAPOOL**

By bus Buses stop at the pier, near the ferry dock.
Destinations Durness (school summer holidays: Mon–Sat

1 daily; 3hr); Inverness (Mon–Sat 3 daily, Sun 1 daily; 1hr 30min); D&E bike-carrying bus from Inverness (mid-May to

4

ULLAPOOL

Ullapool River
MOSS ROAD
A835 NORTH ROAD

0   250
yards

Loch Broom FM

RIVERSIDE TERRACE

CASTLE TERRACE

LADYSMITH STREET

MILL STREET

Library

N

WEST TERRACE

QUAY STREET

MARKET STREET

Tesco

PULTENEY STREET

SEAFORTH ROAD

Ullapool Clock ⓘ

ARGYLE STREET

GARVE ROAD

Museum

WEST ARGYLE STREET

SHORE STREET

Pier

Loch Broom

WEST SHORE STREET

Cruise Booking Office

CalMac Terminal

Pier

●EATING
The Arch Inn	4
The Ceilidh Place	2
Seafood Shack	3
West Coast Delicatessen	1

■ ACCOMMODATION
Ardmair Point	1
Broomfield Holiday Park	6
The Ceilidh Place	3
Tanglewood House	2
Ullapool Youth Hostel	4
West House	5

■ DRINKING
Ferry Boat Inn	1

Stornoway

WALKS AND HIKES AROUND ULLAPOOL
Ordnance Survey Explorer maps 439, 436 & 435
Ullapool lies at the start of several excellent **hiking trails**, from sedate shoreside ambles to strenuous ascents of Munros. As ever, be aware the weather here changes quickly, so take necessary precautions (see page 42). Northwest Outdoors on West Argyle Street stocks a fair selection of kit, plus OS maps. More detailed descriptions of the routes below are available from the hostel on Shore Street.

An easy **half-day ramble** begins at the north end of Quay Street: cross the walkway/footbridge and follow the river beyond towards the sea. Walk past the golf course and follow the shore for around two miles to reach a hilltop lighthouse for fine views across the Summer Isles. For a harder **half-day hike**, head north along Mill Street on the east edge of town to Broom Court retirement home, trailhead for the Ullapool hillwalk. A rocky path zigzags steeply up to the summit of Meall Mòr (886ft) for great views of the area's major peaks. Botanists love the place for its insect-eating sundews and butterworts. The path then drops sharply down the northeast side into **Glen Achall**, where you turn left onto a surfaced road running past a limestone quarry; the main road back to Ullapool lies thirty minutes' walk west.

A right turn where the path meets the road takes you through the **Rhidorroch** estate to Loch Achall, the start of a **two-day wilderness hike** along an old drovers' trail to **Croick**. Don't tackle this alone or without proper gear, and provide details of your route to someone before setting off – and call them to confirm your safe arrival. Start off at *East Rhidorroch Lodge* and camp halfway at **Knockdamph bothy** (closed for stag stalking mid-Oct to mid-Sept) by Loch nan Daimh.

Sept Mon–Sat 1 daily; 1hr 30min).
By ferry CalMac (☎ 01854 612358, ✆ calmac.co.uk) sails to Stornoway, Lewis (2 daily; 2hr 30min).
Tourist office Argyle St (April, May & mid-Sept to March Mon–Sat 9.30am–5pm, Sun 10am–3pm; June to mid-

Sept Mon–Sat 9am–6pm, Sun 9.30am–4.30pm; ☎ 01854 612486, ✆ ullapool.com). This friendly, well-run tourist office also offers an accommodation booking service and you can also book CalMac ferry tickets here.

4

ACCOMMODATION
SEE MAP PAGE 238

Ullapool has a good stock of accommodation but gets very busy from Easter through until September, so booking in advance is essential.

HOTELS, GUESTHOUSES AND B&BS
★ **The Ceilidh Place** 14 West Argyle St ☎ 01854 612103, ✆ theceilidhplace.com. Antique bed frames, old books on vintage cabinets and Roberts Radios (no TVs) add character to rooms of this lovely small hotel, some of which are pepped up with stylish wallpaper; otherwise modern-rustic rules. The lounge and library, with honesty bar, offers sophisticated relaxation. Also manages a bunkhouse (£24, includes linens) directly opposite. **£140**
★ **Tanglewood House** 1 mile south off A835 ☎ 01854 612059, ✆ tanglewoodhouse.co.uk. Charm and character in an extraordinary, curved house full of art and antiques. Rooms (red, green and blue) are individually furnished, though the Green Room, with a terrace to enjoy the position above Loch Broom, is worth its extra £16. Factor in a rocky beach beneath for a dip and a warming lounge/library, and this is a truly memorable stay. May–Oct. **£99**
West House West Argyle St ☎ 01854 613126. A former manse, with all the handsome proportions that suggests, though accommodation (four rooms) is on a room only

basis; that said, plenty of beverages are supplied, including orange juice, fresh milk and a cafetiere and there are some decent breakfast options hereabouts. Two night-minimum stay. May–Sept. **£75**

HOSTEL AND CAMPSITES
★ **Ardmair Point** 3.5 miles north of Ullapool ☎ 01854 612054, ✆ ardmair.com. This is a truly wonderful spot, with large pitches curving around the peninsula, and a big, central grassy field for tents. A pebble beach below and fantastic sunsets round things off. Reception doubles up as a well-stocked shop where you can also get hot drinks. Per pitch **£19**
Broomfield Holiday Park West Shore St ☎ 01854 612020, ✆ broomfieldhp.com. Hurrah: a campsite in the centre of town with loch views and space galore at the tip of Ullapool, plus standard facilities and all a short walk to the heart of Ullapool. Mid-April to Sept. Per pitch **£21**
Ullapool Youth Hostel Shore St ☎ 01854 612254, ✆ hostellingscotland.org.uk. Busy hostel bang on the seafront, where prints and murals of seaside scenes help add a cheerful holiday atmosphere. There are dorms of various sizes, doubles, twins, two lounges and laundry plus lots of good information about local walks. April–Oct. Dorms **£20**, doubles **£45**

CEILIDHS

The **ceilidh** is essentially an informal, homespun kind of entertainment, the word being Gaelic for a "visit". In remote Highland communities, talents and resources were pooled, people gathering to play music, sing, recite poems and dance. The dances themselves are thought to be ancient in origin; the Romans wrote that the Caledonians danced with abandon round swords stuck in the ground, a practice echoed in today's traditional sword dance, where the weapons are crossed on the floor and a quick-stepping dancer skips over and around them.

Highland ceilidhs, fuelled by whisky and largely extemporized, must have been an intoxicating, riotous means of fending off winter gloom. Like much of clan culture, however, the traditions died or were forced underground after the defeat of the Highlanders at **Culloden** and the passing of the 1747 Act of Proscription, which forbade the wearing of the plaid and other expressions of Highland identity.

Ceilidhs were enthusiastically revived in the reign of tartan-fetishist **Queen Victoria**, and in the twentieth century became the preserve of the village hall and hotel ballroom, buoyed to some extent by the popularity of jaunty 1950s TV programmes. More recently, though, the ceilidh has thrown off its dated associations, with places such as *The Ceilidh Place* in Ullapool (see below) and the *Taybank Hotel* in Dunkeld restoring some of its spontaneous, infectious fun to a night of Scottish music and dancing.

Whether performed by skilled traditional musicians or in more rollicking form by younger players, ceilidh music is irresistible, and it's common to find all generations gathering. Ceilidh dances look complex. Actually most are reasonably simple and are explained or "called" beforehand by the bandleader. We find a whisky or two earlier on helps.

EATING
SEE MAP PAGE 238

The Arch Inn 10–11 West Shore St ☎01854 612454, ⓦ thearchinn.co.uk. Ullapool's liveliest pub divides between a popular bar and informal restaurant with Scottish-European cooking: starters like sautéed scallops with parma ham and pea shoots (£7.95), then sirloin steak (£19.95) alongside the usual fish and chips (£10.95). Mon–Thurs 11am–11pm, Fri & Sat 11am–1am, Sun 12.30–11pm; food served noon–2.30pm & 5–9pm.

The Ceilidh Place 14 West Argyle St ☎01854 612103, ⓦ theceilidhplace.com. Barn-like venue remains one of the best in town. After breakfasts, it shifts to a bistro menu with anything from home-made burgers and mussels to a forest mushroom risotto or chilli crab baked with a herb and garlic crust (mains £10.50–20) – and its bar hosts regular live music. Fantastic bookshop (with CDs) attached. Daily 8am–11pm; food served 8am–11am, 11.30am–4pm & 5–9pm.

★ **Seafood Shack** West Argyle St ☎07876 142623, ⓦ seafoodshack.co.uk. Garnering plaudits left, right and centre, the open-air *Shack* is a must visit when in town; you'll need to be quick mind, as folk flock here as soon as the doors open at midday and the most popular dishes (especially the scallops and lobster burger) get snapped up in no time – there are, though, other delicious morsels, such as tempura haddock wrap with pesto and lemon mayo, and hot crab claws with red cabbage slaw and spicy salsa, all of which go for around £8–12. There is covered outdoor seating. Cash only. Apr–Oct daily noon–6pm, July & Aug till 8pm.

West Coast Delicatessen 5 Argyle St ☎01854 613450, ⓦ westcoastdeli.co.uk. Fine food deli serves up proper coffees, home-made houmous and fresh salads, tarts and cakes, plus unmissable "pakora Fridays". Mon–Sat 8.30am–5pm.

DRINKING
SEE MAP PAGE 238

Ullapool has no shortage of decent boozers, many of which – including the *Arch Inn* (see above) – offer live music. It's also worth checking out what's on at *The Venue*, a dedicated live music venue inside the bunkhouse building run by *The Ceilidh Place* – it has an excellent roster of high class acts with, typically, at least two gigs a week.

Ferry Boat Inn 26–27 Shore St ☎01854 612431, ⓦ fbiullapool.com. Popular with locals, the *FBI* is a fine spot to swig a pint of ale at the lochside (midges permitting) and watch the boats. Live music on Saturdays, and also at sister pub *The Argyll* round the corner. Daily 11am–11pm.

Assynt

If the landscape before Ullapool was impressive, the **Assynt** region just north has an epic, almost cinematic, quality. Marking the transition from Wester Ross into Sutherland, this region is one of the least populated areas in Europe and its landscape consists not of mountain ranges but of extraordinary peaks which rise individually from the moorland. See a mountain like **Suilven** and you understand why the name is said to derive from "A-ssynt", meaning seen from afar, or "ass" – Old Norse for rocky. Certainly, Assynt boasts some of the world's oldest rock formations, and roadside signs highlight the region's geological importance as the **Northwest Highlands Geopark** (ⓦnwhgeopark.com).

Lochinver, the main settlement, makes a fine base – it puts peaks like Suilven within reach and is also acquiring a foodie reputation. Without transport it's almost your only option. With wheels, this is splendid touring country: an area of peaceful backroads which twist past crofts to deserted beaches or headlands with superb views to the Outer Hebrides and those shapely mountains. There are appealing crofting villages to discover around **Achiltibuie**, scenic backroads to tour and two Munros to bag above **Inchnadamph**.

Coigach

Coigach is the peninsula immediately north of Loch Broom, accessible via a road off the A835. It's a beautiful drive, squeezing between the northern shore of Loch Lurgainn and mountains like mammoths, including **Cul Beag** (2523ft), craggy **Stac Pollaidh** (2012ft) and the awesome bulk of **Ben More Coigach** (2439ft), southeast, which presides over the area. There's some spectacular coastal scenery too. It's a place to unwind, with gorgeous views of the Summer Isles scattered offshore and signposted trails along coastal moors and mountains. If the steep Ben More Coigach–Sgurr an Fhidhleir horseshoe (7 miles; 7hr) seems too tough, the Culnacraig circuit (5 miles; 2hr) between Achduart and Culnacraig offers great views. Coigach's main settlement is **ACHILTIBUIE**, a crofting village spread above beaches and rocks. Sunsets here can be astonishing.

ARRIVAL AND INFORMATION COIGACH

By bus The Scotbus service from Ullapool to Achiltibuie (Mon–Fri 2–3 daily, Sat 1 daily; 1hr 15min) doubles as the school bus, so services are scheduled around the start and end of the school day.

Tourist information A useful website is ⓦcoigach.com.

ACCOMMODATION AND EATING

Am Fuaran Bar Althandhu ☎01854 622339, ⓦam fuaran.co.uk. A lovely pub whatever the exterior suggests, as cosy as a cabin inside – log-burner and all – and with a fine seafood which, depending upon the day's catch, might include smoked haddock chowder or Summer Isles scallops in ginger and lemon butter (£7.20). Mon–Sat noon–11.45pm, Sun 12.30–11pm; food served 12.30–2.30pm & 6–8.30pm, till 8pm Sun.

★**Port A Bhaigh Campsite** Althandhu ☎01854 622339, ⓦportabhaigh.co.uk. Spread behind the beach with mesmerizing sea views to the Summer Isles and excellent facilities that include a laundry, this is as fine a campsite as you'll find in the Highlands. Midges can be horrendous but the *Am Fuaran Bar* is literally over the road. Per pitch **£10**

Summer Isles Hotel Achiltibuie ☎01854 622282, ⓦsummerisleshotel.com. A stylish hideaway with a superb setting, fresh modern-country decor and lovely simple rooms, all but four of which are in adjoining annexes. Its handsome restaurant, all crisply laid white tablecloths, offers genuinely exciting plates of food like gin cured Hebridean salmon with quail's egg, and cider cured sea trout in a shellfish bisque (£21.50), while the attached former crofters' pub serves up ales from the Orkney Brewery and a less glitzy bar menu plus occasional live music in the evenings. Easter–Oct; bar open noon–11pm; food served in bar noon–2.30pm & 6–9pm, in restaurant 6–9pm. **£150**

Lochinver and around

It's hard to think of a more beautiful route than the single-track road that wriggles north from Coigach towards Inverkirkaig. Unremittingly spectacular, the journey is the Highlands in miniature, threading through stunted beech woods, heaving valleys, open moorland and bare rock, past the startling shapes of Cul Beag (2523ft), Cul Mor (2785ft) and the distinctive sugar-loaf **Suilven** (2398ft) until it slaloms along the sea shore to Inverkirkaig, the start of two fantastic walks (see below). **LOCHINVER**, another two miles north, marks the return to civilization. One of the busier fishing harbours in Scotland, the small town (oversized village, really) has a pleasingly down-to-earth atmosphere. Factor in excellent budget and high-end accommodation and an established reputation for food, and it makes a natural base for the area.

Inverkirkaig Falls and Suilven

A car park at the south end of Inverkirkaig, three miles south of Lochinver, marks the start of a **walk** upriver to **Falls of Kirkaig**, itself the start of a long but gentle walk to the base of **Suilven** – its huge sandstone dome is as much of a landmark today as it was for Viking sailors. Serious hikers use the path as an approach to scale the peak (10–12hr), but you can also follow it for an easy five-mile, three-hour (return) ramble, taking in a waterfall and a secluded loch.

ARRIVAL AND INFORMATION   LOCHINVER AND AROUND

By bus Lochinver may be large by local standards, but connections are not great.

Destinations Ullapool (Mon–Sat 2 daily; 1hr).

Tourist information There's no longer a tourist office here, so consult ⓦ discoverassynt.co.uk.

ACCOMMODATION AND EATING

Some of the local accommodation is in a conjoined village, **Baddidarrach**, on the north side of the loch; from Lochinver, cross the bridge and turn left. On selected dates between April and October, the village hall hosts an excellent craft and produce market (ⓦ madeinassynt. co.uk), which is well worth attending if you can't make one of the restaurants.

An Cala Café & Bunkhouse Lochinver harbour ☏ 01571 844598, ⓦ ancalacafeandbunkhouse.co.uk. The former seamen's mission by the harbour houses a cosy hostel and great café serving the likes of battered monkfish scampi (£11.95) or tandoori veggie masala (£9.95). It has fourteen beds in three modern dorms – spotless if a bit tight for space in the six-bed – plus a good kitchen and laundry facilities. May–Sept Mon–Sat 8am–9pm; Oct–April Wed & Thurs 9am–5pm, Fri & Sat 9am–7.30pm; Dorms £25, doubles £45

Inver Lodge Signed off Main St, Lochinver ☏ 01571

844496, ⓦ inverlodge.com. Refurbishment of a hillside hotel has created a five-star (and very expensive) stay, featuring relaxed contemporary decor with a nod to Highlands country style and loch views. The latter are at their best from the restaurant, an outpost of *Chez Roux*, with French-inspired seafood dishes like pan fried grey mullet with sauce *vierge* (£21.50); there's also a cheaper lunchtime bar menu (steak sandwiches, £10) April–Oct daily noon–2.30pm & 7–9.30pm. £300

Lochinver Larder Main St, near bridge ☏ 01571 844356, ⓦ piesbypost.co.uk. Sensational home-made pies, including exotics like wild boar and saag paneer, have made it famous, but this fine bistro prepares other food too: think smoked fish linguini, home-made fishcakes (both £13.95) or langoustine in lime, ginger and chilli butter (£20). Takeaway available. Easter–Oct Mon–Sat 10am–7.45pm, Sun 10am–5.30pm; Nov–March daily 10am–4pm.

North of Lochinver

There are two routes **north** from Lochinver: the fast A837 along the shore of Loch Assynt (see below) to join the A894, or the scenic B869 coast road. Hugging the indented shoreline, the latter offers coastal views, superb **beaches** and high cliff walks. The first village worth a detour is **ACHMELVICH**, four miles northwest of Lochinver, where a tiny bay cradles a white-sand beach lapped by azure water. It's popular (relatively speaking), but there are equally seductive beaches up the coast, including a tiny, hidden cove, **Port Alltan na Bradhan**, a mile north, plus a beautiful strand at **CLACHTOLL** a couple of miles beyond.

WALKS IN COIGACH AND ASSYNT

Ordnance Survey Explorer map 442

Of Coigach's and Assynt's spectacular array of idiosyncratic peaks, **Stac Pollaidh** (2011ft) counts as the most accessible and popular hike – so much so that the path is often repaired and re-routed up the mountain from a car park on the Achiltibuie Road. It now leads walkers around the northern side of the hill before climbing steeply. You'll need a head for heights on the jagged summit ridge – turn back from the summit if you feel uncertain about basic rock-climbing.

Suilven (2398ft) is the most memorable of the Assynt peaks – "one sandstone chord that holds up time in space", said poet Norman McCaig of its weird sugar-loaf profile. The ascent is a tough eight-hour trip that starts with a boggy five-mile walk to the base. From the A837 at Elphin, head around the north of Cam Loch then through the glen between Canisp and Suilven, to pick up a path that aims for the saddle – Bealach Mor – in the middle of Suilven's summit ridge, from where the path to the top is straightforward. The return is by the same route, although at the saddle you could choose to turn southwest for the route to Inverkirkaig.

The highest peaks in Assynt are **Conival** (3238ft) and **Ben More Assynt** (3274ft), often climbed as Munros (see page 41) even though they're less distinctive than their neighbours, and are known for their bleak landscapes. The route follows the track up Glen Dubh from Inchnadamph; stay to the north of the river and aim for the saddle between Conival and the peak to the north, Beinn an Fhurain. On the ridge, turn southeast to climb to the summit of Conival then east along a high ridge to the top of Ben More. The entire walk, including the return to Inchnadamph, takes five to six hours.

For something less testing there are some classic **coastal walks** immediately north of Lochinver. From **Baddidarrach**, a path with fantastic views of the Assynt peaks leads over heather slopes to Loch Dubh and down to **Achmelvich** (1hr). From here there's a sporadically signposted but reasonable path to **Clachtoll** (about 2hr) past delightful sandy coves, grassy knolls, old watermills and rocks at low tide. More dramatic still is the ninety-minute clifftop circuit from Stoer lighthouse to the famous stack, **The Old Man of Stoer**.

Old Man of Stoer

A side road that branches north off the B869 between **STOER** and **CLASHNESSIE** ends abruptly by a lighthouse at **Raffin**. The reason to come is a two-mile stroll along a boggy track to reach the **Old Man of Stoer**, a 197ft rock stack just off the Point of Stoer, the headland's tip, surrounded by sheer cliffs and occasionally scaled by climbers. It's worth a circuit around the south side of the headland to return with a vast view of the mountains of Assynt, after which you'll deserve a cuppa in the tea van at the car park (April–Sept Mon–Fri & Sun 11am–5pm, except in high winds and heavy rain).

ACCOMMODATION AND EATING   **NORTH OF LOCHINVER**

Achmelvich Beach Youth Hostel Achmelvich ☎ 01571 844480, ⓦ hostellingscotland.org.uk. Although the open-plan lounge-kitchen of this 20-bed hostel (eight- and five-bed dorms plus a private twin) in a former school and cottage struggles when full, most people are outside anyway – just 100yds away are the white sands of the beach. April–Sept. Dorms £22, twin £55

Clachtoll Beach Campsite Clachtoll ☎ 01571 855377, ⓦ clachtollbeachcampsite.co.uk. This simple, neat site at the heart of the crofting village is all about its location right behind one of the most appealing stretches of powder white sand on the west coast. Easter–Sept. Per pitch £19

Loch Assynt and around

Bounded by peaks of the Ben More Assynt massif, the area inland from Lochinver is a wilderness of mountains, moorland, mist and scree. Anglers love it because of the brown trout in its lochs and lochans, while the toothy remains of **Ardveck Castle**, a MacLeod stronghold from 1597 that fell to the Seaforth Mackenzies after a siege in 1691, add romance. The region's other claim to fame is **Knockan Crag** (Creag a' Chnocain; ⓦ knockan-crag.co.uk), eleven miles south of Loch Assynt on the A835 to

Ullapool, one of the world's most important geological sites. In 1859 geologist James Nicol came up with the theory of thrust faults from its geology. Two interpretive **trails** (15min and 1hr) highlight the movement of rock plates for novices and there's information on the area in an unstaffed **visitor centre**.

Kylesku and around

Until a road bridge swept over the mouth of lochs Glencoul and Glendhu, **KYLESKU**, 33 miles north of Ullapool, was the embarkation point for a ferry that was the only link from the west Highlands to north Scotland. Off the main road since the bridge's construction in 1984, it's now a beautiful, soporific spot, where interlocking slopes plunge into the deep waters. Marking a last hurrah before the Assynt's sharp sandstone gives way to rounded quartzite, Kylesku is popular with walkers due to its proximity to **Quinag** (2651ft), less a single peak than several peaks reached by a **ridge walk**. The easiest ascent is from a car park on the A894 a few miles south of Kylesku. Also in the area is Britain's highest waterfall, **Eas a Chùal Aluinn** (650ft), at the head of Loch Glencoul. It's five miles return east of a car park two miles south of Kylesku or a full day on a track around the north side of both lochs. Alternatively, boat tours run from the wharf.

ARRIVAL AND INFORMATION

KYLESKU AND AROUND

By bus D&E Coaches' (☎01463 222444) summer-only service from Inverness to Durness via Ullapool stops at Kylesku. It can carry bikes with a reservation (mid-May to Sept Mon–Sat 1 daily).

Destinations Inverness (late May to Sept 1 daily Mon–Sat, plus Sun 1 daily in July & Aug; 4hr); Lochinver (same times; 30min).

Tourist information The North West Highlands Geopark visitor centre and café, *The Rock Stop* (April–Oct daily 10am–4.30pm; ☎01971 488765; ☯nwhgeopark.com), is based in the old Unapool School Building; as well as loads of great information, there's an exhibition on the region's geology and a super little café with stunning views from its big windows.

ACTIVITIES

Tours Run by the *Hotel Kylesku*, Kylesku Boat Tours offers gentle cruises into lochs Glendhu and Glencoul (April, May & Sept 11am daily; June–Aug 11am & 1pm daily; round trip 1hr 45min; £30; ☎01971 502231, ☯kyleskuboattours.com).

ACCOMMODATION AND EATING

Kylesku Hotel Kylesku ☎01971 502231, ☯kylesku hotel.co.uk. A small hotel of crisp, modern style beside the loch, with rooms in the main building and a handful more in a newer wing called "Willy's Hoose", some of which have a private balcony and loch views. The very accomplished restaurant provides by far the best food in the area, all sourced locally – from the vegetables to the seafood; expect the likes of hake fillet with pea puree and pickled mussels (£19.95) and venison haunch. Restaurant 8–10am & noon–9pm; bar noon–11pm. Feb–Nov. __£120__

The far northwest coast

The **far northwest coast** in Sutherland is a trip too far for some, but those who make the journey will find that this area captures the stark, elemental beauty of the Highlands like nowhere else. Here, as the geology shifts into ice-scoured pinkish quartzite barely covered by a thin skin of moorland, peaks become more widely spaced and settlements smaller and fewer, linked by twisting roads and shoreside footpaths. Up here, life feels exhilaratingly on the edge of civilization. The flip side is that accommodation and food are sparse; be prepared that places get booked up fast in season and the options are thin on the ground during the winter.

Scourie and around

Ten miles north of Kylesku, **SCOURIE** lies among a landscape marbled with lochs and lochans. This is prime Scottish **fly-fishing** territory; permits (£5–20) are available from the Fishing Tackle Shop in the garage (Mon–Fri 9am–1pm & 2–5.30pm; ⓦscouriefillingstation.uk). There's also some terrific **walking** hereabouts up mountains like Ben Stack (2359ft) – locals yarn that its pyramidal peak inspired a visiting Hollywood executive to create the logo for Paramount Pictures – and a beautiful beach makes it a good choice for families.

Handa Island

Managed by the Scottish Wildlife Trust (ⓦ scottishwildlifetrust.org.uk) • No charge to visit, but donations encouraged • Ferries operate April–Sept Mon–Sat 9am–2pm (the last ferry back to the mainland is at 5pm), every 20–30min (£15) • ☎ 07780 967800

Reason enough to come through Scourie is **Handa Island**, the huge chunk of red Torridon sandstone just offshore. Carpeted with machair and purple heather, the island is maintained as a **wildlife reserve** by the Scottish Wildlife Trust and supports one of the largest seabird colonies in northwest Europe – razorbills and Britain's largest breeding colony of guillemots on ragged sandstone cliffs during summer, and puffins in clifftop burrows from late May to mid-July. Until the mid-nineteenth century, Handa supported a community of crofters who survived on fish, potatoes and seabirds and devised their own government system, with a "queen" (Handa's oldest widow) and male "parliament" who met each morning. Uprooted by potato famine in 1847, most villagers emigrated to Cape Breton, Canada.

Ferries shuttle regularly in summer from **Tarbet**, a six-mile drive north of Scourie. When you arrive on Handa Island you will be greeted by a volunteer, who offers an introductory talk on the history and ecology of the island. Allow three hours at least to follow a **footpath** around the island – an easy and enjoyable walk taking in Great Stack, a 361ft rock pillar on the north shore, and fine views across the Minch.

ARRIVAL AND DEPARTURE   **SCOURIE AND AROUND**

By bus Scourie is on the summer-only bike-carrying Inverness–Durness service of D&E Coaches (☎01463 222444) via Ullapool and Lochinver (mid-May to Sept Mon–Sat 1 daily). Durness Bus (☎01971 511223) runs from Lairg to Durness, stopping at Scourie (Mon–Fri).

Destinations Durness (Mon–Sat 1 daily; 1hr); Inverness (late May to Sept Mon–Sat 1 daily, plus Sun 1 daily in July & Aug; 4hr 10min); Lochinver (same times; 50min); Ullapool (same times; 1hr 10min).

ACCOMMODATION AND EATING

Scourie Caravan and Camping Park Scourie ☎01971 502060, ⓦscouriecampsitesutherland.com. Spread behind the beach, this well-maintained site provides sea views to go with its flat pitches and tidy amenities block. On-site café-bar, *The Anchorage* (daily May–Sept 8am–10pm), rustles up food and drinks and has a lounge area in case of bad weather. April to early Oct. Per pitch __£16__

Scourie Hotel Scourie ☎01971 502396, ⓦscouriehotel. com. A traditional, family-run coaching inn whose fishing obsession only adds character. There are taxidermied trout in the wood-panelled cocktail bar, real ales in the public bar, and enormous maps of Scotland in the entrance

hall. Themed Highlands headboards are a nice touch in the simple, elegant rooms. Seasonal four-course dining menu for £32, or bar meals like fish and chips from £12. A memorable stay. April–Sept. __£150__

★ **Shorehouse** Tarbet wharf ☎01971 502251, ⓦshorehousetarbet.co.uk. With its views of pristine shore, Handa and the Old Man of Stoer beyond, this feels like the restaurant at the end of the world. Nautical and airy inside, serving home-made soups and sandwiches, plus mains of salmon, hot mackerel and seafood platters, around £13. Couldn't be much fresher – they catch their own shellfish. Easter–Sept Mon–Sat noon–7pm.

Kinlochbervie

North of Scourie, the road sweeps through the Highlands at its starkest – rocks piled on rocks, bog and water, and a bare, stony coastline that looks increasingly inhospitable. For some that's a call to adventure: sailor and adventurer John Ridgway established an outdoor school on an isolated sea loch off **Loch Laxford** in the 1960s. The largest settlement here, reached on the B801, is **KINLOCHBERVIE**, where a huge fish market and harbour reveal this as the premier fishing port in the area, reduced in stature since its heyday in the late 1980s, but still serviced by trucks from all over Europe. Otherwise it's a scruffy, utilitarian place, usually visited only as a launchpad for Sandwood Bay (see below).

ARRIVAL AND DEPARTURE · KINLOCHBERVIE

By bus Kinlochbervie is on the summer-only Inverness– Durness service of D&E Coaches (☏ 01463 222444) via Ullapool and Lochinver (mid-May to Sept Mon–Sat 1 daily).

Destinations Durness (40min); Scourie (30min); Ullapool (1hr 50min).

ACCOMMODATION AND EATING

Old School Restaurant and Rooms Inshegra, 1 mile before Kinlochbervie on B801 ☏ 01971 521383, ⓦ oldschoolklb.co.uk. By far the most comfortable accommodation option in the area, with a handful of rather smart rooms, including a cute separate en-suite single. Guests are treated to good-value evening meals of home cooking: expect haddock chowder, cullen skink, venison casserole or veggie lasagne (£13–16). **£75**

Sandwood Bay

A single-track road continues northwest of Kinlochbervie through **OLDSHOREMORE**, an isolated crofters' village above a stunning white-sand beach (a magic spot to wild camp), then on to **BLAIRMORE**, start of the four-mile walk to **Sandwood Bay**. The shell-white **beach** beyond the peat moors is one of the most beautiful in Scotland, flanked by rolling dunes and lashed by gales for much of the year. Vikings beached their longships here over a millennium ago – the name is a corruption of "sand" and "vatn", meaning sand and water. Good luck with them both if you decide to wild camp here.

It's possible to trek overland from Sandwood Bay north to Cape Wrath (see page 248), the northwestern tip of mainland Britain, a full day's walk away. If you're planning to meet the Cape Wrath minibus to Durness (see page 248), contact them first since it won't run if the weather turns bad.

The north coast

For years, very few visitors would travel the length of Scotland's isolated, wild north coast. Those who did get this far would most likely head for John O'Groats, take a photo, have a cuppa then head back. But these days the north coast has become a destination in its own right. The soaring popularity of the North Coast 500 route (see page 216) has brought an influx of tourers – cyclists, drivers, caravans and all – to Scotland's rugged northern shore, and few go home disappointed. This gorgeous stretch of road is backed by steep mountains in the west and by lochs and open rolling grasslands in the east, while between them is mile upon mile of crumbling cliffs, sheer rocky headlands and perfect white beaches that are nearly always deserted except for intrepid surfers who come for the best waves in Scotland. Visit between January and March and there's a chance you might witness the Northern Lights, too.

Wee **Durness** is a good jumping-off point for **Cape Wrath**, the windswept promontory at Scotland's tip which has retained an end-of-the-world mystique lost long ago by John O'Groats. Continuing east, **Tongue** enjoys an attractive setting and a Munro to climb nearby, while **Thurso**, the largest town on the north coast, is acclaimed by surfers. For everyone else it's a gateway to some of Scotland's most populous seabird colonies around **Dunnet Head** and **Duncansby Head**.

Durness and around

Scattered over sheltered sandy coves and grassy clifftops, **DURNESS** is the most northwesterly village on the British mainland, straddling the point where the road swings from peat bogs to the fertile limestone machair of the north coast. The village sits above Sango Sands bay, whose fine beach has made it a modest resort. Beatle **John Lennon** came here as a teenager on family holidays to stay with his Auntie Lizzie (Elizabeth Parkes) – his memories later went into the song *In My Life*, and he revisited in 1969 with Yoko. Parkes is buried in the graveyard at Balnakeil, and there is a slightly bizarre memorial to Lennon at the Durness Village Hall which still attracts a trickle of die-hard Beatles fans throughout the year.

Smoo Cave

1 mile east of Durness • Always open; tours daily: April, May & Sept 11am–4pm; June–Aug 10am–5pm • Free (tours £6) • ☎ 01971 511492, ⓦ smoocavetours.weebly.com

A mile east of the village is **Smoo Cave**, a gaping hole in a limestone cliff created by the sea and a small burn. Tucked at the end of a narrow sea cove, the main chamber is accessible via steps from the car park. The much hyped rock formations are quite impressive and if you wish to see more, then between April and September you can join twenty-minute tours into two further caverns led by a member of the Scottish Caving Association; note that advance bookings are not possible and if it has been raining, tours may not be run so do call in advance.

Balnakeil

A mile northwest of Durness, the white sands of **Balnakeil Bay** are stunning in any weather, but especially spectacular when sunny days turn the sea a brilliant Mediterranean turquoise. A path winds north through the dunes behind to reach **Faraid Head** – fine views east to the mouth of Loch Eriboll and west to Cape Wrath make this circuit (3–4hr) the best in the area. While here, drop by the Balnakeil Craft Village, a hippie commune borne out of a disused 1970s military camp (see below).

Cape Wrath

Closer to Iceland than to London, the headland takes its name not from stormy seas but from the Norse word *hvarf* ("turning place"), a throwback to the days when Viking warships passed en route to raid the Scottish coast. Yet **Cape Wrath** still exudes a powerful sense of nature in the raw. The British mainland's most northwesterly point – and one of only two capes in the country – is tipped by a Stevenson lighthouse and stands above **Clo Mor cliffs**, the highest sea cliffs in Britain and a prime breeding site for seabirds. On a clear day you'll gaze out to Orkney and the Outer Hebrides.

The surprise is that Cape Wrath is so easily reached on a day-trip from Durness. The journey begins two miles southwest at **Keoldale**. A foot-passenger **ferry** crosses the Kyle of Durness estuary to link with a **minibus** for the fourteen-mile run to Cape Wrath and the *Ozone* café at the lighthouse (open daily year-round; ☎ 01971

THE FAR NORTH PROJECT

In the midst of the Cold War, the Ministry of Defence built an early warning station up in this lonely, blustery corner of Scotland. It was never commissioned, and when the Sutherland District Council failed to sell the units to local businesses, the "Far North Project" was born. In the early 1960s artists and craftspeople moved into the village, paying an annual rent of just £5, and Scotland's first hippie commune was born. Fifty years on, Balnakeil Craft Village continues to thrive. The free-spirited mentality remains intact, although these days the village contains a mix of private residences and small businesses, including ceramicists, potters and woodturners; most of the businesses are open from Easter till September.

511314). With two to three days to spare, you could catch the ferry (the running of which is very much weather dependent) then walk a circuit to Sandwood Bay, catching a bus back to Durness from Kinlochbervie. There's a basic free bothy at Kearvaig. Note that the Ministry of Defence maintains Garvie Island (An Garbh-eilean) as an air bombing range and so occasionally closes the road to Cape Wrath. At the time of research the Durness Development Group (ⓦcommunitylandscotland. org.uk) was raising funds to purchase the 110 acres of land surrounding the lighthouse at Cape Wrath.

ARRIVAL AND DEPARTURE
DURNESS AND AROUND

DURNESS
By bus Public transport is sparse; the key service is the D&E Coaches (mid-May to Sept Mon–Sat 1 daily). It goes from Inverness (4hr 15min) via Ullapool (2hr 25min) and Scourie (1hr 5min) and has a cycle carrier.

CAPE WRATH
By ferry and minibus The foot-passenger ferry from Keoldale runs from Easter to Oct (in theory daily at 11am, plus June–Aug 9am; £7.50 return; ⓣ07719 544207); call to confirm tides and Ministry of Defence schedules. It drops you on the opposite bank of the kyle to connect with a minibus to Cape Wrath (£13 return).

INFORMATION AND ACTIVITIES

Tourist office In the absence of a tourist office consult ⓦvisitcapewrath.com.
Golf Durness golf course (ⓣ01971 511364, ⓦdurness golfclub.org), the most northwesterly course on mainland

Britain, is a nine-hole with two tee-off options per hole to create 18 holes (£20). Closed to visitors Sun morning, equipment rental from clubhouse (from £5).

4

ACCOMMODATION AND EATING

DURNESS
Lazy Crofter Bunkhouse ⓣ01971 511202, ⓦvisit durness.com/bunkhouse. Run year-round by *Mackay's* next door, this is the finest bunkhouse on the north coast, far more appealing than the hostel by Smoo Cave. Has a snug cabin atmosphere and gets extra marks for individual reading lights in compact twins and two dorms, the hostel sleeping twenty in total. Well equipped kitchen, bike storage and drying room. The terrace has sea views. __£22__
★ **Mackay's** ⓣ01971 511202, ⓦvisitdurness.com/rooms. Handmade and vintage furniture, luxury linen, natural colours and genuine hospitality make this one of the best stays on the north coast. It also manages weekly self-catering options: from a sweet cabin to carbon-negative Croft 103's eco-chic. No dinners, but they compensate for it with superb breakfasts, plus nibbles and wine in the evenings. May–Sept. __£149__
Sango Sands Oasis ⓣ01971 511726, ⓦsangosands. com. This flat, spacious site spreads over cliffs above the turquoise waters of its namesake offering the most spectacular views; try and bag a cliff edge pitch if you can.

The adjoining pub is now the only place in Durness serving dinner, hence is usually rammed, with hearty bar standards from £10–16.50. Free out of season, though cold-water showers only. April–Oct. Per person __£9__

BALNAKEIL
Cocoa Mountain Balnakeil Craft Village ⓣ01971 511233, ⓦcocoamountain.co.uk. "The Best Hot Chocolate", a rich bitter-sweet hot chocolate topped off by white chocolate, is the speciality in the bright modern café of this chocolatier. There's much more besides though, including sweet and savoury tarts, and chocolates and truffles made on site. A real treat after time in the wilds. March–Oct daily 9am–6pm.

CAPE WRATH
Daill Camping Pods Daill beach ⓣ01971 511314. Cape Wrath's first non-bothy accommodation offering. A couple of basic camping pods (both doubles) with outdoor kennels for hardy companions. £6 extra for bedding, cooking equipment and crockery. __£22__

Tongue to Thurso
Vast and empty, the landscape between Tongue and Thurso has considerable drama. It's a bleak moorland intercut with sandy sea lochs and with few inhabitants: tiny **Tongue** is pleasant enough, as is **Bettyhill**, further east. But the

real reason to venture this far is the landscape: a dead-end **coast road** west of Tongue; **Ben Hope** (3040ft), the most northerly Munro; or the blanket bog of the **Flow Country** inland.

Tongue and around

Having taken a slow, circuitous route around Loch Eriboll and east over the moors of A'Mhoine, you roll finally into the pretty crofting township of **TONGUE**. Dominated from a hillside spur by the ruins of **Castle Varrich** (Caisteal Bharraich), a medieval stronghold of the Mackays (three-mile return walk), the village is strewn above the east shore of the **Kyle of Tongue**, which you can cross either via a causeway or by a longer and more scenic single-track road around its southern side. When the tide recedes, this shallow estuary becomes a mass of golden sand flats, superb on sunny days, with the sharp profiles of **Ben Hope** (3040ft) and **Ben Loyal** (2509ft) looming like twin sentinels to the south, and the Rabbit Islands a short way out to sea. A dead-end road offers views of the islands, plus superb seascapes and scenery as it threads through Talmine towards a beach at **Strathan**; take the left turn to Melness before Tongue causeway.

ACCOMMODATION AND EATING — TONGUE AND AROUND

Ben Loyal Tongue ☎ 01847 611216, �🌐 benloyal.co.uk. Seafood fresh off the owner's boat is served in a relaxed pub along with favourites such as haggis bon bons in peppercorn sauce, and venison pie. With decent prices (mains £11–17) and live music most Saturdays, this is the choice of many locals. Daily 11.30am–3pm & 5–11.30pm; food served noon–2.30pm & 6–9pm.

Kyle of Tongue Hostel & Holiday Park East of Kyle of Tongue Bridge ☎ 01847 611789, �🌐 tongue hostelandholidaypark.co.uk. The Duke of Sutherland's old shooting lodge has been repurposed as a large, well-equipped hostel with spacious dorms and family rooms, plus great mountain views. Extensive facilities include kitchen, lounge, laundry, bike shed and shop. Mid-April to Sept. Dorms **£19**, twins **£44**

Tongue Hotel Tongue ☎ 01847 611206, �🌐 tonguehotel. co.uk. This nineteen-bedroom small hotel marries relaxed modern taste with the architectural heritage of a former ducal hunting lodge. There are antiques in the best rooms, even the odd marble washstand, and spacious proportions throughout. The Superior rooms are worth the extra £20. Closed Jan to mid-Feb. **£120**

NORTH-COAST WALKING AND CYCLING

Ordnance Survey Explorer maps 447 & 448

Rising up from the southern end of the Kyle of Tongue, Ben Hope and Ben Loyal offer moderate-to-hard walks, rewarded on a decent day by vast views over the empty landscape. **Ben Hope** (3040ft), which was given its name ("Hill of the Bay") by the Vikings, is the most northerly of Scotland's Munros – they say that from its summit at the summer equinox, the sun never vanishes entirely beneath the horizon. It's surprisingly accessible – the best approach is a four-hour round trip from the road that runs down the west side of Loch Hope. Start at a sheep shed by the roadside, just under two miles beyond the southern end of Loch Hope.

Ben Loyal (2506ft), though lower, is a longer hike at around six hours. To avoid the worst of the bogs, follow the northern spur from Ribigill Farm, a mile south of Tongue. At the end of the southbound farm-track, a path emerges; follow this up a steepish slope to gain the first peak on the ridge from where the walking to the top is easier.

For **shorter walks** or **cycles**, there are well-marked woodland trails at **Borgie Forest**, six miles west of Tongue, and **Truderscraig Forest** by Syre, twelve miles south of Bettyhill on the B871. Near the entrance to Borgie Forest is the *a'chraobh*, a spiral feature created using native trees and carved local stone. If you follow the signs to "**Rosal Pre-Clearance Village**", a stop on the Strathnaver Trail (see page 251), you'll find an area clear of trees with what little remains of the village – fifteen families were evicted between 1814 and 1818. Information boards explain the crofters' lifestyles in the eighteenth century before the upheavals of the Highland Clearances.

JACOBITES IN THE KYLE OF TONGUE

The Kyle of Tongue was the location of the naval engagement reputed to have sealed the fate of Bonnie Prince Charlie's **Jacobite rebellion** in 1746. In response to pleas for help from the prince, the King of France dispatched a sloop, *Hazard*, and £13,600 in gold coins to Scotland. However, the Jacobite ship was spotted by the English frigate HMS *Sheerness* and fled into the Kyle, where it was forced aground. Pounded by English cannons, the Jacobite crew slipped ashore at night in an attempt to smuggle the treasure to Inverness. However, the rebels were ambushed by the anti-Jacobite MacKay clan, and threw the gold into **Lochan Hakel**, southwest of Tongue. On the prince's behest, Lord Cromartie sent 1500 men to rescue the treasure. They too were defeated and taken prisoner. Historians still debate whether the extra men might have altered the outcome of the Battle of Culloden three weeks later. The gold, meanwhile, was recovered later. Or most of it – they say cows still wander out of the loch's shallows with gold pieces stuck in their hooves.

Bettyhill and around

Twelve miles east of Tongue, **BETTYHILL** is a major crofting village, set among rocky green hills. In Gaelic it was known as *Am Blàran Odhar* ("Little Dun-coloured Field"). The origins of the English name are unknown, but it was definitely not named after Elizabeth, Countess of Sutherland, who presided over the Strathnaver Clearances whose sorry tale is told in the town museum. The village is also surrounded on either side by beautiful beaches: **Farr beach**, a splendid crescent of white sand, is behind the museum, while the unbroken arc of **Torrisdale Bay** sweeps west of the town beyond the Naver River. Both receive good surf. For more cerebral stuff, the 24-mile **Strathnaver Trail** runs south along the B873 to Altnaharra, past historical sites from the Neolithic, Bronze and Iron Age periods, as well as the remains of crofting villages cleared in the early 1800s. Free printout area guides are available from the museum (donations welcome).

Strathnaver Museum

In the old Farr church, east of the main village • April–Oct Mon–Sat 10am–5pm • £3 • ✆ 01971 521418, ⓦ strathnavermuseum.org.uk

The volunteer-run **Strathnaver Museum** houses exhibits of ethnological and archeological interest – crofting items including a bizarre fishing buoy made from a dogskin, Pictish stones and a 3800-year-old early Bronze Age beaker – and also narrates the Sutherland Clearances through a short film. Its most famous item is free to view – the **Farr stone**, a ninth-century engraved Pictish gravestone, is in the west end of the graveyard.

| ACCOMMODATION AND EATING | BETTYHILL AND AROUND |

Bettyhill Hotel Main road ✆ 01641 521202, ⓦ bettyhill hotel.com. Two-hundred year old coaching inn sporting twenty contemporaneously furnished, individually-designed rooms plus the excellent *Eilean Neave restaurant*, which serves up Scottish dishes like Highland chicken in a whiskey cream sauce (mains £15–22); you can also get more pub-style grub in the convivial bar which also hosts live, folksy music. Restaurant 6–9pm; bar 11am–11pm. **£85**

Thurso

THURSO feels like a metropolis after the wild west. In reality it's a modest administrative service centre, most of whose visitors only pause before catching the ferry to Orkney from its port, **Scrabster**. Yet it makes a good base for the area and is legendary among British **surfers**, drawn to a wave which barrels off a reef just east of the harbour. One of the most powerful waves in Europe, "Thurso East" is not a break for beginners.

The town's name derives from the Norse word *Thorsa*, literally "River of the God Thor", and in Viking times this was a major gateway to the mainland. Later, ships set sail for the Baltic and Scandinavian ports loaded with meal, beef, hides and fish. Much

THE FLOW COUNTRY

A detour inland on the A897 east of Bettyhill towards Helmsdale heads south into the **Flow Country** tundra. The name (pronounced to rhyme with "now") derives from *flói*, an Old Norse word meaning "marshy ground", and this 1544-square-mile expanse of "blanket bog" – the largest in the world, says UNESCO, which has it filed under "possible" on its World Heritage status list – is both a valuable carbon sink and a home to a wide variety of birdlife. The RSPB's **Forsinard Flows Visitor Centre** (Easter–Oct daily 9am–5pm; free; ☎01641 571225, ⓦrspb. org.uk/forsinard), at the train station in **FORSINARD**, is the gateway to the so-called Forsinard Flows. Pick up a leaflet then follow the mile-long **Dubh Lochan Trail**. Follow the boardwalk to the Flows Lookout Tower before walking over flagstones to learn about its blanket bog. En route, you get to see bog asphodel, bogbean, and insect-trapping sundew and butterwort; you've also got a good chance of spotting greenshanks, golden plovers and hen harriers. During the summer, the visitor centre runs **guided walks** through the area to explain the wonders of peat; wellies or walking boots are recommended.

of the town, however, dates from the 1790s, when Sir John Sinclair built a large new extension to the old fishing port. Consequently, Thurso's grid-plan streets have some rather handsome Victorian architecture in local, greyish sandstone, not least the recently refurbished **Thurso Library**, opened in 1862 as the Miller Institute and complete with clocktower and a pillared facade. There's little sign of the town's older roots, except for **Old St Peter's Church** up the High Street, a substantial ruin with origins in the thirteenth century. Sadly, the town's once excellent museum has also closed.

4

ARRIVAL AND DEPARTURE   THURSO

By train Trains to Thurso leave from Inverness and go up the east coast via Lairg. The following services are all Mon–Sat 4 daily, Sun 1 daily.
Destinations Inverness (3hr 50min); Lairg (2hr 5min); Wick (30min).
By bus Buses depart from the train station, Olrig St and Sir George's St.

Destinations Inverness (4–5 daily; 3hr); John O'Groats (Mon–Fri 6–10 daily, Sat 5 daily; 1hr); Wick (Mon–Fri 8–10 daily; 35min).
By ferry NorthLink ferries (ⓦnorthlinkferries.co.uk) operate ferries to Stromness, Orkney (2–3 daily; 2hr 15min), from Scrabster, a mile west of town, linked by buses from the train station.

ACTIVITIES

North Coast Watersports Dunnet Campsite (☎07982 649635, ⓦnorthcoastwatersports.com. Offers equipment rental, including boards (£20/day), wetsuits (£20/day), and boots and gloves (£5/day), as well as 2hr lessons (£30).

ACCOMMODATION   SEE MAP PAGE 253

Forss House Hotel 5 miles west of Thurso on A836 ☎01847 861201, ⓦforsshousehotel.co.uk. Built in 1810 as a hunting lodge, this fourteen-bedroom hotel offers an upmarket stay, with a choice of traditional accommodation in the main house or more modern rooms in annexes. The Forss River, which wends through the grounds, offers fine salmon fishing. **£145**
The Marine 38 Shore St ☎01847 890676, ⓦthemarine thurso.co.uk. Modern furnishings and tweed headboards make for a relaxed, contemporary style in this lovely little hotel comprising five rooms. More appealing than the rooms, though, is the small conservatory off the gorgeous breakfast room with sea views – surfers take note. **£99**
Pennyland House B&B West of Town on A9 ☎01847 891194, ⓦpennylandhouse.co.uk. Thurso's best B&B, each of the six rooms here is named after a Scottish golf course,

and retains has its own character, whether it be a sea view or an eighteenth-century fireplace. King-size beds, excellent breakfast and en-suites seal the deal. In a nice touch of history, the house happens to be the birthplace of Sir William Alexander Smith, founder of the Boys Brigade. **£90**
Sandra's Backpackers Hostel 24–26 Princes St ☎01847 894575, ⓦsandras-backpackers.co.uk. The only hostel in town is a clean enough, zero-frills but well-run place with four-bed dorms, triples and en-suite doubles. Kitchen, lounge and laundry facility. Dorms **£20**, doubles **£46**
Thurso Bay Camping & Caravan Park Scrabster Terrace ☎01847 892244, ⓦthursobaycamping.co.uk. Large, trim site a 5min walk west from the town centre. As well as views to Dunnet Head and Orkney, it has an on-site coffee shop/diner and a laundry. Mid-April to Sept. Per pitch **£17.50**

EATING

SEE MAP PAGE 253

★ **Captain's Galley** Harbour, Scrabster ☎01847 894999, ⊛captainsgalley.co.uk. Fish fresh off the boat is the speciality – razor clams in vegetable vermouth, and queen scallops with quails eggs and sweet chilli are typically exciting dishes that form part of an ever-inventive menu that win awards for sustainability as much as flavour. Reservations essential. Easter–Oct Thurs–Sat 6.30–10pm.

Tempest Café Thurso Harbour ☎01847 892500. Home baking, toasties and home-made burgers (£5–8) served in a harbourside café with a laidback surf-shack vibe: think surf newspaper cutouts, colourful surfboards and driftwood art on the walls. Bring-your-own drinks on Saturday evenings during the summer (£3 corkage). May–Sept daily 10am– 7.30pm. April–Dec Mon–Fri 10am–6pm, Sat 10am– 8pm, Sun 10am–4pm; Jan–March daily 10am–4pm.

Y Not Bar and Grill Meadow Lane ☎01847 892272. Rock'n'roll memorabilia, sizzling steaks (£19–25) and stacked burgers for under a tenner in this split-level diner and live-music venue (gigs weekends only). Daily 8.30am– late.

Dunnet and around

Despite the publicity given to John O'Groats, the most northerly point of mainland Britain is actually **Dunnet Head** four miles north of the sleepy village of **DUNNET**. Here there's not a great deal to do beyond popping in to Britain's most northerly micro-

THURSO

■ ACCOMMODATION	
Forss House Hotel	2
The Marine	4
Pennyland House B&B	3
Sandra's Backpackers Hostel	5
Thurso Bay Camping & Caravan Park	1

● EATING	
Captain's Galley	1
Tempest Café	2
Y Not Bar and Grill	3

4

distillery, the Dunnet Bay Distillers (☎01847 851287, ⓦdunnetbaydistillers.co.uk) – who are to thank for the fantastic Rock Rose gin and Holy Grass vodka; between mid-March and November, distillery tours (£15) take place at 11am & 2pm Monday to Saturday. It's an evocative spot up at the Dunnet Head, covered in heather and bog and plummeting in red cliffs at the headland, marked by a Stevenson lighthouse, and with the whole north coast spread out before you from Cape Wrath to Duncansby Head on a clear day.

Dunnet Bay

Just south of Dunnet lies **Dunnet Bay**, a vast, golden beach backed by huge dunes. Surfers come for a smattering of reef breaks plus a beach break that offers shelter for beginners depending on whereabouts on the bay you tuck in. At the northeast end of the bay, the **Seadrift Visitor and Ranger Centre** (May–June & Sept Mon, Tues, Thurs, Fri & Sun 2–5pm; July–Aug from 10.30am; free; ☎01847 821531) holds an exhibition about the fauna of the northwest coast and ecology of its sand dunes. It also stocks information leaflets on local history and nature walks.

Mary-Ann's Cottage

South end of Dunnet • June–Sept daily 2–4.30pm • £3 • ☎01847 851765

Signposted off the through road in Dunnet, **Mary-Ann's Cottage** is a farming croft vacated in 1990 by the then 93-year-old Mary-Ann Calder, who eventually passed away in 1996, aged 98. Her grandfather built the cottage and today it is maintained as she left it, full of mementos of the three generations who lived and worked there over 150 years. With its antique rocking chair before a blackened hearth, still with its old metal teapot, and family photos, it's a very intimate portrait of a recent past that already feels distant.

Castle of Mey

5 miles east of Dunnet • May–lateJuly & early-Aug–Sept daily 10.20am–4pm • £11.95, gardens & grounds only £6.50 • ☎01847 851473, ⓦ castleofmey.org.uk

The handful of houses that make up the village of Mey whizz past in a moment – yet it was here that the late Queen Mother had her Scottish home. The original **Castle of Mey** was a sixteenth-century Z-plan affair, owned by the earls of Caithness until 1889, and bought in a state of disrepair in 1952, the year the Queen Mother's husband, George VI, died. She spent her summer holidays here each August, which may help explain why it's a modest wee place, unstuffy inside despite the facade that bristles with turrets. The walls are hung with works by local amateur artists and watercolours by Prince Charles (who still visits in late July, when it's closed for two weeks), and personal mementos of the Queen Mum remain on show – guides are more than happy to explain their significance. The **gardens** outside are a lovely spot for an amble on a sunny day, not least for their views across the Pentland Firth.

ARRIVAL AND DEPARTURE   DUNNET AND AROUND

By bus Bus #80 between Thurso (stops at train station and Olrig St) and John O'Groats passes through Dunnet and Mey (Mon–Fri 8–9 daily, Sat 6 daily).

ACCOMMODATION AND EATING

Castle Arms Hotel Mey ☎01847 851244, ⓦcastlearms hotel.co.uk. A simple but comfortable stay almost opposite the castle entrance whose seven en suite rooms – including a family suite and a room for disabled persons – represent very good value. The restaurant prepares good pub grub such as Scrabster haddock with chips, and Highland chicken with haggis (mains £12–14). April–Oct daily 6–10pm. **£90**

Dunnet Bay Caravan Club Dunnet Bay ☎01847 721319, ⓦcaravanclub.co.uk. On the plus side are the position behind the dunes and immaculate facilities. The bad news is it's geared to motorhomes and is expensive due to a £12 surcharge for non-Caravan Club members. March–Oct. Per pitch **£31**

John O'Groats and around

Snap-happy tourists, windswept pilgrims and knackered cyclists convene at **JOHN O'GROATS**, the most northeasterly settlement on mainland Britain. Consisting of a car park, a souvenir village and not much else, the place has never quite lived up to its folkloric name, although a recent regeneration project has brought some new life to the place with the opening of a technicoloured seafront hotel and a sparkly new café. There are plenty of prettier places to see the sea in north Scotland, but as one end of the Land's End to John O'Groats tour, there's always a happy flow of people either beginning or ending a life-affirming journey here.

Duncansby Head

Marked by a lonely square-towered lighthouse and spectacular cliffs, **Duncansby Head** is the actual northeastern point of mainland Britain, and offers the edge-of-the-world experience that you might have hoped for at John O'Groats, two miles west. The birdlife here is prolific – fulmars, razorbills, puffins, guillemots and kittiwakes in their thousands – and south of the headland lie spectacular 200ft-high cliffs, cut by sheer-sided clefts known locally as *geos*, and several impressive sea stacks. Ask nicely at the tourist information office and somebody might be able to take you on a free guided tour.

ARRIVAL AND INFORMATION   JOHN O'GROATS AND AROUND

By bus John O'Groats has regular bus services from Thurso (Mon–Fri 6–10 daily, Sat 5 daily; 1hr) and Wick (Mon–Fri 7 daily, Sat 5 daily; 50min).

By ferry The John O'Groats passenger ferry (☎01955 611353, ⓦjogferry.co.uk) sails to Burwick, Orkney (May & Sept 2 daily, June–Aug 3 daily; 45min; £24 return). It also offers afternoon cruises around the seabird colonies and stacks of Duncansby Head or the Atlantic grey seal colonies of Stroma (mid-June to Aug daily 2.30pm; 1hr 30min; £19).

Tourist office Beside the main car park (March–Oct daily 9am–5pm; ☎01955 611373, ⓦvisitjohnogroats.com).

ACCOMMODATION AND EATING

The Inn at John O'Groats ☎01955 698583, ⓦtogether travel.co.uk. A multi-million-pound regeneration has brought a tired old seafront hotel back to life as *The Inn at John O'Groats*, with neat self-catering apartments and a brightly coloured, Scandi-style extension to boot; there are also 23 high-spec wooden lodges facing out to sea. Their *Storehouse Café* offers sandwiches, pizzas and the like (£6.50–10), great coffee (best enjoyed in front of the log burner), or champagne for those with something to celebrate. Daily: Easter–May 9am–5pm, June–Oct 8am–7pm, Nov–Easter 9am–5pm. **£185**

The Black Isle and around

The **east coast** of the Highlands is nowhere near as spectacular as the west, and feels more lowland than highland. Heading north from Inverness, you're soon into the **Black Isle** – not an island at all, but a peninsula whose rolling hills, prosperous farms and deciduous woodland make it more reminiscent of Dorset or Sussex than the Highlands. It probably gained its name because of its mild climate: there's rarely frost, which leaves the fields "black" all winter. Another explanation is that the name derives from the Gaelic word for black, *dubh* – a possible corruption of St Duthus.

The Black Isle is littered with **prehistoric sites**, but the main incentive to detour east off the A9 is **Cromarty**, a picturesque fishermen's town that is arguably the highlight of the entire Highlands' east coast. There are, though, plenty of other villages – Fortrose and Rosemarkie among them – that are well worth a visit, while this is also a fabulous spot for dolphin-spotting.

Fortrose and Rosemarkie

FORTROSE, ten miles northeast of Inverness, is a quietly elegant village dominated by the beautiful ruins of a once huge, early thirteenth-century **cathedral** (open access) founded by King David I. It languishes on a pretty green bordered by red-sandstone and colourwashed houses. **ROSEMARKIE** a mile on is equally appealing, with its neat high street of stone houses and a terrific little museum. On sunny days local families descend on the sandy beach, where a cheap-and-cheerful caff has picnic benches looking out to sea. Further along the coast at **Chanonry Point**, roughly midway between Rosemarkie and Fortrose, crowds gather daily to spot **dolphins**, this being home to the northernmost colony of bottlenose dolphins in the world; do check tide times ahead of a visit though. Because of the crowds that descend here, parking (£3) can be tricky, but in July and August there's a free shuttle bus between Fortrose, Rosemarkie and Chanonry Point.

Groam House Museum

High St, Rosemarkie • April–Oct Mon–Fri 11am–4.30pm, Sat & Sun 2–4.30pm • Free • ☎ 01381 620961, ⓦ groamhouse.org.uk

At the lower end of Rosemarkie's high street, **Groam House Museum** displays fifteen intricately carved **Pictish standing stones** (among them the famous Rosemarkie Cross Slab) dating from as early as the eighth century. It also screens a video that highlights other sites in a region that was a stronghold of Pictish culture – a primer to tempt any history buff into a visit to Portmahomack. There's also a harp to pluck, and kids can "build their own" digital Rosemarkie Stone and print it out.

By bus Stagecoach bus #26 from Inverness to Cromarty stop at both Fortrose and Rosemarkie (Mon–Sat every 30min, Sun 6 daily; 30–35min).

ACCOMMODATION

★ **Fortrose Bay Campsite** Wester Greengates ☎ 01381 621927, ⓦ fortrosebaycampsite.co.uk. This superbly-run campsite has neat grassy pitches, somewhat unusually, positioned either side of a (not very busy) through road, and while this doesn't detract from its appeal, you'd do well to try and bag a waterfront spot. Facilities are excellent, and the hospitable owners are a font of local knowledge. April–Oct. Per pitch £25

Cromarty

An appealing jumble of handsome Georgian townhouses and pretty workers' cottages knitted together by a cat's-cradle of lanes, **CROMARTY**, the Black Isle's main settlement, is simply a joy to wander around. An ancient ferry crossing on the pilgrimage trail to Tain, it became a prominent port in 1772, fuelling a period of prosperity that gave Cromarty some of the Highlands' finest Georgian houses. The railways poached that trade in the nineteenth century – a branch line to the town was begun but never completed – but the flip side of stagnation is preservation. Out of town, there's a fine four-mile circular coastal **walk**: leave town to the east on Miller Road and turn right when the lane becomes "The Causeway". For a simpler shoreline walk, turn left here, following the path to the water.

Cromarty Courthouse

Church St • April–Oct daily noon–4pm • free; donations welcome • ☎ 01381 600418, ⓦ cromarty-courthouse.org.uk

The streets are gorgeous, but to help bring Cromarty's past alive try this child-friendly **museum** in the old **Courthouse**, which tells the history of the courthouse and town using audiovisuals and slightly haunting "talking" mannequins in period costume. You are also issued with an audio handset and a map for an excellent **walking tour** around the town.

Hugh Miller's Birthplace Cottage and Museum

Church St • Late March–Sept daily noon–5pm; Oct Tues, Thurs & Fri noon–5pm • £6.50; NTS • ☎ 01381 600245, ⓦ hughmiller.org

Cromarty's most celebrated son is **Hugh Miller**, a nineteenth-century stonemason turned author, journalist, geologist, folklorist and Free Church campaigner. His thatched cottage **birthplace** has been restored to give an idea of what Cromarty must have been like in his day, with decor that swings between cosy rustic and rather formal Victoriana, and displays that highlight his efforts as a social reformer. The building now housing the **museum** was built by his father, though in the event Miller only lived here for three years. On display are a handful of personal effects, including his desk, mallet and shepherd's plaid (he was a prolific walker), as well as a mourning brooch containing a lock of his hair. Upstairs you'll find a collection of his fossils, though the majority of these are on display in the National Museum in Edinburgh. Friendly staff and a pretty garden make this a most enjoyable visit. Useful if you want to delve further still into Miller's life, the free *Hugh Miller Cromarty Trail* leaflet guides you to important spots around the village.

ARRIVAL AND DEPARTURE   CROMARTY

By bus Stagecoach bus #26 runs from Inverness main bus station (Mon–Sat every 30min, Sun 5 daily; 50min).

ACTIVITIES

EcoVentures Off Bank St, next to Sutor Creek ☎ 01381 600323, ⓦ ecoventures.co.uk. Between April and October sails from the harbour in a powerful RIB out through the Sutor stacks to the Moray Firth to see the resident bottlenose dolphins and other wildlife up to three times daily (2hr; £31).

ACCOMMODATION AND EATING

Royal Hotel Marine Terrace ☎ 01381 600217, ⓦ royalhotel-cromarty.co.uk. On the seafront just behind the harbour, this traditional inn provides fairly bland but perfectly acceptable rooms which overlook the Firth. Superiors provide the most character through a mix and match of antique furnishings and more modern decor. One of two options for a pint in town. Mon–Fri 11am–11pm, Sat & Sun till 1am. **£90**

★ **Sutor Creek** 21 Bank St ☎ 01381 600855, ⓦ sutorcreek.co.uk. A lovely café-restaurant full of laidback seaside charm that focuses on local and seasonal food, whether light lunches (£10–12) or excellent dinners like Shetland scallops with pork belly and baby leeks (£24). The same ethos carries into wood-fired pizzas (£12–14), best washed down with Cromarty Brewery beers. A gem. May–Sept daily 10am–9pm; Oct–April Wed 5–9pm & Thurs–Sun 11am–9pm.

Sydney House High St ☎ 01381 600451, ⓦ sydneyhouse.co.uk. Antique wood or wrought-iron beds and pretty dressing tables are typical of the furnishings picked up over the years by the owners to lend character to the three en-suites in their smart redbrick house just off High St. The best rooms look out over the rear gardens. **£80**

Strathpeffer

Visitors first came to this leafy Victorian spa town to take the waters. In the 1970s and 1980s they arrived with coach tours to wallow in its faded glamour. Now **STRATHPEFFER** is restyling itself again as a place for activities in the surrounding hills, with a focus – ironically – on "wellbeing" that sees it return to its origins as a renowned European **health resort**. All manner of guests disembarked from the *Strathpeffer Spa Express* train: George Bernard Shaw, Emmeline Pankhurst (who caused a scandal with a lecture on women's rights) and Franklin and Eleanor Roosevelt on honeymoon.

Renovation has transformed the town's Victorian grand hall into an arts centre and upgraded the adjacent **Upper Pump Room** (April–Sept Mon–Sat 10am–5pm, Sun 1–5pm; donation), where displays narrate the spa town's fascinating history.

For all the appeal of the town's faded grandeur, it's the hills that will make you stay. Within striking distance is **Ben Wyvis**, an approachable Munro usually scaled without complication from **GARBAT**, six miles west of Strathpeffer, in five hours. Another excellent hike in the area is up Cnoc Mor hill, where the Iron Age hillfort of **Knock Farril** affords superb panoramic views to the Cromarty Firth and surrounding mountains.

WALKS AND RIDES AROUND STRATHPEFFER

Ordnance Survey Explorer map 437

From the southern end of Strathpeffer, a two- to three-hour walk leads to the remains of a vitrified Iron Age fort at **Knock Farril**. The first part of the walk is through woodland; after a mile, turn up onto the ridge above and follow it northeast along the crest of the hill known as the Cat's Back. The trees thin out to offer great views of the Cromarty Firth as you reach the hillfort. Before you get to the ridge is **Touchstone Maze**, built as a local arts project in 1992 – its eighty stones are intended to represent the rock types of the Highlands. A path also leads directly to the maze from near the old train station in Strathpeffer.

The **Rogie Falls** are two miles north of Contin on the main A835 to Braemore. They're well signposted and it's a short walk from the car park to where the Black Water froths down a stretch of rocks and mini-gorges, in one place plunging 26ft. Salmon leap upriver in high summer, particularly at a fish ladder built next to the toughest rapids. A suspension bridge over the river leads to some waymarked forest trails, including a five-mile loop to **View Rock**, at a point only 160ft above sea level, but which has great views of the local area. Contin Forest holds several fun **mountain-bike trails** too, including a rooty, rocky, red-grade ten-mile track.

The most ambitious hike in this area is up **Ben Wyvis**, a huge mass of mountain just north. The high point is Glas Lethad Mor (3432ft), which means, rather prosaically, "Big Greenish-Grey Slope". The most common route is through Garbat Forest, leaving the road just south of Garbat itself, staying on the north bank of the Allt a'Bhealaich Mhoir stream to get onto the southwestern end of the long summit ridge at the minor peak of An Cabar.

ARRIVAL AND GETTING AROUND   STRATHPEFFER

By bus Stagecoach bus #27 from Inverness drops passengers in the town square (Mon–Sat hourly, Sun 5 daily; 50min).

Bike rental The excellent Square Wheels (☎ 01997 421000, ⊛ squarewheels.biz; closed Sun & Mon) on the main square rents out bikes and offers good advice on local trails.

ACCOMMODATION AND EATING

Craigvar The Square ☎ 01997 421622, ⊛ craigvar. com. As central as it gets, this B&B provides two beautifully furnished rooms and a suite, all with great outlooks and some thoughtful touches like fresh fruit and decanters of sherry. Good breakfasts set you up for a day in the hills and a relaxing atmosphere to settle into afterwards **£110**

Red Poppy Main St ☎ 01997 423332, ⊛ redpoppy restaurant.co.uk. Bright, modern bistro serving up well-manicured dishes like lamb cutlets on colcannon with minted hollandaise, and hand dived scallops on a cauliflower risotto and pea puree. Good value lunch, High Tea, and early evening (5–6pm) menus too. Tues–Sat 11.30am–8.30pm, Sun 12.30–3pm.

The Dornoch Firth and around

For centuries, visitors on the pilgrim trail to the **Fearn peninsula** came from the south by ferry from Cromarty. Nowadays the area north of **Dornoch Firth** is linked by the A9, skirting past the quiet town of **Tain**, best known as the home of Glenmorangie whisky, and the neat town of **Dornoch** itself, an unexpected pleasure known for its cathedral and golf courses.

Tain

There's a sense of having arrived somewhere as you swing through the handsome buildings of central **TAIN**. Reputedly Scotland's oldest Royal Burgh, it was the birthplace of **St Duthus**, an eleventh-century missionary. Many a medieval pilgrim came to venerate his miracle-working relics enshrined first in a sanctuary then in fourteenth-century **St Duthus Collegiate Church**. James IV visited annually, usually fresh from the arms of his mistress, Janet Kennedy, whom he had installed in nearby Moray.

Tain Through Time

Tower St • April–Oct Mon–Fri 10am–5pm, June–Aug also Sat & Sun 10am–5pm • £3.50 • ☎ 01862 894089, ⊛ tainmuseum.org.uk

Installed in three buildings of St Duthus church and graveyard, the town museum, **Tain Through Time**, is a good place to gen up on the Fearn peninsula's Pictish past and Tain's pilgrimage history, the latter taking in King James's guilty conscience. The dressing-up box is handy if you have kiddies to entertain, and the ticket price includes an audio **walking tour** of the town (set aside twenty minutes). The same ticket gets you into a neighbouring **museum** with a dry display of Tain silver, alongside clan memorabilia.

Glenmorangie Distillery

On the A9, 1 mile northwest of Tain • Tours June–Aug daily 10am–4pm every 30min, April–May & Sept–Oct Mon–Sat 10am–3pm hourly, Nov–March 10am or 2pm by appointment; shop Mon–Fri 10am–5pm, April–Oct also Sat 10am–4pm, June–Aug also Sun noon–4pm • £7 (book ahead) • ☎ 01862 892477, ⊛ glenmorangie.com

Whatever the history, Tain's most popular attraction is the **Glenmorangie Distillery**. Tours of the whisky distillery and warehouses explain the alchemic process that ferments mashed malt, distils the liquid in Scotland's tallest stills then matures it in oak casks to create a delicate, vanilla-y malt. There's a dram or two to finish, naturally. Die-hard whisky aficionados should consider the more comprehensive tasting session on the Signet Tour (£35).

ARRIVAL AND DEPARTURE   TAIN

By train Tain is on the Inverness–Thurso Far North Line (6 daily; Inverness, 1hr 10min; 4 daily Thurso 2hr 35min).

By bus Stagecoach east coast buses from Inverness to

Thurso (#X99) stop in Tain (Mon–Sat 3–5 daily; Sun 4 daily; Inverness 50min; Thurso 2hr 15min).

ACCOMMODATION

Golf View House 13 Knockbreck Rd ☎ 01862 892856, ⊛ bedandbreakfasttain.co.uk. Just south of the centre, this former manse offers a lovely B&B stay in its five rooms. Decor is relaxed contemporary Scottish with a touch of romance and en-suite bathrooms are excellent. Factor in fine views to the Dornoch Firth and full Scottish breakfasts. **£85**

Portmahomack and around

The fishing village of **PORTMAHOMACK**, strung out around a curving sandy beach, is a surprise after the rolling fields of the **Fearn peninsula** east of Tain. Though all but empty nowadays, this was a heartland of eighth-century Picts before Viking raids became too much.

Tarbat Discovery Centre

Tarbatness Rd • April–Sat 2–5pm; May Mon–Sat 10am–5pm; June–Sept Mon–Sat 10am–5pm, Sun 2–5pm; Oct daily 2–5pm • £4 • ☎ 01862 871351, ⊛ tarbat-discovery.co.uk

Archeological digs in the church at the edge of the village have unearthed sculpted artefacts, including some fine gravestones decorated with Celtic animals or mythical beasts, all well presented in the church as the **Tarbat Discovery Centre**. It marks the first stop on a trail of other Pictish sites south on the peninsula – pick up their handy leaflet to locate other standing stones, including those at Hilton and Shandwick.

Tarbat Ness

North of Portmahomack lies **Tarbat Ness**, a gorse-covered point with one of the tallest lighthouses in Britain at its tip. Come for sea views and a seven-mile stroll (2–3hr round trip). The **walk** heads south from Tarbat Ness for three miles, following a narrow passage between the cliffs and foreshore, to the hamlet of Rockfield. A road leads past fishermen's cottages to Portmahomack to rejoin the road back to the lighthouse.

ARRIVAL AND DEPARTURE   PORTMAHOMACK AND AROUND

By bus Buses from Tain, Lamington St, go east to Portmahomack (Mon–Fri 6 daily; 20min), and to Shandwick,

Hill and Fearn (Mon–Fri 7–8 daily, Sat 5 daily).

4

ACCOMMODATION AND EATING

Caledonian House Main St, Portmahomack ☎ 01862 870169, ⊛ caledonian-house.co.uk. Exposed bricks, log-burner and pastel blue and white tones in the bistro, decked out with local artwork and serving the likes of Moroccan spiced salmon (£11.70) and Sunday roasts. The three en-suite rooms have enormous beds, and there are sea views over the breakfast table. Thurs 11am–7pm, Fri & Sat 11am–3pm & 6–10pm, Sun 11am–3pm. __£75__

Oystercatcher Main St, Portmahomack ☎ 01862 871560, ⊛ the-oystercatcher.co.uk. This pretty place in a harbour-side cottage prepares bistro lunches, then dinner menus specializing in seafood, including a cheeky house Bloody Mary – crab with spiced tomato frappé with a zing of vodka; two courses £35.50. Bed and outstanding breakfast is available in three pretty en-suites above. Reservations recommended. Wed–Sat 6.30–11pm, Sun 12.30–3pm. __£112__

SHOPPING

Anta Fearn ☎ 01862 832477, ⊛ anta.co.uk. While you're in the area, pay a visit to Fearn village (signposted) for the workshop outlet of Anta, manufacturer of contemporary fine tweeds and tartans plus pottery and homeware; entertain the kids on a rainy day with painting mugs. Daily 10am–4pm.

Bonar Bridge and around

The A9 across the Kyle of Sutherland has left **BONAR BRIDGE** out on a limb. Yet in the fifteenth century this was a heart of industry because of a large iron foundry. James IV passed through and was so shocked to find the forest virtually clear-felled that he ordered oak saplings to be planted – the ancient woodland east of Bonar Bridge dates from this era. Several miles of **mountain-biking trails** run through nearby Forestry Commission woodland, blue and black grade at Balblair two miles north, and blue and red beneath Carbisdale Castle (see below).

Croik

CROIK is well worth a detour for its humble **church**, which illuminates the tragedy of the Clearances. Evicted from their homes in 1845, ninety villagers from Glencalvie took shelter in the churchyard and scratched poignant messages on the east window of the church. Inside is a facsimile of a contemporary report of their plight by a *Times* journalist.

Carbisdale Castle

A daunting neo-Gothic pile northwest of Bonar Bridge, **Carbisdale Castle** was erected between 1906 and 1917 for the dowager Duchess of Sutherland; it is designed in three styles to give an impression of long heritage. It was eventually acquired by a Norwegian shipping magnate in 1933 until gifted with all its marble statues and gilt mirrors to the SYHA as one of the most opulent **hostels** in the world. The duchess would've been livid. However, protracted expensive repairs saw it closed for years, and in March 2016 it hit the newspapers when it was put on the market for £900,000 before it was duly snapped up by a private investor.

A SCOTTISH SAFARI PARK

The Clearances, rampant forestry and sheep-grazing have conspired to change much of the Highlands beyond recognition. Though not, perhaps, permanently, believes **Paul Lister**, a millionaire entrepreneur turned conservationist who hopes to return the great Caledonian woodland that existed two thousand years ago to his estate near Croik. His high-profile plan to reintroduce predators such as **wolves**, **bears** and **lynx** ran up against local opposition when he bought the £3.2m, 23,000-acre estate in 2003, yet the **Alladale Wilderness Reserve** (☎ 01863 755338, ⊛ alladale.com) has enjoyed some success as a conservation project. Alongside a **reforestation** programme, it nurtures iconic **Highland species** such as red and roe deer, red squirrel, Scottish wildcats, otters and golden eagles as well as reintroduced elk and bison. The estate is run as a Scottish safari park for well-funded guests or groups and provides activities such as fly-fishing, 4WD tours, pony trekking, or survival camps set up by adventurist Bear Grylls. If you're interested in its conservation programme, call to see if you can join a group tour with a ranger.

Lairg and around

North of Bonar Bridge, the A836 parallels the River Shin to **LAIRG**, scattered at the eastern end of **Loch Shin**. It's predominantly a transport hub, with little of interest unless your visit coincides with the annual lamb sale in mid-August, one of the largest one-day markets in Europe.

Falls of Shin

4 miles south of Lairg • Visitor centre daily 10am–5pm • ☎ 01549 402888

The reason to come this way is the **Falls of Shin** in Achany Glen, one of the best places in Scotland to see **salmon** leap on their upstream migration between March and November. Rebuilt anew following a fire in 2013, the superb wood-clad **visitor centre** has outdoor information panels documenting the Falls, as well as the lifecycle of the salmon, and inside a smart café/restaurant and shop; if you don't fancy eating there, there's a pleasant picnic area adjoining a children's playground. From the visitor centre, a short path winds its way down to a viewing platform above the falls, where a 12ft cascade is on the cusp of the maximum leap for fish, so most end up tumbling back into the river; the best time to view this remarkable spectacle is late summer/early autumn.

Dornoch

DORNOCH, a genteel, villagey town eight miles north of Tain, lies on a headland overlooking the **Dornoch Firth**. Blessed with good looks and a sunny climate (by Scottish standards) and surrounded by sand dunes, it has morphed into a modest upmarket resort: all antiques shops and fine accommodation in the historic sandstone centre, one of Scotland's most prestigious **golf courses** plus miles of sandy beaches just outside.

The Cathedral

Castle St • Visitor times mid-May–mid-Sept Mon–Fri 10am–4pm; services Sun 11am • ☎ 01862 810296, ⓦ dornoch-cathedral.com

Dating from the twelfth century, Dornoch became a royal burgh in 1628. Pride of place among its oldest buildings grouped around the square is the imposing **Cathedral**, founded in 1224 and built of local sandstone. The original was horribly damaged by marauding Mackays in 1570, and much of what you see today was restored by the Countess of Sutherland in 1835, though the worst of her Victorian excesses were removed in the twentieth century, when the interior stonework was returned to its original state. The stained-glass windows in the north wall were later additions. The counterpart to the cathedral is the fortified sixteenth-century **Bishop's Palace** opposite, now refurbished as a hotel.

Historylinks

The Meadows • April–Oct daily 10am–4pm: Nov–March by appointment • £4 • ☎ 01862 811275, ⓦ historylinks.org.uk

A block behind the Bishop's Palace on the high street, **Historylinks** is a small museum which tells the story of Dornoch, from local saints and the last witch burning in Scotland, which occurred here in 1727, to the history of the local Royal Dornoch golf course; look out for a beautiful cast iron illuminated clock that once graced the tower of the clubhouse. Around the village, the signposted Historylinks Trail takes you on a tour around Dornoch's historic sights.

ARRIVAL AND DEPARTURE
DORNOCH

By bus Stagecoach's Inverness–Thurso service (via Helmsdale) stops at Dornoch.

Destinations Inverness (5 daily; 1hr 10min); Thurso (Mon–Sat 4 daily, Sun 3 daily; 1hr 45min).

INFORMATION AND ACTIVITIES

Tourist office In the courthouse building next to the Dornoch Castle Hotel (Mon–Fri 9am–6pm, plus Sat June– Aug and Sun July & Aug, same hours; ☎ 01862 810594, ⓦ visitdornoch.com), this is one of few tourist offices in the region, and accordingly has loads of info.

Royal Dornoch Golf Club Golf Rd ☎01862 810219, ⓦroyaldornoch.com. Opened four hundred years ago, this golf club maintains a par 70 Championship links course (£180 April–Sept, £100 rest of year), rated among the world's best by many golf media, and the easier par 71 Struie course (£50). Booking is essential to play. Note that it has a dress code of no T-shirts (except polo shirts).

ACCOMMODATION AND EATING

2 Quail Castle St ☎01862 811811, ⓦ2quail.com. What it lacks in size this three-room B&B makes up in traditional country character and charm. Decor is beautiful, featuring tartan fabrics and paint shades of mossy green and soft mustard, old pine furnishings and oil paintings by local artists. The owner is a chef so breakfasts are excellent, and two- or three-course dinners are available on request. **£120**

Dornoch Castle Hotel Castle St ☎01862 810216, ⓦdornochcastlehotel.com. This smart hotel has modern spacious superior rooms with pillow chocolates and whisky miniatures or comfy but somewhat bland garden-facing rooms; for a splurge though, choose the fabulous historic deluxe rooms in the turreted tower of the Bishop's Palace. Fine dining available in the *Grant MacNicol at the Castle* restaurant (venison loin with artichoke puree, Scrabster halibut with iced vegetables and seaweed spaghetti), as well as a well-stocked

whiskey bar. They've even got their own whiskey distillery on site, housed inside the old fire station building. Bar: daily noon–11pm; Restaurant: daily noon–2pm & 6.30–9pm. **£140**

Luigi's 1 Castle St ☎01862 810893, ⓦluigidornoch. com. A modern metropolitan-styled bistro focusing on soups, ciabattas and pizzas for lunch, and in the evenings upscale mains (£12–18) like seared scallops with pancetta, and loin of lamb with minted pea puree. Lunch daily 11am–2pm; dinner Easter–Oct Sat & Sun 6.45–9pm, & daily during peak months.

Trevose Cathedral Square ☎01862 810269. Centrally placed directly opposite the *Dornoch Castle Hotel* but at a fraction of the price of its neighbour, this detached nineteenth-century B&B swathed in roses beside the cathedral is all warm golds and creams in its two rooms, decorated with country style. May–Sept. **£66**

North to Wick

North of Dornoch, the A9 hugs the coast for most of the sixty miles to **Wick**, the principal settlement in the far north of the mainland. The most telling landmark in the stretch is the **Sutherland Monument** near Golspie, erected to the first duke of Sutherland, the landowner who oversaw the eviction of thousands of tenants during the Clearances. That bitter memory haunts the small towns and villages of this stretch, including **Brora**, **Dunbeath**, **Lybster** and pretty **Helmsdale**. Nonetheless, many of these settlements went on to flourish through a thriving fishing trade, none more so than Wick, once the busiest herring port in Europe.

Golspie and around

Ten miles north of Dornoch the A9 rolls through the red-sandstone town of **GOLSPIE**. It's a pleasantly bustling if fairly forgettable place, and for most visitors serves only as a gateway to good mountain-bike trails or the grandest castle of this coastline.

Dunrobin Castle

A9, 1 mile north of Golspie • Daily: April, May & Oct 10.30am–4.30pm; June–Sept 10am–5pm • £12 • ☎01408 633177, ⓦdunrobincastle.co.uk

Mountain-biking aside, the reason to stop in Golspie is to tour the largest house in the Highlands, **Dunrobin Castle**, north of the centre. Modelled on a Loire chateau by Sir Charles Barry, the architect behind London's Houses of Parliament, it is the seat of the Sutherland family, once Europe's biggest landowners with a staggering 1.3 million acres. They were also the driving force behind the Clearances here – it's worth remembering that such extravagance was paid for by evicting thousands of crofters.

Only a tenth of the 189 furnished rooms are visited on tours of the **interior**, as opulent as you'd expect with their fine furniture, paintings (including works by Edwin Landseer, Allan Ramsay and Sir Joshua Reynolds), tapestries and objets d'art. Alongside, providing a venue for falconry displays (11.30am & 2pm daily), the attractive **gardens** are pleasant to wander en route to Dunrobin's **museum**, housed in the former summerhouse and the repository of the Sutherlands' vulgar hunting trophies – heads and horns on the walls plus displays of everything from elephants' toes to rhinos' tails – and ethnographic holiday souvenirs from Africa.

The last extravagance is that the castle has its own **train** station (summer only) on the Inverness–Wick line; no surprise, considering that the duke built the railway.

The Sutherland Monument

Approaching Golspie, you can't miss the **monument** to the first duke of Sutherland on the summit of **Beinn a'Bhragaidh** (Ben Bhraggie). A 30ft-high statue on a 79ft column, it bears an inscription which recalls its creation in 1834 by "a mourning and grateful tenantry [to] a judicious, kind and liberal landlord", and quietly overlooks the fact that the duke forcibly evicted fifteen thousand crofters from his million-acre estate. The stiff **climb** to the monument (round trip 1hr 30min) provides vast coast views, but the steep path is tough going and there's little view until the top. Head up Fountain Road and pass (or park at) Rhives Farm, then pick up signs for the Beinn a'Bhragaidh footpath (BBFP).

ARRIVAL AND DEPARTURE   **GOLSPIE AND AROUND**

By bus Stagecoach's Inverness–Thurso service stops at Golspie.
Destinations Inverness (Mon–Sat 5 daily, Sun 4 daily; 1hr 25min); Thurso (Mon–Sat 5 daily, Sun 4 daily; 1hr 35min).

By train Dunrobin Castle is a summer stop on the Inverness–Thurso line (April–Oct Mon–Sat 3 daily; 2hr 15min from Inverness, 1hr 35min from Thurso).

ACTIVITIES

Highland Wildcat Trails (ⓦ highlandwildcat.com) have information on the area's black-, red- and blue-graded mountain-biking trails, including a huge single-track

descent from the summit of Ben Bhraggie to sea level. All trails are accessed from the end of Fountain Rd.

4

ACCOMMODATION AND EATING

Coffee Bothy Fountain Rd ☏ 01408 633022. A cabin-style café popular with bikers and walkers. Fill up on all-day breakfasts, fresh soups and ciabattas beforehand (£4–5), and reward yourself with home baking afterwards. Feb–Dec Mon–Fri 9am–4pm, Sat 10am–4pm.
Sleeperzzz Rogart, 8 miles west of Golspie ☏ 01408

641343, ⓦ sleeperzzz.com. Sleep in the quirkiest accommodation for miles around, namely a first-class railway carriage parked in a siding beside the Inverness–Thurso line; there's also a 1950s goods van (sleeping two) and a B&B (sleeping three) occupying the old waiting room. Carriage and van March–Sept only Per person **£20**, B&B **£69**

Helmsdale

HELMSDALE is one of the largest villages between Golspie and Wick. It's certainly the most picturesque: a tight little grid of streets set above a river-mouth harbour. Romantic novelist Barbara Cartland was a frequent visitor and must have looked as exotic as a flamingo in its grey stone streets. For all its charm, it's a newcomer, founded in the nineteenth century to house the evicted inhabitants of Strath Kildonan, which lies behind it, and which subsequently flourished as a herring port.

Timespan Heritage Centre

Dunrobin St • Mid-March–Oct daily 10am–5pm; Nov–mid-March Tues noon–4pm, Sat & Sun 10am–3pm • £4 • ☏ 01431 821327, ⓦ timespan.org.uk

Good looks and sleepy ambience aside, the appeal of Helmsdale is the **Timespan Heritage Centre** beside the river. An ambitious venture for a place this size, the modern museum tells the story of Viking raids, crofting in re-created houses, the Kildonan Gold Rush, the Clearances, and fishing through high-tech displays, a movement sensor to navigate animations of local yarns, and audio-tours. It also has an art gallery-and-café serving up soups and cakes, with lovely views out to the river.

By train On the Inverness–Thurso line (4 daily; 2hr 35min from Inverness, 1hr 10min from Thurso).

Tourist information Strath Ullie Crafts on the harbour doubles as a source of tourist information (Mon–Sat 10am–5.30pm; ☎ 01431 821402, ⓦ helmsdale.org).

ACCOMMODATION AND EATING

Helmsdale Hostel Stafford St ☎ 07971 516287, ⓦ helmsdalehostel.co.uk. Superbly renovated hostel in the old school gymnasium now offering six en suite rooms each sleeping four people (two bunks); self-catering kitchen, lounge, cycle shed and drying facilities. April–Oct. Dorms __£25__

La Mirage 7–9 Dunrobin St ☎ 01431 821615, ⓦ lamirage.org. Not quite "The North's Premier Restaurant" as it claims, but possibly the most bizarre due to the tastes in decor of a former proprietor who styled herself after Barbara Cartland. The menu, although as dated as Babs herself, is solid: fish or scampi and chips, gammon steaks, even chicken Kiev (mains £10–12). Daily 11am–9pm.

Dunbeath and around

The landscape becomes wilder north of Helmsdale. Once over the long haul up the **Ord of Caithness** – a steep hill which used to be a major obstacle and is still blocked by snowstorms – the scenery switches from heather-clad moors to treeless grazing lands, dotted with derelict crofts and dry-stone walls.

Dunbeath

DUNBEATH was another village founded to provide work in the wake of the Clearances, laid along the glen beside the river. The local landlord built a harbour at the river mouth in 1800, at the start of the herring boom, and the settlement briefly flourished. It now suffers the indignity of an A9 flyover soaring over much of the village.

The novelist Neil Gunn was born in one of the terraced houses under the flyover and his tale is told in the **Dunbeath Heritage Centre** (April–Sept Mon & Fri 10am–4pm, Wed 10am–1pm, other times by appointment; £2.50; ☎ 01593 731233, ⓦ dunbeath-heritage.org.uk) alongside exhibits of local Pictish and Viking history, plus a painted river on the floor featuring quotes from Gunn's *Highland River*.

Laidhay Croft Museum

Easter–Sept Mon–Sat 9am–5pm • £3 • ☎ 07563 370231

Just north of Dunbeath is the simple **Laidhay Croft Museum**, housed in an eighteenth-century longhouse which incorporated dwelling, stable and byre. Restored from a ruin in 1971, its re-creation of life in the early 1900s offers a useful riposte to the often over-romanticized life of a Highlander before the Clearances.

Lybster and around

Another neat planned village, **LYBSTER** (pronounced "libe-ster") was established at the height of the nineteenth-century herring boom. Two hundred boats once worked out of its picturesque small harbour, a story told in the **Waterlines** heritage centre here (May–Oct daily 11am–5pm; £2.50 donation requested, ☎ 01593 721520) – there are modern displays about the "silver darlings" and the fishermen who pursued them, plus a smokehouse and a café.

Seven miles north of Lybster, the **Grey Cairns of Camster** are the most impressive of the prehistoric burial sites that litter this stretch of coast. Surrounded by moorland, these two enormous reconstructed burial chambers were originally built five thousand years ago with corbelled dry-stone roofs in their hidden chambers. A few miles further north on the A99, the 365 uneven **Whaligoe Steps** lead steeply down to a natural harbour surrounded by high cliffs.

Wick

Since it was founded by Vikings as *Vik* (meaning "bay"), **WICK** has lived by the sea. It's actually two towns: Wick proper and, south across the river, **Pultneytown**, created by the British Fisheries Society in 1806 to encourage evicted crofters to take up fishing. By the mid-nineteenth century, Wick was the busiest herring port in Europe, with a fleet of more than 1100 boats exporting fish to Russia, Scandinavia and the West Indian slave plantations. The demise of its fishing trade has left Wick down at heel, reduced to a mere transport hub. Yet the huge harbour in Pultneytown and a walk around the surrounding area – scruffy rows of fishermen's cottages, derelict net-mending sheds and stores – gives an insight into the scale of the former fishing trade.

Wick Heritage Centre

Bank Row, Pultneytown • Easter–Oct Mon–Sat 10am–5pm, last entry 3.45pm • £4 • ☎ 01955 605393, ⊛ wickheritage.org

The volunteer-maintained **Wick Heritage Centre** is the best place to evoke the heyday of the fishing boom. Deceptively labyrinthine, it contains a fascinating array of artefacts from the old days, including fully rigged boats, boat models and reconstructed period rooms, plus a superb archive of photographs from the Johnstone Collection captured by three generations of a local family between 1863 and 1975.

Old Pulteney Distillery

Huddart St • May–Sept Mon–Fri 10am–5pm, Sat 10am–4pm; Oct–April Mon–Fri 10am–4pm; tours at 11am & 2pm or by arrangement (£10) • ☎ 01955 602371, ⊛ oldpulteney.com

Until city fathers declared Wick dry in the 1920s, fishermen consumed three hundred gallons of whisky a day. The last distillery in town – and second most northerly in Scotland – distils more refined malts nowadays; most are light or medium-bodied, with a hint of sea salt. The tours give a close-up glimpse of a functioning distillery, which is less polished than some of the others in the Highlands and more charming for it. Needless to say, it ends with a dram or full tastings.

4

ARRIVAL AND DEPARTURE
WICK

By plane Wick John O'Groats Airport (☎ 01955 602215, ⊛ hial.co.uk/wick-airport), just north of town, has flights to and from Edinburgh (Mon, Wed–Fri & Sun 1 daily; 1hr) and Aberdeen (Mon–Fri 2 daily; 35min) with Loganair and Eastern Airways respectively.

By train The train station is immediately south and west of the central bridge. Trains from Inverness (Mon–Sat 4 daily, 4hr 20min) make a long but scenic journey via Lairg,

Helmsdale, then the Flow Country inland.

By bus Local buses depart just south and west of the central bridge. They run to John O'Groats then Thurso; long-distance routes to and from Inverness involve a coordinated change at Dunbeath.

Destinations Inverness (Mon–Sat 6 daily, Sun 4 daily; 3hr); John O'Groats (Mon–Fri 7 daily, Sat 5 daily; 35min); Thurso (Mon–Sat hourly, Sun 5 daily; 30–35min).

ACTIVITIES

Caithness Sea Coast ☎ 01955 609200, ⊛ caithness-seacoast.co.uk. Harbour cruise (30min; £11) plus longer tours to spot wildlife and admire the high cliffs south

(from £21) in a fast RIB. The operator also runs longer trips to Lybster (3hr; £55), including one-way trips in either direction (£33). April–Oct.

ACCOMMODATION AND EATING

Bord de l'Eau Market St ☎ 01955 604400. Riverside bistro offers a slice of France, with a changing menu of Gaelic and seafood dishes, plus some French classics (£14–20). The best seats are in the airy conservatory. Tues–Sat noon–2.30pm & 6–9pm, dinner only Sun.

Mackays Union St ☎ 01955 602323, ⊛ mackayshotel.

co.uk. Oversized headboards, streamlined oak furnishings and iPod docks make this Wick's prime accommodation option; first- and second-floor rooms are our pick. The acclaimed *No. 1 Bistro* serves the likes of barbary duck breast with butternut fondant, pak choi and ginger jus, plus superb fish and chips (mains £14–18). Daily 8am–9pm. **£125**

Skye and the Small Isles

SEA-KAYAKER, LOCH SCAVAIG

5 | Skye and the Small Isles

For many visitors the Isle of Skye (An t-Eilean Sgiathanach) is the Highlands in miniature. With its shapely summits and shifting seascapes, its superb hiking routes, wildlife and crofting villages, it crams much of the region's appeal into one manageable island. It even has classic Highlands weather. According to one theory, Skye is named after the Old Norse for "cloud" (*skuy*), earning itself the Gaelic moniker *Eilean a' Cheò* (Island of Mist). Despite unpredictable weather, tourism has been an important part of the economy since the railway reached Kyle of Lochalsh in 1897. The Edwardian bourgeoisie swarmed to its mountains, whose beauty had been proclaimed by the Victorians ever since Sir Walter Scott visited in 1814, arguably the most successful tourism PR campaign in Scottish history. People still come in droves, yet Skye is deceptively large. You'll get the most out of it – and escape the worst crowds – if you explore the remoter parts of the island, and visit outside of the tourist season which enters full-throttle between June and August.

The Clearances saw an estimated thirty thousand indigenous *Sgiathanachs* (pronounced "ski-anaks") emigrate in the mid-nineteenth century; today, the population is just over nine thousand. Tourism is now by far the island's biggest earner and has attracted hundreds of incomers from the rest of Britain over the last couple of decades, including an increasing quota of artists and first-time B&B owners. Nevertheless, Skye remains the most important centre for **Gaelic culture** and language outside the Western Isles. Over a third of the population is fluent in Gaelic, the Gaelic college on Sleat is the most important in Scotland, and the Free Church maintains a strong presence.

In contrast to the crowds on Skye, the so-called **Small Isles** – the improbably named Rùm, Eigg, Muck and Canna – to the south only receive a trickle of visitors. Each with a population of fewer than a hundred and with its own identity, they are easily accessible by ferry from Mallaig and Arisaig, though limited accommodation means an overnight visit requires planning.

Skye

Skye ranks among Scotland's most visited destinations, with all the summer coach tours that suggests. Yet Scotland's second-largest island also has twenty Munros to bag, and year-round hikers and climbers pay homage to the **Cuillin** ridge, whose peaks dominate the island; you'll need experience and determination to explore them. For years, the hiking-and-heather view of Skye was all you'd get, but over the last decade a new generation of islanders, including an influx of younger settlers, has introduced a vibrant arts and crafts scene and revolutionized the food and accommodation on offer. Nowadays, Skye holds its own against anywhere in Scotland. In fact, so sophisticated is some of the relaxation on offer that the island is no longer the preserve of hikers and coach tours. The former congregate around Cuillin or the impressive rock formations of the **Trotternish** peninsula, the latter **Dunvegan** and its castle or **Portree**, the island's capital, with modest charm and amenities. And if the summer crush really gets too much, there's always the peaceful **Isle of Raasay** off the east coast.

BUTCHER WITH HAGGIS, SKYE

Highlights

① Skye crafts From eccentric weavers to unbeatable locally brewed craft beer, via Scotland's only working tannery, Skye has an abundance of rainy-day activities. See page 271

② Food on Skye Whether you opt for silver service at *Kinloch Lodge* (see page 273), cosy seafront dining at *Loch Bay Restaurant* (see page 280) or alfresco lobster and chips at *The Oyster Shed* (see page 276), you'll eat well on Skye.

③ Skye Cuillin Countless lochans, eleven Munros, one challenging seven-mile ridge trail – and the mountains are almost as impressive seen on the road to Glenbrittle as up on the trail. See page 274

④ Loch Coruisk Few sights in Scotland prepare you for the drama of this glacial loch in the Cuillin – the boat ride there from Elgol just adds to the fun. See page 274

⑤ Trotternish Take a walk into the bizarre, Tolkienesque landscapes of the Quiraing or say hello to the Old Man; this peninsula has some of Skye's most distinctive scenery. See page 281

⑥ Isle of Eigg Sample off-grid island living in the most compelling of the Small Isles, with sandy beaches, an easy climb and peace everywhere. See page 287

HIGHLIGHTS ARE MARKED ON THE MAP ON PAGE 270

ARRIVAL AND DEPARTURE

By car The Skye Bridge sweeps across from Kyle of Lochalsh. If driving, don't underestimate the size of Skye. Fuel is available 24hr at Broadford, as well as at Portree, Armadale, Dunvegan and Uig.

By ferry From Mallaig, Caledonian MacBrayne (☎ 0800 066 5000, ⓦ calmac.co.uk) operates regular car ferries across to

Armadale on the Sleat peninsula (Mon–Sat 9 daily, Sun 6 daily; 35min). In addition, a tiny community-run car ferry called the Glenachulish (☎ 01599 522313, ⓦ skyeferry.co.uk) hops across to Kylerhea from Glenelg, south of Kyle of Lochalsh (Easter to mid-Oct daily 10am–6pm, June–Aug till 7pm; every 20min; 5min).

SKYE & THE SMALL ISLES

N

HIGHLIGHTS

1 Skye crafts
2 Food on Skye
3 Skye Cuillin
4 Loch Coruisk
5 Trotternish
6 Isle of Eigg

0 — 10
miles

SKYE CRAFTS

Skye has a growing number of independent craft traders, each offering a great opportunity to pick up some unique, high-quality local produce (that isn't fudge or whisky). Some offer a free tour without prior arrangement; the perfect remedy to a rainy day. Here are a few of our favourites:

Isle of Skye Brewing Co Uig harbour ☎01470 542477, ⓦskyeale.com. In 1992 a few Skye locals joked that the only solution to the island's poor standard of beers would be to brew their own. Three years later those same locals set up this brewery, and these days any self-respecting Skye pub has their ales on tap. You can pop into their brewery in Uig to have a taster and pick up a bottle or two. Mon–Fri 10am–6pm, Sat 10am–4pm, Sun noon–4pm.

Skyeskyns Stein ☎01470 592237, ⓦskyeskyns. co.uk. The friendly folk at Scotland's only functioning tannery offer informative, witty (and free) tours explaining the whole process of leather making.

Upstairs, you can browse the final products, from surprisingly affordable woolly rugs right up to tailored gilets pushing the £1000 mark. Daily: April–Oct 9am–6pm, Nov–March 9.30am–5.30pm; last tours 30min before closing.

Skye Weavers Signposted off the B884, 1 mile east of Glendale ☎01470 511201, ⓦskyeweavers.co.uk. Stop by Skye Weavers and you may well catch Roger or Andrea pedalling on their extraordinary bicycle-powered loom. They'll happily talk you through the weaving process, and you can browse their exquisite shawls, scarves and other items in the small shop next door. April–Oct Tues–Sat 10am–6pm.

By train and ferry or bus Mallaig (departure point for ferries to Skye) is served by direct trains from Fort William (3–4 daily; 1hr 20min) and Glasgow Queen St (Mon–Sat 3 daily, Sun 2 daily; 5hr 10min). There are also trains from Inverness to Kyle of Lochalsh (Mon–Sat 3–4 daily, Sun 1–2 daily; 2hr 40min). Stagecoach operate a service from Kyle of Lochalsh, stopping at Kyleakin, Broadford and Elgol (Mon–

Fri 3 daily, Sat 1 daily).

Moving on to the Western Isles It's 57 miles from Armadale and 49 miles from Kyleakin to Uig, from where CalMac ferries leave for Tarbert on Harris (2 daily Mon, Tues, Thurs & Sat; 1 daily Wed, Fri & Sun) and Lochmaddy on North Uist (2 daily Mon, Wed & Fri; 1 daily Tues, Thurs, Sat & Sun).

GETTING AROUND AND INFORMATION

By bus Bus services peter out in more remote areas and don't run on Sundays. Skye Dayrider tickets for unlimited one-day travel cost £9.50 (☎0871 200 2233, ⓦstagecoachbus.com).

Tourist information The only remaining tourist office on the island is in Portree. A useful website about the island is ⓦskye.co.uk.

The Sleat peninsula

Thanks to the CalMac ferry from Mallaig to **ARMADALE**, many people's introduction to Skye is the **Sleat** (pronounced "Slate") **peninsula** at the southern tip of the island. The irony is that it's unlike almost anywhere else hereabouts – an uncharacteristically fertile area branded "The Garden of Skye". The main attraction is the **Armadale Castle** estate, which, along with the new Torobhaig Distillery just up the road, makes for an entertaining few hours.

Armadale Castle

On A851, half a mile north of Armadale • April–Oct daily 9.30am–5.30pm; Nov & March Mon–Fri 10am–3pm • £8.75 • ☎01471 844305, ⓦarmadalecastle.com

Armadale Castle, a mile north of the ferry terminal, is the shell of the neo-Gothic seat of the MacDonald clan – the laird moved into the gardeners' cottage when the kelp fertilizer market collapsed in the 1920s. As evocative as the remains are, far more worthwhile is the comprehensive **Museum of the Isles**, which, although intended as an account of the clan, is actually more interesting for its perspectives on Highland history, with sections on the Jacobite period and its aftermath, featuring Bonnie Prince Charlie keepsakes such as his shoe buckles worn in battle at Culloden, his snuff mull, and a set of three firing glasses he once owned. Elsewhere, there's a stash of fearsome looking weaponry – including a magnificent studded targe (shield) and some gorgeous gilt brass and blue steel flintlock pistols – a display of Highland bagpipes, and a couple of cannonballs fired at the castle by HMS *Dartmouth*, sent by William III. Just as appealing is the castle's forty-acre wooded **garden**, from where there are splendid views back across to the mainland.

Torobhaig Distillery

On A851, four miles north of Armadale Castle • Mon–Fri 10am–5pm, Sat & Sun 10am–4pm • tours £10 • ☎ 01471 833447, ⊛ torobhaig.com

Converted from a 200-year old farmstead, **Torobhaig distillery** became only the second ever licensed distillery on Skye upon its opening in 2017, hence its first single malt – a medium-peated version – only came into production in 2020. An old viking name meaning "Bay of God", Torobhaig was the brainchild of Sir Iain Noble, founder of Noble Grossart (Scotland's first modern merchant bank) and prominent Gaelic language activist, but following his death in 2010 it was left to his wife Lucilla to pressed ahead with plans for its completion. Given the early stages of the distillery's development, there's relatively little to see here on a standard tour, though that doesn't make it any less enjoyable; what you will get to see are the eight Douglas fir washbacks and the two magnificent copper stills, named after Sir Iain and his wife – and of course you get to try a dram at the end. Should you wish to hang around, the café here is very good.

Isleornsay

Having retired as Skye's main fishing port, **ISLEORNSAY** (Eilean Iarmain), six miles north of Armadale, is these days just a pretty, secluded village. Come for views: out across the bay to a necklace of seaweed-encrusted rocks and the tidal **Isle of Ornsay**, and behind it all a dramatic panorama of peaks on the mainland.

The west coast of Sleat

A narrow, up-and-down single-track road loops off the A851 to the wilder west coast of Sleat. Turning at Kilbeg, you ascend over moorland past somnambulant sheep before arriving into **TARSKAVAIG**, scattered behind a little beach. Further up the coast, the stony beach at **TOKAVAIG** is overlooked by ruined Dunscaith Castle and enjoys views over the Cuillin range – this, and neighbouring **ORD**, with a sandy beach, offer a superb panorama of the mountains (if the weather plays ball).

ARRIVAL AND DEPARTURE | THE SLEAT PENINSULA

By ferry Reservations are pretty much essential in peak season (☎ 0800 066 5000, ⊛ calmac.co.uk) for the Mallaig–Armadale crossing (Mon–Sat 9–11 daily, Sun 6–8 daily; 35min).

By bus All bus services from/to Armadale are via Broadford. Destinations Broadford (Mon–Fri 5 daily, Sat 2 daily; 30min); Portree (Mon–Fri 2 daily; 1hr 20min); Sligachan (Mon–Fri 2 daily; 1hr).

GETTING AROUND AND ACTIVITIES

Bike rental You can rent bikes from South Skye Cycles (☎ 01471 833464, ⊛ southskyecycles.co.uk; £20/day), based at the Westmans Pottery in Teangue; they also do repairs and cycle tours.

Sea-kayaking Based in Kilmore, South Skye Sea Kayak (☎ 07592 059577, ⊛ southskyeseakayak.co.uk) runs half- and full-day sea-kayaking trips (£60–90) for all abilities.

ACCOMMODATION, EATING AND DRINKING

ARMADALE AND ARDVASAR

The Inn @ Àird a' Bhàsair Ardvasar, 0.5 miles south of Armadale ☎ 01471 844223, ⊛ the-inn-at-ardvasar. co.uk. This pretty little inn – one of the oldest on Skye – has benefited from refurbishment to create comfortable, contemporary accommodation as well as a smart restaurant specializing in local seafood – scallops and crab, plus Speyside beef for around £15. **£155**

ISLEORNSAY AND AROUND

★ **Eilean Iarmain** Isleornsay ☎01471 833332, ⓦ eileaniarmain.co.uk. This small hotel in a whitewashed hamlet is a charmer, romantically furnished in cosy country style: antiques, pretty fabrics, awesome views and not a TV in sight. The restaurant serves fine-food dining such as venison with garlic and white truffle mash (two courses £25), or there's informal eating in the delightful bar (beer battered haddock; £12.95). Meanwhile, folk music sessions are held in the adjoining Am Pràban bar on Fridays. Kitchen open daily 7.30–9.30am, noon–2.30pm & 5.30–9pm. **£190**

★ **Kinloch Lodge** 1 mile north of Isleornsay ☎01471 833333, ⓦ kinloch-lodge.co.uk. The island's smartest hotel remains the home of Lord and Lady MacDonald of MacDonald, and as such is furnished with antiques and clan mementos. It may no longer hold a Michelin star, but chef Marcello Tully's cooking remains outstanding: three-course lunch (£45) and five-course dinner (£85) menus are likely to feature fabulous morsels like warm crab mousse and langoustines with white wine and dill sauce, and Shetland cod in Harris gin and citrus sauce. Expect silver service, and up-to-the-nines clientele. The public drawing rooms and Whisky Bar are another experience altogether. Daily 12.30–2pm & 6.30–9pm. Dinner, bed and breakfast **£340**

Kyleakin

The **Skye Bridge** that rendered the ferry crossing redundant in 1995 has been a mixed blessing for the old port of **KYLEAKIN** (pronounced "ka*la*kin", with the stress on the second syllable). On the one hand, it's now bypassed; on the other, that leaves its neat centre that bit quieter, even in high season. Bizarrely, it's also evolved into something of a backpackers' hangout.

The bridge has been less kind to **Eilean Bàn**, an island from which the bridge leapfrogs to cross Loch Alsh. From 1968 to 1969, its lighthouse keeper's cottage was briefly the home of Gavin Maxwell, author of *Ring of Bright Water*. The island now serves as a nature reserve and can be visited on tours booked through the Bright Water Visitor Centre (see below) in Kyleakin.

ARRIVAL AND INFORMATION **KYLEAKIN**

By bus There are buses from and to Kyle of Lochalsh (6 daily; 5min) and Portree via Broadford (6 daily; 55min).
Tourist information Available in the Bright Water Visitor Centre, The Pier (Easter–Sept, generally Mon–Fri 10am–4pm but phone for times; ☎01599 530040, ⓦ eileanban. org).

ACCOMMODATION AND EATING

Skye Backpackers Kyleakin ☎01599 534510, ⓦ skye backpackers.com. The quirkier and better-equipped of Kyleakin's two hostels. Dorms, doubles, and a couple of stationary hippie caravans out the back offer a basic night's sleep. The Groove Lounge has a log burner and board games. Doubles **£53**; dorms **£20**; caravan dorm **£15**

Broadford

Skye's second-largest village, **BROADFORD** (An t-Àth Leathann), strung out along the main road, has a traffic problem and a charm bypass. It is indeed handy for its full quota of facilities – not least a large supermarket and 24-hour fuel – but you won't want to hang around here for too long. Fill the tank, load up the boot with supplies and go explore the island.

ARRIVAL AND DEPARTURE **BROADFORD**

By bus Broadford is served by local buses from and to Kyle of Lochalsh (Mon–Sat 6–7 daily; 25min), Kyleakin (Mon– Fri 5 daily, Sat 2 daily; 15min) and Portree (Mon–Sat 5–6 daily; 40min).

ACCOMMODATION AND EATING

Café Sia On the A87, Broadford ☎01471 822616, ⓦ cafesia.co.uk. The best pizzas (including takeaways) on Skye, wood-fired to perfection, and probably one of the best coffees too; they offer much more besides, including breakfasts, some terrific seafood dishes and beers from half a dozen Scottish microbreweries. Daily 9.30am–9.30pm.
Creelers Seafood Restaurant Lower Harrapool ☎01471 822281, ⓦ skye-seafood-restaurant.co.uk. No fuss, no highfalutin' foams, this wee restaurant is all about local seafood simply but superbly prepared – a rich

5

WALKING IN THE CUILLIN

Ordnance Survey Explorer map 411

For many walkers and climbers, there's nowhere in Britain to beat **the Cuillin**. The main ridge is just eight miles long, but with its immediate neighbours it is made up of over thirty peaks, twelve of them Munros. Those intent on doing a complete traverse of the Cuillin ridge usually start at **Gars-bheinn**, at the southeastern tip, and finish off at **Sgùrr nan Gillean** (3167ft), descending on the famous *Sligachan Hotel* for a well-earned pint. The entire journey takes a minimum of sixteen hours, which either means a very long day or two days and a bivouac. A period of settled weather is pretty much essential, and only experienced walkers and climbers should attempt it. Take note of all the usual safety precautions and be aware that **compasses** are unreliable in the Cuillin, due to the magnetic nature of the rocks.

If you're based in Glenbrittle, one of the more straightforward walks is the five-mile round trip from the campsite up **Coire Làgan**, to a crystal-cold lochan squeezed in among the sternest of rockfaces. If you simply want to bag one or two of the peaks, several corries provide relatively straightforward approaches to the central Munros. From the hostel, a path heads west along the southern bank of the stream that tumbles down from the **Coire a' Ghreadaidh**. From the corrie, you can climb up to An Dorus, the obvious gap in the ridge, then ascend **Sgùrr a' Mhadaidh** (3012ft) or **Sgùrr a' Ghreadaidh** (3192ft) to the south. Alternatively, before Coire a'Ghreadaidh, you can head south to the Coir' an Eich, from which you can easily climb **Sgùrr na Banachdaich** (3166ft) via its western ridge. To the south of the youth hostel, the road crosses another stream, with another path along its southern banks. This path heads west past the impressive **Eas Mòr** (Great Waterfall), before heading up to the **Coire na Banachdaich**. The pass above the corrie is the main one over to Loch Coruisk, but also gives access to Sgùrr Dearg, best known for its great view of the **Inaccessible Pinnacle** or "In-Pin" (3235ft) – it doesn't actually live up to the name, but Scotland's most difficult Munro requires good rock-climbing skills. Back at Eas Mòr, paths head off for Coire Làgan, by far the most popular corrie thanks to its steep sides and tiny lochan. If you're unsure about any hike or want help, hire a guide: try Skye Guides (☎01471 822116, ⊕skyeguides.co.uk).

bouillabaisse, pan sautéed crayfish tails, or mussels in dry white wine, butter, garlic and parsley (mains average £20). March–Oct Mon–Sat noon–2.30pm & 5–9.30pm.

★ **Tigh an Dochais** 13 Harrapool ☎01471 820022, ⊕skyebedbreakfast.co.uk. Jaw-dropping views down Broadford Bay through walls of glass are the draw at this striking B&B (just three rooms), although streamlined contemporary style and a calm, grown-up vibe are just as good reasons to check in. March–Nov. **£120**

The Cuillin and Red Hills

They have razor-edge ridges, the slopes plummet in scree fields and the lonely lochs are imbued with an almost tangible magic. Small wonder that, for many people, the spectacular **Cuillin** range is the sole reason to visit Skye. When – if – the cloud disperses, these spectacular peaks dominate the island. There are three **approaches**: from the south, by foot or by boat from Elgol; from *Sligachan Hotel* to the north; or from Glenbrittle to the west of the mountains. Glen Sligachan is one of the most popular routes as it divides the granite of the round-topped **Red Hills** (sometimes referred to as the Red Cuillin) to the east from the Cuillin themselves – sometimes known as the **Black Cuillin** on account of the colour of their coarse-grained jagged gabbro. With twenty Munros between them, these are mountains to take seriously. There are around five fatalities a year here and many routes are for experienced climbers only. If you're unsure, hire a guide.

Elgol, Loch Coruisk and Glen Sligachan

The road to **ELGOL** (Ealaghol) at the tip of the Strathaird peninsula is one of the most impressive on Skye, swooping into the heart of the Red Hills to culminate in beautiful views of the Small Isles above Elgol pier.

The chief reason for visiting Elgol is to take a boat, whether a wildlife cruise or a trip across Loch Scavaig to visit **Loch Coruisk**. This isolated, glacial loch lies beneath the highest peaks of the Cuillin and is a superb trip, about an hour by boat then up to a half-day ashore. **Walkers** use the boat simply to begin hikes in the Red Hills or over the pass into **Glen Sligachan**. Alternatively, you can walk round the coast to the bay of **Camasunary**, over two miles to the east – a difficult walk that involves a tricky river crossing and negotiating "The Bad Step", an overhanging rock with a 30ft drop to the sea – and head north to Glen Sligachan. Conversely, a time-honoured approach into Glen Sligachan is from the north via the *Sligachan Hotel* (see below), a popular hikers' base.

Glenbrittle

Yet another route into the peaks is from **Glenbrittle** on the west side. The valley edges the most spectacular peaks of the **Cuillin**, a semicircle of mountains which ring Loch Coruisk, before it runs to a beach at Loch Brittle. One of the least demanding walks is a five-mile round trip (3hr) from *Glenbrittle Campsite* (see below) up Coire Làgan to a lochan squeezed among stern rock faces. An equally good reason to come is the **Fairy Pools**, one of Britain's most celebrated wild swimming destinations. The scenery is superb as the river tumbles beneath peaks – the downside is water temperature of 8–10°C at best, and it gets incredibly busy during the summer. The pools are signposted from Glumagan Na Sithichean car park.

ARRIVAL AND DEPARTURE   THE CUILLIN AND RED HILLS

By bus Elgol is accessed most easily from Broadford (Mon–Fri 3–5 daily, Sat 2 daily; 40min). Sligachan is a stop on the Portree–Broadford route (Mon–Sat 6–7 daily; Broadford 30min, Portree 15min).

ACTIVITIES

Boat trips From Easter to Oct, two operators offer superb trips from Elgol to Loch Coruisk: *Bella Jane* offers a 3hr return trip, including 90mins ashore (4 daily; £15 single, £28 return; ☎01471 866244, ⊛bellajane.co.uk) and the *Misty Isle* (Mon–Sat; £14 single, £28 return; ☎01471 866288, ⊛mistyisleboattrips.co.uk). The owner of *Bella Jane* also runs wildlife-watching and walking trips to the Small Isles in a fast RIB as Aquaxplore (Easter–Oct daily; from £30).

ACCOMMODATION AND EATING

★ **Coruisk House** Elgol ☎01471 866330, ⊛coruiskhouse.com. A taste of Skye on unfussy super-fresh menus – fillet of cod with Orbost Iron Age pork belly, or Sconser king scallops with wild mushrooms (two courses cost £39). Above are two beautiful suites of understated luxury: expect dinner, a relaxing night and an awesome breakfast. Perfect. Reservations essential. March to mid-Oct Daily noon–2pm & 7–10pm. **£130**

Glenbrittle Campsite End of road, Glenbrittle ☎01478 640404, ⊛dunvegancastle.com/glenbrittle/campsite. With sea views and the beach in front, and mountains behind, this spacious, remote site is the best of both worlds. The bad news is midges. Thousands of them, though they vanish with a breeze. On-site shop and café sells camping essentials and proper coffee. April–Sept. Per person **£10**

Glenbrittle Youth Hostel Glenbrittle ☎01478 640278, ⊛hostellingscotland.org.uk. Mountain chalet vibe in this modern hostel popular with climbers and whose excellent facilities include laundry, drying room, bike storage and an open lounge arrangement; its old wood panelling and leather sofas combine into a sort of rugged Scandi chic. Offers frozen prepared meals. April–Sept. Dorms **£18**, doubles **£53**

Rowan Cottage Glasnakille, 1 mile east of Elgol ☎01471 866312, ⊛rowancottage-skye.co.uk. Go across the moors from Elgol pier then left at the T-Junction to find Christine and Jim's place – the end of the road bar 100 yards. It's a homely B&B with a big welcome and sea views to Sleat from rooms. **£70**

Sligachan Bunkhouse On A87 ☎01478 650458, ⊛sligachanselfcatering.com. There are peaks just beyond the back door from this modern, clean, no-frills bunkhouse adjacent to the *Sligachan Hotel*. Within are four dorms sleeping four or six, plus a laundry, a spacious kitchen and a small lounge with a fireplace. Dorms **£22**

Sligachan Hotel and Campsite On A87 ☎01478 650204, ⊛sligachan.co.uk. This long-standing launchpad for hikers is almost embraced beneath Cuillin's peaks. Alongside dated but comfy enough en-suite rooms, it maintains the barn-like *Seumas' Bar* which serves dishes like homemade steak and Cuillin ale pie (£14.95), and which is stocked with over 400 whiskies and serves beer from the on-site Cuillin Brewery. A campsite is over the road (07786 435294). Hotel: March–Oct; campsite: April to mid-Oct. Doubles **£140**, camping per person **£8**

5

Minginish

If the Cuillin has disappeared into the mist for the day and you have your own transport, you can while away a happy afternoon exploring the nearby **Minginish** peninsula, north of Glen Brittle.

Talisker whisky distillery

By Loch Harport, Carbost • March–Oct Mon–Sat 9.30am–5pm, Sun 10am–5pm; Nov–Feb Mon–Sat 10am–4.30pm, Sun 10.30am– 4.30pm • Tours from £10, adults only • ☏ 01478 614308, ⓦ malts.com

One ideal wet-weather activity is a guided tour of the **Talisker whisky distillery**, which produces a sweet full-bodied single malt with a whiff of smoke and peat. Skye's oldest distillery is situated on the shores of Loch Harport at **CARBOST**, not at the village of Talisker itself, which lies on the west coast of Minginish. Proper whisky fanatics will splash out for the excellent two-hour Talisker Masterclass Tour (£45).

ACCOMMODATION AND EATING MINGINISH

Old Inn and Waterfront Bunkhouse Carbost ☏ 01478 640205, ⓦ theoldinnskye.co.uk. A chalet-style building and lochside location lend this bunkhouse a cheerful holiday atmosphere; it also has five well-appointed B&B rooms and a family chalet It's managed by the historic *Old Inn* next door, which provides good bar meals – the likes of beer battered cod, and haggis, neaps and tatties in a whisky cream sauce – for around £12 a main. Daily 8am–9pm. Dorms £25, doubles £90

Oyster Shed Carbost ☏ 07751 025074. This artisanal farm shop serves some of the freshest, best-value seafood anywhere on Skye as well as smoking their own salmon, oysters and shellfish; half lobster and chips (£8.50), pan-fried scallops in garlic butter (from £6.50). Take away, or eat on the picnic benches overlooking Loch Harport. Mon–Sat 11am–5pm.

Skyewalker Hostel Portnalong, 2 miles north of Carbost ☏ 01478 640250, ⓦ skyewalkerhostel.com. Housed in a converted school, this consistently excellent hostel it's an appealing blend of the practical – solid bunks, an outstanding modern kitchen – and the charming – pretty vintage-style bathroom, a lounge that hosts the occasional music evening, a wonderful garden solar dome and marvellous owners. Book one of their "Jedi Huts" (sleeping two) for something completely special. Over 18s only. Easter to mid-Oct. Dorms £20, Jedi Hut £70

Dunvegan

DUNVEGAN (Dùn Bheagain) is something of a letdown after the route there, skirting the bony sea cliffs and stacks of the west coast. Yet it has one of Skye's most famous traditional sights, plus two of the island's more interesting peninsulas, Duirinish and Waternish, in its backyard.

Dunvegan Castle

1 mile north of Dunvegan • Easter–mid-Oct daily 10am–5.30pm • £14, or £12 for gardens only • ☏ 01470 521206, ⓦ dunvegancastle.com

Just north of the village, **Dunvegan Castle** sprawls over a rocky outcrop, sandwiched between the sea and several acres of attractive **gardens**. It's been the seat of the Clan MacLeod since the thirteenth century – and the chief still lives here with his family today – but the present facade is a product of Victorian romanticism. Older architecture remains inside, where you get the usual furniture and oil paintings alongside some more noteworthy items, with tour guides on-hand to bring the history to life. The most intriguing display is the shabby remnants of the **Fairy Flag**, carried back to Skye, they say, by the Gaelic boatmen of King Harald Hardrada after the Battle of Stamford Bridge in 1066. MacLeod tradition states that the flag was the gift of a fairy to protect the clan – as late as World War II, MacLeod pilots carried pictures of it for luck. Between April and September seal-spotting boat trips (£9.50 with a valid castle or garden ticket) are available from the grounds during the summer.

Claigan Coral Beaches

3 miles north of Dunvegan

Keep it quiet, but these **beaches** in Claigan, three miles north of Dunvegan, might be as good a reason to visit as the castle. The strands are not coral but calcified maerl (seaweed) and tiny sea shells. On a sunny day, the white sands and aqua water could almost be the Caribbean, and the sunset over the Duirinish peninsula is as good as any on Skye. From the car park it's a one-mile walk to the beaches, with a few streams to hop over and some muddy fields to traverse, so wear appropriate shoes.

ARRIVAL AND INFORMATION   DUNVEGAN

By bus Dunvegan is served by buses that loop around northern Skye from Portree (Mon–Fri 6 daily, Sat 3 daily; 45min); half of them stop at the castle.

ACCOMMODATION

★ **Greshornish House** Greshornish, 9 miles northeast of Dunvegan ☎01470 582266, ⍟greshornishhouse. co.uk. This wonderful small hotel – half country hotel, half family home of its charming owners – has cosy, traditional rooms, period charm and a relaxed atmosphere that's difficult to leave. £150

Kinloch Campsite Loch Dunvegan ☎01470 508009, ⍟kinloch-campsite.co.uk. Spreads across the head of Loch Dunvegan just as its name (literally "loch head")

suggests, although motorhomes and caravans claim the prime waterfront – campers pitch at the sides and on a low hill. April–Oct. Per person £10

Roskhill House Roskhill, 3 miles south of Dunvegan ☎01470 521317, ⍟roskhillhouse.co.uk. Stone walls, crafts and home-made cake bring charm to this old crofthouse, whose modern oak furnishings and bed throws over crisp white linen lend understated style to your stay. Great breakfasts too. £105

EATING

Edinbane Inn Edinbane, 8 miles east of Dunvegan ☎01470 582414, ⍟edinbaneinn.co.uk. Proper restaurant dishes such as herb-crust lamb with root veg, pea puree and red wine gravy (£17.95) meets local vibe in a pub that wins plaudits from locals. Folk music on Tues and Fri evenings and Sun afternoons. Daily noon–11pm; food served noon–2pm & 5.30–9pm.

Jann's Cakes Dunvegan ☎01470 521730. This tiny place on the high street is a Skye legend for its cakes and home-made chocolates, and also prepares fresh sandwiches and

soups, plus hot organic meals like tagine and curries. Not cheap – £5 for a slice of cake or £6 for smoked haddock chowder – but the quality is high. Tues–Sat 11am–5pm.

The Old School Dunvegan ☎01470 521421, ⍟old schoolrestaurant.co.uk. Offers a strong Scottish menu with the likes of Mallaig peat smoked salmon and beetroot salad, and mushroom, potato and Isle of Arran smoked cheddar in a puff pastry pie (£17.95). Raw stone walls add character to a lofty and rather smart dining room. Live traditional music every other Saturday. Easter–Dec daily noon–3pm & 6–10pm.

The Duirinish peninsula

Much of the **Duirinish peninsula**, west of Dunvegan, is inaccessible to all except walkers prepared to scale or skirt the area's twin flat-topped basalt peaks: Healabhal Bheag (1600ft) and Healabhal Mhor (1538ft). The mountains are better known as **MacLeod's Tables** – the story goes that the MacLeod chief held a royal feast on the lower of the two for James V.

Glendale

West from Loch Dunvegan, the broad, green sweep of **Glendale** feels instantly wilder after Dunvegan. Its moment in history came in 1882, when local crofters staged a rent strike against their landlords, the MacLeods. Five locals, who became known as the "Glendale Martyrs", were given two-month prison sentences, and in 1904 the crofters became the first owner-occupiers in the Highlands.

Colbost Folk Museum

Colbost village • Easter–Oct daily 9.30am–5.30pm • £1.50 • ☎01470 521296

Local history plus information about nineteenth-century crofting is told through news cuttings in this restored blackhouse, four miles up the road from Dunvegan. A guide is usually on hand to answer questions, and the peat fire is often lit.

5

The west coast of Duirinish

A bumpy road leads up the west coast of Duirinish to Ramasaig, continuing five miles to the deserted village of **Lorgill** where, on August 4, 1830, every crofter was ordered to board the *Midlothian* in Loch Snizort to go to Nova Scotia or go to prison (those over the age of 70 were sent to the poorhouse). It's a great place for walkers, though, with easy, blustery footpaths to **Neist Point**, Skye's most westerly spot, a spectacular end-of-the-world headland with high sea cliffs, and wonderful views to the Western Isles.

ARRIVAL AND INFORMATION · THE DUIRINISH PENINSULA

By bus Buses go to Colbost from Portree via Dunvegan (schooldays only; Mon–Fri 2 daily; 1hr 10min).

Tourist information A useful website on the area is ⓦ glendaleskye.com.

ACCOMMODATION AND EATING

Carter's Rest 8/9 Upper Milovaig, 4 miles west of Colbost ☎ 01470 511272, ⓦ cartersrestskye.co.uk. Little touches like a digital radio impress almost as much as furnishings such as super-king beds and locally woven blankets in this luxury four-star B&B with astonishing coast views. **£130**

★ **Red Roof Gallery** Holmisdale, 3 miles west of Colbost ☎ 01470 511304, ⓦ redroofskye.co.uk. This cosy little café owned by an artist-musician couple has a loyal fan base for its superb lunches (average £6–8) of local cheese or seafood platters with home-made breads, plus home baking with great coffee. Occasionally holds intimate live music nights. Tues–Fri noon–8pm.

★ **Three Chimneys** Colbost ☎ 01470 511258, ⓦ three chimneys.co.uk. An intimate, gourmet restaurant at the vanguard of Skye's foodie revolution offering food as bold as it is brilliant. Whether you opt for the three-course dinner menu (£69) or the Skye, Land and Sea tasting menu (£98), expect stunning plates such as scorched Dunvegan langoustines with smoked mussel ketchup and roast sweetbread, and Soay lamb with black garlic and miso glased rib and anchovy fritters. Six sumptuous rooms are available across the courtyard, the price of which includes a marvellous breakfast and an afternoon tea tray. Mid-Jan to mid-Dec daily 6.30–9.30pm; also open for lunch April–Oct daily noon–2.30pm. Doubles **£360**

Waternish

Waternish is a backwater by Skye's standards. Though not as spectacular as Duirinish or Trotternish, it provides equally good views over to the Western Isles, and, with fewer visitors, feels appealingly remote. To reach the peninsula, you cross the **Fairy Bridge** (Beul-Ath nan Tri Allt or "Ford of the Three Burns"), at the junction of the B886. Legend has it that the fourth MacLeod clan chief was forced to say farewell to his fairy wife here when she had to return to her kind – her parting gift was the Fairy Flag (see page 276).

Stein

STEIN, looking out over Loch Bay to the Western Isles, is Waternish's prettiest village, a row of whitewashed cottages built in 1787 by the British Fisheries Society. The place never really took off and was more or less abandoned within a couple of generations. Today it's a little livelier, thanks to its world-class restaurant and historic pub – there are few nicer places on Skye for a pint on a sunny summer evening.

Trumpan Church

At the end of the road that continues north from Stein is the medieval shell of **Trumpan Church**. Its beautiful location belies one of the bloodiest episodes in Skye's history. In a revenge attack in 1578, the MacDonalds of Uist set fire to the church while numerous MacLeods were attending a service within. Everyone perished except one young girl, who squeezed through a window and raised the alarm. The MacLeods rallied and slaughtered the MacDonalds, then threw their bodies into a nearby dyke. In the graveyard is the **Trial Stone** – in the fourteenth century, accused criminals were blindfolded and if they could fit their fingers in its hole they were deemed innocent. Otherwise, ouch.

5

★ **Loch Bay Restaurant** Stein ☎ 01470 592235, ⓦ lochbay-restaurant.co.uk. With Michelin-starred chef Michael Smith at the helm, this tiny, romantic restaurant continues to set the standard for this part of Scotland; the focus of both the lunch (£29.50–34) and dinner (£43.50–70) menus is mainly on fresh seafood (turbot and oyster with velvet crab sauce), but there's much more besides, for example Highland wood pigeon with neep roumelade and wild garlic. Reservations advised. March–Oct Wed–Fri & Sun 12.15–1.45pm, Tues–Sat 6.15–8.45pm, plus Nov–Xmas Wed–Sat 6.15–8.45pm.

Stein Inn Stein ☎ 01470 592362, ⓦ thesteininn.co.uk. This eighteenth-century waterfront inn – the oldest on Skye – is as traditional as you would hope. Come for local ales, an impressive array of malts, and simple but delicious dishes like Skye scallops in oatmeal and Highland venison pie (mains around £13). Above are five cheerful en-suite rooms with sea views. Restaurant Mon–Thurs 11am–11pm/midnight, Fri & Sat 11am–midnight/1am; food served Easter–Oct daily noon–3pm & 6–9pm; Oct–Easter Wed–Sat noon–2.30pm. **£80**

Portree

With a population of around 2500, **PORTREE** is something of a metropolis by Skye's standards. That said, the town still has a small-village feel and is one of the most attractive ports in northwest Scotland, its deep, cliff-edged harbour filled with fishing boats and circled by multicoloured houses. Originally known as Kiltaraglen, it takes its current name – some say – from Port Rìgh (Port of the King), after the state visit James V made in 1540 to assert his authority over the chieftains of Skye.

The focus of activity for many visitors is the **harbour**, with an attractive wharf that dates from the early nineteenth century and a fishing fleet that still lands a modest catch. Looming behind is **The Lump**, a steep and stumpy peninsula on which public hangings once attracted crowds of up to five thousand. The tidy town centre spreads around **Somerled Square**, built in the late eighteenth century as the island's administrative and commercial centre. Rather sadly, it now serves as Portree's bus station and car park.

ARRIVAL AND DEPARTURE PORTREE

By bus Portree is the hub of all transport on the island and has mainland connections from Glasgow with CityLink. Destinations Broadford via Sligachan (Mon–Sat 4–6 daily; 50min); Dunvegan (Mon–Sat 3–6 daily; 45min); Glasgow (Mon–Sat 3 daily; 6hr 15min); Glenbrittle (Mon–Sat 2 daily; 50min); Trotternish circuit via Old Man of Storr, Staffin and Uig (Mon–Sat 6 daily; 2hr total circuit).

INFORMATION AND GETTING AROUND

Tourist office Just off Bridge St (July & Aug Mon–Sat 9am–6pm, Sun 9am–5pm; April, May, Sept & Oct Mon–Sat 9am–5pm, Sun 10am–4pm; Nov–March Mon–Sat 9.30am–4.30pm; ☎ 01478 612992), this is now the island's sole tourist office, hence has loads of information and can book accommodation.

Bike rental Skye Bike Shack, The Old Croft House, 6 Carbost, Skeabost Bridge (Tues–Sat 9am–1pm; ☎ 01470 532375, ⓦ skyebikeshack.com) has top notch bikes for hire (£30/day) as well as offering a repairs service.

ACCOMMODATION

★ **Ben Tianavaig** 5 Bosville Terrace ☎ 01478 612152, ⓦ ben-tianavaig.co.uk. The best B&B in the centre, with a warm welcome from your hosts and three cottagey en-suites that are modern and bright, with unrestricted harbour views from the top-floor rooms. Sociable atmosphere over breakfast, which includes a daily special – such as eggs Benedict – as well as the usual options. Two-night minimum stay. May–Sept. **£85**

Bosville Hotel Bosville Terrace ☎ 01478 612846, ⓦ bosvillehotel.co.uk. Central, boutique hotel offering sleek, comfortable rooms with vintage touches, textiles from Skye Weavers and colourful ceramics from Katharina Lenz in Teangue. Downstairs, the restaurant and bar are among the finest in town. **£165**

Cuillin Hills Hotel Turn left at end of Bosville Terrace ☎ 01478 612003, ⓦ cuillinhills-hotel-skye.co.uk. Lord MacDonald's old hunting lodge secluded in fifteen acres is the smartest formal hotel in Portree, and with views over the Sound of Raasay makes a luxurious country stay with town facilities to hand. Accommodation is spacious and comfortable, refurbished into a sort of Highlands chic. **£240**

Portree Youth Hostel Centre of town, on Bridge Rd ☎ 01478 612231, ⓦ hostellingscotland.org.uk. This sparkling hostel is one of the best equipped on the island, with some 55 beds across bunk dorms and private doubles with en-suites; lounge, kitchen and laundry facilities too Dorms £26, doubles £72

Torvaig Campsite 2 miles north of Portree on A855 ☎01478 611849, ⓦportreecampsite.co.uk. Views of mountains and flat pitches appeal at this family-run site on the road to Staffin, with decent facilities. Easter–Oct. Per person £9

★ **Viewfield House** Signposted off A87 ☎01478 612217, ⓦviewfieldhouse.com. The last word in Scots Baronial style is this pile on the southern edge of town which is almost eccentric in its Victorian grandeur – all fabulous floral wallpaper, hunting trophies, stuffed polecats and antiques. Rooms are individually furnished; some tranquil, some gloriously over the top. Easter to early Oct. £180

EATING AND DRINKING

Café Arriba Quay Brae ☎01478 611830, ⓦcafearriba. co.uk. This local institution packs in the punters, who come for a gossip over coffee or tea served in large china pots as much as the globe-trotting lunch menu of home-made soups, wraps, pastas or creative fast food like wild-boar hot dogs (mains around £10). Good veggie options available. Easter–Oct daily 7am–6pm.

Dulse and Brose Bosville Hotel ☎01478 612846, ⓦbosvillehotel.co.uk. The name translates as "seaweed and oatmeal" and the menu is as varied as this suggests; everything from smoked trout rillettes to duck breast with haggis bon bon, all served in sophisticated, chic surroundings. The neighbouring *Merchant Bar* is the best boozer in town, serving Skye beers and a wealth of whiskies

in an understated, cool space. Bar daily noon–5pm, restaurant serves lunches noon–3pm & dinner 6–10pm.

Isles Inn Somerled Square ☎01478 612129, www. accommodationskye.co.uk. With its log fire and flagstone floors, this rough-and-ready pub has the occasional ceilidh band. Alongside Skye ales, it serves no-nonsense pub grub for around a tenner. Daily 11am–1am.

★ **Scorrybreac** Bosville Terrace ☎01478 612069, ⓦscorrybreac.com. Just eight tables in what could be somebody's front room, but is in fact one of Skye's most exciting restaurants. Chef Calum Munro serves the likes of rib with truffle and toast, and dark chocolate with lavender ice cream (3 courses £48) in charmingly intimate quarters. Feb–Nov Tues–Sat 5–9.30pm.

Trotternish

Protruding twenty miles north of Portree, the **Trotternish peninsula** has some of the island's most bizarre scenery, particularly on the east coast, where volcanic basalt has pressed down on softer sandstone and limestone, causing massive landslides. These, in turn, have created sheer cliffs, peppered with outcrops of hard, wizened basalt – pinnacles and pillars that are at their most eccentric in the **Quiraing**, above Staffin Bay, a long arc of beach just north of Staffin village.

Old Man of Storr
6 miles north of Portree along the A855

The most celebrated column of rock on Skye, the **Old Man of Storr** is all that is left after one massive landslip. Huge blocks of stone still occasionally break off the cliff of the Storr (2358ft) above. A half-hour trek from a car park ascends to the pillar, but don't expect to have it to yourself – this is one of the island's signature sights, and will be busy whatever the weather.

Lealt Falls
Off the A855, east of Lealt

Five miles north of the Old Man, a signposted turn goes west to the **Lealt Falls**, at the head of a gorge which is largely in shadow (and home to crack squadrons of midges). The views across to Raasay and Rona from the first stage of the path can be spectacular. The coast here is worth exploring, too, especially the track leading to **Rubha nam Brathairean** (Brothers' Point).

Kilt Rock
Off the A855, southeast of Staffin

With spectacular tubular, basalt columns that plummet into the sea – like the folds in a kilt, apparently – and cliffs dotted with fulmar and kittiwake, it's little surprise **Kilt Rock** is a popular call on the tourist route. A waterfall which falls 170ft to the sea only adds to the appeal. The car park is a few miles north of the Lealt Falls turn.

5

Quiraing

Just past Staffin Bay, a single-track road cuts east across the peninsula into the **Quiraing**, a spectacular area of rock pinnacles, sheer cliffs and strange rock formations produced by rock slips. There are two **car parks**: from the first, beside a cemetery, it's a steep half-hour climb to the rocks; from the second, on the saddle, it's a longer but more gentle traverse. Once you're among the rocks, you can make out "The Prison" to your right, and the 131ft "Needle" to your left. "The Table", a sunken platform where locals used to play shinty, lies a further fifteen-minute scramble up the rocks.

Duntulm

Beyond Flodigarry, four miles further along the A855, lies **DUNTULM** (Duntuilm), whose heyday as a MacDonald power base is recalled by the shattered remains of a headland fortress abandoned by the clan in 1732; they say a clumsy nurse dropped the baby son and heir from a window onto the rocks below. They also say you can see the keel marks of Viking longships scoured into the rocks.

Skye Museum of Island Life

On the A855, 2 miles southwest of Duntulm • Easter–Sept Mon–Sat 9.30am–5pm • £3 • ☎ 01470 552206, ⓦ skyemuseum.co.uk

It's a short trip from Duntulm to the best of the island's folk museums. Run by a local family, the **Skye Museum of Island Life** – an impressive collection of eight thatched blackhouses decorated with home furnishings and farming tools – provides an insight into a way of life commonplace only a century ago. Behind the museum are the graves of **Flora MacDonald**, heroine during Bonnie Prince Charlie's flight, and her husband. Such was her fame that the original mausoleum fell victim to souvenir hunters and had to be replaced. The Celtic cross headstone is inscribed with a tribute by Dr Johnson, who visited her in 1773: "Her name will be mentioned in history, if courage and fidelity be virtues mentioned with honour."

Uig

Skye's chief ferry port for the Western Isles is **UIG** (Uige; pronounced "oo-ig"), which curves its way round a dramatic horseshoe bay. In the past most folk would just pass through here, but with a clutch of excellent places to stay and eat now, as well as the chance to pop into the Skye Brewing Co on the harbour, this is becoming a destination in its own right. Don't miss the lovely, gentle **walk** up Glen Uig, better known as the **Faerie Glen**, a Hobbity landscape of miniature hills at the east end of the bay.

ARRIVAL AND GETTING AROUND — TROTTERNISH

By ferry CalMac (☎ 0800 066 5000, ⓦ calmac.co.uk) sails between Uig and Tarbert on the Isle of Harris (1–2 daily; 1hr 40min).

By bus A circular bus route (service #57A and #57C) loops around the peninsula from Portree via Old Man of Storr, Staffin and Uig (Mon–Sat 6 daily; 2hr total circuit).

ACCOMMODATION AND EATING

STAFFIN AND AROUND

Ellishadder Art Café Culnacnoc, 3 miles south of Staffin ☎ 01470 562734, ⓦ ellishaddergallery.co.uk. Superb light lunches of savoury tarts like courgette, fennel and goats' cheese (£8.90) plus exquisite cakes for afternoon nibbles in a gallery/café that sells the owners' beautiful hand-weavings and paintings. Easter–Oct Mon–Thurs noon–4.30pm.

Staffin Campsite Staffin ☎ 01470 562213, ⓦ staffin campsite.co.uk. A spacious site with a relaxed vibe and a good location spread beneath the Trotternish Ridge, with glimpses of the sea a 10min walk away. There's plenty of flat

ground and a simple amenities block. Bike rental available (£5/half day). Per person **£5**

UIG

★ **Cowshed Bunkhouse** Just south of Uig, off the A87 ☎ 07917 536820, ⓦ skyecowshed.co.uk. Closer to chic hotel than banged-up bothy, this "boutique bunkhouse" offers four- and six-bed dorms (all with privacy curtains and underfloor heating), and posh pods sleeping four with heating and kitchenette. The relaxed, open-plan living and dining area is kitted out with log-burner and Space Invaders gaming table, with views of Uig harbour. Dorms **£18**, pods **£60**

RAASAY IN HISTORY

Raasay's woes began after the staunchly Jacobite MacLeods of Lewis sent a hundred local men and 26 pipers to Culloden. Bonnie Prince Charlie later spent a miserable night on Raasay in a "mean low hut" during his flight and swore to replace the turf cottages with proper stone houses (he never did). Raasay was practically destroyed by **government troops** in the aftermath of the 1745 uprising, then when the MacLeods were forced to sell up in 1843, the Clearances started in earnest. In 1921, seven ex-servicemen and their families from neighbouring **Rona** illegally squatted crofts on Raasay, and were imprisoned, causing a public outcry. As a result, both islands were **bought** by the government the following year. Rona now has one permanent resident while Raasay's population stands at around two hundred.

★ **Ferry Inn** On the A87 ☎01470 542300, ⓦtheferry innskye.com. This sophisticated, luxury inn has four en-suite doubles – two with bay views and two with woodland views – above one of Skye's best pubs. The long, impressive bar was made from elm wood salvaged from the Clan Donald estate, and the cask Isle of Skye Brewing Co ales are brewed just a few hundred yards away. Two-night minimum stay and no under 18s £185

The Sheiling & Ella's Café ☎01470 542797. Within a former crofters' warehouse behind Uig garage, Ella serves home-made toasted focaccia, smoked salmon and crowdie pâté and delicious baking (£5–8). It doubles as a local crafts outlet to feel like a village hall on fête day. Tues–Sat 10am–4pm.

Woodbine House ☎01470 542243, ⓦwoodbineskye. co.uk. In a late nineteenth-century house on the Duntulum Road, this smart B&B has five tasteful en-suite rooms, some of which benefit from ace sea views, along with a cosy lounge and roaring log fire. The helpful owners also arrange activities, including wildlife-spotting trips (from £20) and kayak rental (£35 for 3 people, half day). March–Sept. £72

Isle of Raasay

The hilly, fourteen-mile island of **Raasay** (Ratharsair) – meaning "Isle of the Roe Deer" – sees few visitors. Yet in many ways it's the ultimate Skye escape, with plenty of walks – intimate strolls compared to the wide spaces of Skye – and rich flora and fauna, including golden eagles, snipe, orchids and the unique Raasay vole, not to mention the castaway thrill of a small island. Most visitors come on foot – if you come by car, be aware there's no filling station. The ferry docks in Churchton Bay, near **INVERARISH**, the island's tiny village set within thick woods on the southwest coast. The chief – indeed only – attraction here is the **Isle of Raasay Distillery** (01478 470178; raasaydistillery.com), a state of the art facility which began distilling in 2017, hence its first single malt, a lightly-peated version, only rolled off the production line in 2020; you can partake in one of three different tours (£10–15); the views from here are fantastic. You can stay here, too, at **Borodale House** (see page 284).

Dun Caan

Most visitors come to walk into the island's interior – a rugged terrain of sandstone in the south and gneiss in the north. The obvious destination is the flat-top volcanic plug of **Dun Caan** (1456ft) where Boswell "danced a Highland dance" when he visited with Dr Johnson in 1773. The five-mile trail to the top is easy to follow; a splendid trek along the burn through forest behind Inverarish, culminating in epic 360-degree views of Skye and the mainland from the top. The quickest return is down the northwest slope, but you can also get back to the ferry along the path by the southeast shore, passing the abandoned crofters' village of Hallaig. Keep your eyes peeled for roaming eagles overhead and the odd scuttling grouse.

North Raasay

On a fine day the north provides fine views across to the Cuillin, Portree and the Trotternish peninsula. Where the road dips to the east coast the stark remains of fifteenth-century **Brochel Castle** stand overlooking the shore. The final two-mile stretch

5

of the road to Arnish is known as **Calum's Road**: in the 1960s the council refused to extend the road, so Calum MacLeod decided to build it himself. It took him ten years, and by the time he'd finished he and his wife were the only people left in the village.

ARRIVAL AND INFORMATION

ISLE OF RAASAY

By ferry The CalMac ferry (Mon–Sat 8–10 daily, Sun 2 daily; 25min; ☎ 01687 462403, ⓦ calmac.co.uk) to Raasay

departs from Sconser, 3 miles northeast of *Sligachan Hotel*.
Tourist information ⓦ raasay.com.

ACCOMMODATION AND EATING

Borodale House Short walk from ferry pier ☎ 01478 470178, ⓦ raasaydistillery.com. Luxury accommodation within the Isle of Raasay Distillery building itself. The six en-suite bedrooms have all the comforts of a boutique hotel, from feather pillows to fluffy towels, and three are blessed with sensational views of the Isle of Skye. Guests have exclusive access to a lounge-bar; continental breakfast included. Open Feb–Nov (distillery tours run year-round). **£215**

Raasay House 5-minute walk from Distillery ☎ 01478 660300, ⓦ raasay-house.co.uk. The MacLeods' rebuilt

manor offers everything from four-star deluxe rooms with balconies and views to the Cuillins to modern bunkrooms. The convivial bar/restaurant is the best place to eat and drink on the island, offering comforting dishes such as wild Raasay venison pie (£18.95). Among activities on offer (Easter–Oct, weather-dependent other months) are guided walks and canyoning, coasteering, kayaking and sailing (all £45–50), and boat trips (from £30). Bike rental available for £15/half day. Dorms **£25**, doubles **£95**

The Small Isles

Seen from southern Skye or the west coast of the Highlands, the **Small Isles** – **Rùm**, **Eigg**, **Muck** and tiny **Canna** – lie scattered in a silver-grey sea like a siren call to adventure. After centuries of being passed between owners, most islands have stabilized into tight-knit communities of crofters. While Muck is still privately owned, Eigg was bought out by its islanders in 1997, ending more than 150 years of property speculation, while other islands have been bequeathed to national agencies: Rùm, by far the largest and most visited of the group, passed to the Nature Conservancy Council (now Scottish Natural Heritage) in 1957; and Canna has been in the hands of the National Trust for Scotland since 1981.

Many people come on a day-trip from Mallaig, but the Small Isles deserve longer. They are an opportunity to experience some off-grid island life while walking, birdwatching or simply admiring seascapes. Accommodation requires **forward planning**, and public transport on the islands is nonexistent. But regular ferries mean you're not as cut off as the atmosphere suggests. Better still, services link all islands for a happy week of island-hopping.

Brief history

The history of the Small Isles is typical of the Hebrides: early Christianization, followed by Norwegian rule, ending in 1266 when the islands fell into Scottish hands. Their support for the Jacobites resulted in hard times after the failed 1745 rebellion, but the biggest problems came in the mid-eighteenth century. The success of potatoes grown with traditional cereals eliminated famine at a stroke, prompting a population explosion. In 1750, there were a thousand islanders. By 1800 that number had almost doubled. At first, the problem of **overcrowding** was camouflaged by a kelp boom, but the economic bubble burst with the end of the Napoleonic Wars and, to maintain profit margins, the owners resorted to drastic action. The first to **sell** was Alexander MacLean. Having acquired quotations to ship its people to Nova Scotia, he gave islanders a year's notice and sold Rùm as grazing land. He also cleared Muck to graze cattle, as did the MacNeills on Canna. Only on Eigg was compassion shown: the new owner, a certain Hugh MacPherson, who bought the island in 1827, offered some tenants extended leases.

ARRIVAL AND DEPARTURE   **THE SMALL ISLES**

Be aware that boats are frequently cancelled by bad **weather**, so check forecasts.

By ferry CalMac (☎01687 462403, ⓦcalmac.co.uk) sails from Mallaig (late March to mid-Oct daily, otherwise Mon–Sat), although doesn't sail to all islands each day.

Long day-trips are possible on Sat. Sheerwater (☎01687 450224, ⓦarisaig.co.uk) sails return trips daily from Arisaig to Eigg (£18), plus Rùm (£20) or Muck (£25) from late April to late Sept. The ride doubles as a wildlife cruise so, while enjoyable, is more expensive than travelling with CalMac.

Rùm

After almost a century as the "Forbidden Isle" – the exclusive sporting estate of self-made Lancastrian industrialists the Bulloughs – **Rùm** has opened up. Indeed, since it passed to Scottish Natural Heritage (SNH) in 1957, visitors are positively encouraged. Many come to hike the eight-mile **Rùm Cuillin Ridge Walk**, tracking a crown of peaks that are modest by Skye's standards – the summit of Askival is only 2663ft – but every bit as impressive in looks. And in recent years, crofting land has been released as Scottish Natural Heritage tries to encourage a community. Most of the island's twenty or so inhabitants live around **KINLOCH** on the east coast, and many are employed by SNH, which runs the island as a National Nature Reserve. SNH have reintroduced native woodland and **white-tailed (sea) eagles**, most of which promptly flew to neighbouring islands. The island is renowned for its **Manx shearwaters**, which nest in burrows on high peaks. You can learn more about the flora and fauna in an unmanned **visitor centre** halfway between the wharf and castle.

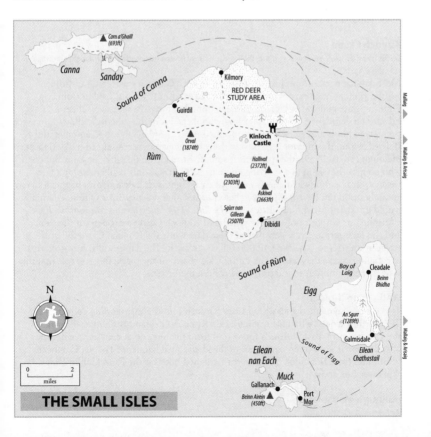

> ### HIKING IN THE RÙM CUILLIN
> *Ordnance Survey Explorer map 397*
>
> Rùm's **Cuillin** may not be as famous as Skye's, but in fine weather offers equally exhilarating **hiking** possibilities. Whatever route you choose, be sure to take all the usual safety precautions (see page 42).
>
> The most popular walk is to traverse most or part of the **Cuillin Ridge**, around a twelve-hour round trip from Kinloch. The most frequent route is via Coire Dubh, then on to the saddle of Bealach Bairc-mheall. From here, you can either climb Barkeval to the west, or go for **Hallival** (2372ft) southeast, which looks daunting but is only a mild scramble. South of Hallival, the ridge is grassy, but the north ridge of **Askival** (2663ft) needs to be taken carefully, sticking to the east side. Askival is the highest mountain on Rùm, and if you're thinking of heading back, or the weather's closing in, Glen Dibidil provides an easy descent.
>
> To continue along the ridge, head west to the double peak of **Trollaval** (or Trallval). The descent to Bealach an Fhuarain is steep, after which it's another scramble to reach the top of **Ainshval** (2562ft). Depending on the time and weather, you can continue along the ridge to **Sgùrr nan Gillean**, descend via Glen Dibidil and take the coastal path back to Kinloch, or skip the Sgùrr and go straight on to the last peak of the ridge, **Ruinsival**.

The best **beach** is **Kilmory** in the north of the island, a flattish walk on tracks through Kinloch then Kilmory glens (10 miles, 5hr return from Kinloch). Bear in mind that Rùm is the wettest of the Small Isles, and is notorious for midges (see page 39) – come prepared.

Kinloch Castle

Kinloch, signposted 15min walk from ferry • March–Oct Mon–Sat 45min guided tours coincide with the ferry, though do check in advance • £9 • ☎ 01254 823323

Most day-trippers to Rùm head straight for **Kinloch Castle**, a squat, red-sandstone edifice. Built at huge expense in 1900 – the red sandstone was shipped in from Dumfriesshire and the soil for the gardens from Ayrshire – its interior is sheer Edwardian decadence. It's also appealingly bonkers. From the galleried hall, with its tiger rugs, stags' heads and giant Japanese incense burners, to the Soho snooker table in the Billiard Room, the interior is packed with technical gizmos accumulated by **Sir George Bullough** (1870–1939), the spendthrift son of self-made millionaire, Sir John Bullough, who bought the island as a sporting estate in 1888. It was only really used for a few weeks each autumn, when guests were woken at eight each morning by a bagpiper; later, an orchestrion (an electrically driven barrel organ) that was made for Queen Victoria would grind out pre-dinner ditties like *The Ride of the Valkyries* and *Ma Blushin' Rosie*.

During our last visit only the downstairs of Kinloch Castle was open for the tour, and the orchestrion rarely gets played these days while the Kinloch Castle Friends Association tries to raise the £40,000 bill to restore it. The damp walls, furniture rips and ceiling cracks may add to the ramshackle charm of the place, but you feel that the sooner the £5 million restoration fund comes, the better.

Walks from Kinloch

Two gentle waymarked **walks** head from Kinloch into the surrounding countryside. The **Northside nature trail** (1hr) circuits via Kinloch Glen and is signposted from the visitor centre. In addition, a forest trail from the ferry dock reaches an otter hide (15min return walk) then continues to the abandoned hamlet of Port na Caranean (40min on from the hide). The goal for hardened hikers is the Rùm Cuillin Ridge Walk (see box above).

Bullough Mausoleum

Harris, 8 miles southwest of Kinloch

When the island's head count peaked at 450 in 1791, the hamlet of **HARRIS** on the southwest coast (a 3–4hr walk from Kinloch) housed a crofting community. All that remains are ruined blackhouses, which makes the Neoclassical **Bullough Mausoleum** all the more extraordinary. It was built by Sir George for his father and is actually the second family mausoleum here: the first was lined with Italian marble, but dynamited after a friend remarked it looked like a public lavatory.

ARRIVAL AND INFORMATION — RÙM

By ferry The longest day-trip possibilities from Mallaig are on Sat (just under 11hr). Note that overnight visitors cannot bring dogs, but day-trippers can. Summer timetables are: Arisaig–Rùm (Tues, Thurs & Sat 1 daily; 1hr 45min–2hr 30min); Canna–Rùm (Mon, Wed, Fri & Sat 1 daily; 55min); Eigg–Rùm (Mon & Sat 1 daily; 1hr–3hr 30min); Mallaig–

Rùm (Mon, Wed, Fri, Sat & Sun 1 daily; 1hr 20min–2hr 30min).

Tourist information There is an unmanned visitor centre on the way from the ferry to Kinloch Castle. Another good source of information is ⓦisleofrum.com.

ACCOMMODATION AND EATING

Visitors are permitted to **wild camp** and there are two simple **bothies** (three nights maximum) in Dibidil, on the southeast coast, and Guirdil, on the northwest coast. You'll find a shop/post office/off-licence in Kinloch, beside the community hall, which serves **teas** and **snacks** (during summer open 10am–noon on ferry days, and 5–7pm most evenings).

Ivy Cottage Kinloch ☏01687 462744, ⓦivycottage isleofrum.co.uk. Delivers loch views from two pleasant en-suite rooms (one of which can be used as a family room) and the conservatory where you have breakfast and dinner, both of which are included in the price. Bikes to rent, and a craft shop next door. Two-night minimum stay April–Sept. £150

Kinloch Campsite ☏01687 460328. A community-run campsite with an appealing location spread along the shore on the south side of Kinloch Bay. Also on site are four tiny, insulated camping cabins with four mattresses each. Camping per person £8; cabins for two £35

Rum Bunkhouse Kinloch ☏01687 460318, ⓦrum bunkhouse.com. This impressive bunkhouse is the most comfortable option on the island for walking groups who don't want to brave the bothies. Twenty beds (one twin, three four-beds and a six-bed dorm), plus a large living area with sofas and a wood-burning stove, and two well equipped kitchens. Per person £23, twin £50

Eigg

Eigg – which measures just five miles by three – does little to conceal its volcanic origins. It is made of a basalt plateau, and a great stump of pitchstone lava, known as An Sgùrr, rises in the south. Geology aside, Eigg has an appealingly strong sense of community among its hundred-odd residents. This was given an enormous boost in 1997 when they (alongside the Scottish Wildlife Trust) pulled off the first **buyout** of a Highlands estate, thereby ending Eigg's unhappy history of private ownership. The anniversary is celebrated with an all-night **ceilidh** on the weekend nearest June 12. Its other world-first is that its electricity grid is powered entirely by renewable sources.

Galmisdale

Ferries arrive into **Galmisdale Bay**, in the southeast corner of the island. Head up through woods for superb sea views, or track the shore south to see crofting ruins before the Sgùrr cliffs – the remains of Upper and Lower Grulin settlements. If the tide is low you can scramble along the shore into Cathedral Cave or Massacre Cave (**Uamh Fhraing**), where all but one of Eigg's 396 inhabitants died in 1577, suffocated by the MacLeods of Skye, who lit a fire in the cave mouth. Bring a torch and prepare to feel spooked.

An Sgùrr

The largest piece of pitchstone in the UK, **An Sgùrr** (1289ft) is the obvious destination for a hike. Actually, the route up is not as daunting as the cliffs suggest; the path is signposted left from the main road, crossing boggy moor to approach the summit from the north via a saddle (3–4hr return). The rewards are wonderful views to Muck and Rùm.

5

Cleadale

For an easy stroll, strike out to **CLEADALE**, the main crofting settlement in north Eigg. It's spectacularly sited beneath the island's basalt ridge, **Ben Bhuidhe**, and above a beach known as Camas Sgiotaig, or the **Singing Sands**, because the quartz grains squeak underfoot. The views from here to Rùm, its peaks often cloaked by clouds, are unforgettable.

Museum of Crofting Life

Croft 6 • Always open • Free • ☎ 01687 482410

While in Cleadale, poke your head into the community-run **Museum of Crofting Life** to see what life would have been like for the Campbell family, who moved here in 1907. Laminated print-outs bring context to the building's items, which include an old hot-water bottle, an original Singer sewing machine and hundreds of tools and cast iron utensils laid out in the attic.

ARRIVAL AND DEPARTURE   EIGG

By ferry Summer timetables are: Canna–Eigg (Mon & Sat 1 daily; 2hr 10min); Mallaig–Eigg (Mon, Thurs, Sat & Sun 1hr 15min); Muck–Eigg (Thurs 1 daily; 35min); Rùm–Eigg (Mon & Sat 1 daily; 1hr–3hr 20min). Note that visitors (except for disabled badge holders, are not permitted to bring vehicles onto the island.

GETTING AROUND AND INFORMATION

By minibus or bike A minibus is scheduled around ferries (☎ 01687 482494; £2). Bike rental is available from Eigg Adventures (☎ 01687 347007, ⊛ eiggadventures.co.uk; £15/day), based at the harbour. They also offer kayak rental (£20 for 2hr), archery sessions (£12; 50min) and guided walks (from £15).

Tourist information The friendly folk at the *An Laimhrig* complex will give you all the information you need. Alternatively, visit ⊛ isleofeigg.org.

ACCOMMODATION AND EATING

There's an excellent **wild camp** on north Galmisdale Bay. A craft and produce **market** in the community hall uphill from Galmisdale (June–Aug Mon noon–4pm; occasionally during winter) is a great spot to pick up lunch.

An Laimhrig Harbour. Island ingredients go into home-made soups, quiche, pizza, lamb or venison burgers, plus blackboard specials such as fishcakes – all for under £10. Craft shop and well-stocked mini-supermarket in the same complex. Summer open 10am (Sun 11.30am), evening meals available during peak months, winter open around ferry schedules.

Glebe Barn Galmisdale ☎ 01687 482417, ⊛ glebebarn. co.uk. Eigg's hostel on the hill above the harbour has a spacious lounge with awesome coast views and pleasant wee dorm rooms. Better still is the self-contained cottage *Glebe Apartment* – a superb stay for up to three people. April–Oct. Dorms **£21**, twins **£47**, apartment from **£62**

Kildonan House Down a long, unmarked road, north side of Galmisdale Bay ☎ 01687 482446, ⊛ kildonan houseeigg.co.uk. A traditional stay in an eighteenth-century farmhouse, whose warm and welcoming host Marie offers three pleasingly simple pine-panelled rooms, one with an en-suite shower, all with sea views and dinners (usually catch-of-the-day) included. **£120**

★ **Lageorna** Cleadale ☎ 01687 460081, ⊛ lageorna. com. Two beautiful, modern rooms full of contemporary crafts – think rustic wooden beds (built on Rùm) and knitted throws – and astonishing views, plus a lovely vintage cottage that sleeps six. The owner also prepares superb three-course set menus for just £30. Closed over Christmas and New Year, open by arrangement over winter months. Doubles **£110**, cottage **£650**

Sue Holland's Croft Cleadale ☎ 01687 482480, ⊛ eiggorganics.co.uk. On an organic croft, this is the only designated campsite and it's a belter, with views and sunsets to inspire poetry. The old cowshed is now a basic bothy for up to four, or for more comfort choose a yurt; for all accommodation, guests are free to avail themselves of the shower and toilet facilities in the house. Sue also runs crofting tours and courses on growing vegetables. Camping per person **£5**, bothy and yurt **£50**

Muck

Barely two miles long, tiny **Muck** is the smallest and most southerly of the Small Isles. Low-lying and almost treeless, it is extremely fertile, so has more in common with Coll and Tiree than with its neighbours. Its name derives from *muc*, the Gaelic for "pig" (or possibly *muc mara*, "sea pig" or porpoise, which are plentiful), and has long caused embarrassment to lairds – they preferred to call it the "Isle of Monk" because it briefly belonged to the medieval church.

PORT MÓR is the hub of all activity, where visitors arrive and just about all of the thirty or so residents live – a tenth of the 320 of the early 1800s. A mile-long road connects Port Mór with the island's main farm, **Gallanach**, which overlooks rocky skerries on the north side. The nicest sandy **beach** is Camas na Cairidh, to the east of Gallanach. For a stiffer challenge, **Beinn Airein** (2hr return), in the southwest corner of the island, is worth climbing, despite being only 450ft above sea level, for a 360-degree panorama of surrounding islands from its summit.

ARRIVAL AND INFORMATION
MUCK

By ferry Summer timetables are: Canna–Muck (Sat 1 daily; 1hr 35min); Eigg–Muck (Thurs, Sat & Sun 1 daily; 45min); Mallaig–Muck (Tues & Thurs–Sun 1 daily; 1hr 30min–2hr).

Tourist information The Craft Shop & Tea Room (see below) doubles as an information point. See also ⓦ isleofmuck.com.

ACCOMMODATION AND EATING

To **wild camp** on the island, check in at The Craft Shop & Tea Room to find out about any areas currently off-limits.

The Craft Shop & Tea Room Port Mór ☎ 07908 956822. The only shop on the island prepares daily soups and sandwiches made from fresh home-baked bread, plus afternoon teas and dinners of fresh shellfish prepared on request. April, May & Sept days & hours vary; June–Aug daily except Thurs 11am–4pm.

Gallanach Lodge Gallanach Bay ☎ 01687 462365, ⓦ gallanachlodge.co.uk. A purpose-built luxury lodge that takes full advantage of a superb position above the beach to provide fantastic views to Rùm. The style is island boutique – rustic, handmade beds in eight rooms (a mixture of doubles and twins) with hotel-style mod cons. Full board only. **£180**

Isle of Muck Bunkhouse Port Mór ☎ 07833 195654, ⓔ bunkhouse@isleofmuck.com. Two bunkrooms and two doubles in the island's simple wee hostel, sited near the port. Life revolves around the Raeburn stove in the simple living room and the kitchen. Hardly luxurious but full of character. Extra £5 for bedding. Per person **£22**

Canna

Measuring a mere five miles by one, **Canna** is managed as a **bird sanctuary** by the National Trust for Scotland (NTS). There are no roads, just open moorland stretched over a basalt ridge, and few people now that the population has dwindled to eight. While Canna doesn't receive many visitors by ferry, plenty come by yacht for the best harbour in the Small Isles, a sheltered bay off Canna's main hamlet, **A'Chill**. Notwithstanding walks (see below), you come to Canna for birdlife; this has been a sanctuary since 1938, and 157 species have been recorded, including golden and white-tailed eagles, and Manx shearwaters, razorbills and puffins on cliffs at the western end.

Although less obviously scenic than the other Small Isles, the flat(ish) terrain makes for enjoyable **walks**. You can circuit the entire island on a long day (10hr; 12 miles), or from the dock it's about a mile across a grassy plateau to the cliffs on the north shore and Compass Hill, named because its high iron content distorts compasses. A mile west is Carn a'Ghaill, Canna's summit at a heady 688ft.

ARRIVAL AND INFORMATION
CANNA

By ferry Summer timetables are: Eigg–Canna (Mon & Sat; 1 daily; 2hr 20min); Mallaig–Canna (Mon, Wed, Fri & Sun 1 daily, Sat 2 daily; 2hr 30min–3hr 45min); Muck–Canna (Sat 1 daily; 1hr 35min); Rùm–Canna (Mon, Wed & Fri–Sun 1 daily; 1hr 5min).

Tourist information ⓦ theisleofcanna.com.

ACCOMMODATION

With permission from the NTS, you may **wild camp** on Canna, though bring supplies.

Tighard ☎ 01687 462474, ⓦ tighard.com. The Sanday room is the pick – spacious, traditional and with sweeping sea views – in the only B&B on Canna. Its other two smaller and simpler twins also enjoy sea views. Friendly host Fiona also offer packed lunch and dinner with prior arrangement. **£110**

The Western Isles

BLACKHOUSE, GARENIN (GEARRANNAN)

The Western Isles

Beyond Skye, across the unpredictable waters of the Minch, lie the wild and windy Outer Hebrides, officially known as the Western Isles. A 130-mile-long archipelago stretching from Lewis and Harris in the north to the Uists and Barra in the south, the islands appear as an unbroken chain when viewed from across the Minch, hence their nickname, the Long Isle. In reality there are more than two hundred islands, although only a handful are inhabited, with the total population around 28,000. This is truly a land on the edge, where the turbulent seas of the Atlantic smash up against a geologically complex terrain whose coastline is interrupted by a thousand sheltered bays and sweeping sandy beaches. The islands' interiors are equally dramatic, veering between flat, boggy, treeless peat moor and bare mountaintops soaring high above a host of tiny lakes, or lochans.

The major difference between the Western Isles and much of the Hebrides is that the islands' fragile economy is still mainly concentrated around crofting, fishing and weaving, and the percentage of incomers is low. In fact, the Outer Hebrides remain the heartland of **Gaelic** culture, with the language spoken by the majority of islanders. Its survival is partly thanks to the efforts of the Western Islands Council, the Scottish parliament and the influence of the Church in the region: the Free Church and its various offshoots in Lewis, Harris and North Uist, and the Catholic Church in South Uist and Barra.

Lewis and Harris form two parts of the same island. The interior of the northernmost, **Lewis**, is mostly peat moor, a barren and marshy tract that gives way to the bare peaks of **North Harris**. Across a narrow isthmus lies **South Harris**, with wide beaches of golden sand trimming the Atlantic in full view of the rough boulder-strewn mountains to the east. Across the Sound of Harris, to the south, a string of tiny, flatter isles linked by causeways – **North Uist**, **Benbecula**, **South Uist** – offers breezy beaches, whose fine sands front a narrow band of boggy farmland, which, in turn, is bordered by a lower range of hills to the east. Finally, tiny **Barra** contains all the above landscapes in one small Hebridean package and is connected by causeway to even tinier **Vatersay**.

In contrast to their wonderful surroundings, villages in the Western Isles are seldom picturesque in themselves, and are usually made up of scattered, relatively modern crofthouses dotted about the elementary road system. The Outer Hebrides' only sizeable settlement is Stornoway, a town which retains a modicum of charm thanks to what's left of its old harbour frontage and traditional and Victorian buildings in the near vicinity. Many visitors, walkers and nature-watchers forsake the main settlements altogether and retreat to secluded cottages, simple hostels and B&Bs.

GAELIC IN THE WESTERN ISLES

All Ordnance Survey maps and many **road signs** are exclusively in **Gaelic**, a difficult language to the English-speaker's eye, with complex pronunciation, though the English names sometimes provide a rough guide. If you're driving, it's a good idea to pick up a bilingual Western Isles **map**, available at most tourist offices. We've put the English equivalent first in the text, with the Gaelic in parentheses.

Highlights

❶ Garenin, Lewis An abandoned crofting village whose thatched blackhouses have been beautifully restored: some are now self-catering cottages, one is a café, and a couple have been left as they were when they were last inhabited. See page 304

❷ Callanish standing stones, Lewis Scotland's finest standing stones have a serene lochside setting on the west coast of the Isle of Lewis. See page 305

❸ Boat trip to St Kilda Permanently inhabited until 1930, now a UNESCO World Heritage Site; getting to this tiny, remote island chain forty miles north-west of North Uist is an adventure in

itself. See page 307

❹ St Clement's Church, Harris Rodel's pre-Reformation church, at the southernmost tip of Harris, boasts the most ornate sculptural decoration in the Outer Hebrides. See page 313

❺ Barra and Vatersay beaches Barra and its tiny neighbour, Vatersay, are dotted with stunning, deserted golden-sand beaches backed by flower-cloaked machair. See pages 321 and 324

❻ Cycling the Hebridean Way Usually tackled south–north to make use of the prevailing wind, the scenic 185-mile Hebridean Way crosses ten islands from Vatersay to the Butt of Lewis. See page 325

HIGHLIGHTS ARE MARKED ON THE MAP ON PAGE 294

THE WESTERN ISLES

0 ————————————— 25
miles

N

Sula Sgeir
Butt of Lewis
Port of Ness

Flannan Isles

A857

Barvas

Garenin ❶ A858
Carloway
❷ Callanish
Standing
Stones

Arid Uig

Bernera

A857

Stornoway

A858

A859

A866

L e w i s

A859

U l l a p o o l

HIGHLIGHTS

❶ Garenin, Lewis

❷ Callanish standing stones, Lewis

❸ Boat trip to St Kilda

❹ St Clement's Church, Harris

❺ Barra and Vatersay beaches

❻ Cycling the Hebridean Way

Scarp

*An Cliseam
(2619ft)*

Taransay

Tarbert

*Shiant
Isles*

T h e   M i n c h

Scalpay

Harris

A859

Leverburgh
❹ † St Clement's
Church, Harris

Berneray

North Uist

A867
Lochmaddy

T h e   L i t t l e   M i n c h

Uig

*Monach
Islands*

Benbecula

A865

*Neist
Point*

Portree

Skye

Raasay

*South
Uist*

*Beinn Mhor
(2034ft)*

❻

Lochboisdale

A87
Broadford

Canna

Armadale

Eriskay

winter only

winter only

Hyskeir

Rùm

S M A L L   I S L E S

Mallaig

Barra

Castlebay

Vatersay

❺ *Sandray*

Pabbay

Mingulay
Barra Head

Eigg

Muck

Arisaig

W E S T E R N   I S L E S

❸ ◄ St Kilda

▼ Tiree

◆ Oban

Brief history

The Western Isles were first settled by Neolithic farming peoples around 4000 BC. They are remembered by scores of remains, from passage graves through to stone circles – most famously at **Callanish** (Calanais) on Lewis. Viking colonization gathered pace from 700 AD onwards – as evidenced by the islands' place names, the majority of which are of Norse, not Gaelic, origin – and it was only in 1266 that the islands were returned to the Scottish Crown. James VI (and I of England), a Stuart and a Scot, though no Gaelic-speaker, was the first to put forward the idea of clearing the Hebrides, though it wasn't until after the Jacobite uprisings, in which many Highland clans disastrously backed the wrong side, that the **Clearances** began in earnest.

The isolation of the Outer Hebrides exposed them to the whims and fancies of merchants and aristocrats who caught "island fever" and bought them up. From the mid-eighteenth century onwards, the land and its people have been sold to the highest bidder. Some proprietors have been well-meaning but insensitive – like **Lord Leverhulme**, who had no time for crofting and wanted to turn Lewis into a centre of the fishing industry in the 1920s. Others have simply been autocratic, such as **Colonel Gordon of Cluny**, who bought Benbecula, South Uist, Eriskay and Barra, and forced the inhabitants onto ships bound for North America at gunpoint. Almost everywhere crofters were driven from their ancestral homes, robbing them of their particular sense of place. Today, memorials and cairns dot the landscape, commemorating the often violent struggle which accompanied this period.

ARRIVAL AND DEPARTURE   THE WESTERN ISLES

By plane There are scheduled flights from Glasgow, Edinburgh, Inverness and Aberdeen to Stornoway on Lewis, and from Glasgow to Barra and Benbecula. Be warned: weather conditions are notoriously changeable, making flights prone to delay and even cancellation. On Barra, the plane lands on the beach, so the timetable is adjusted with the tides.

By ferry CalMac car ferries run two services daily from Ullapool to Stornoway; one or two daily from Uig, on Skye, to Tarbert and Lochmaddy; and operate daily from Oban to Barra and Mallaig to South Uist. The timetables quoted in the text are summer frequencies – check ⓦ calmac.co.uk for the latest and always book ahead.

GETTING AROUND

By car and by ferry A series of causeways makes it possible to drive from one end of the Western Isles to the other with just two interruptions – the ferry from Harris to Berneray, and from Eriskay to Barra. If you're going to take the ferry, it's advisable to book in advance. Note that petrol stations can be a long distance apart (and might be closed on Sundays).

By bus The islands have a decent bus service, though there are no buses on Sundays.

By bike The wind makes cycling something of a challenge – head from south to north to catch the prevailing wind. It's free to take bikes on all ferry services, or if you prefer to rent there are rental outlets in Barra and Stornoway.

Lewis (Leodhas)

Shaped rather like the top of an ice-cream cone, **Lewis** is the largest and most populous of the Western Isles. Nearly half of the island's inhabitants live in the crofting and fishing villages strung out along the northwest coast, between **Callanish** (Calanais) and **Port of Ness** (Port Nis), in one of the country's most densely populated rural areas. On this coast you'll also find the best-preserved **prehistoric remains** – Dun Carloway (Dùn Charlabhaigh) and the Callanish standing stones. The landscape is mostly peat bog – hence the island's Gaelic name, from *leogach* (marshy) – but the shoreline is more dramatic, especially around the Butt of Lewis, the island's northernmost tip. The rest of the island's population live in **Stornoway**, on the east coast, the only real town in the Western Isles. To the south, where Lewis is physically joined with Harris, the land rises to over 1800ft, providing an exhilarating backdrop for the excellent beaches that pepper the isolated western coastline around **Uig**.

6

RELIGION IN THE WESTERN ISLES

It's difficult to overestimate the importance of **religion** in the Western Isles, which are divided – with very little enmity – between the **Catholic** southern isles of Barra and South Uist, and the **Protestant** islands of North Uist, Harris and Lewis. Church attendance is higher than anywhere else in Britain and in fact, Barra, Eriskay and South Uist are the only parts of Britain where Catholics are in a majority, and where you'll see statues of the Madonna by the roadside. In the Presbyterian north, the creed of **Sabbatarianism** is strong. Here, Sunday is the Lord's Day, and the whole community (irrespective of their degree of piety) stops work – shops close, pubs close, garages close and there's very little public transport. Visitors should check whether it's OK to arrive at or leave their accommodation on a Sunday, to avoid causing offence.

The main area of division is, paradoxically, within the Protestant Church itself. Scotland's national church, the **Church of Scotland**, is Presbyterian (ruled by the ministers and elders of the church) rather than Episcopal (ruled by bishops). At the time of the main split in the Presbyterian Church – the so-called **1843 Disruption** – a third of its ministers left the Church of Scotland, protesting at a law that allowed landlords to impose ministers against parishioners' wishes, and formed the breakaway **Free Church of Scotland** – sometimes referred to as the "**Wee Frees**", though this term is also used for members of the Free Presbyterian Church of Scotland. Since those days there have been several amalgamations and reconciliations with the Church of Scotland, as well as further splits.

The various brands and subdivisions of the Presbyterian Church may appear trivial to outsiders, but to the churchgoers of Lewis, Harris and North Uist (as well as much of Skye and Raasay) they are still keenly felt. In part, this is due to social and cultural reasons: Free Church elders helped organize resistance to the Clearances, and the Wee Frees have contributed greatly to preserving the **Gaelic language**. A Free Church service is a memorable experience – there's no set service or prayer book and no hymns, only biblical readings, psalm singing and a sermon; the pulpit is the architectural focus of the church, not the altar, and communion is taken only on special occasions. If you want to attend a service, the Free Church on Kenneth Street in Stornoway has one of the UK's largest Sunday-evening congregations, with up to 1500 people attending.

Brief history

After Viking rule ended in 1266, Lewis became a virtually independent state, ruled over by the **MacLeod clan** for several centuries. In 1610, however, King James VI declared the folk of Lewis to be "void of religion", and attempted to establish a colony, as in Ulster, by sending Fife Adventurers to attack Lewis. They were met with armed resistance by the MacLeods, so, in retaliation, James VI granted the lands to their arch rivals, the MacKenzies of Kintail. The MacKenzie chiefs – the Earls of Seaforth – chose to remain absentee landlords until 1844, when they sold Lewis to **Sir James Matheson**, who'd made a fortune from pushing opium on the Chinese. Matheson was relatively benevolent when the island was hit by potato famine in the mid-1840s, but ultimately opted for solving the problem through eviction and emigration. His chief factor, Donald Munro, was utterly ruthless, and was only removed after the 1874 Bernera Riot. The 1886 Crofters' Act greatly curtailed the power of the Mathesons; it did not, however, right any of the wrongs of the past. Protests, such as the 1887 Pairc Deer Raid, in which starving crofters killed two hundred deer from one of the sporting estates, and the Aignish land raids of the following year, continued against the Clearances of earlier that century.

When **Lord Leverhulme**, founder of the soap empire Unilever, acquired the island (along with Harris) in 1918, he was determined to drag Lewis out of its cycle of poverty by establishing an integrated fishing industry. To this end he founded MacFisheries, a nationwide chain of retail outlets for the fish which would be caught and processed on the islands: he built a cannery, an ice factory, roads, bridges and a light railway; he bought boats, and planned to use spotter planes to locate the shoals of herring. But the dream never came to fruition. Unfortunately, Leverhulme regarded the island's centuries-old tradition of crofting as inefficient and "an entirely impossible way of life". In 1923, financial difficulties prompted Leverhulme to pull out of Lewis and concentrate on Harris. He gifted Lews Castle and Stornoway to its inhabitants and offered free crofts to those islanders who had not been involved in land raids. In the event, few crofters took up the offer – all they wanted was security of tenure, not ownership. Whatever the merits of Leverhulme's plans, his departure left a huge gap in the non-crofting economy, and between the wars thousands emigrated.

Stornoway (Steòrnabhagh)

In these parts, **STORNOWAY** is a buzzing metropolis, with around eight thousand inhabitants, a one-way system, a pedestrian precinct and all the trappings of a large

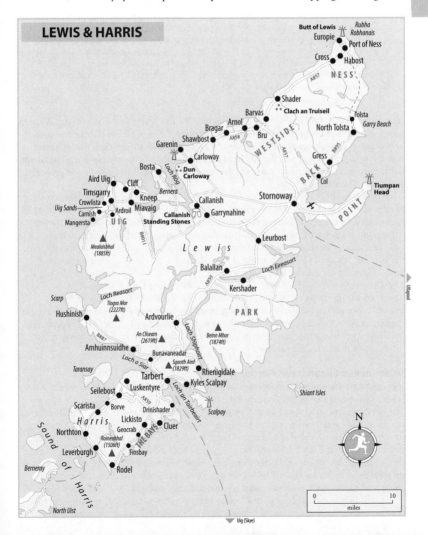

LEWIS & HARRIS

6

THE IOLAIRE DISASTER

Of the 6200 men from the Western Isles who served in World War I, around a thousand died – the highest casualty rate per capita in the British Empire. Yet, on **New Year's Day 1919**, in the single most terrible tragedy to befall Lewis, another 208 perished. Some 530 servicemen were gathered at Kyle of Lochalsh to return home to Lewis and their families on the mailboat. As there were so many of them, an extra boat was called into service, the **Iolaire**, originally built as a luxury yacht in 1881. The boat left at 7.30pm heavily overloaded, carrying 284 young men and veterans, friends and relatives, to cross the Minch. In the early hours of the morning as the boat approached Stornoway harbour, it struck a group of rocks called Blastan Thuilm (Beasts of Holm). In the darkness, it was impossible for those on board to see that they were in fact only twenty yards from the shore.

One man, a boatbuilder from Ness (Nis), a village that was to lose 21 men that night, fought his way ashore with a lifeline which saved the lives of forty others. Another was saved by clinging to the mast for seven hours, but he lost his elder brother, who'd postponed his return so that they could come back together. Another man, when on active service, had spent 36 hours in the sea, the sole survivor of his torpedoed ship; now he drowned within sight of his home. Every village in Lewis lost at least one returning loved one, and this, together with the losses in the war and the mass emigration that followed, cast a shadow over life on Lewis for many years. It was the worst peacetime shipping disaster in home waters that century. There's a **monument** at Holm Point (Rubha Thuilm), overlooking the rocks, and the ship's bell is in the Museum nan Eilean in Stornoway.

---

town. It's a centre for employment, a social hub for the island and home to the Western Isles Council, or **Comhairle nan Eilean Siar**, set up in 1974, which has done so much to promote Gaelic language and culture. Aesthetics are not its strong point, however, and the urban pleasures on offer are limited, but in July Stornoway hosts the **Hebridean Celtic Festival** (⊕hebceltfest.com), a Celtic music festival held in Lews Castle grounds, and at An Lanntair arts centre.

For centuries, life in Stornoway has focused on its **harbour**, whose quayside was once filled with barrels of pickled herring, and whose deep and sheltered waters were thronged with coastal steamers and fishing boats in their nineteenth-century heyday, when over a thousand boats were based at the port. Today, most of the catch is landed on the mainland, and, despite the daily comings and goings of the CalMac ferry from Ullapool, the harbour is a shadow of its former commercial self – the nicest section is Cromwell Street Quay, by the tourist office, where the remaining fishing fleet ties up for the night.

Stornoway's commercial centre, to the east, is little more than a string of unprepossessing shops and bars. The one exception is the old **Town Hall** on South Beach, a splendid Scots Baronial building from 1905, its rooftop peppered with conical towers, above which a central clocktower rises. One block east along South Beach, and looking rather like a modern church, you'll find **An Lanntair** (Gaelic for "lantern"), Stornoway's modern cultural centre.

Museum nan Eilean (Lews Castle)

Across the bay from the town centre • Grounds open 24hr; Museum April–Sept Mon–Wed, Fri & Sat 10am–5pm, Oct–March Mon–Wed, Fri & Sat 1–4pm • Free • ☎ 01851 822750, ⊕ lews-castle.co.uk

The castellated pomposity of **Lews Castle** was built by Sir James Matheson in 1863 after resettling the crofters who used to live here. As the former laird's pad, it has long been seen by many as a symbol of old oppression: it was here, in the house's now-defunct conservatory, that Lady Matheson famously gave tea to the Bernera protesters, when they marched on Stornoway prior to rioting; when the eccentric Lord Leverhulme took up residence, he had unglazed bedroom windows which allowed the wind and rain to enter, and gutters in the asphalt floor to carry off the residue.

The building was closed for over 25 years before undergoing a £14 million makeover that included a new extension to house a state-of-the-art bilingual museum, telling the story of the islands' geology, Gaelic culture and struggles of the nineteenth century. The museum has long-term loan of six Lewis Chessmen, twelfth-century Viking chess-pieces, which were carved from walrus ivory and whale teeth. Lews Castle's external attraction is its mature wooded **grounds**, a unique sight on the Western Isles, for which Matheson imported thousands of tons of soil. Hidden among the trees is the **Woodland Centre**, which has a straightforward exhibition on the history of the castle and the island, and a decent café serving soup, salads and cakes.

ARRIVAL AND GETTING AROUND   STORNOWAY

By plane Stornoway Airport (☎01851 702256, ⓦhial. co.uk) is 4 miles east of the town centre: the hourly bus takes 15min (Mon–Sat only), or it's a £5 taxi ride into town.
By ferry Ferries between Stornoway and Ullapool (Mon–Sat 2–3 daily, Sun 1 daily; 2hr 30min; ☎0800 0665000) run

from the octagonal CalMac ferry terminal on South Beach, near the bus station.
By bus The bus station (☎01851 704327) is on South Beach in the town centre.
Destinations Arnol (Mon–Sat 4–7 daily; 30min); Barvas

STORNOWAY

ACCOMMODATION
Cabarfeidh Hotel	1
Heb Hostel	5
Hebridean Guest House	4
Jannel	2
Laxdale Holiday Park	3

DRINKING
The Criterion Bar	1

EATING
An Lanntair	4
Digby Chick	3
Thai Café	1
The Good Food Boutique	2

(Mon–Sat 4–7 daily; 20min); Callanish (Mon–Sat 3–6 daily; 32min); Carloway (Mon–Sat 2–6 daily; 45min); Garenin (Mon–Sat 3–4 daily; 1hr); Great Bernera (Mon–Sat 4 daily; 1hr); Leverburgh (Mon–Sat 4–5 daily; 2hr); Port of Ness (Mon–Sat 6–8 daily; 1hr); Shawbost (Mon–Sat 6–9 daily; 45min); Tarbert (Mon–Sat 5 daily; 1hr); Tolsta (Mon–Sat hourly; 40min); Uig (Mon–Sat 4 daily; 1hr–1hr 30min).

By car Car rental is available from Mackinnon Self-Drive, 18 Inaclete Rd (☎01851 702984, ⌨mackinnonselfdrive.co.uk) from around £25/day – they're based in Stornoway and local deliveries are free (but let them know if you're taking the car off Lewis and Harris).

INFORMATION AND ACTIVITIES

Tourist office 26 Cromwell St (April to mid-Sept Mon–Sat 9am–5.45pm; mid-Sept to Oct Mon–Sat 9am–4.45pm; Nov–March Mon–Fri 9am–5pm; ☎01851 703088).

Bike hire Alex Dan's Cycle Centre, 67 Kenneth St (☎01851 704025, ⌨stornowaycyclehire.co.uk; closed Sun), offers bike rental from £20/day to £60/week; panniers and car racks are also available.

Surfing Surf Lewis at 10 East St, Sandwick (☎07920 427194, ⌨surflewis.com) offers beginner lessons (£40/2hr 30min) and equipment hire (wetsuit £10/day).

ACCOMMODATION
SEE MAP PAGE 299

Cabarfeidh Hotel Manor Park ☎01851 702604, ⌨cabarfeidh-hotel.co.uk. Large, reasonably upmarket hotel near Lews Castle with an excellent choice of cooked breakfasts including kippers, pancakes with syrup and the full Scottish fry-up. **£115**

Heb Hostel 25 Kenneth St ☎01851 709889, ⌨heb hostel.co.uk. A clean, centrally located terrace house in salmon pink, converted into a simple hostel, with free breakfast, wi-fi, laundry and kitchen facilities. Run by a friendly resident warden. Dorms **£19**, shepherds hut **£50**

Hebridean Guest House 61 Bayhead St ☎01851 702268, ⌨hebrideanguesthouse.co.uk. Whitewashed property, a 5min walk from the harbour and within easy reach of Lews Castle with a large range of en-suite and tastefully decorated rooms. **£120**

Jannel 5 Stewart Drive ☎01851 705324, ⌨jannel-stornoway.co.uk. A short walk from the town centre, this B&B is run by a delightful landlady, and offers five immaculate en-suite rooms. **£89**

Laxdale Holiday Park Laxdale Lane ☎01851 703234, ⌨laxdaleholidaypark.com. The well-equipped campsite has caravans, a self-catering lodge (week-long stays only), a wigwam for groups and a purpose-built bunkhouse, as well as a sheltered spot for tents. It lies a mile or so along the road to Barvas. Bunkhouse per person **£18**, wigwam **£40**, camping per pitch **£18**

EATING
SEE MAP PAGE 299

An Lanntair Kenneth St ☎01851 703307, ⌨lanntair.com. Arts venue with a stylish, modern café-bar-restaurant that serves food all day. Light lunches start at £4 for soup and bread, or for more substantial eating, they do burgers, fish and chips and pastas from £10. Food served Mon–Sat 10am–8pm.

★ **Digby Chick** 5 Bank St ☎01851 700026, ⌨digby chick.co.uk. Smart, modern, buzzy little bistro with a real emphasis on using local produce, such as the famous Stornoway black pudding. There are some interesting options on offer here like their Indian-French fusion of salmon with curried bisque, tandoori onions and coconut bonbons, or ordinary battered fish 'n' chips if curry's not your thing. Two-course lunch menu costs £15.95. Mon–Sat noon–2pm & 5.30–9pm.

Thai Café 27 Church St ☎01851 701811. Despite the name, this is actually a restaurant, serving authentic no frills Thai food. The lunchtime pad Thai is particularly good value at £5, while evening mains like the spicy Jungle Curry – stir-fried beef and peppers in a spicy cocount gravy – cost around £9. No licence, so bring your own bottle (£1 corkage). Mon–Sat noon–2.30pm & 5–11pm.

The Good Food Boutique 59 Cromwell St ☎01851 701394, ⌨thegoodfoodboutique.co.uk. Deli counter and storeroom with quality international and local produce. Takeaway sandwiches and salad boxes are available from £4.50 (think *porcetta* with apple and chilli chutney) or there's everything you need for a picnic or barbecue (cheese, olives, meat, marinades, bread, wine…). Mon–Sat 8.30am–5.30pm.

DRINKING
SEE MAP PAGE 299

The Criterion Bar 32 Point St ☎01851 701990. A tiny, authentic no-frills Stornoway pub, where they have regular informal (music) sessions – if nothing's going down, try nearby *MacNeill's*. Mon–Thurs 11am–11pm, Fri & Sat 11am–1am.

Back (Am Bac)

The dead-end B895 that runs along Lewis's east coast, north of Stornoway – an area known as **Back** – boasts excellent golden beaches and marks the starting point of a lovely coastal walk to Ness.

Griais Memorial
The legacy of Lord Leverhulme's brief ownership of Lewis is recalled by the striking **Griais Memorial** to the Lewis land-raiders, situated by Griais Bridge, above Gress Sands. It was here that Leverhulme's plans came unstuck: he wanted to turn the surrounding crofting land into three big farms, which would provide milk for the workers of his fish-canning factory; the local crofters just wanted to return to their traditional way of life. Such was Leverhulme's fury at the land-raiders from Gress (Griais) and nearby Coll (Col), a mile to the south, that, when he offered to gift the crofts of Lewis to their owners, he made sure the offer didn't include Gress and Coll. The stone-built memorial is a symbolic croft split asunder by Leverhulme's interventions.

6

The path to Ness
Further north, beyond Tolsta (Tolastadh), is the finest of the coast's sandy **beaches**, Garry (Gheardha), and the beginning of the footpath to Ness. Shortly after leaving the bay, the path crosses the **Bridge to Nowhere**, built by Leverhulme as part of an unrealized plan to forge a new road along the east coast to Ness. Further along the track, there's a fine waterfall on the River of Stones (Abhainn na Cloich). The makeshift road peters out, but a waymarked path continues for another ten miles via the old sheiling village of Diobadail, to Ness. It's very boggy, and badly churned up in places, so make sure you've got proper footwear.

ARRIVAL AND DEPARTURE   BACK
By bus There's a regular bus from Stornoway to Back (Mon– Sat hourly; 25min).

ACCOMMODATION

Broad Bay House On the B895 just south of Gress ☏01851 820990, ⓦbroadbayhouse.co.uk. Thirteen years ago, this place raised the bar exponentially both in terms of standards and price and it still leads the way: quality furnishings, patio doors leading to private decking areas, free laundry and exceptionally good home cooking with set dinners (from £25). <u>£189</u>

Seaside Villa Just off the B895 just south of Gress ☏01851 820208, ⓦseasidevilla.co.uk. Good budget B&B option, with clean, small rooms, a real peat fire and a friendly Gaelic welcome. There's great views down to the easily accessible sandy beach. No credit cards. <u>£80</u>

The road to Barvas (Barabhas)
The A857 crosses the vast, barren **peat** bog (see page 302) that characterizes the interior of Lewis, an empty, undulating wilderness riddled with stretch marks formed by peat cuttings and pockmarked with freshwater lochans. The whole area was once covered by forests, but these disappeared long ago, leaving a deposit of peat that continues to serve as a valuable energy resource, with each crofter being assigned a slice of the bog.

Twelve miles across the peat bog the road approaches the west coast of Lewis and divides, heading southwest towards Callanish, or northeast through **BARVAS** (Barabhas), which has a handy shop and petrol station. Just beyond Barvas, a signpost points to the pleasant **Morven Gallery** (Easter–Sept Mon–Sat 10.30am–5pm; free; ⓦmorvengallery.com), which hosts exhibitions by local artists and photographers and has a handy café too, serving great coffee, where you can hole up during bad weather. Three miles further up the road, you pass the 20ft monolith of **Clach an Truiseil**, the first of a series of prehistoric sights between the crofting and weaving settlements of **Ballantrushal** (Baile an Truiseil) and **Shader** (Siadar) .

Ness (Nis)
At the northern tip of Lewis, **NESS** (Nis) is made up of a string of densely populated, fervently Presbyterian villages. Ness has the highest percentage of Gaelic-speakers in

6

PEAT

One of the characteristic features of the landscape of the Highlands and Islands is **peat** (*mòine*) – and nowhere is its presence more keenly felt than on Lewis. Virtually the whole interior of the island is made up of one vast blanket bog, scarred with lines of peat banks old and new, while the pungent smell of peat smoke hits you as you pass through the villages. Peat is made up of **dead vegetation** that has failed to rot completely because the sheer volume of rainfall has caused the soil acidity to reach a level that acts as a preservative. In other words, organic matter – such as sphagnum moss, rushes, sedges and reeds – is dying at a faster rate than it is decomposing. This means, of course, that peat is still (very slowly) forming in certain parts of Scotland, at an inch or less every fifty years. In the (mostly treeless) islands, peat provided an important source of fuel, and the cutting and stacking of peats in the spring was part of the annual cycle of crofting life. Peat cutting remains embedded in the culture, and is still practised on a large scale, particularly in the Hebrides. It's a social occasion as much as anything else, which heralds the arrival of the warmer, drier days of late spring.

Great pride is taken in the artistry and neatness of the **peat banks and stacks**. In some parts, the peat lies up to 30ft deep, but peat banks are usually only cut to a depth of around 6ft. Once the top layer of turf has been removed, the peat is cut into slabs between two and four peats deep, using a traditional *tairsgeir* (pronounced "tushkar"). Since peat is **ninety percent water** in its natural state, it has to be carefully "lifted" in order to dry out. Peats tend to be piled up either vertically in "rooks", or crisscrossed in "windows"; either way, the peat will lose three quarters of its water content, and shrink by about a quarter. Many folk wonder how on earth the peat can dry out when it seems to rain the whole time, but the wind helps, and eventually a skin is formed that stops any further water from entering the peats. After three or four weeks, the peats are skilfully "grieved", like the slates on a roof, into round-humped stacks or onto carts that can be brought home. Traditionally, the peat would be carried from the peat banks by women using "creels", baskets that were strapped on the back. Correctly grieved peats allow the rain to run off, and therefore stay dry for a year or more outside the croft.

---

the country (75 percent), but the locals are perhaps best known for their annual culling of young gannets on **Sula Sgeir** (see page 303). These scattered settlements have none of the photogenic qualities of Skye's whitewashed villages: the churches are plain and unadorned; the crofters' houses relatively modern and smothered in grey pebbledash rendering or harling; the stone cottages and enclosures of their forebears often lie half-abandoned in the front garden: a rusting assortment of discarded cars and vans store peat bags and the like. The road terminates at the fishing village of **PORT OF NESS** (Port Nis), with a tiny harbour and lovely golden beach. It's worth noting that there are few shops (other than mobile ones) in these parts, so it's as well to stock up in Stornoway before you set out.

Comunn Eachdraidh Nis

Cross School, North Dell (Dail bho Thuath), Cross • Café open Mon–Fri 10.30am–4.30pm • ☎ 01851 810377, ⓦ cenonline.org

For an insight into the social history of the area, take a look inside **Comunn Eachdraidh Nis** (the Ness Historical Society). The museum, housed in the village school, contains a large collection of photographs, religious artefacts and local antiques as well as a decent World War I exhibition. There's good café here too, serving light lunches.

Europie (Eoropaidh)

Shortly before you reach Port of Ness, a minor road heads two miles northwest to the hamlet of **EUROPIE** (Eoropaidh) – pronounced "Yor-erpee". By the road junction that leads to the Butt of Lewis stands the simple stone structure of **St Moluag's Church** (Teampull Mholuaidh), amid the runrig fields, now acting as sheep runs. Thought to date from the twelfth century, when the islands were still under Norse rule, but restored in 1912 (and now used once a month by the Scottish Episcopal Church for sung Communion), the church features a strange south chapel with only a squint window connecting it to the nave. In the late seventeenth century, the traveller Martin Martin noted: "They all went to church… and then standing silent for a little time, one of them gave a signal… and immediately all of them went into the fields, where they fell a drinking their ale and spent the remainder of the night in dancing and singing, etc." Church services aren't what they used to be.

Butt of Lewis (Rubha Robhabais)

From Eoropaidh, a narrow road twists to the bleak and blustery northern tip of the island, **Rubha Robhanais** – well known to devotees of the BBC *Shipping Forecast* as the **Butt of Lewis** – where a redbrick lighthouse sticks up above a series of sheer cliffs and stacks, alive with kittiwakes, fulmars and cormorants, with skuas and gannets feeding offshore; it's a great place for spotting marine mammals. The lighthouse is closed to the public, and there's no way down to the sea, but backtrack half a mile or so, and there's a path down to the tiny sandy bay of **Port Sto**, a more sheltered spot for a picnic than the Butt itself.

6

OFFSHORE ISLANDS

Though three men dwell on Flannan Isle
To keep the lamp alight,
As we steer'd under the lee, we caught
No glimmer through the night.   *Flannan Isle* by Wilfred Wilson Gibson

On December 15, 1900, a passing ship reported that the lighthouse on the **Flannan Isles**, 21 miles west of Aird Uig on Lewis, was not working. The lighthouse had been built the previous year by the Stevenson family (including the father and grandfather of author Robert Louis Stevenson). Gibson's poem goes on to recount the arrival of the relief boat from Oban on Boxing Day, whose crew found no trace of the three keepers. More mysteriously still, a full meal lay untouched on the table, one chair was knocked over, and only two oilskins were missing. Subsequent lightkeepers doubtless spent many lonely nights trying in vain to figure out what happened, until the lighthouse went automatic in 1971.

Equally famous, but for different reasons, is the tiny island of **Sula Sgeir**, also known as "The Rock", 41 miles north of the Butt of Lewis. Every August, the men of Ness (known as Niseachs) set sail from Port of Ness to harvest the young gannets or guga that nest in their thousands high up on the islet's sea cliffs. It's a dangerous activity, but boiled gannet and potato are a popular Lewis delicacy (the harvest is strictly rationed), and there's no shortage of volunteers for the annual two-week cull. For the moment, the Niseachs have a licence to harvest up to two thousand birds, granted by Scottish Natural Heritage who manage the island.

Somewhat incredibly, the island of **Rona** (sometimes referred to as North Rona), ten miles east of Sula Sgeir, was inhabited on and off until the nineteenth century, despite being less than a mile across, with up to thirty inhabitants at one time. The island's St Ronan's Chapel is one of the oldest Celtic Christian ruins in the country. St Ronan was, according to legend, the first inhabitant, moving here in the eighth century with his two sisters, Miriceal and Brianuil, until one day he turned to Brianuil and said, "My dear sister, it is yourself that is handsome, what beautiful legs you have." She apparently replied that it was time for her to leave the island, and made her way to neighbouring Sula Sgeir where she was later found dead with a shag's nest in her ribcage. The island is now owned by Scottish Natural Heritage and is an important breeding ground for Leach's storm petrel.

Clearly visible from the ferry to Lewis and Harris, the **Shiant Isles** (w shiantisles.net), whose name translates as "the enchanted islands", sit in the middle of the Minch, five miles off the east coast of Lewis. Inhabited on and off until the beginning of the last century, the islands were bought by the author Compton MacKenzie in 1925, and then sold on to the publisher Nigel Nicolson, whose family still owns them. The Shiants have wonderful cliffs of fluted basalt columns that shelter thousands of seabirds, including puffins, in the breeding season.

By bus There's a regular bus service between Stornoway   and Port of Ness (Mon–Sat 6–9 daily; 50min).

ACCOMMODATION

The Decca Ness, two miles south of the Butt of Lewis Lighthouse ☎ 01851 810571, ⓦ thedecca.co.uk. This converted radio navigation station is predominantly a tearoom that also does B&B and a wide repertoire of meals for £20 if booked in advance. The en-suite rooms are attractive enough and there's a living room for guests with maps of the area, books, games and DVDs. Up for sale at the time of writing. £90

Galson Farm South Galson (Gabhsann Bho), eight miles north east of Barvas ☎ 01851 850492, ⓦ galsonfarm. co.uk. An attractive converted eighteenth-century farmhouse with two sitting rooms, which offers generous portions of Aga-cooked dinner (for £20), bed and breakfast, and runs a 6-bunk hostel close by. Hostel per person £20, doubles £95

Westside (An Toabh Siar)

Heading southwest from the crossroads near Barvas brings you to the **Westside**. The main road lies a mile or so inland from the coast, but several villages meander down towards the sea. At **Arnol** and **Garenin** (Gearrannan) there are beautifully preserved blackhouses to explore, and, at **Callanish** (Calanais), the islands' justifiably popular standing stones.

Arnol Blackhouse

42 Arnol • April–Sept Mon–Sat 9.30am–5.30pm; Oct–March Mon–Tues & Thurs–Sat 10am–4pm • £6 • ☎ 01851 710395

In Arnol, the remains of numerous blackhouses lie abandoned by the roadside. One, however, has been very carefully preserved to show exactly how a true blackhouse, or *taigh-dubh*, would have been. The dark interior is lit and heated by a small peat fire, kept alight in the central hearth of bare earth; smoke drifts up through the thatch, helping to keep out the midges and turn the heathery sods and oat-straw thatch itself into next year's fertilizer. The animals would have slept in the byre, separated only by a low partition, while potatoes and grain were stored in the adjacent barn. The elderly woman who lived here moved out very reluctantly in 1964, only after the council agreed to build a house with a byre for her animals (the building now houses the ticket office). Across the road is a ruined blackhouse, abandoned in 1920 when the family moved into no. 39, the white house, or *taigh-geal*, next door. A little beyond the blackhouse, a path leads down to **Loch na Muilne**, where you've a good chance of spotting the very rare red-necked phalarope (May–Aug).

Shawbost (Siabost) museum

Old School Centre, Shawbost • April–Sept Mon–Sat noon–4pm • Free • ☎ 01851 710212

Two miles west of Bragar, at **SHAWBOST** (Siabost) – home to one of the main Harris Tweed mills in the Outer Hebrides – there's a tiny **museum** in the **Old School Centre**, across the road from the new school. The exhibits – most of them donated by locals – include a rare Lewis brick from the short-lived factory set up by Lord Leverhulme.

Norse Mill and Kiln

Signposted off the A858 at Shawbost • Open 24hr • Free

Just outside Shawbost, to the west, there's a sign to the restored **Norse Mill and Kiln**. It's a ten-minute walk over a small hill to the two thatched bothies beside a little stream; the nearer one's the kiln, the further one's the horizontal mill. Mills and kilns of this kind were common in Lewis up until the 1930s, and despite the name are thought to have been introduced here from Ireland as early as the sixth century.

Garenin (Gearrannan)

Garenin • May–Sept Mon–Sat 9.30am–5.30pm • £3.60 • ☎ 01851 643416, ⓦ gearrannan.com

In the parish of Carloway (Carlabhagh), with its crofthouses, boulders and hillocks rising out of the peat moor, a mile-long road leads off north to the beautifully remote coastal settlement of **GARENIN** (Gearrannan). Here, rather than re-create a single museum-piece blackhouse as at Arnol, a whole cluster of nine thatched crofters' houses – the last of which was abandoned in 1974 – has been restored and put to use as accommodation for holiday-makers and a museum. As an ensemble, they give a great impression of what a **Baile Tughaidh**, or blackhouse village, must have been like. The first house you come to houses the ticket office and **café**. The second house has been restored to its condition at the time of abandonment, so there's electric light but no running water, lino flooring, but a peat fire and box-beds – and a weaving machine in the byre. The third house has interpretive panels and a touch-screen computer telling the history of the village and the folk who lived there. Next door, there are toilets, while the rest have been converted into **self-catering cottages** and a **hostel**.

Dun Carloway (Dùn Charlabhaigh)

Signposted off the A858 • Open 24hr • ☎ 01851 710395

Just south of Carloway village, **Dun Carloway** (Dùn Charlabhaigh) perches on top of a conspicuous rocky outcrop overlooking the sea. One of Scotland's best-preserved **brochs**, or fortified towers, its dry-stone circular walls reach a height of more than 30ft on one side. The broch consists of two concentric walls, the inner one perpendicular, the outer one slanting inwards, the two originally fastened together by roughly hewn flagstones, which also served as lookout galleries reached via a narrow stairwell. The only entrance to the roofless inner yard is through a low doorway set beside a crude and cramped guard cell. As at Callanish, there have been all sorts of theories about the purpose of the brochs, which date from between 100 BC and 100 AD; the most likely explanation is that they were built to provide protection from Roman slave-traders.

Callanish (Calanais) standing stones

Loch Roag • **Stones** Open 24hr • Free • **Callanish Visitor Centre** April, May, Sept & Oct Mon–Sat 10am–6pm; June–Aug Mon–Sat 9.30am–8pm; Oct–March Tues–Sat 10am–4pm • £3.50 • ☎ 01851 621422, ⓦ callanishvisitorcentre.co.uk

Overlooking the sheltered, islet-studded waters of Loch Roag (Loch Ròg) on the west coast, are the islands' most dramatic prehistoric ruins, the **Callanish standing stones**. These monoliths – nearly fifty slabs of gnarled and finely grained gneiss up to 15ft high – were transported here between 3000 BC and 1500 BC, but their exact function remains a mystery. No one knows for certain why the ground plan resembles a colossal Celtic cross, nor why there's a central burial chamber. It's likely that such a massive endeavour was prompted by the desire to predict the seasonal cycle upon which these early farmers were entirely dependent, and indeed many of the stones are aligned with the positions of the sun and the stars. Whatever the reason for their existence, there's certainly no denying the powerful primeval presence, not to mention sheer beauty, of the stones.

You can visit the stones at any time, but if you need shelter or some simple sustenance, head to the nearby **Callanish Visitor Centre**, which has a small museum that explores the theories about the stones. If you want to commune with standing stones in solitude, head for the smaller circles in more natural surroundings a mile or two southeast of Callanish, around Garynahine (Gearraidh na h-Aibhne).

ARRIVAL AND DEPARTURE	WESTSIDE

By bus A circular bus service connects Callanish, Carloway and Garenin to Stornoway (Mon–Sat 3–6 daily; Callanish 32min, Carloway 45min, Garenin 1hr).

ACCOMMODATION

Eilean Fraoich Campsite Shawbost (Siabost) ☎ 01851 710504, ⓦ eileanfraoich.co.uk. Located behind the old village church, this pristine, flat, grassy campsite is in complete contrast with the surrounding undulating

6

BOAT TRIPS

There's a wide choice of **boat trips** offered around the Western Isles. Prices start at around £50 per person for a short RIB wildlife cruise to around £190 for a day-trip to St Kilda. Sea Trek (☎01851 672469, ⍟seatrek.co.uk), who leave from Miavaig (Miabhaig) in Uig, go regularly to St Kilda (and occasionally to Sula Sgeir and Rona), as do Kilda Cruises (☎01859 502060, ⍟kildacruises.co.uk), who operate a 55ft motor cruiser from West Tarbert on Harris, and also offer charter trips to the likes of the Shiant Isles. Hebridean Sea Tours (☎01871 817803, ⍟hebrideanseatours.co.uk) run day trips from Ardmhor on Barra to St Kilda, Canna, Mingulay and several other Barra isles. For longer trips around the islands, contact Island Cruising (☎01851 672381, ⍟island-cruising.com), based at Miavaig (Miabhaig) in Uig.

---

landscape. The site offers a kitchen with the usual appliances, a dining room attached and laundry facilities and quoted price includes a car and two adults. April–Oct. Per pitch £18

The Gearrannan Hostel/Taigh Dhonnchaidh 7a Callanish (Calanais) ☎01851 643416, ⍟gearrannan. com/hostel. Taigh Dhonnchaidh or "Duncan's House" is a converted thatched blackhouse that's part of a sort of living museum (with an actual museum in the village, too). The hostel has one room with 10 bunks, plus a family room for 3. It's cosy and warm, and walk-ins are accepted if they have space. Dorms £20, triple £65

Bernera (Bearnaraigh)

Dividing Loch Roag (Loch Ròg) in two is the island of Great Bernera, usually referred to simply as **Bernera**. Joined to the mainland since 1953 via a narrow bridge that spans a small sea channel, Bernera is a rocky island, dotted with lochans, fringed by a few small lobster-fishing settlements and, until recently, owned by Robin Ian Evelyn Milne Stuart le Comte de la Lanne Mirrlees, the Queen's former herald, who also claimed the title Prince of Incoronata (an area of former Yugoslavia gifted to the count by King Peter II).

Bernera has an important place in Lewis history due to the **Bernera Riot** of 1874, when local crofters successfully defied the eviction orders delivered to them by the landlord, Sir James Matheson. In truth, there wasn't much of a riot, but three Bernera men were arrested and charged with assault. The crofters marched on the laird's house, Lews Castle in Stornoway, and demanded an audience with Matheson, who claimed to have no knowledge of what his factor, Donald Munro, was doing. In the subsequent trial, Munro was exposed as a ruthless tyrant, and the crofters were acquitted. A stone-built cairn now stands as a memorial to the riot, at the crossroads beyond the central settlement of **BREACLETE** (Brecleit), which sits beside one of the island's many lochs.

Bernera Museum

Breacleit Community Centre • Mid-May–Sept Mon–Fri noon–4pm, Oct–mid-May Tues & Thurs noon–4pm • Free • ☎01851 612331

Housed in the local community centre, the **Bernera Museum** has a small exhibition on lobster fishing, a mysterious five-thousand-year-old Neolithic stone ball, a room dedicated to an Iron Age village discovered at Bosta and, of course, a genealogy section.

Iron Age House

Bosta (Bostadh) • Mid-May–Aug Mon–Fri noon–4pm • £3 • ☎01851 612314

Much more interesting than the Bernera Museum is the replica **Iron Age House** that's been built above a precious little bay of golden sand beyond Bosta (Bostadh) cemetery, three miles north of Breaclete – follow the signs "to the shore". In 1992, gale-force winds revealed an entire late Iron Age or Pictish settlement hidden under the sand; due to its exposed position, the site has been refilled with sand, and a full-scale mock-up built instead, based on the "jelly baby" houses – after the shape – that were excavated. Inside, the house is incredibly spacious, and very dark, illuminated only by a central hearth and a few chinks of sunlight. If the weather's fine and you climb to the top of the nearby hills, you should get a good view over the forty or so islands in Loch Roag (Loch Ròg), and maybe even the Flannan Isles (see page 303) on the horizon.

ARRIVAL AND DEPARTURE
BERNERA

By bus There are regular buses from Stornoway to Bernera   (Mon–Sat 4 daily; 1hr).

Uig (Uuige)

6

It's a long drive along the B8011 to the remote district of **UIG**, which suffered badly from the Clearances. The landscape here is hillier and more dramatic than elsewhere, a combination of myriad islets, wild cliff scenery and patches of pristine golden sand.

Timsgarry (Timsgearraidh)

The main road takes you through the narrow canyon of Glen Valtos (Glèann Bhaltois) to **TIMSGARRY** (Timsgearraidh), overlooking **Uig Sands** (Tràigh Uuige), the largest and most prized of all Lewis's golden strands, where the sea goes out for miles at low tide; the best access point is from the cemetery car park in Ardroil (Eadar Dha Fhadhail), a couple of miles south of Timsgarry.

Comunn Eachdraidh Uig

Timsgarry, just off the B8011 at the Aird Uig turn-off • Easter–Sept Mon–Sat noon–5pm • £2 • ☎ 01851 672223

A giant wooden statue of one of the **Lewis Chessmen**, which were found in a local sandbank in 1831, heralds the **Comunn Eachdraidh Uig** in Timsgarry. Inside, you can see some replicas of the twelfth-century Viking chess-pieces, six of which now reside in Museum nan Eilean (Lewis Museum). As well as putting on some excellent temporary exhibitions, the museum has bits and bobs from blackhouses and is staffed by locals, who are happy to answer any queries you have; there's also a welcome **tearoom** attached.

ARRIVAL AND DEPARTURE
UIG

By bus There are regular buses from Stornoway to Uig   (Mon–Sat 4 daily; 1hr–1hr 30min).

ACCOMMODATION AND EATING

Ardroil campsite Ardroil (Eadar Dha Fhadhail) ☎ 01851 672248. The location, by one of the most remote and incredible sandy beaches in the Western Isles, is unbeatable. There's a small utilities block with showers and

---

ST KILDA (HIORT)

Britain's westernmost island chain is the **St Kilda** (⊛ kilda.org.uk) archipelago, forty miles from North Uist. Dominated by Britain's highest cliffs and sea stacks, Hirta, the main island, was occupied until 1930 when the last 36 Gaelic-speaking inhabitants were evacuated at their own request. The island was then bought by the Marquess of Bute, to protect the island's millions of nesting seabirds. In 1957, having agreed to allow the army to build a missile-tracking radar station here linked to South Uist, the marquess bequeathed the island to the NTS. St Kilda is one of only two dozen **UNESCO World Heritage Sites** with a dual status reflecting its natural and cultural significance. Despite its inaccessibility, several thousand visitors make it out here each year; if you get to land, you can see the museum, send a postcard and enjoy a drink at the army's pub, the *Puff Inn*. Between mid-May and mid-August, the NTS organizes volunteer **work parties**, which either restore and maintain the old buildings or take part in archeological digs – for more information, contact the NTS (☎ 0844 493 2100, ⊛ nts.org.uk). For the armchair traveller, the best general book on St Kilda is Tom Steel's *The Life and Death of St Kilda*, or else there's the classic 1937 film *The Edge of the World* by Michael Powell (which was actually shot on Foula in Shetland). Several companies offer **boat day-trips** for around £190/ person plus £5 landing fee. The sea journey (8hr return) is not for the faint-hearted and there's no guarantee that you'll be able to land.

sinks for washing dishes plus a very handy electric socket. Nearest shop is a 10min walk. Per person **£5**

Baile na Cille Timsgarry (Timsgearraidh) ☎ 01851 672242, ⊛ bailenacille.co.uk. A chaotic kind of place, run by an eccentric couple who are very welcoming to families and dogs and dish up wonderful set-menu dinners for £30 a head. Mid-April to mid-Sept. **£130**

Kneep campsite Kneep (Cnip) ☎ 01851 6722332. Small campsite beside the wonderful sandy Reef Beach (Tràigh na Beirghe) and an ideal place to take a kayak (if you have one) to explore the tiny islands nearby. The site is run by the local community and the only facilities are a small unisex toilet block with coin-operated showers (£1 a shower). Easter to mid-Sept. Per person **£10**

Suainaval 3 Crowlista (Cradhlastadh) ☎ 01851 672386, ⊛ suainaval.com. The best B&B in the whole area, run by a truly welcoming couple; rooms have pine floors and furnishings, Harris Tweed chairs and fabulous views over the golden sands of Uig. **£80**

Harris (Na Hearadh)

Harris, whose name derives from the Old Norse for "high land", is much hillier, more dramatic and much more immediately appealing than Lewis, its boulder-strewn slopes descending to aquamarine bays of dazzling white sand. The shift from Lewis to Harris is almost imperceptible, as the two are, in fact, one island, the "division" between them embedded in a historical split in the MacLeod clan, lost in the mists of time. The border was also, somewhat crazily, a county boundary until 1975, with Harris lying in Invernessshire, and Lewis belonging to Ross and Cromarty. Nowadays, the dividing line is rarely marked even on maps; for the record, it comprises Loch Reasort in the west, Loch Seaforth (Loch Shìphoirt) in the east, and the six miles in between. Harris itself is more clearly divided by a minuscule isthmus, into the wild, inhospitable mountains of **North Harris** and the gentler landscape and sandy shores of **South Harris**.

Brief history

Along with Lewis, Harris was purchased in 1918 by **Lord Leverhulme**. In contrast to Lewis, though, Leverhulme and his ambitious projects were broadly welcomed by the people of Harris. His most grandiose plans were drawn up for Leverburgh, but he also purchased an old Norwegian whaling station in Bunavoneadar (Bun Abhàinn Eadarra) in 1922, built a spinning mill at Geocrab and began the construction of four roads. Financial difficulties, a slump in the tweed industry and the lack of market for whale products meant that none of the schemes was a wholehearted success, and when he died in 1925 the plug was pulled on all of them by his executors.

Since the Leverhulme era, unemployment has been a constant problem in Harris. Crofting continues on a small scale, supplemented by the Harris Tweed industry, though the main focus of this has, in fact, shifted to Lewis. Fishing continues on **Scalpay**, while the rest of the population gets by on whatever employment is available: roadworks, crafts, hunting and fishing and, of course, the one growth industry, tourism.

Tarbert (An Tairbeart)

Sheltered in a green valley on the narrow isthmus, **TARBERT** (An Tairbeart) is the largest settlement on Harris and a wonderful place to arrive by boat. The port's mountainous backdrop is impressive, and the town is attractively laid out on steep terraces sloping up from the dock.

Isle of Harris Distillery

Tarbert • Year-round Mon–Sat 10am–5pm; tours March–Oct (1hr 15min; see online for times) • Tours £10 • ☎ 01859 502212, ⊛ harrisdistillery.com

Islanders are justifiably proud of the award-winning **Isle of Harris Distillery** gin, which is infused with hand-harvested local sugar kelp (you'll see the distinct rippled bottles

GIANT WOODEN CHESSMAN OUTSIDE UIG MUSEUM

6

HARRIS TWEED

Far from being a picturesque cottage industry, as it's sometimes presented, the production of **Harris Tweed** is vital to the local economy, with a well-organized and unionized workforce. Traditionally the tweed was made by women, from the wool of their own sheep, to provide clothing for their families, using a 2500-year-old process. Each woman was responsible for plucking the wool by hand, washing and scouring it, dyeing it with lichen, heather flowers or ragwort, carding (smoothing and straightening the wool, often adding butter to grease it), spinning and weaving. Finally the cloth was dipped in stale urine and "waulked" by a group of women, who beat the cloth on a table to soften and shrink it while singing Gaelic waulking songs. Harris Tweed was originally made all over the islands, and was known simply as *clò mòr* (big cloth).

In the mid-nineteenth century, Catherine Murray, **Countess of Dunmore**, who owned a large part of Harris, started to sell surplus cloth to her aristocratic friends; she then sent two sisters from Strond (Srannda) to Paisley to learn the trade. On their return, they formed the genesis of the modern industry, which continues to serve as a vital source of employment, though demand (and therefore employment levels) can fluctuate wildly as fashions change. To earn the official **Harris Tweed Authority (HTA)** trademark of the Orb and the Maltese Cross – taken from Lady Dunmore's coat of arms – the fabric has to be hand-woven on the Outer Hebrides from 100 percent pure new Scottish wool, while the other parts of the manufacturing process must take place only in the local mills.

The main **mills** are actually in Carloway and Shawbost, in Lewis, where the wool is dyed, carded and spun. In the last few decades, there has been a revival of traditional tweed-making techniques, with several small producers following old methods, using indigenous plants and bushes to **dye** the cloth: yellow comes from rocket and broom; green from heather; grey and black from iris and oak; and, most popular of all, reddish brown from crotal, a flat grey lichen scraped off rocks.

everywhere you go in the Outer Hebrides). They also are also a whisky distillery, and tastings of their single malt is available during tours. The distillery has a community feel and a relaxed canteen perfect for tea and cake.

ARRIVAL AND INFORMATION

TARBERT

By ferry There are CalMac car ferries to and from Uig on Skye (Mon–Sat 1–2 daily; 1hr 45min).

By bus Tarbert is served by six different bus routes and is reachable from Stornoway and all the nearby coastal settlements.

Destinations Hushinish (schooldays Mon–Fri 2–3 daily; school holidays Tues & Fri 3 daily; 40min); Leverburgh (Mon–Sat 6–8 daily; 45min–1hr); Leverburgh via the Bays (Mon–Sat 2–4 daily; 1hr); Rhenigdale (by request 07769 159218; Mon–Sat 2–3 daily; 30min); Scalpay (Mon–Sat 4–6 daily; 20min).

Tourist information There's a welcome point at the Essence of Harris retail shop at the pier (Mon–Sat 9am–5pm; 01859 502011).

ACCOMMODATION

Coel na Mara 7 Direcleit 01859 502464, ceolnamara. com. With your own transport, this secluded B&B, just south of Tarbert, is a good choice. Nicely furnished throughout, with great views over East Loch Tarbert. The smallest and cheapest room doesn't have en-suite facilities. **£108**

Harris Hotel Scott Rd 01859 502154, harrishotel. com. Just a 5min walk from the harbour, this is Tarbert's longest-established and largest hotel. The 23 en-suite rooms are tastefully furnished, and some have sea views.

The hotel is also open to the public for food – even on a Sunday – with a lunch menu that includes a generous portion of venison burger for £12. **£119**

No. 5 hostel 5 Drinishader (Drinisiadar) 01851 511255, number5.biz. A converted cottage, 3 miles south of Tarbert, offering bed linen and laundry service along with canoes, kayaks (£15/half day) and cycles (£15/day) for rent. The hostel has twin rooms, plus one 4-bed dorm; there's also a 5-bed croft house that can be booked as one unit. Dorms **£21**

EATING AND DRINKING

Pierhouse Restaurant Hotel Hebrides, Pier Rd 01859 502364. There aren't many options in Tarbert, but this smart hotel restaurant is just around the corner from the ferry terminal. Local produce with an emphasis on sustainability (Isle of Lewis Lamb with mashed potato, Colcannon cabbage, red wine and mint jus, £21.50) and attentive service. April–Sept.

North Harris (Ceann a Tuath na Hearadh)

Mountainous **North Harris** was run like some minor feudal fiefdom until 2003, when the locals managed to buy the land for a knock-down £2 million. If you're coming from Stornoway on the A859, it's a spectacular introduction to Harris, its bulging, pyramidal mountains of ancient gneiss looming over the dramatic fjord-like **Loch Seaforth** (Loch Shìphoirt). From **ARDVOURLIE** (Aird a' Mhulaidh), you weave your way over a boulder-strewn saddle between mighty **Sgaoth Aird** (1829ft) and An Cliseam or the **Clisham** (2619ft), the highest peak in the Western Isles. This bitter terrain, littered with debris left behind by retreating glaciers, offers but the barest of vegetation, with an occasional cluster of crofters' houses sitting in the shadow of a host of pointed peaks, anywhere between 1000ft and 2500ft high.

The road to Hushinish (Huisinis)

The winding, single-track B887, which clings to the northern shores of West Loch Tarbert (Loch a Siar), gives easy access to the awesome mountain range of the (treeless) Forest of Harris to the north. Immediately as you turn down the B887, you pass through **Bunavoneadar** (Bun Abhàinn Eadarra), where some Norwegians established a short-lived whaling station – the slipways and distinctive redbrick chimney can still be seen. Seven miles further on, you pass **Abhainnsuidhe Castle** (pronounced "avan-soo-ee"), designed by David Bryce in Scottish Baronial style in 1865 for the Earl of Dunmore. The main road takes you right past the front door, much to the annoyance of the castle's successive owners – as you do, be sure to admire the lovely salmon-leap waterfalls and pristine castle grounds. It's another five miles to the end of the road at the small crofting community of **Hushinish** (Huisinis), where you are rewarded with a south-facing beach of shell sand that looks across Hushinish Bay to South Harris.

Scarp

A slipway north of Hushinish Bay serves the nearby island of **Scarp**, a hulking mass of rock rising over 1000ft, once home to over two hundred people but abandoned in 1971 (it's now a private holiday hideaway). The most bizarre moment in its history – subject of the 2002 film *The Rocket Post* – was undoubtedly in 1934, when the German scientist **Gerhardt Zucher** experimented in sending mail by rocket. Zucher made two attempts at launching his rocket from Scarp, but the letter-laden missile exploded before it got off the ground, and the idea was shelved.

ACCOMMODATION   **NORTH HARRIS**

Rhenigidale (Reinigeadal) Hostel 4 miles off the A859 ⊕ gatliff.org.uk. A member of the Gatliff Hebridean Hostels Trust, this well-equipped 12-bed hostel also has camping space for three small tents outside. It's situated in an isolated coastal community – there's a (request-only: call ☎ 07769 159218 by 8pm the day before) bus connection or else it's a magnificent six-mile (3hr) hike over the rocky landscape from Tarbert: ask at the tourist office for directions. No advance booking and no phone. Dorms **£16**, camping **£10**

SCALPAY (SCALPAIGH)

A high-flying, single-track bridge, erected in 1997, connects Harris to the island of **Scalpay** (Scalpaigh) – from the Norse "*skalp-ray*" (the island shaped like a boat), off the east coast of Harris. Scalpay is the place where Bonnie Prince Charlie is thought to have tried unsuccessfully to get a boat to take him back to France after the defeat at Culloden. On a good day, it's a pleasant and fairly easy three-mile hike along the island's north coast to the **Eilean Glas** lighthouse, which looks out over to Skye. This was the first lighthouse to be erected in Scotland, in 1789, though the present Stevenson-designed granite tower dates from 1824.

South Harris (Ceann a Deas na Hearadh)

The mountains of **South Harris** are less dramatic than in the north, but the scenery is no less attractive. There's a choice of routes from Tarbert to the ferry port of **Leverburgh**, which connects with North Uist: the east coast, known as **The Bays** (Na Baigh), is rugged and seemingly inhospitable, while the **west coast** is endowed with some of the finest stretches of golden sand in the whole of the archipelago, buffeted by the Atlantic winds.

6

The Bays (Na Baigh)

Paradoxically, most people on South Harris live along the harsh eastern coastline of **The Bays** rather than the more fertile west side. But not by choice – they were evicted from their original crofts to make way for sheep-grazing. Despite the uncompromising lunar landscape – mostly bare grey gneiss and heather – the crofters managed to establish "lazybeds" (small labour-intensive, raised plots between the rocks fertilized by seaweed and peat), a few of which are still in use even today. The narrow sea lochs provide shelter for fishing boats, while the interior is speckled with freshwater lochans, and the whole coast is now served by the endlessly meandering **Bays Road**, often wrongly referred to as the "Golden Road", though this, in fact, was the name given to the sideroad to Scadabay (Scadabhagh), coined by a local councillor who disapproved of the expense.

The west coast

The main road from Tarbert into South Harris snakes its way west for ten miles across the boulder-strewn interior to reach the coast. Once there, you get a view of the most stunning **beach**, the vast golden strand of **Luskentyre** (Tràigh Losgaintir). The road continues to ride above a chain of sweeping sands, backed by rich **machair**, that stretches for nine miles along the Atlantic coast. In good weather the scenery is particularly impressive, foaming breakers rolling along the golden sands set against the rounded peaks of the mountains to the north and the islet-studded turquoise sea to the west – and even on the dullest day the sand manages to glow beneath the waves. A short distance out to sea is the island of **Taransay** (Tarasaigh), which once held a population of nearly a hundred, but was abandoned as recently as 1974. South of Luskentyre lies **Scarista** (Sgarasta), where one of the first of the Hebridean Clearances took place in 1828, when thirty families were evicted and their homes burnt.

Seallam!

Northton (Taobh Tuath) • Mon–Sat 10am–5pm • £2.50 • ☎ 01859 520258

There's loads of information on local history, geology, flora and fauna at **Seallam!**, a purpose-built heritage centre close to the village of **Northton** (Taobh Tuath), overlooked by the round-topped hill of Chaipabhal at the westernmost tip of South Harris. As well as detailing the area's history of emigration, it's a useful centre for ancestor-hunters, and there's a good section on St Kilda (see page 307).

Leverburgh (An t-Ob)

From Northton the road veers to the southeast to trim the island's south shore, eventually reaching the sprawling settlement of **LEVERBURGH** (An t-Ob). Named after Lord Leverhulme, who planned to turn the place into the largest fishing port on the west coast of Scotland, it's the terminal for the CalMac **car ferry** service to Berneray and the Uists. The hour-long journey across the skerry-strewn Sound of Harris is one of Scotland's most tortuous ferry routes, with the ship taking part in a virtual slalom-race to avoid numerous hidden rocks – it's also a great crossing from which to spot seabirds and sea mammals.

Rodel (Roghadal)

A mile or so from Renish Point (Rubha Reanais), the southern tip of Harris, is the old port of **RODEL** (Roghadal), where a smattering of picturesque ancient stone houses lies among the hillocks. Down by the old harbour where the ferry from Skye used to arrive, you'll find the former *Rodel Hotel*, a solid, stone-built hotel originally erected in 1781 and slated for redevelopment by the owners of the Harris Distillery.

St Clement's Church (Tur Chliamainn)

Rodel • Generally open at all times • Free; HES • Ⓦ historicenvironment.scot

On top of one of the grassy humps, with sheep grazing in the graveyard, is **St Clement's Church** (Tur Chliamainn), burial place of the MacLeods of Harris and Dunvegan in Skye. Dating from the 1520s – in other words pre-Reformation, hence the big castellated tower (which you can climb) – the church was saved from ruination in the eighteenth century, and fully restored in 1873 by the countess of Dunmore. The bare interior is distinguished by its wall tombs, notably that of the founder, Alasdair Crotach (also known as Alexander MacLeod), whose heavily weathered effigy lies beneath an intriguing backdrop and canopy of sculpted reliefs depicting vernacular and religious scenes – elemental representations of, among others, a stag hunt, the Holy Trinity, St Michael and the devil, and an angel weighing the souls of the dead. Look out, too, for the *sheila-na-gig* halfway up the south side of the church tower; unusually, she has a brother displaying his genitalia, below a carving of St Clement on the west face.

ARRIVAL AND INFORMATION

SOUTH HARRIS

By ferry There's a daily ferry between Leverburgh and Berneray, North Uist (1–2 daily in winter, 3–4 daily in summer; 1hr).

By bus There's a regular bus service along the west coast between Leverburgh and Tarbert (Mon–Sat 6–8 daily; 45min–1hr), and a less frequent one via The Bays on the east coast (Mon–Sat 2–4 daily; 1hr).

ACCOMMODATION AND EATING

THE BAYS

★ **Lickisto Blackhouse Camping** Lickisto (Liceasto) Ⓣ 01859 530359, Ⓦ lickistoblackhousecamping. co.uk. Beautiful campsite by a rocky bay with a restored blackhouse for the campers' use. A couple of renovated thatched byres house basic washing facilities, while the blackhouse is the place to cook, eat and congregate with other campers by the peat fire. Yurts also available. March–Oct. Yurts **£70**, camping per pitch **£24**

Old School House Finsbay (Fionnsbhagh) Ⓣ 01859 530420, Ⓦ theoldschoolhousefinsbay.com. Attractive Victorian former village schoolhouse with two en-suite twin rooms. It's run by a very friendly couple who provide good home cooking and generous portions for dinner (£20–30) and breakfast. **£90**

Skoon 4 Geocrab Ⓣ 01851 530268, Ⓦ skoon.com. There aren't too many places to stop and have a bite to eat, so *Skoon Gallery and Studio* is something of a boon. There's always soup and bread, both home-made, for £5, or from time to time they do a full afternoon tea for £10. April–Sept Tues–Sat 10am–4.30pm; Oct–March Fri–Sat 10am–4.30pm.

THE WEST COAST

Beul-na-Mara Seilebost Ⓣ 01859 550205, Ⓦ beulna mara.co.uk. This is a perfectly decent B&B run by an excellent host, but what makes it particularly special is the stunning location, overlooking the golden sands of Luskentyre Bay (Tràigh Losgaintir). **£95**

Pairc an t-Srath Borve (Na Buirgh) Ⓣ 01859 550386, Ⓦ paircant-srath.co.uk. A working crofthouse, tastefully furnished with antiques and Harris tweeds that has a superb view from the dining room, particularly at sunset. Guests can recover from a hard day's hiking in the in-house sauna. Book into the dining room for dinner (open to all limited number of non-residents), where three beautifully prepared courses are served for £38. **£108**

★ **Temple Café** Northton (Taobh Tuath) Ⓣ 07876 340416. Great waterside café in a unique stone and timber building resembling a hobbit house. They offer tasty deep-filled pies and quiches that come with a crunchy salad for £8.50. There's a good selection of tray bakes and scones too. April–Sept Tues–Sun 10.30am–5.30pm, Thurs & Fri & Sun 6.30–9pm; Oct–March same hours, Sat & Sun only.

LEVERBURGH

★ **Am Bothan** Ferry Rd Ⓣ 01859 520251. Quirky, bright-red timber-clad bunkhouse that makes for a pretty luxurious, very welcoming hostel close to the ferry. Lovely big kitchen/living room, plus laundry and drying facilities too. April–Oct. Dorms **£22.50**

The Anchorage Ferry Terminal Ⓣ 01859 520225, Ⓦ anchoragerestaurant.co.uk. Lots of locally sourced seafood on offer in this lively bar/restaurant by the ferry slipway. Considerably more expensive than your average Hebridean eatery (seafood linguine for £21.50), but there are cheaper options like roast vegetable fregola for £11.50. Reservations essential summer evenings. Mon–Sat noon–11pm; food served noon–9pm.

Carminish House 1a Strond ☎01859 520400, ⓦcarminish.com. Modern guesthouse with bright, ensuite rooms and a residents' lounge, which has an open fire and some fabulous views over the Sound. April–Oct. £100

North Uist (Uibhist a Tuath)

Compared to the mountainous scenery of Harris, **North Uist** – seventeen miles long and thirteen miles wide – is much flatter and for some comes as something of an anti-climax. Over half the surface area is covered by water, creating a distinctive peaty-brown lochan-studded "drowned landscape". Most visitors come here for the trout- and salmon-fishing and the deerstalking, all of which (along with poaching) are critical to the survival of the island's economy. Others come for the smattering of prehistoric sites, the birds, the otters, or the sheer peace of this windy isle and the solitude of North Uist's vast sandy beaches, which extend – almost without interruption – along the north and west coasts.

Lochmaddy (Loch nam Madadh) and around

Despite being situated on the east coast, some distance away from any beach, the ferry port of **LOCHMADDY** – "Loch of the Dogs" – makes a good base for exploring the island. Occupying a narrow, bumpy promontory, overlooked by the brooding mountains of North Lee (Lì a Tuath) and South Lee (Lì a Deas) to the southeast, it's difficult to believe that this sleepy settlement was a large herring port as far back as the seventeenth century. While there's not much to see in Lochmaddy itself, there are several prehistoric sites in the surrounding area.

Taigh Chearsabhagh

Mon–Sat 10am–5pm (4pm in winter) • £3 • ☎01876 603970, ⓦtaigh-chearsabhagh.org

The only thing to keep you in Lochmaddy is **Taigh Chearsabhagh**, a converted eighteenth-century merchant's house, now home to a community arts centre, with a simple airy café, post office, shop and excellent museum, which puts on some worthwhile exhibitions. Taigh Chearsabhagh was one of the prime movers behind the commissioning of a series of seven sculptures dotted about the Uists. Ask at the arts centre for directions to the ones in and around Lochmaddy, the most interesting of which is the **Both nam Faileas** (Hut of the Shadow), half a mile or so north of the town. The hut is an ingenious dry-stone, turf-roofed camera obscura built by sculptor Chris Drury that projects the nearby land-, sea- and skyscape onto its back wall – take time to allow your eyes to adjust to the light. On the way back, keep a lookout for otters, which love the tidal rapids hereabouts.

North Uist's Neolithic sights

The most remarkable of North Uist's Neolithic sights is **Barpa Langass**, a huge, chambered burial cairn a short walk from the A867, seven barren miles southwest of Lochmaddy. The stones are visible from the road and, unless the weather's good, it's not worth making a closer inspection as the chamber has collapsed and is now too dangerous to enter.

A mile further down the A867, a side road leads off to *Langass Lodge*. Beside the hotel, a rough track leads to the small stone circle of **Pobull Fhinn** (Finn's People), which enjoys a much more picturesque location overlooking a narrow loch. The circle covers a large area and, although the stones are not that huge, they occupy an intriguing amphitheatre cut into the hillside.

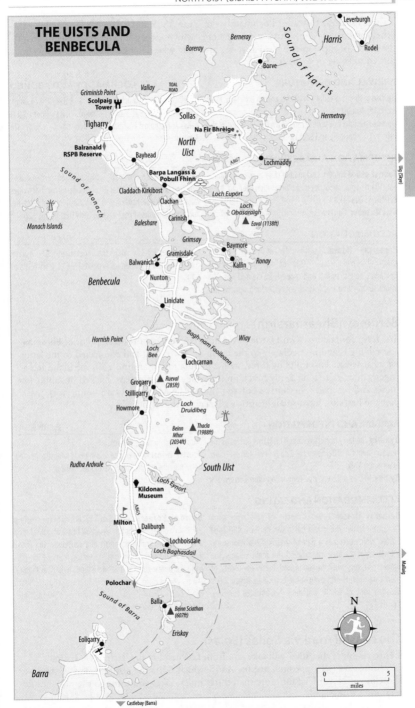

**THE UISTS AND
BENBECULA**

Leverburgh

Berneray

Boreray

Harris

Rodel

Borve

Sound of Harris

Hermetray

Griminish Point
**Scolpaig
Tower**

Vallay

TIDAL
ROAD

Sollas

*North
Uist*

Na Fir Bhrèige

Tigharry

**Balranald
RSPB Reserve**

Bayhead

A867

Lochmaddy

**Barpa Langass &
Pobull Fhinn**

Sound of Monach

Claddach Kirkibost

Clachan

Loch Euport

*Loch
Obasaraigh*

▲ *Eaval (1138ft)*

Monach Islands

Baleshare

Carinish

Grimsay

Baymore

Balwanich

Gramisdale

Kallin

Ronay

Benbecula

Nunton

Liniclate

Hornish Point

Bagh-nam Faoileann

Wiay

*Loch
Bee*

Lochcarnan

Grogarry

▲ *Rueval
(285ft)*

Stilligarry

Howmore

*Loch
Druidibeg*

▲ *Thacla
(1988ft)*

*Beinn
Mhor
(2034ft)* ▲

▲

Rudha Ardvule

South Uist

**Kildonan
Museum**

Loch Eynort

Milton

A865

Daliburgh

Lochboisdale

Loch Baghasdail

Polochar

Balla

▲ *Beinn Sciathan
(607ft)*

Sound of Barra

Eoligarry

Eriskay

Barra

N

0   5
miles

Castlebay (Barra)

6

Uig (Skye)

Mallaig

Three miles northwest of Lochmaddy along the A865 you'll find Na Fir Bhreige (The Three False Men), three standing stones which, depending on your legend, mark the graves of three spies buried alive or three men who deserted their wives and were turned to stone by a witch.

ARRIVAL AND DEPARTURE

LOCHMADDY AND AROUND

By ferry There's a daily ferry from and to Uig, Skye (1–2 daily; 1hr 40min).

By bus A regular bus service runs down the backbone of the Uists to Lochboisdale and Eriskay.

Destinations Balivanich (Mon–Sat 6–8 daily; 30–45min); Balranald (Mon–Sat 3 daily; 50min); Eriskay (Mon–Sat 3 daily; 2hr 20min); Lochboisdale (Mon–Sat 5–6 daily; 1hr 30min).

INFORMATION AND ACTIVITIES

Tourist office Pier Rd, Lochmaddy (July to mid-Oct Mon–Sat 10am–5pm; Also opens to greet the evening ferry; ☎ 01876 500321).

Uist Outdoor Centre Lochmaddy, 100yds north of the village ☎ 01876 500480, ⓦ uistoutdoorcentre.co.uk. Outdoor centre with hostel accommodation and activities ranging from sea-kayaking to rock climbing for residents and non-residents alike. March to early Dec. Dorms **£20**

ACCOMMODATION

Hamersay House Lochmaddy ☎ 01876 500700, ⓦ hamersayhouse.co.uk. One of the region's more upmarket hotels; stylish and modern inside and out. The in-house brasserie has lots of pricey seafood options like langoustines for £20 while the vegetarian option usually comes for a more economically palatable £13. Daily 6–9pm. **£145**

Berneray (Bhearnaraigh)

The ferry connection with Harris leaves from the very southeastern point of **Berneray**, a low-lying island immediately to the north of North Uist and connected to the latter via a causeway. Two miles by three, with a population of around 140, the island has a superb three-mile-long sandy beach on the west and north coast, backed by rabbit-free dunes and machair. The **Nurse's Cottage** (June–Aug Mon–Fri 11am–3pm; free), just past the harbour, has a small historical display on the island.

ARRIVAL AND INFORMATION

BERNERAY

By ferry The ferry from Leverburgh on Harris arrives at the very southern tip of Berneray (1–2 daily in winter, 3–4 daily in summer; 1hr).

By bus There's a decent bus connection with Lochmaddy (Mon–Sat 5–6 daily; 20min).

Tourist information The community website ⓦ isleofberneray.com is a useful source of information.

ACCOMMODATION AND EATING

Berneray Hostel 2 miles north of the ferry port ⓦ gatliff.org.uk. The island has a wonderful Gatliff Trust hostel, which occupies a pair of thatched blackhouses in a lovely spot by a beach, beyond the main village. The property is very well equipped and there are plenty of tourist pamphlets and even some binoculars if you fancy doing a spot of whale watching. No advance booking. Dorms **£16**

Bistro on Berneray ☎ 01876 540288, ⓦ bernerayshopandbistro.co.uk. Bright blue licensed bistro and local shop a few minutes from the north Uist causeway. The menu includes sandwiches and grilled wraps from £4.95, plus fresh Berneray crab and langoustines (when available). Shop year-round Mon–Sat 9.30am–5.30pm; Bistro Mon–Sat: April–Sept 10am–4pm & 5.30–8.30pm, Oct–March 10am–3pm.

The coastal road via Sollas (Solas)

In just six miles the A867 will take you from Lochmaddy to Clachan via several Neolithic sites (see opposite), but the A865, which skirts the northern and western shoreline of North Uist for more than thirty miles, takes you through the most scenic sections of the island.

Sollas (Solas)

Once you've left the boggy east coast and passed the turning to Berneray and the Harris ferry, the road reaches the parish of **SOLLAS** (Solas), which stands at the centre of a couple of superb tidal strands – sea green at high tide, sandy and golden at low tide – backed by large tracts of machair that are blanketed with wild flowers in summer. A memorial opposite the local co-op recalls the appallingly brutal Clearances undertaken by Lord MacDonald of Sleat in Sollas.

Vallay (Bhalaigh)

6

Visible across the nearby sandy strand is the tidal island of **Vallay** (Bhalaigh), on which stands the ruined mansion of wealthy textile manufacturer and archeologist Erskine Beveridge (cousin of Lord William) – check tide times before setting out.

Scolpaig Tower and Griminish Point

Beyond Solas, the rolling hills that occupy the centre of North Uist slope down to the sea. Here, in the northwest corner of the island, you'll find **Scolpaig Tower**, a castellated folly on an islet in Loch Scolpaig, erected as a famine-relief project in the nineteenth century – you can reach it, with some difficulty, across stepping stones. A tarmac track leads down past the loch and tower to Scolpaig Bay, beyond which lies the rocky shoreline of **Griminish Point** (Rubha Griminis), the closest landfall to St Kilda (see page 307), clearly visible on the horizon in fine weather, looming like some giant dinosaur's skeleton emerging from the sea.

Balranald RSPB Reserve

Visitor centre April–Aug daily 9am–6pm

Roughly three miles south of Scolpaig Tower, through the sand dunes, is the **Balranald RSPB Reserve** where, if you're lucky, you should be able to encounter corncrakes, once common throughout the British countryside, but now among the country's rarest birds. Unfortunately, the birds are very good at hiding in long grass, so you're unlikely to see one; however, the males' loud "craking" is relatively easy to hear from May to July throughout the Uists and Barra. In fact, there are usually one or two making a loud noise right outside the RSPB **visitor centre**, from which you can pick up a leaflet outlining a two-hour loop walk around the headland, marked by posts. A wonderful carpet of flowers covers the machair in summer, and there are usually corn buntings and arctic terns inland, and gannets, Manx shearwaters and skuas out to sea.

ACCOMMODATION   **THE COAST ROAD VIA SOLLAS**

Balranald Hebridean Holidays Balranald ☏ 01876 510304, ⊛ balranaldhebrideanholidays.com. Lovely campsite by the RSPB reserve, surrounded by fields of wild flowers and close to a sandy beach. Clean amenities block, free wi-fi, a washing machine and tumble drier, and the office sells basic provisions. March–Sept. Per pitch **£10**, glamping pod **£50**

Clachan (Clachan na Luib) and around

CLACHAN (Clachan na Luib), centred on the main crossroads of the A865 and the A867 from Lochmaddy, has a post office and general store. Offshore, to the southwest, lie two flat, tidal, dune and machair islands, the largest of which is **Baleshare** (Baile Sear), with its fantastic three-mile-long beach, connected by causeway to North Uist. In Gaelic the island's name means "east village", its twin "west village" having disappeared under the sea during a freak storm in the fifteenth or sixteenth century. The storm also isolated the **Monach Islands** (also known by their old Norse name of Heisker or Heisgeir in Gaelic), once joined to North Uist at low tide, now eight miles out to sea. The islands were inhabited until the 1930s, when the last remaining families moved to Sollas.

Eabhal

For a superb overview of North Uist's watery landscape, it's a boggy but relatively straightforward climb up the island's highest hill, **Eabhal** (1138ft). Just north of Clachan, turn right at the signpost for Loch Euphoirt and follow the road to the end. On foot, skirt round the east side of Loch Obasaraigh and approach the summit from the northeast (return trip 3–4hr).

ACCOMMODATION   CLACHAN AND AROUND

★ **Bagh Alluin** 21 Baleshare (Baile Sear) ☎01876 580370, ⓦjacvolbeda.co.uk. A secluded, beautifully designed modern B&B with large rooms and fantastic views. Run by a friendly Dutch artist, who can point you in the right direction to see the best of the island's wildlife. **£95**

Langass Lodge Loch Eport, just off the A867 ☎01876 580285, ⓦlangasslodge.co.uk. A former hunting lodge beside a small wood (a very rare sight in the Uists). It has reasonably tasteful, spacious rooms, a bar and restaurant that serves excellent local seafood, as well as meat and veggie dishes, for around £25 for main course. Daily 6–8.30pm. **£130**

★ **Moorcroft Holidays** 17 Carinish (Cairinis) ☎01876 580305, ⓦmoorcroftholidays.co.uk. An exposed but flat and very well-equipped campsite, with sea views; the bunkhouse is pretty luxurious with three twin rooms, lovely wooden floors and furnishings, a modern kitchen and a homely living/dining room. If you prefer some privacy, they also rent out little "hobbit homes" for up to three people that have a fridge, sink and cooking facilities. April–Oct. Bunkhouse per person **£25**; camping per person **£8**; hobbit home **£50**

EATING AND DRINKING

Claddach Kirkibost Centre Claddach Kirkibost (Cladach Chireboist) ☎01876 580390, ⓦcladdach-kirkibost.org. Community-centre café in a conservatory with sea views. Soups, sandwiches and simple dishes, even the occasional curry or Tex-Mex dish (£6–7), mostly made from local produce. Mon–Sat 10am–4pm.

Westford Inn Claddach Kirkibost (Cladach Chireboist)

☎01876 580653, ⓦwestfordinn.com. North Uist's only pub – luckily it's a good one – is housed in the eighteenth-century factor's house. There's a wood-panelled bar plus several smaller rooms with real fires in bad weather, Isle of Skye Brewing Company ales on tap and pub food until 9pm. Sun–Thurs noon–11pm, Fri noon–midnight, Sat noon–1am.

Benbecula (Beinn na Faoghla)

Blink and you could miss the pancake-flat island of **Benbecula** (put the stress on the second syllable), sandwiched between Protestant North Uist and Catholic South Uist. Most visitors simply trundle along the main road that cuts across the middle of the island in less than five miles – not such a bad idea, since the island is scarred from the postwar presence of the Royal Artillery, who once made up half the local population. The only reason to come to **BALIVANICH** (Baile a Mhanaich), Benbecula's grim, grey capital, is if you're flying into or out of **Benbecula Airport**, or you need an ATM or a supermarket.

Museum nan Eilean

Liniclate School (Sgoil Lionacleit) • Term time Tues–Sat 10am–1pm & 2–5pm • ☎01870 603692, ⓦcne-siar.gov.uk

The only secondary school (and public swimming pool) on the Uists and Benbecula is in Liniclate (Lionacleit), in the south of the island. The school is home to a small **Museum nan Eilean**, which puts on temporary exhibitions on the history of the islands, as well as occasional live music and other events.

ARRIVAL AND DEPARTURE   BENBECULA

By plane Benbecula Airport (☎01870 602310, ⓦhial. co.uk/benbecula-airport) is just a 10–15min walk north of Balivanich. The airport serves Glasgow and Stornoway and there's a small café inside the terminal building.

By bus Buses en route to and from South or North Uist stop

outside Balivanich's airport.

Destinations Berneray (Mon–Sat 5–7 daily; 1hr 10min); Eriskay (Mon–Sat 5–7 daily; 1hr 30min); Lochboisdale (Mon–Sat 7–8 daily; 1hr); Lochmaddy (Mon–Sat 6–7 daily; 30min).

ACCOMMODATION AND EATING

Nunton House Hostel Nunton ☎01870 602017, ⓦnuntonhousehostel.com. Four small dorm rooms in the eighteenth-century former clan chief's house, where Bonnie Prince Charlie dressed up in Flora MacDonald's maid's clothing before his escape over the sea to Skye. Sadly the prince wouldn't recognize the place these days as all the charm has been modernized out of it, save for the delightful hearth. Dorms **£25**

Shell Bay Caravan Park Liniclate (Lionacleit) ☎01870 602447. Flat, wind-buffeted, grassy field right next to the main school (and museum) on Benbecula – facilities are quite good (including laundry and hot showers), though it's not the most romantic of spots. April–Sept. Per pitch **£14**

Stepping Stone Balivanich (Baile a Mhanaich) ☎01870 603377. A modern café-restaurant that serves cheap sandwiches and soups at lunchtime for around £3 to £4 and more varied dishes in the evening, such as chicken supreme with a whisky sauce for £15. Rooms are £90. Mon–Fri 9am–9pm, Sat 11am–9pm, Sun noon–9pm.

South Uist (Uibhist a Deas)

South Uist is the largest and most varied of the southern chain of islands. The west coast boasts some of the region's finest machair and beaches – a necklace of gold and grey sand strung twenty miles from one end to the other – while the east coast features a ridge of high mountains rising to 2034ft at Beinn Mhòr. There are few places to stop for food and drink, until you get to the south of the island.

The Reformation never took a hold in South Uist (or Barra), and the island remains Roman Catholic, as is evident from the various roadside shrines. The only blot on South Uist's landscape is the Royal Artillery missile range, which dominates the northwest corner of the island. Whatever you do, however, don't make the mistake of simply driving down the main A865 road, which runs down the centre of the island.

The north

The northern half of the island contains the best **mountains** and **beaches**. To climb the mountains, you need a detailed 1:25,000 map, to negotiate the island's maze of lochans; to reach the beaches (or even see them), you have to get off the main road and pass through the old crofters' villages that straggle along the west coast.

One of the best places to reach the sandy shoreline is at **HOWMORE** (Tobha Mòr), a pretty little crofting settlement with a number of restored houses, many still thatched, including one distinctively roofed in brown heather. It's an easy walk from the village church across the flower-strewn machair to the gorgeous beach. In among the crofts are the shattered, lichen-encrusted remains of no fewer than four medieval churches and chapels, and a burial ground now harbouring just a few scattered graves. The sixteenth-century **Clanranald Stone**, carved with the arms of the clan who ruled over South Uist from 1370 until 1839, used to lie here, but is now displayed in the nearby Kildonan Museum (see page 320).

ACCOMMODATION   THE NORTH

Howmore (Tobha Mòr) hostel Howmore (Tobha Mòr) ⓦgatliff.org.uk. Simple Gatliff Trust hostel occupying a lovely cosy thatched crofthouse near the village church, and just a short walk from the beach. Fully equipped kitchen. No advance bookings and bring provisions, as the nearest shop is 7 miles away. Dorms **£16**

Kinloch Grogarry (Groigearraidh) ☎01870 620316, ⓦkinlochuist.com. A fine, modern B&B sheltered by a little patch of woodland and overlooking freshwater Loch Druidibeg – run by a very keen angler, who will do three-course evening meals for £25 or packed lunches for £10. **£100**

Orasay Inn Lochcarnan (Loch a' Charnain) ☎01870 610298, ⓦorasayinn.co.uk. A modern purpose-built hotel and restaurant (evening meals only) off the main road with well-kept rooms, some of which have a private decked area. Daily 6–8.30pm. **£99**

Lochboisdale (Loch Baghasdail) and around

LOCHBOISDALE occupies a narrow, bumpy promontory on the east coast, but, despite being South Uist's chief settlement and ferry port, has only very limited facilities (there's a bank here, but the nearest supermarket is three miles west in Dalabrog).

Kildonan Museum (Taigh-tasgaidh Chill Donnain)

5 miles south of Howmore • April–Oct daily 10am–5pm • £3 • ☎ 01878 710343, ⊛ kildonanmuseum.co.uk

Reasonably large museum featuring mock-ups of Hebridean kitchens through the ages, two lovely box-beds and an impressive selection of old Photos, accompanied by an unsentimental yet poetic text on crofting life in the last two Centuries. Pride of place goes to the sixteenth-century **Clanranald Stone**, carved with the arms of the clan who ruled over South Uist from 1370 to 1839. The museum café serves sandwiches and home-made cakes, and has a choice of historical videos for those really wet and windy days.

ARRIVAL AND INFORMATION   LOCHBOISDALE AND AROUND

By ferry One ferry connects Mallaig to Lochboisdale (winter one on Tues & Sat; summer one daily; 3hr 30min).
By bus There's a regular bus service along the spine road (as they call it) to North Uist (Mon–Sat only).
Destinations Balivanich (Mon–Sat 2–5 daily; 1hr);

Berneray (Mon–Sat 1 daily; 2hr 50min); Eriskay (Mon–Sat 4–6 daily; 40min); Lochmaddy (Mon–Sat 1–2 daily; 1hr 30min).
Tourist office Pier Rd (Easter–Oct Mon–Sat 9am–5pm; also open for an hour to meet the ferry; ☎ 01878 700286).

ACCOMMODATION AND EATING

Heron Point Lochboisdale ☎ 01878 700073, ⊛ heron point.co.uk. Homely B&B just a mile up the road from the ferry terminal with four en-suite bedrooms. Efficiently run by a very friendly host who cooks up a wonderful breakfast of smoked salmon and poached eggs. **£95**
Kilbride Café & Campsite 9 West Kilbride ☎ 07751 251522, ☎ 01878 700008 ⊛ kilbride-campsite.business. site. Tea, coffee, juices and milkshakes, along with home-baking and a basic hot menu of tasty burgers, fish and chips and all-day-breakfasts (nothing over £6.95). The café benefits from the same beautiful views of the Sound of Barra as the adjacent campsite, which has 30 hard pitches and loads of green space for tents. Café daily 11am–3pm. Camping **£10**
Lochboisdale Hotel Lochboisdale ☎ 01878 700332, ⊛ lochboisdale.com. The town's long-established hotel

is a convenient place to shelter if you're waiting for a ferry, and it does fish and chips and other typical bar meals for around £10–14. If you staying over, the accommodation is a bit dated but the rooms are spacious, comfortable and have great views over the harbour. **£100**
Polochar Inn Polochar (Poll a' Charra) ☎ 01878 700215, ⊛ polocharinn.com. One of best places to hole up in, right on the south coast overlooking the Sound of Barra, and with its own sandy beach close by; the rooms all have sea views, and on the ground floor is a good pub, with attached restaurant dishing up creamy pesto gnocchi for £12 or scallops and black pudding for £22. Mon–Thurs 11am–11pm, Fri & Sat 11am–1am, Sun 12.30–11pm; food served Mon–Sat 12.30–2.30pm & 5.30–9pm, Sun 12.30–8.30pm.

Eriskay (Eiriosgaigh)

Famous for its patterned jerseys and a peculiar breed of pony, originally used for carrying peat and seaweed, barren, hilly **Eriskay** has been connected by a causeway to the south of South Uist since 2001. The pretty island, which measures just over two miles by one, and shelters a small fishing community of about 150, makes an easy day-trip from South Uist.

For a small island, Eriskay has had more than its fair share of historical headlines. The island's main beach on the west coast, Coilleag a Phrionnsa (Prince's Cockle Strand), was where **Bonnie Prince Charlie** landed on Scottish soil on July 23, 1745 – the sea bindweed that grows here to this day is said to have sprung from the seeds Charles brought with him from France. The prince, as yet unaccustomed to hardship, spent his first night in a local blackhouse and ate a couple of flounders, though he apparently couldn't take the peat smoke and chose to sleep sitting up rather than endure the damp bed.

> **SS POLITICIAN**
>
> Eriskay's greatest claim to fame came in 1941 when the **SS** *Politician*, or "Polly" as she's fondly known, sank on her way from Liverpool to Jamaica, along with her cargo of bicycle parts, £3 million in Jamaican currency and 264,000 bottles of whisky, inspiring *Whisky Galore*, Compton MacKenzie's book, and the Ealing comedy (filmed on Barra in 1948 and released as *Tight Little Island* in the US). The real story was somewhat less romantic, especially for the 36 islanders who were charged with illegal possession by the Customs and Excise officers. Nineteen of the islanders were found guilty and imprisoned in Inverness. The ship's stern used to be seen at low tide northwest of Calvay Island in the Sound of Eriskay until the sea finally swallowed it up. One of the original bottles (and other memorabilia) can be viewed at *Am Politician* (see below).

St Michael's Church

Near the causeway

Built in 1903, in a vaguely Spanish style on raised ground in the northwest corner of the island, by the causeway, is the Roman Catholic **St Michael's Church**. Its most striking features are the bell, which sits outside the church and comes from the World War I battle cruiser *Derfflinger*, the last of the scuttled German fleet to be salvaged from Scapa Flow, and the altar, which is made from the bow of a lifeboat.

Ben Sciathan

The walk (2hr return from the causeway) up to the island's highest point, **Ben Sciathan** (607ft), is well worth the effort on a clear day, as you can see the whole island, plus Barra, South Uist, and across the sea to Skye, Rùm, Coll and Tiree. On the way up or down, look out for the diminutive Eriskay ponies, which roam free on the hills but tend to graze around Loch Crakavaig, right in the centre of the island and its only freshwater source.

ARRIVAL AND DEPARTURE   ERISKAY

By ferry CalMac run a small car ferry between Eriskay and Ardmhor on Barra (5 daily except Sun in winter when there's 2; 40min).

By bus There's a regular bus service between Eriskay and Lochboisdale (Mon–Sat 4–6 daily; 40min).

ACCOMMODATION AND EATING

Am Politician Rubha Ban ☎ 01878 720246. The island's purpose-built pub named after the SS *Politician* (see above) is unlikely to win any design awards. However, it offers great views out to sea from its conservatory where you can dine on scallops with black pudding for £8.50 as well as the usual pub grub options. Easter–Oct Mon–Sat 11.30am–11pm (sometimes later), Sun noon–11pm; Oct–Easter open some weekends 11.30am–11pm; food served noon–7.45pm.

Oir na Mara ☎ 01878 720216. This plain, modern bungalow B&B is kept by a true perfectionist; the rooms are spotlessly clean and the bedding is high quality. Tea and home-made cakes are offered to guests on arrival, and Eriskay's pub is conveniently nearby for meal times. **£70**

Barra (Barraigh)

Four miles wide and eight miles long, **Barra** is the Western Isles in miniature: sandy beaches backed by machair, mountains of Lewisian gneiss – the oldest rock in Britain – prehistoric ruins, Gaelic culture and a laidback, welcoming population of around 1200. A kind of feudal island state, it was ruled over for centuries, with relative benevolence, by the MacNeils. Unfortunately, the family sold the island in 1838 to Colonel Gordon of Cluny, who had also bought Benbecula, South Uist and Eriskay. The colonel deemed the starving crofters "redundant" and offered to turn Barra into a state penal colony. The government declined, so the colonel called in the police and proceeded with some of the most cruel forced Clearances in the Hebrides. In 1937, the 45th chief of the MacNeil clan bought back most of the island, and in 2003 the estate was gifted to the Scottish government.

Castlebay (Bàgh a Chaisteil)

The only settlement of any size is **CASTLEBAY** (Bàgh a Chaisteil), which curves around the barren rocky hills of a wide bay on the south side of the island. It's difficult to imagine, but Castlebay was a herring port of some significance back in the nineteenth century, with hundreds of boats in the harbour and curing and packing factories ashore. Barra's religious allegiance is immediately announced by the large Catholic church, Our Lady, Star of the Sea, which overlooks the bay; to underline the point, there's a Madonna and Child on the slopes of **Sheabhal** (Heaval; 1260ft), the largest peak on Barra and a fairly short hike from Castlebay – although there's no marked path and the ground is steep and can be boggy.

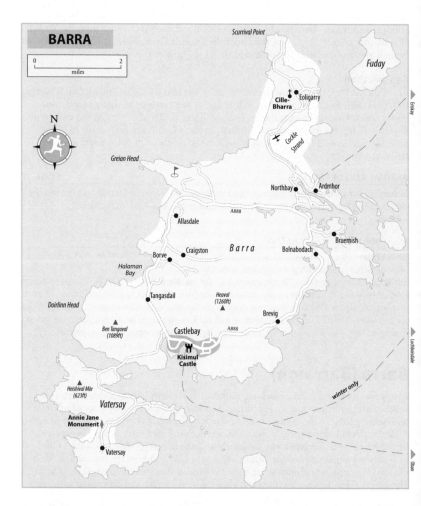

MINGULAY AND THE SMALLER BARRA ISLES

Several of the **Barra Isles**, also known as the Bishop's Isles, to the south of Vatersay were inhabited until just before World War II. The largest of the islands is **Mingulay** (Miùghlaigh), which once had a population of 160 and, with its large seabird colonies, spectacular sea cliffs and stacks, is often compared to St Kilda. The crofters of Mingulay began a series of land raids on Vatersay from 1906, and by 1912 the island had been abandoned, with none of the publicity later given to St Kilda. The most southerly of the Barra Isles is Berneray (Bearnaraigh) – not to be confused with the Berneray north of North Uist – best known for its lighthouse, **Barra Head**, which stands on cliffs over 620ft high. For details of boat trips to Mingulay and the other islands, phone Donald (☎01871 890384, ⊕barrafishingcharters.com) or contact the tourist office in Castlebay (see page 324).

Kisimul Castle

April–Sept Tues–Sun 9.30am–5.30pm • £5.50; HES • ☎01871 810313, ⊕historicenvironment.scot • Access by ferry from Castle Slip Landing, Castlebay (call for sailing times), weather permitting • In 2019, the Great Hall was closed for maintenance until further notice (entry fee discounted)

As its name suggests, Castlebay has a castle in its bay, the picturesque medieval islet-fortress of Caisteal Chiosmuil, or **Kisimul Castle**, ancestral home of the MacNeil clan. The castle burnt down in the eighteenth century, but when the 45th MacNeil chief – conveniently enough, a wealthy American and trained architect – bought the island back in 1937, he set about restoring the castle. There's nothing much to see inside, but the whole experience is fun – head down to the slipway at the bottom of Main Street, where the ferryman will take you over.

Dualchas

The Square • April–Sept Mon, Tues & Wed 10am–1pm • £4 • ☎01871 810413

The Barra Heritage Centre, known as **Dualchas** (Gaelic for Heritage), is on the road that leads west out of town. It's an unpretentious little museum, housing the odd treasure like the monstrance from St Barr's Church in Northbay. There are lots of old newspapers, photo archives and local memoirs to trawl through; the museum also has a handy **café** serving soup, toasties and cakes.

The north

If you head to the north end of the island from Castlebay, you have a choice of taking the west- or east-coast road. The west-coast road takes you past the island's finest sandy beaches, particularly those at **Halaman Bay** and near the village of Allasdale (Allathasdal). The east-coast road wends its way in and out of various rocky bays, one of which, **Northbay** (Bàgh a Tuath), shelters a small fishing fleet and a little island sporting a statue of St Barr, better known as Finbarr, the island's Irish patron saint.

Cockle Strand

At the north end of the island, Barra is squeezed between two sandy bays: the dune-backed white sand west side takes the full force of the Atlantic breakers and is a wonderful hidden spot for a stroll, while the east side boasts the crunchy shell sands of Tràigh Mhòr, better known as **Cockle Strand**. The beach is also used as the island's **airport**, with planes landing and taking off according to the tides, since at high tide the beach (and therefore the runway) is covered in water. As its name suggests, the strand is also famous for its cockles and cockleshells, the latter being used to make harling (the rendering used on most Scottish houses).

Eoligarry (Eòlaigearraidh)

To the north of the airport is the scattered settlement of **EOLIGARRY** (Eòlaigearraidh), which boasts several sheltered sandy bays. Here, too, is **St Barr's Church** (Cille-Bharra), burial ground of the MacNeils (and the author Compton MacKenzie). The ground lies beside the ruins of a medieval church and two chapels, one of which has been reroofed to provide shelter for several carved medieval gravestones and a replica of an eleventh-century rune-inscribed cross, the original of which is in the National Museum of Scotland in Edinburgh.

Vatersay (Bhatarsaigh)

To the south of Barra is the island of **Vatersay** (Bhatarsaigh), shaped rather like an apple core, and since 1991 linked to its neighbour by a causeway – a mile or so southwest of Castlebay. The island is divided into two peninsulas connected by a slender isthmus, whose dunes feature the **Annie Jane Monument**, a granite needle erected to commemorate the 350 emigrants who lost their lives when the *Annie Jane* ran aground off Vatersay in 1853 en route to Canada. The main settlement (also known as Vatersay) has little charm, but it does have a lovely **sandy beach** to the south; another fine beach, visible from Castlebay, is situated at the eastern end of the northern half of the island. Climb up the chief hill, **Heiseabhal Mòr** (623ft), to get an overview of the uninhabited islands to the south of Vatersay.

ARRIVAL AND GETTING AROUND
BARRA

By plane Barra Airport (☎01871 890212, ⊕hial.co.uk) has direct flights from and to Glasgow, timetables depend on tide times.

By ferry The main ferry terminal on Barra is in Castlebay where the ferry from Oban arrives: from Eriskay, you arrive at at Ardmhor, an uninhabited spot on the northeast of the island.

Destinations Coll (Wed; 4hr); Eriskay (5 daily, 2 in winter on Sun; 40min); Oban (summer daily, winter Wed & Fri–Mon; 5hr); Tiree (Wed; 2hr 45min).

By bus There's a fairly decent bus service out of Castlebay,

which does the rounds of the island daily except Sunday. Book in advance for the Vatersay bus; ask at the Tourist office for details.

Destinations Airport (Mon–Sat 4–7 daily; 30min); Eriskay ferry (Mon–Sat 2–5 daily to coincide with ferry timetable; 25min); Eoligarry (Mon–Sat 3–6 daily; 35min); Vatersay (Mon–Sat 2–3 daily; 20min).

By car or bike Barra Car Hire (☎01871 890313) will deliver cars to either ferry terminal or the airport, and Barra Cycle Hire (☎01871 810846, ☎07876 402842) will do the same with bikes (from £10/day).

INFORMATION AND ACTIVITIES

Tourist office Bùth Bharraigh, Main St, Castlebay (⊕barrashop.co.uk; ☎01871 817948; April–Sept Mon–Sat 10am–7.15pm, Sun noon–4pm & 6–7.15pm). Visitor information (including hotel booking) and a shop with a

range of local produce, wholefoods and crafts. Barra Cycle Hire stores bikes here, too.

Sea-kayaking Guided tours available from the *Dunard Hostel* (see below); arrange in advance.

ACCOMMODATION

Castlebay Hotel Castlebay ☎01871 810223, ⊕castlebay-hotel.co.uk. The *Castlebay* is the more welcoming of the town's two hotels – a grey Victorian pile, with spectacular views over the bay from the restaurant and some of the rooms. The six rooms vary in price considerably and all are in desperate need of modernisation. **£90**

★ **Dunard Hostel** Castlebay ☎01871 810443, ⊕dunardhostel.co.uk. A relaxed, family-run place just west of the ferry terminal in Castlebay, that has twins, dorm beds and a family room. There's a well-equipped kitchen, a long dining table and a cosy living room with resident cats snoozing by the fire. They also offer a range of guided

sea-kayaking trips posted up on the noticeboard (average around £20). Dorms **£20**, twins **£45**

Heathbank Hotel Northbay (Bagh a Tuath) ☎01871 890266, ⊕barrahotel.co.uk. Converted mission church, now home to a comfortable hotel and unpretentious local watering hole and upmarket restaurant. **£150**

Northbay House Northbay (Bagh a Tuath) ☎01871 890255. The old schoolhouse in Northbay, originally built in 1888, is now a B&B run by a friendly couple – breakfast menu includes local smoked haddock and poached egg. **£76**

Tigh-na-Mara Castlebay ☎01871 810304, ⊕tighna mara-barra.co.uk. For value and location – just a few

THE HEBRIDEAN WAY

A dual aspect long-distance route has traversed the Western Isles archipelago since 2017. The 156-mile **walking trail** and 185-mile **cycle trail** (National Cycling Route 780) cover different ground but each stretches from Vatersay in the south to Lewis in the north (the walk ends in Stornoway and the cycle at the Butt of Lewis). The Hebridean Way is astonishingly varied and flower strewn machair, white sand beaches, craggy mountains and lochs zip by, as Golden and even White-tailed Eagles fly overhead. You'll need to know the ferry schedules – passengers can take bikes aboard for free – and although it's remote, there are places to rest and pick up supplies. For a stress-free trip, allow 4–6 days for cycling and 10–12 days for walking (see ⓦ visitouterbrides.co.uk for details).

6

minutes from the pier in Castlebay – you can't beat this simple Victorian guesthouse overlooking the sea. April–Oct. **£80**

CAMPING

Croft 183 Balnabodach (Buaile nam Bodach) ☎ 01871 810846, ⓦ croft183.com. A well-equipped campsite on the rocky eastern side of the island, with kitchen and laundry facilities, plus a hostel building with twin-bed hostel rooms, private doubles and family rooms. Per pitch **£14**, dorms **£18**, doubles **£46**, family room **£65**

★ **Scurrival campsite** 3 Eoligarry (Eòlaigearraidh) ☎ 01871 890292. This is a lovely, simple site with showers and toilet facilities, overlooking the sea and close to the wide sandy beach of Scurrival (Tràigh Sgurabhal) in the north of the island. April–Oct. Dorms **£5**

EATING AND DRINKING

★ **Café Kisimul Castlebay** ☎ 01871 810645, ⓦ cafe kisimul.co.uk. As well as offering Italian comfort food and great music, the *Kisimul* also cooks up the best curry in northwest Scotland (mains £13–18) – try the unique scallop pakora starter for £7.95. Mon–Sat 10am–4pm & 6–9pm, Sun 5.30–9pm.

Barra Airport Café Tràigh Mhòr ☎ 07855 143545. Wonderful little café with views of the planes landing and taking off from the beach airport. Coffee, cake and specials including soup of the day (£4.95) and falafel wrap (£6.50). Open for fish suppers on Friday and Saturday nights in summer (5–7pm). Daily 10am–4pm.

ENTERTAINMENT AND SPORT

Films are occasionally shown on Saturday evenings at the **local school** – look out for the posters – where there is also a **swimming pool** (Tues–Sun), **library** and **sports** **centre**, all of which are open to the general public. A mobile "screen machine" also rolls into Castlebay from time to time (ⓦ screenmachine.co.uk).

Orkney

STROMNESS

Orkney

Orkney is a captivating and fiercely independent archipelago made up of seventy or so mostly low-lying islands, with a population of around twenty two thousand. The locals tend to refer to themselves first as Orcadians, regarding Scotland as a separate entity, and proudly flying their own red, yellow and blue flag. For an Orcadian, the Mainland invariably means the largest island in Orkney rather than the rest of Scotland, and throughout their distinctive history the islands have been linked to lands much further afield, principally Scandinavia.

7

The islands offer excellent coastal **walking**, abundant birdlife and beautiful white-sand beaches that could easily be mistaken for the Caribbean. Orkney has two chief settlements: **Stromness**, an attractive old fishing town on the far southwestern shore, and the capital, **Kirkwall**, at the dividing point between East and West Mainland. The Mainland is relatively heavily populated and farmed throughout, its green fields dotted with sandstone farmhouses. To the southeast, it's joined by causeways to a string of islands, the largest of which is **South Ronaldsay**. The island of **Hoy**, the second largest in the archipelago, south of Mainland, presents a superbly dramatic landscape, with some of the highest sea cliffs in the country. Hoy, however, is atypical: Orkney's smaller, much quieter **northern islands** are low-lying, fertile outcrops of rock and sand, scattered across the ocean.

Brief history

Small communities began to settle in the islands by 4000 BC; **Skara Brae** on the Mainland is one of the best-preserved Stone Age settlements in Europe. Elsewhere the islands are scattered with chambered tombs and stone circles, proof of the well-developed religious and ceremonial practices taking place here from around 2000 BC. More sophisticated **Iron Age** inhabitants built fortified villages incorporating stone towers known as brochs, the finest of which is the **Broch of Gurness**. Later, **Pictish** culture spread to Orkney and the remains of several early Christian settlements can be seen, the best at the **Brough of Birsay**. Around the ninth century, settlers from Scandinavia arrived and the islands became **Norse** earldoms, forming outposts of a powerful, expansive culture. The last of the Norse earls was killed in 1231, but their lasting legacy was not only their language but also Kirkwall's great medieval **St Magnus Cathedral**.

Sea trading and whaling

After Norse rule, the islands became the preserve of **Scottish earls**, who exploited and abused the islanders, although a steady increase in sea trade did offer some chance of escape. French and Spanish ships sheltered here in the sixteenth century, and the ships of the **Hudson's Bay Company** recruited hundreds of Orcadians to work in the Canadian fur trade. The islands were also an important staging post in the **whaling industry** and the herring boom, which drew great numbers of Dutch, French and Scottish boats. The choice of **Scapa Flow**, Orkney's natural harbour, as the Royal Navy's main base brought plenty of money and activity during both world wars, and left the clifftops dotted with gun emplacements and the sea bed scattered with wrecks – which today make for wonderful diving opportunities.

The oil boom

After the war, things quietened down, although since the mid-1970s the large **oil terminal** on the island of Flotta, and the establishment of the Orkney Islands Council

ST MAGNUS CATHEDRAL, KIRKWALL

Highlights

❶ Maeshowe Orkney's – and Europe's – finest Neolithic chambered tomb. See page 334

❷ Skara Brae Older than Stonehenge or the Great Pyramids, Skara Brae is a mesmerizing Neolithic settlement, crammed with domestic detail. See page 336

❸ St Magnus Cathedral, Kirkwall Beautiful red-sandstone Romanesque cathedral in miniature, built by the Vikings in the twelfth century. See page 340

❹ Tomb of the Eagles Fascinating, privately owned Neolithic chambered tomb on the south-eastern tip of South Ronaldsay. See page 346

❺ Rackwick Experience the splendid isolation of this tiny settlement on the island of Hoy, with its rumbling rocky beach, and walk over to the famous Old Man of Hoy. See page 348

❻ Scapa Flow Visitor Centre Learn about the wartime history of Orkney's great natural harbour – once Britain's chief naval base and site of the scuttling of the German Fleet in 1919. See page 349

❼ Westray Thriving Orkney island with seabird colonies, sandy beaches, a sixteenth-century ruined castle and a figurine that's one of the earliest representations of the human form found in the UK. See page 354

❽ North Ronaldsay Orkney's northernmost island features a world-renowned bird observatory, seaweed-eating sheep and Britain's tallest land-based lighthouse. See page 363

HIGHLIGHTS ARE MARKED ON THE MAP ON PAGE 330

(OIC), combined with EU development grants, have brought surprise windfalls, stemming the exodus of young people. Meanwhile, many disenchanted southerners have become "ferryloupers" (incomers), moving to Orkney in search of the simplicity of island life.

ARRIVAL AND DEPARTURE

By plane Loganair (☏ 0344 800 2855, ⓦ loganair.co.uk) operate direct flights to Kirkwall from Inverness, Aberdeen, Edinburgh, Glasgow and Sumburgh in Shetland. Be warned: weather conditions are notoriously changeable, making flights prone to delay and even cancellation.

By ferry NorthLink run car ferries daily from Scrabster (with a shuttle bus from Thurso) to Stromness and less frequently from Aberdeen and Lerwick (in Shetland) to

ORKNEY

0 ——————————— 10
miles

N

HIGHLIGHTS

1 Maeshowe

2 Skara Brae

3 St Magnus Cathedral, Kirkwall

4 Tomb of the Eagles

5 Rackwick

6 Scapa Flow Visitor Centre

7 Westray

8 North Ronaldsay

7

ORKNEY FESTIVALS

The **Orkney Folk Festival** (Ⓦorkneyfolkfestival.com) is a four-day music festival, held at the end of May and centred on Stromness but with gigs all over the Mainland – it's very popular with locals and visitors alike, so expect tickets to sell out fast. The biggest cultural event by far, however, is the week-long **St Magnus Festival** (Ⓦstmagnusfestival.com), a superb arts festival held towards the end of June, with events held all over the Mainland and the outer islands. July is peppered with several island regattas and agricultural shows, culminating in the agricultural **County Show** held in Kirkwall on the second Saturday of August.

To find out **what's on** (and the weather forecast), tune in at 7.30am to *Around Orkney* (Mon–Fri) on Radio Orkney (93.7FM), and buy yourself a copy of *The Orcadian*, which comes out on Thursdays (Ⓦorcadian.co.uk).

Kirkwall; Pentland Ferries run daily car ferries from Gills Bay (near John O'Groats) to St Margaret's Hope; and John O'Groats Ferries run a small passenger ferry to Burwick.

The timetables in the text are summer frequencies – check online for the latest sailing schedule and always book ahead.

GETTING AROUND AND TOURS

By plane Loganair (Ⓣ0344 800 2855, Ⓦloganair.co.uk) run flights from Kirkwall to most of the outer isles, using an eight-seater plane, with discounted fares to North Ronaldsay and Papa Westray and between the islands if you stay over.

By ferry Getting to the other islands by ferry from the Mainland isn't difficult, but travel between individual islands isn't straightforward. Ask Orkney Ferries (Ⓣ01856 872044, Ⓦorkneyferries.co.uk) about additional Sunday sailings in summer, which often make useful inter-island connections. Tickets are expensive. Book ahead if you're taking a vehicle.

By bus The bus service on Orkney Mainland is pretty good overall. Except in Stromness and Kirkwall, there are no scheduled bus stops so just stand at a safe, visible spot and

flag the bus down. On the smaller islands, a minibus usually meets the ferry and will take you to your destination. Check Ⓦorkney.gov.uk for bus timetables.

By bike Cycling is an option if the weather holds, since there are few steep hills and distances are modest, though the wind can make it hard going. For Orkney Cycle Hire in Stromness; for Cycle Orkney in Kirkwall.

Tours There's a whole range of escorted tours around the Mainland, which are great for those without a vehicle. Wildabout Orkney (Ⓣ01856 877737, Ⓦwildaboutorkney. com) offer a variety of tours of the Mainland, with departures from Stromness and Kirkwall, and there are several other companies specializing in particular islands, as listed throughout this chapter.

Stromness

STROMNESS is a quite enchanting port at which to arrive by boat, its picturesque waterfront a procession of tiny sandstone jetties and slate roofs nestling below the green hill of Brinkies Brae. It's well worth spending a day exploring, or using as a base in preference to Kirkwall. Its natural sheltered harbour (known as Hamnavoe) was probably used in Viking times, but the town itself only really took off in the eighteenth century when the **Hudson's Bay Company** made Stromness its main base from which to make the long journey across the North Atlantic. Crews from Stromness were also hired for herring and whaling expeditions – and press-ganged into the Royal Navy.

By 1842, the town boasted forty or so pubs, and reports circulated of "outrageous and turbulent proceedings of seamen and others who frequent the harbour". The **herring boom** brought large numbers of small boats, along with thousands of young women who gutted, pickled and packed the fish in barrels. Things got so rowdy by World War I that the town voted in a referendum to ban the sale of alcohol, leaving Stromness dry from 1920 until 1947. Nowadays, Stromness is very quiet, though it remains an important fishing port and **ferry terminal** and is the focus of the popular four-day **Orkney Folk Festival**, held at the end of May.

Unlike Kirkwall, the old town of Stromness still hugs the shoreline, its one and only street a narrow winding affair, paved with great flagstones and fed by a tight network of alleyways or closes. The central section, which begins at the imposing sandstone *Stromness Hotel*, is known as **Victoria Street**, though in fact it takes on several other names as it threads its way southwards. On the east side of the street the houses are gable-end-on to the waterfront, and originally each one would have had its own pier, from which merchants would trade with passing ships.

Pier Arts Centre

Victoria St • Tues–Sat 10.30am–5pm • Free • ☎ 01856 850209, ⓦ pierartscentre.com

A warehouse on one of the old jetties on Victoria Street now forms half of the **Pier Arts Centre**; the other half is a modern glass-and-steel structure framing views of the harbour. The gallery has a remarkable permanent collection of twentieth-century British art, including work by Scottish sculptor Eduardo Paolozzi, and, most notably, by members of the Cornish group such as Barbara Hepworth, Ben Nicholson, Terry Frost, Patrick Heron and the self-taught Alfred Wallis. The collection is constantly being added to, with contemporary works by the likes of Anish Kapoor enhancing the original bequest.

Stromness Museum

52 Alfred St • April–Sept daily 11am–5pm; Oct–March Mon–Sat 11am–3.30pm • £5 • ☎ 01856 850025, Ⓦ stromnessmuseum.co.uk

At the junction of Alfred Street and South End stands the **Stromness Museum**, built in 1858, partly to house the collections of the local natural history society. The natural history collection is still here – don't miss the pull-out drawers of birds' eggs, butterflies and moths. Look out for the Halkett cloth boat, an early inflatable like the one used by John Rae, the Stromness-born Arctic explorer, whose fiddle, octant and shotgun are also on display. Amid the beaver furs and model boats are numerous salty artefacts gathered from shipwrecks, including some barnacle-encrusted crockery from the German High Seas Fleet that was sunk in Scapa Flow in 1919.

Ness Battery

1 mile south of Stromness • Guided hour-long tours all year (check website for Nov–March) • £6 • ☎ 07759 857298, Ⓦ nessbattery.co.uk

Erected in World War I to guard the western entrance to Scapa Flow, **Ness Battery** is one of the most interesting of Orkney's coastal gun emplacements. On the tour you hear stories of the lives of the soldiers who manned the six-inch guns, and see several of the original wooden huts, one of which served as the Mess Hall and retains the idiosyncratic wartime murals painted there during World War II.

ARRIVAL AND DEPARTURE

STROMNESS

By ferry Car ferries operated by NorthLink (☎ 0845 600 0449, Ⓦ northlinkferries.co.uk) arrive in the centre of Stromness from Scrabster (2–3 daily; 1hr 30min), which is connected to nearby Thurso by shuttle bus. The tiny passenger ferry to Moaness Pier on Hoy (via Graemsay), run by Orkney Ferries (☎ 01856 872044, Ⓦ orkneyferries.co.uk), departs from the old harbour in Stromness (Mon–Fri 4–5

daily, Sat & Sun 2 daily; 25min).
By bus Buses depart from Stromness Ferry Terminal. Call ☎ 01856 873535 or check Ⓦ orkney.gov.uk for timetables. Destinations Houton (Mon–Fri 2 daily; 15min); Kirkwall (Mon–Sat 2 hourly, Sun every 2hr; 30min); Skara Brae (Mon, Thurs & Sat 1 daily; 20min, also hop-on hop-off bus 1 daily April–Oct); St Margaret's Hope (Mon–Sat hourly; 1hr 5min).

INFORMATION AND GETTING AROUND

Tourist information Local information can be found in various venues throughout the town including the Pier Arts Centre and Stromness Museum, Ⓦ visitorkney.com).

By bike Orkney Cycle Hire, 54 Dundas St (☎ 01856 850255, Ⓦ orkneycyclehire.co.uk) rent bikes from £10 a day.

ACCOMMODATION

SEE MAP PAGE 332

Brinkies Guest House Innertown ☎ 01856 851881. A substantial double-bay-fronted Victorian guesthouse located a 10min walk up from the town. Rooms enjoy fantastic views and the residents' lounge has loads of reading matter. **£70**

Brown's 47 Victoria St ☎ 01856 850661, Ⓦ browns orkney.co.uk. A family-run place overseen by the very friendly Mrs Brown and situated right in the centre of town. There are twins, triples and quads as well as regular bunk beds in very small dorms. Single £22.50; dorms **£20**; doubles en suite **£50**

Burnside Farm 1 mile north of Stromness on A965 ☎ 01856 850723, Ⓦ burnside-farm.com. A cracking B&B run by a local couple on a working farm. The views are

great, and the furnishings and facilities are truly top-notch: en-suite wet-rooms, plus bere bannocks for breakfast. **£80**
Hamnavoe Hostel 10a North End Rd ☎ 01856 851202, Ⓦ hamnavoehostel.co.uk. A good 10min walk from the ferry terminal and no beauty from the outside, but inside it's all spotlessly clean, welcoming and well equipped. There's a choice of small dorms or singles, some en suite, some not. Dorms **£20**; singles **£22**
Point of Ness Campsite A mile south of the ferry terminal at Point of Ness ☎ 01856 873535. Busy council-run campsite in a superb (though extremely exposed) setting, with great views over to Hoy; facilities include a TV lounge and a washing machine. April to Sept. Per pitch for large tent/caravan with electricity **£20.20**

EATING

SEE MAP PAGE 332

Hamnavoe Restaurant 35 Graham Place ☎ 01856 850606. Friendly little front-room restaurant, with a real fire burning. The menu concentrates on nicely presented

local produce – try the tusk or hake straight off the boats – main courses start at around £16.50 and booking is essential. May–Sept Tues–Sun only.

7

Julia's Café and Bistro 20 Ferry Rd ☎ 01856 850904, ⓦ juliascafe.co.uk. Daytime café right opposite the ferry terminal, with a sunny conservatory and tables outside if the weather's good enough. It's comfort food for the most part, including a decent home-made fish pie, all for under £10. Mon–Sat 9am–5pm, Sun 10am–5pm (longer hours in the summer).

DRINKING

SEE MAP PAGE 332

Ferry Inn 10 John St ☎ 01856 850280, ⓦ ferryinn. com. Situated opposite the ferry terminal, this is the most popular and welcoming pub in town, serving up classic pub grub as well as local scallops, Orkney steak and ale pie (all around £12), washed down with Orkney beer on draught. Daily 7am–midnight; food served until 9pm.

West Mainland

The great bulk of the **West Mainland** – west of Kirkwall, that is – is fertile farmland, fenced off into a patchwork of fields used either to produce crops or for cattle-grazing. Fringed by a spectacular western coastline, West Mainland is littered with some of the island's most impressive prehistoric sites, such as the village of **Skara Brae**, the standing **Stones of Stenness**, the chambered tomb of **Maeshowe** and the **Broch of Gurness**, as well as one of Orkney's best-preserved medieval castles at **Birsay**. Despite the intensive farming, some areas are too barren to cultivate, and the high ground and wild coastline include several interesting **wildlife reserves**.

Stenness

The parish of **Stenness**, northeast of Stromness along the main road to Kirkwall, slopes down from Ward Hill (881ft) to the lochs of Stenness and Harray; the first is tidal, the second is a freshwater trout loch. The two lochs are joined by a short causeway that may well have been a narrow isthmus around 3000 BC, when it stood at the heart of Orkney's most important Neolithic ceremonial complex, centred on the burial chamber of **Maeshowe**.

Stones of Stenness

Guided tours June–Aug Mon, Wed & Fri 10am; Sept & May Wed 10am • Free; HES • ☎ 01856 841732, ⓦ historicenvironment.scot

The most visible part of the complex between lochs Stenness and Harray is the **Stones of Stenness**, originally a circle of twelve rock slabs, now just four, the tallest of which is a real monster at over 16ft, and remarkably slender. A broken tabletop lies within the circle, surrounded by a much-diminished henge (a circular bank of earth and a ditch) with a couple of entrances.

Ring of Brodgar

Guided tours June–Aug daily 1pm; Sept & May Thurs 1pm • Free; HES • ☎ 01856 841732, ⓦ historicenvironment.scot

Less than a mile to the northwest of the Stones of Stenness, past the huge **Watch Stone** which stands beside the road, at over 18ft in height, the **Ring of Brodgar** is a much wider circle dramatically sited on raised ground. There were originally sixty stones, 27 of which now stand; of the henge, only the ditch survives. At the height of summer, go early (or late), so as to avoid the coach parties – or arrive in time for one of the guided tours.

Maeshowe

If arriving in your own vehicle, you'll need to book a car park space several days in advance • Daily: April–Sept 10am–5pm; Oct–March 10am–4pm; guided tours only, best to book in advance • £9; HES • ☎ 01856 851266, ⓦ historicenvironment.scot

Several large burial mounds are visible to the south of the Ring of Brodgar, but these are eclipsed by one of Europe's most impressive Neolithic burial chambers, **Maeshowe**, less than a mile northeast of the Stones of Stenness. Dating from 3000 BC, its excellent state of preservation is partly due to its construction from massive slabs of sandstone weighing up to thirty tons. The tours (lasting in total around 55 minutes) start on the hour at Stenness visitor centre, where a shuttle bus takes visitors to the tomb and back.

You enter the **central chamber** of Maeshowe down a low, long passage, one wall of which consists of a single immense stone. The entrance is narrow and not suitable for those who suffer from claustrophobia. Once inside, you can stand upright and admire the superb masonry of the lofty corbelled roof. Remarkably, the tomb is aligned so that the rays of the winter solstice sun hit the top of the Barnhouse Stone, half a mile away, and reach right down the passage of Maeshowe to the ledge of one of the three cells built into the walls of the tomb. When Maeshowe was opened in 1861, it was virtually empty, thanks to the work of generations of grave-robbers, who had left behind only a handful of human bones. The Vikings entered in the twelfth century, probably on their way to the Crusades, leaving copious runic graffiti, including cryptographic twig runes, cut into the walls of the main chamber. They include phrases such as "Many a beautiful woman has stooped in here, however pompous she might be", and the more prosaic "Thor and I bedded Helga".

7

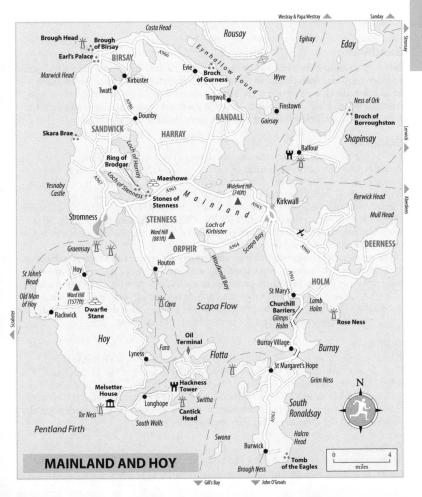

MAINLAND AND HOY

By bus Buses from Stromness to Kirkwall (Mon–Sat hourly, Sun every 2hr; 15min) to Stenness Visitor Centre with shuttle

bus to Maeshowe. The hop-on, hop-off open-top bus runs daily April–Oct (Stromness to Kirkwall) and visits all the sites.

ACCOMMODATION AND EATING

Hammersmith Bed and Breakfast Harray ☎ 01856 771838, ⓦ hammersmithbb.co.uk. Located closed to the World Heritage Neolithic sites this B&B offers a high standard of accommodation and a warm and friendly welcome. Good hearty breakfasts. **£85**

Merkister Hotel Harray Loch ☎ 01856 771366, ⓦ merkister.com. Substantial hotel on the northeastern shore of the Loch of Harray, popular with the locals and visiting anglers. The bar's lively and does reliable, locally sourced dishes such as fish and chips (around £13) or steak (around £20), but there's a restaurant too, offering a wider range of local seafood (mains £15–24). Food served daily noon–2pm & 6–9pm.

Mill of Eyrland 4 miles southwest of Maeshowe on the A964 to Orphir ☎ 01856 850136, ⓦ millofeyrland.co.uk. Carefully converted former mill by a little stream; it's filled to the brim with wonderful antiques and old machinery, as well as all mod cons; and enormous breakfasts at the communal dining table. Free wi-fi is patchy in the rooms. **£80**

Standing Stones Hotel ☎ 01856 850449, ⓦ standing stoneshotel.co.uk. This welcoming hotel and hostelry with great views over Stenness Loch has seventeen en-suite rooms. Food is served in a comfortable lounge and features dishes highlighting Orkney produce such as steak and Orkney ale pie (£13.95). Food served daily noon–9.30pm. **£120**

Sandwick

North of Stromness, the parish of **Sandwick** contains the best known of Orkney's prehistoric monuments, **Skara Brae**, beautifully situated beside the white curve of the Bay of Skaill. In addition, the cliffs either side of the bay provide some of the most spectacularly rugged **coastal walks** on Orkney's Mainland. The other good reason for exploring Sandwick is to visit the wonderful **Orkney Brewery** in the old schoolhouse in Quoyloo.

Skara Brae

Daily: April–Sept 9.30am–5.30pm; Oct–March 10am–4pm • £9; HES • ☎ 01856 841815, ⓦ historicenvironment.scot

At **Skara Brae**, the extensive remains of a small Neolithic fishing and farming village, dating back to 3000 BC, were discovered in 1850 after a fierce storm ripped off the dunes covering them. The village is amazingly well preserved, its houses huddled together and connected by narrow passages, which would originally have been covered over with turf. The houses themselves consist of a single, spacious living room, filled with domestic detail, including dressers, fireplaces, built-in cupboards, beds and boxes, all ingeniously constructed from slabs of stone.

The **visitor centre** houses an excellent **café/restaurant** and an introductory **exhibition**, with a few replica finds, and some hands-on stuff for kids. You then proceed to a full-scale replica of House 7 (the best-preserved house), complete with a fake wood-and-skin roof. It's all a tad neat and tidy, with fetching uplighting – rather than dark, smoky and smelly – but it gives you the general idea, and makes up for the fact that, at the site itself, you can only look down on the houses from the outer walls.

Skaill House

In the summer months, your ticket also covers entry to nearby **Skaill House** (April–Oct), an extensive range of buildings 300 yards inland, home of the laird of Skaill. The original house was a simple two-storey block, built for Bishop George Graham in the 1620s, but it has since been much extended. The house's prize possession is Captain Cook's dinner service from the *Resolution*; it was delivered after Cook's death when the *Resolution* and the *Discovery* sailed into Stromness in 1780.

Yesnaby

At **Yesnaby**, to the south of the Bay of Skaill, the sandstone cliffs have been savagely eroded into stacks and geos by the force of the Atlantic. Come here during a westerly

KITCHENER MEMORIAL

Marwick Head, an RSPB reserve renowned as a seabird nesting spot, is clearly visible to the south of Birsay Bay thanks to the huge castellated tower of **Kitchener Memorial**. Raised by the people of Orkney, it commemorates the Minister of War, Lord Kitchener (of "Your Country Needs You!" poster fame), who drowned along with all but 12 of the 655 men aboard the cruiser HMS *Hampshire* when the ship struck a mine just off the coast on June 5, 1916. There has been much speculation about the incident over the years, because Kitchener was on a secret mission to Russia to hold talks with the Tsar. A German spy claimed to have sabotaged and sunk the ship, and rumours abounded that Kitchener had been deliberately sent to his death (he was extremely unpopular at the time). In reality, it appears to have been a simple case of naval incompetence: the weather forecast of severe northwesterly gales was ignored, as were the reports of submarine activity in the area.

gale and you'll see the waves sending sea spray shooting over the wartime buildings and the neighbouring fields. The clifftops support a unique plant life, which thrives on the salt spray, including the rare, and very small, purple Scottish primrose, which flowers in May and from July to late September. The walk south along the coast from here is exhilarating: the Old Man of Hoy is visible in the distance and, after a mile and a half, you come to an impressive sea stack known as Yesnaby Castle.

ARRIVAL AND DEPARTURE
SKARA BRAE

By bus Services are limited (Mon, Thurs & Sat only, also hop-on hop-off bus 1 daily April–Oct). Alternatively, since it's only 7 miles from Stromness, you could just rent a bike.

EATING AND DRINKING

★ **Orkney Brewery** Quoyloo ☎ 01856 841777, ⊕ orkneybrewery.co.uk. The old schoolhouse in Quoyloo has been tastefully converted into a state-of-the-art microbrewery, with tasting tours (£5) and also a great café where local produce is very much to the fore – try the home-made bere bannock burgers – and all dishes are under £12 (platters £9–15). April–Oct daily 10am–4.30pm.

Birsay and around

Occupying the northwest corner of the Mainland, the parish of **BIRSAY** was the centre of Norse power in Orkney for several centuries before Kirkwall got its cathedral.

Earl's Palace

A tiny cluster of homes is gathered around the imposing sandstone ruins of the **Earl's Palace**, built in the late sixteenth century by Robert Stewart, Earl of Orkney, using the forced labour of the islanders, who weren't even given food and drink for their work. By all accounts, it was a "sumptuous and stately dwelling", built in four wings around a central courtyard, its upper rooms decorated with painted ceilings and rich furnishings; surrounding the palace were flower and herb gardens, a bowling green and archery butts. The palace appears to have lasted barely a century before falling into ruin; the crumbling walls and turrets retain much of their grandeur, although inside there is little remaining domestic detail. However, its vast scale makes the Earl's Palace in Kirkwall seem almost humble in comparison.

Brough of Birsay

Accessible 2hr either side of low tide • Tide times available at Kirkwall tourist offices and on Radio Orkney (93.7FM; Mon–Fri 7.30–8am) or ☎ 01856 841815.

Just over half a mile northwest of Birsay village is the **Brough of Birsay**, a substantial Pictish settlement on a small tidal island. On the island, by St Peter's Church, is a small ticket office (see below), where you have to pay an entrance fee in season.

St Peter's Church

Mid-June–Sept daily 9.30am–5.30pm • £6; HES • ☎ 01856 761606, ⓦ historicenvironment.scot

The focus of the village of Brough of Birsay was – and still is – the sandstone-built twelfth-century **St Peter's Church**, which stands slightly higher than the surrounding buildings; the stone seating along the walls is still in place, and there are a couple of semicircular recesses for altars, and a semicircular apse. The church is thought to have stood at the centre of a monastic settlement. Close by are remains of a large complex of Viking-era buildings, including several houses, a sauna and some sophisticated stone drains. At the ticket office, you can inspect a few artefacts gathered from the site, including a game made from whalebone, and an antler pin.

The northern coastline

The Brough of Birsay is a popular day-trip, partly due to the fun of dodging the tides, but few bother to explore the rest of the island, whose gentle green slopes, as viewed from the mainland, belie the dramatic, rugged cliffs that characterize the rest of the coastline. In winter, sea spray from the crashing waves can envelop the entire island. In summer, the cliffs are home to various seabirds, including a few puffins, making the half-mile walk to the island's castellated **lighthouse** and back along the northern coastline well worth the effort. While there, spare a thought for the lighthouse keepers on the **Sule Skerry** lighthouse from 1895 to 1982 – the most isolated in Britain – which lies on a piece of bare rock just visible some 37 miles west across the sea, and whose only contact with the outside world was via carrier pigeon.

Barony Mills

May–Sept daily 11am–5pm • Free • ☎ 01856 721439, ⓦ birsay.org.uk/baronymill.htm

Half a mile southeast of Birsay, up the burn, is the **Barony Mills**, Orkney's only working nineteenth-century watermill. The mill specializes in producing traditional stoneground beremeal, essential for making bere bannocks. Bere is a four-kernel barley crop with a very short growing season, perfectly suited for the local climate and once the staple diet in these parts. The miller on duty will give you a guided tour and show you the machinery going through its paces, though milling only takes place in the autumn.

Kirbuster Museum

Birsay • March–Oct Mon–Sat 10.30am–1pm & 2–5pm, Sun 2–5pm • Free • ☎ 01856 771268

Lying between the Loch of Boardhouse and the Loch of Hundland, the **Kirbuster Museum** offers an insight into life on an Orkney farmstead in the mid-nineteenth century. Built in 1723, the farm is made up of a typical, though substantial, collection of flagstone buildings, with its own, very beautiful, garden. Ducks, geese and sheep wander around the grassy open yard, entered through a whalebone archway. The farm has retained its firehoose, in which the smoke from the central peat fire was used to dry fish fillets, before drifting up towards a hole in the ceiling.

ARRIVAL AND DEPARTURE   BIRSAY AND AROUND

By bus Bus services from Kirkwall (Mon–Sat 2 daily; 30–   40min) will get you to Birsay.

ACCOMMODATION AND EATING

Barony Hotel 1 mile east of Birsay ☎ 01856 721327, ⓦ baronyhotel.com. Stark hotel overlooking the Loch of Boardhouse. The hotel bar is the only watering hole around – decor in the rooms is a bit dated, but it's clean and comfy enough and the trout from the loch is worth sampling. **£90**

Birsay Bay Tearoom 500yd south of the Earl's Palace

☎ 01856   721399, ⓦ birsaybaytearoom.co.uk. For light snacks and home-made cake, head for the modern tearoom, at the southern edge of the village, which boasts superb views of the Brough (binoculars provided). April–Sept Thurs–Mon 10.30am–5pm; shorter hours in winter.

Birsay Outdoor Centre 1 mile southeast of Birsay at junction of A967 and B9056 ☎ 01856 873535 ext 2415, ⓦ www.orkney.gov.uk. A large council-run hostel with

a fully equipped kitchen and a drying room; there's also a campsite alongside. April–Sept. Dorms £18; per pitch for large tent/caravan with electricity. £20

Broch of Gurness

Evie • April–Sept daily 9.30am–12.30pm & 1.30–5.30pm • £6; HES • ☎ 01856 751414, ⓦ historicenvironment.scot

Near the village of Evie, on the north coast, is the **Broch of Gurness** (also known as Aikerness Broch), the best-preserved broch on Orkney, still surrounded by a remarkable complex of later buildings. As at Birsay, the sea has eaten away half the site, but the broch itself, dating from around 100 BC, still stands, its walls reaching a height of 12ft in places, its inner cells still intact. Clustered around the broch, the compact group of homes has also survived amazingly well, with much of their original and ingenious stone shelving and fireplaces still in place. The best view of the site is from the east, where you can clearly make out the "main street" leading towards the broch. Also worth a look is the **visitor centre** where you can try your hand at the quernstone corn grinder. The broch is clearly signposted from Evie, the road skirting the pristinely white **Sands of Evie**, a perfect picnic spot in fine weather, with great views across the turbulent waters of Eynhallow Sound towards the island of Rousay.

7

ARRIVAL AND DEPARTURE
BROCH OF GURNESS

By bus Bus services from Kirkwall get you to Evie (Mon–Sat   5 daily; 30min), from which it's a 30min walk to the broch.

ACCOMMODATION

Castlehill Evie ☎ 01856 751228, ⓦ castlehillorkney. co.uk. This modern crofthouse under Burgar Hill looks nothing special from the outside but it's well decked out inside, with pleasant wooden furnishings and quality bedding. Great views and top-notch home cooking. £100
Howe Bothy Evie ☎ 01856 751449. Comprises a tiny

four-bunk bothy (groups only) in an old cart shed and a little en-suite double with a kitchen in the old cow byre – both beautifully converted by local artist, John Vincent. Use of a boat if you fancy some trout fishing. Minimum of 2 nights for both. Bothy £55, double £45

Orphir

The southern shores of the West Mainland, overlooking Scapa Flow, are much gentler than the rest of the coastline, and have fewer of Orkney's premier-league sights. However, if you've time to spare, or you're heading for Hoy from the car ferry terminal at Houton, there are a couple of points of interest in the neighbouring parish of **ORPHIR**.

Orkneyinga Saga Centre

Gyre Rd • daily 9am–6pm • Free

Beside the parish cemetery in Orphir, you'll find the **Orkneyinga Saga Centre**, containing a small exhibition with a fifteen-minute audiovisual show which gives you a taste of the *Orkneyinga Saga*, the bloodthirsty Viking tale written around 1200 AD by an unnamed Icelandic author, which described the conquest of the Northern Isles by the Norsemen. The **Earl's Bu** (or farm) at Orphir features in the saga as the home of Earl Thorfinn the Mighty, Earl Paul and his son, Håkon, who ordered the murder of Earl (later St) Magnus on Egilsay (see page 353). The foundations of what was probably the Earl's Bu have been uncovered just outside the cemetery gates, while inside the cemetery is a section of the round church, built by Håkon after his pilgrimage in penance to Jerusalem.

Kirkwall

Initial impressions of **KIRKWALL**, Orkney's capital, are not always favourable. It has nothing to match the picturesque harbour of Stromness, and its residential sprawl is far less appealing. However, it does have one great redeeming feature – its sandstone **cathedral**, without doubt the finest medieval building in the north of Scotland. In any case, if you're staying any length of time on Orkney you're bound to find yourself in Kirkwall at some point, as it's home to the islands' better-stocked shops, including the only large supermarket, and is the departure point for most of the ferries to Orkney's northern isles.

Nowadays, the town is very much divided into two main focal points: the old harbour, at the north end of the town, where visiting yachts moor and the small inter-island ferries come and go all year round; and the flagstone **main street**. Despite the latter taking four different names as it winds through the town, orientation is easy with the prominent spire of St Magnus Cathedral clearly marking the town centre.

St Magnus Cathedral

Broad St • April–Sept Mon–Sat 9am–6pm, Sun 1–6pm; Oct–March Mon–Sat 9am–1pm & 2–5pm • Free • Guided upper-level tours Thurs & Sat 11am & 2pm • £8.60 • ☎ 01856 874894, ⦾ stmagnus.org

Standing at the very heart of Kirkwall, **St Magnus Cathedral** is the town's most compelling sight. This beautiful red-sandstone building was begun in 1137 by the Orkney Earl Rögnvald (aka St Ronald), spurred on by the growing cult surrounding the figure of his uncle Magnus, killed by his cousin Håkon in 1117. When Magnus's body was buried in Birsay, a heavenly light was said to have shone overhead, and his grave soon drew pilgrims from far afield. When Rögnvald took over the earldom, he built the cathedral in his uncle's honour, moving the centre of religious and secular power from Birsay to Kirkwall, before he himself was murdered.

Built using yellow sandstone from Eday and red sandstone from the Mainland, the cathedral has been added to and extended over the centuries. Today much of the detail in the soft sandstone has worn away – the capitals around the main doors are reduced to artistically gnarled stumps – but it's still an immensely impressive building, its shape and style echoing the great cathedrals of Europe. Inside, the atmosphere is surprisingly intimate, the bulky sandstone columns drawing your eye up to the exposed brickwork arches, while around the walls is a series of mostly seventeenth-century tombstones, many carved with a skull and crossbones and other emblems of mortality, alongside chilling inscriptions calling on the reader to "remember death waits us all, the hour none knows".

In the square pillars on either side of the high altar, the bones of Magnus and Rögnvald are buried. In the southeastern corner of the cathedral lies the tomb of the Stromness-born Arctic explorer John Rae, who tried to find Sir John Franklin's expedition; he is depicted asleep, dressed in moleskins and furs, his rifle and Bible by his side. Beside Rae's tomb is Orkney's own Poets' Corner, with memorials to, among others, George Mackay Brown, Eric Linklater, Edwin Muir and Robert Rendall (who was also an eminent conchologist). Another poignant monument is the one to the dead of HMS *Royal Oak*, which was torpedoed in Scapa Flow in 1939 with the loss of 833 men.

Bishop's and Earl's Palaces

Palace Rd • April–Oct daily 9.30am–5.30pm • £6; HES • ☎ 01856 871918, ⦾ historicenvironment.scot

South of the cathedral are the ruined remains of the **Bishop's Palace**, traditional residence of the Bishop of Orkney from the twelfth century. Here, the Norwegian king Håkon died in 1263 on his return from the Battle of Largs. Most of what you see now, however, dates from the time of Bishop Robert Reid, founder of Edinburgh University, in the mid-sixteenth century. The walls still stand, as does the tall round tower housing the bishop's private chambers. The ticket for the Bishop's Palace also covers entry to the neighbouring **Earl's Palace** – better preserved and more fun to explore – built by the infamous Earl Patrick Stewart around 1600 using forced labour. With its grand entrance, fancy oriel windows, dank dungeons, massive fireplaces and magnificent central hall, it has a confident solidity, and is a fine example of Scottish Renaissance architecture. The roof is missing but many domestic details remain, including a set of toilets and the stone shelves used by the clerk to do his filing. Earl Patrick enjoyed his palace for only a very short time before he was imprisoned and charged with treason. The earl might have been acquitted, but he foolishly ordered his son, Robert, to organize an insurrection; he held out for four days in the palace against the Earl of Caithness, before being captured and sent to Edinburgh to be hanged; his father was beheaded there five weeks later.

Orkney Museum

Broad St • Mon–Sat 10.30am–5pm (closed for lunch Oct–April) • Free • ☎ 01856 873535

Opposite the cathedral stands the sixteenth-century **Tankerness House**, a former home for the clergy, and now home to the **Orkney Museum**. A couple of rooms have been

KIRKWALL

0   100
yards

EATING
Dil Se	2
Helgi's	1
Lucano	6
Real Food Café	5
The Reel	4
Trenabies Bistro	3

ACCOMMODATION
2 Dundas Crescent	5
Albert Hotel	3
Avalon House	1
Kirkwall Youth Hostel	7
Lynnfield Hotel	8
Peedie Hostel	2
Pickaquoy Campsite	4
West End Hotel	6

SCAPA FLOW

Apart from a few oil tankers, there's very little activity in the great natural harbour of **Scapa Flow**, yet for the first half of the twentieth century, it served as the main base of the Royal Navy, with over a hundred warships anchored here at any one time. The coastal defences required to safeguard Scapa Flow as the country's chief naval headquarters were considerable, and many are still visible all over Orkney, ranging from half-sunk blockships to the **Churchill Barriers** (see page 345) and the gun batteries that pepper the coastline. Unfortunately, these defences weren't sufficient to save **HMS *Royal Oak*** from being torpedoed by a German U-boat in October 1939, but they withstood several heavy German air raids during the course of 1940. Ironically, the worst disaster the Flow ever witnessed was self-inflicted, when **HMS *Vanguard*** sank on July 9, 1917, after suffering an internal explosion, killing 843 crew and leaving only two survivors.

Scapa Flow's most celebrated moment in naval history, however, was when the entire **German High Seas Fleet** was interned here immediately after World War I. A total of 74 ships, manned by several thousand German sailors, was anchored off the isle of Cava awaiting the outcome of the Versailles Peace Conference. At around noon on Midsummer's Day 1919, believing either that the majority of the German fleet was to be handed over, or that hostilities were about to resume, the commanding officer, Admiral von Reuter, ordered the fleet to be scuttled. By 5pm, every ship was beached or had sunk and nine German sailors had lost their lives, shot by outraged British servicemen. The British government was publicly indignant, but privately relieved since the scuttling avoided the diplomatic nightmare of dividing the fleet among the Allies.

Between the wars, the largest **salvage operation** in history took place in Scapa Flow, with the firm of Cox & Danks alone raising 26 destroyers, one light cruiser, four battlecruisers and two battleships. Despite this, seven ships – three battleships and four light cruisers – remain on the seabed of Scapa Flow, along with four destroyers and a U-boat. For more on Scapa Flow's wartime role, visit the museum on Hoy. Scapa Flow is one of the world's greatest **wreck dive sites**, and Scapa Scuba (☎01856 851218, ⓦscapascuba.co.uk), based in Stromness, offer one-to-one scuba-diving tuition from £80 for half a day. The land-based Wartime Orkney Explorer private tour (☎01856 878822, ⓦorkneyuncovered.co.uk) gives expert insight into the history of Scapa Flow and beyond, showing what life was like for civilians and military personnel guarding Orkney's shores during two world wars (7hr; £380 for two).

restored as they would have been in 1820, when it was the Baikie family's private home. The rest houses some of the islands' most treasured finds, among the more unusual of which are a witch's spell box and a lovely whalebone plaque from a Viking boat grave discovered on Sanday. On a warm summer afternoon, the museum **gardens** are thick with the buzz of bees and vibrantly coloured flora.

Orkney Wireless Museum

Kiln Corner, Junction Rd • April–Sept Mon–Sat 10am–4.30pm, Sun 2.30–4.30pm • £3 • ☎01856 871400, ⓦ orkneywirelessmuseum.org.uk

At the harbour end of Junction Road, you can browse around the tiny **Orkney Wireless Museum**, a single room packed to the roof with every variety of antique radio equipment imaginable. The museum is particularly strong on technical flotsam from the two world wars, and there's even a working crystal set that you can listen to.

Highland Park distillery

Holm Rd, 1 mile south of Kirkwall along the A961 • April & Sept Mon–Fri 10am–5pm hourly tours; May–Aug Mon–Sat 10am–5pm, Sun noon–5pm hourly tours; Oct–March Mon–Fri tours at 2 & 3pm • £7.50 • ☎01856 874619, ⓦ highlandpark.co.uk

The **Highland Park distillery** has been in operation for more than two hundred years, and still has its own maltings, although it was closed during World War II, when the army used it as a food store and the huge vats served as communal baths. The standard tour takes around an hour (and includes a tasting), but there are lengthier, pricier tours available – see the website for details.

Scapa Bay

If the weather is unusually good and you're moved to consider a swim, follow the locals and head a mile south of town on the B9148 to **Scapa Bay**, Kirkwall's very own sandy beach. Briefly a naval headquarters at the outbreak of World War I, Scapa's pier is now used by the council tugs and pilot launches servicing the oil tankers out in Scapa Flow. Visible from the beach is the green Admiralty wreck buoy marking the position of **HMS Royal Oak**, torpedoed by a German U-boat on October 14, 1939, with the loss of 833 men (out of a total crew of around 1400). A small display shed at the eastern end of the bay tells the full story, and has photos of the wreck (still an official war grave) as it looks today.

ARRIVAL AND INFORMATION   KIRKWALL

By plane Kirkwall Airport (☎01856 886210, ⓦhial.co.uk) is 3 miles southeast of town on the A960; take the hourly bus (15min), or a taxi (£10).

Destinations within Orkney Eday (Mon & Wed 1–2 daily; 10–30min); North Ronaldsay (Mon–Sat 3 daily, 2 on Sun; 20–30min); Papa Westray (Mon–Fri 3 daily, Sat & Sun 2 daily; 15–35min); Sanday (Mon–Fri 2 daily, Sat & Sun 1 daily; 15min); Stronsay (Mon–Fri 2 daily, Sat & Sun 1 daily; 10–25min); Westray (Mon–Fri 2 daily, Sat & Sun 1 daily; 15–25min).

By ferry NorthLink Ferries (☎0845 600 0449, ⓦnorthlinkferries.co.uk) run services from Shetland (3 weekly; 5hr 30min) and Aberdeen (3–4 weekly; 6hr), and all cruise ships dock at the Hatston terminal, a mile northwest of town; a shuttle bus takes you into Kirkwall (or Stromness if you prefer). Ferries for Orkney's northern isles leave from the town pier in Kirkwall.

Destinations within Orkney (ⓦorkneyferries.co.uk). Eday (2–3 daily; 1hr 15min–2hr 25min); North Ronaldsay (Tues & Fri; 2hr 40min); Papa Westray (Tues & Fri; 2hr 15min);

Sanday (2 daily; 1hr 25min); Shapinsay (3–5 daily; 45min); Stronsay (1–3 daily; 1hr 40min–2hr); Westray (2–3 daily; 1hr 25min). Reduced service in winter.

By bus ☎01856 870555, ⓦstagecoachbus.com. The bus station is behind the Kirkwall Travel Centre, West Castle St.

Destinations Birsay (Mon–Sat 2 daily; 30–40min); Burwick (2–3 daily; 40min); Deerness (Mon–Sat 3–4 daily; 30min); Evie (Mon–Sat 4–5 daily; 30min); Houton (5–6 daily; 25min); Kirkwall Airport (Mon–Sat every 30min, 10 on Sun; 15min); Skara Brae (Mon, Thurs & Sat only; 50min, also hop-on hop-off bus 1 daily April–Oct); St Margaret's Hope (Mon–Sat hourly; 35min); Stromness (Mon–Sat 2 hourly, Sun every 2hr; 30min); Tingwall (Mon–Sat 3–5 daily; 25min).

Tourist office Kirkwall Travel Centre, West Castle St, houses the tourist office (daily 9am–5pm; ☎01856 872856, ⓦvisitorkney.com).

Bike rental Cycle Orkney, Tankerness Lane (☎01856 875777, ⓦcycleorkney.com), rents bikes from £25/day – children's bikes (£10) and some electrics (£35) available.

ACCOMMODATION   SEE MAP PAGE 341

HOTELS AND B&BS

2 Dundas Crescent 2 Dundas Crescent ☎01856 874805, ⓦtwodundas.co.uk. Run by an Orcadian couple and situated just behind the cathedral, this Victorian former manse is grand and tastefully decorated, with four spacious rooms and period fittings. **£80**

Albert Hotel Mounthoolie Lane ☎01856 876000, ⓦalberthotel.co.uk. Great central location, lively *Bothy Bar* (with disco attached) and contemporary furnishings: this is Kirkwall's hippest hotel (all things being relative). **£148**

Avalon House Carness Rd ☎01856 876665, ⓦavalon-house.co.uk. Don't judge a B&B by its drab, modern exterior; this is a comfortable, purpose-built guesthouse run efficiently by a very welcoming couple, and situated a pleasant 20min coastal walk from the town centre. **£90**

Lynnfield Hotel Holm Rd ☎01856 872505, ⓦlynnfield.co.uk. Small ten-room hotel in a quiet spot a mile or so out of town near the distillery – the dark wood furnishings make the place seem really quite grand in style, and the food is excellent – try the North Ronaldsay mutton, which comes from the island's famous seaweed-eating flock (mains £16–25). **£125**

West End Hotel 14 Main St ☎01856 881201, ⓦwestendkirkwall.co.uk. Orkney's first hospital is now a good, old-fashioned hotel located in a quiet street, just a few minutes' walk south of the centre. **£125**

HOSTELS AND CAMPSITES

Kirkwall Youth Hostel Old Scapa Rd ☎01856 872243, ⓦhostellingscotland.org.uk. A good 10min walk out of

7

the centre on the road to Orphir – the welcome at this former World War II military base is friendly enough, but it's no beauty outside or in. April–Sept. Dorms **£18.50**, twins **£48**

Peedie Hostel 1 Ayre Houses ☎01856 881201, ⓦkirkwall peediehostel.com. Centrally located overlooking the old harbour and out to sea, this is a clean and comfortable hostel

with just eight beds. Washing machine and tumble dryer available. Dorms **£18**, twin **£35**

Pickaquoy Campsite Ayre Rd ☎01856 879900, ⓦpick aquoy.campmanager.com. Central and well equipped, since it is behind (and run by) the local leisure centre, but not exactly picturesque. March–Dec. Per pitch **£23.85**

EATING AND DRINKING
SEE MAP PAGE 341

Dil Se 7 Bridge St ☎01856 875242. Kirkwall's Indian restaurant has won numerous awards since it opened – tandooris and baltis are superb, with lots of veggie options (sides £4–8, mains £11–18). Daily 4–11pm.

Helgi's 14 Harbour St ☎01856 879293, ⓦhelgis.co.uk. Popular modern pub on the harbourfront serving nicely presented bar food, from burgers/fish and chips to fajitas (all for around £11). Free wi-fi. Mon–Wed 11am–midnight, Thurs–Sat 11am–1am, Sun 12.30pm–midnight; food served daily noon–9pm.

Lucano 31 Victoria St ☎01856 875687. Busy, bright, modern, authentic Italian – the family hail from Basilicata – offering 10-inch pizzas, fresh pasta and risotto with an Orcadian angle for all around £10. It's popular so book ahead. Breakfast available, too. Daily 7.30am–9pm.

Real Food Café 25 Broad St ☎01856 874225, ⓦwww. judithglue.com. Cheery cream and sky-blue wood-

panelling decor at this small café at the back of Judith Glue's gift shop, opposite the cathedral. Try the Westray crab as a starter (£6.50) or main course salad (£16) and bere bannocks (£5.50). June–Sept daily 9am–10pm; shorter hours in the low season. Judith also owns the excellent Storehouse Restaurant with Rooms in Bridge Street.

★ **The Reel** 6 Broad St ☎01856 871000, ⓦwrigley andthereel.com. The old customs house near the cathedral is now a fabulous, laidback self-service café, run by the musical Wrigley Sisters, serving great coffee, sandwiches, toasties, panini and cakes, and offering free wi-fi and regular live music (Wed, Thurs & Sat; bar open). Mon–Sat 9am–6pm; in summer also Sun 10am–5pm.

Trenabies Bistro Albert St ☎01856 874336. This cosy, old-fashioned café with booths is a classic Kirkwall institution – order Cajun fries and a panino for around £5. Mon–Fri 8.30am–5.30pm, Sat 9am–5.30pm.

ENTERTAINMENT

New Phoenix Cinema Pickaquoy Centre ☎01856 879900, ⓦpickaquoy.net. The "Picky" is a modern leisure centre, but its 1600-seat hall also serves as the town's main

large-scale venue for a whole variety of events – it also houses the 250-seat New Phoenix cinema.

East Mainland and South Ronaldsay

Southeast from Kirkwall, the **East Mainland** juts out into the North Sea, its northern coastline consisting of three exposed peninsulas that jut out like giant claws. The East Mainland is joined, thanks to the remarkable Churchill Barriers, to several smaller islands, the largest of which are **Burray** and **South Ronaldsay**. The heavily farmed land contains few of Orkney's more famous sights but there are some good coastal walks and several unusual prehistoric sites, in particular the **Tomb of the Eagles** near Burwick.

Deerness

The easternmost peninsula of **Deerness** is joined to the Mainland only by a narrow, sandy isthmus. From the car park at its northeastern corner, a short walk eastwards will bring you to **The Gloup**, an impressive collapsed sea-cave, whose name stems from the Old Norse *gluppa*, or "chasm"; the tide still flows in and out through a natural arch, making strange gurgling noises. From here, you can walk along the tops of the collapsing sandstone coastline half a mile north to the **Brough of Deerness**, a grassy promontory now accessible only via a precipitous path; the ruins are thought to have once been a Norse or Pictish monastic site. Another half-mile will bring you to the sea cliffs of **Mull Head**, home to nesting seabirds from May to August, including fulmars, kittiwakes, guillemots, razorbills and puffins, plus, inland, arctic terns that swoop and screech threateningly.

THE CHURCHILL BARRIERS

The southeastern corner of Orkney Mainland is connected to the islands of Burray and South Ronaldsay by four causeways known as the **Churchill Barriers**, built during World War II as anti-submarine barriers. It was an astonishing feat of engineering considering the strength of Orkney tides, and also an extremely expensive undertaking, costing an estimated £2.5 million (more than £150 million in today's money). The Admiralty (under Churchill) were only prompted into action by the sinking of the battleship HMS *Royal Oak* on October 14, 1939. Despite the presence of blockships, deliberately sunk during World War I in order to close off the eastern approaches, one German U-boat captain managed to get through and torpedo the *Royal Oak*, before returning to a hero's welcome in Germany. As you cross the barriers – don't cross them during high winds – you can still see the rusting blockships, even at low tide, an eerie reminder of Orkney's important wartime role.

Lamb Holm: the Italian Chapel

June–Aug daily 9am–6.30pm; May & Sept 9am–5pm, April & Oct 10am–4pm; Nov–March 10am–1pm • £3

Special camps were built on the uninhabited island of Lamb Holm, to accommodate the 1700 men involved in building the Churchill Barriers, 1200 of whom were Italian POWs. The camps have long since disappeared, but the Italians left behind the extraordinary **Italian Chapel** on **Lamb Holm**, by the main road (A961). This, the so-called "Miracle of Camp 60", must be one of the greatest adaptations ever, made from two Nissen huts, concrete, barbed wire and parts of a rusting blockship. It has a great false facade, and colourful trompe-l'oeil decor, lovingly restored by the chapel's original architect, Domenico Chiocchetti, in 1960.

Burray

Largest of the little islands between the Mainland and South Ronaldsay, **Burray** has a population of around 400. The main village expanded enormously in the nineteenth century during the boom years of the herring industry, but was badly affected by the sinking of the blockships during World War I. The two-storey warehouse, built in 1860 in order to cure and pack the herring, has since been converted into the *Sands Hotel*.

Orkney Fossil and Heritage Centre

Easter–Sept daily 10am–5pm • £4.75 • 01856 731255, orkneyfossilcentre.co.uk

The **Orkney Fossil and Heritage Centre** is in a converted farm on the main road that crosses the island. Most of the fossils downstairs have been found locally, and largely feature fish and sea creatures, since Orkney was at the bottom of a tropical sea in Devonian times (400 million years ago). The UV "glow room", where the rocks reveal their iridescent colours, is a hit with kids, though be sure to show them the coprolite (fossilized poo) among the main displays, too. Upstairs, there's much wartime memorabilia and a whole section on the Churchill Barriers – kids can build their own – while the ground floor has a community-run café.

ARRIVAL AND DEPARTURE BURRAY

By bus Buses from Kirkwall to St Margaret's Hope call in at Burray village shop (Mon–Sat hourly; 30min).

ACCOMMODATION AND EATING

Sands Hotel 14 Main St 01856 731298, thesands hotel.co.uk. An imposing former fish warehouse overlooking Burray harbour – now a hotel with simple pine furnishings and a few original features. The bar menu dishes (all under £12) include herring in oatmeal, and mince and tatties; the restaurant serves up local scallops and black pudding (mains £15.50–22.50). Food served Mon–Sat noon–2pm & 6–9pm, Sun noon–2pm & 5.30–8.30pm. **£135**

South Ronaldsay

At the southern end of the barriers is low-lying **South Ronaldsay**, the largest of the islands linked to the Mainland and, like the latter, rich farming country. It was traditionally the chief crossing point to the Scottish mainland, as it's only six miles across the Pentland Firth from Caithness. Today, car **ferries** arrive at St Margaret's Hope, and a small passenger ferry links John O'Groats with Burwick, on the southernmost tip of the island (see page 347 for details).

St Margaret's Hope

The main settlement on South Ronaldsay is **ST MARGARET'S HOPE**, which local tradition says takes its name from Margaret, the Maid of Norway, daughter of the king of Norway, who is thought to have died here aged 8 in November 1290. As granddaughter of Alexander III, Margaret had already been proclaimed queen of Scotland and was on her way to marry the English prince Edward (later Edward II), thereby unifying the two countries. Today, St Margaret's Hope – or "The Hope", as it's known locally (from the Norse *hyop* meaning "bay") – is a peaceful little gathering of pleasant stone-built houses overlooking a sheltered bay, and is by far the largest settlement.

Smiddy Museum

Cromarty Square • May–Aug daily 2–4.30pm • Free • ☎ 01856 831331

The village smithy is now a **Smiddy Museum**, particularly fun for kids who enjoy getting hands-on with the old tools, drills and giant bellows. There's also a small exhibition on the annual **Boys' Ploughing Match**, in which local boys compete with miniature hand-held ploughs on the third Saturday in August, at the beautiful golden beach at the **Sands O'Right** in Hoxa, a couple of miles west of The Hope. Simultaneously a **Festival of the Horse** takes place, with the local children, mostly girls, dressed in spectacular costumes and harnesses.

Tomb of the Eagles

Daily: March 10am–noon; April–Sept 9.30am–5.30pm; Oct 9.30am–12.30pm • £7.80 • ☎ 01856 831339, ⓦ tomboftheeagles.co.uk

One of Orkney's most enjoyable archeological sights is the Isbister Chambered Cairn at the southeastern corner of South Ronaldsay, also known as the **Tomb of the Eagles**. The cairn was discovered in 1958 and excavated by a local farmer, Ronald Simpson of Liddle, whose family still own it, so a visit here makes a refreshing change from Historic Environment Scotland sites. First, you get to look round the family's private museum of prehistoric artefacts; you can actually touch and admire the painstaking craftsmanship of Neolithic folk, and pick up a skull. Next there's a brief guided tour of a nearby Bronze Age **burnt mound**, which is basically a Neolithic rubbish dump. Finally you get to walk the mile or so out to the **chambered cairn**, by the cliff's edge, where human remains were found alongside talons and carcasses of sea eagles. To enter the cairn, you must lie on a trolley and pull yourself in using an overhead rope – something guaranteed to put a smile on every visitor's face. The cairn's clifftop location is spectacular, and walking along the coast in either direction is rewarding.

Tomb of the Otters

Mid-April–Sept daily 1am–5pm • £6 • ☎ 01856 831605, ⓦ bankschamberedtomb.co.uk

A Neolithic stone's throw from the Tomb of the Eagles, another chambered cairn was discovered in 2010 near Banks farmhouse by local farmer Hamish Mowatt, having lain undisturbed for five thousand years. The Banks Chambered Cairn, or **Tomb of the Otters** as it's been dubbed, is unique on Orkney as it was cut directly into the bedrock. Layers of human bones within the tomb were found to be mixed with vast quantities of otter spraint, hence the name. You can examine some of the skulls and teeth found, and, if possible, you get to crawl into the waterlogged tomb – waterproofs and boots are a good idea. There's also the excellent *Skerries Bistro* on site (see page 347).

ARRIVAL AND DEPARTURE

By ferry Pentland Ferries (☎ 01856 831226, ⊚ pentland ferries.co.uk) operates car catamarans from Gill's Bay (3–4 daily; 1hr), near John O'Groats (linked by bus to Wick and Thurso). John O'Groats Ferries (☎ 01955 611353, ⊚ jogferry. co.uk) runs a passenger ferry from John O'Groats to Burwick on South Ronaldsay (May–Sept 2–3 daily; 40min). Its departure is timed to connect with the arrival of the Orkney Bus from Inverness; there's also a free shuttle service from

SOUTH RONALDSAY

Thurso train station for certain sailings. The ferry is small and, except in fine weather, is recommended only for those with strong stomachs.

By bus There is a regular bus service from Kirkwall to St Margaret's Hope (Mon–Sat hourly; 30min), and a summer-only one to Burwick, which connects with the John O'Groats ferry (May–Sept 2–3 daily; 40min).

ACCOMMODATION AND EATING

ST MARGARET'S HOPE

Bankburn House 0.5 miles south of the Hope on the A961 ☎ 01856 831310, ⊚ bankburnhouse.co.uk. Solid Victorian sea captain's house, just outside the Hope, with a variety of rooms, some en suite, some with shared facilities, all with high ceilings and period features. **£56**

The Creel Front Rd ☎ 01856 831284, ⊚ thecreel.co.uk. There are just three lovely sea-view rooms at this quality B&B, all beautifully furnished with light pinewood fittings. The breakfasts are superb, non-residents can usually drop in for tea and cakes, and evening meals can be arranged too. **£110**

Murray Arms Hotel Back Rd ☎ 01856 831 205, ⊚ the murrayarmshotel.com. This popular eaterie and watering hole has six en-suite rooms, some with garden views. Substantial breakfasts and meals showcasing local seafood are available in the bar (mains from £8). Food served Mon–Fri 2–9pm, Sat & Sun noon–9pm. **£100**

St Margaret's Cottage Church Rd ☎ 01856 831637. Handsome sandstone house on the edge of The Hope, run by a genuine Orcadian couple, with three rooms available – very handy for the Pentland ferry. **£70**

Wheems 2 miles southeast of the Hope ☎ 01856 831556, ⊚ wheemsorganic.co.uk. Rambling old crofthouse and organic farm with a couple of wooden bothies, a stone cottage and a yurt for hire, plus a sloping field for camping, with all the usual facilities. April to October or by prior arrangement. Per pitch **£20**, yurt **£50**, cottage **£70**

BURWICK

Sea View Cottage B9041 five minutes' drive from Burwick ☎ 01856 831329, ⊚ banksoforkney.co.uk. This charming self-catering 100-year old stone cottage for two overlooking the Pentland Firth has a fully modernised interior. Also available is Banks Barn which sleeps five people. Minimum 3 nights. Prices per week Sea View **£330**, Banks Barn **£500**

Skerries Bistro Banks ☎ 01856 831605, ⊚ skerries bistro.co.uk. Ultra-modern bistro, with its own chambered cairn nearby, overlooking the Pentland Firth, offering local fish and king scallops as big as steaks (evening mains around £18), plus delicious home-made puddings and cakes. April–Oct Sun–Fri except Tues eve noon–4pm & 6–9pm.

Hoy

Hoy, Orkney's second-largest island, rises sharply out of the sea to the southwest of the Mainland. The least typical Orkney island, but certainly the most dramatic, it has north and west sides made up of great glacial valleys and mountainous moorland rising to over 1500ft, dropping into the sea off red sandstone cliffs, and forming the landmark sea stack known as the **Old Man of Hoy**. The northern half of Hoy is virtually uninhabited, with just the tiny village of Hoy opposite Stromness, and the cluster of houses at **Rackwick** nestling dramatically in a bay between the cliffs. Meanwhile, most of Hoy's four hundred or so residents live on the gentler, more fertile land in the southeast, in and around the villages of **Lyness** and **Longhope**. This part of the island is littered with buildings dating from the two world wars, when Scapa Flow served as the main base for the Royal Navy (see page 342).

North Hoy

Much of **North Hoy**'s magnificent landscape is made up of rough grasses and heather, which harbour a cluster of arctic plants (and a lot of midges) as well as a healthy population of mountain hares and birdlife. Facilities are minimal, however, with the nearest shop in Longhope (see page 350), and both Hoy and Rackwick are absolutely tiny, with very little in the way of transport. If you're walking to Rackwick from Hoy, take the well-marked footpath past Sandy Loch and along the large open valley of **Berriedale** (1hr 30min).

Dwarfie Stane

Halfway along the road from Hoy to Rackwick, duckboards head across the heather to the **Dwarfie Stane**, Orkney's most unusual chambered tomb, cut from a solid block of sandstone and dating back to 3000 BC. The tomb is decorated with copious Victorian graffiti, the most interesting of which is on the northern exterior, where Major Mouncey, a former British spy in Persia and a confirmed eccentric who dressed in Persian garb, carved his name backwards in Latin and also carved in Persian the words "I have sat two nights and so learnt patience". Since 2015, however, most of the visitors descending on the Dwarfie Stane car park are here to see a young pair of **sea eagles** – the first to nest on Orkney for 142 years – who have chosen a nearby site to attempt to breed. In 2018 two chicks were successfully hatched for the first time in 140 years.

Rackwick

RACKWICK is an old crofting and fishing village squeezed between towering sandstone cliffs on the west coast. In an area once quite extensively cultivated, Rackwick went into a steady decline in the middle of the twentieth century: its school closed in 1953 and the last fishing boat put to sea in 1963. Electricity finally arrived in 1980 but these days only a few of the houses are inhabited all year round (the rest serve as holiday homes), though the savage isolation of the place has provided inspiration for a number of artists and writers, including Orkney's George Mackay Brown, who wrote "When Rackwick weeps, its grief is long and forlorn and utterly desolate". A small farm building beside the hostel has a tiny **museum** with a brief rundown of Rackwick's rough history, but for a deeper insight into how folk used to live in these parts, head over to the **Craa Nest**, the oldest crofthouse in the village, just up the path to the Old Man; last occupied in 1940, the place still has its box-beds, barn and kiln intact. A short stroll away is the sandy beach, backed by giant sandstone pebbles.

The Old Man of Hoy

Rackwick has a steady stream of walkers and climbers passing through en route to the **Old Man of Hoy**, a great sandstone stack 450ft high, perched on an old lava flow which protects it from the erosive power of the sea. The Old Man is a popular challenge for rock climbers, and a 1966 ascent, led by the mountaineer Chris Bonington, was the first televised climb in Britain. The well-trodden footpath from Rackwick is an easy three-mile walk (3hr round trip) – although the great skuas will dive-bomb you during the nesting season (May–Aug) – and rewards you with a great view of the stack. The surrounding cliffs provide ideal rocky ledges for thousands of nesting seabirds, including guillemots, kittiwakes, razorbills, puffins and shags.

Continuing north along the clifftops from the Old Man, the path peters out before **St John's Head**, which, at 1136ft, is one of Britain's highest sea cliffs. Another, safer, option is to hike to the top of **Ward Hill** (1577ft), the highest peak in Orkney, from which on a fine day you can see the whole archipelago.

ARRIVAL AND GETTING AROUND   NORTH HOY

By ferry The passenger ferry from Stromness to Moaness Pier, by Hoy village (Mon–Fri 4–6 daily, Sat & Sun 2 daily; 25min; ☏ 01856 872044) also serves the island of Graemsay en route.

By bus A Hoy Community bus operates a hail and ride service on two routes, Longhope to Lyness and Moaness Pier to Longhope (limited service check; ☏ 01856 701356, ⓦ hoyorkney.com).

ACCOMMODATION AND EATING

Beneth'ill Café Hoy ☎ 01856 791119, ⓦ benethillcafe. co.uk. Friendly, simple café, a short walk from Moaness Pier, offering sandwiches, paninis and salads along with home-made puddings, proper coffee, teas, hot chocolate, juices and alcoholic drinks. April–Sept daily 10am–6pm.

Hoy Centre 1 mile west of Moaness Pier ☎ 01856 873535 ext 2417. A council-run, SYHA-affiliated hostel in an old school. Situated in Hoy village, this place is large and modern,

with a well-equipped kitchen, washing and drying facilities and all rooms en-suite. Dorms £20.60, family rooms £48

Rackwick Outdoor Centre Signposted at entrance to village, 0.5 miles north of the beach ☎ 01856 873535 ext 2901. Housed in Rackwick's tiny little former schoolhouse, this simple hostel has just eight beds in two rooms and a small kitchen. The central location in Rackwick village is great. Camping permitted. April–Sept. Dorms £16.40

Lyness

Along the sheltered eastern shore of Hoy, high moorland gives way gradually to a gentler environment. Hoy defines the western boundary of Scapa Flow, and LYNESS played a major role for the Royal Navy during both world wars. Most of the old wartime buildings have been cleared away, but the harbour and hills around Lyness are still scarred with scattered concrete structures that once served as hangars and storehouses, and are now used as barns and cowsheds. Among these are the remains of what was – incredibly – once the largest cinema in Europe, but perhaps the most unusual building is the monochrome Art Deco facade of the old **Garrison Theatre** (now a private home) where the troops were entertained, on the main road to the south. Lyness also has a large **naval cemetery**, where many of the victims of the various disasters that have occurred in the Flow, such as the sinking of the *Royal Oak* (see page 342), now lie, alongside a handful of German graves.

Scapa Flow Visitor Centre and Museum

March, April & Oct Mon–Sat 10am–4pm; May–Sept daily 10am–4pm; Nov–Feb limited opening check in advance • Free • ☎ 01856 791300, ⓦ orkney.com

The old oil pumphouse, standing opposite Lyness ferry terminal, has been turned into the **Scapa Flow Visitor Centre**, giving a fascinating insight into wartime Orkney – even the **café** has an old NAAFI feel about it. As well as the usual old photos, torpedoes, flags, guns and propellers, there's a paratrooper's folding bicycle, and a whole section devoted to the scuttling of the German High Seas Fleet and the sinking of the *Royal Oak*. The pumphouse itself retains much of its old equipment used to pump oil from tankers into sixteen tanks, and into underground reservoirs cut into the neighbouring hillside. You can also wander over to the Romney Hut, where Admiral von Reuter's *Chefboot* resides along with engines from the old wartime railway, and to the air-raid shelter beyond. From April to October there are regular guided walks around the former naval base.

ARRIVAL AND DEPARTURE
LYNESS

By ferry The roll-on/roll-off car ferry to/from Houton on the Mainland (Mon–Fri 6 daily, Sat & Sun 2–5 daily; 35min–1hr; ☎ 01856 811397) sometimes calls in at the

oil terminal island of Flotta, and begins and ends its daily schedule at Longhope – if you're taking a vehicle over, you should book in advance.

ENTERTAINMENT

Gable End Theatre 1.5 miles south of Lyness Pier ⓦ orkneycommunities.co.uk/iohdt. Established in the old North Walls school buildings, this community-run theatre

(with its own wind turbine) shows regular films and puts on the occasional theatre piece and gig – check their Facebook page for the latest information.

Melsetter House

4 miles southwest of Lyness • May, June & Sept Fri & Sat by appointment • ☎ 01856 791352

The finest architecture on Hoy is to be found at **Melsetter House**, overlooking the deep inlet of North Bay. Originally built in 1738, it was bought by Thomas Middlemore, heir to a Birmingham leather tycoon, who commissioned Arts and Crafts architect William Lethaby to transform the house in 1898. The owners will happily take you round a handful of rooms in the house itself, all of which are simply decorated with white wood panelling, floral plasterwork and William Morris-style fabrics, and leave you to wander freely around the very beautiful grounds. Don't miss the little **Chapel of St Margaret and St Colm** that Lethaby fashioned from the Melsetter outhouses, which features four tiny stained-glass windows by, among others, Ford Madox Brown and Edward Burne-Jones.

Longhope

East of Melsetter House, a causeway built during World War II connects Hoy with South Walls (pronounced "Waas"), a fertile tidal island which is more densely populated than Hoy. Along the north coast is the main settlement of **LONGHOPE**, an important safe anchorage even today.

Longhope Lifeboat Museum

Southeast of the causeway • By appointment • Free • ☎ 01856 701333, ⓦ longhopelifeboat.org.uk

The **Longhope Lifeboat Museum** houses the *Thomas McCunn*, a lifeboat in service from 1933 to 1962 and still launched for high days and holidays. The Longhope lifeboat capsized in gale-force winds in 1969 on its way to the aid of a Liberian freighter. The entire eight-man crew died, leaving seven widows and ten fatherless children; the crew of the freighter, by contrast, survived. There's a moving memorial to the men – six of whom came from just two families – in **Kirkhope churchyard** on the road to Cantick Head Lighthouse.

Hackness Martello Tower

Point of Hackness • April–Oct daily 9.30am–5.30pm • £6; HES • ☎ 01856 701727, ⓦ historicenvironment.scot

Longhope's strategic importance during the Napoleonic Wars is evident at the Point of Hackness, where the **Hackness Martello Tower** stands guard over the entrance to the bay, with a matching tower on the opposite promontory of Crockness. Built in 1815, these two circular, sandstone Martello towers are the northernmost in Britain, and protected merchant ships from American and French privateers. You enter Hackness Tower via a steep ladder connected to the upper floor, where nine men and one officer shared the circular room. The walls are up to 9ft high on the seaward side, and the tower even had its own water supply.

ARRIVAL AND DEPARTURE   LONGHOPE

By ferry The roll-on/roll-off car ferry from Houton on the Mainland to Lyness begins and ends each day at Longhope – book ahead if you're taking a vehicle over (1 daily, 1hr 20min; ☎ 01856 811397).

ACCOMMODATION

Old Hall Cottage 2 miles southeast of Longhope ☎ 07735 326606, ⓦ oldhallcottage.co.uk. Lovely 200-year-old converted byre sleeps six at a squeeze and is let out on a nightly basis or as a B&B; lovely sheltered garden overlooking Scapa Flow. **£60**

Stromabank Hotel 1.5 miles southeast of Longhope ☎ 01856 701494, ⓦ stromabank.co.uk. This small, unpretentious hotel is housed in the old schoolhouse on the hill above Longhope, with views over the Pentland Firth – there are four en-suite rooms available and the bar serves as the local pub. Bar food available in the evening. **£90**

Shapinsay

Just a few miles northeast of Kirkwall, **Shapinsay** (population 300) is the most accessible of Orkney's northern isles. A gently undulating grid-plan patchwork of rich farmland, it's a bit like an island suburb of Kirkwall, which is clearly visible across the bay.

Balfour

Shapinsay's only village is **BALFOUR**, named after the family who owned the local castle and the island, reformed the island's agricultural system and rebuilt the village – previously known as Shoreside – as a neat and disciplined cottage development, to house their estate workers. The family's grandiose efforts in estate management have left some appealingly eccentric relics around the village. Melodramatic fortifications around the harbour include the huge and ornate **gatehouse**. There's also a stone-built coal-fired **gasometer**, which once supplied castle and harbour with electricity and, southwest of the pier, the castellated **Douche** or Dishan Tower, a seventeenth-century doocot, converted into a saltwater toilet and shower in Victorian times.

Balfour Castle

Shapinsay's chief landmark is **Balfour Castle**, an imposing baronial pile visible as you approach on the ferry and a short walk from the village. Designed by David Bryce, it was completed in 1848 by the Balfour family of Westray, who had made a small fortune in India the previous century. The Balfours died out in 1960, and for the last few years the castle had been used as an exclusive-use holiday or dining retreat. The house is now privately owned and not open to the public.

Shapinsay Heritage Centre

The Smithy • May–Sept daily 2–4pm • Free • ☎ 01856 711246

The old smithy, halfway along Balfour's main street, houses the volunteer-run **Shapinsay Heritage Centre**, where there is information about the island, and a series of workshops held during the summer, plus a range of arts and crafts for sale. Tea and cakes are also available. Check their Facebook page for what's on.

ARRIVAL AND DEPARTURE   SHAPINSAY

By ferry Shapinsay is an easy day-trip from Kirkwall (3–5   daily; 30min; ☎ 01856 872044).

ACCOMMODATION AND EATING

★ **Iona Cottage** a few minutes east of Balfour on B9059 ☎ 01224 867184, ⊕ islandselfcatering.co.uk. This self-catering cottage for up to 6 people has three en-suite bedrooms and features a spacious sun porch with views across Elwick Bay to Kirkwall. Green energy is supplied via a wind turbine and local produce is available from a village shop. From **£300** per week.

Rousay, Egilsay and Wyre

The hilly island of **Rousay** is one of the more accessible northern isles as well as being home to a number of intriguing prehistoric sites. The group of a dozen or so houses above the ferry terminal is the only settlement of any size, but a single road runs around the edge of the island, connecting a string of small farms which make use of the more cultivable coastal fringes. Many visitors come on a day-trip, as it's easy enough to reach the main points of archeological interest on the south coast by foot from the ferry terminal.

Rousay's diminutive neighbours, **Egilsay** and **Wyre**, contain a few medieval attractions of their own, which can either be visited on a day-trip from Rousay itself, or from the Mainland.

Rousay

Despite its long history of settlement, **Rousay** today is home to little more than two hundred people (many of them incomers), as this was one of the few parts of Orkney to suffer Highland-style clearances, initially by George William Traill at Quandale in the northwest. His successor and nephew, Lieutenant General Sir Frederick William Traill-Burroughs, built a wall to force crofters onto a narrow coastal strip and eventually provoked so much distress and anger that a gunboat had to be sent to restore order. You can learn about the history and wildlife of the island from the well-laid-out display room of the **Rousay Heritage Centre** housed in the back of the ferry waiting room.

Trumland House

Gardens May–Oct daily 10am–5pm • £2.50 • ☎ 01856 821322

The island's laird, Lieutenant General Traill-Burroughs, built **Trumland House**, the forbidding Jacobean-style pile designed by David Bryce, in the 1870s, hidden in the trees half a mile northwest of the ferry terminal. The house is currently undergoing much-needed restoration, as are the landscaped **gardens**: the rhododendrons have been pushed back and there are now lovely wooded walks and a walled garden.

The three cairns

The road west from Trumland House is bordered over the next couple of miles by a trio of intriguing prehistoric cairns, starting with **Taversoe Tuick**. Dating back to 3500 BC, it's remarkable in that it exploits its sloping site by having two storeys, one entered from the upper side and one from the lower.

A little further west is the **Blackhammar Cairn**, which is more promising inside than it looks from the outside. You enter through the roof via a ladder; the long interior is divided into "stalls" by large flagstones, rather like the more famous cairn at Midhowe (see page 353).

Finally, there's the **Knowe of Yarso**, another stalled cairn dating from the same period. It's worth the stiff climb up the hill from the road, if only for the magnificent view. The

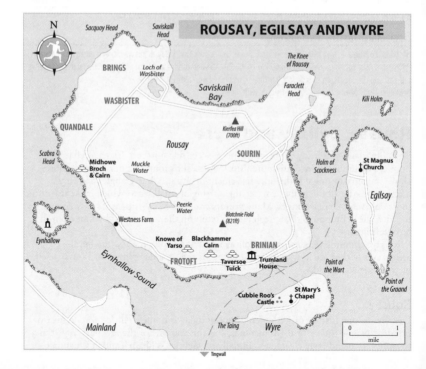

remains of 29 individuals were found inside, with the skulls neatly arranged around the walls; the bones of 36 deer were also buried here.

Trumland RSPB reserve

A footpath sets off from beside the Taversoe Tuick tomb into the **RSPB reserve** that encompasses most of the nearby heather-backed hills, the highest of which is **Blotchnie Fiold** (821ft). This high ground offers good hillwalking, with superb panoramic views of the surrounding islands, as well as excellent birdwatching. If you're lucky, you may well catch a glimpse of merlins, hen harriers, short-eared owls and red-throated divers, although the latter are more widespread just outside the reserve on one of the island's three freshwater lochs, which also offer good trout fishing.

Westness Walk

The southwestern side of Rousay is home to the most significant and impressive of the island's archeological remains, strung out along the shores of Eynhallow Sound, which runs between the island and the Mainland. Most lie on the mile-long **Westness Walk** that begins at Westness Farm, four miles west of the ferry terminal. This scramble along the shore is rewarded with a kaleidoscope of history, with remains of an Iron Age cairn, a Viking farm, a post-Reformation church, a medieval tower, and crofts from which the tenants were evicted in the nineteenth century. Half a mile further, you'll reach the impressive clifftop scenery around **Scabra Head**, where numerous seabirds nest in summer.

Midhowe Cairn

Towards the end of the walk, **Midhowe Cairn** comes as something of a surprise, both for its immense size – it's known as "the great ship of death" and measures nearly 100ft in length – and because it's now entirely surrounded by a stone-walled barn with a corrugated roof. Unfortunately, you can't actually explore the roofless communal burial chamber, dating back to 3500 BC, but only look down from the overhead walkway. The central corridor, 25 yards long, is partitioned with slabs of rock, with twelve compartments on each side, where the remains of 25 people were discovered in a crouched position with their backs to the wall.

Midhowe Broch

A couple of hundred yards beyond Midhowe Cairn is Rousay's finest archeological site, **Midhowe Broch**, whose compact layout suggests that it was originally built as a sort of fortified family house, surrounded by a complex series of ditches and ramparts. The broch itself looks as though it's about to slip into the sea: it was obviously shored up with flagstone buttresses back in the Iron Age, and has more recently been given extra sea defences by Historic Scotland. The interior of the broch, entered through an impressive doorway, is divided into two separate rooms, each with its own hearth, water tank and quernstone, all of which date from the final phase of occupation around the second century AD.

Egilsay

Egilsay, the largest of the low-lying islands sheltering close to the eastern shore of Rousay, makes an easy day-trip. Egilsay is almost entirely inhabited by incomers, and a large slice of the island's farmland is managed by the RSPB in a vain attempt to encourage corncrakes. If you're just here for the day, walk due east from the ferry terminal to the coast, where there's a beautiful sandy bay overlooking Eday.

St Magnus Church

The island is dominated by the ruins of **St Magnus Church**, with its distinctive round tower, venue for Egilsay's ever more popular summer-solstice celebrations. Built around

7

the twelfth century in a prominent position in the middle of the island, probably on the site of a much earlier version, the roofless church is the only surviving example of the traditional round-towered churches of Orkney and Shetland. It is possible that it was built as a shrine to Earl (later Saint) Magnus, who arranged to meet his cousin Håkon here in 1117, only to be treacherously killed on Håkon's orders by the latter's cook, Lifolf.

Wyre

The tiny island of **Wyre**, to the southwest of Egilsay and directly opposite Rousay's ferry terminal, is another possible day-trip, and is best known for **Cubbie Roo's Castle**, the "fine stone fort" and "really solid stronghold" mentioned in the *Orkneyinga Saga*, and built around 1150 by local farmer Kolbein Hruga. The castle gets another mention in *Håkon's Saga*, when those inside successfully withstood all attacks. The outer defences have survived well on three sides of the castle, which has a central keep, with walls to a height of around 6ft, its central water-tank still intact. Close by the castle stands **St Mary's Chapel**, a roofless twelfth-century church founded either by Kolbein or his son, Bjarni the Poet, who was Bishop of Orkney. Kolbein's permanent residence or **Bu** is recalled in the name of the nearby farm, the Bu of Wyre, where the poet **Edwin Muir** (1887–1959) spent his childhood, described in detail in his autobiography. To learn more about Muir, Cubbie Roo or any other aspect of Wyre's history, pop into the **Wyre Heritage Centre**, near the chapel.

ARRIVAL AND DEPARTURE   ROUSAY, EGILSAY AND WYRE

By ferry Rousay makes a good day-trip from the Mainland, with car ferries from Tingwall (5–6 daily; 30min) linked to Kirkwall by bus (5 daily; 30min–1hr). Most of the Rousay ferries call in at Egilsay and Wyre, but some are request journeys and must be booked the day before (☎ 01856 751360).

By bus A bus runs every Thursday (7am–7pm; book ahead on ☎ 01856 821360, ⓦ aroundrousay.co.uk/bus). Minibus tours are available on demand (☎ 01856 821234; £35; 5–7hr) from the ferry terminal on Rousay.

ACCOMMODATION AND EATING

ROUSAY

Accommodation and eating options on Rousay are very limited. If you're coming for the day or self-catering, bring your own provisions, as Rousay Stores, the island's main general store, is in the northeastern corner of the island.

The Space The Old Kirk On the B9604 2 miles east of the ferry terminal ⓔ info@thespaceorkney ⓦ thespace orkney.com. Sleeping 6–8 people, this fantastic conversion of an old chapel is stunningly set in a secluded spot on the hillside above the sea. Popular with musicians and artists (it has its own recording studio) it is also available for families

or friends. Minimum stay four days £500

The Taversoe 3 miles west of ferry terminal ☎ 01856 821325, ⓦ taversoehotel.co.uk. Unpretentious accommodation in four rooms (all with sea views). Serves classic pub meals – fish and chips, scampi or burgers (all under £10). Free wi-fi. £95

Trumland Farm 0.5 miles west of ferry terminal ☎ 01856 821252. This working organic farm has a couple of dorms and a family room – you can also camp here, and they offer bike rental (£8/day). Camping per person £6, dorms £14

Westray

Although exposed to the full force of the Atlantic weather in the far northwest of Orkney, **Westray** shelters one of the most tightly knit, prosperous and independent island communities, numbering some six hundred Old Orcadian families who give the island a strongly individual character. Fishing, farming and tourism are the mainstays of the economy. The landscape is very varied, with sea cliffs and a trio of hills in the west, and rich low-lying pastureland and sandy bays elsewhere. However, given that it's about twelve miles from the ferry terminal in the south to the cliffs of Noup Head in the far northwest – and that the boat from Kirkwall takes nearly an hour and a half, Westray is an island that repays a longer stay, especially as there's lots of good accommodation and the locals are extremely welcoming.

Pierowall

The main village and harbour is **PIEROWALL**, set around a wide bay in the north of the island, eight miles from Rapness ferry terminal on the island's southernmost tip. Pierowall is a place of some considerable size, relatively speaking, with a school, several shops and a bakery (Orkney's only one off the Mainland).

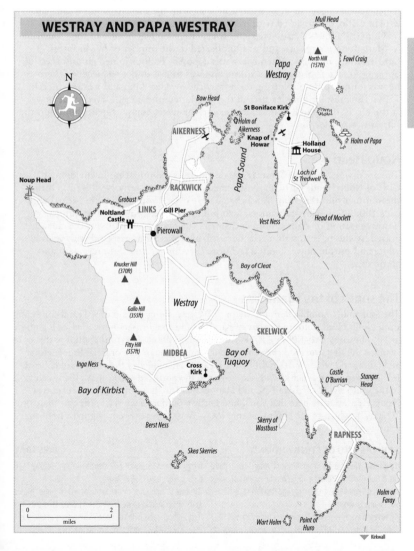

WESTRAY AND PAPA WESTRAY

Mull Head

Papa Westray

North Hill (157ft)   Fowl Craig

Bow Head

St Boniface Kirk

Holm of Aikerness

AIKERNESS

Knap of Howar

Holland House

Papa Sound

Holm of Papa

Loch of St Tredwell

Noup Head

Grobust

RACKWICK

LINKS   Gill Pier

Noltland Castle

Vest Ness   Head of Moclett

Pierowall

Knucker Hill (370ft)

Bay of Cleat

Gallo Hill (355ft)

Westray

SKELWICK

Fitty Hill (557ft)

MIDBEA

Bay of Tuquoy

Inga Ness

Cross Kirk

Castle O'Burrian   Stanger Head

Bay of Kirbist

Berst Ness

Skerry of Wastbust

RAPNESS

Skea Skerries

Holm of Faray

0   2   miles

Wart Holm   Point of Huro

Kirkwall

7

Westray Heritage Centre

May–Sept Mon 11.30am–5pm, Tues–Sat 10am–noon & 2–5pm, Sun 1.30–5pm, Oct–April by appointment, open most Wed 2–4pm • £3 • ☎ 01857 677414, ⊛ westrayheritage.co.uk

The village's **Westray Heritage Centre** is a very welcoming wet-weather retreat, and a great place to gen up on (and with any luck catch a glimpse of) the Westray Wife or **Orkney Venus** – a remarkable, miniature Neolithic female figurine found in 2009 in the dunes to the northwest of Pierowall – along with her incomplete companion, and the recently discovered Grobust Grandad.

Noltland Castle

April–Sept daily 9.30am–5.30pm; Oct–March 10am–4pm • Free • HES • ☎ 0131 668 8600

The island's most impressive ruin is the colossal sandstone hulk of **Noltland Castle**, which stands above the village half a mile west up the road to Noup Head. This Z-plan castle, pockmarked with over seventy gun loops, was begun around 1560 by Gilbert Balfour, a shady character from Fife, who was Master of the Household to Mary, Queen of Scots, and was implicated in the murder of her husband, Lord Darnley, in 1567. When Mary was deposed, Balfour joined an unsuccessful uprising in favour of the exiled queen and was forced to flee to Sweden. There he was found guilty of plotting to murder the Swedish king and was executed in 1576. The most striking features of the interior are the huge, carved stone newel at the top of the grand, main staircase, and the secret compartments built into the sills of two of the windows.

Noup Head

The northwestern tip of Westray rises up sharply, culminating in the dramatic sea cliffs of **Noup Head**, particularly spectacular when a westerly swell is up. During the summer months (May–Aug) the guano-covered rock ledges are packed with over 100,000 nesting guillemots, razorbills, kittiwakes, fulmars and puffins: a heady sensation of sight, sound and smell. The open ground above the cliffs, grazed by sheep, is superb maritime heath and grassland, carpeted with yellow, white and purple flowers, and a favourite breeding ground for arctic tern and arctic skua.

The south of the island

The four-mile coastal walk in the **south** of Westray, along the top of red-sandstone cliffs from Noup Head south to the Bay of Kirbist, is thoroughly recommended, as is a quick ascent of nearby **Fitty Hill** (557ft), Westray's highest point. Also in the south of the island is the tiny **Cross Kirk**, which, although ruined, retains an original Romanesque arch, door and window. It's right by the sea, and on a fine day the nearby sandy beach is a lovely spot for a picnic, with views over to the north side of Rousay. The sea cliffs in the southeast of the island around **Stanger Head** are not quite as spectacular as at Noup Head, but it's here that you'll find **Castle o'Burrian**, a sea stack, the best place on Westray at which to see **puffins** nesting (May–Aug) – there's even a signpost from the main road.

ARRIVAL AND GETTING AROUND
WESTRAY

By plane You can fly from Kirkwall (Mon–Fri 2 daily, Sat & Sun 1 daily; 15min) and go on the world's shortest scheduled flight between Westray and Papa Westray (Mon–Sat 1 daily; 2min).

By ferry Westray is served by car ferry from Kirkwall (2–3 daily; 1hr 25min; ☎ 01856 872044), and there's a passenger ferry between Pierowall (Westray) and Papa Westray (3–6 daily; 25min; ☎ 01856 872044).

By bus A minibus (May–Sept; at other times phone ☎ 07789 034289, ⊛ westraybusservice.co.uk) meets the ferry and connects with the Papa Westray ferry at Gill Pier in Pierowall; book a seat for the bus on the ferry.

INFORMATION AND TOURS

Tourist information ⓦ westraypapawestray.co.uk.
Tours Guided tours of the island by minibus can be arranged with Westraak (☎01857 677777, ⓦ westraak. co.uk), who will meet you at the ferry.

ACCOMMODATION AND EATING

★ **Chalmersquoy** Pierowall ☎01857 677214, ⓦ chalmersquoywestray.co.uk. The barn ls a converted farm hostel at the southern edge of Pierowall; it's luxurious inside, with family rooms and twin bunks available, has a small campsite, Chalmersquoy, adjacent to it and a games room – run by a genuinely friendly Westerly family. Bed and breakfast and self-catering are also available. Dorms £24; camping per pitch £12

Haff Yok ☎01857 677767. Pop-up café in a little shed in Pierowall itself (opposite the Lady Kirk). Great for soup, toasties and cakes, with a few tables in a south-facing suntrap.

May–Sept Mon–Sat 10.30am–5pm, Sun noon–4pm.
No. 1 Broughton Pierowall ☎01857 677726, ⓦ no1 broughton.co.uk. Top-notch, good-value B&B in a renovated mid-nineteenth-century house with views across the bay, with three en-suite rooms, a lovely conservatory and even a small sauna. £60

Pierowall Hotel Pierowall ☎01857 677472, ⓦ pierowallhotel.co.uk. The social hub of Pierowall itself is unpretentious and very welcoming – the cheaper rooms have shared facilities. The popular bar has excellent fish and chips, fresh off the boats. £96

Papa Westray

Across the short Papa Sound from Westray is the island of **Papa Westray**, known locally as "Papay". With a population hovering around ninety, Papay has had to fight hard to keep itself viable over the last couple of decades, helped by a hefty influx of outsiders. With one of Orkney's best-preserved Neolithic settlements, and a large nesting seabird population, Papay is worthy of a stay in its own right or an easy day-trip from its big neighbour.

As the name suggests – *papøy* is Old Norse for "priest" – the island was once a medieval pilgrimage centre, focused on a chapel dedicated to **St Tredwell**, now reduced to a pile of rubble on a promontory on the loch of the same name just inland from the ferry terminal. St Tredwell (Triduana) was a plucky young local girl who gouged out her eyes and handed them to the eighth-century Pictish king Nechtan when he attempted to rape her. By the twelfth century, the chapel had become a place of pilgrimage for those suffering from eye complaints.

Holland House

Central point of the island • Farm buildings always open • Free

The island's visual focus is **Holland House**, occupying the high central point of the island and once seat of the local lairds, the Traill family, who ruled over Papay for three centuries. The main house, with crow-stepped gables, is still in private hands, but the owners are happy for visitors to explore the old buildings of the home farm, on the west side of the road, which include a kiln, a doocot and a horse-powered threshing mill. An old bothy for single male servants, decorated with red horse-yokes, has been restored and made into a small **museum** filled with bygone bits and bobs, from a wooden flea-trap to a box-bed.

Knap of Howar

From Holland House, it's around half a mile to the western shore, and to Papay's prime prehistoric site, the **Knap of Howar**. Dating from around 3500 BC, this Neolithic farm building makes a fair claim to being the oldest-standing house in Europe. It's made up of two roofless buildings, linked by a little passageway; one has a hearth and copious stone shelves, and is thought to have been some kind of storehouse.

St Boniface Kirk

St Boniface Kirk is a pre-Reformation church three-quarters of a mile north of the Knap of Howar. Inside, it's beautifully simple, with a bare flagstone floor, dry-stone walls, a little wooden gallery and just a couple of surviving box pews. The church is known to have seated at least 220, which meant they would have been squashed in, fourteen to a pew. In the graveyard is a Viking **hogback grave**, decorated with carvings imitating the wooden shingles on the roof of a Viking longhouse.

North Hill

Guided walks in summer • Free • ☎ 01856 850176, www.rspb.org.uk

The northern tip of the island around **North Hill** (157ft) is an RSPB reserve. During the breeding season you're asked to keep to the coastal fringe, where razorbills, guillemots, fulmars, kittiwakes and puffins nest, particularly around Fowl Craig on the east coast, where you may spot the rare Scottish primrose, which flowers in May and from July to late September. If you want to explore the interior of the reserve, which has one of the largest arctic tern colonies in Europe as well as numerous arctic skuas, contact the RSPB.

The Kelp Store Heritage & Craft Centre

0.5 miles east of the Papay Co-op • Contact Papay Ranger for opening times • ☎ 07931 235213

This stone building down by the old pier was once used for storing kelp, but these days it is home to the **Old Kelp Store Heritage Centre**, a great wet-weather retreat and place to learn about the history of the island. As well as acting as the island's heritage centre, the place also puts on various events from musical evenings to whisky-tasting sessions.

Holm of Papay

Boat trips by arrangement • ☎ 07931 235213• £25

Papay's Ranger can take **visitors** by boat to the **Holm of Papay**, the little island off the east coast. Despite its tiny size, the Holm boasts several Neolithic chambered cairns, one of which, occupying the highest point, is extremely impressive. Descending into the tomb via a ladder, you enter the main rectangular chamber, which is nearly 70ft in length, with no fewer than twelve side-cells, each with its own lintelled entrance.

ARRIVAL AND DEPARTURE   PAPA WESTRAY

By plane You can fly direct from Kirkwall to Papa Westray (Mon–Fri 3 daily, Sat & Sun 2 daily; 25min) for around £15 return if you stay overnight. Papay is also connected to Westray by the world's shortest scheduled flight (Mon–Sat 1 daily) – 2min or less with a following wind.

By ferry The passenger ferry from Gill Pier in Pierowall (3–6 daily; 25min; ☎ 01856 677216) also takes bicycles.

Car ferries On Tuesdays, the car ferry goes from Kirkwall to Papa Westray via North Ronaldsay, taking over four hours; on Fridays, the car ferry from Kirkwall to Westray continues to Papa Westray; at other times, you must catch a bus to connect with the Papa Westray ferry from Pierowall. The bus should be booked ahead, while on the Westray ferry (☎ 01857 677758); it accepts a limited number of bicycles.

GETTING AROUND AND INFORMATION

Guided tours The Papay Ranger offers Papay Peedie Tours by minibus (☎ 07931 235213) – full-days with lunch (May–Aug Wed, Thurs & Sat; £50, children £25) – you can even do it from Kirkwall as a 12hr day-trip. The tour takes you through history from Neolithic times to Celtic origins and Christian influence. Then after a three-course lunch at the Heritage centre you take a walk around the RSPB reserve. At other times, you can arrange bespoke tours with the Ranger.

Tourist information ⊕ papawestray.co.uk.

ACCOMMODATION AND EATING

Beltane House East side of the island ☎ 01857 644224, ⊕ papawestray.co.uk. The Papay Community Co-op offers six private single, double, twin and family rooms (*Papa Westray Hostel*), a place to camp, and a shop, all within the old estate workers' cottages at Beltane, east of Holland House. Attractive camping bothies resembling upturned wooded boat shelters are also available. *Beltane House* runs a self-service café for all island visitors to use and also opens its "bar cupboard" every Saturday night from 8pm, with bar meals available. Camping per person £10, bothies per person £25 (two people £45), private rooms £50, shared rooms £22

Eday

A long, thin island at the centre of Orkney's northern isles, **Eday** shares more characteristics with Rousay and Hoy than with its immediate neighbours, dominated as it is by heather-covered upland, with farmland confined to a narrow strip of coastal ground. However, Eday's hills have proved useful in their own way, providing huge quantities of peat, which has been exported to other peatless northern isles for fuel, and was even, for a time, exported to various whisky distillers. Eday's yellow sandstone has also been extensively quarried, and was used to build the St Magnus Cathedral in Kirkwall.

Eday is sparsely inhabited, with a population of around 150, the majority of them incomers, and there's no main village as such; the island post office, petrol pump and community shop all cluster in Hammerhill. The ferry terminal is at the south end of the island, whereas the chief points of interest (and most of the amenities) are all in the northern half, about four miles away. The name Eday comes from the Norse for "isthmus" and, indeed, the island is almost divided in two by its thin waist. On either side are sandy bays, between which lies the airfield (known as London Airport). To the south, around Flaughton Hill (328ft), there's a large breeding population of whimbrels.

Eday Heritage Centre and HMS Otter

May–Sept daily 10am–4pm; Nov–March by appointment • Free, donation requested • Heritage Centre ☎ 01857 622331; North School ☎ 01857 622225

Eday Heritage Centre, in an old Baptist chapel a mile north of the island's airport, has historical displays on Eday, with information on the island's tidal energy testing centre in the Fall of Warness. Perhaps the most unusual attraction, however, is in the nearby former North School, where several internal sections of the Cold War-era **submarine** HMS *Otter* have been reassembled in the old school hall.

Eday Heritage Walk: Mill Loch to Red Head

The clearly marked **Eday Heritage Walk** (4hr 30min return) begins at Mill Loch, which is a breeding ground of several pairs of **red-throated divers** where a bird hide overlooks the loch. Clearly visible over the road is the 15ft **Stone of Setter**, Orkney's most distinctive standing stone, weathered into three thick, lichen-encrusted fingers. From here, passing the less spectacular Braeside and Huntersquoy chambered cairns en route, you can climb the hill to reach Eday's finest, the **Vinquoy Chambered Cairn**, which has a similar structure to that of Maeshowe. You can crawl into the tomb through the narrow entrance: a skylight inside lets light into the main, beehive chamber but not into the four side-cells. From the cairn, you can continue north to the viewpoint on the summit of **Vinquoy Hill** (248ft), and to the very northernmost tip of the island, where lie the dramatic red-sandstone sea cliffs of **Red Head**, where numerous seabirds nest in summer.

Carrick House

Open by appointment • ☎ 01857 622260

The grandest home on Eday is Carrick House, on the northeast coast. Built by the Laird of Eday in 1633, it was extended in the original style by successive owners, but is best known for its associations with the pirate **John Gow** – on whom Sir Walter Scott's

7

novel *The Pirate* is based – whose ship *The Revenge* ran aground on the **Calf of Eday** in 1725. He asked for help from the Laird, but was taken prisoner in Carrick House, before being sent off to London, where he was tortured and executed. The highlight of the tour is the bloodstain on the floor of the living room, where John Gow was detained and stabbed while trying to escape.

ARRIVAL AND INFORMATION   EDAY

By plane You can make a day-trip by plane from Kirkwall to Eday on Wednesdays (2 on Wed; 10min).

By ferry Eday is served by regular car ferry from Kirkwall (2–3 daily; 1hr 15min–2hr; ☎01856 872044). The ferry

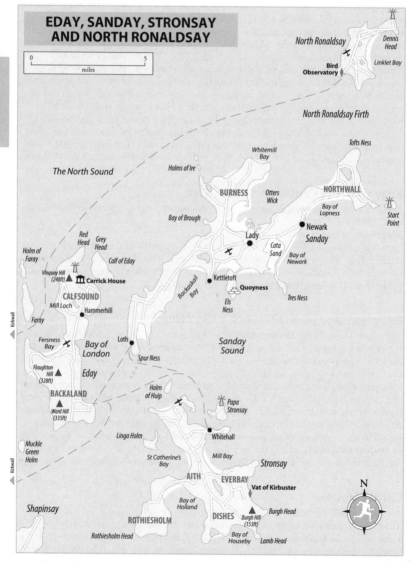

EDAY, SANDAY, STRONSAY AND NORTH RONALDSAY

0 _____ 5
miles

North Ronaldsay

Dennis Head

Bird Observatory

Linklet Bay

North Ronaldsay Firth

The North Sound

Holms of Ire

Whitemill Bay

Tofts Ness

BURNESS

Otters Wick

NORTHWALL

Bay of Brough

Bay of Lopness

Start Point

Newark

Lady

Sanday

Cata Sand

Bay of Newark

Red Head

Grey Head

Calf of Eday

Holm of Faray

Vinquoy Hill (248ft)

Carrick House

Backaskail Bay

Kettletoft

Quoyness

CALFSOUND

Mill Loch

Hammerhill

Els Ness

Tres Ness

Faray

Fersness Bay

Bay of London

Loth

Sanday Sound

Flaughton Hill (328ft)

Eday

Spur Ness

BACKALAND

Ward Hill (335ft)

Holm of Huip

Papa Stronsay

Muckle Green Holm

Linga Holm

Whitehall

St Catherine's Bay

Mill Bay

Stronsay

AITH

EVERBAY

Vat of Kirbuster

Shapinsay

Bay of Holland

DISHES

Burgh Hill (153ft)

Burgh Head

ROTHIESHOLM

Rothiesholm Head

Bay of Houseby

Lamb Head

N

Kirkwall

Kirkwall

terminal is at Backaland pier in the south, although you should be able to get a lift to the north of the island with someone off the ferry if you ask around.

Tourist information ⓦ visiteday.wordpress.com.

GETTING AROUND AND TOURS

Guided tour Eday's minibus (May to mid-Sept Mon, Wed & Fri or by appointment; 2hr 30min; £15; ☎ 01857 622206) will collect you from the ferry, take you on a tour of the island and deposit you wherever you want; every Thursday it will simply take you wherever you wish to go (without the tour). Eday also has a Ranger service, offering weekly guided walks – check Eday Scarfs Facebook page.

ACCOMMODATION AND EATING

Eday Community Hostel, London Bay Just south of the airport ☎ 07447 460169, ⓦ hostellingscotland.org. uk. An SYHA-affiliated, community-run hostel, situated in an exposed spot – phone ahead as there's no resident warden. Washing machine and dryer, bike rental and free wi-fi, and guided walks can be arranged. Dorms **£20**

Stronsay

7

A low-lying, three-legged island, **Stronsay** is strongly agricultural, its interior an almost uninterrupted collage of green pastures. The island features few real sights, but the coastline has enormous appeal: a beguiling combination of sandstone cliffs, home to several seabird colonies, interspersed with wide white sands and (in fine weather) clear turquoise bays. The most dramatic section of coastline, featuring great, layered slices of sandstone, lies in the southeast corner of the island. Stronsay has a population of around 350 and has seen two economic booms in the last 300 years. The first took place in the eighteenth century, employing as many as 3000 people; it was built on collecting vast quantities of seaweed and exporting the **kelp** for use in the chemical industry, particularly in making iodine, soap and glass. In the following century, **fishing** came to dominate life here, as Whitehall harbour became one of the main Scottish centres for curing the herring caught by French, Dutch and Scottish boats. By the 1840s, up to 400 boats were working out of the port, attracting hundreds of female herring-gutters. By the 1930s, however, the herring stocks had been severely depleted and the industry began a long decline.

Whitehall

WHITEHALL, in the north of the island, is the only real village on Stronsay, made up of rows of stone-built fishermen's cottages set between two large piers. Wandering along the tranquil, rather forlorn harbour-front today, you'll find it hard to believe that the village once supported 5000 people in the fishing industry during the summer season, as well as a small army of coopers, coal merchants, butchers, bakers, several Italian ice-cream parlours and a cinema. It was said that, on a Sunday, you could walk across the decks of the boats all the way to **Papa Stronsay**, the tiny island that shelters Whitehall from the north. The old Fish Mart by the pier houses a small **museum**, with a few photos and artefacts from the herring days – ask at the adjacent café for access.

Papa Stronsay

Ferry The island's monks take visitors to the island by boat, by prior arrangement • ☎ 01857 616210, ⓦ papastronsay.com

Clearly visible from the harbour-front at Whitehall is the tiny island of **Papa Stronsay**, which features in the *Orkneyinga Saga* as the place where Earl Rognvald Brusason was murdered by Earl Thorfinn Sigurdarson. Later, during the herring boom, it was home to five fish-curing stations. The island is thought originally to have been a **monastic retreat**, a theory given extra weight by the discovery of an eighth-century chapel during recent excavations. In 2000, Papa Stronsay was bought by Transalpine Redemptorist monks, who had broken with the Vatican over their refusal to stop celebrating Mass in Latin. They have subsequently built themselves the multi-million-pound Golgotha Monastery, with a creamery for making their Monastery Cheese. Since 2008, they have been accepted into the Roman Catholic Church and renamed the Sons of the Most Holy Redeemer.

Vat of Kirbuster to Lamb Head

Signposts show the way to Orkney's biggest and most dramatic natural arch, the **Vat of Kirbuster**. Before you reach it there's a seaweedy, shallow pool in a natural sandstone amphitheatre, where the water is warmed by the sun, and kids and adults can safely wallow: close by is a rocky inlet for those who prefer colder, more adventurous swimming. You'll find nesting seabirds, including a few puffins, as you approach **Burgh Head**. Meanwhile, at the promontory of **Lamb Head**, there are usually loads of seals, a large colony of arctic terns, and good views out to the lighthouse on the outlying island of **Auskerry**.

ARRIVAL AND GETTING AROUND   STRONSAY

By plane Flights from Kirkwall (Mon–Fri 2 daily, Sat 1 daily; 25min) and from Sanday (Mon–Sat 1 daily; 6min).
By ferry Stronsay is served by a regular car ferry service from Kirkwall to Whitehall (1–3 daily; 1hr 40min–2hr;

☎01856 872044).
By taxi/car There's no bus service, but D.S. Peace (☎01857 616335) operates taxis and offers car rental.

ACCOMMODATION AND EATING

Storehouse Whitehall ☎01857 616263. A good alternative to the *Stronsay Hotel* is this welcoming little B&B in Whitehall, with en-suite rooms, a guest lounge and full board on request. £65
Stronsay Fish Mart Whitehall ☎01857 616401. The old fish market, by the ferry terminal, has been refurbished as a hostel, a heritage centre and a cheap and cheerful daytime

café serving tea, sandwiches and delicious home-made cakes – check Facebook for the latest opening hours. Free wi-fi available. Dorms £20
Stronsay Hotel Whitehall ☎01857 616213. Stronsay's only hotel, right by the ferry terminal, has modern en-suite rooms, while the hotel bar serves up generous portions of cheap and cheerful pub food. £80

Sanday

Despite being the largest of the northern isles, and the most populous after Westray, **Sanday** is the least substantial, a great low-lying, drifting dune strung out between several rocky points. The island's sweeping aquamarine bays and vast stretches of clean white sand are the finest in Orkney, and in good weather it's a superb place to spend a day or two. The sandy soil is very fertile, and the island remains predominantly agricultural even today, holding its own agricultural show each year at the beginning of August. The shoreline supports a healthy seal, otter and wading bird population, and behind the sandy beaches are stretches of beautiful open machair and grassland, thick with wild flowers during spring and summer. The entire coastline offers superb walks, with particularly spectacular sand dunes to the south of the vast, shallow, tidal bay of **Cata Sand**.

Start Point Lighthouse

Accessible only during low tide

The island has a long history as a shipping hazard, with many wrecks smashed against its shores, although the construction of the **Start Point Lighthouse** in 1802 on the island's exposed eastern tip reduced the risk for seafarers. Shipwrecks were, in fact, not an unwelcome sight on Sanday, as the island has no peat, and driftwood was the only source of fuel other than cow dung – it's even said that the locals used to pray for shipwrecks in church. The present 82ft-high Stevenson lighthouse, dating from 1870, now sports very natty, unusual, vertical black-and-white stripes. It actually stands on a tidal island, so ask locally for the tide times before setting out (it takes an hour to walk there and back). Better still, phone and arrange a tour, which allows you to climb to the top of the lighthouse.

Quoyness Chambered Cairn

Sanday is rich in archeology, with hundreds of mostly unexcavated sites including brochs, burnt mounds and cairns, the most impressive of which is **Quoyness Chambered Cairn**, on the fertile farmland of Els Ness peninsula. The tomb, which dates from before 2000 BC, has been partially reconstructed, and rises to a height of around 13ft. The imposing, narrow entrance, flanked by high dry-stone walls, would originally have been roofed for the whole of the way into the 13ft-long main chamber, where skeletal remains were discovered in the six small side-cells.

ARRIVAL AND DEPARTURE

SANDAY 7

By plane The airfield is in the centre of the island and there are regular flights to Kirkwall (Mon–Fri 2 daily, Sat 1 daily; 10min) some flights to Stronsay (check website 🌐 loganair. co.uk; 6 min).

By ferry Ferries from Kirkwall to Sanday (2 daily; 1hr 25min) arrive at Loth Pier, at the southern tip of the island.

By bus All sailings are met by the Sanday Bus (📞 07513 084777), which will take you to most points on Sanday, but advance reservation is recommended.

INFORMATION AND TOURS

Tourist information 🌐 sanday.co.uk, 🌐 sandayorkney. co.uk.

Tours The Sanday Ranger (📞 07496 011705, 🌐 sanday ranger.org) organizes activities and guided walks throughout the summer, as well as regular Sanday Bus Tours (May–mid-Sept Wed; £35; 📞 07513 084777).

ACCOMMODATION AND EATING

Ayre's Rock 6 miles northeast of the ferry terminal 📞 01857 600410, 🌐 ayres-rock-hostel-orkney.com. If you're on a budget, this is a great place to stay: a well-equipped hostel, a couple of caravans and a small campsite (with several wooden camping pods for rent) overlooking the bay, with washing and laundry facilities, a cooked breakfast (£8) and bike rental. Per pitch £10, dorms £19.50, caravans £15, static caravan £50, single pods £18.50 (two people £35)

Backaskaill Farmhouse 5 miles northeast of ferry terminal 📞 01857 600305. Lovely solid stone-built farmhouse overlooking Backaskaill Bay, run by a very welcoming and helpful Manx couple – views over the bay from the conservatory – full board available on request. £80

Belsair Hotel Kettletoft 📞 01857 600206. The Belsair is one of two pubs in Kettletoft, Sanday's original fishing port. Decent pub food is on offer (fish and chips, burgers and the like for under £10) on a daily basis. Opening hours vary; check ahead. Accommodation also available.

Braeswick 2 miles north of the ferry terminal 📞 01857 600708, 🌐 braeswick.co.uk. Despite the rather plain exterior, this B&B is a good choice with three very pleasantly decorated rooms and a breakfast room with lovely views over the bay and an excellent base for birdwatching. £75

North Ronaldsay

North Ronaldsay – or "North Ron" as it's fondly known – is Orkney's most northerly island, with a population of around fifty. Separated from Sanday by some treacherous waters, it has an outpost atmosphere, brought about by its extreme isolation. Measuring just three miles by one, and rising only 66ft above sea level, the only features to interrupt the flat horizon are **Holland House** – built by the Traill family, who bought the island in 1727 – and the two lighthouses at **Dennis Head**. The rest of the island is almost overwhelmed by the magnitude of the sky, the strength of the wind and the ferocity of the sea so that its very existence seems an act of tenacious defiance. Despite this, North Ronaldsay has been inhabited for centuries, and continues to be

> ### NORTH RONALDSAY SHEEP
>
> The island's **sheep** are a unique, tough, goat-like breed, who feed mostly on seaweed, giving their flesh a dark tone and a rich, gamey taste, and making their thick wool highly prized. A high **dry-stone dyke**, completed in the mid-nineteenth century and running the thirteen miles around the edge of the island, keeps them off the farmland, except during lambing season, when the ewes are allowed onto the pastureland. North Ronaldsay sheep are also unusual in that they can't be rounded up by sheepdogs like ordinary sheep, but scatter far and wide at some considerable speed. Instead, once a year the islanders herd the sheep communally into a series of **dry-stone "punds"** near Dennis Head, for clipping and dipping, in what is one of the last acts of communal farming practised in Orkney.

heavily farmed, from old-style crofts whose roofs are made from huge local flagstones. With no natural harbours and precious little farmland, the islanders have been forced to make the most of what they have, and **seaweed** has played an important role in the local economy. During the eighteenth century, kelp was gathered here, burnt in pits and sent south for use in the chemicals industry.

Bird Observatory

The most frequent visitors to the island are ornithologists, who come in considerable numbers to clock the rare migrants that land here briefly on their spring and autumn migrations. The peak times of year for migrants are from late March to early June, and from mid-August to early November. However, many breeding species spend the spring and summer here, including gulls, terns, waders, black guillemots, cormorants and even the odd corncrake. The permanent **Bird Observatory** (see page 365), in the southwest corner of the island, can give advice on recent sightings.

The Lighthouses and the Wool Mill

Exhibition May–Aug daily 10am–5pm • Free • **Guided tours** by appointment • £6 or £9 with the Mill • ☎ 01857 633257, ⓦ northronaldsay.co.uk

The attractive, stone-built **Old Beacon** was first lit in 1789, but the lantern was replaced by the huge bauble of masonry you now see as long ago as 1809. The **New Lighthouse**, designed by Alan Stevenson in 1854 half a mile to the north, is the tallest land-based lighthouse in Britain, rising to a height of over 100ft. There's an exhibition on the lighthouse in one of the keepers' cottages, as well as an exhibition on the history of life on the island and a café (see below). You can also climb to the top of the lighthouse, don white gloves (to protect the brass) and admire the view – on a clear day you can see Fair Isle, and even Sumburgh and Fitful Head on Shetland. Finally, you can combine this with a tour of the island's **Wool Mill** where they turn the North Ron fleeces into yarn and felt (ⓦ northronaldsayyarn.co.uk).

ARRIVAL
NORTH RONALDSAY

By plane Your best bet is to catch a flight from Kirkwall (Mon–Sat 3 daily, 2 on Sun; 15min): if you stay the night on the island, you're eligible for a bargain £21 return fare.
By ferry The ferry direct from Kirkwall to North Ronaldsay runs just once a week (Fri; 2hr 40min), though there are also summer sailings via Papa Westray (Tues; 3hr 10min; ☎ 01856 872044).

GETTING AROUND

By minibus A minibus usually meets the ferries and planes (☎ 01857 633244) and will take you off to the lighthouse, but phone ahead to make sure.
Bike rental Bikes can be hired at the Lighthouse Visitor Centre and dropped off at the airport or ferry terminal, or at your holiday accommodation (☎ 07809 770082, ⓦ northronaldsay.co.uk; £10/day).

ACCOMMODATION AND EATING

Bird Observatory ☎01857 633200, ⓦnrbo.co.uk. You can stay at the ecofriendly bird observatory, either in an en-suite guest room or in a hostel bunk bed, or you can camp. The *Obscafé* serves decent evening meals (£15.50 for two courses) – try the mutton, washed down with Dark Island beer. Food served daily noon–2pm & evenings by arrangement. Camping per person £5, dorms £19, doubles £87

The Lighthouse ☎01857 633297, ⓦnorthronaldsay. co.uk. Great little café in the old lighthouse keepers' cottages serving snacks and affordable evening meals (by arrangement) – sample one of their North Ronaldsay mutton pies. May–Aug daily 10am–5pm; Sept–April phone ahead.

7

Shetland

FAIR ISLE

Shetland

Shetland is surprisingly different from neighbouring Orkney. While the latter lies within sight of the Scottish mainland, Shetland lies beyond the horizon, closer to Bergen in Norway than to Edinburgh, and to the Arctic Circle than to Manchester. With little fertile ground, Shetlanders have traditionally been crofters, often looking to the sea for an uncertain living in fishing and whaling or the naval and merchant services. The 23,000 islanders tend to refer to themselves as Shetlanders first, and, with the Shetland flag widely displayed, they regard Scotland as a separate entity. As in Orkney, the Mainland is the one in their own archipelago, not the Scottish mainland.

Most folk come here for the unique **wildlife** and **landscape**. Smoothed by the last glaciation, the coastline's crust of cliffs, with caves, blowholes and stacks, testifies to the continuing battle with the weather. Inland (a relative term, since you're never more than three miles from the sea), the treeless terrain is a barren mix of moorland, studded with peaty lochs.

The islands' capital, **Lerwick**, is a busy little port and the only town of any size; many parts of Mainland can be reached from here on a day-trip. **South Mainland**, a narrow finger of land that runs 25 miles from Lerwick to **Sumburgh Head**, is an area rich in archeological remains, including the offshore Iron Age **Mousa Broch** and the ancient settlement of **Jarlshof**. A further 25 miles south of Sumburgh Head is the remote but thriving **Fair Isle**, synonymous with knitwear and exceptional birdlife. The **Westside** of Mainland is sunnier but also more sparsely inhabited, as is **North Mainland**. A mile off the west coast, **Papa Stour** boasts some spectacular caves and stacks; much further out are the distinctive peaks and precipitous cliffs of the remote island of **Foula**. Shetland's three **North Isles** bring Britain to a dramatic, windswept end: **Yell** has the largest population of otters in Scotland; **Fetlar** is home to the rare red-necked phalarope; north of **Unst**, there's nothing until you reach the North Pole.

SHETLAND PONIES, SHEEP AND SHEEPDOGS

Shetland is famous for its diminutive **ponies**, but it is still a surprise to find so many of them on the islands. A local ninth-century carving shows a hooded priest riding a very small pony, but traditionally they were used as pack animals, and their tails were essential for making fishing nets. During the Industrial Revolution, Shetland ponies were exported to work in the mines in England, being the only animals small enough to cope with the low galleries. Shetlands then became the playthings of the English upper classes (the Queen Mother was patron of the Shetland Pony Stud Book Society) and they still enjoy the limelight at the Horse of the Year show. You can see them in action at the annual Viking **Shetland Pony Show** in August, or phone ahead and visit Robins Brae Shetland pony stud in Dunrossness (☎01950 460539, ⊛robinsbraeshetlandponystud.com).

Shetland sheep are also less substantial than their mainland counterparts, and are thought to be descended from those brought by the Vikings. Shetland wool comes in a wide range of colours, is very fine and is used to make the famous "Fair Isle" patterns and shawls so gossamer-thin that they can be passed through a wedding ring. To round up Shetland's small sheep, an even smaller **sheepdog** was bred, crossed with rough-coated collies. These dogs are now recognized as a separate breed, called "shelties", known for their gentleness and devotion as well as their agility and obedience. Their coat is distinctive, being long, straight and rough over a dense, furry undercoat – perfect for Shetland weather.

SHETLAND FOLK FESTIVAL

Highlights

❶ Shetland Museum Beautifully designed modern waterside museum, with imaginative displays telling the story of Shetland, and a great café too. See page 374

❷ Traditional music Catch some local music at the regular informal sessions in Lerwick, or at the annual Shetland Folk Festival. See page 375

❸ Isle of Noss Traffic-free island nature reserve where you're guaranteed to see seals, guillemots, gannets and puffins. See page 377

❹ Mousa Take a short boat trip to this remote islet, which boasts Scotland's finest 2000-year-old broch and nesting storm petrels. See page 381

❺ Jarlshof Crowd-free archeological site

mingling Iron Age, Bronze Age, Pictish, Viking and medieval settlements. See page 383

❻ Sumburgh Head Explore Shetland Mainland's southernmost lighthouse, and then enjoy the spectacular view out to Fair Isle from the lighthouse café. See page 383

❼ Fair Isle Magical little island halfway between Shetland and Orkney, with a lighthouse at each end and a world-famous bird observatory in the middle. See page 384

❽ Hermaness Run the gauntlet of the dive-bombing "bonxies" for spectacular views of nesting seabirds and Muckle Flugga, Britain's most northerly point. See page 401

HIGHLIGHTS ARE MARKED ON THE MAP ON PAGE 370

Weather has a serious influence in these parts. In winter, gales are routine, and even in the summer months it'll often be windy and rainy. The wind-chill factor is not to be taken lightly, and there's often a dampness in the air, even when it's not actually raining. While there are some good spells of dry, sunny weather (often bringing in sea mist) from May to September, it's the **simmer dim**, the twilight which lingers through the small hours at this latitude, which makes Shetland summers so memorable.

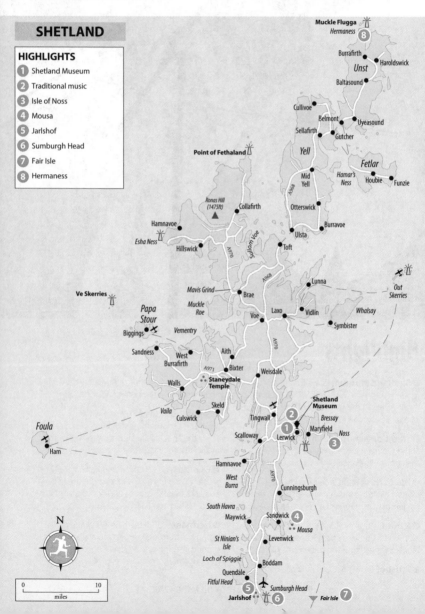

SHETLAND

HIGHLIGHTS

1. Shetland Museum
2. Traditional music
3. Isle of Noss
4. Mousa
5. Jarlshof
6. Sumburgh Head
7. Fair Isle
8. Hermaness

BÖDS

With only one Hostelling Scotland in Shetland, it's worth knowing about the islands' unique network of **camping böds** (March–Oct). Traditionally, a böd was a small building beside the shore, where fishermen stored their gear and occasionally slept; the word was also applied to trading posts established by Hanseatic merchants. Today, the tourist board uses the term pretty loosely: the places they run range from stone-built cottages to weatherboarded sail lofts. To stay at a böd, you must **book in advance** with the Shetland Amenity Trust (☏01595 694688, ⓦcamping-bods.com), as there are no live-in wardens. The more basic böds have no cooking facilities or electricity, but all have a solid fuel stove, cold water, toilets and bunk beds with mattresses – those with electricity have a meter, for which you need £1 coins. If you're camping, they're a great way to escape the wind and rain.

Brief history

Since people first began to explore the North Atlantic, Shetland has been a stepping stone on routes between Britain, Ireland and Scandinavia; people have lived here since **prehistoric times**, certainly from about 3500 BC. The **Norse settlers** began to arrive from about 800 AD, and established Shetland first as part of the Orkney earldom, ruling it directly from Norway after 1195. The Vikings left the islands with a unique cultural character, most evident today in the place names and in the **dialect**, which contains many words from **Norn**, the language spoken here until the nineteenth century. Shetland was never part of the Gaelic-speaking culture of Highland Scotland, and the later Scottish influence is essentially a Lowland one.

Scottish takeover

In 1469, Shetland followed Orkney in being **mortgaged to Scotland**, Christian I of Norway being unable to raise the dowry for the marriage of his daughter, Margaret, to James III, who annexed Shetland in 1472: the mortgage was never redeemed. Though Shetland retained links with other North Sea communities, religious and administrative practice gradually became Scottish, and **mainland lairds** set about grabbing what land and power they could. The economy soon fell into the hands of **merchant lairds**; they controlled the fish trade and the tenants who supplied it through a system of truck, or forced barter. It wasn't until the 1886 Crofters' Act and the simultaneous rise of **herring fishing** that ordinary Shetlanders gained some security. However, the boom and the prosperity it brought were short-lived and the economy soon slipped into depression.

The world wars and the oil boom

During the two world wars, thousands of naval, army and air force personnel were drafted in, and some notable relics, such as huge coastal guns, remain. **World War II** also cemented the old links with Norway, Shetland playing a remarkable role in supporting the Norwegian Resistance (see page 378). Since the 1970s, the **oil industry** has provided a substantial income, which the Shetland Islands Council (SIC) have wisely reinvested in the community, building roads, improving housing and keeping the price of ferry tickets down. In Shetland, at least, the oil boom seems set to continue for some time, with **tourism** playing only a minor role in the economy. Comparatively few travellers make it out here, and those who do are as likely to be Faroese or Norwegian as British.

ARRIVAL AND DEPARTURE   SHETLAND

By plane Loganair (☏0344 800 2855, ⓦloganair.co.uk) operate direct flights to Sumburgh airport (ⓦhial.co.uk), 25 miles south of Lerwick, from Inverness, Aberdeen, Edinburgh, Glasgow, Manchester and Kirkwall in Orkney, plus summer flights from Bergen in Norway.

By ferry NorthLink (ⓦnorthlinkferries.co.uk) runs an overnight car ferry daily from Aberdeen to Lerwick (12hr 30min), sometimes calling in at Kirkwall in Orkney on the way (14hr 30min).

GETTING AROUND AND TOURS

By plane Airtask (☎01595 840246, ⓦairtask.com/shetland-islands-Inter-island-service /shetland) runs flights from Tingwall airport, 5 miles west of Lerwick, to the more remote islands. To reach Tingwall airport, either take the bus from Lerwick bus station (Mon–Fri 10 daily, 2 on Sat; 15min), or there's a dial-a-ride taxi service, which must be booked a day in advance (☎01595 745745).

By ferry The council-run inter-island ferries (☎01595 745804, ⓦwww.shetland.gov.uk/ferries) are excellent and fares are very low.

By bus The bus network (☎01595 744868, ⓦzettrans.org.uk) is pretty good in Shetland, with buses from Lerwick to every corner of Mainland, and even via ferries across to Yell and Unst.

Car rental It's worth considering car rental once on the islands. Bolts Car Hire (☎01950 693636, ⓦboltscarhire.co.uk) and Star Rent-a-Car (☎01595 692075, ⓦstarrentacar.co.uk) have vehicles available at Sumburgh airport and in Lerwick.

Tours There's a range of escorted tours and boat trips around the Mainland, great for those without a vehicle. Specific tours are mentioned throughout the text, but Shetland Wildlife (☎01950 460939, ⓦshetlandwildlife.co.uk) offer a variety of tours and holidays, while the more adventurous might consider Sea Kayak Shetland (☎01595 840272, ⓦseakayakshetland.co.uk).

Lerwick

The focus of Shetland's commercial life, **LERWICK** is home to a third of the islands' total population. Its sheltered **harbour** is busy with ferries, fishing boats, and oil-rig supply vessels. In summer, the quayside comes alive with visiting yachts, cruise liners, historic vessels such as the *Swan* and the occasional tall ship. Behind the old harbour is the compact town centre, made up of one long main street, Commercial Street; from here, narrow lanes, known as "**closses**", rise westwards to the late Victorian new town.

Established in the seventeenth century as *Leir Vik* ("Muddy Bay") to cater for the **Dutch** herring fleet, the town was burnt down in 1614 and 1625 by the jealous folk of Scalloway, and again in 1702 by the French fleet. During the nineteenth century, with the presence of ever-larger Scottish, English and Scandinavian boats, it became a major **fishing** centre, and whalers called to pick up crews on their way to the northern hunting grounds. Business was from the jetties of buildings known as **lodberries**, several of which survive beyond the *Queen's Hotel*. **Smuggling** was part of the daily routine, and secret tunnels – some of which still exist – connected the lodberries to illicit stores. Lerwick expanded in the Victorian era, and the large houses and grand public buildings established then still dominate, notably the **Town Hall**. Another period of rapid growth began during the oil boom of the 1970s, with the farmland to the southwest disappearing under a suburban sprawl, the town's northern approaches becoming an industrial estate.

Commercial Street

Lerwick's attractive main street is the narrow, winding, flagstone-clad **Commercial Street**, whose buildings exhibit a mixed bag of architectural styles, from the powerful neo-Baroque of the Bank of Scotland at no. 117 to the plainer houses and old lodberries at the south end, beyond the *Queen's Hotel*. Here, you'll find **Bain's Beach**, a small, hidden stretch of golden sand that's one of the prettiest spots in Lerwick.

The closses

Although the narrow lanes, or **closses**, that connect the Street to Hillhead are now desirable, it's not so long ago that they were regarded as slum-like dens of iniquity, from which the better-off escaped to the Victorian new town laid out to the west on a grid plan. The steep stone-flagged lanes are fun to explore, each one lined by tall houses with trees, fuchsias, flowering currants and honeysuckle pouring over the garden walls. If you look at the street signs, you can see that all the closses have two names: their former ones and their current titles, chosen in 1845 by the Police Commissioners –

Reform, Fox and Pitt, reflecting the liberal political culture of the period – or derived from the writings of Sir Walter Scott.

Fort Charlotte

Commercial St • Daily: April–Sept 9.30–5.30pm; Oct–March 10am–4pm • Free; HES • ⓦ historicenvironment.scot

Commercial Street's northern end is marked by the towering walls of **Fort Charlotte**, which once stood directly above the beach. Begun for Charles II in 1665, the fort was attacked and burnt down by the Dutch in August 1673. In the 1780s it was repaired and named in honour of George III's queen. Since then, it's served as a prison and a Royal Navy training centre; it's now open to the public, except when used by the Territorial Army.

Town Hall

HIllhead • Mon–Fri 9am–5pm • Free • ☎ 01595 693535, ⓦ shetland.gov.uk

The Victorian new town, on the hill above the harbour, is dominated by the splendid **Town Hall**, a Scottish Baronial monument to civic pride, built by public

LERWICK

■ DRINKING & NIGHTLIFE
The Lounge	2
Mareel	1

■ ACCOMMODATION
Brentham House	1
Fort Charlotte Guest House	3
Isleburgh House Hostel	4
The Queens	6
Rockvilla Guest House	2
Woosung	5

● EATING
Fjarå	4
Fort Café	2
Gurkha Kitchen	1
Peerie Shop Café	3

8

subscription. Providing there are no functions going on, you are free to wander round the building to admire the stained-glass windows in the main hall, which celebrate Shetland's history, and to climb the castellated central tower that occupies the town's highest point.

Shetland Museum

Hay's Dock • Easter-Sept Mon–Sat 10am–5pm, Sun noon–5pm; Jan–Easter Tues–Sat 10am-4pm • Free • ☎ 01595 695057, Ⓦ shetlandmuseumandarchives.org.uk

Lerwick's chief tourist sight is the **Shetland Museum**, housed in a stylishly modern waterfront building, off Commercial Road. The permanent exhibition begins in the Lower Gallery, where you'll find replicas of the hoard of Pictish silver found at St Ninian's Isle (see page 382); the Monks Stone, thought to show the arrival of Christianity in Shetland; and a block of butter, tax payment for the King of Norway, found preserved in a peat bog. Kids can try grinding flour with a quernstone, and visit a dark "trowie knowe" where the trows live. Among the boats artistically suspended in the Boat Hall is a sixareen, once used as a mailboat to Foula. The Upper Gallery concentrates on the last two centuries of the islands' social history, from knitting and whaling to the oil industry. The museum also hosts temporary art exhibitions, puts on events and demonstrations and shows archive films. Meanwhile, out on the waterfront, the wacky Shetland Receivers emit snippets of Shetland conversation.

8 Böd of Gremista

May–Sept Tues–Sat noon–5pm • £3 • ☎ 01595 694386, Ⓦ shetlandtextilemuseum.com

Just beyond Lerwick's main ferry terminal, a mile and a half north of the town centre, stands the **Böd of Gremista**, the birthplace of **Arthur Anderson** (1792–1868), naval seaman, businessman, philanthropist, Shetland's first native MP and founder of Shetland's first newspaper, the *Shetland Journal*. The building has been completely restored and now houses the **Shetland Textile Museum**, which puts on special exhibitions on the heritage of the islands' knitting culture.

Clickimin Broch

A mile southwest of Lerwick town centre on the road leading to Sumburgh, the much-restored **Clickimin Broch** stands on what was once a small island in Loch Clickimin.

UP HELLY-AA

On the last Tuesday in January, Lerwick plays host to **Up Helly-Aa** (Ⓦ uphellyaa.org), the largest of the fire festivals held in Shetland (Jan–March). Around nine hundred torch-bearing participants, all male and all in extraordinary costumes, march in procession. The annually appointed Guizer Jarl and his "squad" appear as Vikings brandishing shields and silver axes; the other squads are dressed randomly as giant insects, space invaders, ballet dancers and the like. They all congregate at the King George V Playing Field where, after due ceremony, the torches are thrown into the longship. A firework display follows, then the squads do the rounds of a dozen "halls" (including the Town Hall) from around 8.30pm until the early hours, giving comic performances at each.

Up Helly-Aa dates from Victorian times, when it was introduced to replace the banned Christmas tradition of rolling burning tar-barrels through the streets. Although this is essentially a community event with entry by invitation only, visitors are welcome at the Town Hall – contact the tourist office in advance. To find out more, head over to the **Galley Shed** (mid-May to mid-Sept Tues 2–4 & 7–9pm, Fri 7–9pm, Sat 2–4pm; £3), on St Sunniva St, where you can view this year's longship and the costumes, shields and photographs.

LERWICK'S OTHER FESTIVALS

After the antics of Up Helly-Aa (see page 374), the **Shetland Folk Festival** (☎01595 694757, ⓦshetlandfolkfestival.com) features four days of musical mayhem, spread across the archipelago, with everything from local groups to international folk bands; book early as gigs sell out. Held over a week at Mareel, Lerwick, in July, **Fiddle Frenzy** (☎01595 743843, ⓦshetlandarts.org) shows how fiddling is central to Shetland's musical culture. It's curated by different musicians each year and includes classes for budding fiddlers. The **Shetland Accordion and Fiddle Festival** (☎01595 693162, ⓦshetlandaccordionandfiddle. com) is organized by the local accordion and fiddle club over a long weekend in mid-October. Threatening to eclipse even the Shetland Folk Festival is **Shetland Wool Week** (ⓦshetlandwoolweek.com), a week-long celebration of all things knitty in late September/ early October.

The settlement here began as a small farmstead around 700 BC and was later enclosed by a defensive wall. The main tower served as a castle and probably rose to around 40ft, as at Mousa (see page 381), though the remains are now around 10ft high. There are two small entrances, one at ground level and the other on the first floor, carefully protected by outer defences and smaller walls. With the modern housing in the middle distance, it's pretty hard to imagine the original setting.

ARRIVAL AND DEPARTURE   LERWICK

By plane Flights from outside Shetland land at Sumburgh airport, 25 miles to the south. Flights within Shetland depart from Tingwall airport.

Destinations within Shetland Fair Isle (Mon, Wed & Thurs 2–3 daily, 1 on Tues, Fri & Sat; 25min); Foula (Mon 1 daily, Tues, Wed & Fri 2 daily; 15min); Out Skerries, calling at Whalsay on request (Mon & Wed 1 daily, Thurs 2 daily; 20min); Papa Stour (Tues 2 daily; 10min). Weather conditions can affect the schedule which is reduced in winter.

By ferry NorthLink ferries (☎0845 600 0449, ⓦnorthlink ferries.co.uk) from Aberdeen (daily; 12hr 30min) and Orkney (3–4 weekly; 6hr) arrive at Lerwick's ferry terminal, about a mile north of the town centre. Ferries to other islands within Shetland leave from the town harbour.

Destinations Bressay (approximately every 30min–1hr daily; 7min); Fair Isle (alternate Thurs; 5hr); Skerries (Wed; 2hr 30min).

By bus Buses stop on the Esplanade, close to the old harbour, or at the Viking Bus Station on Commercial Rd, north of the town centre. Call ☎01595 744868 or visit ⓦzettrans.org.uk for timetables and more information.

Destinations Brae (Mon–Sat 8 daily; 45min); Hamnavoe (2–3 daily; 30min); Hillswick (Mon–Sat 3 daily; 1hr 40min); Laxo (Mon–Sat 2 daily; 40min); Levenwick (Mon–Sat 6–8 daily, 5 on Sun; 30min); Scalloway (Mon–Sat hourly, 4 on Sun; 20min); Sumburgh airport (Mon–Sat 6–7 daily, 5 on Sun; 45min); Tingwall (Mon–Fri 7 daily, Sat 4 daily; 10min); Toft (Mon–Sat 5–6 daily; 50min); Vidlin (Mon–Sat 3 daily; 45min); Voe (Mon–Fri 5 daily, 3 on Sat; 35min); Walls (Mon–Sat 6 daily; 50min).

INFORMATION

Tourist office The tourist office is at the Market Cross, Commercial St (April–Sept Mon–Sat 9am–5pm, Sun 10am–4pm; Oct–March Mon–Sat 9am–4pm; ☎01595 693434, ⓦvisitshetland.com).

Websites/newspaper For accommodation check out ⓦshetlandvisitor.com. For what's on, consult ⓦwhatson shetland.com or buy the *Shetland Times* on Fridays (ⓦshetlandtimes.co.uk).

TOURS AND ACTIVITIES

Another Shetland passion is **boating**, and regattas take place most summer weekends, throughout the islands. The sport of yoal racing has a big following, too, and teams from different districts compete in sixareens, large six-oared boats, which replaced yoals as the backbone of Shetland's fishing fleet.

Dim Riv, takes passengers on regular trips around Bressay Sound (£10).

Swan ☎01595 695193, ⓦswantrust.com. If you plan ahead, you could take a trip on the *Swan*, a restored wooden sailing ship from 1900, which undertakes trips lasting from one to nine days (from £80 for a day).

BOAT TOURS

Dim Riv ☎07901 588168. The replica Viking longship,

8

ACCOMMODATION   SEE MAP PAGE 373

Brentham House 7 Harbour St ☎01950 460201, ⓦbrenthamhouse.co.uk. Spacious, newly furnished rooms and apartments in a Victorian, bay-fronted terrace; no reception, and no proper breakfast – bookings and key pickups are organised through the sister hotel, the Sumburgh Hotel. **£85**

Fort Charlotte Guest House 1 Charlotte St ☎01595 692140, ⓦfortcharlotte.co.uk. Small guesthouse with great central location (on the south side of the fort), spacious rooms and a welcoming host. **£85**

Islesburgh House Hostel King Harald St ☎01595 745100, ⓦhostellingscotland.org.uk. Hostelling Scotland-affiliated, spacious Victorian hostel offering well-worn but comfortable accommodation, family rooms, a café, free wi-fi and laundry facilities. Dorms **£22; doubles £45**

The Queens 24 Commercial Street ☎01595 692826, ⓦkgqhotels.co.uk. In existence since the early 1860s, The Queens has an old-fashioned charm. Situated in Lerwick's conservation area, it offers comfortable rooms with most overlooking the picturesque harbour and easy access to town centre amenities. Doubles **£95**

Rockvilla Guest House 88 St Olaf St ☎01595 695804, ⓦrockvillaguesthouse.com. Refurbished in 2015, this guesthouse in one of the handsome Victorian houses in the upper part of town, is run by a very hospitable couple, who keep the place spotless and serve up top-notch breakfasts – fast, free wi-fi throughout the building. Doubles **£80**

Woosung 43 St Olaf St ☎01595 693687, ⓦshetland visitor.com/woosung. Family-run B&B, up on the hill above the harbour, run by a very friendly local landlady. The whole place is kept spotlessly clean, but not all rooms are en suite. Doubles **£60**

EATING   SEE MAP PAGE 373

Fjarå Sea Rd ☎01595 697388, ⓦfjaracoffee.com. Unlikely location (by the big Tesco), 15min walk from town, this modern, buzzy café has been a big hit with the locals – it's right by the shoreline so the views are great and sandwiches and salads (for under £10) are imaginative. Booking advised for the evening when the menu gets more adventurous (mains £14–16). Tues–Sat 8am–10pm, Sun 10am–6pm.

Fort Café 2 Commercial St ☎01595 693125. Lerwick's best fish-and-chip shop, situated below Fort Charlotte: takeaway or eat inside in the small café. Mon–Fri 11am–10.30pm, Sat 11am–7pm, Sun 4–10.30pm.

Gurkha Kitchen 33 North Rd ☎01595 690400. Reliably good curry house, with cheerful, efficient service and reasonable prices – try the Nepalese roti or the mixed balti and mop it up with some garlic naan (mains under £10), or go for the all-day Sunday buffet (£10 per person). Mon–Sat noon–2pm & 4.30–11pm, Sun 1–11pm.

Peerie Shop Café Esplanade ☎01595 692816, ⓦpeerieshop.co.uk. Designer shop/gallery/café in an old lodberry, with a good range of cakes, soup and sandwiches; and what is probably Britain's northernmost latte. Mon–Sat 9am–5.30pm.

DRINKING AND NIGHTLIFE   SEE MAP PAGE 373

The Lounge 4 Mounthooly St ☎01595 692231. Lerwick's friendliest pub, where local musicians often gather for a session in the upstairs room. Thursday night is quiz night. Daily 11am–1am.

Mareel North Ness ☎01595 745500, ⓦshetlandarts. or/venues/mareel. Lerwick's modern cultural complex is the place to come for films and gigs – and also to sink into one of the leather sofas and enjoy views over the north bay, while tucking into burger and chips, ciabatta sandwiches and salads (until 4pm), or nachos and other bar snacks. Sun–Thurs 9am–11pm, Fri & Sat 9am–1am.

Bressay and Noss

Shielding Lerwick from the full force of the North Sea is the island of **Bressay**, dominated at its southern end by the conical Ward Hill (744ft) – "da Wart" – and accessible on a regular car and passenger ferry from Lerwick (takes about 7min). The chief reason for visiting Bressay is the tiny but spectacular island of **Noss**, off the east coast, whose high cliffs support a huge seabird colony in breeding season.

Bressay Heritage Centre

Maryfield • May–Sept Tues, Wed, Fri & Sat 10am–4pm, Sun 11am–5pm • Free • ☎01595 820750

If you've time to kill before the ferry, pop into the **Bressay Heritage Centre**, by the ferry terminal, where there are temporary exhibitions on the island's history. A Bronze Age **burnt mound** – essentially a pile of discarded rocks and charcoal used in fires – has been reconstructed next to the centre. Visible to the north is **Gardie House**, built in 1724 and, in its Neoclassical detail, one of the finest of Shetland's laird houses, where the likes of Sir Walter Scott and minor royalty once stayed, and now home to the Lord Lieutenant of Shetland.

Noss

Appropriately enough for an island that slopes gently into the sea at its western end, and plunges vertically 500ft at its eastern end, **Noss** has the dramatic and distinctive outline of a half-sunk ocean liner, while its name means "a point of rock". Inhabited until World War II, it's now a nature reserve and sheep farm, managed by Scottish Natural Heritage, who operate a RIB **ferry** from Bressay.

On the island, the old farmhouse contains a small visitor centre, where the warden will give you a quick briefing and a free map. Nearby is a sandy beach, while behind the haa (laird's house) is a **Pony Pund**, a square stone enclosure built for the breeding of Shetland ponies. The most memorable feature of Noss is its eastern **sea cliffs**, rising to a peak at the massive Noup (500ft), from which can be seen vast colonies of cliff-nesting gannets, puffins, guillemots, shags, razorbills and fulmars: one of the highlights of Shetland. As Noss is only a mile or so wide, it's easy enough to walk to the sea cliffs and back (allow 4hr), but make sure you keep close to the coast, since otherwise the great skuas (locally known as "bonxies") may well dive-bomb you.

ARRIVAL AND GETTING AROUND   BRESSAY AND NOSS

By ferry The car ferry to Bressay departs from the town harbour in Lerwick (every 30min–1hr; 7min; ☎ 01595 743974) and arrives in Maryfield on the west coast. The RIB ferry to Noss (mid-April–Aug); £3 return; before setting out phone ☎ 0800 107 7818 to check times, ⓦ nature-shetland. co.uk) leaves from the east coast, 3 miles from Maryfield – an easy walk or short journey by bike, bus or car.

By bus No direct buses cross Bressay to the Noss ferry, but the bus that meets the Monday, Wednesday and Friday ferry at 1pm from Lerwick will take you part of the way.

Boat trips Shetland Seabird Tours run a 3hr sightseeing boat from Lerwick (April–Oct daily 9.45am & 2.15pm; £45; ☎ 07767 872260, ⓦ shetlandseabirdtours.com), allowing you a sea view of the vast bird colonies.

Central Mainland

The districts of Tingwall and Weisdale, plus the old capital of **Scalloway**, make up the **Central Mainland**, an area of minor interest in the grand scheme of things, but very easy to reach from Lerwick. In fine weather, it's a captivating mix of farms, moors and lochs, and includes Shetland's only significant woodland. The area also holds strong historical associations, with the Norse parliament at **Law Ting Holm**, unhappy memories of Earl Patrick Stewart's harsh rule at Scalloway and nineteenth-century Clearances at Weisdale.

Scalloway

Approaching **SCALLOWAY** from the east, there's a dramatic view over the town and the islands beyond. Once the capital of Shetland, Scalloway's importance waned through the eighteenth century as Lerwick, just six miles to the east, grew in trading success and status. Nowadays, Scalloway is fairly sleepy, though its harbour remains busy enough, with a small fishing fleet and the North Atlantic Fisheries College (NAFC) on the far side.

THE SHETLAND BUS

The story of the **Shetland Bus** – the link between Shetland and Norway that helped to sustain the Norwegian Resistance through the years of Nazi occupation – is quite extraordinary. Under threat of attack by enemy aircraft or naval action, small Norwegian fishing boats set out from Shetland to run arms and resistance workers into lonely fjords. The trip took at least 24 hours and on the return journey boats brought back Norwegians in danger of arrest by the Gestapo, or those who wanted to join Norwegian forces fighting with the Allies. For three years, through careful planning, the operation was remarkably successful: instructions to boats were passed in cryptic messages in BBC radio broadcasts. Local people knew what was going on, but the secret was generally well kept. In total, 350 refugees were evacuated, and more than 400 tons of arms, large amounts of explosives and 60 radio transmitters were landed in Norway.

Originally established at **Lunna** in the northeast of the Mainland, the service moved to **Scalloway** in 1942, partly because the village offered good marine-engineering facilities at Moore's Shipyard on Main Street, where a plaque records the morale-boosting visit of the Norwegian Crown Prince Olav. Explosives and weapons were stored in the castle, and **Kergord House** in Weisdale was used as a safe house and training centre for intelligence personnel and saboteurs. The hazards, tragedies and elations of the exercise are brilliantly described in David Howarth's book, *The Shetland Bus*; their legacy today is a heartfelt closeness between Shetland and Norway.

Scalloway Castle

If the door is locked, get the key from Scalloway Museum or Scalloway Hotel • Free; HES • ⓦ historicenvironment.scot

In spite of modern developments nearby, Scalloway is dominated by the imposing shell of **Scalloway Castle**, a classic fortified tower-house built with forced labour in 1600 by the infamous Earl Patrick Stewart, and thus seen as a powerful symbol of oppression. Stewart, who'd succeeded to the Earldom of Orkney and Lordship of Shetland in 1592, held court here, reputedly increasing his power and wealth by using harsh justice to confiscate assets. He was eventually arrested and imprisoned in 1609 for his aggression toward his fellow landowners; his son, Robert, attempted an insurrection and both were executed in Edinburgh in 1615. The castle was used for a time by Cromwell's army, but had fallen into disrepair by 1700; what remains is well preserved and fun to explore.

Scalloway Museum

Castle Street • Mid-April–Sept Mon–Sat 11am–4pm, Sun 2–4pm • £3 • ☏ 01595 880734, ⓦ scallowaymuseum.org

The **Scalloway Museum**, in an old knitwear outlet, has a café overlooking the adjacent castle. The displays range from Neolithic finds to the impact of modern aquaculture, and there's a replica wheelhouse and a longship for the kids to play with, but the most interesting section tells the story of the **Shetland Bus** (see above). There are models of some of the fishing boats that made the trip across the North Sea, a replica of the Lewis guns that were hidden in oil drums aboard the ships and a miniature radio receiver supplied to the Norwegian Resistance.

ARRIVAL AND DEPARTURE   SCALLOWAY

By bus There are regular buses to Scalloway from Lerwick (Mon–Sat hourly, 4 on Sun; 20min) and a less frequent service from Scalloway to Trondra and Burra (Mon–Sat 4 daily; 20min).

ACCOMMODATION AND EATING

The Cornerstone ☏ 01595 880346, ⓦ thecornerstonebandb.com. Bright, modern café and B&B on the corner of the main street, with five modern rooms. Café serves breakfast fry-ups until 11.30am, comfort food until 2pm, then scones and cakes after that. Café Mon–Sat 9.30am–5pm, Sun noon–5pm. Doubles __£80__

Da Haaf ☏ 01595 772480, ⓦ nafc.uhi.ac.uk/facilities. Unpretentious restaurant in the NAFC with views over Scalloway

harbour. Simple, super-fresh grilled fish dishes (£12–16), high-quality fish and chips and tasty home-made puddings (£6–7). Mon–Fri 8.30am–4pm, Fri & Sat 5.30–9pm.

Scalloway Hotel ☎ 01595 880444, ⓦ scallowayhotel. com. Well-established hotel on the harbour front – ask for a harbour-view room if possible. The hotel restaurant serves up pretty impressive dishes (mains around £22), but you can also eat well in the bar (mains £14–18) – both menus feature lots of local fish and seafood. Food served Mon–Sat noon–3pm & 5–9pm, Sun noon–8pm. Doubles <u>£140</u>

Trondra

Southwest of Scalloway – and connected to the Mainland by a bridge since 1971 – is the island of **Trondra**, where you can visit a working crofthouse. Pick up a leaflet and a bucket of feed for the hens from the barn, and head off along the **Croft Trail**, which takes you to see the ducks, down to the shore (a good picnic spot), over to a restored watermill and then through a field of orchids and other wild flowers.

Burra

Burra Bridge connects Trondra with the twin islands of East and West **Burra**, which have some beautiful beaches and some fairly gentle coastal walks.

West Burra

West Burra has the largest settlement in the area, **HAMNAVOE**, unique in having been planned by the local landlord as a fishing port. Just south of Hamnavoe, a small path leads down from the road to the white sandy beach at **Meal**. At the southern end of West Burra, at **Banna Minn**, is another fine beach, with excellent walking nearby on the cliffs of Kettla Ness, linked to the rest of West Burra only by a sliver of tombolo.

East Burra

East Burra, joined to West Burra at the middle like a Siamese twin, ends at the hamlet of **HOUSS**, distinguished by the tall, ruined laird's house or haa. From the turning place outside the cattle-grid, continue walking southwards, following the track to the left, down the hill and across the beach, and after about a mile you'll reach the deserted settlement of **Symbister**, inhabited until the 1940s. You can now see ancient field boundaries and, just south of the ruins, a **burnt mound**. Half a mile further south, the island ends in cliffs, caves and wheeling fulmars.

Tingwall and around

TINGWALL, the name for the loch-studded, fertile valley north of Scalloway, takes its name from the **Lawting** or Althing (from *thing*, the Old Norse for "parliament"), in existence from the eleventh to the sixteenth century, where local people and officials gathered to make or amend laws and discuss evidence. The Lawting was situated at **Law Ting Holm**, the small peninsula at the northern end of the Loch of Tingwall that was once an island linked to the shore by a causeway. Structures on the holm have long since vanished, but an information board helps in visualizing the scene. At the southwest corner of the loch, a seven-foot **standing stone** by the roadside is said to mark the spot where, after a dispute at the Lawting in 1389, Earl Henry Sinclair killed his cousin and rival, Marise Sperra, together with seven of his followers.

Tingwall Kirk

Just north of the Loch of Tingwall is **Tingwall Kirk**, unexceptional from the outside, but preserving its simple late eighteenth-century interior. In the burial ground, a dank, turf-covered **burial aisle** survives from the medieval church demolished in 1788. Inside are several very old gravestones, including one to a local official called a *Foud* – a representative of the king – who died in 1603.

Weisdale Mill

May–Oct Mon–Sat 10.30am–5pm, Sun 11am–5pm; Nov–April Wed–Fri 11am–3pm, Sat & Sun 11am–4pm • Free • ☎ 01595 745750, ⓦ shetlandarts.org

The parish of **WEISDALE**, five miles northwest of Tingwall, is notable primarily for **Weisdale Mill**, situated up the B9075 from the head of Weisdale Voe. Built for milling grain in 1855, this is now an attractively converted arts centre, housing the small, beautifully designed **Bonhoga Gallery**, in which touring and local exhibitions of painting, sculpture and other media are shown.

ARRIVAL AND DEPARTURE TINGWALL AND AROUND

By plane Tingwall airport (☎ 01595 840246), about a mile north of the Loch of Tingwall, is the main airport for flights to other islands within Shetland.

By bus There are buses from Lerwick's Viking Bus Station to Tingwall (Mon–Fri 5 daily, Sat 2 daily; 10min) and to Weisdale (Mon–Sat 2–5 daily; 20min). To get to Tingwall airport, you can either walk the half mile from the Tingwall crossroads or pre-order the Dial-a-Ride scheduled service (☎ 01595 694617).

ACCOMMODATION AND EATING

Herrislea House Hotel Veensgarth ☎ 01595 840208, ⓦ herrisleahouse.co.uk. North of the loch and a stone's throw from the airport, this large hotel has nine, individually decorated, en-suite bedrooms. The husband and wife team serve an excellent breakfast to see you on your way before your flight the next morning. Doubles **£125**

Weisdale Mill ☎ 01595 745750, ⓦ shetlandarts. org. Weisdale Mill has a lovely little café, serving soup, quiches and snacks in a suntrap south-facing conservatory overlooking the stream. May–Oct Tues–Sat 10.30am–5pm, Sun 11am–5pm; Nov–April Wed–Fri 11am–3pm, Sat & Sun 11am–4pm.

8

South Mainland

Shetland's **South Mainland** is a long, thin finger of land, only three or four miles wide but 25 miles long, ending in the cliffs of **Sumburgh Head** and **Fitful Head**. It's a beautiful area with wild undulating landscapes, lots of good green farmland, fabulous views out to sea and the mother of all brochs on the island of **Mousa**, just off the east coast in **Sandwick**. The most concentrated points of interest are in **Dunrossness**, at the southern end of the peninsula, with its seabird colonies, crofting museum, and **Jarlshof**, Shetland's most impressive archeological site.

Sandwick

SANDWICK is a township made up of a number of close but distinct settlements, about halfway down the east coast of South Mainland. Most visitors come here to take a boat from Leebotton to the island of **Mousa**, under a mile off the coast, which boasts the most amazingly well-preserved broch in the whole of Scotland.

Mousa

Day-trip April–mid-Sept Mon–Fri 11.30am, Sun 1.30pm; takes 15min • £16 • **Storm petrel trip** Late-May–mid-July Mon, Wed & Sat 10.30pm; 2hr 30min • £25 • Advance booking necessary; ☎ 07901 872339, ⓦ www.mousa.co.uk

If the weather's fine, you could easily spend the whole day on **Mousa**, watching the seals sun themselves on the rocks in the southeastern corner of the island, and looking out for black guillemots (or "tysties" as they're known locally) and arctic terns, which breed here.

Mousa Broch

Mousa's main attraction is **Mousa Broch**, which features in both *Egil's Saga* and the *Orkneyinga Saga*, contemporary chronicles of Norse exploration and settlement. In the former, a couple eloping from Norway to Iceland around 900 AD take refuge in it after being shipwrecked, while in the latter the broch is besieged by an Earl Harald Maddadarson when his mother is abducted and brought here from Orkney by Erlend the Young, who wanted to marry her. Rising to more than 40ft, and looking rather like a Stone Age cooling tower, Mousa Broch has a remarkable presence, its low entrance-passage passing through two concentric walls to a central courtyard, divided into separate beehive chambers. Between the walls, a rough (very dark) staircase leads to the top parapet; a torch is provided for visitors.

Thousands of **storm petrels** breed around the broch, fishing out at sea during the day and only returning to the nests after dark. The ferry runs special late-night trips, setting off in the "simmer dim" twilight around 11pm. Even if you've no interest in the storm petrels, which appear like bats as they flit about in the half-light, the chance to explore the broch at midnight is worth it alone.

Sandsayre Interpretive Centre
April–mid-Sept daily 10am–5pm • Free • ⓦ shetlandheritageassociation.com

Beside the Stevenson-built Sandsayre Pier, from which you catch the boat to Mousa, is an **interpretive centre**. It's really just a glorified waiting room (handy in bad weather) with some local history displays, but there's also an old boatshed with a restored flitboat, originally used to transport sheep to Mousa for grazing, and a good account of the remarkable story of Betty Mouat who survived nine days lost at sea, at the age of sixty.

Hoswick Visitor Centre
May–Sept Mon–Sat 10am–5pm, Sun 11am–5pm • Free • ☎ 01950 431406, ⓦ shetlandheritageassociation.com

In Hoswick, a mile or so southwest of Leebotton, **Hoswick Visitor Centre** has a fantastic collection of vintage radios, and a permanent exhibition on crofting, haaf fishing, whaling, and the copper and iron mines beyond Sand Lodge. The Betty Mouat story (see above) is also told here, and a café serves cakes, tea and coffee.

Dunrossness

Shetland's southernmost parish is known as **DUNROSSNESS** or "The Ness", a rolling agricultural landscape (often likened to that of Orkney), dominated in the southwest by the great brooding mass of Fitful Head (929ft). The main road leads eventually to **Sumburgh**, whose **airport** is busy with helicopters and aircraft shuttling to and from the North Sea oilfields, as well as passenger services, and **Grutness**, the minuscule **ferry terminal** for Fair Isle. It's worth venturing this far to see the Neolithic and Viking remains at **Jarlshof** and the lighthouse and the seabirds (including puffins) at **Sumburgh Head**.

St Ninian's Isle

On the west coast of South Mainland, a signposted track leads down from the village of **BIGTON** to a spectacular sandy causeway, or **tombolo**, which connects the Mainland to **St Ninian's Isle**. The tombolo – a concave strip of shell sand with Atlantic breakers crashing on either side – is usually exposed; you can walk over to the island, where there are the ruins of a church probably dating from the twelfth century and built on the site of an earlier, Pictish, one. Excavated in the 1950s, a hoard of 28 objects of Pictish silver was found beneath a slab in the floor of the earlier building. It included bowls, a spoon and brooches, thought to date from around 800 AD. Replicas are in the Shetland Museum and the originals in the Museum of Scotland in Edinburgh.

Loch of Spiggie

South of Bigton, the coast is attractive: cliffs alternate with beaches and the vivid greens and yellows of the farmland contrast with black rocks and a sea which may be grey, deep blue or turquoise. The **Loch of Spiggie**, which used to be a sea inlet, attracts large autumn flocks of some two hundred whooper swans. A track leads from the east side of the loch to a long, reasonably sheltered sandy beach known as the **Scousburgh Sands** or Spiggie Beach.

Crofthouse Museum

May–Sept daily 10am–1pm & 2–5pm • Free (donations welcomed) • ☎ 01950 460557, ⊕ shetlandheritageassociation.com

Housed in a well-to-do thatched croft in Southvoe, built around 1870, the **Crofthouse Museum** re-creates the feel of crofting life, with a peat fire, traditional box-beds and so forth. Adjacent to the living quarters is the byre for the cows and tatties, and the kiln for drying the grain. Crofting was mostly done by women in Shetland, while the men went out haaf-net fishing for the laird. Down by the nearby burn, there's also a restored thatched horizontal mill.

Quendale Mill

Mid-April–mid-Oct daily 10am–5pm • £4 • ☎ 01950 460969, ⊕ quendalemill.co.uk

A few miles south of the Loch of Spiggie lies the beautifully restored full-size **Quendale Mill**, in the village of the same name, overlooking a sandy south-facing bay. It was built in the 1860s but not in operation since the early 1970s; you can explore the interior and watch a short video of the mill working, and there's a tearoom attached.

Old Scatness Broch and Iron Age Village

Mid-May–Aug Fri 10.15am–4.30pm (check ahead) • £5 • ☎ 01595 694688, ⊕ shetlandamenity.org

Extending the airport revealed a vast Iron Age archeological site known as **Old Scatness Broch and Iron Age Village**. At the centre of the site are the remains of an Iron Age broch, surrounded by a settlement of interlocking wheelhouses – so-called because of their circular ground plan – two of which have been either partially or wholly reconstructed.

Jarlshof

Daily: April–Sept 9.30am–5.30pm; Oct–March (restricted hour call ahead) • £6; HES • ☎ 01856 841815, ⊕ historicenvironment.scot

Of all the archeological sites in Shetland, **Jarlshof** is the largest and most impressive. What makes Jarlshof so amazing is the fact that you can walk right into a house built 1600 years ago, which is still intact to above head height. The site is big and confusing, scattered with the ruins of buildings dating from the Bronze Age to the early seventeenth century. The name, which is misleading as it is not primarily a Viking site, was coined by Sir Walter Scott, who used the ruins of the Old House in his novel *The Pirate*. However, it was only at the end of the nineteenth century that the Bronze Age, Iron Age and Viking settlements were discovered, after a violent storm ripped off the top layer of turf.

The Bronze Age smithy and Iron Age dwellings nearest the entrance, dating from the second and first millennia BC, are nothing compared with the cells which cluster around the **broch**, close to the sea. Only half of the original broch survives, and its courtyard is now an Iron Age aisled roundhouse, with stone piers. It's difficult to distinguish the broch from the later Pictish **wheelhouses** that now surround it, but it's all great fun to explore, as you're free to roam around the cells, checking out the in-built stone shelving, water tanks, beds and so on. Inland lies the maze of grass-topped foundations marking out the **Viking longhouses**, from the ninth century AD. Towering over the whole complex are the ruins of the laird's house, built by Robert Stewart, Earl of Orkney and Lord of Shetland, in the late sixteenth century, and the **Old House of Sumburgh**, built by his son, Earl Patrick.

Sumburgh Head Lighthouse

Daily: April–Sept 11am–5.30pm • Entry £6 • ☎ 01595 694688, ⊕ sumburghhead.com

8

The Mainland comes to a dramatic end at **Sumburgh Head** (262ft), which rises sharply out of the land only to drop vertically into the sea. The road up to it is the perfect site for watching nesting seabirds such as kittiwakes, fulmars, shags, razorbills and guillemots, as well as gannets diving for fish. This is also the easiest place in Shetland to get close to **puffins**: during the nesting season (May to early Aug), you simply need to look over the western wall, just before you enter the lighthouse complex, to see them arriving at their burrows a few yards below with beaks full of sand eels or giving flying lessons to their offspring.

You can visit the clifftop lighthouse, built by Robert Stevenson in 1821, and explore some of the outbuildings, including the reconstructed World War II secret radar hut which helped protect the Royal Navy anchored in Scapa Flow. As well as a visitor centre with an exhibition on the history of the lighthouse, there's a **Marine Life Centre**, with hard-hitting displays on the worrying recent decline in seabird numbers. After roaming the complex, you can settle down and enjoy the sea views from the lighthouse's **café** (closed for refurbishment at time of writing).

ARRIVAL AND DEPARTURE   SOUTH MAINLAND

By plane Sumburgh airport, at the southernmost tip of South Mainland, is Shetland's main airport. There's a bus service to Lerwick (Mon–Sat 6–7 daily, 5 on Sun; 45min) or else it's a £44 taxi ride (☎01950 460560).

By bus There are regular buses from Lerwick to Levenwick (Mon–Sat 7–8 daily, 5 on Sun; 30min); Sandwick (Mon–Sat 8–10 daily, 5 on Sun; 25min); Sumburgh (Mon–Sat 6–7 daily, 5 on Sun; 45min).

ACCOMMODATION AND EATING

Betty Mouat's Cottage Scatness ☎01595 694688, ⓦcamping-bods.com. Next to an excavated broch and not far from the airport, this stone-built cottage is a camping böd with two bedrooms, hot water, a solid-fuel stove and an electricity meter (£1 coins needed). March–Oct. Dorms £12
Levenwick Campsite Levenwick ☎01950 422320, ⓦlevenwick.shetland.co.uk. Small, terraced campsite run by the local community with hot showers and laundry facilities and a superb view over the east coast. May–Sept. Per pitch £11
★ **Mucklehus** Levenwick ☎01950 422370, ⓦmucklehus.co.uk. A lovely B&B run by a local artist in a former Master Mariner's house built in 1890 near the sandy beach in Levenwick, 18 miles south of Lerwick; the rooms

are small, but stylish. Doubles £80
Solbrekke B&B Park Rd, Sandwick ☎01950 431410. Surrounded by lovely gardens overlooking the island of Mousa Broch, this two double-bedroom property is in an ideal spot from which to explore South Mainland's attractions. Doubles £100
The Spiggie Dunrossness ☎01950 460409, ⓦthespiggie hotel.co.uk. Guesthouse with six en-suite rooms and two self-catering apartments. The restaurant has great views out to Foula and, if you're lucky, incredible sunsets. Bar meals are priced around £12, or you can have well-presented dishes such as lobster or whatever the local catch is, à la carte in the restaurant (mains £14–20). Food served Mon & Tues 6–10pm, Wed–Sun noon–2.30pm & 6–10pm. Doubles £125

Fair Isle

Marooned in the sea halfway between Shetland and Orkney, **Fair Isle** is very different from both. The weather reflects its isolated position: you can almost guarantee that it'll be windy, though if you're lucky your visit might coincide with fine weather – what the islanders call "a given day". Fair Isle's population had tumbled from 400 to 44 by the 1950s, at which point evacuation was seriously considered. The laird, **George Waterston**, who'd set up a bird observatory in 1948, passed it into the care of the NTS in 1954 and rejuvenation began. Today, Fair Isle supports a community of around sixty.

The north end of the island rises like a wall, while the Sheep Rock, a sculpted stack of rock and grass on the east side, is another dramatic feature. The croft land and the island's scattered white houses are concentrated in the south. Fair Isle has two **lighthouses**, one at either end of the island, both designed by the Stevenson family and erected in 1892. Earlier, the Vikings used to light beacons to signal an enemy fleet advancing, and in the nineteenth century a semaphore consisting of a tall wooden pole was used; it can still be seen on the hill above South Lighthouse. The North Lighthouse was considered to be on such an exposed spot that the foghorn was operated from within. The South Lighthouse has the distinction of having a short, very challenging, six-hole golf course, and can be visited by appointment (Info@ southfairisle.scot; £5).

Fair Isle Bird Observatory

01595 760258, fairislebirdobs.co.uk

A devastating fire destroyed the Fair Isle Bird Observatory (FIBO) in March 2019. The building will be reconstructed in 2022 and hopefully open to the public in 2023 – check the website for updates. Standing just above the sandy bay of North Haven, where the ferry from Shetland Mainland arrives, it housed an exhibition on the island past and present, and served as one of the major European centres for ornithology. Fair Isle is a landfall for a huge number and range of migrant birds during the spring and autumn passages. Migration routes converge here, and more than 345 species, including many rarities, have been noted. As a result, Fair Isle is a haven for twitchers, who descend on the island in planes and boats whenever a major rarity is spotted; for more casual birders, however, there's also plenty of summer resident birdlife to enjoy.

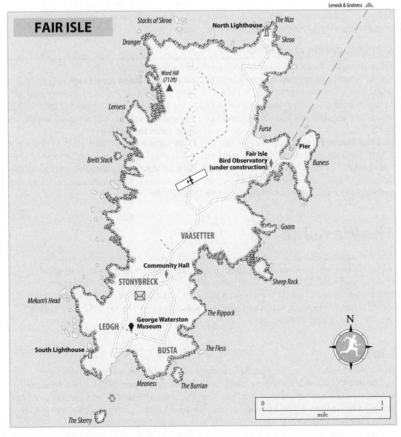

The high-pitched screeching that fills the sky above the airstrip comes from hundreds of **arctic terns**, and arctic skuas can also be seen here. Those in search of **puffins** should head for the cliffs around Furse, while to find **gannets** aim for the spectacular Stacks of Scroo.

George Waterston Museum

May–Sept Mon, Tues & Thurs 2–4pm, Wed 10am–noon • Free • ☎ 01595 760244 ⓦ shetlandheritageassociation.com

Fair Isle is known for its **knitting** patterns, still produced with great skill by the local knitwear cooperative. There are samples on display at the **George Waterston Museum**, next to the Methodist Chapel. Particularly memorable are stories of shipwrecks; in 1868 the islanders undertook a heroic rescue of all 465 German emigrants aboard the *Lessing*. More famously, *El Gran Grifon*, part of the retreating Spanish Armada, was lost here in 1588 and three hundred Spanish seamen were washed up on the island. Food was in such short supply that fifty died of starvation before help could be summoned from Shetland.

ARRIVAL AND DEPARTURE
FAIR ISLE

By plane Airtask (☎ 01595 840246, ⓦ airtask.com) flies from Tingwall to Fair Isle April-Oct (Mon–Sat 1–3 daily) and from Sumburgh (Sat only) for around £90 return.

By ferry The passenger ferry connects Fair Isle with either Lerwick (alternate Thurs; 4–5hr) or Grutness in Sumburgh (Tues, alternate Thurs & Sat; 3hr); since the boat only takes a limited number of passengers, it's advisable to book in advance (☎ 01595 760363). The crossing can be rough, so if you're susceptible to seasickness it's worth considering flying.

ACCOMMODATION AND EATING

If you're staying over, book accommodation in advance and note that camping is not permitted. There are no eating out options hence all accommodation is booked on a full-board basis. There is a shop/post office, Stackhoull Stores, in the south of the island (closed Tues & Sat afternoon, and all day Thurs & Sun).

Auld Haa Guesthouse Close to the Museum ☎ 01595 760349. The accommodation may not be fancy but the warm-hearted, easy-going host offers tasty nutritious food and great local knowledge. Excellent views from the garden include the chance to see gannets plunging into the shimmering sea. Doubles **£150**

Fair Isle Guest House Upper Leogh 1.5 miles south of the airport ☎ 01595 760248, ⓦ kathycoull.com. You'll be well looked after at this whitewashed crofthouse B&B by spinning and weaving expert, Kathy Coull, who also runs textile courses. Doubles **£100**

South Light House 2 miles south of the airport ☎ 07755 2566231. B&B at the southernmost tip of the island, not literally in the lighthouse, but in the adjacent keepers' cottages – note bathrooms are not en suite. Doubles **£140**

The Westside

The western Mainland of Shetland – known as the **Westside** – stretches west from Weisdale and Voe to Sandness. Although there are some important archeological remains and wildlife in the area, its greatest appeal lies in its outstanding **coastal scenery** and walks. Cut by several deep voes, the coastline is very varied; aside from dramatic cliffs, there are intimate coves and some fine beaches, as well as, just offshore, the stunning island of **Papa Stour**.

Sandsting

In the south, on the picturesque **Sandsting** peninsula, there's a very sheltered voe (inlet) by **SKELD**, with a working harbour and a marina. There are also two beautiful terracotta-coloured **sandy bays** just a mile to the east at **REAWICK**, and excellent **coastal walks** to be had, to the southwest, around Westerwick and Culswick, past red-granite cliffs, caves and stacks.

Walls and around

Once an important fishing port, **WALLS** (pronounced *waas*), appealingly set round its harbour, is now a quiet village which comes alive once a year in the middle of August for the Walls Agricultural Show, the biggest farming bash on the island. If you're just passing by, you might like to stop by the **bakery and tearoom**, but Walls also has several good **accommodation** options.

Stanydale Temple

Three miles east of Walls lies the finest Neolithic structure in the Westside, dubbed the **Stanydale Temple** by the archeologist who excavated it because it resembled a temple on Malta. Whatever its true function, it was twice as large as the surrounding oval-shaped houses (now in ruins) and was certainly of great importance, perhaps as some kind of community centre. The horseshoe-shaped foundations measure more than 40ft by 20ft internally, with immensely thick walls, still around 4ft high, whose roof would have been supported by spruce posts (two postholes can still be clearly seen). To reach the temple, take the path marked out by black-and-white poles across the moorland for half a mile from the road.

Vaila

A short distance across the sea south of Walls lies the island of **Vaila**, from where in 1837 Lerwick philanthropist Arthur Anderson operated a fishing station in an unsuccessful attempt to break down the system of fishing tenures under which tenants were forced to fish for the landlords under pain of eviction. The ruins of Anderson's fishing station still stand on the shore, but the most conspicuous monument is **Vaila Hall**, the largest laird's house on Shetland, originally built in 1696, but massively enlarged by a wealthy Yorkshire mill-owner, Herbert Anderton, who bought the island in 1893. Anderton also restored the island's ancient watchtower of Mucklaberry Castle, built a Buddhist temple (now sadly in ruins), and had a cannon fired whenever he arrived on the island. The island is currently owned by Dorota Rychlik, an equally eccentric Polish émigré, and her husband, Richard Rowland. They welcome visitors, who should make a point of popping into the Whalehouse at Cloudin, where they'll find the 42ft skeleton of a young male **sperm whale** – nicknamed "Bony Dick" – who washed up on the island in 2000. Enquire at *Burrastow House* (☎01595 809307) about transport.

8

Sandness

At the end of a long winding road across an undulating, uninhabited, boulder-strewn landscape, you eventually reach the fertile scattered crofting settlement of **SANDNESS** (pronounced "saaness"), which you can also reach by walking along the coast from Walls past the dramatic Deepdale and across Sandness Hill. It's an oasis of green meadows in the peat moorland, with a nice beach, too.

Jamieson's Spinning Mill

ⓦ jamiesonsofshetland.co.uk

The family-run **Jamieson's Spinning Mill** at Sandness is the only one on Shetland producing pure Shetland wool. Sadly, the modern factory is no longer open for tours but there is a shop (often unmanned) where you can buy a range of products. If you ask, they might even give you a quick glimpse behind the scenes.

ARRIVAL AND DEPARTURE   **THE WESTSIDE**

By bus There's an infrequent bus service between Lerwick and Skeld (Mon–Sat 1–3 daily; 1hr), and between Lerwick and Walls (Mon–Sat 5–6 daily; 45min), with a feeder service from Sandness (Mon–Sat 2–3 daily; 45min) – some journeys are dial-a-ride and need to be booked in advance (☎01595 745745).

ACCOMMODATION AND EATING

SKELD

Skeld böd ☎ 01595 694688, ⓦ camping-bods.com. A lovely old whitewashed building overlooking the campsite and the harbour, with one room and six beds; there's electricity, a solid-fuel stove and a small shop and café in the local creamery. March–Oct. Dorms £̲1̲2̲

Skeld campsite ☎ 01595 860287 ⓦ skeldcaravanpark. co.uk. A flat patch of grass (with hard standing and electric points), right by the pier and marina in the sheltered port of Skeld. The campsite's little, white, weatherboarded amenity block (with kitchen) is positively picturesque. Per pitch £̲1̲4̲

WALLS AND AROUND

Bo's B&B 1.5 miles southwest of Walls ☎ 01595 809258, ⓦ bosimmons.wix.com/bosbandb. One double room for

B&B in a newly built ecofriendly house, a glamping-style bothy and a wooden camping pod for the hardy, situated on the road from Walls to Burrastow. May–Sept. B&B £̲8̲0̲, bothy £̲2̲0̲, pods £̲1̲0̲

★ **Burrastow House** 3 miles southwest of Walls ☎ 01595 809307, ⓦ burrastowhouse.co.uk. Beautifully situated off the beaten track southwest of Walls, parts of the house date back to 1759 and have real character; others are more modern. The cooking is superb and evening meals are available for non-residents, too. Doubles £̲1̲2̲0̲

Voe House Walls ☎ 01595 694688, ⓦ camping-bods. com. This five-bedroom camping böd is Shetland's largest, with its own peat fire. Note that *Voe House*, confusingly, is not in Voe but in Walls. March–Oct. Dorms £̲1̲2̲

Papa Stour

A mile offshore from Sandness is the rocky island of **Papa Stour**, formed of volcanic lava and ash and subsequently eroded into some of the most impressive coastal scenery in Shetland. In good weather, it makes for a perfect day-trip, but in foul weather or a sea mist it can certainly appear pretty bleak. Its name, meaning "big island of the priests", derives from its early Celtic Christian connections, and the island was home, in the eighteenth century, to people who were mistakenly believed to have been lepers (it seems more likely they were suffering from vitamin deficiency).

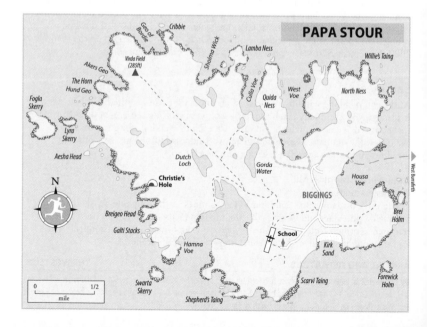

8

WALKING ON PAPA STOUR

Ordnance Survey Explorer map 467

The chief attraction of Papa Stour is **walking**; to reach the best of the coastal scenery, head for the far west of the island. From **Virda Field** (285ft), the highest point, in the far northwest, you can see the treacherous rocks of **Ve Skerries**, where a lighthouse was erected as recently as 1979. The couple of miles of coastline from here southeast to **Hamna Voe** has some of the island's best stacks, blowholes and natural arches. The most spectacular is **Kirstan's Hole**, a group of partly roofed clefts, extending far inland, where shags nest on precipitous ledges. Other points of interest include a couple of defunct horizontal click-mills, below **Dutch Loch**, and the remains of a "meal road", so-called because the workmen were paid in oatmeal or flour. In addition, several pairs of red-throated divers regularly breed on inland lochs such as **Gorda Water**.

The land is fertile, and in the nineteenth century Papa Stour supported a community of three hundred, but by the early 1970s there was a population crisis. With just sixteen inhabitants, and no children, the islanders made appeals for new blood to revive the fragile economy and staged a dramatic recovery, releasing croft land to young incomers. Papa Stour was briefly dubbed "the hippie isle". A new harbour and roll-on-roll-off ferry in 2005 gave the island some hope, but the school is currently closed, there is no accommodation apart from wild camping and the population is now around 20 people.

Papa Stour's main settlement, **BIGGINGS**, lies in the east near the pier, and it was here that excavation in the early 1980s revealed the remains of a thirteenth-century Norse house or "**stofa**", thought to have belonged to the future King Haakon V of Norway. In 2008, the house was partially reconstructed; an explanatory panel explains its significance.

ARRIVAL AND DEPARTURE   PAPA STOUR

By plane Airtask (☎ 01595 840246, ✈ airtask.com) flies from Tingwall twice every Tuesday (around £75 return).

By ferry The ferry runs from West Burrafirth, 5 miles north of Walls, to Papa Stour (Wed, Fri & Sat 2 daily, Sun 1 daily; 40min; ☎ 01955 745804) – book in advance, and reconfirm the day before departure.

Foula

Separated from the nearest point on Shetland's Mainland by about fourteen miles of often turbulent ocean, **Foula** is without a doubt the most isolated inhabited island in the British Isles. Seen from the Mainland, its distinctive mountainous form changes subtly, depending upon the vantage point, but the outline is unforgettable. Its western **cliffs**, the second highest in Britain after those of St Kilda, rise at **The Kame** to some 1220ft above sea level; a clear day at The Kame offers a magnificent panorama stretching from Unst to Fair Isle. On a bad day, the isolation and exposure are complete and the cliffs generate turbulent blasts of wind known as "flans", which rip through the hills with tremendous force.

Arriving on Foula, you can't help but be amazed by the sheer size of the island's immense, bare mountains, whose summits are often hidden in cloud, known on the Mainland as "Foula's hat". The gentler eastern slopes provide good crofting land, and plentiful peat, and it is along this "green belt" that the island's population is scattered. The only road runs along the eastern side of the island, and is used by Foula's remarkable fleet of clapped-out vehicles.

Foula's name is derived from the Old Norse for "bird island" and it's home to a quarter of a million **birds**. Arctic terns wheel overhead at the airstrip, red-throated divers can usually be seen on the island's smaller lochs, while fulmars, guillemots, razorbills, puffins and gannets cling to the rock ledges. However, it's the island's colony of **great skuas** or "bonxies" that you can't fail to notice, with an estimated 3000 pairs on Foula, making it the largest colony in the world. During the nesting season (May–Aug), they attack anyone who comes near. Although their dive-bombing antics are primarily meant as a threat, they can make walking across the moorland fairly stressful: the best advice is to hold a stick above your head or stick to the road and the coast.

Brief history

Foula has been inhabited since prehistoric times, and the people here take pride in their separateness from Shetland, cherishing local traditions such as the observance of the **Julian calendar** (officially dropped in Britain in 1752), where Old Yule is celebrated on January 6 and New Year doesn't arrive until January 13. Foula was also the last place that **Norn**, the old Norse language of Orkney and Shetland, was spoken as a first language, in the eighteenth century, and more of the Shetland dialect survived here than elsewhere. Foula's population peaked at two hundred at the end of the nineteenth century, and today numbers around forty.

ARRIVAL AND DEPARTURE   FOULA

By plane Airtask (☎01595 840246, ⌨airtask.com) flies from Tingwall (Mon 1 daily, Tues, Wed & Fri 2 daily, 15min); tickets cost around £86 return.

By ferry Be sure to book and reconfirm your journey by ferry (☎01595 840208, ⌨bkmarine.org), which departs from Walls (Tues & Thurs; additional sailings in summer subject to weather conditions; 2hr). The ferry arrives at Ham, in the middle of Foula's east coast.

INFORMATION AND TOURS

Tourist information Foula has its own resident part-time Rangers, who usually greet new arrivals and offer local advice (mid-April to Oct). It's also possible to arrange for guided walks with a Ranger (Wed & Fri; ☎01595 753236, ⌨foulaheritage.com), or you can download self-guided walk leaflets from the website. There's no shop on the

WALKING ON FOULA

Ordnance Survey Explorer map 467
Many people come to Foula to view the island's famous cliffs – though in actual fact they are very difficult to appreciate except from the air or the sea. If the weather's fine, though, it's worth climbing to the top of **The Sneug** (1373ft), for the views stretching from Unst to Fair Isle. From the airstrip, climb up the southeast ridge of **Hamnafield** (1130ft), and then continue along the ridge of Brustins to The Sneug itself. From The Sneug, drop down to **The Kame** (1220ft), Foula's sheer cliff, the best view of which is from Nebbiefield, to the south. Return via Da Nort Bank to Soberlie Hill, from where you can pick up the island's road. In total it's only a walk of five or six miles, but it'll take three to four hours. If you're coming from the ferry at Ham, it's probably best to do the circuit in reverse, which is no bad thing, as the climb from Soberlie Hill up Da Nort Bank is one of the most exhilarating on the island, as the edge of the hill is an ever-increasing vertical drop.

There are other, more gentle, walks on Foula. The coastal scenery to the north of the island, beyond Mucklegrind, features several stacks and natural arches, with the waves crashing over skerries, and seals sunning themselves. One of the easiest places to spot seabirds is from beyond the graveyard in Biggings, past Hametoun. The nearby hill of **The Noup** (803ft) is a relatively easy climb, compared to The Sneug, and, if you descend to the northwest, it brings you to **Sneck o' da Smallie**, where there's a narrow slit in the cliffs, some 200ft high. You can return to the airstrip by heading back down the valley known as The Daal, although the bonxies are pretty thick on the ground. All Foula's cliffs are potentially lethal, especially in wet weather, and all the usual safety precautions should be taken (see page 42).

island, so bring your own supplies.
Boat trips Day-trips are not possible on the regular ferry, but The Swan Trust (☎ 01595 695193, ⌨ swantrust.com) do boat trips on Wednesdays from Walls.

8

ACCOMMODATION

Leraback Foula ☎ 01595 753226. Other than self-catering, the only accommodation on Foula is at this B&B near Ham. It's a simple but very welcoming place to stay; full board only and they'll collect you from the airstrip or pier. Doubles **£80**

North Mainland

The **North Mainland**, stretching over thirty miles from the central belt around Lerwick, is wilder than much of Shetland, with relentlessly bleak moorland and some rugged and dramatic coastal scenery. It's all but split in two by the isthmus of **Mavis Grind**: to the south lies **Sullom Voe**, Shetland's oil terminal, and **Brae**, the area's largest town; to the north is the remote region of **Northmavine**, boasting some of Shetland's most scenic cliffs.

Voe

If you're travelling north, you're bound to pass by **VOE**, but if you stay on the A970 it's easy to miss the picturesque old village, a tight huddle of homes and workshops down below the road around the pier (signposted "Lower Voe"). Set at the head of a deep, sheltered sea loch, Voe has a Scandinavian appearance, helped by the presence of the **Sail Loft**, painted in a rich, deep red. The building was originally used by fishermen and whalers for storing their gear; later, it became a knitwear workshop, and it was here that woollen jumpers were knitted for Edmund Hillary's 1953 Mount Everest expedition. Today, the building has been converted into a large **camping böd**.

ACCOMMODATION AND EATING   VOE

Sail Loft By the harbour ☎ 01595 694688, ⌨ camping-bods.com. Originally a giant storeroom, this enormous böd is situated right by the loch and has hot showers, a kitchen and a solid-fuel fire in the smaller of the two rooms. Bring £1 coins for the electricity meter. March–Oct. Dorms **£12**

Lunnasting

Lunnasting is the area to the northeast of Voe, on the east coast. The main town is **VIDLIN**, departure point for the Out Skerries (see page 395), three miles east of Laxo, which is the ferry terminal for Whalsay (see page 394).

The Cabin Museum

Tues, Thurs, Sat & Sun 1–5pm • Free • ☏ 01806 577232 ⓦ shetlandheritageassociation.com

Halfway between Laxo and Vidlin, the B9071 passes **The Cabin Museum**, a modern barn packed to the rafters with wartime memorabilia collected by the late Andy Robertson. You can try on some of the uniforms and caps or pore over the many personal accounts of the war written by locals.

Lunna

The long, thin peninsula of Lunna Ness, to the northeast of Vidlin, is pinched in the middle at the tiny remote settlement of **LUNNA**. It was here, at **Lunna House**, originally built in 1660, that the Shetland Bus made its headquarters during World War II (see page 378). Down the hill from Lunna House lies the little whitewashed **Lunna Kirk**, built in 1753, with a simple, tiny interior including a carved hexagonal pulpit. On the outside wall is a "lepers' squint", through which those believed to have the disease (then believed to be highly contagious) could participate in the service without risk of infecting the congregation; there was, however, no leprosy here, the outcasts in fact suffering from a hereditary, non-infectious skin condition brought on by malnutrition. In the graveyard, several unidentified Norwegian sailors, torpedoed by the Nazis, are buried.

8

Brae

BRAE, a sprawling settlement that still has the feel of a frontier town, was expanded hastily in the 1970s to accommodate the workforce for the **Sullom Voe Oil Terminal**, the largest of its kind in Europe, situated just to the northeast of the town. During World War II Sullom Voe was home to the Norwegian Air Force and a base for RAF seaplanes.

ACCOMMODATION AND EATING   BRAE

★ **Busta House** ☏ 01806 522506, ⓦ bustahouse.com. A laird's house with stepped gables that sits across the bay from Brae. Even if you're not staying the night here, it's worth coming for lunch in the Long Room, for a stroll around the wooded grounds, or for the excellent set-menu meal (£35) in the Pitcairn Restaurant. Doubles £120

Frankie's ☏ 01806 522700, ⓦ frankiesfishandchips.com. A popular fish and chip café with great views over Busta Voe. As well as fish straight off the boats, you can get king scallops, smoked haddock and mussels. Mon–Sat 9am–8pm, Sun noon–8pm.

Northmavine

Northmavine, the northwest peninsula of North Mainland, is unquestionably one of the most picturesque areas of Shetland, with its often rugged scenery, magnificent coastline and wide-open spaces. The peninsula begins a mile west of Brae at **Mavis Grind**, a narrow isthmus at which it's said you can throw a stone from the Atlantic to the North Sea, or at least to Sullom Voe. Just by the roadside here, there's a great little display on the area's incredible **geodiversity**, thanks to its violent, volcanic past.

Hillswick

HILLSWICK, the main settlement in the area, is situated on another narrow isthmus, and was once a centre for deep-sea or haaf fishing, and later a herring station. In

1900, the North of Scotland, Orkney & Shetland Steam Navigation Company built the **St Magnus Hotel** to house their customers, importing it in the form of a timber kit from Norway. Despite various alterations over the years, it still stands overlooking St Magnus Bay, rather magnificently clad in mustard plasterwork and black timber.

Down by the ancient harbour, **Da Böd** was founded by a Hanseatic merchant in 1684, later became Shetland's oldest pub and is now the Hillswick Wildlife sanctuary (ⓦhillswickwildlifesanctuary.org), where visitors are welcome to visit from May to September after 2pm. The sanctuary is embarking on a major project to upgrade the facilities that will provide a visitor centre with art, crafts, photos and literature on an environmental and wildlife theme. The stony beach by the harbour is very sheltered, but the sandiest **beach** is on the west side of the Hillswick isthmus, overlooking Dore Holm.

Esha Ness

Just outside Hillswick, a side road leads west to the exposed headland of **Esha Ness**, celebrated for its splendid coastline views. Spectacular red-granite **cliffs**, shaped into fantastic forms by the elements, spread out before you as the road climbs away from Hillswick: to the south, out at sea, are the stacks known as **The Drongs** off the Ness of Hillswick, while in the distance the Westside and Papa Stour are visible. After three miles, you reach *Braewick* café and campsite, where there's a great view over the wide bay of Brae Wick, from which several small dead-end roads lead off to the coast.

Tangwick Haa Museum

Easter–Sept daily 11am–5pm • Free • ☎ 01806 503389, ⓦ tangwickhaa.org.uk

One small dead-end road, off the main road, leads south to the **Tangwick Haa Museum**, housed in a seventeenth-century building, which, through photographs, old documents and fishing gear, tells the often moving story of this remote corner of Shetland and its role in the dangerous trade of deep-sea fishing and whaling. All ages will also enjoy the shells and the Shetland wool and sand samples.

Stenness fishing station

West of Braewick, the road divides, with the southern branch leading to the remains of **Stenness fishing station**, once one of the most important haaf-fishing stations in Shetland. A few ruined böds used by the fishermen are still visible along the sloping pebbly beach where they would dry their catch. In the early nineteenth century, as many as eighteen trips a year were made in up to seventy open, six-oared boats, known as "sixareens", to the fishing grounds thirty or forty miles to the west. A Shetland folk song, *Rowin' Foula Doon*, recalls how the crews rowed so far west that the island of Foula began to sink below the eastern horizon.

Esha Ness Lighthouse

West of Braewick, where the road divides, the northernmost branch ends at **Esha Ness Lighthouse**, a great place to view the red-sandstone cliffs, stacks and blowholes of this stretch of coast. An information board at the lighthouse details some of the dramatic geological features here, and if the weather's a bit rough you should be treated to some spectacular crashing waves. One of the features to beware of here are the blowholes, some of which are hidden far inland. The best example is the **Holes of Scraada**, a partly roofed cleft, half a mile north of the lighthouse, where the sea suddenly appears three hundred yards inland from the cliff line. The incredible power of the sea can be seen in the various giant boulder fields above the cliffs: these **storm beaches** are formed by rocks torn from the cliffs in storms and deposited inland.

8

HILLSWICK AND AROUND

Almara Urafirth ☎01806 503261, ⓦwww.almara. shetland.co.uk. This modern B&B – up on a hill overlooking Ura Firth – serves up a friendly family welcome, big breakfasts and excellent views. £80

St Magnus Bay Hotel Hillswick ☎01806 503372, ⓦstmagnusbayhotel.co.uk. Large, distinctive mustard and black hotel with large, high-ceilinged public rooms, and rooms ranging from the spacious to the cosy. The restaurant serves generous and filling portions – the Sunday carvery is particularly popular. £130

ESHA NESS

Braewick café and campsite Braewick, 4 miles northwest of Hillswick ☎01806 503345, ⓦeshaness. moonfruit.com. Café with great views of the Drongs, serving soup, sandwiches and toasties, plus home-made cakes and scones (daily 10am–5pm. The campsite is pretty exposed but you can always book one of the four wooden wigwams if the wind gets too much. Food served daily 10am–5pm. Wigwams £48; camping per pitch £12

Johnnie Notions Böd Hamnavoe, 1.5 miles north of Braewick ☎01595 694688, ⓦcamping-bods.com. One of the few places to stay in Esha Ness, this tiny four-bed böd – the birthplace of a pioneer in smallpox inoculation – is in a remote hamlet of Hamnavoe, north of Braewick. There's no electricity and cold water only, but there is a solid-fuel stove. March–Oct. Dorms £10

Whalsay

The island of **Whalsay**, known in Shetland as the "Bonnie Isle", is in a world of its own, with a friendly community of over a thousand, devoted almost entirely to fishing, and a dialect even other Shetlanders struggle to fathom. The islands' fishing crews operate a very successful pelagic fleet of immense super-trawlers which can fish far afield in all weathers, catching a wide range of species. The island is also extremely fertile, but crofting takes second place to fishing here; there are also plentiful supplies of peat, which can be seen in spring and summer, stacked neatly to dry out above huge peat banks, ready to be bagged for the winter.

Although the majority of folk live in or around Symbister, the rest of Whalsay – which measures roughly two miles by eight – is quite evenly and fairly densely populated. Of the prehistoric remains, the most notable are the two **Bronze Age houses** on the northeastern coast of the island, half a mile south of Skaw, known respectively as the "Benie Hoose" and "Yoxie Biggins". The latter is also known as the "Standing Stones of Yoxie", due to the use of megaliths to form large sections of the walls, many of which still stand.

Symbister

Ferries from the Mainland arrive at **SYMBISTER** in the southwest, whose harbour is usually dominated by the presence of several of the island's sophisticated, multi-million-pound purse-netters, some over 180ft long; you'll also see smaller fishing boats and probably a few "fourareens", which the locals race regularly in the summer months.

Pier House

Mon–Sat 9am–1pm & 2–5pm, Sun 2–4pm • Free

Across the busy harbour from the ferry berth stands the tiny grey-granite **Pier House**, the key for which resides in the shop opposite. This picturesque little building, with a hoist built into one side, is thought to have been a Hanseatic merchants' store, and contains a good display on how the Germans traded salt, tobacco, spirits and cloth for Whalsay's salted, dried fish from medieval times until the eighteenth century; close by is the Harbour View house, thought to have been a Hanseatic storehouse or booth.

Whalsay Heritage Centre

May–Sept Wed & Fri–Sun 2–5pm; Oct–April Thurs 7–9pm • £3 • ☎01806 566397, ⓦ whalsayheritage.co.uk

Overlooking the town is the imposing Georgian mansion of **Symbister House**, built in grey granite and boasting a Neoclassical portico. It was built in the 1830s at great expense by the laird Robert Bruce, reputedly not because he wanted to live on Whalsay but because he wanted to deprive his heirs of his fortune. It's now part of the local school, though you can still see the old doocot behind the house, and various outbuildings in the Midden Court, one of which houses a **heritage centre** on the history of the island.

Grieve House

About half a mile east of Symbister at the hamlet of **SODOM** – an anglicized version of Sudheim, meaning "South House" – is **Grieve House** (now a camping böd but temporarily closed), the modest former home of celebrated Scots poet, writer and Communist **Hugh MacDiarmid** (1892–1978), born Christopher Grieve in the Borders town of Langholm. He stayed here from 1933 until 1942, writing about half of his output, including much of his best work: lonely, contemplative poems honouring fishing and fishermen, with whom he sometimes went out to sea. At first, he seems to have fallen in love with the islands, but poor physical and mental health, exacerbated by chronic poverty, dogged him. Eventually, unwillingly conscripted to work in a Glasgow munitions factory, he left with his new wife and young son, never to return.

ARRIVAL AND DEPARTURE | WHALSAY

By ferry Car ferries run regularly to Whalsay from Laxo on the Mainland (☎01595 743973; 30min) – book ahead to take a car. In bad weather, especially southeasterly gales, the service operates from Vidlin instead. Laxo–Symbister (roughly every 45min; 30min).

8

ACCOMMODATION AND EATING

Oot Ower Lounge and Campsite Huxter ☎01806 566658. A family-run pub overlooking the Loch of Huxter – this is pretty much the only place to eat and drink on the island (phone ahead to check they're open and serving food), with fish and chips for around £10, and somewhere to camp. Per pitch £10

SHOPPING

Shoard Brough, 2 miles northeast of Symbister. The country's remotest charity and recycling shop is in Brough, halfway between Symbister and the golf course. It has limited opening hours, but is a must if you're in the area. Shetland's take on Aladdin's Cave. Wed, Thurs & Sat 2–4pm.

Out Skerries

Four miles out to sea, off the northeast tip of Whalsay, the **Out Skerries** ("Oot Skerries" or plain "Skerries" as the locals call them) consist of three tiny low-lying rocky islands, Housay, Bruray and Grunay, the first two linked by a bridge, with a population of around seventy. That people live here at all is remarkable, and that it is one of Shetland's more robust communities is astonishing, its livelihood based on fishing from a superb, small natural harbour and on salmon farming in a nearby inlet. There are good, if short, walks, with a few prehistoric remains, but the majority of visitors are divers exploring the wreck-strewn coastline, and ornithologists who come here when the wind is in the east, hoping to catch a glimpse of rare migrants.

The Skerries' jetty and airstrip are both on the middle island of **Bruray**, which boasts the Skerries' highest point, Bruray Wart (173ft), an easy climb, and home to the islands' ingenious spiral-channel collection system for rainwater, which can become scarce in summer. The easternmost island, **Grunay**, is now uninhabited, though the abandoned lighthouse keepers' cottages on the island's chief hill remain; despite appearances, the Stevenson-designed lighthouse itself sits on the outlying islet of Bound Skerry. The largest of the Skerries, **Housay**, has the most indented and intriguing coastline, to which you should head if the weather's fine.

ARRIVAL AND DEPARTURE | OUT SKERRIES

By ferry Ferries to and from Skerries leave from Vidlin on the Mainland (Mon & Fri–Sun; 1hr 30min) and Lerwick (Wed; 2hr 30min), but day-trips are only possible from Vidlin (Fri & Sun). Make sure you book your journey by 5pm the previous evening (☎01595 745804), or the ferry might not run. You can take your car over, but, with less than a mile of road to drive along, it's not necessary.

ACCOMMODATION

Camping is allowed, with permission. There is a shop, and a shower/toilet block by the pier.

Rocklea ☎01806 515228, ⊕rockleaok.co.uk. The only B&B on the islands is a modern crofthouse on Bruray run by the very welcoming Johnsons, who offer optional full board. Doubles £100

The North Isles

Many visitors never make it out to Shetland's trio of **North Isles**, thinking that they are too remote, which is a shame, as the ferry links are, in fact, frequent and inexpensive, and the roads fast. Much of the scenery is the familiar Shetland landscape of undulating peat moorland, dramatic coastal cliffs and silent glacial voes. However, with Lerwick that much further away, the spirit of independence and self-sufficiency in the North Isles is much more keenly felt. **Yell**, the largest of the three, is best known for its vast otter population, but is otherwise often overlooked. **Fetlar**, the smallest of the trio, is home to the rare red-necked phalarope, but **Unst** has probably the widest appeal, partly as the most northerly landmass in the British Isles, but also for its nesting seabird population. Note that **public transport** on all three islands is very limited, and that often it's necessary to book your journey the day before to ensure that the service runs.

Yell

Historically, **Yell** hasn't had good write-ups. The writer Eric Linklater described it as "dull and dark", while the Scottish historian George Buchanan claimed it was "so uncouth a place that no creature can live therein, except such as are born there". If you keep to the fast main road, which links the island's two ferry terminals of **Ulsta** and **Gutcher**, you'll pass a lot of uninspiring peat moorland. Get onto the minor roads, though, and you'll begin to appreciate the island and have more chance of spotting one of Yell's numerous **otters**. The coastline is gentler and greener than the interior, and is relieved by several voes, natural harbours used as hiding places by German submarines during World War II.

Burravoe and around

At **BURRAVOE**, in the southeastern corner of Yell, there's a lovely whitewashed laird's house dating from 1672, with crow-stepped gables, that now houses the **Old Haa Museum** (April–Sept Mon–Thurs & Sat 10am–4pm, Sun 2–5pm; free; ☎01957 722339, ⊕oldhaa.com), which is stuffed with artefacts, and has lots of material on the history of the local herring and whaling industry; there's a very pleasant wood-panelled café on the ground floor, too. Back at the crossroads stands **St Colman's Kirk**, completed in 1900, featuring an apsed chancel and several winsome Gothic windows, and surmounted by a tiny little spire. From May to August, you'll find thousands of **seabirds** (including puffins) nesting in the cliffs above Ladies Hole, less than a mile to the northeast of the village.

YELL, UNST & FETLAR

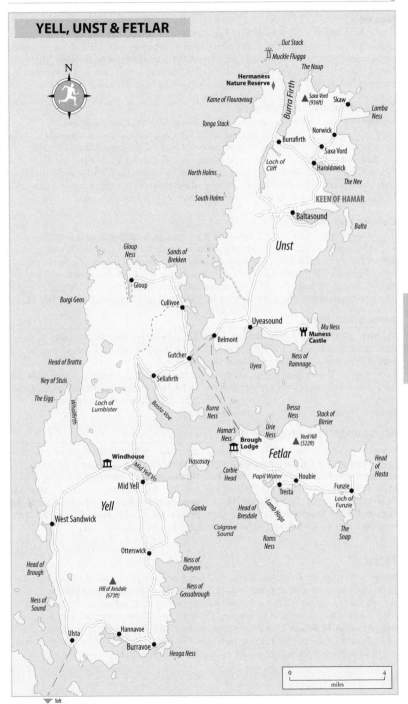

N

Out Stack
Muckle Flugga
The Noup

**Hermaness
Nature Reserve**
Kame of Flouravoug

Saxa Vord
(936ft)

Skaw

Lamba
Ness

Norwick

Tonga Stack

Burrafirth

Saxa Vord

Loch of
Cliff

Haroldswick

The Nev

North Holms

KEEN OF HAMAR

South Holms

Baltasound

Balta

Unst

Gloup
Ness

Sands of
Brekken

Gloup

Burgi Geos

Cullivoe

Uyeasound

Mu Ness
**Muness
Castle**

Belmont

Head of Bratta

Gutcher

Uyea

Ness of
Ramnage

Ney of Stuis

Sellafirth

The Eigg

Loch of
Lumbister

Bosta Voe

Burra
Ness

Tressa
Ness

Stack of
Birrier

Hamar's
Ness

Urie
Ness

Vord Hill
(522ft)

**Brough
Lodge**

Fetlar

Windhouse

Hascosay

Head
of
Hosta

Yell

Mid Yell Vo

Corbie
Head

Papil Water

Houbie

Mid Yell

Tresta

Funzie

Loch of
Funzie

West Sandwick

Gamla

Head of
Bresdale

Lamb Hoga

The
Snap

 Otterswick

Colgrave
Sound

Rams
Ness

Head of
Brough

Ness of
Queyon

Hill of Arisdale
(673ft)

Ness of
Gossabrough

Ness of
Sound

Ulsta

Hannavoe

Burravoe

Heoga Ness

8

0   4
miles

Toft

Mid Yell

The island's largest village, **MID YELL**, has a small marina, a couple of shops and a leisure centre with a swimming pool. A mile northwest of the village, on a hill above the main road, stands the spooky, abandoned eighteenth-century **Windhouse**; skeletons were found under the floor and in its wood-panelled walls, and the house is now believed by many to be haunted (its ghost-free lodge is a camping böd; see page 371).

Shetland Gallery and Global Yell

Shetland Gallery · Easter–Sept Tues–Sat 11am–5pm, Sun 2–5pm · Free · ☎ 01957 744386, ⓦ shetlandgallery.com

Two miles east of Gutcher, the ferry terminal for Unst, the main road passes the diminutive Sellafirth Business Park, where you'll find the **Shetland Gallery**, Britain's northernmost art gallery, a pleasant, modern space displaying local artists' works. Across the car park is **Global Yell** (ⓦ globalyell.org), a Centre for Creative Industries in Shetland, specifically weaving (and singing); they're extremely welcoming and you can have a go at a miniature loom, or sign up for one of their longer courses.

Cullivoe and around

To the north of Gutcher, around **CULLIVOE** the landscape is relatively gentle, with attractive coastal scenery. The **Sands of Brekken** are made from crushed shells, and are beautifully sheltered in a cove a mile or two north of Cullivoe. A couple of miles to the west, the road ends at **GLOUP**, with its secretive, narrow voe. In the nineteenth century, this was one of the largest haaf-fishing stations in Shetland; a memorial commemorates the 58 men who were lost when a great storm overwhelmed six of their sixareens in July 1881.

8

ARRIVAL AND TOURS
YELL

By ferry ☎ 01595 745804, ⓦ www.shetland.gov.uk. Ferries to Ulsta (Yell) from Toft on the Mainland are very frequent (every 30min–1hr; 20min), as are ferries from Gutcher across the Bluemull Sound to Belmont (Unst) and Hamar's Ness (Fetlar) – note it's cash or cheque only on the ferries.

By bus An integrated bus and ferry service from Lerwick goes all the way to Gutcher (Mon–Sat 1 daily; 2hr 10min). On Yell, buses from Ulsta run to Gutcher (Mon–Sat 3–4 daily; 30min).

Guided tours Local otter spotter John Campbell (☎ 01806 577358) takes groups of two or three in search of otters (£150 a day for a couple) – book in advance.

ACCOMMODATION AND EATING

Quam West Sandwick ☎ 01957 766256, ⓦ quambandbyellshetland.co.uk. Large, kit-built Scandinavian-style working croft with sheep, ducks, hens and Shetland ponies on site. There are wonderful sea views across Yell Sound, and dinner is available for an extra £15 a head. Doubles £80

Tearoom Old Haa Museum ☎ 01957 722339. Enjoy home-baked cakes and a welcome cup of tea or coffee beside a lovely old fireplace adorned with fire irons. April–Sept Mon–Thurs & Sat 10am–4pm, Sun 2–5pm.

Windhouse Lodge camping böd Mid Yell ☎ 01595 694688, ⓦ camping-bods.com. The Windhouse gatehouse, on the main road near Mid Yell, has a wood- and peat-fired heater and hot showers. Bring £1 coins for the electricity meter. March–Oct. Dorms £12

Fetlar

Fetlar is the most fertile of the North Isles, much of it grassy moorland and lush green meadows with masses of summer flowers. It's known as "the garden of Shetland", though that's pushing it a bit, as it's still a fairly unforgiving, treeless landscape. Around nine hundred people once lived here and there might well be more than sixty now, were it not for **Sir Arthur Nicolson** who, in the first half of the nineteenth century, cleared many of the people at forty days' notice to make room for sheep. Today Fetlar's population lives on the southern and eastern sides of the island.

Brough Lodge
Sir Arthur Nicolson's architectural tastes were rather more eccentric than some other local tyrants; but still astonishing **Brough Lodge**, a rambling castellated composition built in stone and brick in the 1820s, can be seen about a mile south of the ferry terminal, and owes something – perhaps an apology – to Gothic, Classical and maybe even Tudor styles. Nicolson is also responsible for the nearby round-tower folly, which was built with stone from the abandoned crofthouses. The building has been left to rot but attempts to raise funds to breath life back into Brough Lodge are underway (⊛broughlodge.org).

Vord Hill
Much of the northern half of the island around Fetlar's highest point, **Vord Hill** (522ft), is now an RSPB reserve. As well as harbouring important colonies of arctic skua and whimbrel, Fetlar is perhaps best known for having harboured Britain's only breeding pair of **snowy owls**, which bred on Stackaberg, to the southwest of Vord Hill, from 1967 to 1975.

Houbie and around
At the tiny main settlement, **HOUBIE**, in the centre of the island on the south coast, there's a rather less adventurously styled laird's house called Leagarth, with an impressive conservatory, built by Fetlar's most famous son, Sir William Watson Cheyne (1852–1932), who, with Lord Lister, pioneered antiseptic surgery. You can learn more about Cheyne's colourful life from the nearby **Fetlar Interpretive Centre** (May–Sept Mon–Sat 11am–4pm, Sun 12.30–4pm; £2; ☎01957 733206, ⊛fetlar. org), a welcoming museum with information on Fetlar's outstanding birdlife and the archeological excavations that took place near Houbie. For a sandy bay in which to relax, the **Sand of Tresta** is less than a mile to the west

Loch of Funzie
Fetlar is one of very few places in Britain where you'll see the graceful **red-necked phalarope** (late May–early Aug): the birds are unusual in that the female does the courting and then leaves the male in charge of incubation. A hide has been provided overlooking the marshes (or mires) to the east of the **Loch of Funzie** (pronounced "Finny"); the loch itself is also a good place at which to spot the phalaropes, and is a regular haunt of red-throated divers.

8

ARRIVAL AND GETTING AROUND
FETLAR

By ferry Ferries to Fetlar (Mon–Sat 6–9 daily; Sun 5 daily; 25–40min) depart regularly from both Gutcher (Yell) and Belmont (Unst), and dock at Hamar's Ness, three miles northwest of Houbie.

By bus There's a Funzie to Hamar's Ness service (Mon–Sat 3–4 daily), which is a dial-a-ride electric minibus service

– to use it you must book your journey the day before (☎01595 745745).

By car If you do have your own vehicle, bear in mind that there's no petrol station on Fetlar, so fill up before you come across.

ACCOMMODATION AND EATING

Aithbank Böd Aith ☎01595 694688, ⊛camping-bods. com. A cosy wood-panelled cottage, a mile east of Houbie, with two rooms, sleeping a total of seven. Hot water and kitchen including cooker with grill and hotplates. March–Oct. Dorms **£10**

Fetlar Café Houbie ☎01957 733227. The island's only café lives inside the island shop/post office in Houbie. Cooked breakfasts, soup, sandwiches, toasties or an omelette all for £4 or under. Daily 10am–4.30pm, shorter hours in winter.

Gord Houbie ☎01957 733227, ✉gord@fetlarshetland. co.uk. The modern house attached to the island shop in Houbie is also a B&B with great sea views from all the rooms. All guests are full board only, and they do meals for non-residents by arrangement. Doubles **£150**

Unst

Much of **Unst** is rolling grassland – a blessed relief for some after the peaty moorland of Yell – but the coast is more dramatic: a fringe of cliffs relieved by some beautiful sandy beaches. As Britain's most northerly inhabited island, there is a surfeit of "most northerly" sights, and many visitors only come here in order to head straight for Hermaness, to see the seabirds and look out over Muckle Flugga and the northernmost tip of Britain, to the North Pole beyond. The island's population plummeted in 2006 following the closure of the local RAF radar base at Saxa Vord, which used to employ a third of the population.

Uyeasound and around

On the south coast, not far from the ferry terminal, is **UYEASOUND**, with Greenwell's Booth, an old Hanseatic merchants' warehouse by the pier, sadly now roofless. Further east lie the ruins of **Muness Castle**, a diminutive defensive structure, with matching bulging bastions and corbelled turrets at opposite corners. It was built in 1598 by the Scots incomer, Laurence Bruce, stepbrother and chief bullyboy of the infamous Earl Robert Stewart, and probably designed by Andrew Crawford, who shortly afterwards built Scalloway Castle for Robert's son, Patrick. The inscription above the entrance asks visitors "not to hurt this vark aluayis", but the castle was sacked by Danish pirates in 1627 and never really re-roofed. A little to the north is a vast sandy beach, backed by the deserted crofting settlement of Sandwick.

Baltasound and around

Unst's main settlement is **BALTASOUND**, five miles north of Uyeasound; its herring industry used to boost the local population of around five hundred to as much as ten thousand during the fishing season. As you leave Baltasound, heading to Haroldswick, be sure to take a look at **Bobby's bus shelter**, an eccentric, fully furnished, award-winning Shetland bus shelter on the edge of town.

The **Keen of Hamar**, east of Baltasound, and clearly signposted from the main road, is one of the largest expanses of serpentine debris in Europe, and is home to an extraordinary array of plant life. It's worth taking a walk on this barren, exposed, almost lunar landscape that's thought to resemble what most of northern Europe looked like at the end of the last Ice Age. With the help of one of the Scottish Natural Heritage leaflets (kept in a box by the stile or download it from www.nature.scot) you can try to identify some of the area's numerous rare and minuscule plants, including Norwegian sandwort, frog orchid, moonwort and the mouse-eared Edmondston's chickweed, which flowers in June and July and is found nowhere else in the world.

From the Keen of Hamar to Haroldswick, the main road crosses a giant boulder field of **serpentine**, a greyish-green, occasionally turquoise rock found widely on Unst, and which weathers to a rusty orange.

Haroldswick

Beyond the Keen of Hamar, the road drops down into **HAROLDSWICK**, where near the shore you'll find the **Unst Boat Haven** (May–Sept Mon–Sat 11am–4pm, Sun 2–4pm; ☎01957 711809; £3; ⓦunstheritage.com), displaying a beautifully presented collection of historic boats with many tools of the trade and information on fishing. If you want to learn about other aspects of Unst's history, head for the nearby **Unst Heritage Centre** (May–Sept Mon–Sat 11am–4pm, Sun 2–4pm; £3; ☎01957 711528 ⓦunstheritage. com), housed in the old school building by the main crossroads, where they also put on have-a-go activities such as spinning, knitting and potting.

Saxa Vord

Just north of Haroldswick is **SAXA VORD** (also, confusingly, the name of the nearby hill), home to the eyesore former **RAF base**, containing self-catering accommodation, a restaurant, bar and hostel, where there's also a basic café and an **exhibition** on the history of the RAF on Unst (☎01957 711711; ⌨saxavord.com). The former base is also home to Britain's most northerly brewery, the **Valhalla Brewery**, source of Shetland Ales (visits by appointment; ☎01957 711658, ⌨valhallabrewery.co.uk), and **Shetland Reel**, its most northerly gin distillery (April–Sept Tues, Thurs & Sat visits by appointment; ☎01957 711217, ⌨shetlandreel.com).

Hermaness Nature Reserve

To the west of Burra Firth lies the bleak headland of **Hermaness**, now a National Nature Reserve and home to more than 100,000 nesting seabirds (May–Aug). There's an excellent **visitor centre** in the former lighthouse keepers' shore station, where you can pick up a leaflet showing the marked routes across the heather, which allow you access into the reserve. Whatever you do, stick to the path so as to avoid annoying the vast numbers of nesting great skuas.

From Hermaness Hill, you can look down over the jagged rocks of the wonderfully named Vesta Skerry, Rumblings, Tipta Skerry and **Muckle Flugga**. There are few more dramatic settings for a lighthouse than Muckle Flugga, and few sites could ever have presented as great a challenge to the builders, who erected it in 1858. Beyond Muckle Flugga is **Out Stack**, the most northerly bit of Britain, where Lady Franklin landed in 1849 in order to pray (in vain, as it turned out) for the safe return of her husband from his expedition to discover the Northwest Passage, undertaken four years previously. The views from here are inevitably marvellous, as is the birdlife; there's a huge gannetry on one of the stacks, and puffins burrow all along the clifftops. The walk down the west side of Unst towards Westing is one of the finest in Shetland: if the wind's blowing hard, the seascape is memorably dramatic.

8

ARRIVAL AND INFORMATION   UNST

By ferry Ferries (☎01595 745804) shuttle regularly across Bluemull Sound from Gutcher on Yell over to Belmont on Unst (every 30min–1hr; 10min).

By bus An integrated bus and ferry service goes from Lerwick to Baltasound on Unst (Mon–Sat 1–2 daily; 2hr 40min). From Belmont, Unst's ferry terminal, buses run to Baltasound (Mon–Sat 3–4 daily; 15min), Haroldswick (Mon–Sat 3–4 daily; 30min) and Uyeasound (Mon–Sat 3–4 daily; 10min).

Tourist Information See ⌨visit-unst.com for detailed up-to-date information.

ACCOMMODATION

Bordanoost Lodge Haroldswick ☎07792 384625; ⌨bordanoostlodge.co.uk. Newly renovated, three en-suite double rooms with quality furnishings and extra special touches have views over either the cliffs or beach and gardens. Doubles **£90**

Gardiesfauld Uyeasound ☎01957 755279, ⌨www. gardiesfauld.shetland.co.uk. A large, clean, modern hostel near Uyeasound pier which allows camping, and offers bike rental. April–Sept. Dorms **£16**; camping per person **£8**

EATING AND DRINKING

Baltasound Hotel Baltasound ☎01957 711334, ⌨baltasoundhotel.co.uk. Wherever you stay, it's a good idea to book yourself in for dinner or self-cater – the only other option is the bar food at the *Baltasound Hotel* (mains £12–18). Food served daily 5.45–8.15pm.

Saxa Vord Restaurant ☎01957 711711; ⌨saxavord. com. Delicious and homely meals incorporate only the best local produce: mains (£10–18.50) might include Shetland lamb shank or Highland chicken breast stuffed with haggis. A hearty carvery is served on Sundays. May–Sept daily 6–9pm.

Skibhoul Café & Stores Baltasound ☎01957 711444. The island's main shop is attached to the local bakery (founded in 1885). As well as freshly made bread and cakes, the speciality pizzas and quiche are popular – there's also a self-service café and reading corner in the store. Mon–Sat 9.30am–5.30pm.

Victoria's Vintage Tea Room Haroldswick ☎01957 711885, ⌨victoriasvintagetearooms.co.uk. Bone china, patterned bunting and checked tablecloths for a surreal "high tea" experience in this cheerful tearoom close to Unst Boat Haven, with views across the bay. April–Sept Tues–Sat 11am–5pm, Sun noon–4pm (call to check in winter).

LEWIS CHESSMEN

Contexts

History

It's hard to look at a landscape in the Scottish Highlands and Islands and not have a sense of the stories from history swirling around, from the ancient Stone Age settlers whose dwellings and stone circles are still so well preserved around the Northern and Western Isles, to the empty villages and lonely glens depopulated during the Clearances. Unusually for Europe, the history of the region is dominated more by the wildness of the sea and harshness of the landscape than by the politics of London or Paris, and even Edinburgh has often felt distant, another landscape, another language and another difficult journey away.

Prehistoric Scotland

Scotland's first inhabitants were Mesolithic **hunter-gatherers**, who arrived as the last Ice Age retreated around 8000 BC. They lived initially in the area south of Oban, where heaps of animal bones and shells have been excavated in the caves on the Mull of Kintyre and on the plains north of Crinan. From here there is evidence of their moving onto the islands of Arran, Jura, Rùm, Skye and Lewis, where the damp and relatively warm coastal climate would have been preferable to the harsher inland hills and glens. Around 4500 BC, **Neolithic farming peoples** from the European mainland began moving into Scotland. To provide themselves with land for their cereal crops and grazing for their livestock, they cleared large areas of upland forest, usually by fire, and in the process created the characteristic moorland landscapes of much of modern Scotland. These early farmers established permanent settlements, some of which, like the well-preserved village of **Skara Brae** on Orkney, were near the sea, enabling them to supplement their diet by fishing and to develop their skills as boatbuilders. The Neolithic settlements were not as isolated as was once imagined: geological evidence has, for instance, revealed that the stone used to make axe heads found in the Hebrides was quarried in Northern Ireland.

Settlement spurred the development of more complex forms of religious belief. The Neolithic peoples built large chambered burial mounds or **cairns**, such as Maeshowe in Orkney (see page 334) and the Clava Cairns near Inverness. This reverence for human remains suggests a belief in some form of afterlife, a concept that the next wave of settlers, the **Beaker people**, certainly believed in. They built the mysterious **stone circles**, thirty of which have been discovered in Scotland. Such monuments were a massive commitment in terms of time and energy, with many of the stones carried from miles away, just as they were at Stonehenge in England. The best-known Scottish circle is that of **Callanish** (Calanais) on the Isle of Lewis (see page 305), where a dramatic series of monoliths forms avenues leading towards a circle made up of thirteen standing stones. The exact function of the circles is still unknown, but many of the stones are aligned with the position of the sun at certain points in its annual cycle, suggesting that the monuments are related to the changing of the seasons.

4500 BC	3000 BC	2000 BC
Neolithic people move into Scotland	Neolithic township of Skara Brae built	Callanish standing stones erected on Lewis in the Western Isles

The Beaker people also brought the **Bronze Age** to Scotland. New materials led directly to the development of more effective weapons, and the sword and the shield made their first appearance around 1000 BC. Agricultural needs plus new weaponry added up to a state of endemic warfare as villagers raided their neighbours to steal livestock and grain. The Bronze Age peoples responded to the danger by developing a range of defences, among them the spectacular **hillforts**, great earthwork defences, many of which are thought to have been occupied from around 1000 BC and remained in use throughout the Iron Age, sometimes far longer. Less spectacular but equally practical were the **crannogs**, smaller settlements built on artificial islands constructed of logs, earth, stones and brush, such as those found on Loch Tay.

The Celts and the Picts
Conflict in Scotland intensified in the first millennium BC as successive waves of **Celtic** settlers, arriving from the south, increased competition for land. Around 400 BC, the Celts brought the technology of **iron** with them. These fractious times witnessed the construction of hundreds of **brochs** or fortified towers. Concentrated along the Atlantic coast and in the Northern and Western Isles, the brochs were dry-stone fortifications (built without mortar or cement) often over 40ft in height. Some historians claim they provided protection for small coastal settlements from the attentions of Roman slave-traders. Much the best-preserved broch is on the Shetland island of **Mousa** (see page 381); its double walls rise to about 40ft, only a little short of their original height. The Celts continued to migrate north almost up until Julius Caesar's first incursion into Britain in 55 BC.

At the end of the prehistoric period, immediately prior to the arrival of the Romans, Scotland was divided among a number of warring Iron Age tribes, who, apart from the raiding, were preoccupied with wresting a living from the land, growing barley and oats, rearing sheep, hunting deer and fishing for salmon. The Romans were to write these people into history under the collective name Picti, or **Picts**, meaning "painted people", after their body tattoos.

The Romans
The **Roman conquest** of Britain began in 43 AD, almost a century after Caesar's first invasion. By 80 AD the Roman governor Agricola felt secure enough in the south of Britain to begin an invasion of the north, building a string of forts along the southern edge of the Highlands and defeating a large force of Scottish tribes at Mons Graupius. Precisely where this is remains a puzzle for historians, though most place it somewhere in the northeast, possibly on the slopes of Bennachie, near Inverurie in Aberdeenshire. The long-term effect of his campaign, however, was slight. Work on a major fort – to be the base for 5000 soldiers – at Inchtuthill, north of Perth on the Tay, was abandoned before it was finished, and the legions withdrew south. In 123 AD **Emperor Hadrian** decided to seal the frontier against the northern tribes and built **Hadrian's Wall**, which stretched from the Solway Firth to the Tyne and was the first formal division of the mainland of Britain. Twenty years later, the Romans again ventured north and built the **Antonine Wall** between the Clyde and the Forth rivers, a clear statement of the hostility they perceived to the north. This was occupied for about forty years, but thereafter the

100 BC–100 AD	43 AD	83
Fortified Iron Age brochs built across Scotland	Britain is invaded by the Romans	British tribes defeated by the Romans at the Battle of Mons Graupius in northeast Scotland

Romans, frustrated by the inhospitable terrain of the Highlands, largely gave up their attempt to subjugate the north, and instead adopted a policy of containment.

The Dark Ages

In the years following the departure of the Romans in 410 AD, the population of Scotland changed considerably. By 500 AD there were four groups of people, or nations, dominant in different parts of the country. The **Picts** occupied the Northern Isles, the north and the east as far south as Fife. Today their settlements can generally be identified by place names with a "Pit" prefix, such as Pitlochry, and by the existence of carved symbol stones, like those found at Aberlemno in Angus. To the southwest, between Dumbarton and Carlisle, was a population of **Britons**. Many of the Briton leaders had Roman names, which suggests that they were a Romanized Celtic people, possibly a combination of tribes maintained by the Romans as a buffer between the Wall and the northern tribes, and peoples pushed west by the Anglo-Saxon invaders landing on the east coast. Both the Britons and the Picts spoke variations of P-Celtic, from which Welsh, Cornish and Breton developed.

On the west coast, to the north and west of the Britons (in what is now Argyll), lived the **Scotti**, Irish-Celtic invaders who would eventually give their name to the whole country. The first Scotti arrived in the Western Isles from Ireland in the fourth century AD, and about a century later their great king, Fergus Mor, moved his base from Antrim to Dunadd, near Lochgilphead, where he founded the Kingdom of Dalriada. The Scotti spoke Q-Celtic, the precursor of modern Scottish Gaelic. On the east coast, the Germanic **Angles** had sailed north along the coast to carve out an enclave around Dunbar in East Lothian.

Within three centuries, another non-Celtic invader was making significant incursions. From around 795 AD, **Norse** raids began on the Scottish coast and Hebrides, soon followed by the arrival of settlers, mainly in the Northern Isles and along the Caithness and Sutherland coastline. In 872 AD, the king of Norway set up an earldom in **Orkney**, from which **Shetland** was also governed, and for the next six centuries the Northern Isles took a path distinct from the rest of Scotland, becoming a base for raiding and colonizing much of the rest of Britain and Ireland – and a link in the chain that connected the Faroes, Iceland, Greenland and, more tenuously, North America.

The next few centuries saw almost constant warfare among the different groups. The main issue was land, but this was frequently complicated by the need of the warrior castes, who dominated all of these cultures, to exhibit martial prowess. Military conquests did play their part in bringing the peoples of Scotland together, but the most persuasive force was **Christianity**. Many of the Britons had been Christians since Roman times and it had been a Briton, St Ninian, who conducted the first missionary work among the Picts at the end of the fourth century. Attempts to convert the Picts were resumed in the sixth century by St Columba, who, as a Gaelic-speaking Scot, demonstrated that Christianity could provide a bridge between the different tribes.

Columba's establishment of the island of **Iona** (see page 82) as a centre of Christian culture opened the way for many peaceable contacts between the Picts and the Scotti. Intermarriage became commonplace, so much so that the king of the Scotti, Kenneth

142	162	410
The Romans build the Antonine Wall between the Firth of Forth and the Firth of Clyde	The Roman army retreat behind Hadrian's Wall	The Romans withdraw from Britain

MacAlpine, who united Dalriada and Pictland in 843, was the son of a Pictish princess – the Picts traced succession through the female line. Similarly, MacAlpine's creation of the united kingdom of **Alba**, later known as **Scotia**, was part of a process of integration rather than outright conquest, though it was the Scots' religion, Columba's Christianity and their language (Gaelic) that were to dominate the merger, allowing many aspects of Pictish life, including their language, to fall forgotten and untraceable into the depths of history. Kenneth and his successors gradually extended the frontiers of their kingdom by marriage and force of arms until, by 1034, almost all of what we now call Scotland – on the mainland, at least – was under their rule.

The Middle Ages

By the time of his death in 1034, **Malcolm II** was recognized as the king of Scotia. He was not, though, a national king in the sense that we understand the term, as under the Gaelic system kings were elected from the *derbfine*, a group made up of those whose great-grandfathers had been kings. The chosen successor, supposedly the fittest to rule, was known as the tanist (*tànaiste*). By the eleventh century, however, Scottish kings had become familiar with the principle of heredity, and were often tempted to bend the rules of tanistry. Thus, Malcolm secured the succession of his grandson **Duncan** by murdering a potential rival tanist. Duncan, in turn, was killed by **Macbeth** near Elgin in 1040. Macbeth was not, therefore, the villain of Shakespeare's imagination, but simply an ambitious Scot of royal blood acting in a relatively conventional way.

The Canmores

The victory of **Malcolm III**, known as Canmore (Bighead), over Macbeth in 1057 marked the beginning of a period of fundamental change in Scottish society. Having avenged his father Duncan, Malcolm III, who had spent the previous seventeen years at the English court, sought to apply to Scotland a range of ideas he had brought back with him. He and his heirs established a secure dynasty based on succession through the male line and introduced **feudalism** into Scotland, a system that was diametrically opposed to the Gaelic system, which rested on blood ties: the followers of a Gaelic king were his kindred, whereas the followers of a feudal king were vassals bought with land. The Canmores successfully feudalized much of southern and eastern Scotland by making grants to their Norman, Breton and Flemish followers; they preferred to make their capital in Edinburgh, and in these regions, Scots – a northern version of Anglo-Saxon – pushed out Gaelic as the lingua franca. They also began to reform the **Church**, a development started with the efforts of Margaret, Malcolm III's second wife, who, though English, had been brought up in Hungary, and brought Scottish religious practices into line with those of the rest of Europe, for which she was eventually canonized.

The policies of the Canmores laid the basis for a **cultural rift** in Scotland between the Highland and Lowland communities. Factionalism between various chiefs tended to distract the Highland tribes from their widening differences with the rulers to the south, while the ever-present Viking threat also served to keep many of the clans looking to the west and north rather than the south.

563	**795**	**843**	**872**
St Columba founds a monastery on Iona and begins to convert the Picts	Viking raids on the Scottish coast and islands begin	Kenneth MacAlpine becomes the first King of the Scots and the Picts	Orkney and Shetland come under Viking rule

Norwegian rule over the islands

In 1098, a **treaty** between Edgar, King of Scots, and Magnus Bareleg, King of Norway, ceded sovereignty of all the islands to the Norwegians – Magnus even managed to include Kintyre in his swag by being hauled across the isthmus at Tarbet sitting in a boat, thus proving it an "island", as it could be circumnavigated. In practice, however, power in this Viking kingdom of *Súðreyjar* (Southern Islands) was in the control of local chiefs, lieutenants of a king on the Isle of Man who was himself subordinate to the king of Norway. By marrying the daughter of one of the Manx kings and skilful raiding of neighbouring islands, **Somerled**, King of Argyll, established himself and his successors as Lords of the Isles. Their natural ally was to the Scottish rather than the Norwegian king, and when **Alexander III** (1249–86), Scotland's strongest king in two centuries, sought to buy back the Hebrides from King Håkon of Norway in 1263, the offended Norwegian king sent a fleet of 120 ships to teach the Scots a lesson and drag the islands back into line. Initially the bullying tactics worked, but the fleet lingered too long, was battered by a series of autumnal storms, and retreated back to Orkney in disarray following a skirmish with Alexander's army at the **Battle of Largs** on the Clyde coast. While in Orkney, King Håkon died, and three years later the **Treaty of Perth** of 1266 returned the Isle of Man and the Hebrides to Scotland in exchange for an annual rent.

The Wars of Scottish Independence

In 1286 **Alexander III** died, and a hotly disputed succession gave Edward I, King of England, an opportunity to subjugate Scotland. In 1291 Edward presided over a conference where the rival claimants to the Scottish throne presented their cases. Edward chose **John Balliol** in preference to Robert the Bruce, his main rival, and obliged John to pay him homage, thus turning Scotland into a vassal kingdom. Bruce refused to accept the decision, thereby continuing the conflict, and in 1295 Balliol renounced his allegiance to Edward and formed an alliance with France – the beginning of what is known as the "**Auld Alliance**". In the conflict that followed, the Bruce family sided with the English, Balliol was defeated and imprisoned, and Edward seized control of almost all of Scotland.

Edward had shown little mercy during his conquest of Scotland – he had, for example, had most of the population of Berwick massacred – and his cruelty seems to have provoked a truly national resistance. This focused on **William Wallace**, a man of relatively lowly origins from southwest Scotland who forged an army of peasants, lesser knights and townsmen that was fundamentally different to the armies raised by the nobility. Figures like Balliol, holding lands in England, France and Scotland, were part of an international aristocracy for whom warfare was merely the means by which they struggled for power. Wallace, by contrast, led proto-nationalist forces drawn from both Lowlands and Highlands determined to expel the English from their country. Probably for that very reason Wallace never received the support of the nobility and, after a bitter ten-year campaign, he was betrayed and executed in London in 1305.

With Wallace out of the way, feudal intrigue resumed. In 1306 **Robert the Bruce**, the erstwhile ally of the English, defied Edward and had himself crowned king of Scotland. Edward died the following year, but the unrest dragged on until 1314, when Bruce decisively defeated a huge English army under Edward II at the **Battle of Bannockburn**.

1040	1156	1266	1286
Macbeth crowned King of Scotland	Somerled seizes the Kingdom of the Isles	The Treaty of Perth hands the Hebrides back to Scotland from the Norwegians	Death of Alexander III sparks the Wars of Scottish Independence

THE HIGHLAND CLANS

The term "**clan**", as it is commonly used to refer to the quasi-tribal associations found in the Highlands of Scotland, only appears in its modern usage in the sixteenth century. In theory, the clan bound together blood relatives who shared a common ancestor, a concept clearly derived from the ancient Gaelic notion of kinship. But in practice many of the clans were of non-Gaelic origin – such as the Frasers, Sinclairs and Stewarts, all of Anglo-Norman descent – and it was the mythology of a common ancestor, rather than the actuality, that cemented the clans together. Furthermore, clans were often made up of people with a variety of surnames, and there are documented cases of individuals changing their names when they swapped allegiances. At the upper end of Highland society was the clan chief (who might have been a minor figure, like MacDonald of Glencoe, or a great lord, like the Duke of Argyll, head of the Campbells), who provided protection for his followers: they would, in turn, fight for him when called upon to do so. Below the clan chief were the chieftains of the septs, or subunits of the clan, and then came the tacksmen, major tenants of the chief to whom they were frequently related. The tacksmen sublet their land to tenants, who were at the bottom of the social scale. The Highlanders wore a simple belted plaid wrapped around the body – rather than the kilt – and not until the late seventeenth century were certain tartans roughly associated with particular clans. The detailed codification of the tartan was produced by the Victorians, whose romantic vision of Highland life originated with George IV's visit to Scotland in 1822, when he appeared in an elaborate version of Highland dress, complete with flesh-coloured tights.

At last Bruce was firmly in control of his kingdom, and in 1320 the Scots asserted their right to independence in a successful petition to the pope, now known as the **Declaration of Arbroath**.

The Stewarts

In the years following Bruce's death in 1329, the Scottish monarchy gradually declined in influence. The last of the Bruce dynasty died in 1371, to be succeeded by the "Stewards", hence **Stewarts**. The reign of **James IV** (1488–1513), the most talented of the early Stewarts, ended in a terrible defeat for the Scots – and his own death – at the **Battle of Flodden Field**.

Meanwhile, the shape of modern-day Scotland was completed when the Northern Isles were gradually wrested from Norway. In 1469, a marriage was arranged between Margaret, daughter of the Danish king, Christian I, and the future **King James III** (1460–88) of Scotland. Short of cash for Margaret's dowry, Christian mortgaged Orkney to Scotland in 1468, followed by Shetland in 1469; neither pledge was ever successfully redeemed. The laws, religion and administration of the Northern Isles became Scottish, though their Norse heritage is still very evident in place names, dialect and culture. Meanwhile, the MacDonald Lords of the Isles had become too unruly for the more unified vision of James IV, and in 1493 the title reverted to the Crown. It still remains there: the current Lord of the Isles is Prince Charles.

The religious wars

In many respects the **Reformation** in Scotland was driven as much by the political intrigue of the reign of **Mary, Queen of Scots** (1542–67), as it was by religious

1314	1320	1371
Under Robert the Bruce, the Scots defeat the English at the Battle of Bannockburn	The Declaration of Arbroath, asserting Scottish independence, is sent to the pope	Robert II becomes the first of the Stewart (Stuart) kings to rule Scotland

conviction. Although in later years the hard-line Presbyterianism of the Highlands and Hebrides would triumph over political expediency, the revolutionary thinking of **John Knox** and his Protestant die-hards initially made little impact in the north. If some of the Lowland lords were still inclined to see religious affiliation as a negotiable tool in the quest for power and influence, the loyalty – if not, perhaps, the piety – of many of the Highland chiefs to both their monarch and the Catholic faith was much more solid.

James VI (1567–1625), who in 1603 also became James I of England, disliked Presbyterianism because its quasi-democratic structure – particularly the lack of royally appointed bishops – appeared to threaten his authority. In 1610 he restored the Scottish bishops, leaving a legacy that his son, **Charles I** (1625–49), who was raised in Episcopalian England, could not handle. He provoked the **National Covenant**, a religious pledge that committed the signatories to "labour by all means lawful to recover the purity and liberty of the Gospel as it was established and professed".

Charles declared all the "**Covenanters**" to be rebels, a proclamation endorsed by his Scottish bishops. The Covenanters, well financed by the Kirk, assembled a proficient army under Alexander Leslie. In desperation, Charles summoned the English Parliament, the first for eleven years, hoping it would pay for an army. But the decision was a disaster and Parliament was much keener to criticize his policies than to raise taxes. In response Charles declared war on Parliament in 1642.

The Civil War

The major conflicts of the ensuing **Civil War** were mostly confined to England. In Scotland, the English Parliamentarians made an uneasy alliance with the Covenanters, who ruled over Scotland until 1650. During this period, the power of the Presbyterian Kirk grew considerably: laws were passed establishing schools in every parish and, less usefully, banning trade with Catholic countries. The only effective opposition to the theocratic state came from the **Marquis of Montrose**, who had initially supported the Covenant but lined up with the king when war broke out. Montrose was a gifted campaigner whose army was drawn from the Highlands and Islands, where the Kirk's influence was still weak, and included a frightening rabble of islanders and Irishmen under the inspiration of Colonsay chief Alasdair MacDonald, or **Colkitto**, whose appetite for the fray was fed by Montrose's willingness to send them charging into battle at the precise moment they could inflict most damage. For a golden year Montrose's army roamed the Highlands undefeated, scoring a number of brilliant tactical victories over the Covenanters, but the reluctance of his troops to stay south of the Highland Line made it impossible for him to capitalize on his successes and, as the clansmen dispersed with the spoils of victory back to their lands, Montrose was left weak and exposed. Unfailingly loyal to a king who was unwilling to take the same risks for his most gifted general, Montrose was eventually captured and executed in 1650.

Many English Parliamentarians suspected the Scots of hankering after the return of the monarchy, a suspicion confirmed when, at the invitation of the earl of Argyll, the future **Charles II** came back to Scotland in 1650. To regain his Scottish kingdom, Charles was obliged to renounce his father and sign the Covenant, two bitter pills taken to impress the population. In the event, the "Presbyterian restoration" was short-lived. Cromwell invaded, defeated the Scots at Dunbar and forced Charles into exile.

1468	1488	1513	1560
James III marries Margaret of Denmark and receives Orkney and Shetland as part of her dowry	The Western Isles come under the rule of the Scottish Crown	The Scots are defeated by the English at the Battle of Flodden Field	The Scottish Church breaks with the Roman Catholic Church

Until the Restoration of 1660, Scotland was united with England and governed by seven commissioners.

The Restoration

The Restoration brought bishops back to the Kirk, integrated into an essentially Presbyterian structure of Kirk sessions and presbyteries. Over three hundred clergymen, a third of the Scottish ministry, refused to accept the reinstatement of the bishops and were edged out of the Church, and forced to hold open-air services, called **Conventicles**, which Charles did his best to suppress.

When **James VII** (James II of England), whose ardent Catholicism caused a Protestant backlash in England, was forced into exile in France in 1689, the throne passed to **Mary**, his Protestant daughter, and her Dutch husband, **William of Orange**. In Scotland there was a brief flurry of opposition to William when **Graham of Claverhouse**, known as "Bonnie Dundee", united the Jacobite clans against the government army at the **Battle of Killiecrankie**, just north of Pitlochry. However, the inspirational Claverhouse was killed on the point of claiming a famous victory, and again the clans, leaderless and unwilling to press south, dissipated and the threat passed.

William and Mary quickly consolidated their position, restoring the full Presbyterian structure in Scotland and abolishing the bishops, though they chose not to restore the political and legal functions of the Kirk, which remained subject to parliamentary control. It was sufficient, however, to bring the religious wars to a close, essentially completing the Reformation in Scotland and establishing a platform on which political union would be built.

The Union

Highland loyalty to the Stewart line lingered on into the eighteenth century, something both William and the political pragmatists saw as a significant threat. In 1691, William offered pardons to those Highland chiefs who had opposed his accession, on condition that they took an oath of allegiance by New Year's Day 1692. Alastair Maclain, one of the MacDonalds of Glencoe, had turned up at the last minute, but his efforts to take the oath were frustrated by the king's officials, who were determined to see his clan, well known for their support of the Stewarts, destroyed. In February 1692, Captain Robert Campbell of Glenlyon quartered his men with the MacDonalds of Glencoe and, two weeks later, in the middle of the night, his troops acted on their secret orders, turned on their hosts and carried out the infamous **Massacre of Glencoe**. Thirty-eight MacDonalds died, and the slaughter caused a national scandal, especially among the clans, where "murder under trust" – killing those offering you shelter – was considered a particularly heinous crime.

The situation in Scotland was further complicated by the question of the succession. Mary died without leaving an heir and, on William's death in 1702, the crown passed to her sister **Anne**, James VII's second daughter, who was also childless. In response, the English Parliament secured the Protestant succession by passing the **Act of Settlement**, which named the Electress Sophia of Hanover, a granddaughter of James VI (I), as the next in line to the throne. The Act did not, however, apply in Scotland, and the English feared that the Scots would invite James Edward Stewart, the son of James VII

1567	1587	1603	1638
Abdication of Mary, Queen of Scots, and accession of James VI (aged 1)	Mary, Queen of Scots, is executed on the orders of Queen Elizabeth I	James VI of Scotland becomes James I of England	National Covenant proclaimed by Scottish Presbyterians

(II) by his second wife, back from France to be their king. Consequently, Parliament appointed commissioners charged with the consideration of "proper methods towards attaining a union with Scotland". The project seemed doomed to failure when the Scottish Parliament passed the **Act of Security**, in 1703, stating that Scotland would not accept a Hanoverian monarch unless they had first received guarantees protecting their religion and their trade.

The Act of Union

Despite the strength of anti-English feeling, the Scottish Parliament passed the **Act of Union** by 110 votes to 69 in 1707. Some historians have explained the vote in terms of bribery and corruption, but there were other factors. Scottish politicians were divided between the Cavaliers – Jacobites (supporters of the Stewarts) and Episcopalians – and the Country party, whose Presbyterian members dreaded the return of the Stewarts more than they disliked the Hanoverians. To the Highlands and Islands, however, the shift of government four hundred miles further south from Edinburgh, itself distant enough for many, was to make relatively little difference to their lives for the best part of the rest of the century.

The country that was united with England in 1707 contained three distinct cultures: in south and east Scotland, they spoke Scots; in Shetland, Orkney and the far northeast, the local dialect, though Scots-based, contained elements of Norn (Old Norse); in the rest of north and west Scotland, including the Hebrides, Gaelic was spoken. These linguistic differences were paralleled by different forms of social organization and customs. The people of north and west Scotland were mostly pastoralists, moving their sheep and cattle to Highland pastures in the summer, and returning to the glens in the winter. They lived in single-room dwellings, heated by a central peat fire and sometimes shared with livestock, and in hard times they would subsist on cakes made from the blood of their live cattle mixed with oatmeal. Highlanders supplemented their meagre income by raiding their clan neighbours and the prosperous Lowlands, whose inhabitants regarded their northern compatriots with a mixture of fear and contempt. This was the background for the exploits of Scotland's very own Robin Hood character, **Rob Roy** (see page 138).

The Jacobite uprisings

When James VII (II) was deposed, he had fled to France, where he planned the reconquest of his kingdom with the support of the French king. When James died in 1701, the hopes of the Stewarts passed to his only son, James Edward Stewart, the "Old Pretender" ("Pretender" in the sense of having pretensions to the throne; "Old" to distinguish him from his son Charles, the "Young Pretender"). James's followers became known as **Jacobites**, derived from Jacobus, the Latin equivalent of James.

The Fifteen

After the accession to the British throne of the Hanoverian George I, son of Sophia, Electress of Hanover, it sparked the **Jacobite uprising of 1715** (also known as The Fifteen): its timing appeared perfect. Scottish opinion was moving against the Union, which had failed to bring Scotland any tangible economic benefits. The English had

1650	1689	1692	1698
The Scots Royalist army is defeated at the Battle of Dunbar by the English under Oliver Cromwell	Unsuccessful Jacobite uprising against William of Orange	Glencoe massacre: 38 members of the MacDonald clan murdered by anti-Jacobite Campbells	1200 Scots leave to establish a colony in Panama

also been accused of bad faith when, contrary to their pledges, they attempted to impose their legal practices on the Scots. Neither were Jacobite sentiments confined to Scotland. There were many in England who toasted the "King across the water" and showed no enthusiasm for the new German ruler. In September 1715, the fiercely Jacobite John Erskine, Earl of Mar, raised the Stewart standard at Braemar Castle. Just eight days later, he captured Perth, where he gathered an army of over 10,000 men, drawn mostly from the Episcopalians of northeast Scotland and from the Highlands. Mar's rebellion took the government by surprise. They had only 4000 soldiers in Scotland, under the Duke of Argyll, but Mar dithered until he lost the military advantage. The **Battle of Sheriffmuir** in November was indecisive, but by the time the Old Pretender arrived the following month, 6000 veteran Dutch troops had reinforced Argyll. The rebellion disintegrated rapidly and James slunk back to exile in France in February 1716.

The Forty-Five

Led by James's dashing son, Charles Edward Stewart (Bonnie Prince Charlie), the **Jacobite uprising of 1745** (known as The Forty-Five), though better known, had even less chance of success than the 1715 rising. In the intervening thirty years, the Hanoverians had consolidated their hold on the English throne, Lowland society had become uniformly loyalist and access into the Highlands for both trade and internal peacekeeping had been vastly improved by the military roads built by General Wade. Even among the clans, regiments such as the Black Watch were recruited, which drew on the Highlanders' military tradition, but formed part of the government's standing army. Despite a promising start to his campaign, Charles met his match at the **Battle of Culloden**, near Inverness, in April 1746, the last set-piece battle on British soil, the last time a claymore-wielding Highland charge would be set against organized ranks of musket-bearing troops, and the last time a Stewart would take up arms in pursuit of the throne. As with so many of the other critical points in the campaign, the Jacobite leadership at Culloden was divided and ill-prepared. When it came to the fight, the Highlanders were in the wrong place, exhausted after a forced overnight march, and seriously outnumbered and outgunned. They were swept from the field, with over 1500 men killed or wounded compared to Cumberland's 300 or so. After the battle, many of the wounded Jacobites were slaughtered, an atrocity that earned Cumberland the nickname "Butcher".

In the aftermath of the uprising, the wearing of tartan, the bearing of arms and the playing of bagpipes were all banned. Rebel chiefs lost their land and the Highlands were placed under military occupation. Most significantly, the government prohibited the private armies of the chiefs, thereby effectively destroying the clan system. Within a few years, more Highland regiments were recruited for the British army, and by the end of the century thousands of Scots were fighting and dying for their Hanoverian king against Napoleon.

The Highland Clearances

Once the clan chief was forbidden his own army, he had no need of the large tenantry that had previously been a vital military asset. Conversely, the second half of the

1707	1715	1746	1762
The Act of Union unites the kingdoms of Scotland and England	Jacobite uprising against the accession of Hanoverian King George I	Bonnie Prince Charlie's Jacobite army is defeated at the Battle of Culloden	Beginning of the Highland Clearances

BONNIE PRINCE CHARLIE

Prince Charles Edward Stuart – better known as **Bonnie Prince Charlie** or "The Young Pretender" – was born in 1720 in Rome, where his father, "The Old Pretender", claimant to the British throne (as the son of James VII), was living in exile with his Polish wife. At the age of 25, with no knowledge of Gaelic, an imperfect grasp of English and a strong attachment to the Catholic faith, the prince set out for Scotland with two French ships, disguised as a seminarist from the Scots College in Paris. He arrived on the Hebridean island of **Eriskay** on July 23, 1745, with just seven companions, and was immediately implored to return to France by the clan chiefs, who were singularly unimpressed by his lack of army. Charles was unmoved and went on to raise the royal standard at **Glenfinnan**, thus signalling the beginning of the **Jacobite uprising**. He only attracted less than half of the potential 20,000 clansmen who could have marched with him, and promises of support from the French and English Jacobites failed to materialize. Nevertheless, after a decisive victory over government forces at the **Battle of Prestonpans**, near Edinburgh, Charles made a spectacular advance into England, getting as far as Derby. London was in a state of panic: its shops were closed and the Bank of England, fearing a run on sterling, slowed withdrawals by paying out in sixpences. But Derby was as far as Charles got. On December 6, threatened by superior forces, the Jacobites decided to retreat to Scotland against Charles's wishes. Pursued back to Scotland by the Duke of Cumberland, he won one last victory, at Falkirk, before the final disaster at **Culloden** in April 1746.

The prince spent the following five months in hiding, with a price of £30,000 on his head, and literally thousands of government troops searching for him. He certainly endured his fair share of cold and hunger while on the run, but the real price was paid by the Highlanders themselves, who risked their lives (and often paid for it with them) by aiding and abetting the prince. The most famous of these was, of course, 23-year-old **Flora MacDonald**, whom Charles first met on South Uist in June 1746. Flora was persuaded – either by his looks or her relatives, depending on which account you believe – to convey Charles "over the sea to Skye", disguised as an Irish servant girl by the name of Betty Burke. She was arrested just seven days after parting with the prince in Portree, and held in the Tower of London until July 1747. She went on to marry a local man, had seven children, and in 1774 emigrated to America where her husband was taken prisoner during the American War of Independence. Flora returned to Scotland and was reunited with her husband on his release; they resettled in Skye and she died at the age of 68.

Charles eventually boarded a ship back to France in September 1746, but, despite his promises – "For all that has happened, Madam, I hope we shall meet in St James's yet" – never returned to Scotland, nor did he ever see Flora again. After mistreating a string of mistresses, he eventually got married at the age of 52 to the 19-year-old **Princess Louise of Stolberg-Gedern** in an effort to produce a Stuart heir. They had no children, and she eventually fled from his violent drunkenness; in 1788, a none-too-"bonnie" Prince Charles died in the arms of his illegitimate daughter in Rome. Bonnie Prince Charlie became a legend in his own lifetime, but it was the Victorians who really milked the myth for all its sentimentality, conveniently overlooking the fact that the real consequence of 1745 was the virtual annihilation of the Highland way of life.

eighteenth century saw the Highland **population increase** dramatically after the introduction of the easy-to-grow and nutritious potato. Between 1745 and 1811, the population of the Outer Hebrides, for example, rose from 13,000 to 24,500. The clan chiefs adopted different policies to deal with the new situation. Some encouraged

1843	1846	1886	1914–18
The Great Disruption: a third of the Church of Scotland leave to form the Free Church of Scotland	Highland potato famine: 1.7 million Scots emigrate	Crofters' Holdings Act grants security of tenure in the Highlands and Islands	100,000 Scots lose their lives in World War I

emigration, and as many as 6000 Highlanders left for the Americas between 1800 and 1803 alone. Other landowners saw the economic advantages of developing alternative forms of employment for their tenantry, mainly fishing and kelping. **Kelp** (brown seaweed) was gathered and burnt to produce soda ash, which was used in the manufacture of soap, glass and explosives. There was a rising market for soda ash until the 1810s, with the price increasing from £2 a ton in 1760 to £20 in 1808, making a fortune for some landowners and providing thousands of Highlanders with temporary employment. Fishing for **herring** – the "silver darlings" – was also encouraged, and new harbours and coastal settlements were built all around the Highland coastline. Other landowners developed **sheep runs** on the Highland pastures, introducing hardy breeds like the black-faced Linton and the Cheviot. But extensive sheep-farming proved incompatible with a high peasant population, and many landowners decided to clear their estates of tenants, some of whom were forcibly moved to tiny plots of marginal land, where they were to farm as **crofters**.

The pace of the **Highland Clearances** accelerated after the end of the Napoleonic Wars in 1815, when the market price for kelp, fish and cattle declined, leaving sheep as the only profitable Highland product. The most notorious Clearances took place on the estates of the Countess of Sutherland, who owned a million acres in northern Scotland. Between 1807 and 1821, around 15,000 people were thrown off her land, evictions carried out with considerable brutality. A potato famine followed in 1846, forcing large-scale emigration to America and Canada and leaving the huge uninhabited areas found in the region today.

The crofters fight back

The crofters eked out a precarious existence, but they hung on throughout the nineteenth century, often by taking seasonal employment away from home. In the 1880s, however, a sharp downturn in agricultural prices made it difficult for many crofters to pay their rent. This time, inspired by the example of the Irish Land League, they resisted eviction, forming the **Highland Land League** or **Crofters' Party**, and taking part in direct action protests, in particular land occupations, or **land raids**, as they became known. In 1886, in response to the social unrest, Gladstone's Liberal government passed the **Crofters' Holdings Act**, which conceded three of the crofters' demands: security of tenure, fair rents to be decided independently, and the right to pass on crofts by inheritance. But Gladstone did not attempt to increase the amount of land available for crofting, and shortage of land remained a major problem until the **Land Settlement Act** of 1919 made provision for the creation of new crofts. Nevertheless, the population of the Highlands continued to fall into the twentieth century, with many of the region's young people finding city life more appealing.

The world wars

Depopulation of an all-too-familiar kind was present in the early decades of the twentieth century, with Highland regiments at the vanguard of the British Army's infantry offensives in both the Anglo-Boer wars at the start of the century and **World War I**. The months after hostilities ended also saw one of the most remarkable spectacles in Orkney's long seafaring history, when 74 vessels from the German naval fleet,

1928	1939	1939–45	1961
The National Party of Scotland is formed	The population of Scotland reaches five million	34,000 Scottish soldiers lose their lives in World War II; 6000 civilians die in air raids	The US deploy Polaris nuclear missiles in Holy Loch

lying at anchor in **Scapa Flow** having surrendered to the British at the armistice, were scuttled by the skeleton German crews that remained aboard.

The same harbour was immediately involved in **World War II**, when a German U-boat breached the defences around Orkney in October 1939 and torpedoed HMS *Royal Oak*, with the loss of 833 men. Many more ships and lives were lost in the waters off the Hebrides during the hard-fought Battle of the Atlantic, when convoys carrying supplies and troops were constantly harried by German U-boats. Various bases were established in the Highlands and Islands, including a flying-boat squadron at Kerrera, by Oban, with Air Force bases on Islay, Benbecula, Tiree and Lewis, and a Royal Naval anchorage at Tobermory; on the mainland, commandos were trained in survival skills and offensive landings in the area around lochs Lochy and Arkaig, near Fort William. Though men of fighting age again left the Highlands to serve in the forces, the war years were not altogether bleak, as the influx of servicemen ensured a certain prosperity to the places where they were based, and the need for the country to remain self-sufficient meant that farms and crofts – often worked by the women and children left behind – were encouraged to keep production levels high.

Even before the war, efforts had been made to recognize the greater social and economic needs of the Highlands and Islands with the establishment of the **Highlands and Islands Medical Service**, a precursor to the National Health Service introduced by the first postwar Labour government. Other agencies were set up in the 1940s, including the **North of Scotland Hydro Electric Board** and the **Forestry Commission**, both of which were tasked to improve the local infrastructure and create state-sponsored employment.

The Highlands and Islands today

After Britain joined the EEC in 1972, the Highlands and Islands were identified as an area in need of special assistance and, in harness with the **Highlands and Islands Development Board**, significant investment was made in the area's infrastructure, including roads, schools, medical facilities and harbours. European funding was also used to support the increased use and teaching of **Gaelic**, and the encouragement of Gaelic broadcasting, publishing and education. At the same time there was a renaissance of Gaelic culture across Scotland as a whole, from the annual National Mod to the nationwide success of folk-rock bands such as Runrig and Capercaillie, with the result that the indigenous language and culture of the Highlands and Islands, while still vulnerable, are as healthy now as they have been for a century.

As the world acknowledged the urgency of reacting to the climate crisis in 2019, Scotland declared its commitment to ending its own contribution to global climate change by 2045. The Highlands and Islands is on its way to becoming the world's first net zero aviation region, by 2040.

Employment in the Highlands and Islands

The strength of cultural identity – even in its more clichéd forms – has always been a vital aspect of the Highlands and Islands' attraction as a tourist destination. **Tourism** remains the dominant industry in the region, despite the furrowed brows of, on the one hand, businesses vulnerable to dips in numbers and spending, and on the other,

1979	1996	1999	2009
Scottish referendum for devolution fails to gain the required forty percent	The Stone of Scone is returned to Scotland	Labour win the most seats in Scotland's first-ever general election	Carol Ann Duffy becomes the first Scottish Poet Laureate

conservationists concerned by the impact of increased numbers. The main traditional industries, **farming** and **fishing**, continue with European support to struggle against European competition, while others, such as **whisky** and **tweed making**, remain prominent in certain pockets although they have never, in fact, been large-scale employers. Few of the region's new industries have quite fulfilled the initial hopes raised of them, but most remain to contribute to the economic diversity of the region. **Forestry**, for example, has seen large tracts of the Highlands planted, more sensitively now than in the past; North Sea **oil** has brought serious economic benefits not just to the northeast coast but also to Orkney and Shetland; **salmon farming** has become widespread, tainting many otherwise idyllic west-coast scenes, but long accepted as a vital part of numerous coastal communities. The new growth industry is **alternative energy**, such as large wind farms and schemes to harness tidal and wave energy; Scotland's Green Deal announcement suggests the eco-industry will generate broad employment opportunities in the future. Increasingly popular, especially among young adults, is "**cyber-crofting**" – essentially the operation of internet-based businesses or services from remoter areas. The possibilities thrown up by the communications revolution have also led to the establishment of the **University of the Highlands**, with various colleges linked to each other and to outlying students by networked computers.

Immigration and land ownership

As remote living is made more viable, however, it is not just the indigenous population who benefit, and **immigration** into the Highlands now matches the long-term trend of emigration, with Inverness ranking as one of the fastest-growing urban areas in Britain and most islands enjoying a steady increase in population (the 2011 Census revealed a rise of four percent). The incomers – invariably called "white settlers" – are now an established aspect of Highland life, often providing economic impetus in the form of enthusiastically run small businesses, though their presence can still rankle in the intimate lives of small communities. Any prejudicial control from outside the region is looked on suspiciously, not least in the question of **land ownership**, which remains one of the keys to Highland development – some would say the most important of all. Some of the largest Highland estates continue to be owned and managed from afar, with little regard to local needs or priorities; two-thirds of the private land in Scotland is owned by a mere 1250 people, many of them aristocrats or foreign nationals. However, the success of groups of crofters in buying estates in Assynt and Knoydart, as well as the purchase of the islands of Eigg and Gigha by their inhabitants, hints at a gradual broadening of land ownership.

Devolution and independence

With so many unique issues to tackle, it is perhaps not surprising that the Highlands and Islands have always maintained an independent and generally restrained voice in Scottish politics. Far removed from the Central Belt, the region has remained largely ambivalent to the surges of nationalism in other parts of the country. **Devolution**, which led to the establishment of the Scottish Parliament in Edinburgh in 1999, was initially regarded with scepticism in the Highlands and Islands, and, in the 2014 referendum, the region voted decisively against **independence**, particularly in Orkney and Shetland. Despite this, the area has not been immune to the rise of the

2011	2013	2014
The Scottish National Party win a majority in the Scottish Parliament	Andy Murray becomes the first Scot to win Wimbledon men's singles title since 1896	Scotland votes to remain part of the United Kingdom in an independence referendum

Scottish National Party, and now only Orkney and Shetland remain Liberal Democrat strongholds. The impact of the 2016 **Brexit** referendum, in which 52 percent of UK voters opted to leave the EU, has yet to be played out. In the Highlands and Islands, as in Scotland as a whole, around 60 percent voted to remain in the EU, prompting many to call for another independence referendum. So far the polls suggest no post-Brexit surge of support for Scottish independence. Nicola Sturgeon proposed that a second referendum be held, which will take place in May 2021. According to her, another aspect has made Scots rethink independence, and that is the Covid-19 pandemic. She claimed that Covid-19 has made Scots realize the 'benefits' of being independent from the UK. At the time of writing, there had been over 220,000 cases of Covid-19 and 7,500 deaths in Scotland. The rates are much less than the rest of the UK, with England having around 3.8 million cases and 112,000 deaths, along with roughly 210,000 cases in Wales and just under 120,000 cases in Northern Ireland.

2016	**2019**	**2021**
Scotland votes to remain within the EU, but the UK as a whole votes to leave	The Scottish Green Deal outlines world-leading strategies in the face of Earth's climate crisis	At the time of writing Scotland emerges from a lockdown in response to the Covid-19 pandemic

Books

We've highlighted a selection of books below that will give you a flavour of the Scottish Highlands and Islands, past and present; books marked with ★ are particularly recommended.

HISTORY, POLITICS AND CULTURE

★**Neal Ascherson** *Stones Voices*. Intelligent, thought-provoking ponderings on the nature of Scotland and the road to devolution from Scots-born *Observer* journalist, interspersed with personal anecdotes.

Joni Buchanan *The Lewis Land Struggle*. A history of crucial encounters between the crofters of Lewis and their various landlords, written from the crofters' point of view using contemporary sources.

Tom Devine *The Scottish Nation 1700–2000*. Best post-Union history from the last Scottish Parliament to the new one.

★**David Howarth** *The Shetland Bus*. Wonderfully detailed story of the espionage and resistance operations carried out from Shetland by British and Norwegian servicemen, written by someone who was directly involved.

Fitzroy Maclean *Bonnie Prince Charlie*. Very readable and more or less definitive biography of Scotland's most romantic historical figure written by the "real" James Bond.

John Prebble *Glencoe*, *Culloden* and *The Highland Clearances*. Emotive and subjective accounts of key events in Highland history, which are very readable.

★**Author unknown** *Orkneyinga Saga*. Probably written about 1200 AD, this is a Norse saga which sheds light on the connection between Norway and the Northern Isles, still felt strongly today; contains history of the early earls of Orkney, and is, incidentally, a stirring, bloodthirsty thriller.

GUIDES AND PICTURE BOOKS

George Mackay Brown *Portrait of Orkney*. A personal account by the famous Orcadian poet of the island, its history and way of life, illustrated with photographs and drawings.

Sheila Gear *Foula, Island West of the Sun*. An attempt to convey what it is like to live far out in the sea on an island of savage beauty.

★**Hamish Haswell-Smith** *The Scottish Islands*. An exhaustive and impressive gazetteer with maps and absorbing information on all the Scottish islands. Filled with attractive sketches and paintings, the book is breathtaking in its thoroughness and lovingly gathered detail.

Charles Maclean *St Kilda*. Traces the social history of the island, from its earliest beginnings to the seemingly inevitable end of the community, with moving compassion.

Magnus Magnusson *Rùm: Nature's Island*. A detailed history of Rùm from earliest times up to its current position as a National Nature Reserve.

Peter May *Hebrides*. A journey in prose and photographs around the islands, which inspired May to write his best-selling *Lewis* trilogy.

MEMOIRS AND TRAVELOGUES

Patrick Baker *The Cairngorms: A Secret History*. Compelling account of this spellbinding, yet still relatively little known about, mountain range, incorporating nuggets like the search for the elusive wildcat to the discovery of aircraft wreckage. A terrific companion if you're planning to spend any time in the area.

Patrick Barkham *Islander*. In this wonderful book, the acclaimed natural history writer embarks upon an enlightening trawl around some of Britain's smaller islands, including, in Scotland, Barra, Eigg and Orkney – and you'll want to visit them too after reading this.

Madeleine Bunting *Love of Country: A Hebridean Journey*. A thoughtful, and thought-provoking, book about the Hebrides, with chapters on Jura, Iona, Staffa, Rùm, Eriskay, Lewis and St Kilda.

Jim Crumley *The Great Wood*. The history, wildlife and folklore of the 5000-year-old Caledonian forest is the latest work from this prolific author who writes with a poetic intensity. Also *Among Islands*, *The Isle of Skye* and *Gulfs of Blue Air*.

David Duff (ed.) *Queen Victoria's Highland Journals*. The daily diary of the Scottish adventures of "Mrs Brown" – Victoria's writing is detailed and interesting without being twee, and she lovingly conveys her affection for Deeside and the Highlands.

Rowena Farre *Seal Morning*. An absorbing account of a young girl growing up on a remote croft in the Highlands towards the beginning of the last century and the wildlife she adopted. Eight-year-olds and upwards will love it and so will adults.

★**Elizabeth Grant of Rothiemurchus** *Memoirs of a Highland Lady*. Hugely readable recollections, written with wit and perception at the beginning of the eighteenth century, charting the social changes in Edinburgh, London and particularly Speyside.

Peter Hill *Stargazing*. Engaging account of being a tyro lighthouse-keeper on three of Scotland's most famous lighthouses: Pladda, Ailsa Craig and Hyskeir.

★ **Samuel Johnson & James Boswell** *A Journey to the Western Isles of Scotland* and *The Journal of a Tour to the Hebrides*. Lively accounts of a famous journey around the islands taken by the noted lexicographer Dr Samuel Johnson, and his biographer and friend.

Alasdair Maclean *Night Falls on Ardnamurchan*. First published in 1984 but frequently reprinted, this is a classic and moving story of the life and death of the Highland community in which the author grew up.

Gavin Maxwell *Ring of Bright Water*. Heart-warming true tale of a man's relationship with three otters. Suitable for 7-year-olds upwards.

Alastair McIntosh *Poacher's Pilgrimage: An Island Journey*. The author, who grew up on Lewis, undertakes a return pilgrimage to the island, as well as Harris to the south, in what is a warm, poetic, and occasionally very funny, book.

★ **Iain Mitchell** *Isles of the West; Isle of the North*. In the first book, Mitchell sails round the Inner Hebrides, talking to locals and incomers, siding with the former, caricaturing the latter, and, with a fair bit of justification, laying into the likes of the RSPB and SNH. *Isles of the North* gives Orkney and Shetland the same treatment, before heading off to Norway to find out how it can be done differently.

★ **Alistair Moffat** *The Hidden Ways*. In this eminently readable book, the insatiable historian sheds fascinating light on some of Scotland's lesser known drove roads, walking a dozen or so of them from the Borders to the Highlands; by turns informative and engaging.

Edwin Muir *Scottish Journey*. A classic travelogue written in 1935 by the troubled Orcadian writer on his return to Scotland from London.

Sir Walter Scott *The Voyage of the Pharos*. In 1814 Scott accompanied Stevenson senior on a tour of the northern lighthouses, visiting Shetland, Orkney, the Hebrides and even nipping across to Ireland; he wrote a lively diary of their adventures, which included dodging American privateers.

FICTION

George Mackay Brown *Beside the Ocean of Time*. A child's journey through the history of an Orkney island, and an adult's effort to make sense of the place's secrets in the late twentieth century. *Magnus* is his retelling of the death of St Magnus, with parallels for modern times.

Ann Cleeve *Blue Lightning*. The latest in her detective series, which conveys a great sense of Shetland, and has become a popular TV series.

★ **Lewis Grassic Gibbon** *Sunset Song, Cloud Howe* and *Grey Granite*. This trilogy, known as *A Scots Quair* and set in northeast Scotland, has become a classic, telling the story of the conflict in one woman's life between Scottish and English culture.

★ **Neil M. Gunn** *The Silver Darlings*. Probably Gunn's most representative and best-known book, evocatively set on the northeast coast and telling the story of the herring fishermen during the great years of the industry. Other examples of his romantic, symbolic works include *The Lost Glen*, *The Silver Bough* and *Wild Geese Overhead*.

Eric Linklater *The Dark of Summer*. Set on the Faroes, Shetland, Orkney (where the author was born), and in

theatres of war, this novel exhibits the best of Linklater's compelling narrative style, although his comic novel *Private Angelo* is better known.

Compton MacKenzie *Whisky Galore*. Comic novel based on a true story of the wartime wreck of a cargo of whisky off Eriskay. Full of predictable stereotypes, but still funny.

Peter May *The Blackhouse, The Lewis Man* and *The Chessmen*. A trilogy of dark detective stories set on the Isle of Lewis featuring a policeman from Edinburgh who grew up on the island. Good on atmosphere.

Sir Walter Scott *The Pirate*. Inspired by stories of Viking raids and set in Orkney and Shetland, this novel was very popular in Victorian times.

★ **Iain Crichton Smith** *Consider the Lilies*. Compassionate story about an old woman evicted during the Highland Clearance, by Scotland's finest bilingual (English and Gaelic) writer.

Robert Louis Stevenson *Kidnapped*. A thrilling historical adventure set in the eighteenth century, every bit as exciting as the better-known *Treasure Island*.

POETRY

★ **George Mackay Brown** *Selected Poems 1954–1992*. Brown's work is as haunting, beautiful and gritty as the Orkney islands which inspire it. *Travellers* – compiled after his death – features work either previously unpublished or appearing only in newspapers and periodicals.

★ **Norman MacCaig** *Selected Poems*. This selection includes some of the best work from this important Scottish poet, whose deep love of nature and of the Highland landscape is always evident. *Norman MacCaig: A Celebration*, an anthology

written for his 85th birthday, includes work by more than ninety writers, including Ted Hughes and Seamus Heaney.

★ **Sorley Maclean (Somhairle Macgill-Eain)** *From Wood to Ridge: Collected Poems*. Written in Gaelic, his poems have been translated into bilingual editions all over the world, dealing as they do with the sorrows of poverty, war and love.

Edwin Morgan *New Selected Poems*. A love of words and their sounds is evident in Morgan's poems, which are refreshingly varied and often experimental. He comments on the Scottish scene with shrewdness and humour.

Edwin Muir *Collected Poems*. Muir's childhood on Orkney at the turn of the twentieth century remained with him as a dream of paradise from which he was banished to Glasgow. His poems are passionately concerned with Scotland.

Iain Crichton Smith *Collected Poems*. Born on the Isle of Lewis, Iain Crichton Smith wrote with feeling, and sometimes bitterness, in both Gaelic and English, of the life of the rural communities, the iniquities of the Free Church, the need to revive Gaelic culture and the glory of the Scottish landscape.

Language

Language is a thorny, complex and often highly political issue in Scotland. If you're not from Scotland yourself, you're most likely to be addressed in a variety of English, spoken in a Scottish accent. Even then, you're likely to hear phrases and words that are part of what is known as Scots, now officially recognized as a distinct language in its own right. To a lesser extent, Gaelic, too, remains a living language, particularly in the *Gàidhealtachd* or Gaelic-speaking areas of the northwest Highlands, Western Isles, parts of Skye and a few scattered Hebridean islands. In Orkney and Shetland, the local dialect of Scots contains many words carried over from Norn, the Old Norse language spoken in the Northern Isles from the time of the Vikings until the eighteenth century.

Scots

Scots began life as a northern branch of Anglo-Saxon, emerging as a distinct language in the Middle Ages. From the 1370s until the Union in 1707, it was the country's main literary and documentary language. Since the eighteenth century, however, it has been systematically repressed to give preference to English.

Rabbie Burns is the most obvious literary exponent of the Scots language, but there was a revival in the last century led by poets such as Hugh MacDiarmid. Only recently has Scots enjoyed something of a renaissance, getting itself on the Scottish school curriculum in 1996, and achieving official recognition as a distinct language in 1998. Despite these enormous political achievements, many people (rightly or wrongly) still regard Scots as a dialect of English. For more on the Scots language, visit ⓦsco.wikipedia.org.

Gaelic

Scottish **Gaelic** (*Gàidhlig*, pronounced "gallic") is one of the only four Celtic languages to survive into the modern age (Welsh, Breton and Irish Gaelic are the other three). Manx, the old language of the Isle of Man, died out early last century, while Cornish was finished as a community language in the eighteenth century. Scottish Gaelic is most closely related to Irish Gaelic and Manx – hardly surprising since Gaelic was introduced to Scotland from Ireland around the third century BC. Some folk still argue that Scottish Gaelic is merely a dialect of its parent language, Irish Gaelic, and indeed the two languages remain more or less mutually intelligible. From the fifth to the twelfth centuries, Gaelic enjoyed an expansionist phase, thanks partly to the backing of the Celtic Church in Iona.

Since then, Gaelic has been in steady decline. Even before Union with England, power, religious ideology and wealth gradually passed into non-Gaelic hands. The royal court was transferred to Edinburgh and an Anglo-Norman legal system was put in place. The Celtic Church was Romanized by the introduction of foreign clergy, and, most important of all, English and Flemish merchants colonized the new trading towns of the east coast. In addition, the pro-English attitudes held by the Covenanters led to strong anti-Gaelic feeling within the Church of Scotland from its inception.

The two abortive Jacobite rebellions of 1715 and 1745 furthered the language's decline, as did the Clearances that took place in the Gaelic-speaking Highlands from the 1770s to the 1850s, which forced thousands to migrate to central Scotland's new industrial belt or emigrate to North America. Although efforts were made to halt the decline in the first half of the nineteenth century, the 1872 Education Act gave no official recognition to Gaelic, and children were severely punished if they were caught speaking the language in school.

The 2011 census put the number of Gaelic-speakers at under 60,000 (just over one percent of the population), the majority of whom live in the **Gàidhealtachd**, though there is thought to be an extended Gaelic community of perhaps 250,000 who have some understanding of the language. Since the 1980s, great efforts have been made to try and save the language, including the introduction of bilingual primary and nursery schools, and a huge increase in the amount of broadcasting time given to Gaelic-language and Gaelic music programmes, and the establishment of highly successful Gaelic colleges such as Sabhal Mòr Ostaig (@smo.uhi.ac.uk).

Gaelic grammar and pronunciation

Gaelic is a highly complex tongue, with a fiendish, antiquated **grammar** and, with only eighteen letters, an intimidating system of spelling. **Pronunciation** is easier than it appears at first glance; one general rule to remember is that the stress always falls on the first syllable of a word. The general rule of syntax is that the verb starts the sentence whether it's a question or not, followed by the subject and then the object; adjectives generally follow the word they are describing.

SHORT AND LONG VOWELS

Gaelic has both short and long vowels, the latter being denoted by an acute or grave accent.

a as in cat; before nn and ll, as in cow
à as in bar
e as in pet
é like rain
i as in sight

i like free
o as in pot
ò like enthral
ó like cow
u like scoot
ù like loo

VOWEL COMBINATIONS

Gaelic is littered with diphthongs, which, rather like in English, can be pronounced in several different ways depending on the individual word.

ai like cat, or pet; before dh or gh, like street
ao like the sound in the middle of colonel
ea like pet, or cat, and sometimes like mate; before ll or nn like cow

èa as in hear
ei like mate
eu like train, or fear
ia like fear
io like fear, or shorter than street
ua like wooer

CONSONANTS

The consonants listed below are those that differ substantially from the English.

b at the beginning of a word like the **b** in big; in the middle/end of a word like the **p** in pair
bh at the beginning of a word like the **v** in van; elsewhere it is silent
c as in cat; after a vowel it has aspiration before it
ch always as in loch, never as in church
cn like the **cr** in crowd
d like the **d** in dog, but with the tongue pressed against the back of the upper teeth; at the beginning of a word or before e or i, like the **j** in jam; in the middle or at the end of a word like the **t** in cat; after i like the **ch** in church

dh before and after a, o or u is an aspirated **g**, rather like a gargle; before e or i like the **y** in yes; elsewhere silent
fh usually silent; sometimes like the **h** in house
g at the beginning of a word as in get; before e like the **y** in yes; in the middle or end of a word like the **ck** in sock; after i like the **ch** in loch
gh at the beginning of a word as in get; before or after a, o or u rather like a gargle; after i sometimes like the **y** in gay, but often silent
l after i and sometimes before e like the **l** in lot; elsewhere a peculiarly Gaelic sound produced by flattening the front of the tongue against the palate
mh like the **v** in van

p at the beginning of a word as in pet; elsewhere it has aspiration before it

rt pronounced as **sht**

s before e or i like the **sh** in ship; otherwise as in English

sh before a, o or u like the **h** in house; before e like the **ch** in loch

t before e or i like the **ch** in church; in the middle or at the end of a word it has aspiration before it; otherwise as in English

th at the beginning of a word, like the **h** in house; elsewhere, and in the word *thu* (you), silent

GAELIC PHRASES, VOCABULARY AND COURSES

One of the best introductory **teach-yourself Gaelic** courses is *Speaking Our Language* by Richard Cox, based on the TV series, much of which you can watch on YouTube. If you just want to get better at pronouncing Gaelic words, try *Blas na Gàidhlig* by Michael Bauer, or for a phrasebook, your best bet is *Everyday Gaelic* by Morag MacNeill. You can also do some self-learning on the Gaelic section of the BBC website ⊕ bbc.co.uk.

BASIC WORDS AND GREETINGS

yes tha
no chan eil
hello hallo
how are you? ciamar a tha thu?
fine tha gu math
thank you tapadh leat
welcome fàilte
come in thig a-staigh
good day latha math
goodbye mar sin leat
good night oidhche mhath
who? cò?
where is...? càit a bheil...?
when? cuine?
what is it? dé tha ann?
morning madainn
evening feasgar
day là
night oidhche
tomorrow a-màireach
tonight a-nochd
cheers slàinte
yesterday an-dé
today an-diugh
tomorrow maireach
now a-nise
food lòn
bread aran
water uisge
milk bainne
beer leann
wine fion
whisky uisge beatha
Edinburgh Dun Eideann
Glasgow Glaschu
America Ameireaga
Ireland Eire
England Sasainn
London Lunnain

SOME USEFUL PHRASES

How much is that? Dè tha e 'cosg?
What's your name? Dè 'n t-ainm a th'ort?
Excuse me Gabh mo leisgeul
I'd like a double room 'Se rùm dùbailte tha mi'giarraigh
Do you speak Gaelic? A bheil Gàidhlig agad?
What is the Gaelic for ...? Dé a' Ghàidhlig a tha ... air?
I don't understand Chan eil mi 'tuigsinn
I don't know Chan eil fhios agam
It doesn't matter 'S coma
I'm sorry Tha mi duilich

NUMBERS AND DAYS

1 aon
2 dà/dhà
3 trì
4 ceithir
5 còig
6 sia
7 seachd
8 ochd
9 naoi
10 deich
11 aon deug
20 fichead
21 aon ar fhichead
30 deug ar fhichead
40 dà fhichead
50 lethcheud
60 trì fichead
100 ceud
1000 mìle
Monday Diluain
Tuesday Dimàirt
Wednesday Diciadain
Thursday Diardaoin
Friday Dihaoine
Saturday Disathurna
Sunday Didòmhnaich/La na Sàbaid

GAELIC GEOGRAPHICAL AND PLACE-NAME TERMS

The purpose of the list below is to help with place-name derivations from Gaelic and with more detailed map-reading.

abhainn river

ach or auch, from achadh field

ail, aileach rock

Alba Scotland

aonach ridge

ard, ardan or arden, àird from a point of land or height

aros dwelling

ault, from allt stream

bad brake or clump of trees

bagh bay

bal or bally, from baile town, village

balloch, from bealach mountain pass

ban white, fair

bàrr summit

beg, from beag small

ben, from beinn mountain

blair, from blàr field or battlefield

cairn, from càrn pile of stones

camas bay, harbour

cnoc hill

coll or colly, from coille wood or forest

corran a spit or point jutting into the sea

corrie, from coire round hollow in mountain-side, whirlpool

craig, from creag rock, crag

cruach bold hill

drum, from druim ridge

dubh black

dun or dum, from dùn for

eilean island

ess, from eas waterfall

fin, from fionn white

gair or gare, from geàrr short

garv, from garbh rough

geodha cove

glen, from gleann valley

gower or gour, goat **from gabhar**

inch, from innis meadow or island

inver, from inbhir river mouth

ken or kin, from ceann head

knock, from cnoc hill

kyle, from caolas narrow strait

lag hollow

larach site of an old ruin

liath grey

loch lake

meall round hill

mon, from monadh hill

more, from mór large, great

rannoch, from raineach bracken

ross, from ros promontory

rubha promontory

sgeir sea rock

sgurr sharp point

sron nose, prow or promontory

strath, from srath broad valley

tarbet, from tairbeart isthmus

tigh house

tir or tyre, from tìr land

torr hill, castle

tràigh shore

uig shelter

uisge water

Norn (Orkney and Shetland)

Between the tenth and seventeenth centuries, the chief language of Orkney and Shetland was **Norn**, a Scandinavian tongue close to modern Faroese and Icelandic. After the end of Norse rule, and with the transformation of the Church, the law, commerce and education, Norn gradually lost out to Scots and English, eventually petering out completely in the eighteenth century. Today, Orkney and Shetland have their own dialects, and individual islands and communities within each group have local variations. The **dialects** have a Scots base, with some Old Norse words; however, they don't sound strongly Scottish, with the Orkney accent – which has been likened to the Welsh one – especially distinctive. Listed below are some of the words you're most likely to hear, including some birds' names and common elements in place names.

NORN PHRASES AND VOCABULARY

aak guillemot

alan storm petrel

ayre beach

bister farm

böd fisherman's store

bonxie great skua

bruck rubbish
burra heath rush
crö sheepfold
eela rod-fishing from small boats
ferrylouper incomer (Orkney)
fourareen four-oared boat
foy party or festival
geo coastal inlet
gloup blowhole, behind a cliff face, where spray is blasted out from the cave below (from Old Norse glup, a throat)
haa laird's house
haaf deep-sea fishing. Lit. "heave" (Shetland)
hap hand-knitted shawl
howe mound
kame ridge of hills
kishie basket
maa seagull
mool headland
moorit brown
mootie tiny

muckle large
noost hollow place where a boat is drawn up
norie (or tammie-norie) puffin
noup steep headland
peerie/peedie small
plantiecrub (or plantiecrö) small dry-stone enclosure for growing cabbages
quoy enclosed, cultivated common land
roost tide race
scattald common grazing land
scord gap or pass in a ridge of hills
setter farm
shaela dark grey
simmer dim summer twilight
sixern/sixareen six-oared boat
solan gannet
soothmoother incomer (Shetland)
udal Norse law designating land as a freehold without any charter or feudal-type arrangement
voe sea inlet
yoal rowing boat used for fishing (Shetland)

Glossary

Auld Old

Bairn Baby

Bannock Unleavened bread made from oats or barley

Ben Hill or mountain

Blackhouse Thick-walled traditional dwelling

Bonnie Pretty

Bothy Primitive cottage, hut or mountain shelter

Brae Slope or hill

Brig Bridge

Broch Circular prehistoric stone fort

Burn Small stream or brook

Byre Shelter for cattle; cottage

Cairn Mound of stones

CalMac Caledonian MacBrayne ferry company

Ceilidh (pronounced "kay-lee"). Social gathering involving dancing, drinking, singing and storytelling

Central belt Central Scotland between the Forth and Clyde including Edinburgh and Glasgow

Clan Extended family

Clearances Evictions from the Highlands

Corbett A mountain between 2500ft and 3000ft high

Covenanters Supporters of the Presbyterian Church in the seventeenth century

Crannog Celtic lake or bog dwelling

Croft Small plot of farmland with house, common in the Highlands

Dirk A long dagger

Dolmen Grave chamber

Doocot Dovecot

Dram Literally, one-eighth of a fluid ounce. Usually refers to any small measure of whisky

Dun Fortified mound

Episcopalian A church which has bishops in its organizational structure

Firth A wide sea inlet or estuary

Gillie Personal guide used on hunting or fishing trips

Glen Deep, narrow mountain valley

Harling Limestone and gravel mix used to cover buildings

Henge Circular ditch with a bank

Hogmanay New Year's Eve

Howe Valley

Howff Meeting place; pub

HES Historic Environment Scotland, a government-funded heritage organization

Kilt Knee-length tartan skirt worn by Highland men

Kirk Church

Laird Landowner; aristocrat

Law Rounded hill

Links Grassy coastal land; coastal golf course

Loch Lake

Lochan Little loch

Mac/Mc These prefixes in Scottish surnames derive from the Gaelic, meaning "son of". In Scots "Mac" is used for both sexes. In Gaelic "Nic" is used for women: Donnchadh Mac Aodh is Duncan MacKay, Iseabail Nic Aodh is Isabel MacKay

Machair Sandy, grassy, lime-rich coastal land, generally used for grazing

Manse Official home of a Presbyterian minister

Munro A mountain over 3000ft high

Munro-bagging The sport of trying to climb as many Munros as possible

Neuk Corner

NTS The National Trust for Scotland, a heritage organization

Pend Archway or vaulted passage

Presbyterian The form of church government used in the official (Protestant) Church of Scotland, established by John Knox during the Reformation

RIB Rigid Inflatable Boat

Runrig A common form of farming in which separate ridges are cultivated by different occupiers under joint agreement

Sassenach Derives from the Gaelic *Sasunnach*, meaning literally "Saxon"; used by Scots to describe the English Scottish Baronial style of architecture favoured by the Scottish landowning class, featuring crow-stepped gables and round turrets

Sheila na gig Female fertility symbol, usually a naked woman displaying her vulva

Shieling Simple huts or shelters used by shepherds during summer grazing

Shinty Stick-and-ball game played in the Highlands, with similarities to hockey

Smiddy Smithy

SNH Scottish Natural Heritage, a government-funded conservation body

SNP Scottish National Party

Sporran Leather purse worn in front of, or at the side of, a kilt

Tartan Check-patterned woollen cloth, particular patterns being associated with particular clans

Thane A landowner of high rank; the chief of a clan

Tombolo A spit of sand connecting an island to the mainland

Trews Tartan trousers

Wee Small

Wee Frees Followers of the Free Presbyterian or Free Church of Scotland

Wynd Narrow lane

Yett Gate or door

Small print and index

A ROUGH GUIDE TO ROUGH GUIDES

Published in 1982, the first Rough Guide – to Greece – was a student scheme that became a publishing phenomenon. Mark Ellingham, a recent graduate in English from Bristol University, had been travelling in Greece the previous summer and couldn't find the right guidebook. With a small group of friends he wrote his own guide, combining a contemporary, journalistic style with a thoroughly practical approach to travellers' needs.

The immediate success of the book spawned a series that rapidly covered dozens of destinations. And, in addition to impecunious backpackers, Rough Guides soon acquired a much broader readership that relished the guides' wit and inquisitiveness as much as their enthusiastic, critical approach and value-for-money ethos. These days, Rough Guides include recommendations from budget to luxury and cover more than 120 destinations around the globe, from Amsterdam to Zanzibar, all regularly updated by our team of roaming writers.

Browse all our latest guides, read inspirational features and book your trip at **roughguides.com**.

Rough Guide credits

Editors: Siobhan Warwicker and Zara Sekhavati
Cartography: Katie Bennett
Picture editor: Aude Vauconsant

Head of DTP and Pre-Press: Rebeka Davies
Layout: Ruth Bradley
Head of Publishing: Sarah Clark

Publishing information

Ninth Edition 2021

Distribution

UK, Ireland and Europe
Apa Publications (UK) Ltd; sales@roughguides.com
United States and Canada
Ingram Publisher Services; ips@ingramcontent.com
Australia and New Zealand
Woodslane; info@woodslane.com.au
Southeast Asia
Apa Publications (SN) Pte; sales@roughguides.com
Worldwide
Apa Publications (UK) Ltd; sales@roughguides.com

Special Sales, Content Licensing and CoPublishing

Rough Guides can be purchased in bulk quantities at discounted prices. We can create special editions, personalised jackets and corporate imprints tailored to your needs. sales@roughguides.com.
roughguides.com

Printed in Poland

The publishers and authors have done their best to ensure the accuracy and currency of all the information in **The Rough Guide to Scottish Highlands and Islands**, however, they can accept no responsibility for any loss, injury, or inconvenience sustained by any traveller as a result of information or advice contained in the guide.

Help us update

We've gone to a lot of effort to ensure that this edition of **The Rough Guide to Scottish Highlands and Islands** is accurate and up-to-date. However, things change – places get "discovered", opening hours are notoriously fickle, restaurants and rooms raise prices or lower standards. If you feel we've got it wrong or left something out, we'd like to know, and if you can remember the address, the price, the hours, the phone number, so much the better.

Please send your comments with the subject line **"Rough Guide Scottish Highlands and Islands Update"** to mail@uk.roughguides.com. We'll credit all contributions and send a copy of the next edition (or any other Rough Guide if you prefer) for the very best emails.

ABOUT THE AUTHOR

Norm Longley has spent most of his working life in central/ eastern Europe – he is the author of the Rough Guides to Slovenia and Romania – but more recently has turned his hand to home shores, contributing to Scotland, Wales and Ireland guides. He lives in Somerset and can occasionally be seen erecting marquees on the Rec in Bath.

Rachel Mills is a freelance writer and editor based by the sea in Kent. She is a co-author for Rough Guides to New Zealand, India, Canada, Ireland and Great Britain; a regular contributor to Telegraph Travel and loveEXPLORING.com; and an expert in sustainable, responsible tourism. Follow her @rachmillstravel.

Hilary Weston and **Jackie Staddon** have combined their skills as travel writers, updaters and editors for over 25 years. In that time, they have contributed to a host of guidebooks on destinations from around the world but their great passion for Italy dominates. Now semi-retired, in more recent times they have devoted a lot of their writing to promoting the wonderful destinations that the UK has to offer.

Photo credits

(Key: T-top; C-centre; B-bottom; L-left; R-right)

Index

Map symbols

The symbols below are used on maps throughout the book

——— - -	International boundary	✈	International airport	🍶	Whisky distillery	⚓	Swimming
— — —	Chapter boundary	✗	Domestic airport	⛷	Skiing	⛽	Petrol station
▨▨▨▨	Motorway	🅿	Parking	⛳	Golf course	🏛	Abbey
....	Major road	♦	Point of interest	▲	Peak	✝	Chapel
....	Minor road	∴	Ruins/archeological site	�530	Viewpoint		Building
●━●━●━●	Unpaved road	🏛	Stately home	⁀⁀	Rocks	⇄	Church
▭▭▭▭	Pedestrian road	♖	Castle	🗼	Lighthouse	⊞	Cemetery
⊥⊥⊥⊥⊥⊥	Steps	♦	Museum	🗲	Waterfall		Park
- - - - -	Footpath	♈	Gardens	◠	Cave	▦	Forest
▬▬▬▬▬	Railway	✂	Battlefield	⌂	Cairn(s)		Beach
— —	Ferry route	🛆	Campsite	ᛦᛦ	Standing stones		
+++++++	Canal	ⓘ	Tourist office	⁝⁝	Stone circle		
●- - -●	Cable car	✉	Post office	◎	Cup- and ring-marked rocks		

Listings key

◼	Accommodation
●	Eating
◼	Drinking/nightlife